MODERN LEARNING THEORY

THE CENTURY PSYCHOLOGY SERIES

RICHARD M. ELLIOTT, *Editor*
KENNETH MacCORQUODALE, *Assistant Editor*

WILLIAM K. ESTES
SIGMUND KOCH
KENNETH MacCORQUODALE
PAUL E. MEEHL
CONRAD G. MUELLER, Jr.
WILLIAM N. SCHOENFELD
WILLIAM S. VERPLANCK

•

with the editorial assistance of
A. T. POFFENBERGER

Modern Learning Theory

➤➤➤➤➤➤➤❯❮❰❮❰❮❰❮

A CRITICAL ANALYSIS
OF FIVE EXAMPLES

New  York

APPLETON-CENTURY-CROFTS, Inc.

PRINTED IN THE UNITED STATES OF AMERICA
E 29223

FOREWORD

THIS VOLUME is one tangible product of an interesting experiment in education. Other products, tangible and intangible, are materializing and will continue to do so over the years.

The problem of the production of scientific men in greater numbers and of a higher quality is a matter of great concern to leaders in education. Although the need is more spectacular in the physical sciences, it is no less pressing in the social sciences. Social scientists who have been studying the problem of increasing output in the social sciences have noted an unfortunate trend in the scientific careers of young people. They have seen that the rise in the cost of living during this period has left the college and university instructors in an increasingly unfavorable financial position. The consequence in many instances has been that the long vacations which academic people had been accustomed to devote to research training and study must now be spent in supplementing academic salaries through teaching in academic summer sessions or other routine gainful employment. The situation of the serious minded scholar is well described in the following words of one of them:

The routine responsibilities and pressures of the academic year leave far too little time for the sort of leisurely, contemplative, intellectual activity which was once so much more a part of the academic life than it is today and it is not a question of "time to think." Even when one finds a little time, the whole problem of shifting gears from class work, thesis conferences, administrative responsibilities, yes, even laboratory work on one's own experimental program, makes good thinking difficult. The whole atmosphere and frame of mind is too permeated by the intrusions of these other things, so the teacher often feels mentally tired, or irritable, or in need of some thoroughly avocational activity when the daily tasks are finished.

The writer has heard numerous discussions among fellow members of the Social Science Research Council who were searching for some feasible program through which promising young social scientists could be given freedom for study and research during summer vacations while receiving the equivalent of their teaching or other salaries. He happened also to know about a group of young psychologists who were engaged in research upon the theory of learning and who at considerable financial sacrifice to themselves had been meeting during two summers for periods of group discussion of their common problems. These men were invited to submit a proposal for a summer "seminar," the proposal to comprise a detailed statement of organization, purpose, procedure, membership, together with a budget covering all expenses of travel and maintenance in addition to the equivalent for each participant of the usual academic stipend for summer teaching.

A concise and informative prospectus of such a program was prepared by the group and submitted in the fall of 1949 by the Social Science Research Council to the Carnegie Corporation of New York, which provided funds for the "seminar" to be conducted under the general sponsorship of the Council.

Dartmouth College through Dean Donald M. Morrison generously offered the facilities of its campus for the experiment, including offices, meeting rooms, and most excellent library services. The physical conditions on this cool, quiet campus were nearly ideal for such a project. The vital part played by the college is most clearly seen in the spontaneous adoption of the name, "Dartmouth group" and "Dartmouth book on theory." The financial arrangements gave to each person the equivalent of a summer session salary, plus travel and other incidental expenses.

In the prospectus it was proposed that a group of psychologists meet with the purpose of discussing the status and current problems of learning theory:

Such a conference would be the first of its kind. Customarily, work such as that envisaged is found only in university seminars guided by individual teachers or theorists. This plan is very different; it proposes that a conference of theorists, assembled from different universities, meet together and attack theoretical problems through cooperative effort. The field of learning seems an appropriate one to attack because of its central importance in behavioral science; because learning is a field in which there is an accumulation of soundly established experimental information; because attempts at the theoretical organization of basic data have been prominent so that particular formulations are most open to examination; and finally it was the common interest of the group in which the seminar idea originated.

The "seminar" consisted of seven men, all young and of approximately the same age, academic rank, and prestige. Their attitudes toward science in general and toward psychology in particular were sufficiently uniform to furnish a common basis for group discussion. It was presumed that they were reasonably free from preconceived alliances and were not partisans or spokesmen for any one theory or theorist. Undoubtedly there were differences among them in academic background and research interest and there were undoubtedly some individual preferences for one theory or another. But the uniformity of aim and interests underlying the diversities had much to do with the success of the conference.

The seven members were: William K. Estes, Indiana University; Sigmund Koch, Duke University; Kenneth MacCorquodale, University of Minnesota; Paul E. Meehl, University of Minnesota; Conrad G. Mueller, Jr., Columbia University; William N. Schoenfeld, Columbia University; and William S. Verplanck, Harvard University.

There were in addition three assistants with graduate training in psychology who gave invaluable help during the summer, namely, Frances Clayton, John Courtney, and Paul Hutt.

It was obviously impossible to cover the whole range of learning theory except in a most superficial fashion, so that the problem of selecting theories for examination had to be met at the outset. Five theories were finally chosen which seemed to occupy a dominant position in the field of learning theory in terms of their popularity, their contemporaneousness, and their influence upon current writing and research. These were the theories of Clark L. Hull, Edward C. Tolman, Burrhus F. Skinner, Kurt Lewin, and Edwin R. Guthrie. A different set of five theories might have been selected on the basis of other criteria such as correctness or completeness. What part special prejudices and preferences of the members of the group may have had to do with the final choice of theories is not easy to determine. Whatever the basis for selection, the outcome would seem to indicate that the choice was a fortunate one.

The success of any conference depends to a great extent upon the preliminary work that is done in preparation for it, and this seminar is no exception. The group had met in the winter of 1949 in order to prepare plans and to consider possible procedures. It was decided that each member should come to the conference with two or more "papers" sufficiently well prepared to present for informal discussion. This was a fortunate provision inasmuch as it gave some immediate direction to the deliberation, while it in no way hampered the freedom to speak or to bring up other questions. Furthermore, each member or pair of conferees accepted the primary responsibility for analysis and final report on one of the theories. Such a division of labor was a most flexible one, however, and was not intended to interfere with the range of participation of any member in the discussion.

It might be supposed that there would crystallize out from such a critical and unbiased analysis of theories and the experimental evidence on which they rest, some one basic theory of the learning process which all reasonable persons could accept. If there were any such expectations among the members of the group they were soon dissipated. Each theory appeared to exist within its own closed system and to defy direct comparison and the pooling of data. Concepts, techniques, apparatus, units of measurement, and definition of terms were peculiar to a given theory and could not safely be lifted out of their own frame of reference. Each theory, then, had to be examined and analyzed separately for internal consistency and the degree to which it satisfied the logic of science.

For this reason, if for no other, it would have been too much to expect that there would emerge a final and unified report on learning theory, resembling a unanimous supreme court decision or even a majority opinion. It seemed proper, therefore, that the reports on each of the theories as they appear here should be signed by the persons who prepared them and each author would assume sole responsibility for his work even though each report was the outcome of some weeks of joint deliberation during the seminar, supplemented by extensive exchanges of comment among members of the group in the interval between the seminar and the completion of the manuscript for publication.

No attempt was made to obtain uniformity among the final written reports of the different theories. Beyond the general framework set up for the analysis of the theories, and certain agreed specifications for citation of references, contributors were free to write and arrange their material as they chose. After careful consideration of all the factors involved it was decided to allow for each report its own set of references immediately following the report, in spite of the repetition of certain references which this procedure entailed.

It should be clearly understood that it was not the main purpose of the project to produce a book on learning theory, although it was the expectation of the group that results of the summer's work would be published in some form. The program was directed toward providing promising young investigators with the time and opportunity for advancing their interest and ability in research. Only upon completion of the program was publication of a major report proposed.

As there is no similar intensive treatment of learning theory available, it should be found useful wherever advanced courses in learning are given. There are other tangible by-products of this experiment. Most notable is the financial support and sponsorship by another foundation of several similar seminars in other fields of research. The intangible products may, however, become the most important ones if in any small degree they contribute to the progress of the social sciences.

The authors wish to express their appreciation to the many persons and institutions who gave assistance in the course of their work, and particularly to Dartmouth College for serving as host; to Dr. Donald R. Young, Director of the Russell Sage Foundation, for his constructive criticism of the original proposal; to the Social Science Research Council for its encouragement and assistance during the course of its sponsorship; and to the Carnegie Corporation for its financial support.

A. T. POFFENBERGER

CONTENTS

INTRODUCTION

THE MAJOR contributions of the outstanding theorists of our time have been made. Their offerings have set the framework of the larger part of our current theoretical literature, and have placed their stamp on the vigorous output of our experimental laboratories. Within their limits lie the controversies and issues that engage most of our theoretical attention. Yet, these theories are commonly said to have irreconcilable differences among them. The truth of this can be revealed only by a detailed analysis of their structure and content.

The procedures we have adopted for our critical examination of contemporary learning theory sought to make the best use of past experience as a basis for evaluation, and to draw some lessons for the further development of learning theory. We followed several avenues of approach to these goals. First, we asked what lines of attack have been employed by influential learning theorists in the past. Then, we attempted to determine the merits of these strategies as they have proved themselves in actual use. Finally, we looked for additional guides to theory construction in the experience of the more advanced sciences.

With this orientation, we proceeded as empirically as possible. Just as the learning theorist initiates his enterprise with observations of his subjects, we took our start from detailed consideration of the activities of theorists. And just as any empirical investigator, we were faced at the outset with the problem of sampling. The project had to be trimmed to manageable proportions, and we could not undertake any attempt to do justice to the work of all the individuals who are actively contributing to current learning theory. Believing that a cursory or superficial treatment of theoretical systems would be worse than none at all, we decided to limit ourselves to those that we could subject to a reasonably exhaustive analysis. Accordingly, we selected for study five theories which have seemed for the past two decades to occupy a prominent, even dominant, position in the field of learning: namely those developed by Clark L. Hull, Edward C. Tolman, Burrhus F. Skinner, Kurt Lewin, and Edwin R. Guthrie.

In approaching the work of each theorist, we wanted to consider: (1) what his program for a learning theory is insofar as he has one, that is, how he conceives the whole undertaking; and, (2) what his actual theory is insofar as he has one, together with the adequacy of his theory by either logical or pragmatic standards. In addition, we did not wish to overlook entirely the influence that each theorist's conception and work may have exerted upon contemporary psychology. Certain difficulties arise, however, when one attempts to exhibit a theory in a not-merely-reportorical way. It is not enough simply to repeat the theorist's words. We need to analyze what he said, and on occasion to reconstruct what he must have meant if he were to be consistent with himself. Now this is clearly a touchy business. One must draw the line between a deliberate knowledgeable reconstruction and unwitting additions, between recasting and supplementing a formulation, between necessary and possible inference, between actual and desirable interpretations. In all this, we have tried to be careful. We well knew how delicate was the balance we were striking, and how easily are prompted the charges of misrepresentation and miscomprehension. We proceeded cautiously, sifting everything we could find of the men's writings, and ignoring hearsay accounts. But we did not hesitate to take this approach since we were unanimous in feeling that unless we did so we would not be giving our theorists a complete hearing. Their work had to be fairly put before it could be fairly evaluated.

We have attempted to make progress toward several objectives:

(1) Evaluation of the impression held by many psychologists that there are a number of competing theories in the area of learning. Here we are using the term theory, in accordance with general understanding among scientists, to denote a conceptual apparatus mediating scientific explanation and prediction in an empirical area.

(2) Appraisal of the different theories, or of the different programs for theory construction, with respect to their fruitfulness in generating research. A number of individuals—for example, Tolman and Lewin—have attempted comprehensive formulations of broad areas of psychology, laying down the pretheoretical framework or attitudes which were to guide their theory construction, adopting a characterization of the subject matter of their theories, identifying the kind of empirical data to be sought, and exhibiting the kinds of theoretical concepts and principles which they believe to be required in the area. While it was necessary to consider the influence of some of these programs upon the current status of the science of learning, it was equally important, we felt, to distinguish a program from a theory in the more technical sense.

(3) Possible location, within the theoretical systems under consideration, of limited theories which have been formalized to the extent of being testable and which may provide material for the synthesis of more comprehensive theories.

(4) The illustration of a somewhat more intensive analysis of theoretical materials than has been customary in psychology. The exploitation of whatever is of value in the theory of the past requires that the analysis of theory be approached with the same discipline as the construction of

theory. Only when practiced at such a level can theoretical analysis provide the clues needed for continuing theoretical progress.

We have not fully accomplished our desire to clarify differences among current theories and to abstract features which they hold in common. But our wish to do so, and the little we did achieve on this score must not be taken as implying that we feel any of the existing lines of attack upon problems of learning should be scrapped. On the one hand, we appreciate the need for a common theoretical structure to facilitate the ordering and application of our knowledge of learning. On the other, we recognize the complexity of the material which must be handled by a behavior theory. Vigorous individual attempts at theory construction along a wide variety of fronts are probably not only desirable but necessary for continued progress in this area. The present reviews reflect our belief that we may expect to learn as much from the errors and the failures of these attempts as from their successes.

In the following section, we indicate in outline form the "dimensions" along which we have evaluated our five selected theories. The main aspects of theory included in this outline are those which we believe one must consider in examining a proposed theory and trying to make clear its structure and content. This outline was collaboratively devised by us, and a common understanding of the various rubrics was arrived at in group discussion. Because extant theories differ so widely in organization, the analytic outline has been used flexibly in preparing the critiques of the several theories. Thus, where the nature of a theoretical system required or recommended it, the topics of the outline were rearranged in sequence, or differentially emphasized, or refined still further. Always, however, the outline was kept in mind during the course of an analysis so that the various treatments would be comparable on fundamental points. The working outline is given below, along with examples of the types of questions asked in connection with certain of the rubrics.

OUTLINE FOR REVIEWS OF THEORIES

I. Structure of the Theory.
   A. Delineation of empirical area.
      1. Data language.
         Is the data language explicit and theoretically neutral?
         How does the theorist relate his empirical variables to the data language?
      2. Dependent and independent variables.
         How does the selection of variables compare with those of other learning theories?
         What influence does the choice of variables exert upon the form of the theory?
      3. Relation between empirical areas covered and orientative attitudes exhibited by the theorist.

B. Theoretical concepts.
1. Primitive terms.
Are the primitive terms of the theory reducible to physical or object language?
Is the usage of primitive terms fixed by implicit or explicit definitions?
2. Principal constructs.
Do these serve only a summarizing function or are they related by definition or by hypothesis to terms of other disciplines (e.g., physiology)?
3. Relations assumed among constructs.
How are the major theoretical variables interrelated in the foundation assumptions of the theory?
How are such interrelations constructed from the observation base of the theory?
4. Relations assumed or derived between constructs and experimentally defined variables.

II. Methodologic Characteristics.
A. Standing of the theory on principal methodologic "dimensions."
1. Explicit axiomatization.
2. Quantitativeness.
3. Consistency and independence of principal theoretical assumptions.
4. Use of physical or mathematical models.
B. Techniques of derivation.
Are the empirical consequences of the theory developed by informal arguments or formal derivations?

III. Empirical Content and Adequacy.
A. Range of data for which interpretation or explanation in terms of the theory has been claimed.
B. Specificity of prediction demonstrated.
C. Obvious failures to handle facts in the area III A.
D. Tours-de-force.
Has it been possible to predict new experimental phenomena?
Have any predictions of this sort been confirmed?
Does the theory account for facts not predictable from competing theories in the same area?
E. Sensitivity to empirical evidence.
F. Programmaticity.
G. Special virtues or limitations; techniques which may prove useful outside the context of the specific theory.

The foregoing outline is undoubtedly somewhat arbitrary insofar as the breakdown into dimensions or categories is concerned. Despite the arbitrariness of the classification, however, we believe wide agreement would obtain among current writers in the logic of science that an adequate review of any scientific theory must include essentially the same features.

The rather formal and categorical appearance of the outline should not be taken to mean that we were preoccupied entirely with the morphological aspects of the theories. Scientific theories are evaluated, not on some absolute scale of "theoryness," but with respect to what we expect them to do. Some of the functions of a useful theory are: (1) clarifying the description of the world possible in ordinary language, (2) summarizing existing knowledge, (3) mediating applications of our knowledge to new situations, (4) leading to fruitful lines of experimental inquiry. Even usefulness is not absolute; one can well ask, useful to whom, or useful for what? A theory which in one form is satisfactory for the purposes of a practitioner may not be useful in that form for a research scientist. Nor can we agree with the view, commonly advanced, that theories which account for the same set of known facts are identical except for a matter of taste in the choice of words; they may, in fact, be quite disparate as instruments for guiding further inquiry and developing linkages with theories in related areas.

Our primary concern in the present reviews is with the learning theory as it may function in the long-range development of a science of behavior. Thus, our five selected theories are for their most part formulations which have grown out of experimental fact and which are actually influencing research upon problems of learning. If some of our reviews appear unduly harsh, it is simply because we feel that the strictest criticism of current formulations is necessary to facilitate further development. Since our purposes are entirely constructive, it is necessary to evaluate current theories against principles of theory construction as we understand them at present, not, as an historian would do, against the views of theory generally accepted at the time these theoretical formulations were initiated. We appreciate fully the position of the theorist who perforce works with the knowledge and methods available in his day, but who inevitably faces criticism arising from advances in knowledge and method that have resulted from his own efforts. With generous spirit, he hopes that his work will be a temporary stage in the development of more adequate theory.

THE AUTHORS

MODERN LEARNING THEORY

SECTION 1

Clark L. Hull

SIGMUND KOCH

INTRODUCTION

FROM 1929 until his death in 1952, Hull was ceaselessly dedicated to the construction of his theory of behavior. The theory was developed in a tortuous, piecemeal way. General hypotheses advanced in the early phase of the program were under continuous revision and extension, and, from time to time, major modifications or realignments of the emerging theoretical structure were put forward.

Three principal periods in the development of the theory may be roughly distinguished. During the interval 1929-1943, key concepts were informally elaborated, and "miniature" formalizations of parts of the total projected theory were put forward. The second period, 1943-1949, begins with the publication in *Principles of Behavior* (56) of the first "complete" postulate set tentatively believed adequate to the major phenomena of behavior, and ends with the distribution of a memorandum (62) setting forth a radical revision of the 1943 postulate set. Finally, there is the brief terminal phase of Hull's career, during which the 1949 postulates were further revised, and published in the small 1951 volume, *Essentials of Behavior* (75).

Published sources, at each stage of the development of the theory, tended to lag behind the actual status of Hull's thinking. Indeed, Hull informs us that the "most detailed record" of the growth of the theory may be found "scattered through twenty-five volumes of hand-written notebooks" which "began in October, 1915, and extend to the present time" (1951) (75, p. 120). At all periods, published sources have represented only a sample of the available materials comprising the completed portion of the theory. Other sources include: (1) the long series of mimeographed seminar notes and "memoranda concerning behavior theory" (e.g., 46, 51, 57) which Hull sent to interested people in the profession, at sporadic intervals; (2) unpublished manuscripts circulated by Hull among students and associates; (3) pre-publication drafts of manuscripts which often contained materials not included in the published versions. It should be recorded here that, at the time of Hull's death, the manuscript for an extended book concerned with "concrete deductions of the systematic details of individual (nonsocial) behavior" (70, p. 174) from the new theory, was nearing completion.

All the above considerations complicate the problems faced by the analyst of Hullian theory. In order to facilitate meaningful treatment within manageable scope, the field of the present analysis has been circumscribed in a number of ways.

1) The most influential form of the theory, in its *effect* on the psychological public, has certainly been that contained in *Principles of Behavior*. It is also the only formulation of a "complete" (i.e., "non-miniature") Hullian postulate set put forward with sufficient indication of the inductive basis and general rationale of the main assumptions to permit detailed and determinate analysis. For these reasons, the *pivot* of any comprehensive examination of Hull's theoretical effort must be the formulations of *Principles of Behavior*. Nevertheless, the postulate set of 1949, as later elaborated in the 1951 book, *Essentials of Behavior*, defines a set of assumptions so radically different from those of *Principles of Behavior* as to constitute an essentially new theory. Although there is reason to believe that the 1943 version of the system will remain a more influential formulation, no adequate evaluation of the *consequences* of Hull's theoretical objectives and methods can be made without serious consideration of the later work. Indeed, insight into the full significance of the orienting commitments and methods which underlie the theory of *Principles of Behavior,* only becomes possible through the backward illumination cast by the 1949-1951 postulates. Thus, consideration of the 1943 theory demands supplementation by analysis of the theory of 1949-1951, and we must accept the paradox of reporting on two theories in order to appreciate the significance of one of them.

2) The central references, then, on which this report is based are *Principles of Behavior* and *Essentials of Behavior*.[1] The long series of journal articles germane to the theory (1929-1951) and the book, *Mathematico-Deductive Theory of Rote Learning* (51) will also be tapped. For the most part, the report will be based on published, rather than informally circulated, materials. Mimeographed "memoranda concerning behavior theory" will necessarily figure in the discussion of the 1949-1951 postulate sets, but other mimeographed materials and unpublished

---

[1] In all further references to these volumes, *Principles of Behavior* will be abbreviated to *Pr.B.* and *Essentials of Behavior* to *Essentials.*

sources will not be used. Much of this material overlaps with published sources, and much represents trial-error theoretical sallies later abandoned by Hull. As for the remainder, the fact that Hull has withheld or postponed public commitment makes its status with respect to the published theory indeterminate.

3) Despite the above restrictions, any attempt to deal analytically with a set of formulations so extensive as Hull's must proceed from a selective incidence. At this moment in the history of psychology, a report on Hull's work could be slanted in any one of a number of directions. One of these might be an evaluation of the empirical evidence for or against the major Hullian hypotheses which are deemed most valuable. Another might be an assessment of the survival prospects of various components of the system, or an estimate of what modifications and creative refinements might be made in order to insure the perpetuation of the "theory" as a coherent systematic approach to the analysis of behavior. The present report takes quite another question as its primary concern. It asks: *what kind of a theory can Hull be said to have; what are the orienting commitments and methods which underlie its construction; what is the degree of correspondence between Hull's theoretical objectives and the resulting theoretical structure?*

Hull's theory is the product of a period of heroic optimism in recent theoretical psychology. The keynote of this era is the belief in the imminent feasibility of comprehensive theory, having an unrestricted range of application to the major phenomena of organismic behavior. This era—dating roughly from 1930—seems distinctly on the wane. Yet, it would not be quite correct to say that it is over. If, within recent years, we have learned that the major "theories" which dominated psychology during the thirties and forties were, in reality, over-extended *programs* towards theory, we have not yet arrived at a clear perception of the enormity of the distance separating such programs from theory, nor have we settled on the characteristics of those programs and objectives which might mediate realistic progress. Perhaps the single greatest barrier to appreciation of the need for reassessment of where we stand today is the belief that the heroic era has given us *one* formulation which is a *theory* in the most rigorous natural science connotation of the word. Not only Hull's supporters, but even many of his critics, seem unquestioningly agreed that Hull has put forward a detailed, high order, determinate theoretical structure. Curiously enough, Hull's followers are likely to argue that, even if Hull is wrong, he *at least* has a determinate theory, while opponents are likely to urge that Hull must be wrong, *because* he has a determinate theory. *For these reasons, it is of the first importance to test Hull's formulations against the criteria of rigorous natural science theoretical procedure—eminently fair criteria, in Hull's case, because he explicitly adopted them.*

The foregoing objectives have determined the form and level of this report. Part I applies to the formulations of *Pr.B.*, a set of analytic rubrics deemed adequate to characterize the methodological status of any scientific formulation having theoretical intentions. Part II compares the theory of *Pr.B.* with the markedly different formulations of the 1949-1951 postulate sets, and inquires into the grounds for the difference. Part I seeks to cover maximum ground, in its application to the theory of the manifold analytic rubrics, by adhering to a pattern of widespread but brief sampling; Part II can only realize its objective by means of a more discursive mode of presentation. Part III adds a brief set of sum- marizing evaluations.

In general, the presentation presupposes familiarity with the material under analysis, and frequent reference, on the part of the reader, to the cited sources is desirable. The presentation is frankly evaluative in in- tent: Hull's writings are quoted or summarized only to an extent that makes evaluative analysis possible, and evaluative discussion is not par- celed into special sections, but is interlarded throughout the exposition.

There is a sense in which a distinction may be made between Hull's theory and *Hullian* theory. Certain of Hull's core hypotheses have re- ceived significant independent elaboration by such people as Spence, Miller, Dollard, Mowrer and others. It is entirely possible that Hull's future impact on the field may be registered primarily through the efforts of such workers. Nevertheless, consideration of the various brands of Hullian deviationism or neo-Hullianism is not within the province of this report.

Part I. The Theory of Principles of Behavior

A. HULL'S ORIENTATIVE ATTITUDES

Connected with the formulation of any empirical theory is a set of statements which talk about the theory. In an explicitly formalized theory, the statements which refer to the elements of the theory, rather than to whatever constitutes the objects of the theory, comprise the *metatheory* of the system in question. No theory can be constructed, interpreted, or applied without the specification of a metatheory. In unformalized, quasi-formalized, and partly formalized "theories," what- ever corresponds to metatheory becomes of very great importance, for such formulations must be understood largely as proposals for the con- struction of theories, rather than fully realized theories. Indeed, in most of the nonformal and incomplete "theories" characteristic of present psychology, the formulations consist mainly of statements ultimately rele- vant to the metatheory rather than the object-language of the projected "theory." It is thus essential, in any analysis of such "theories," to examine with care statements which the theorist makes about the aims of his "theory," the nature and level of the concepts he employs, the grounds for the selection of concepts, and principles, etc. Should the theorist proceed to the detailed development of any part of a projected "theory," it becomes critically important to compare this realized portion of the theoretical program with what the theorist has *said* about the proposed "theory." In this way, valuable information about the feasibility of the program, the potential fruitfulness of the theorist's orientative proposals, and even the degree of intellectual responsibility of the theorist, may be gained.

In this section, we itemize those of Hull's orientative attitudes which we believe to be of importance in characterizing the nature of his theoretical program. This itemization of orienting attitudes will make available a condensation of Hull's professed theoretical intentions which can be related to the discussion of specific aspects of the theory, later in the report. The characterizations of these orientative commitments are inferences based, so far as possible, on concrete metatheoretical statements made by Hull.

Getting the orienting attitudes of a theorist into focus demands that they be seen in relation to the influences which serve as the theorist's point of departure. For this reason, we attempt an initial delineation of Hull's more general orienting notions by examining (1) *his relation to the behaviorist tradition*. We then summarize more specific orienting commitments with respect to: (2) *formal characteristics of adequate theory*, (3) *level of descriptive and explanatory concepts*, and (4) *background considerations used as accessory criteria for hypothesis formation*.

1. Relations to Behaviorist Tradition

It is fashionable to label Hull a "neo-behaviorist." In order to understand his most general orientative ideas, it becomes necessary to determine wherein Hull is a "behaviorist," and wherein "neo."

The "classical" behaviorism of Watson, Weiss, Holt, etc., which achieved the peak of its influence in the mid-twenties, was itself little more than a set of orientative attitudes. Behaviorism was a vocal and energetic movement towards theory, but not a single behavioristic writer put forth a concrete theory, or even a particularly detailed program for theory. Individual early behaviorists were often far apart on concrete empirical issues. The core of the movement was a common set of orientative attitudes, the most prominent of which were the following.

1) *The insistence on inter-subjective (objective) techniques for securing and expressing empirical data*. This was held to be incompatible with the continued use of "introspective," "subjective," or "anthropomorphic" methods.

2) *The advocacy of stimulus and response variables as the only legitimate independent and dependent variables in which to express the re-*

sults of psychological research, and formulate theory. In line with this, the task of psychology was represented (by Watson and others) in some such way as "given the stimulus, to predict the response, and given the response, to infer the stimulus."

3) *The commitment to conditioned response principles, or some related form of S-R associationism, as the basic laws of learning.* In writers like Watson, this commitment went little further than the assertion that learning could be accounted for by *C.R.* principles, and the absence of an attempt to elaborate conditioning theory in a systematic or detailed way was conspicuous. Writers like Guthrie (by no means a *typical* early behaviorist) and Holt did carry out applications of associationistic principles to concrete learning phenomena, but their attempts were of an informal and exploratory character.

4) *A strong emphasis on "peripheral" determinants of behavior.* This emphasis is, of course, related to the *S-R* orientation, the plausibility of which behaviorists tried to buttress by showing how all effective behavior determinants and processes could be gotten into *S-R* terms. Thus we find the peripheral or motor theory of thinking, the preoccupation with the explanatory possibilities of proprioceptive and internal stimulus factors, and the general devaluation of the importance of central processes —all characteristic of early behaviorism. It is not unfair to note a certain coherence between the behavioristic insistence on "objective" methods and the stress on peripheral theorizing.

5) *An emphasis on extreme environmentalism.*

Hull operates within the general frame of reference defined by the first four behavioristic orientative attitudes. He is: (1) an objectivist, (2) an *S-R* theorist, (3) a user of *C.R.* principles, and (4) a peripheralist —but he holds and applies all these attitudes with a *difference.*[2] Hull is not at all coy about explicitly pointing up these differences. As early as 1930, in the second article devoted to the exposition of his theory, Hull wrote:

Perhaps no theorists have been more naive in their attempts at system construction than those who seek in the principles of stimulus-response the main explanation of those forms of behavior called mental. It may even be that, thus far, none have failed much worse in achieving the solid substance of genuine

---

[2] The degree of a theorist's "environmentalism" is a tenuous (and rather futile) thing to measure, but it is safe to say that Hull recognizes the efficacy of innate behavior determinants to a greater degree than writers like Watson and Holt. Hull has stated: "There is much reason to believe . . . that even if organisms could be subjected to identical environmental conditions from the moment of conception, great differences would still be displayed in the behavior of different species as a whole and in the behavior of the individual organisms of each species. Such differences must presumably be regarded as dependent upon, i.e., derived from, differences in the innate or original nature and constitution of the individual organism. We shall accordingly call them *innate* differences" (59, p. 56).

explanation. Even so, the author has considerable confidence in the possibilities of this point of view (28, pp. 242-243).

Perhaps the single most general difference between Hull's approach and that of classical behaviorism is implied in the above quotation (and related passages in the same article). Hull is self-consciously setting himself within the behaviorist framework. Yet he is sharply criticizing earlier behaviorism for its failure to exploit this point of view in a systematic and detailed way. In its most general sense, the "neo" part of Hull's "neo-behaviorism" is based on his firm intention to assume intellectual responsibility for developing the orienting principles of behaviorism by means of detailed hypothetico-deductive procedures. The strength of Hull's conviction is indicated by the fervor with which he advertises the merits of strict postulational procedures not only in this early article, but in virtually every one of his subsequent theoretical publications.

We will now outline certain of the more specific contrasts between Hull's approach and the several orientative attitudes of earlier behaviorism from which his approach stems.

a. Objectivism. The objectivism of early behaviorism was partly a methodological, partly a metaphysical thesis. Methodologically, the behaviorists' insistence on "objective observation" seemed motivated mainly by the aim to insure inter-subjective definition and application of psychological concepts. This methodological proposal was in certain conspicuous cases presented along with a denial of the "existence of consciousness."

Hull explicitly rejects the metaphysical component of the thesis. In *Mind, Mechanism and Adaptive Behavior,* he writes:

What, then, shall we say about consciousness? Is its existence denied? By no means. But to recognize the existence of a phenomenon is not the same thing as insisting upon its basic, i.e., logical, priority. Instead of furnishing a means for the solution of problems, consciousness appears to be itself a problem needing solution (42, p. 30).

Hull's *methodological* objectivism is, on the other hand, compatible with the methodological aspect of the early behavioristic thesis, but it is developed more sharply. Early behaviorism was concerned mainly with guaranteeing the inter-subjectivity of the descriptive (first-order) concepts used to express empirical data in psychology. It was implicitly committed to what we can now characterize as some form of the "physical thing language," as a reduction basis for psychological statements. Hull, too, is committed, by declared intention, to a physicalism in this sense, but Hull, with his more sophisticated conception of theory, and his more explicit use of intervening variables, has taken greater pains to trace out the consequences of objectivism at the level of explanatory theory. His major concern, in this connection, is to point out the danger in the use of intervening variables which are not "securely anchored" by explicit functional relationships to antecedent independent, and consequent dependent, variables. For instance, in *Pr.B.*, he states:

This surreptitious substitution and acceptance of one's knowledge of what needs to be done in a biological emergency for a theoretical deduction is the essence of what we shall call *anthropomorphism*, or the *subjective*, in behavior theory. . . . The only known cure for this unfortunate tendency to which all men are more or less subject is a grim and inflexible insistence that all deductions take place according to the explicitly formulated rules stating the functional relationships of A to X and of X to B. This latter is the essence of the scientifically *objective* (56, p. 24; Cf. also pp. 23-28, and the 2nd note, p. 30).

b. *S-R* orientation. Hull is, of course, committed to the use of stimulus and response terms as the basic conceptual units for the designation of the independent and dependent variables of his theory. So were early behaviorists. But from this point on, a number of differences arise.

(*a*) Classical behaviorists were notoriously vague about their conception of theory, and insensitive to the nature of the theoretical procedures either embodied in or implied by their own theoretical efforts. For instance, in writers like Watson, it is difficult to tell whether the intention is to proceed in terms of direct *S-R* correlations, or to admit mediating concepts of the sort that we now call intervening variables. Whatever the intention, there is good evidence to suggest that certain intervening variables are implied in Watson's formulations (e.g., "reflex connections," hypothetical proprioceptive stimulus factors, etc.). Insofar as early behaviorists acknowledged or presupposed intervening variables, however, they tended to be few in number and to *represent either inferred stimulus factors, or factors uniquely determined by independent "stimulus" variables.*

Hull, on the other hand, has explicitly introduced a complex array of intervening variables, certain of which are not uniquely determined by independent variables having the nature of a stimulus. Notable among these is the intervening variable of "drive" (D), to which Hull, in *Pr.B.* attributed a "sensitizing" or "energizing" function, in addition to the "persisting stimulus" role formerly assigned to this concept (56, pp. 226-257). Since D, at least partly by virtue of its general energizing function, is assumed to combine multiplicatively with habit strength ($_sH_R$) in the determination of a pivotal intervening variable, reaction potential ($_sE_R$), and since a number of subsequent links in the lengthy intervening variable chain between $_sE_R$ and final response are partly determined by $_sE_R$, it is clear that this non-stimulus determined variable plays an important role in the theory. Another intervening variable which does not seem uniquely determined by antecedent stimulus factors is "reactive inhibition" (I_R). This is conceived as a "primary negative drive" generated by the occurrence of a reaction, and having among its antecedent independent variable conditions, the "work (W) involved in the execution of the response" (56, p. 300). It should be emphasized that the presence of such constructs in Hull's theory constitutes one of the more significant deviations from the traditional behaviorist framework, and even from the earlier (pre-1943) forms of Hull's own theory.

(b) It has become a truism to observe that early behaviorists were systematically ambiguous in their definitions and applications of the concepts "stimulus" and "response." The term "stimulus" was indiscriminately applied to states of affairs ranging from the physical energy change acting on a single receptor to the behavior-evoking effect of a complex social situation, while "response" could designate anything from the contraction of a single muscle cell, to the name of a class of end results brought about by a widely varying range of movement sequences. In his earlier publications, Hull showed an almost comparable indiscriminateness in his use of stimulus and response concepts, but he seemed sensitive to the nature and magnitude of the problems (e.g., 43, p. 219). In any case, unlike earlier behaviorists, Hull has made an explicit attempt to cope with so-called problems of "stimulus equivalence" (47, 50, 56, 60, 63, 67), and (to a lesser extent) "response equivalence" (34, 35). We reserve evaluation of the success of these attempts for later parts of this report.

c. Use of C.R. principles. One of the sharpest contrasts between Hull and early behaviorism may be found in Hull's use of *C.R.* principles. His attitude toward the utility of *C.R.* principles is also of critical significance for delineating the empirical area which Hull feels to be most fruitful in providing inductive materials for the construction of behavior theory.

Differences in Hull's approach to *C.R.* materials and that of earlier behaviorists like Watson may be summarily stated as follows.

(a) Unlike earlier behaviorists, Hull is not in any direct and literal sense a *C.R.* theorist. For Hull, the basic conditions under which learning takes place are not adequately characterized by the principle of conditioning in its Pavlovian form, or indeed any variant form which regards contiguous association of stimulus and response to be a sufficient condition for the occurrence of learning. Rather, Hull feels that the Pavlovian theory of conditioning represents a special case of a principle which, since 1937,[3] has represented the central postulate of his theory—the so-called

---

[3] In early theoretical articles Hull had tended to rely on a principle of "conditioning" or "redintegration" as his primary learning assumption. He first gave evidence of veering towards a "law of effect" position in a review of Thorndike's *Fundamentals of Learning*, published in 1935 (41). The first formal appearance of a principle of reinforcement in a published postulate set appears in 1937 as "postulate 2" of the *Mind, Mechanism and Adaptive Behavior* system (42, p. 16). This postulate was there designated the principle of "positive association," but it makes association contingent on a "reinforcing state of affairs."

"principle of reinforcement." The principle of reinforcement, in turn, represents an objectively retranslated and pseudo-quantitative form of Thorndike's "Law of Effect." In the 1937 miniature formalization of his theory appearing in *Mind, Mechanism and Adaptive Behavior* (42, pp. 17-18), Hull included a "derivation" purporting to show that the Pavlovian *C.R.* was a special case of the law of reinforcement, and his position did not change.

If the *C.R.* is a special case of the law of effect, Hull can then assume that many of the detailed relationships which hold for *C.R.* situations, must also hold for "law of effect" learning situations. Observing that the experimental situation used in *C.R.* work tends to approximate conditions of ideal simplicity, Hull feels that it is fruitful "to combine Thorndike's sounder empirical generalization with the numerous behavioral laws discovered by the economical *C.R.* mode of experimentation" for the development of a comprehensive theory.

(b) It should be clear, then, that for Hull, the empirical generalizations arising from *C.R.* research are of the first importance in providing the raw materials for the postulates of behavior theory. But such generalizations do not function directly, or in an unaltered form, as postulates. Thus, a second contrast arises between the way Hull and earlier behaviorists utilized *C.R.* principles. Insofar as earlier behaviorists tended to use *C.R.* principles in concrete explanatory contexts, there was no thoroughgoing attempt to translate such principles into the system language of a theory. Hull, on the other hand, translates whatever *C.R.* generalizations he uses into the constructs of his system.

(c) Earlier behaviorists were content to use *C.R.* principles in the *qualitative* form in which (for the most part) they arose out of Pavlovian and later research. From his earliest articles on, however, Hull advertised the intention to work towards *quantitative* behavior theory. In line with this, he advocated and applied the procedure of fitting empirical equations to data deriving from conditioning and other types of learning situations.

d. Peripheralism. The peripheralism of earlier behavioristic writers was a major emphasis, manifested by a general tendency to retranslate various classes of phenomena traditionally regarded as "mental," or intimately related to the operation of higher levels of the central nervous system, into "motor," "muscular," and more directly, "kinesthetic" terms. In this way, the roles of possible peripheral mechanisms in the mediation of thinking, imaginal processes, set and attending, emotional behavior, etc. were more or less casually explored. Such analyses were presented in a speculative way, and were not supported by systematic and detailed explorations of the explanatory potentialities of the concepts put forward. One of Hull's central interests was in elaborating the explanatory possibilities of such peripheral mechanisms, in a more concrete way than did his behaviorist predecessors. Accordingly, Hull has deductively explored the possible roles of such conceptual mechanisms as "proprioceptive stimulation," "the drive stimulus" (S_D), and the "fractional anticipatory goal response" (r_G) in the mediation of a wide range of behavior phenomena (e.g., 29, 30, 31, 34, 35, 38, 44, 56). Indeed, the attempt to tease out the possible roles of such mechanisms in the chaining of response sequences, behavioral "short circuiting," "foresight," various forms of "insight," etc., has perhaps been one of Hull's major contributions to the field.

The strength of Hull's predilection for peripheralism seems generally reflected in his writing by a tendency to keep out of the brain everything that he can possibly get into the afferent or efferent segments of the nervous system. Thus, when in 1943, he made provision in his system for the hypothetical process of "neural interaction," he insisted on naming the relevant principle, *"afferent neural interaction."* It is clear, from his discussion of this postulate in the text of *Pr.B.* (56, pp. 42-44; 48-49), that he grants the possibility of such interaction taking place in the cortex, but it seems equally clear in the same discussion that his preference is for such events taking place "in the end organ itself" or "in nuclei lying between the end organ and the brain" (p. 43).

The preceding discussion of Hull's relation to the behaviorist tradition should serve to define the main coordinates of his system of orientative attitudes. To complete the picture, it is now necessary to summarize certain more specific orientative commitments.

2. Formal Characteristics of Adequate Theory

Hull's advocacy of the use in psychology of precise, hypothetico-deductive theoretical techniques has already been noted. But the fervor of the attitudes underlying this objective must be appreciated, if we are to assess adequately the direction of Hull's theoretical efforts, as they developed over the years. Evaluation of Hull's *application* of hypothetico-deductive methods is reseved for a later section of the report. The purpose here is to spell out certain features of the attitudinal orientation towards method, which has determined the development of Hull's theory.

In virtually *every one* of his theoretical publications, Hull felt compelled to include general discussion of the nature of scientific theory, and to lay down corresponding prescriptions for the construction of adequate psychological theory. These discussions have varied in extent, from a few scattered paragraphs (e.g., 28, 29, 30, 34, 38, 44), to detailed analyses of the nature of theory (42, 51, 56).

In his second theoretical article, *Simple Trial and Error Learning* (28), references to theoretical method reveal a number of emphases which reappear, as a kind of obsessive *leit-motif*, in subsequent theoretical publications. These emphases are somewhat as follows.

(a) Legitimate scientific explanation requires the detailed deduction of a "phenomenon" from a set of explicit and unambiguous postulates and definitions.

(b) The capacity of a theory to generate *novel* (i.e., previously unformulated) empirical relationships is a particularly significant measure of its fruitfulness (and even, apparently, its probability value).

(c) Ambiguous, insufficiently explicit, or inadequately stated hypotheses cannot be subjected to determinate experimental test.

(d) Theoretical methods of a precise order can already be used in psychology. (By way of demonstrating this, Hull then puts forward the set of theoretical deductions—at one or another level of specificity and formality—which comprises the main substance of the given publication.)

(e) Theorists of supposedly opposing viewpoints must face the responsibility of showing, in detail, how their own postulates can generate deductions similar to those presented by Hull. If they cannot make determinate derivations from their principles, then they have no theory. If they can perform similar deductions, then to this extent their theories are in agreement with Hull's. If certain of the deductions from the opposing sets of principles are in conflict, then the matter should be resolved in the laboratory.

In the earlier phases of his career as theorist, Hull seemed to be gearing his concrete theoretical efforts to relatively modest objectives. In each of the theoretical articles preceding 1935, Hull explored the consequences of a limited group of tentatively formulated hypotheses. Such hypotheses were stated *qualitatively* and certain of their more important consequences were informally "derived" by a more or less closely reasoned indication of the steps connecting "deductions" with their premises. Nevertheless, the drive toward rigorous formalization and quantification was revealed, even during this period, by frequent comments occurring in the embedding material accompanying the various theoretical analyses.

The second phase in the quest for hypothetico-deductive rigor came into evidence with the publication of the "miniature systems" on *rote learning* in 1935 (39), and *adaptive behavior* in 1937 (42). These "systems" represent crude qualitative formalizations, patterned more or less vaguely on the model of geometry. In each case, a set of verbally stated postulates and definitions are given, and brief theorem sequences are derived, the major steps of the derivations being recorded in greater detail than in the case of the earlier, less formal publications. However, even in the 1935 article which presents the rote learning system, Hull is clearly not satisfied with *non-quantitative* formalization. He writes:

At present . . . the superficial appearance of the concepts regarding learning which are current among our theorists does not suggest ready mathematical treatment. And while this condition is probably more apparent than real, it seems to raise the important question as to whether rigorous logical deductions can be made on the basis of such quasi-mathematical concepts as have so far emerged from behavior experiments (39, p. 498).

By 1939, the "condition" referred to in the above passage is no longer even "apparent." In this year, Hull *et al.* published *Mathematico-Deductive Theory of Rote Learning* (51). This most elaborate of Hull's attempts at formalization puts forward 18 postulates, and the derivations of a large number of theorems in *both* mathematical and verbal form. In addition, the 86 definitions are stated alternately in English, and symbolic logic, and symbolic logical equivalents for the postulates are also given. *From this point on, the preoccupation with quantification becomes the dominant factor in Hull's theoretical work.* By 1943, Hull felt it possible to put forward, in *Pr.B.*, a tentative postulate set for a *comprehensive* theory of behavior, the major postulates of which were formulated in (presumably) quantitative terms. Since much of the "quantitative" material in that work was admittedly *illustrative,* Hull devoted most of his effort from 1943 to his death in 1952, to an attempt to achieve genuine quantification. The results of these endeavors are registered in the revised postulate sets of 1949-1951 (68, 69, 70, 75).

3. Level of Descriptive and Explanatory Concepts

In this section, we ask questions concerning the "level of analysis" to which the conceptual elements of Hull's theory are geared. With regard to a psychological theory, at least two types of questions concerning "level of analysis" may be raised.

(a) What is the level of the elements of the theory, as defined by membership in the language system of one or another of the extant sciences which are believed to concern different "levels" of the same subject matter (e.g., physiology, bio-chemistry, physics)?

(b) What is the "level" of the elements of a theory, as defined by the "specificity-generality" or "fineness-coarseness" of the variables designated by those elements, *within* the scientific language system to which they belong?

It should be clear that discussions of whether a psychological theory (or theorist) is "behavioral" or "physiological," "molecular" or "molar," tend frequently to confuse (a) and (b). It is also evident that such discussions are often further confused by failure to recognize that different elements of the theory may (and usually do) belong to quite different scientific language systems, while two or more elements at the same linguistic level may vary quite widely in "specificity."

In order to avoid complex and extended analysis at this place, we will let Hull speak for himself:

Students of the social sciences are presented with the dilemma of waiting until the physico-chemical problems of neurophysiology have been adequately solved before beginning the elaboration of behavior theory, or of proceeding in a provisional manner with certain reasonably stable principles of the coarse, macroscopic or molar action of the nervous system whereby movements are evoked by stimuli, particularly as related to the history of the individual organism.

There can hardly be any doubt that a theory of molar behavior founded upon an adequate knowledge of both molecular and molar principles would in general be more satisfactory than one founded upon molar considerations alone. But here again the history of physical science is suggestive. Owing to the fact that Galileo and Newton carried out their molar investigations, the world has had the use of a theory which was in very close approximation to observations at the molar level for nearly three hundred years before the development of the molecular science of modern relativity and quantum theory. . . . It is conceivable that the elaboration of a systematic science of behavior at a molar level may aid in the development of an adequate neurophysiology and thus lead in the end to a truly molecular theory of behavior firmly based on physiology.

It happens that a goodly number of quasi-neurological principles have now been determined by careful experiments designed to trace out the relationship of the molar behavior of organisms, usually as integrated wholes, to well-controlled stimulus situations. Many of the more promising of these principles were roughly isolated in the first instance by the Russian physiologist, Pavlov, and his pupils. . . . Because of the pressing nature of behavior problems, both practical and theoretical aspects of behavior science are, upon the whole, being developed according to the second of the two alternatives outlined above. For these reasons the molar approach is employed in the present work.

In this connection it is to be noted carefully that the *alternatives of microscopic versus macroscopic and molecular versus molar, are relative rather than absolute.* In short, there are degrees of the molar, depending on the coarseness of the ultimate causal segments or units dealt with. Other things equal, it would seem wisest to keep the causal segments small, to approach the molecular, the fine and exact substructural details, just as closely as the knowledge of that substructure renders possible. There is much reason to believe that the seeming disagreements among current students of behavior may be largely due to the difference in the degree of the molar at which the several investigators are working (56, pp. 20-21).

The above passages represent Hull's answers to the two questions which we distinguished concerning level of analysis. His replies are Pickwickian to say the least.

To query (a), he answers that the elements of his theory belong to the language of "a systematic science of behavior at a molar level." However, his theory is apparently based on "a goodly number of *quasi-neurological* principles" [italics mine], whatever that means.

To query (b), Hull answers that the "ultimate causal segments" discriminated by his theory are to be kept "small." They are "to approach the molecular, the fine and exact substructural details, just as closely as the knowledge of that substructure renders possible." However, Hull seems to be assuming that the degree of "fineness" or "exactness" of the elements of a behavior theory is identical with, or varies directly with, closeness or fidelity to "substructural" or "molecular" detail, such detail corresponding, no doubt, to neurophysiological subject matter. Such an assumption does not seem reasonable.

Hull's views on the level of analysis at which he approaches his subject matter, insofar as they can be given meaning, should be borne in mind during the examination of his theory. In the light of the indeterminacy of these views, it should not be surprising that a systematic ambiguity has long seemed apparent with respect to the behavioral versus physiological level, and the reality status, of certain of the Hullian concepts. This question will be pursued further, later in the report.

4. Background Considerations Used as Accessory Criteria for Hypothesis Formation

Here it is appropriate to make reference to a background factor in Hull's thinking which has played a role in determining the nature of his theory. This is Hull's constant preoccupation with the conditions of biological adaptation and organismic survival. Such considerations of "adaptive dynamics" seem to have guided the choice of hypotheses throughout the development of the theory.

Hull's emphasis on the necessity of choosing postulates in accordance with their potentialities for mediating deductions of the "adaptive" characteristics of behavior, has been so persistent that some of his readers have been led to believe the concept of "biological adaptation" (and related concepts) to be an integral element of his system. To such an interpretation, Hull has made the following rejoinder (56, p. 66):

The emphasis . . . on the general significance of organic evolution in adapting organisms to meet critical biological emergencies calls for a word of comment. . . . It is the view of the author that adaptive considerations are useful in making a preliminary survey in the search for postulates, but that once the postulates have been selected they must stand on their own feet. This means that once chosen, postulates or principles of behavior must be able to yield deductions in agreement with observed detailed phenomena of behavior; and, failing this, that no amount of *a priori* general adaptive plausibility will save such a postulate from being abandoned.

The importance of the role played by Hull's Darwinianism, is indicated by the following characterization of the *task* of behavior science:

It is the primary task of a molar science of behavior to isolate the basic laws or rules according to which various combinations of stimulation, arising from the state of need on the one hand and the state of the environment on the other, bring about the kind of behavior characteristic of different organisms. A closely related task is to understand why the behavior so mediated is so generally adaptive, i.e., successful in the sense of reducing needs and facilitating survival, and why it is unsuccessful on those occasions when survival is not facilitated (56, p. 19).

In general, Hull has not tended to be a "model" theorist in any explicit or conspicuous sense. Yet, his "adaptive dynamics" criterion of hypothesis selection has tended to perform very much the same role in his thinking as do detailed models in the case of other theorists. Indeed, this criterion serves as the basis of a device which figures prominently in Hull's thinking and which possesses certain of the properties of more formal models. Hull describes this "device" as follows:

A device much employed by the author has proved itself to be a far more effective prophylaxis. This is to regard, from time to time, the behaving organism as a completely self-maintaining robot, constructed of materials as unlike ourselves as may be. In doing this it is not necessary to attempt the solution of the detailed engineering problems connected with the design of such a creature. It is a wholesome and revealing exercise, however, to consider the various problems in behavior dynamics which must be solved in the design of a truly self-maintaining robot (56, p. 27).

The above is the only *published* reference to the Hullian robot which the writer has seen. There is additional evidence, though, that the device played an important heuristic role in Hull's thinking. In about 1941-1942, the writer read a pre-publication draft of *Pr.B.* which had the robot frolicking about through the course of an entire chapter. A series of questions were asked with regard to what conditions the design of a robot would have to satisfy, for various types of behavioral adaptation to occur.

5. Summary of Principal Orientative Commitments

Neglecting certain of the indeterminacies in Hull's statements of objectives, we may reconstruct, from the preceding discussion, the following summary profile of Hull's orientative attitudes.

(a) Hull seeks to construct a "molar science of behavior," the primary task of which is to "isolate the basic laws or rules according to which various combinations of stimulation, arising from the state of need on the one hand and the state of the environment on the other, bring about the kind of behavior characteristic of different organisms."

(b) These laws are to be inter-subjectively stated and validated.

(c) Insofar as possible, "peripheral" behavior determinants are to be employed. The independent and dependent variables are to be expressible mainly in "stimulus" and "response" terms, while the intervening variables may or may not be uniquely determined by antecedent *stimulus* variables.

(d) The inductive basis of these laws is to consist of the empirical generalizations arising from "law of effect" and conditioned response experimentation. Such empirical generalizations are to be translated into the terms of a systematic behavior theory language, and are to be quantified in terms of empirical curve-fitting procedures.

(e) Principles constructed in the above ways are to function as formal postulates, and the major phenomena of organismic behavior are to be derived as theorems by rigorous logical and mathematical techniques. The postulates are to be formulated, at the earliest date possible, as fully quantified mathematical equations.

(f) Terms of the systematic behavior theory referred to in (d), are to be defined at a "molar behavioral" level, but they are to do justice to neurophysiological events, as thoroughly as knowledge permits.

(g) Initial selection of postulates is to be guided by preliminary considerations about the extent to which they seem compatible with the requirements of biological adaptation. The system is to be validated in terms of its success in mediating correct deductions concerning *both* adaptive and maladaptive forms of behavior.

B. STRUCTURE OF THE THEORY

In this section, we will attempt analytic characterization of the theory of *Pr.B.* The structure of this theory is, of course, defined by the postulates, definitions, and textual elucidations of concepts put forward in *Pr.B.* Our intention is *not* expository; it will be assumed that *Pr.B.* or some detailed summary of its postulates (21, 53, 86), is either available, or known to the reader. Rather, the intention is to *abstract* from the postulates and textual embedding materials the major classes of components constitutive of the theory, and examine the methodological status of each. In particular, we will be concerned with evaluating the adequacy of these components in the light of Hull's theoretical intentions. This we proceed to do under the following rubrics: (1) *data language*, (2) *independent and dependent variables*, (3) *intervening variables* and (4) *construct interrelations*.

1. Data Language

Since all empirical definitions of a theory are constructed from a linguistic base that may be called the "data language" of the theory in question, it is well to begin the analysis of Hull's theory by a consideration of his data language. The properties of the theorist's data language may provide valuable clues with regard to the status of the theory. If, for instance, characteristic inadequacies in the use of data language are demonstrable, these must contaminate all empirical (operational) definitions of the theory, and a corresponding limitation is thereby imposed on the significance of all statements made by the theory.

There are two senses in which one may raise questions as to the "data language" of a theory.

(1) One may seek to determine the characteristics of the *immediate data language* in which empirical or operational definitions of theoretical terms are put forward, and against which primitive and derived statements of the theory are compared (observation records).

(2) One may ask questions concerning the proposed or implied *epistemic reduction basis* of the terms of the theory. In this event, one is concerned with a logical reconstruction of the characteristics of the "ultimate" confirmation language (i.e., protocol language) to which all proper statements of the theory are, in principle, reducible.

The empirical definition of terms in a scientific theory is almost never carried to its epistemic reduction basis. Such a procedure would be hopelessly cumbersome, and, for most practical purposes, unnecessary. The practice, rather, is to reduce the term to statements which can be assumed to have the same, unambiguous meaning for all individuals to whom the definition is addressed. In practice, this generally means reduction to statements which are still highly remote from the final reduction basis of the term in question. There are no explicit pragmatic rules for determining at what "level" of reduction does precision of reference become assured for a given audience, but certain obvious inferences about this can be made from the character of the *immediate data language* relative to whatever consensus of language habits exists among the investigators in a given field at a given time. For these reasons, we will concern ourselves primarily with (a) Hull's *immediate data language*. We supplement this with brief consideration of (b) the *epistemic reduction basis* of Hull's theoretical terms.

a. Hull's immediate data language. Immediate data language tends to appear in two contexts in connection with an empirical system: (1) in statements which are explicitly intended to provide operational definitions of terms in the theory language, and (2) in descriptions of experimental conditions, observations, and the results of statistical or mathematical transformations of observations which the theorist is relating in some way to the construct language of the theory. *In Pr.B. no formal operational definitions are given.* The empirical reference of theoretical terms is either informally indicated in the textual discussion, or left to be inferred from use. In later discussion of the mode of definition of theoretical variables, we will have occasion to deal extensively with such informal operational definition. Here, it will be instructive to consider some characteristic examples of Hull's usage of immediate data language in connection with the description of experimental materials (type 2 above). We begin with two exhibits from *Pr.B.*

The first exhibit is of particular interest, because Hull is here introducing a detailed description of a "demonstration experiment" in order to explain the workings of the basic principle of the theory—"primary reinforcement." Thus the use of data language is especially self-conscious and detailed. It reads (p. 70 [4]):

Demonstration Experiment A. The laboratory in which the experiment is performed is without windows and its walls are painted black; this gives the room an appearance of being rather dimly illuminated, though in fact it is not. On a table rests a black wooden apparatus about two feet long, a foot wide, and a foot high. It has a hinged glass lid which permits clear observation of the interior. The floor of the box consists of small transverse rods of stainless steel placed about a quarter inch apart. Midway between the two ends of the box is a partition consisting of the same type of metal rods similarly arranged but placed vertically. This partition or barrier reaches to within about four inches of the lid. A two-throw electric switch permits the charging of the floor rods of either compartment and of the partition with a weak alternating current.

On a second table nearby there rests a wire cage containing a sleek and lively albino rat about one hundred days of age. The laboratory technician opens the lid of the cage and the rat at once stands up on its hind legs with its head and forepaws outside the aperture. The technician grasps the rat about the middle with his bare hand and transfers it to one of the compartments of the apparatus. The animal, after a brief pause, begins moving about the compartment, sniffing and inspecting the various parts, often stretching up on its hind legs to its full length against the walls of the box.

After some minutes the technician throws the switch which charges both the partition and the grid upon which the rat is standing. The animal's behavior changes at once; in place of the deliberate exploratory movements it now displays an exaggeratedly mincing mode of locomotion about the compartment interspersed with occasional slight squeaks, biting of the bars which are shocking its feet, defecation, urination, and leaps up the walls. These reactions are repeated in various orders and in various parts of the compartment; sometimes the same act occurs several times in succession, sometimes not. After five or six minutes of this variable behavior one of the leaps carries the animal over the barrier upon the uncharged grid of the second compartment. Here after an interval of quiescence and heavy breathing the animal cautiously resumes exploratory behavior, much as in the first compartment. Ten minutes after the first leap of the barrier the second grid is charged and the animal goes through substantially the same type of variable behavior as before. This finally results in a second leaping of the barrier and ten minutes more of safety, after which this grid is again charged, and so on. In this way the animal is given fifteen trials, each terminated by a leap over the barrier.

The second exhibit is characteristic of the many brief descriptions of experiments which are scattered through the theoretical discussions of *Pr.B.* It runs (pp. 226-229):

In the present context we are fortunate in having an excellent empirical study which shows the functional dependence of the persistence of food-seeking behavior jointly on (1) the number of reinforcements of the habit in question, and (2) the number of hours of food privation. Perin . . . and Williams . . . trained albino rats on a simple bar-pressing habit of the Skinner type . . . giving

---

[4] Throughout the remainder of Part I, all quotations from *Pr.B.* will be identified in terms of page number only. The bibliographic index number will be omitted.

separate groups different numbers of reinforcements varying from 5 to 90 under a standard 23 hours' hunger. Later the groups were subdivided and subjected to experimental extinction with the amount of food privation varying from 3 to 22 hours.

The gross outcome of this experiment is shown in Fig. 48, where the height of each column represents the relative mean number of unreinforced reactions performed by each group before experimental extinction yielded a five-minute pause between successive bar pressures. The positions of the twelve columns on the base shows clearly the number of reinforcements and the number of hours' food privation which produced each. It is evident from an examination of this figure that *both* the number of reinforcements and the number of hours of food privation are potent factors in determining resistance to experimental extinction. Moreover, it is clear that for any given amount of food privation, e.g., 3 or 22 hours, the different numbers of reinforcements yield a close approximation to a typical positive growth function. On the other hand, it is equally clear that for a given number of reinforcements, e.g., 16, the number of hours of food privation has an almost linear functional relationship to the resistance to experimental extinction.

It is evident from these two exhibits that the "data language" consists of a heterogeneous set of expressions, conforming to the rules of English syntax. The expressions derive from everyday discourse, and from a variety of scientific languages, including physics, mathematics, biology, and psychology. In general, the *psychological* expressions are restricted to terms which derive from a type of uncodified psychological vocabulary more or less common to experimental psychologists (e.g., "reaction," "habit," "bar-pressing habit," "extinction," "learning curves," "threshold"). There are several intrusions of a term from the construct language —"reinforcements"—in the data language of the second exhibit. There is also an occurrence in the first exhibit of a term—"inspecting"—which some investigators may find difficult to apply in a consistent way. In general, though, the data language is such as to satisfy reasonable standards of inter-subjective applicability, and differs in no significant way from the language of any psychological writer when making sense in a theoretically neutral context. When the two above exhibits are supplemented by reference to the data language of Hull's published experimental reports (and those of his students), the same properties are in evidence—except, perhaps, for a greater frequency and range of construct language intrusions.

As soon as we inquire, however, into the *theoretical use* which is made of such apparently innocuous data language expressions, patent difficulties arise. Consider the first exhibit. The purpose of this passage is to demonstrate the operation of the fundamental "law" of primary reinforcement. This law, in the form given in the ensuing discussion in *Pr.B.* (p. 71), states the conditions under which "an afferent receptor impulse ($\dot{s}$) resulting from the impact . . . of a stimulus energy ($\dot{S}$)" comes to evoke a "reaction (R)."

The transition from the demonstration experiment of the first exhibit to this "law" is mediated by the following passage (p. 71):

It is evident from the foregoing that the final successful competition of the reaction of leaping the barrier (R_4) with the various futile reactions of the series such as leaping against the wooden walls of the apparatus (R_1), squeaking (R_2), and biting the floor bars (R_3) must have resulted, in part at least, from a differential strengthening of R_4. It is also evident that each of these competing reactions was originally evoked by the slightly injurious effects of the current on the animal's feet (the condition of need or drive, D) in conjunction with the stimulation (visual, cutaneous, etc.) arising from the apparatus at about the time that the reaction took place. The stimulation arising from the apparatus at the time of the respective reactions needs to be designated specifically: leaping against the wall will be represented by S_A; squeaking, by $S_{A'}$; biting, by $S_{A''}$; and leaping the barrier, by $S_{A'''}$. It is assumed that preceding the learning, the leaping of the barrier was evoked by a compound connection between the receptor discharges s_D and s_A, arising from S_D and S_A respectively, and R_4; i.e., R_4 must have been evoked jointly by the converging connections, $s_D \rightarrow R_4$ and $s_{A'''} \rightarrow R_4$. These are the connections which evidently have been strengthened or reinforced. Because of this, learning is said to be a procss of *reinforcement*.

Note carefully how the various elements of the data language are placed into correspondence with terms in the theory language. R_1 is ordered to "leaping against the . . . walls of the apparatus," R_2 to "squeaking," R_3 to "biting the floor bars," and R_4 to "leaping the barrier." If we now inquire what the construct R means in Hull's *theory language*, we nowhere find an adequately detailed or consistent definition. We are, however, told, in the glossary (p. 406) that "$R = . . .$ reaction or response in general (muscular, glandular, electrical)." We are also informed (p. 25) that, "Our usual thoughtless custom is to speak of cycles of behavior by merely naming their outcome, effect or end result, and practically to ignore the various movements which brought this terminal state about," and that (p. 25) "an ideally adequate theory . . . ought . . . to begin with colorless movement and mere receptor impulses as such." Thus, Hull is here making very inflated theoretical capital out of his data language materials. R_1, R_2, R_3, and R_4 are clearly being identified in terms of "outcome," "effect," or "end result," *and the data language observation records are being placed in correspondence with the construct R in a way which plainly violates the rules of the theory.*

The situation grows worse when we turn to the application of the stimulus (S) and receptor impulse (s) constructs. S is defined, in the first instance, as "stimulus energy in general, e.g., the energy of sound, light, or heat waves, pressure, etc." (p. 407); s is the "afferent neural impulse resulting from the action of a stimulus energy on a receptor" (p. 407). Also, in postulate 1 which formally introduces these constructs into the theory, S is identified as a "stimulus energy" which "impinges on a suitable receptor organ," and s as the resulting "afferent neural impulse . . . propagated along connected fibrous branches of nerve cells in the general direction of the effector organs, via the brain" (p. 47). But, in the case of the first exhibit, S corresponds to whatever stimulation arises "from the apparatus *at the time of the respective reactions*" [ital. mine]. In other words, S is being identified by *reference to response*, according to some such tacit criterion as "any part of the environment, discriminated by the experimenter, which impinges on the organism simultaneously with the occurrence of R." The various S's are certainly *not* being specified in terms of *independent physical energy criteria*. As for s, its use in the quoted passage represents a supererogatory addition to S, on the apparent assumption that whenever an S is, in some way, identified, it is legitimate to interpolate a corresponding s.

Such discrepancies between the data language *realizations* of stimulus and response variables, and the *definitions* of these variables in the construct language of the theory are almost ubiquitous in Hull's writings. The effect is to produce a systematic ambiguity in the basic independent and dependent variables (S and R) of the theory. Such an ambiguity in the terminal empirical constructs of the theory must necessarily ramify into every postulate. We will have occasion to discuss further indeterminacies in Hull's S and R variables, later in the report.

Considering, now, the theoretical exploitation made of the substance of the second exhibit, we run into another far reaching inadequacy in the relations between Hull's data language and his theory language. The second exhibit consists of a very brief paraphrase of the procedures and results of the Perin (103) experiment. If we neglect the forgivable intrusion of "number of reinforcements" as an equivalent for some such expression as "number of rewarded training trials," the exposition is in careful, theoretically neutral terms (e.g., "persistence of food seeking behavior," "number of hours of food privation," etc.). Nevertheless, a few pages after the introduction of the Perin experiment, in a discussion of "primary motivational concepts" we find Hull saying (p. 239):

> Turning now to the concept of reaction-evocation potentiality, we find, thanks to Perin's investigation sketched above . . . that we are able *at once* to define $_sE_R$ as the product of a function of habit strength ($_sH_R$) multiplied by a function of the relevant drive (D) [ital. mine].

In other words, what Hull has *"at once"* done is to set three *data language expressions* which designate the experimental variables whose relations are investigated in the Perin study, into correspondence with three theoretical constructs. The "number of reinforcements" is ordered to habit strength" ($_sH_R$); "the number of hours of food privation" is ordered to "drive" (D); and "persistence of food-seeking behavior" is ordered to "reaction potential" ($_sE_R$). The obtained relations among the experimental variables are then, without more ado, transferred to the theoretical variables, and what results is one of the major principles of the theory (ultimately formalized in postulate 7, p. 254), a principle, moreover, of *unrestricted generality*.

Now, the setting of "data language" expressions into correspondence with construct language expressions is essentially the problem of empirical or "operational" definition. A fully adequate analysis of the logical and practical issues connected with empirical definition still awaits the efforts of methodologists. Any such analysis, however, must respect certain of the elementary revelations yielded by Carnap's formulation in terms of the "reduction sentence" (6, 85). The *typical* form of an empirical definition is a set of *conditional* statements ("reduction pair" or "bilateral reduction sentence") which "reduces" a construct, by *implicative* relations, ultimately to data language statements of the observations which should result under certain specified conditions. In the typical case, a *plurality* of reduction sentences may be written for a term in the construct language. The "richer" the empirical reference of a concept, the greater the number of reduction sentences that can be written at a given time. Further, the class of reduction sentences corresponding to a given concept at a given time is "open"; it is always possible that the growth of relevant empirical knowledge will lead to new "reductive symptoms." In the case of theoretical constructs which appear in statements intended as *general* laws, the actual generality of the law is uniquely determined, at any given time, by the number and variety of reduction sentences which can be written for the construct in question.

Returning to Hull's theoretical utilization of the Perin materials, it is clear that the direct jump from the data language expressions to the corresponding theory language law, is tantamount to assuming an *equation*, rather than a *conditional* relationship, between the theoretical variables ($_sH_R$, D, $_sE_R$) and their reductive "realizations" in the experiment. Hull, of course, does not *intend* such an equation, because the law is offered as quite general in reference, and Hull plainly regards such variables as D, $_sH_R$ and $_sE_R$ as having varied empirical manifestations. But, *in effect*, an equation of construct and data language equivalent exists, because the relationships imputed to the theoretical variables by the "law" are nowhere empirically demonstrated by *further* data language reductions, nor is the need for this pointed up.

In an early phase of the construction of the theory, remote leaps from the data of single defining experiments to general theoretical statements are more or less inevitable. When such a leap is made, it is essential that the theoretical statement be regarded with great tentativeness, and that the conditional and therefore "open" character of the relation between constructs and the original reductive "symptoms" be kept in the foreground. It is essential, in other words, that efforts be made to enlarge the empirical reference of the theoretical variables by the "discovery" of additional reductive symptoms, and this can only be done by testing the "law" in a wide variety of further empirical contexts. Hull, however, tends to suppress precisely such considerations in the theoretical utilization of the Perin data. And, in general, *such considerations are suppressed in most of the instances in which Hull uses experimental materials to suggest construct interrelations.*

In this analysis of Hull's use of data language, we have already come upon one of the central deficiencies of his technique of theory construction —the tendency to base fundamental behavior laws of unspecified generality on single experiments, independently of any analysis of the generalization ranges within which the findings can rationally be expected to hold. There are many facets to this practice. It is evident not only in Hull's use of data language, but in his explicit conception of the status of independent and dependent variables. It is evident in his entire technique of postulate construction; in the mathematical analysis of experimental materials, in the moot status of the constants in empirical equations, and in many other ways. We will come upon such manifestations of the tendency towards uncritical over-generalization repeatedly, in later sections of the report.

b. Epistemic reduction basis of Hull's theoretical terms. This question need not detain us long. We saw in the discussion of Hull's "objectivism" that he is committed to the "intersubjective" definition of all psychological concepts. This means that, by intention at least, he is a thoroughgoing "operationist," although he wisely chooses to ignore the term (p. 30). And this, in turn, means that he must accept some such linguistic base as the "physical thing language" (6, 85) for the ultimate epistemic reduction of all psychological (and, in general, empirically meaningful) terms.

If a theorist's *immediate data language* is such as to have adequate intersubjectivity of reference, it should follow that reduction to the physical thing language is, in principle, possible. Nothing in the nature of Hull's use of theoretically neutral English would seem to preclude the possibility of carrying out such reductions. The deficiencies in Hull's use of data language are of another order. There is nothing which prevents the assignment of *some kind* of consistent empirical reference to each of the theoretical terms. There is much, however, *which prevents reductions which are consistent with implicit (postulational) and explicit definitions of the theoretical terms.*[5] We have seen in the preceding discussion that

---

[5] Issues concerning the interrelations of implicit, explicit and empirical definition are badly in need of analysis by methodologists of science. A term may have adequate "operational" definition in terms of univocality of empirical reference (i.e., reducibility to the physical thing language). Yet, the definition may be entirely inadequate with respect to the role that the term plays within the postulates and explicit definitions of a theory. Analyses of operational or empirical definition have thus far been mainly confined to attempts to formulate criteria for the *conditions under which empirical concepts are meaningful.* Too little attention has been given

Hull's *immediate* data language reductions of, for instance, "stimulus" and "response" are not in accord with the explicit and implicit definitions of these terms given in, or inferable from *Pr.B. In effect,* this means that no "operational" definitions are provided for the S and the R which occur in the construct language. Or contrariwise, the S and the R which occur in the construct language are not "really" in the theory, but rather some other constructs whose theoretical properties require redefinition in a way which is consistent with the data language usage of S and R.

A final difficulty, which has little to do with the properties of Hull's immediate data language, but much to do with the possibility of unambiguous epistemic reduction, should be mentioned here. This is created by Hull's frequent tendency to ascribe different and inconsistent properties to certain of his variables at different points in the postulates, the text, and the explicit definitions (so far as these latter are given or inferable). Thus, for instance, one of the four dependent variables of the theory, "amplitude" (A), is defined in the glossary (p. 403) as "amplitude, magnitude or intensity of a reaction," while, in its *postulated* introduction into the theory (postulate 15, p. 344) it is referred to as "the amplitude (A) of responses *mediated by the autonomic nervous system*" [ital. mine]. To complicate, further, our discussion of S and R variables, it should be recorded that, despite predominant emphasis, in sources which provide implicit and explicit definition, on S as physical energy and R as "movement," there are occasional overtones in the same sources that imply a conception of R as "outcome" or "effect," and S as any part of the environment which bears a demonstrable lawful relation to R. In later parts of the report, we shall meet many additional examples of discrepancies in the theoretical definitions of variables which must lead to alternate and incompatible epistemic reduction of the same variable.

2. Independent and Dependent Variables

The "independent variables" of a theory are the terms referring to the factors available for "measurement," and, when possible, manipulation, which are discriminated by the theory as the antecedent conditions of the events that the theory is designed to predict. The "dependent variables" of a theory are the terms designating the classes of events that the theory is designed to predict. "Intervening variables" are terms interpolated between the independent and dependent variables, and having properties such that a class of empirical relationships describable by a given number of statements which directly relate independent and dependent variables, can be derived from a substantially smaller number

---

to the *interplay between operational and other classes of definition in the construction of theories.*

of statements which relate independent to intervening variables, and these, in turn, to dependent variables.[6] The most direct access to the nature of the empirical materials with which a theory is concerned is afforded by examination of the independent and dependent variables, either explicitly employed, or presupposed, by the theory.

In *Pr.B.*, Hull provided explicit indications of what he regarded as the "antecedent determining condition[s]" and "consequent . . . event[s]" to which his chain of intervening variables is, by intention at least, "securely anchored." Although he makes frequent use of the term "intervening variable" (occasionally alternating this with "logical construct") to designate the term interpolated between such "observable and measurable" antecedent conditions and consequent events, the terms "independent variable" and "dependent variable" are *not* explicitly used. There is, of course, no doubt that Hull was referring, when he used expressions like "antecedent and . . . consequent . . . conditions or events" (e.g., p. 382), to independent and dependent variables, in some such sense as defined in the preceding paragraph. Nevertheless, as we shall later see, the tendency to talk *as if* intervening variables were anchored to "directly observable" *events*, rather than to terms (independent and dependent variables) in the construct language of the theory which may be *reducible* to "observable events," led to (and perhaps reflected) considerable confusion in the definition and general treatment of empirical variables.

It should be recorded that *Pr.B.* is the first of Hull's major publications in which some form of the independent-intervening-dependent variable schema was explicitly followed. In earlier writings, he ran into difficulties time after time because of his inability to make clear distinctions among these three types of variables. This seems particularly to have been the case whenever Hull attempted explication of the status of the so-called "unobservables" within his system (39, p. 510; 42, p. 7; 51, p. 7).

The structural outlines of the postulate set presented in *Pr.B.* may be viewed (and is so viewed by Hull) as a complex chain of intervening variables interpolated between the independent variables which represent the observable antecedents of behavior, and the dependent variables which represent observable aspects of the consequent behavior. As we

---

[6] These are not intended as formally precise statements. Careful logical and epistemological analysis is badly needed in this area, as can be seen from the compounding of confusion resulting from recent methodological discussion of intervening variables. One faces a trying impasse in writing an analytic report of the present sort. If unconscionable discursiveness is to be avoided, one must *apply* methodological tools without sufficient characterization of the tools. In partial solution to this problem, we have adopted the practice of briefly elucidating those methodological concepts which seem particularly fuzzy in current usage, before applying them. Such brief elucidations can only aim for an "intermediate" level of precision; the objective is sufficient characterization to permit meaningful analysis of the theory under scrutiny, not general or ultimate adequacy.

have seen, Hull emphasizes very strongly the point that legitimate intervening variables must be "securely anchored," by explicit functional relationships, to the antecedent independent variables and the consequent dependent variables. The postulates of *Pr.B.*, therefore, are made up of elements which take one of three forms:

(a) They relate an independent variable to an intervening variable.
(b) They relate one or more prior intervening variables to another intervening variable.
(c) They relate the final intervening variable in the chain to one or another dependent variable.

Any *complete list* of independent and dependent variables must accordingly be reconstructed from the postulates. The *definitions* of these variables must be reconstructed from the properties implicitly imputed to them by the postulates in which they occur (implicit definition), and from explicit and "operational" definitions either stated in, or inferable from, the textual embedding discussions, and the "glossary of symbols."

In the following discussions, it is not our purpose to reconstruct a *complete* list of the variables (i.e. the *independent* variables; the few *dependent* variables may be briefly characterized), but rather to examine their definitional and general methodological status, and to test certain of them against Hull's "secure anchorage" criterion. Consequently, in this section, we (a) *examine certain of the independent variables appearing in the theory of Pr.B.*, (b) *record the dependent variables*, and (c) *discuss their systematic status and mode of definition*. The section concludes with (d) a *summary of Hull's treatment of independent and dependent variables*.

a. Independent variables. The expression, "independent variable," has become systematically ambiguous in discussions of psychological methodology. The independent-intervening-dependent variable schema established by Tolman (137, 138) for the analysis of theory implies a sense of the expression, "independent variable," which overlaps only partly with the expression as it is used in mathematics and in general scientific methodology. At least three senses of the expression may be distinguished:

Sense I: Terms in the *construct language* of a theory denoting the chief *classes* of empirical events which serve as the operationally identifiable, or "measurable," and, wherever possible, manipulable, antecedent conditions of the events that the theory is designed to predict. "Antecedent conditions" is, of course, used in the *logical*, not the *temporal* sense. This would seem to be the sense of "independent variable" implicit in the Tolman independent-intervening-dependent variable schema which has become so widely used in analytic discussion of psychological theory. We propose to refer to "independent variables" in this sense as "*systematic independent variables.*"

Sense II: A term or expression denoting any factor in an experimental situation which is systematically varied, or operated upon in some way, with the intent to observe and record a correlated change in another part of the system defined by the experiment. Sense II independent variables may be called "*experimental independent variables.*" It should be noted in passing that Sense I and Sense II of "independent variable" are very frequently confused. *Experimental* independent variables *may* be specific, singular "realizations" (operational or reductive "symptoms") of a *systematic* independent variable; they are not, however, to be identified with the systematic independent variable to which they are ordered. Sense I independents are terms in the *construct language;* Sense II independents are expressions in *immediate data language.* A Sense II independent variable *need not* be a "realization" of a Sense I independent; empirical relations between experimental variables which are ordered to no extant theory are often investigated.

Sense III: All terms in a statement of functional dependency of which a given term (the dependent variable) is a specified function. This corresponds roughly to the usage of "independent variable" in mathematics. Sense III independent variables may be designated "*mathematical independent variables.*" An analogous set of distinctions can, of course, be made for different senses of the term "dependent variable."

Hull apparently regards the principal independent and dependent variables constitutive of the "major" intervening variables of his system to be those put forward in Fig. 84 of *Pr.B.* (p. 383), and represented as Fig. 1 in this report. The independent variables included by Hull in this summarizing diagram, together with elucidations of each derived from the glossary of *Pr.B.*, and indications of the intervening variables to which they are related, are presented in Table 1.

Even superficial collation of the independent variables in the first column of Table 1 with the verbal and the mathematical formulations of the postulates will disclose that the list of independent variables given by Hull, as constitutive of the indicated intervening variables, is highly incomplete. For this reason, we have attempted to exhibit in Table 2 all of the "independent" variables which appear in both the verbal and equational forms of the postulates which introduce the major intervening variables of the theory—$_sH_R$, $_s\bar{H}_R$, $_sE_R$, $\dot{I}_R$, I_R, $_sI_R$, $_s\bar{E}_R$. It should be emphasized that Table 2 excludes breakdowns of the postulates which introduce certain other intervening variables (e.g., s, $\check{s}$, $_sU_R$, $_sO_R$, $_sL_R$, and $_s\dot{\bar{E}}_R$), and thus must not be viewed as a resumé of the entire system. The table does, however, contain the *principal* independent variables discriminated by the theory, because the omitted postulates contain intervening variables, either of a type not linked to independent variables

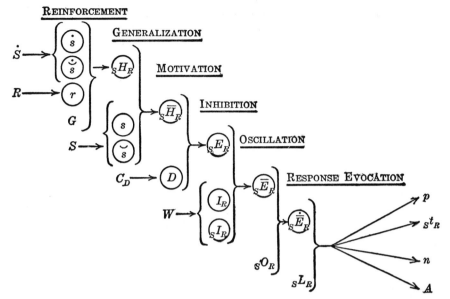

FIG. 1. Hull's summary diagram of the structure of the theory of *Pr.B.*, taken from Clark L. Hull, *Principles of Behavior*. New York: Appleton-Century-Crofts, 1943. P. 383

Diagram summarizing the major symbolic constructs (encircled symbols) employed in the present system of behavior theory, together with the symbols of the supporting objectively observable conditions and events. In this diagram $\dot{S}$ represents the physical stimulus energy involved in learning; R, the organism's reaction; $\dot{s}$, the neural result of the stimulus; $\ddot{s}$, the neural interaction arising from the impact of two or more stimulus components; r, the efferent impulse leading to reaction; G, the occurrence of a reinforcing state of affairs; $_sH_R$, habit strength; S, evocation stimulus on the same stimulus continuum as $\dot{S}$; $_s\bar{H}_R$, the generalized habit strength; C_D, the objectively observable phenomena determining the drive; D, the physiological strength of the drive to motivate action; $_sE_R$, the reaction potential; W, work involved in an evoked reaction; I_R, reactive inhibition; $_sI_R$, conditioned inhibition; $_s\bar{E}_R$, effective reaction potential; $_sO_R$, oscillation; $_s\dot{\bar{E}}_R$, momentary effective reaction potential; $_sL_R$, reaction threshold; p, probability of reaction evocation; $_st_R$, latency of reaction evocation; n, number of unreinforced reactions to produce experimental extinction; and A, amplitude of reaction. Above the symbols the lines beneath the words *reinforcement, generalization, motivation, inhibition, oscillation* and *response evocation* indicate roughly the segments of the chain of symbolic constructs with which each process is especially concerned.

$(_sO_R, _sL_R)$, or they are linked to independents which appear also in connection with postulates that *are* included in the breakdowns of Table 2 $(s, \ddot{s})$.

In accordance with the quantitative intentions of Hull's theory, postulates are stated both verbally and "equationally" in such a way as to define the mathematical function forms interconnecting the theoretical terms. The postulates contain *four* classes of terms which may be regarded as *Sense III* ("mathematical") independent variables.

(a) *Systematic independent variables* of the type already identified as Sense I (e.g., S, N, G, W, etc.).

(b) *Prior intervening variables*, or terms functioning within the theory as intervening variables, each of which has appeared in some previous postulate as a *Sense III dependent variable*. For instance, after $_sH_R$ has appeared as a Sense III *dependent* variable on the left hand side of the equation defined by postulate 4, it appears as a Sense III *independent*

TABLE 1.   The independent variables distinguished by Hull in his summary diagram (Fig. 1) together with the glossary elucidations of each and indications of the related intervening variables

Symbol	Elucidation	Related Intervening Variable
$\dot{S}$	"A stimulus when considered as in the process of being conditioned to the reaction." (p. 407)	
$\dot{R}$	"A reaction which is in the process of being conditioned to a stimulus." (p. 406)	$_sH_R$
G	"A need reduction or a stimulus which has been closely associated with a need reduction; primary reinforcement; also a primary goal reaction." (p. 404)	
S	"Stimulus energy which evokes a response on the basis of a previously formed habit." (p. 407)	$_s\bar{H}_R$
C_D	"Conditions which produce the drive (D), the objective conditions from which D may be calculated." (p. 403)	$D\text{----}{\to}_sE_R$
W	"The amount of work, i.e., $W = F'L$." (p. 408)	I_R , $_s\bar{E}_R$, $_sI_R$

variable on the right hand side of the equation defined by postulate 5 on stimulus generalization. In this context, the previously introduced intervening variable $_sH_R$ becomes one of the variables of which a new intervening variable $_s\bar{H}_R$ (Sense III dependent) is a specified function.

(c) *Empirical constants* appearing on the right hand side of the equations which represent the "mathematical statement" of the postulate (e.g., the exponential constants k, j, u, i, etc.).

(d) *Formal constants* appearing on the right hand side of equations, such as M (the physiological maximum of habit strength) and e (the logarithmic "base").

In Table 2, an attempt has been made to assemble the *Sense III* independent variables of all four classes distinguished above, for each of the theoretical intervening variables listed in column (1). In other words, we have regarded, for purposes of the analysis, the intervening variables introduced by each postulate as Sense III dependent variables which are some function of the Sense III independent variables specified by the relevant postulate. The *systematic independent variables (Sense I)* given for the verbal postulates in column (2), and for the equations in column (4), are the chief "antecedent" empirical variables discriminated by the theory of *Pr.B.*, and it is the exhibition of these that constitutes the primary purpose of Table 2. The additional categories of *Sense III* independent variables given in the table are included in order to provide a relatively complete picture of the factors constitutive of the major intervening variables of the theory. The significance, within the theory, of the *systematic* independent variables cannot be adequately defined without some indication of the prior intervening variables, and the empirical and formal constants, which conjointly determine each of the major intervening variables, according to the functions asserted by the postulates.

Verbal formulations of the major postulates typically include a rough description of the function form linking the intervening variable under introduction to systematic independent variables and prior intervening variables, but *do not include* a specification of empirical and formal constants,[7] as do most of the equations. For this reason, only systematic independent variables and prior intervening variables can be listed for the verbal formulations.

Certain interesting considerations about the structure of the theory emerge, when we supplement the incomplete list of systematic independent variables derived from Hull's diagram (Table 1), by reference to the verbal and mathematical content of the postulates. We will discuss certain of the more noteworthy considerations regarding "independent variables" suggested by Table 2, in the following paragraphs. Certain other considerations, not uniquely relevant to "independent variables," will be discussed in later parts of the report.

(1) *Discrepancies among the independent variables employed in verbal as against equational formulations of the postulates.* Inspection of Table 2 will show that such discrepancies are manifold and frequent.

One class of discrepancies involves the absence of certain of the independent variables given in the verbal formulations from the equations, and *vice versa.* For instance, in verbal postulate 4, systematic independent G is crucial to the specification of the conditions constitutive

---

[7] The single exception to this statement, among the postulates analyzed in Table 2, is the verbal form of Postulate 4 which makes reference to the formal constant M— the "physiological maximum of habit strength."

TABLE 2. "Independent variables" appearing in verbal and mathematical "Principles of Behavior" *

INTERVENING VARIABLE AND POSTULATE IN WHICH IT IS INTRODUCED	"INDEPENDENT VARIABLES" (OF VARIOUS TYPES) OF WHICH	
	Verbal Statement	
	Systematic Independent Variables	Prior Intervening Variables
$_sH_R$ POSTULATE 4 (pp. 178-179)	$\dot{s}C_r$—close temporal contiguity of an effector activity $(r \rightarrow R)$ and a receptor activity $(S \rightarrow s)$ G—diminution of a need $\dot{G}$—a stimulus which has been closely and consistently associated with the diminution of a need N—the number of reinforcements "Magnitude of need reduction" (no symbol given for this in verbal postulate) t—delay in reinforcement t'—degree of asynchronism of $\dot{S}$ and R when both are of brief duration t''—duration of the continuous action of $\dot{S}$ on the receptor when R begins	s—afferent neural impulse (linked to independent variable S by Postulate 1) r—efferent discharge (not formally introduced into theory by any postulated specification or linkage to R)
$_s\bar{H}_R$ POSTULATE 5 (p. 199)	d—the magnitude of the difference on a stimulus continuum between the afferent impulses of $\dot{s}$ (impulse at point of reinforcement) and s (impulse of reaction evocation) in j.n.d. units [The glossary defines d as "the number of j.n.d.'s lying between the two stimulus aggregates $\dot{S}$ and S'' (p. 403).]	$_sH_R$ at $\dot{S}$—the strength of the habit at the point of reinforcement
D, S_D POSTULATE 6 (pp. 253-254)	**None**—C_D is introduced in the *text* and defined in the glossary (p. 403) as "conditions which produce the drive (D), the objective conditions from which D may be calculated." Postulate 6, however, gives no statement of the dependence of D on any independent variable.	None—unless it is assumed that D has been introduced in Postulate 3 (p. 66), or Postulate 4 (p. 178). These Postulates mention D but do not link it to any antecedent variable.

* Wherever page references for the elucidation of symbols are not given, they are either direct quotations from postulated statements in which the symbols appear, or slightly modified paraphrases of such postulated characterizations.

THE CORRESPONDING INTERVENING VARIABLE IS A FUNCTION

	Equational Statement		
Systematic Independent Variables	Prior Intervening Variables	Empirical Constants	Formal Constants
N—the number of reinforcements w—a constant change in a measurable objective criterion which results in a need reduction t—delay in reinforcement t'—$T_R - T_{\dot S} - .66$ where $\dot S$ is of more than instantaneous duration and overlaps the beginning of R t''—$T_R - T_{\dot S} - .44$ where $\dot S$ and R are practically instantaneous T_R—the time of the beginning of R $T_{\dot S}$—the time of the beginning of $\dot S$ [The equation (equation 16, p. 178) is given for the case of t'.]		i—exponential constant in expression containing N K—constant in expression containing w J—constant in expression containing t U—constant in expression containing t'	M—100 habs, the physiological maximum of habit strength (also included in verbal statement) e—mathematical constant taken at 10 (logarithmic base)
d—the difference between S and $\dot S$ in j.n.d.'s	$_SH_R$ at $\dot S$	J'—an empirical constant of the order of .01 in the case where d is a qualitative difference, but of the order of .006 where d is a quantitative difference	e—logarithmic base, taken at 10
None	D—strength of the dominant primary drive	b—constant in the equation for Postulate 6, i.e., $S_D = bf(D)$. It is assumed that "$b > 0$."	

TABLE 2 (*continued*)

INTERVENING VARIABLE AND POSTULATE IN WHICH IT IS INTRODUCED	"INDEPENDENT VARIABLES" (OF VARIOUS TYPES) OF WHICH	
	Verbal Statement	
	Systematic Independent Variables	Prior Intervening Variables
$_sE_R$ POSTULATE 7 (pp. 253-254)	None	$_s\bar{H}_R$ D
	<div>Part (*a*) — I_R</div> R—Reaction	$_sE_R$ D—(but in new sense as "primary negative drive")
	<div>Part (*b*) — $\dot{I}_R$</div>	
$I_R, \dot{I}_R$ $_s\bar{E}_R$ POSTULATE 8 (p. 300) [Verbal form consists of 4 parts, and mathematical statement of 4 equations. Breakdown indicates intervening or other principal variable under definition in each part, and the relevant independent variables.]	*n*—number of reaction evocations	
	<div>Part (*c*) — $\dot{I}_R$</div> W—work involved in the execution of R	
	<div>Part (*d*) — I_R</div> t'''—time since evocation of an R	
$_sI_R, \dot{I}_R$ $_s\bar{E}_R$ POSTULATE 9 (p. 300) [Verbal statement consists of 2 parts; mathematical statement consists of 2 equations. Breakdown as above.]	<div>Part (*a*) — $_sI_R$</div> S—stimuli R—cessation of a response	I_R
	<div>Part (*b*) — $\dot{I}_R$</div> None	$_sI_R$ I_R

Equational Statement

Systematic Independent Variables	Prior Intervening Variables	Empirical Constants	Formal Constants
None	$_s\bar{H}_R$ D		
$\boxed{\text{Equation } (a) \text{ --- } _s\bar{E}_R}$ None	$_sE_R$ I_R --- (not previously introduced)		
Equation (b) --- n (appears here as "mathematical" *dependent* var.) W---"$=F'L$, in which F' represents force and L represents distance or length of the movement" (p. 279)	$\dot{I}_R$ --- (not previously introduced)	B, C	
$\boxed{\text{Equation } (c) \text{ --- } \dot{I}_R}$ W---as above n---number of reaction evocations		B, C	
$\boxed{\text{Equation } (d) \text{ --- } t'''I_R}$ t'''---"The duration in minutes following a sequence of unreinforced evocations of R during which neither reinforced nor unreinforced evocations of R have occurred" (p. 408)	I_R	q---exponential constant	e
$\boxed{\text{Equation } (a) \text{ --- } \dot{I}_R}$ None	$_sI_R$ I_R		M_1---the max. of $_sH_R$ as limited by the amount and quality of the reinforcing agent
$\boxed{\text{Equation } (b) \text{ --- } _s\bar{E}_R}$ None	$_sE_R$ $\dot{I}_R$		

of $_sH_R$, yet no reference to it is made in connection with the equations. In the equations of postulate 8, there is nothing which suggests that I_R (reactive inhibition) "is created whenever a reaction (R) is evoked in an organism," although precisely this latter is asserted in verbal postulate 8. In verbal postulate 9, the generation of conditioned inhibition $(_sI_R)$ is clearly linked to the association of stimuli (S) "with the cessation of a response (R)," but this could hardly be inferred from the equational form of the postulate.[8]

Obvious examples of terms which appear in the equational forms of the postulates, and *not* in the verbal form are, of course, all empirical constants, and all formal constants with the exception of M in postulate 4. The systematic independent variable w in the equation for postulate 4 does not appear in the verbal formulation, although its referent is apparently meant to coincide with the "magnitude of need reduction" factor (and also G, and possibly G) referred to in verbal postulate 4. The definition of w, however, given along with the "mathematical statement" (p. 178) equates w with a hypothetical operational symptom of "magnitude of need reduction," which is insufficiently characterized to permit determinate substitution for w in any attempt to *use* the equation.

Another class of verbal versus equational discrepancies (or perhaps a sub-class of the discrepancies mentioned above) consists in more or less subtle transformations in the meanings ascribed the same independent variable symbols, as they occur in the alternate forms of the same postulates. A conspicuous example of this is d in postulate 5 which, in the verbal postulate, is identified as the "magnitude of the difference" on a stimulus continuum between "the afferent impulses of $\acute{s}$ and s," while in the equation d is a difference, not between afferent impulses, but between stimuli (S and $\acute{S}$). The t' and t'' (asynchronism) variables of postulate 4 provide another example. The reversal of reference as between t' and t'' in the two formulations of the postulate is probably an oversight, and may be easily corrected. Aside from this, however, it should be noted that the equational definitions of t' and t'' involve the introduction of two constants (.66 and .44) which do not appear in the verbal postulates, and the significance of which for the equation in which t' and t'' appear, is far from clear.

(2) *The absence from the postulates of a critical systematic independent variable specified in Hull's diagram (Fig. 1).* The six systematic independent variables which Hull feels of sufficient importance to acknowledge in his summary diagram include C_D, defined in the glossary of *Pr.B.* (p. 403) as, "conditions which produce the drive (D); the ob-

---

[8] Those who advocate an exegesis of Hull's theory which regards the verbal postulates as unnecessary addenda to the equations, should take careful note of such discrepancies as the ones mentioned in the text. It is difficult to see, in any case, what meaning can be assigned to the terms of an equation, without some verbal explication of those terms, *somewhere.*

jective conditions from which D may be calculated." It is clear from Table 2, however, that postulate 6 which introduces D and S_D (the drive stimulus) includes no reference to C_D. There is *no* postulated linkage of D (and in turn S_D) to any systematic independent variable. If the postulates define the content of the "theory" of *Pr.B.*, C_D is not a part of the theory, nor, for that matter is D or S_D, for these intervening variables remain unmoored to *any* antecedent empirical variables.

(3) *Indeterminacy of what constitutes the independent variables for which intervening variables in the case of the inhibition postulates.* This point cannot be discussed independently of a general consideration of postulates 8 and 9, which, both in the verbal and the equational variants, are in a highly unsatisfactory condition. The breakdown in Table 2 can only suggest the magnitude of the confusion.

The *verbal* form of postulate 8 (p. 300) begins with the introduction of I_R (reactive inhibition) which is held either to result from (or to be?) "a primary negative drive (D)" which is "created" whenever "a reaction (R) is evoked." The "primary negative drive . . . has an innate capacity (I_R) to inhibit the reaction potentiality $({}_sE_R)$ to that response." Succeeding parts of the postulate state that the "amount of net inhibition $(\dot{I}_R)$ [not *reactive* inhibition (I_R)] generated by a sequence of reaction evocations" is a specified function of "the number of evocations (n)," *and* "the work (W) involved in the execution of the response" (brackets mine). A final part of the postulate tells us that *reactive inhibition* (not $\dot{I}_R$) "spontaneously dissipates as a simple negative growth function of time (t''')."

In essence, then, the postulate introduces a new intervening variable, "reactive inhibition," which is held to be related to a new usage of what looks like a previously introduced intervening variable (D, as a *primary negative drive*), and this in turn is linked to the perfectly general, *qualitative* independent variable condition of response evocation. A *second* new intervening variable, *net inhibition* (or a third, depending on whether the new usage of D is regarded as a new construct or a special sense of the old), is now *quantitatively* linked to two new systematic independent variables, n and W. Finally the dissipation of *reactive inhibition* is *quantitatively* linked to a new independent time variable, t'''. Since there is no indication, within the postulate, of the relation between *reactive* inhibition and *net* inhibition, the only information that we can derive is that I_R is an inhibitory state, taken against ${}_sE_R$, which accumulates according to some unspecified function of reaction evocation, but which dissipates as a quantitatively specified function of time, while $\dot{I}_R$ is an X which accumulates as a quantitatively specified function of n and W.

If we turn to the *"mathematical statement"* of postulate 8 (p. 300), the situation becomes even more muddy. In the four "equations" of the mathematical statement, I_R is nowhere linked to defining systematic independent variables. Even the single vague linkage to R, asserted in the *verbal* form of postulate 8, is not in evidence. Nevertheless, I_R occurs in two of these equations as a Sense III *independent* variable [equations (a) and (d)], and once [equation (d)] as a Sense III *dependent* variable. This means that equations (a) and (d) must be, strictly speaking, contentless. Equations (b) and (c) reassert, in mathematical form, the functional relations between $\dot{I}_R$ and n and W already defined in verbal postulate 8. Notice that *now* the only one of the intervening variables "introduced" in postulate 8, which is linked to any response variable, is $\dot{I}_R$.

Verbal postulate 9 (p. 300) introduces a third (fourth?) inhibition variable. This is *conditioned inhibition* (sI_R) which is held to "summate physiologically with reactive inhibition (I_R) against the reaction potentiality to a given response." Conditioned inhibitions are implicitly defined as, "stimuli (S) closely associated with the cessation of a response (R)" which "become conditioned to the inhibition (I_R) associated with the evocation of that response." We pass over the fact that Hull here seems to be introducing a very new type of theoretical concept into the system, one involving the association of stimuli not with responses but with *drive states* (let us remember that whatever else I_R may be, it is "an innate capacity" of a "primary negative drive"). More to the point, is the fact that Hull here "introduces" an additional intervening variable (sI_R) which is implicitly defined by reference to a variable, I_R, which, in turn, we have seen to have no adequate empirical definition at all. Further, the systematically indeterminate concept of sI_R is then *linked* to the indeterminate I_R by a specific mathematical function ("physiological summation" as defined earlier in the theory in the case of "positive habit tendencies").

Reference to the "mathematical statement" of postulate 9 (p. 300) helps not at all. Formula (a) relates $\dot{I}_R$ (net inhibition) to a function of the two inadequately defined variables, I_R (reactive inhibition) and sI_R (conditioned inhibition). Formula (b) introduces the new intervening variable of "effective reaction potential" $(s\bar{E}_R)$ as equal to $sE_R - \dot{I}_R$. This, of course, effectively transfers the indeterminacy of $\dot{I}_R$ to $s\bar{E}_R$.

The above analysis has proceeded by an independent examination of postulates 8 and 9, taken separately. If we now consider them as a single interrelated unit, the confusion is not lessened. Thus, equation (a) of postulate 8,

$$s\bar{E}_R = sE_R - I_R,$$

and equation (b) of postulate 9,

$$s\bar{E}_R = sE_R - \dot{I}_R,$$

are flat contraries. And I_R, which "physiologically" summates with $_sI_R$ to form $\dot{I}_R$, according to equation (a) of postulate 9, has as its only independent definition equation (d) of postulate 8:

$$t''' \quad I_R = I_R e^{-qt''''}$$

But, as we have seen, no statements are given (mathematical or verbal) which would make it possible to determine I_R at any given time. Such a statement is given (at least in part) for $\dot{I}_R$ in (b) and (c) of postulate 8, which link $\dot{I}_R$ to n and W. The crux of the difficulty seems to be the failure to specify the extent to which systematic independent variables, n and W differentially affect $\dot{I}_R$ and I_R. We are given certain empirical variables for the quantitative constitution of $\dot{I}_R$; we are told that I_R is some fractional component of $\dot{I}_R$, but there is no way of determining the extent to which what is asserted for $\dot{I}_R$ is meant to hold for I_R. Furthermore, since $_sI_R$ is defined in terms of I_R, we have no way of knowing the extent to which n and W affect $_sI_R$.

Thus, we are left with a horrible indeterminacy as to the status of independent variables n and W within the theory—an indeterminacy which ramifies, of course, directly upon all the "inhibitory" intervening variables, and thence, into the rest of the theory.

b. Dependent variables. The systematic *dependent variables* of the theory of *Pr.B.* may be briefly and unequivocally identified. They are four in number, and the symbols, together with their "glossary" definitions, are as follows:

(1) p or "probability of reaction evocation" (p. 406);
(2) *str* or "latency of a reaction evocation" (p. 408);
(3) n or "number of unreinforced reactions required to produce experimental extinction" (p. 406);
(4) A or "amplitude, magnitude, or intensity of a reaction" (p. 403).

In other words, the entire system of *Pr.B.* is geared to the prediction of reaction (R), as indicated by each of these four dependent variable "measures." The classes of antecedent "data" available for such theoretical prediction are of the variety designated by the systematic independent variables of the theory. Just as the independent variables must be linked by explicit functional relations (preferably quantitative) to the intervening variables, so too, the intervening variables must be linked to the dependent variables.

In the system of *Pr.B.*, the final intervening variables which must be calculated for the prediction of behavior are "effective reaction potential" $(_s\bar{E}_R)$ and "momentary effective reaction potential" $(_s\dot{\bar{E}}_R)$. This means that each of the dependent variable indicators must be quantitatively moored to $_s\bar{E}_R$ or $_s\dot{\bar{E}}_R$, and four postulates appearing in *Pr.B.* (postulates 12 to 15, p. 344) attempt to do precisely this.

Inspection of the *postulated* introductions of the dependent variables immediately discloses a definitional vagary. From postulates 12, 13, and 14 we learn that *p, str* and *n* refer only to "striated-muscle reactions." From postulate 15, we learn that *A* designates "the amplitude . . . of responses mediated by the autonomic nervous system." No such restrictions are imposed on the dependent variables in the glossary definitions, and at various points in the text.

c. Logical status and mode of definition of independent and dependent variables. Since most psychological theorists have made no effort to provide explicit identification of the independent and dependent variables recognized by their theories, certain confusions about the status of such variables would seem to be prevalent. Adequate statement of a theory demands the specification of its independent and dependent variables. The "terms" designating such variables are *within the construct language of the theory,* and are not to be confused with expressions in the data language to which these terms may (and should) be reducible by empirical definition. The *critical empirical or operational definitions of a theory must appear in connection with its independent and dependent variables,* for it is at these points that the theory must establish contact with "observable states of affairs."

Hull's attempt to make explicit his independent and dependent variables is admirable, and almost unique in psychological theory. The only other major psychological theorist who has made an effort in this direction has been Tolman, but the effort has been little more than a gesture. However, Hull's general treatment of his independent and dependent variables shows two closely related defects:

(*a*) He tends to think of these variables as representing "directly observable events" (e.g., p. 29).

(*b*) He fails to provide sufficiently detailed and unambiguous operational or empirical definition of these variables.

It could be argued, of course, that Hull's intent in *Pr.B.* is the *informal* presentation and explication of his postulate set, and consequently, that detailed operational definitions are not to be expected. Unfortunately, however, even at an informal level, elucidation of these variables is both insufficient in detail and ambiguous. We present, in condensed form, a few illustrations of such deficiencies.

(1) *G* is defined in the glossary of *Pr.B.* as "a need reduction or a stimulus which has been closely associated with a need reduction; primary reinforcement; also a primary goal reaction" (p. 404), and in the text has certainly been used in all these contexts. Operationally, such an "elucidation" is double-talk. Obviously, the *process* (or processes?) of "need reduction" or "primary reinforcement" (e.g., changes in a drive state; strengthening of *s-r* or *S-R* connections) must be regarded just

as much as corresponding to "intervening variable" aspects of the system, as do the processes designated by D. A "primary goal reaction" *could* be an independent variable entity, *or*, in certain contexts, it could correspond to a *dependent* variable. Further, the senses in which G as a "primary goal reaction" might serve as an independent variable must be spelled out in more careful operational terms. G as a "stimulus which has been closely associated with a need reduction" seems to represent a genuine independent variable aspect of the theory, but this sense of G *also* requires detailed and determinate operational definition, which, in turn, presupposes a far more adequate specification of the conditions of "secondary reinforcement" than the theory includes. Such specification could conceivably disclose an intervening variable "process" corresponding to "secondary reinforcement," but differing from "primary reinforcement" in certain ways. Thus, a central "independent variable" of the theory turns out to be, by implication, several independent variables, several intervening variables, and at least one dependent variable, no *one* of which "variables" receives even an approximation of adequate empirical definition.

(2) At first blush, it would appear that W (work) is given rather more adequate empirical definition, than most of Hull's independent variables. The definition is formally presented as:

$W = F'L$, in which F' represents force and L represents distance or length of the movement, as in ordinary mechanics (p. 279).

Such a definition relates the independent variable to concepts which have a well-defined operational significance in physical science. But let us recall that W is a variable which serves, in a thoroughly general way, as an antecedent condition to the accumulation of $\dot{I}_R$ (net inhibitory potential) with respect to instances of *any class of reactions, whatsoever*. The operations *equated* to W could hardly be applied to glandular responses, changes in muscular tonicity, etc. Obviously, quite different sets of operations must be specified for the determination of the W (or its equivalent) in these cases. No one can blame a theorist for incapacity to specify details which are beyond the limits of present knowledge. But putting forward a concept like W in the form of an *equation* (reduction sentence having the form of an explicit definition) implies that the operational definition of W is completed, and so tends to gloss over the fact that W (or some set of variables having similar systematic function) must acquire additional operational symptoms, before the concept approximates empirical adequacy. Instead of going out of his way to point up problems of this order, Hull shows a quite general tendency to present formulations which represent half-way solutions of their intended functions, with an air of finality.

(3) Independent variables S,[9] as we know from the discussion of Hull's data language, reflects in its operational usage certain of the most fundamental inadequacies of the theory. These inadequacies ramify throughout the system, and are reflected everywhere in the text of *Pr.B.* Hull's summarizing definition of S in the glossary has previously been quoted in part (cf. p. 21, this report). We now reproduce it in full:

$S =$ 1. stimulus energy in general, e.g., the energy of sound, light, or heat waves, pressure, etc.
　　2. more specifically, stimulus energy which evokes a response on the basis of a previously formed habit (p. 407).

We previously noted that data language *applications* of S show a wide departure from sense 1 above. Just as in the case of W, the sense 1 elucidation of S links the variable to concepts (physical energy sources) which have a well defined operational status in physics. But in Hull's actual *operational practice,* stimuli are characterized not in terms of their physical energy properties, but in terms of some part of the environment, discriminated by the experimenter, which bears (or may bear) a lawful relation to response.

At first blush sense 2 seems interpretable as a formulation at gross variance with sense 1, and in possible accord with data language usage. One might assume that the expression "stimulus energy" is *here* gratuitous, and that S is now being represented as any discriminable x (complex of events, part of the environment) which is an empirically demonstrable antecedent of response (i.e., "evokes a response on the basis of a previously formed habit"). Actually, no such subtlety is intended. Sense 2 merely records Hull's symbolic convention of using S as the sign for "stimulus" as considered in its capacity of *response evocation,* from $\dot{S}$ (p. 407), the "stimulus when considered as in the process of being conditioned to a reaction." In both cases (the S of action evocation, and the $\dot{S}$ of original conditioning) the defining property is sense 1—"stimulus energy . . . the energy of sound, light, or heat waves, pressure, etc."

Hull's emphasis on "physical energy" criteria of S seems enforced by the intention to show that, *in principle,* the theory can derive entities having the characteristics of "stimuli" in the *data language* ("*behavioral*") *sense, via* S as physical energy, the afferent impulse (s), afferent neural interaction, the principle of reinforcement, and, *in particular,* the mechanisms of primary stimulus generalization, secondary generalization, etc. We would be better able to evaluate the fate of this intention *after* analysis of the intervening and other variables introduced in these assumptions. But we may anticipate the results of further analysis to the extent of noting that these additional variables and principles are as

---

[9] The discussion is, of course, intended to hold for all sub-specifications of the stimulus variables in *Pr.B.,* as well as for S (e.g., S_D, S_C, S_u).

programmatic, and empirically unmoored, as is the concept of "stimulus energy" itself.

(4) The discussion of Hull's data language usage of R showed difficulties of the same order as was the case with S. This parallelism with the inadequacies of S continues, when we examine the *general* treatment of R. Before going further, it is well to recall that R is given both an independent and a dependent variable usage in the theory of *Pr.B.* (cf. Fig. 1).

The full glossary elucidation of R is (p. 406):

$R =$ (1) reaction or response in general (muscular, glandular, electrical);
     (2) more specifically, the reaction which occurs as the result of previous conditioning.

This tells us next to nothing. Sense (1) characterizes "reaction" only adjectivally as "muscular, glandular, electrical," but gives us no clue to the circumstances under which the noun "reaction" may be applied. Sense (2) is merely a symbolic discrimination of R as considered in the performance situation from $\dot{R}$ (p. 406), "a reaction which is in the process of being conditioned to a stimulus." The following statements, however, give us further help:

Our usual thoughtless custom is to speak of cycles of behavior by merely naming their outcome, effect, or end result, and practically to ignore the various movements which brought this terminal state about (p. 25).

An ideally adequate theory even of so-called purposive behavior ought, therefore, to begin with colorless movement and mere receptor impulses as such, and from these build up step by step both adaptive behavior and maladaptive behavior. The present approach does not deny the molar reality of purposive acts (as opposed to movement), of intelligence, of insight, of goals, of intents, of strivings, or of value; on the contrary, we insist upon the genuineness of these forms of behavior. We hope ultimately to show the logical right to the use of such concepts by deducing them as secondary principles from more elementary objective primary principles. Once they have been derived we shall not only understand them better but be able to use them with more detailed effectiveness, particularly in the deduction of the movements which mediate (or fail to mediate) goal attainment . . . (pp. 25-26).

These statements, together with the glossary elucidations of R, leave little doubt that Hull proposes to deal with "reaction" or "response" as physically definable "movements" ("muscular, glandular") and associated physical events ("electrical"). But, just as in the case of the S concept, there is a marked deviation from the "definitions" in actual practice. In concrete applicational contexts, Hull assumes an operational correspondence between R and behavioral "outcome, effect, or end result." Hull plainly intends to justify his practice by the derivation of "adaptive . . . and maladaptive behavior" from "colorless movement" —presumably *via* the postulates of *Pr.B.* (as in the derivation of the "behavioral" S). A very important link in such a derivation must, of course, be some analysis of *response generalization*. But here we must note—quite aside from the programmaticity of other postulates that would be necessary—that *Pr.B.* contains *no analysis* of response generalization. Indeed, the only reference to the topic in *Pr.B.* is contained in a footnote (p. 183) which says that "space is not available in the present work for an adequate treatment of it."

(5) The argument developed in (4) above has an obvious bearing on the significance of the four explicit dependent variable R indicators given by Hull: p, $_str$, n, and A. Hull supplies informal operational definitions for each of these which superficially seem adequate. But each of these response "measures" is left in the air, because of failure to characterize that which the measure measures (i.e., R). Obviously, R must be "qualitatively" or topographically delimited in some way before we can determine its probability of occurrence, its latency, etc. But Hull fails to provide adequate conceptual tools for precisely this identification of R. It may be significant, in this connection, that Hull does not even include R as a dependent variable in the diagram of his "major" constructs (Fig. 1), but rather inserts p, $_str$, n and A as directly related to $_s\dot{E}_R$.

d. Summary of Hull's treatment of independent and dependent variables. In the analyses of this section, we have found manifold inadequacies in Hull's treatment of the independent and dependent variables of the theory of *Pr.B.* He begins initially with a defective metatheoretical notion of such systematic empirical variables, which equates them with "directly observable events." Despite Hull's *attempt* to be explicit about these variables, we have found many barriers in the way of unequivocal specification of the total set of such variables presupposed by the theory. There are discrepancies among the *independent variables* identified in verbal, as against mathematical, formulations of the same postulates. There is indeterminacy with regard to which independent variables are linked to which intervening variables in certain of the postulates. One major independent variable (C_D) has no *postulated* linkage to any intervening variable at all. The *dependent variables* are unequivocally specified in *number*, but not in meaning.

No *formal* empirical or "operational" definitions are specified. Whatever operational definitions of major empirical variables such as G, W, S, and R are *informally* suggested in the text, glossary and postulate formulations can be shown either to be inadequate to the theoretical role of the variable in question, inconsistent with data language applications, or insufficiently characterized to permit univocal interpretation. In one conspicuous case, a so-called independent variable G was defined so as to suggest multiple independent, intervening and dependent variable usages.

If the independent and dependent variables of a theory are the factors

TABLE 3. Intervening variables of the theory of *Pr.B.* as represented in Hull's summary diagram (Fig. 1) and classified according to "type"

TYPE I		TYPE II		TYPE III	
Symbol	*Elucidation*	*Symbol*	*Elucidation*	*Symbol*	*Elucidation*
$\dot{s}$	"Afferent neural impulse . . . in the process of being conditioned to a reaction" (p. 407)	$_sH_R$	"Habit strength conceived as a rough or approximate stimulus-response relationship to $_sH_r$" (p. 404)	$_sO_R$	"Behavioral oscillation" (p. 313); "The oscillatory weakening potentiality associated with effective reaction potential" (p. 406)
$\check{s}$	"Afferent neural impulse as modified by afferent neural interaction" (p. 407) (Considered in process of being conditioned to a reaction)	$_s\bar{H}_R$	"Effective habit strength" (p. 404)	$_sL_R$	"Reaction threshold, the minimal amount of effective reaction potential . . . that will mediate reaction evocation" (p. 405)
r	"Efferent discharge" (p. 111)	$_sE_R$	"Reaction potentiality" (p. 253); "Excitatory potential, potentiality of reaction evocation" (p. 404)		
s	"Afferent neural impulse resulting from the action of a stimulus energy on a receptor, as $S \rightarrow s$" (p. 407) (Considered in process of action evocation)	$_s\bar{E}_R$	"Effective reaction potential" (p. 404)		
$\check{s}$	"Afferent neural impulse as modified by afferent neural interaction" (p. 407) (Considered in process of action evocation)	$_s\dot{\bar{E}}_R$	"Momentary effective reaction potential; $_s\bar{E}_R$ as modified by $_sO_R$" (p. 404)		
D	"Strength of the dominant primary drive operative in the primary motivation to action after the formation of the habit involved" (p. 403)				
I_R	Actually Type II: "Amount of reaction inhibition" (p. 404)				
$_sI_R$	"Amount of conditioned inhibitory potential" (p. 404)				

which provide anchorage to empirical states of affairs, the theory of
Pr.B. must already be regarded as badly adrift.

3. Intervening Variables

It is the avowed function of the postulates of *Pr.B.* to introduce successive links of the "intervening variable" chain of the theory, and to relate
this chain to the empirical (independent and dependent) variables. Hull
regards intervening variables or "logical constructs" as "symbols or X's
(that) represent entities or processes which, if existent, would account
for certain events in the observable molar world" (p. 21). He believes
that "their use is attended with certain difficulties and even hazards"
(p. 22):

> At bottom this is because the presence and amount of such hypothetical factors
> must always be determined indirectly. But once (1) the dynamic relationship
> existing between the amount of the hypothetical entity (X) and some antecedent
> determining condition (A) which can be directly observed, and (2) the dynamic
> relationship of the hypothetical entity to some third consequent phenomenon or
> event (B) which also can be directly observed, become fairly well known, the
> scientific hazard largely disappears. . . . When a hypothetical dynamic entity, or
> even a chain of such entities each functionally related to the one logically
> preceding and following it, is thus securely anchored on both sides to observable
> and measurable conditions or events (A and B), the main theoretical danger
> vanishes. This at bottom is because under the assumed circumstances no
> ambiguity can exist as to when, and how much of, B should follow A.

The main purpose of this section is to determine how successfully the
intervening variables of *Pr.B.* have eluded these "hazards" cited by Hull.
The discussion will include (1) a classification of the *chief intervening
variables*, and (2) consideration of their *systematic status*.

a. Chief intervening variables. Hull's summarizing diagram presented
in Fig. 1 (p. 29, this report), gives a bird's-eye view of what he regarded
as the major symbolic constructs" (encircled symbols) of *Pr.B.*, "together
with . . . the supporting objectively observable conditions and events"
(p. 383).

A rough classification of intervening variables, based on the nature of
their relations with independent variables, may be made from this diagram. Type I intervening variables will be those which are *directly* linked
to independent variables (e.g., $\dot{s}$). Type II intervenings are those which
bear *indirect* relations to independent variables, as mediated by their
direct relations to prior intervening variables (e.g., $_sH_R$). Type III
intervenings are those which bear *no relations* to independent variables.
Table 3 presents the intervening variables of the theory as classified
according to *type*.

Presumably, Fig. 1 and Table 3 reveal the intervening variable structure
of the theory as abstracted from the postulates. Careful collation of these

materials with the postulates and embedding discussions, however, will immediately reveal many discrepancies. For instance, $\acute{s}$ and $\check{s}$ cannot possibly be Type I variables, because according to postulate 2 which introduces these variables (p. 47) into the theory, they are linked not to the independent variables $\acute{S}$ and S, but to the prior intervening variables $\acute{s}$ and s. D cannot be regarded as in the theory at all, because there is no postulated linkage to C_D. Similarly, Type I intervening variable r cannot be in the theory because there is no postulated linkage to independent variable R.

The inhibition variables demand special scrutiny. Although Hull treats them in the postulates, diagram, and various other places as Type I (directly related to independents), there are implications to the contrary both in Hull's explicit statements, and in their place in the structure of the theory.

$\acute{I}_R$ and I_R seem, by implication of postulate 8 (p. 300), to be some function of a Type I intervening variable which Hull refers to as "a primary negative drive (D)" produced "whenever a reaction is evoked." By postulate 9, $_sI_R$ arises by virtue of stimuli being "closely associated to the cessation of a response," these stimuli thus becoming "conditioned to the inhibition . . . associated with the evocation of that response" (p. 300). Such conditioning of a stimulus to the reactive inhibition associated with the response is presumed to take place only because cessation of R brings about reduction of the "negative D" posited in postulate 8, thus eventuating in the *process of reinforcement,* or G. Thus, it would seem that $_sI_R$ requires linkage to the prior Type I variable of G, as well as the prior Type I variable of "negative D" implied in postulate 8. Such an analysis would force us to regard $\acute{I}_R$, I_R, and $_sI_R$ as Type II variables on *our definition*—i.e., as intervening variables related mediately to independents via Type I intervenings.

It should further be apparent that certain intervening variables which appear *neither* in the postulates, nor the structural diagram, should be included, if full specification of the variables *presupposed* by the theory were to be achieved. To take but one instance, the highly ambiguous "independent" variable G would seem to demand, at the minimum, the specification of a correlated Type I intervening variable corresponding to the *process* of "need reduction" or "primary reinforcement."

We should also note that Type III intervenings $_sL_R$ and $_sO_R$, whatever their merits, are at variance with Hull's metatheoretical conception of the nature of intervening variables, since they are not linked, either programmatically or actually, to any "observable" antecedent conditions at all.

We will meet additional instances of indeterminacy in the intervening variable chain in the subsequent discussion of construct interrelations.

b. Systematic status of the intervening variables. In the following paragraphs, we will be concerned with two questions: (1) the *mode of definition* of the intervening variables, and (2) their *reality status*.

(1) *Mode of definition.* The postulate set constitutes the *implicit* definition (85) of the intervening variables. As we have already noted, in *Pr.B.* intervening variables are introduced in each case by specified linkages (asserted within postulates) to (1) independent variables, (2) other intervening variables, and (3) dependent variables. These functional relationships are specified in a general way in the verbal formulation of the postulates, and (presumably) more concretely in the "mathematical" statements given for most of the postulates.

In an empirical system, terms given *implicit definition* may also be subjected to other classes of definition: viz., explicit and empirical or operational definitions. In "interpretive" systems, "coordinating definition" may also be distinguished, but Hull's theory is not of this variety (cf. 85).

Since *Pr.B.* is far from a fully formalized theory, it is difficult to determine whether *explicit* definitions are intended for any of the intervening variables. In *Mathematico-Deductive Theory of Rote Learning* (51), which *is* highly formalized, the intervening variables ("symbolic constructs") are introduced "as undefined terms"—i.e., they have the acknowledged role of *"primitives." Pr.B.*, however, states only postulates in "formal" fashion; *definitions* not being *formally* indicated. Nevertheless, the embedding discussion provided by the text attributes many properties to the intervening variables as over and above those assigned by the postulates. We cite but one example:

The drive concept, for example, is proposed as a common denominator of all primary motivations, whether due to food privation, water privation, thermal deviations from the optimum, tissue injury, the action of sex hormones, or other causes (p. 239). . . . Most, if not all, primary needs appear to generate and throw into the blood stream more or less characteristic chemical substances, or else to withdraw a characteristic substance. . . . It appears probable that when blood which contains certain chemical substances thrown into it as the result of states of need, or which lacks certain substances as the result of other states of need, bathes the neural structures which constitute the anatomical basis of habit ($_sH_R$), the conductivity of these structures is augmented through lowered resistance either in the central neural tissue or at the effector end of the connection, or both (pp. 240-241).

Whether certain of these embedding statements could be assigned the status of explicit definitions is an arbitrary matter for a theory in the form of *Pr.B.* Decision would depend on whether Hull regards such statements as "extra-systemic" aids to understanding, or as intrinsic to the theory. It could, we think, be argued that certain of these statements must *necessarily* be regarded as parts of the theory, but which specific statements would constitute *explicit* definitions, which empirical definitions (or parts of empirical definitions), and which would be assimilated into a more adequate statement of postulates, remains moot at this level of formalization.

How do Hull's *intervening* variables stand with respect to empirical or operational definition? There has been much confusion on this question. Hull talks about the desirability of "an empirically workable operational definition" of his "quantitative" intervening variable units (e.g., habs, motes, wats, pavs) in a footnote (p. 281). It must be noted, however, that Hull's metatheoretical view of the nature of an intervening variable precludes *direct operational definitions*. Intervening variables are linked by specified functional relations either immediately or mediately (via other intervenings) to independent and dependent variables. The independent and dependent variables are presumably operationally defined. Insofar as one can legitimately speak of intervening variables as being operationally defined, this can only be *indirectly* in terms of the operational definitions of the independent and dependent variables. The situation is, of course, complicated by the fact that Hull does not seem to remain consistent with his notion of intervening variables as X's which are uniquely characterized by their stated functional relations to "antecedent" and "consequent" conditions. To the extent that Hull treats (explicitly or by implication) specific intervening variables as "existential reals," the possibility of *direct* operational determination must remain open. This question shades over into our next topic.

(2) *"Reality status" of Hull's intervening variables.* Questions having to do with the "reality status" of Hull's theoretical constructs have long been matters of considerable controversy. Those who favor a consistent interpretation of Hull's constructs as "purely behavioral" must maintain that Hull's "intervening variables" are *exclusively* defined in terms of their stated relations to empirical variables which are unique to the language of behavior theory. The alternate possibility is that some or all of what Hull's calls his "intervening variables" are defined in such a way as to assert or imply "existential" referents which correspond to entities dealt with at a different linguistic level (e.g., the language of physiology, biochemistry, etc.). Theoretical variables of this latter variety would correspond to what MacCorquodale and Meehl (93) have termed "hypothetical constructs," in contradistinction to functionally constituted, non-ontologically-significant, "intervening variables."

The only source from which the *meaning* of a theoretical term can be inferred is the totality of its definitional specifications (implicit, explicit and empirical), and its detailed contextual usage within the theory. There is no doubt that the postulates, text and glossary of *Pr.B.* contain many statements which impute physiological referents (and other "existence" properties) to some, and perhaps all, "intervening variables." Although the presence of such existence assertions and implications is easy to detect, the precise content of such ontological attributions, in the case

of each concept, is very difficult to reconstruct. This is only partly because
of the scattered, informal and often inconsistent nature of the definitional
specifications in *Pr.B.*; the difficulty is compounded by Hull's apparent
inability to adopt a determinate metatheoretical position about the
reality status of his concepts. We saw this to be the case in discussing
Hull's orienting attitudes with respect to "level of analysis," earlier in the
report (cf. pp. 13-15, this report). The net result is the paradox of a
"molar behavior" theorist who seeks to derive all behavioral relations
from the "afferent impulse" and the "efferent discharge."

There is no particular point in attempting reconstruction of the physiological existence properties imputed to each concept. Evidence that such
properties *are* introduced is easily marshaled. In summary fashion, we
may cite the following:

(1) Hull leaves little room for doubt that his intention is *at least* to
guide the choice of his concepts by the requirements of extant neurophysiological knowledge (cf. p. 14, this report).

(2) There is no question but that certain of the "sign vehicles" in
the postulates of *Pr.B.* appear also in the language systems of such
disciplines as neurophysiology and neuroanatomy. Take for example:
"afferent impulse," "receptor," "central nervous tissue" (postulate 1, p.
47), "afferent neural impulse," "nervous system" (postulate 2, p. 47),
"effector activity," "receptor activity" (postulate 4, p. 178). There is
also no doubt that the usage of certain of these sign vehicles, within the
postulates, is more than roughly similar to their usage within *physiology*.
We need go no further than the first sentence of postulate 1 (p. 47):

When a stimulus energy (S) impinges on a suitable receptor organ, an
afferent neural impulse (s) is generated and is propagated along connected
fibrous branches of nerve cells in the general direction of the effector organs, via
the brain.

(3) It is evident that many statements may be found at various points
in the textual embedding discussion of key intervening variables which
directly impute physiological referents to such variables. For instance
(p. 102):

. . . it is important to note that habit strength cannot be determined by
direct observation, since it exists as an organization as yet largely unknown,
hidden within the complex structure of the nervous system.

It is evident, further, that in the text Hull discusses, sometimes in considerable detail, possible physiological mechanisms which correspond to
various of his intervening variables. Occasionally, Hull goes out of his
way to show the possibility of deriving "molar behavioral," intervening
variable properties from "neurological" or "submolar" factors (e.g., the
"deduction" of the relations between S-R asynchronism and $_sH_R$ from a

"neurological hypothesis," pp. 167-169; the discussion of the "possible submolar causes" of $_sO_R$, pp. 309-310).

It must be emphasized that the extent to which each of Hull's intervening variables implies "physiological existents" is a separate question, requiring detailed analysis in each case. There are certainly wide differences in specificity of physiological (or ontological) reference. In a general way, one could contend that the Type I intervenings, which clearly function as the immediate intra-organismic surrogates for the independent variable factors of the theory, probably carry the strongest (physiological) existence implications among the three types. An "afferent impulse" would seem to be just *that* (among other things assumed by the postulates in which the expression occurs) and an "effector activity," just *that*. Drive (and "need" [10]) is certainly correlated with a physiological existent, and so, we would contend, is the intervening variable sense of G (the physiological events correlated with need reduction which act so as to strengthen $_sC_R$'s).

Type II and Type III intervenings seem to correspond somewhat more roughly to physiological "reals" than Type I concepts. Type I variables seem to be set up in such a way as to imply physiological referents which "possess" most or all of the properties which the identical sign-vehicles denote when used in the language of physiology. Type II and Type III intervenings, by and large, imply physiological referents of which the variables, *as postulated*, are a highly abstractive or selective function.

4. Interrelations Among Constructs

The relations interconnecting the three classes of variables of the theory of *Pr.B.* are, of course, exhibited by the verbal formulations and the corresponding "mathematical statements" of the postulates. Diagrammatic and tabular recapitulations of the construct interrelations asserted by the postulates which introduce the chief intervening variables of the theory are given in Fig. 1, and Tables 1, 2 and 3 of the present report.

In this section we will (1) summarize certain *general characteristics* of the construct interrelations asserted by the theory of *Pr.B.*, and (2) present an initial survey of certain *indeterminacies in construct interrelations*. The discussions of this section are intended as merely a preliminary limning in of the issues. Many of the problems connected with construct interrelations can only be dealt with in terms of extensive analysis of Hull's techniques of quantification, and the empirical aspects of his methods of postulate construction. These issues will be considered in later parts of the report.

a. **General characteristics of construct interrelations.** The variable linkages asserted by the postulates are constructed from a variety of

---

[10] The relation between "drive" and "need" is one of the enigmas of *Pr.B.*

sources. The majority are based on empirical equations fitted to the data of empirical behavior studies, the *experimental* independent and dependent variables of which are taken as "realizations" of the *theoretical* variables under consideration. In such cases, the particular experiments used to suggest construct interrelations may either be *designed* for the purpose (e.g., Hovland's studies in connection with postulate 5 on "stimulus generalization," pp. 183-190; the Perin-Williams study in connection with postulate 7 on "primary motivation," pp. 226-257), or *selected* as the best available evidence (e.g.,) the Grindley experiment in connection with the relation between $_sH_R$ and "amount of need reduction," pp. 125-127). Some of the construct linkages seem based on a complex admixture of "rational" and "empirical" considerations (cf. discussion of $_sH_R$ as a function of N in section on *quantification* pp. 74-78, this report). A number of postulates which assert only "qualitative" construct interrelations (no "mathematical" statements being given) seem based primarily on rational considerations (e.g., postulate 2 on "neural interaction," pp. 342-347; postulate 3 concerning "innate behavior" as related to "conditions of need," pp. 57-67; postulate 11 on the "reaction threshold," p. 344; and postulate 16, p. 344, on "the competition of . . . incompatible reaction potentials"). Although the inductive basis for most of the postulated functions derives from behavior experimentation, at least one major construct linkage—the relation between "stimulus energy" (S) and the "afferent neural impulse" (s)—seems directly based on neurophysiological evidence.

Much confusion seems to exist about the *degree of quantitative specificity* of the construct linkages in *Pr.B.* This issue will be discussed in some detail in a subsequent consideration of *quantification.* Here we should note that in most instances Hull attempts to specify the *type* of mathematical function form relating the theoretical variables under consideration. In the "mathematical" statements of the postulates, this is done in terms of equations which exhibit the function form in mathematical notation, but do not include values for the various empirical constants. In the verbal formulations of each of the postulates, function forms are identified in terms of a verbal paraphrase having one or another degree of specificity—e.g., "positive growth function," "negative growth function," "negative function," "rises quickly to a maximum . . . following which it gradually falls," "increasing monotonic function," "negatively accelerated decreasing monotonic function." Despite a popular impression to the contrary, the theory of *Pr.B.* does not provide "mathematical statements" for all of its postulates. Three postulates (1, 2 and 3) are given only in the verbal form, without equational supplementation. In the case of two other postulates (11 and 16), the so-called "mathematical statements" are translations of the verbal formulations into symbolic logic.

b. A sampling of indeterminacies in construct-interrelations. Our purpose here is to make an initial test of the extent to which the relationships specified in the postulates conform to Hull's demand that all independent-intervening-dependent variable interconnections be specified by unambiguous functional relationships. We confine the present discussion to a number of brief exhibits which demonstrate a failure to characterize the functions linking the variables in question with sufficient specificity or completeness to permit passage from the antecedent variable(s) to the next in the chain. Many of the grounds for such indeterminacy have, of course, already been considered in previous discussions. Many additional sources and varieties of indeterminacy will be considered in the subsequent division on "Methodological Characteristics," and in further portions of the report.

We should state at the outset that Hull's inability to do more than adumbrate his construct interrelations in a programmatic and indeterminate way may be a reflection of the empirical and methodological limitations on the theoretically feasible in current psychology, rather than an indictment of Hull. But it seems particularly important to point up such indeterminacy because of the danger that it may remain hidden under the apparent formality and detail of Hull's presentation.

We begin with consideration of *postulate* 4 because this critical principle of the theory illustrates several sources of indeterminacy in construct-linkages which are typical of many of the other postulates. We then continue with a sample of further exhibits.

Postulate 4: Perhaps the pivotal intervening variable of the theory— $_sH_R$ (and Δ_sH_R)—cannot be determinately calculated because:

(a) It is expressed in terms of an operationally meaningless programmatic unit—the "hab."

(b) By admission of Hull, the defining functions given both verbally and in the equational form represent only a subset of the functions which generate $_sH_R$ (cf. p. 181). The "intensity of the conditioned stimulus" and "the vigor or intensity of the reaction" are indicated as additional possible systematic independent variables which may require linkage to $_sH_R$.

(c) No adequate explication (operational definition) is given of the significance of certain of the systematic independent variables which appear in postulate 4 as determinants of $_sH_R$—notably G, and $\dot{G}$ in the verbal form of the postulate, and what is apparently the representation of both of these in the mathematical statement —w. The ambiguities of G have already been sampled. $\dot{G}$ is nowhere defined, except implicitly in verbal postulate 4, as a stimulus associated with need diminution. The variable w is variously referred to as "the magnitude of a reinforcing agent" (p. 508) or "a constant change in a measurable objective criterion which results in a need reduction" (p. 178). Actually, w, which elsewhere (Ch. IX of *Pr.B.*) is held to represent all empirical events associated with quantity and quality of reward, is completely programmatic as a *measurable* independent variable.

(d) No adequate discussion is given of the meaning of the critical empirical constants k, j, u, and i. As in the case of all empirical constants of the system, one is left in the dark as to the intended generality of these constants, and as to the method for determining them for any empirical context other than the context of initial determination.

In performing actual derivations, or in any exemplary application of the theory, the most that can be done with postulate 4 is to make an arbitrary estimate of $_sH_R$ on the basis of "intuitive" weightings of the contributions of the determining variables. Or, in concrete experimental contexts, one can assign a rough ordinal "value" to $_sH_R$, based on the "setting" of the experimental independent variable, when conditions are such that the remaining parameters can be regarded as constant.

It would be boresome to spell out similar points for each of the remaining postulates to which they are relevant. In general:

Point (a) (*empirically meaningless units*) holds for all further intervening variables built up from $_sH_R$ in the postulated chain. Further sources of indeterminacy come in with the introduction of the "mote" as the unit of drive intensity, the "wat" as the unit for reaction potential and the "pav" as the unit for I_R (or is it $_iI_R$?—Hull is not clear concerning his intention here).

Point (b) (*specification of a subset of the determining functions*) probably holds for a number of postulates other than those for which Hull explicitly acknowledges such incompleteness. In a very general sense, all of the postulates are suspect from this point of view, since it would indeed be surprising if, in the present state of empirical knowledge, Hull had correctly identified all of the determining variables for each of the intervenings in the theory. It would be still more surprising if some single "standard" function could adequately represent the relations between the independent and intervening variables. Thus, for example, it would seem sanguine to expect that all generalization gradients under all circumstances will assume the form of the "negative growth function" posited in postulate 5.

Point (c) (*inadequate operational definition of independent variables*) holds, as we have seen, for many of the independent variables introduced in connection with other postulates: e.g., W, S, R, C_D, d.

Point (d) (*insufficient explication of empirical constants*) holds for all postulates in which constants appear, i.e., the "mathematical statement" of *every* postulate in which concrete function forms are identified.

Postulate 2: This postulate links s (afferent neural impulse) to $\check{s}$ (afferent neural impulse as modified by neural interaction). The indeterminacy of postulate 2 has often been noted. The "neural interaction" principle fails to specify the *conditions* determining the *amount* and *character* of neural interaction effects beyond:

Other things equal, the magnitude of the interaction effect of one afferent impulse upon a second is an increasing monotonic function of the first (p. 47).

The postulate on neural interaction thus functions as a blank form which must be set at arbitrary values in *ad hoc* fashion any time it is used in derivations. It should also be indicated that this postulate has a peculiar importance in that it must, in principle, be used in *every* derivation of the system (i.e., s must always be transformed into $\check{s}$ at the moment of generation). Indeed s, *per se*, seems to be some kind of limiting abstraction.

Postulate 6: This assumption introduces an intervening variable, D, and links this to another intervening, S_D, but, as has already been indicated, *does not* specify any functional relation linking D to any independent variable. Discussion is given to a number of the relevant problems in the text of *Pr.B.* (p. 239), and in other connections (cf. Fig. 1, also glossary *Pr.B.*, p. 403) a systematic independent variable C_D, presumably constitutive of D, is introduced. But to the extent that the *postulates* define the content of the theory of *Pr.B.*, C_D is not a part of the theory, and hence another relational gap exists in the construct chain.

Postulates 8 and 9: The inhibition postulates are ambiguous with regard to which independent variables are related to I_R as against $\dot{I}_R$ (cf. pp. 37-39, this report). This means that, given the independent variables acknowledged by the theory, we cannot determinately calculate I_R or $\dot{I}_R$, and therefore $_sI_R$ and $_s\bar{E}_R$.

Postulate 16: The assumption about "the competition of . . . incompatible reaction potentials" suffers from much the same order of indeterminacy as does postulate 2. This postulate is admittedly a simplifying assumption which asserts that:

When the reaction potentials . . . to two or more incompatible reactions . . . occur in an organism at the same time, only the reaction whose momentary effective reaction potential . . . is greatest will be evoked (p. 344).

Hull acknowledges that experimentation suggests the occurrence of "associative inhibition" under such circumstances, but he is not prepared to state the function determining "possible generalized inhibitory tendencies." Such caution is highly commendable, but it is easy to forget that the absence of a determinate functional specification at this place makes postulate 16 another "blank form" assumption, in a sense similar to that of postulate 2. And it should be noticed that, like postulate 2, postulate 16 is, from a *literal* point of view, relevant to *every* application of the theory to concrete behavior situations.

Before leaving this section, it should be noted that a multiplication of indeterminacy of construct-interrelations may arise from the possibility that certain members of the postulate set are non-consistent. "Consistency," as we shall later have occasion to note, is extremely difficult to evaluate in a complex empirical postulate set—particularly a tentative and programmatic one. Nevertheless, the part of postulate 8 which assumes that "the amount of net inhibition (I_R) generated by a sequence of reaction evocations is a simple linear increasing function of the number of evocations" seems to imply consequences which could conflict with the implications of the positive growth relationship between habit strength and number of reinforcements (N). In any case, the rules for applying these assumptions jointly in derivations need clarification, if "absurd" results are to be avoided.

C. METHODOLOGICAL CHARACTERISTICS

In the preceding division of the report, we considered, independently, the chief components—*data language, independent and dependent variables, intervening variables, construct interrelations*—which mutually determine the structure of the theory of *Pr.B.* In the present division, we are concerned with certain of the formal and mathematical characteristics of that theoretical structure. Since Hull's theoretical objectives, both in terms of long-range orienting attitudes and specifically in the formulation of *Pr.B.*, are hypothetico-deductive and quantitative, it becomes of the first importance to examine the theory in the light of the criteria of hypothetico-deductive and mathematical procedures. Such inquiry should enable us to test the degree of correspondence between Hull's explicit aims and his achievement in *Pr.B.* It should also give us additional insight into the methods of theory construction which determine the theoretical structure already considered. Accordingly, in this division of the report, we examine the theory of *Pr.B.* in terms of (1) *explicitness of axiomatization*, (2) *techniques of quantification and postulate construction*, and (3) *techniques of derivation*.

1. Explicitness of Axiomatization

If we assign rank-order grades among the influential learning theorists of the past few decades with respect to explicitness of axiomatization, Hull unquestionably comes out as top man in the class. Although it is customary to recognize this, and to point to Hull's work as a *model* of formal precision within the field of behavior theory, it may still be useful to assess the status of Hull's axiomatic procedures on a less relative scale. Indeed, if Hull's formulations are to serve as models of rigor in our field, it becomes essential to determine the limits within which emulation of the model might prove desirable.

There is perhaps some confusion among psychological methodologists as to standards of explicitness of axiomatization in science. Only in certain of the systems of symbolic logic do we find a close approximation to "complete" explicitness of axiomatization (i.e., with full statement of rules of inference, careful distinction between syntax and object language; consistency, independence, and completeness proofs, etc.). Even within symbolic logic, maximum explicitness is found only in the "poorer" systems (e.g., systems like the *sentential calculus*). Mathematical systems vary widely in explicitness of axiomatization, but as a group they are less explicitly formalized than logical calculi. Finally, in general, the empirical systematizations of physical science are considerably less explicit than mathematical systems.

In an *empirical theory*, fullness or explicitness of axiomatization is not, *in itself*, a positive value. Rather, the empirical theorist must carefully balance the evident virtues of fully explicit axiomatization, against the great labor involved in approximating this, and the joint dangers of conceptual inflexibility and empirical hollowness that are attendant upon premature formalization. Although no codified rules exist to facilitate such decisions,[11] a complex of pragmatic criteria must be brought to bear on *adapting* the explicitness of axiomatization to the characteristics of the material under systematization, and to the requirements, existing at the given time, for achieving intersubjectivity of reference among the investigators in the field. It seems fairly evident that the practice in psychology has been to aim for (or achieve) rather less explicitness of axiomatization than such criteria would make desirable. This should not blind us to the fact that it is possible to subject certain classes of empirical relationships to a *more explicit* level of axiomatization than may be desirable.

Recall that different levels of explicitness are characteristic of the four types of theoretical formulations that Hull has put forward: (1) the early informal articles (e.g., 26, 28, 29, 30, 32, 34, 35, 38), (2) the

---

[11] It is naive to expect that complex and subtle decisions of this order can ever be derived from some standard set of methodological rules. Nevertheless, issues having to do with the relations between various components of formal procedure and the pragmatic conditions which justify their application are in need of much further analysis by methodologists of science. Unfortunately, the various models of empirical systematization advocated by philosophers of science have been derived by logical reconstruction from highly advanced theoretical formulations, mainly in physics. The heuristic values of setting such procedural models before psychologists are great. However, attempts must be made to specify the *conditions* under which the applications of such procedures become feasible in various areas of psychology, and the *extent* to which there may be limits, *in principle*, on realizing hypothetico-deductive systems comparable in all respects to the criterion achievements of physics.

verbally formulated, qualitative "miniature" systems (39, 42, 47), (3) the partially "quantified" postulate set of *Pr.B.*, and (4) the highly formalized *Mathematico-Deductive Theory of Rote Learning* (51). Even in the early theoretical articles, Hull attempted greater explicitness of formulation than is evident in the writings of most learning theorists.

It is entirely possible that Hull has in certain contexts aimed for a more explicit degree of axiomatization that would be desirable on the basis of criteria similar to those discussed above. This seems to have been the case in *Mathematico-Deductive Theory of Rote Learning* (51) which represents, by intention at least, a more explicit level of formalization than most theories in physics. In this work, each of the 18 postulates is stated both verbally, and in a combination of the language of symbolic logic and mathematics. Eighty-six explicit definitions are constructed from 16 primitive terms, and are also stated alternately in English and symbolic logic. Theorems are derived mathematically, and these derivations are explicated by alternate ones in English. Only one sample proof is carried out in symbolic logic; it is the proof of "Corollary 1 of Postulate 1," and it requires the prior derivation of *50* theorems before the symbolic expression of the corollary may be written as a derived statement. The obsessive degree of axiomatization of this work can, however, be justified by Hull's desire to put forward a model theory. The subtitle of the book is *A Study in Scientific Methodology*, and as such a study the system represents an important contribution. At the other extreme, it may be significant to note that the least explicitly axiomatized of Hull's formulations—the early articles—seem among his most fruitful and suggestive contributions.

In *Pr.B.*, the status with regard to explicit axiomatic treatment is quite complex. Hull's intention in this book is primarily to present the *postulate set* for a general theory of behavior, and *not* to provide any detailed elaboration of the consequences of this theory. Thus "only a random sampling of some fifty or so secondary principles (corollaries) is included in the . . . volume," and "these are given chiefly for purposes of illustrating the meaning of the primary principles" (p. 398). Since the purpose of the book was *restricted* to the elucidation of postulates, there is every reason to expect great care in insuring the explicitness and univocality of what these postulates assert, and what the text says that they assert. Among other things this would mean the specification of careful and consistent explicit and operational definitions for many of the terms which occur in the postulates. It would have mattered little whether the resources of symbolic logic or other formalistic embellishments were utilized, for there was no evident intention to carry out rigorous formal derivations. The chief requisite would have been consistency and precision of reference within the resources of the English language and the notation of the theory.

In summary fashion, the general situation with regard to explicitness of axiomatization in *Pr.B.* may be stated as follows.

(1) *The level of explicitness aimed at is in some respects too "high" and in some respects too "low"* (in relation both to the character of the material under systematization, and the demands of rigor and communication). Specifically, an unrealistic level of explicitness is attempted in the quantitative formulation of the *postulates,* while the "explicitness" objective seems too modest in the case of *definitions.*

(2) *The over-all level of explicitness achieved falls short of the over-all level aimed for,* or at least it falls short of the *impression* of explicitness that Hull apparently tried to create.

This gap between intended (or suggested) explicitness and achievement is a serious matter. The formalistic impression created by the elaborate verbiage of the postulates, the many symbols, and the mathematical trim tends to obscure many sources of ambiguity in the theory. Specification of formal, *explicit* and *empirical* definitions might either have exposed many of these ambiguities, or eliminated them.

In the consideration of the structure of the theory, we had occasion to note many examples of ambiguity in the definitions of the three classes of theoretical variables, and in the specification of their functional interconnections. Gathering certain of these departures from explicitness together, we may classify some of the principle *sources* of ambiguity in the following way:

(1) Discrepancies between text, verbal formulations of postulates, and mathematical formulations of postulates (in any combination).
(2) Omissions in formulations of postulates of qualifications made in the text.
(3) Surreptitious shifts in the usage of presumably the same variables in different postulates.
(4) Downright ambiguity of the postulates due to insufficient explication of terms *anywhere.*

The first two sources of ambiguity (discrepancies between text, verbal, and mathematical formulations of postulates, and omissions of qualifications) have been amply illustrated in the discussion of *independent and dependent variables* (cf. pp. 25-46, this report), *intervening variables* (pp. 46-51), and *construct interrelations* (pp. 51-56). Similarly, as regards item (4) ("downright ambiguity"), we have seen that certain of the postulates—e.g., postulates 8 and 9 on inhibition—defy unequivocal interpretation, no matter what combination of the relevant formulations (verbal or mathematical postulates, text) are considered. As for item (3)—surreptitious shifts in the use of variables from one postulate to another—our consideration of the "stimulus" and "response" variables has already implied this, but it may prove instructive to assemble the evidence at this place.

Postulate 1, as we already know, links "stimulus energy," S, to the "afferent neural impulse," s. If we take this postulate, together with Hull's declared theoretical intentions (cf. quoted passage, p. 43, this report) seriously, it must follow that *all* other postulates be formulated in terms of s not S, and, whenever *reaction* becomes relevant, in terms of r not R. Postulate 2 on "afferent neural interaction" is, of necessity, consistent with this expectation, being formulated in terms of s. When we get to postulate 3, an ambiguity already creeps in, for although this postulate talks about unlearned "receptor effector connections" (p. 66), the symbol introduced to designate such connections is $_sU_R$, not $_sU_r$. The critical postulate 4 shows a like ambiguity in that an increment of $_sH_R$ is held to result from the temporal contiguity of "a receptor activity" and "an effector activity" ($_sC_r$), and, curiously enough, the symbol $_sH_R$ is implicitly defined as "an increment to a tendency ($\Delta\ _sH_R$) for that *afferent impulse* on later occasions to evoke that *reaction*" (p. 178, ital. mine). Postulate 5 also talks in terms of "afferent impulse $\dot{s}$ and s" (p. 199) as it introduces the concept $_s\bar{H}_R$. Arriving at postulate 6, we find the "afferent impulse" phraseology completely absent as the "drive stimulus (S_D)" is introduced (p. 253). (The "afferent impulse" symbolism would seem particularly appropriate in this case where the stimulation is typically "internal.") Postulate 8 talks in terms of R, while postulate 9 talks about "stimuli (S) closely associated with the cessation of a response (R)" (p. 300). Postulate 11 is formulated in terms of "stimulus (S)" and "reaction (R)," while postulates 12 through 16 are uniformly expressed in terms of "reaction evocation," "reaction," or "responses."

One consequence of this tendency to shift indifferently as between S and s, R and r is the basic ambiguity which is conferred on the central construct of the theory—that of a habit connection ($_sH_R$). Leeper (92) has already indicated that habit connections are treated in at least four different senses in *Pr.B.*, namely as: (1) stimulus-response connections, (2) receptor-effector connections, (3) *zones* of receptor-effector connections and (4) afferent neural impulse and efferent discharge connections (or afferent impulse and reaction connections).

On the basis of all of the foregoing considerations, we should underline a highly instructive paradox. On the surface, the theory of *Pr.B.* with its carefully labeled verbal postulates and their mathematical translations *appears* to be one of the most explicitly axiomatized formulations in psychology. Yet, close analysis brings so many dimensions of ambiguity into view that the apparently crisp contours of each postulate, and the set as a whole, fades away into uncertainty. What a given postulate of *Pr.B.* asserts will depend upon whether the interpretation is based on the verbal or mathematical statement, whether the interpreter wishes to stress one elucidatory passage in the text rather than another (or indeed on whether the text is given weight at all), whether the given postulate is considered in isolation from others or in conjunction with them, whether the interpreter reads one or multiple meanings into a given symbol, and whether the interpreter can construct *some* meaningful interpretation of postulates which seem equivocal in all contexts of the presentation. Such deficiencies of communication are, of course, common in informal and "literary" modes of presentation. It is not our intention to draw an invidious contrast between the theory of *Pr.B.* and certain less "formally" stated competing formulations. In such *informal* presentations, however, one *expects* and is prepared for a certain "hiddenness" of axiomatization. One is *not* comparably prepared for a possible vagueness of assumptional content when the trappings of postulational technique are present. Explicit *identification* of axioms does not necessarily entail explicit *formulation* of axioms. It is important that theorists and analysts of theory guard against mistaking the former for the latter.

This section should not be concluded without brief reference to the problems connected with the *consistency, independence and completeness* of the postulates of *Pr.B.* All three of these desirable properties of postulate sets are very difficult to evaluate even in relatively simple formal systems (of logic and mathematics). So-called "proofs" of consistency, independence and completeness depend, in the first instance, on finding a specific *interpretation* (or set of interpretations) of the axiom set, in terms of a set of entities which are themselves accepted as consistent. In a complex *empirical* postulate set (scientific theory) the problems are of an entirely different order. Finding an alternate empirical "interpretation" of a postulate set initially constructed for purposes of systematizing a complex empirical domain is, in most cases, out of the question. Should such an interpretation be found, the chances of deciding consistency, independence or completeness would be no better than in the case of the original interpretation. In general, in empirical systems of any degree of complexity, whether the postulate set implies contradictory theorems, whether certain of the "postulates" are, in reality, derivable from others, and whether every relationship that can be constructed from the *base* (primitive terms and relations) of the theory is derivable as a theorem, can only be decided by patient inspection as the theory is elaborated.

It is, of course, meaningless to raise questions about the "completeness" of a theory having the status of that of *Pr.B.* With regard to consistency and independence, we may offer the following scattered considerations.

A striking possibility of inconsistency arises as between elements of postulate 4 (reinforcement) and postulate 8 (inhibition). The *growth* relationship linking $_sH_R$ with N, seems capable of generating consequences incompatible with the *linear* relationship assumed to hold between net inhibition (I_R) and the number of reaction evocations (n), without further specification of more detailed characteristics of these two functions.[12]

With regard to possible cases of nonindependence of postulates, it may be of interest to observe that Hull, himself, acknowledges two such instances. The first has to do with postulate 9 which implicitly defines the construct of "conditioned inhibition" $(_sI_R)$. It will be recalled that $_sI_R$ arises by virtue of stimuli "closely associated with the cessation of a response" becoming "conditioned to the inhibition (I_R) associated with the evocation of the response" (p. 300). Since I_R is assumed, in the first instance, to constitute "a primary negative drive" which must diminish with cessation of response, this might be interpreted as providing a source of primary reinforcement for the conditioning of the "closely associated" S to some such entity as the R of "muscular contraction" (thereby generating "negative habits" or tendencies *not* to respond). Indeed, the "alternate" assumption of $_sI_R$ as a *primitive* mechanism in postulate 9, assuming as it does a direct linkage between a stimulus and a *drive* variable, seems to violate an implicit convention of the theory (and a reasonable one) to the effect that R processes and *only* R processes are attachable to S processes. We will later see that, in the theory of 1949-1951, $_sI_R$ actually becomes a *derived* mechanism. So far as can be determined, however, the shift in 1949 is made on no different a basis that it *could* have been made in 1943. In any event, the inhibitory assumptions are so unsatisfactory in form in both theories that the question of whether $_sI_R$ be best treated as primitive or derived becomes an idle concern.

A second principle pointed to by Hull as possibly nonindependent is postulate 10 on "behavioral oscillation." Hull suggests (p. 320) that "in the present system, the principle of oscillation seems to be shifting from the status of a postulate or primitive principle to that of a theorem or secondary principle," but gives no grounds for this belief. If Hull were to remain consistent with the discussion of oscillation in *Pr.B.*, the "derivation" of $_sO_R$ could only have been mediated via such "submolar" considerations as the random "spontaneous firing" of nerve cells and the variability in the reaction thresholds of axon fibers (together with such postulated principles as neural interaction and generalization). Such a "derivation" would entail the introduction into the theory of one or more postulates asserting the existence of these physiological phenomena, or at least defining the characteristics of some variable or variables which

---

[12] It is interesting to note that in the 1949-1951 postulate sets, alterations of a sort which remove this possibility of inconsistency are evident in the inhibition assumptions (cf. Part II, p. 144).

represent some abstractive function of these phenomena. It may be relevant to add that the postulate of behavioral oscillation *remains a postulate* in the 1949 theory.

2. *Techniques of Quantification and Postulate Construction*

No aspect of Hull's procedure is more important for an understanding of the status of the theory of *Pr.B.* than his "quantitative" techniques. In the discussion of *orientative attitudes* (pp. 12-13, this report), and in other places, we have seen that the desire to achieve quantitative behaviorial laws dominated Hull's efforts from the beginning of his theoretical career. By 1940, Hull felt prepared to attempt the specification of quantitative postulates in the context of the *limited-scope* theory represented by *Mathematico-Deductive Theory of Rote Learning* (51). The publication of *Pr.B.*, only two years later, represents Hull's initial attempt to approximate the quantitative specification of a postulate set for a behavioral theory of *unrestricted generality*. As we will later show in detail (cf. Part II), the terminal decade of Hull's career—from 1943 until his death—was ruled by the effort to translate the largely programmatic "quantification" of *Pr.B.* into the substance of "genuine" quantification.

Introductory Considerations. Perhaps the principal reason for the persistence of certain confusions about the status of Hull's theory stems from failure to get the quantitative aspects of his procedure into proper perspective. To some extent, this failure reflects a certain superficiality in recent and current thinking about the place of mathematical and "quantitative" procedures within psychological theory. We stand, at present, very far from the solution of many methodological (and creative mathematical) problems which must be resolved before attempts to achieve quantitative laws of any wide degree of generality can become rational. If these problems are far from solution, they are at least susceptible to formulation. It is to Hull's credit that he apparently perceived *some* of the problems which act as barriers against quantification. Unfortunately, however, his desire to surmount them was so great that a clear definition of the barriers did not always register in his writing. In many cases, the speed and vigor of the jump tended to blur the contours of what was being jumped over.

Any assessment of a theorist's quantitative procedures must start from the recognition that such procedures may figure in a plurality of contexts within any empirical theory. In general, three such contexts may be distinguished:

(1) Procedures for the *measurement* of the (systematic) independent and dependent variables in terms of which the empirical laws of the theory are expressed.

(2) Statement of the *mathematical form,* at one level of determinacy or another, of the *functions* relating any given variable or set of variables to another.

(3) *Rules of inference* in the derivation of theorems from postulates.

The first two contexts of mathematical application are of *primary* importance, because they uniquely determine the manner and extent to which mathematical principles may function as "rules of inference" in mediating derivations. Problems relevant to the construction of quantitative theory center, then, in "contexts" (1) (the mensuration of empirical variables) and (2) (the specification of function forms). Although there are special problems characteristic of each context, fruitful solutions to problems in either can only be achieved in the light of requirements established by the other.

It cannot be our purpose here to consider in detail the problems that confront the behavior theorist with quantitative intentions in each of these areas. Certain of the more conspicuously moot ones must, however, be mentioned. First, it should be noted that systematic independent and dependent variables must be susceptible to an order of "measurement" which might pragmatically legitimate the effort to specify function forms to the degree of mathematical precision sought. Without going into the subtleties of the problem of measurement, this at least means that the theorist must give careful thought to such matters as whether explicit *mathematical functions* fitted to the values of independent and dependent variables having only "ordinal" significance can have *predictive* empirical significance, and if so to what extent. Whatever the level of "measurement" the theorist believes attainable, he must take precautions that the "scale" which is ordered to a given independent or dependent variable is ordered to that variable *as it functions within the theory* (i.e., as it is *applied* in data language usage), and not to a homonym which in practice plays no role within the theory (e.g., independent variable S may appear to be measurable in several extensive dimensions, but this may not hold for S as actually used in the theory). Again, whether the independent or dependent variables be orderable to "ordinal," "interval," or "ratio" scales, the theorist must consider with care the question of whether the scaling procedure holds for a subset (or a single one) of the *experimental* independent or dependent variables to which his *systematic* empirical variables are reducible, or for the systematic variables actually identified in the theory language (e.g., a scale for "differences" in the functional effects of "stimuli" at different points on a stimulus-attribute dimension like frequency, in terms of j.n.d. units, may not be applicable to all differences in stimulation). Further, if the theorist seeks high generality of quantitative lawful relationships, as he must if he adheres to an intervening variable paradigm, he must fulfill some such requirements as the following.

(1) All alternate *experimental* variables to which a given independent variable is reducible (e.g., the various sets of empirical conditions constitutive of hunger, thirst, sex, etc., etc. in the case of such a systematic independent variable as C_D) must be brought to converge by appropriate "scaling" techniques on a common quantitatively constituted *intervening variable* (e.g., "drive").

(2) The intervening variable chain must be so constituted that a terminal value may be calculated (e.g., $_s\bar{E}_R$) which leads by *quantitatively consistent* divergent relations to all empirical instances of all systematic *dependent* variables of the theory (e.g., the scaling of $_s\bar{E}_R$ and its associate dependent variables must be such that any $_s\bar{E}_R$ value is translatable into mensurationally consistent values of p or $_st_R$ or n or A, for any instance of R whatsoever).

From such issues as were mentioned above, it is clear that mensurational problems concerning independent and dependent variables dovetail with problems concerning the nature of the function forms which the theorist seeks to specify in the lawful statements of his theory. In general, what is meant by a "mathematical" or "quantitative" function is itself vague in current usage. Classifying stated function forms as "quantitative" or "qualitative" is to make a very crass dichotomy; the "quantitativeness" of a functional relation may vary over a wide range of *specificity* in the mathematical description of the relationship. Current usage in psychological methodology would probably agree in regarding as a "qualitative" function statements of functional dependency between variables which go no further than an indication of "direction" (e.g., "positive," "negative") of the relationship (although strict adherence to the logistic interpretation of mathematics must demand that even such a function be regarded as "mathematical"). A more "quantitative" specification of function forms might involve a more detailed description of the trend or "shape" of the relation (e.g., "positively accelerated increasing"). Progressively higher degrees of "quantitativeness" may involve an identification of equational type (e.g., "exponential," "positive growth"), or an identification of equational type together with specification of parametric values (i.e., estimates of empirical constants).[13] Clearly, the order of "measurement" to which the independent and dependent variables of the theory seem actually or potentially susceptible will determine the degree of function-quantification which is rationally feasible (e.g., should the type of measurement preclude meaningful "additive" operations, the specification of highly quantitative functions becomes an empty objective). Contrariwise, the level of function-quantification sought must delimit the types of independent and dependent variables which are open to the theorist, and must influence

---

[13] Each degree of the "quantitative" mentioned above must itself be regarded as an interval on a continuum containing further sub-variations.

the theorist's programmatic commitments towards achieving the measurement of these variables.

An important dimension of variation among empirical functions might be loosely characterized as the *generality* of the relationship. This would refer to: (*a*) the range of "reductive symptoms" to which the independent and dependent variables of the function are reducible and for which the asserted relationship holds within "acceptable" probability limits, and (*b*) the range of variation in the empirical conditions, presumably independent of the variables related by the function, over which the function holds. At least in *psychological* theory, a prime difficulty seems to be that the higher the "degree of quantification" of function forms attempted, the lower is the empirical generality of the function likely to be. At bottom, this inverse relation between degree of quantitative specificity and empirical generality is probably related to a failure to identify the "right" empirical variables (if there are "right" variables, in this sense, in psychology), and to the inappropriateness of the order of mensurability of these variables to the mathematical requirements of the function-specifications. Be this as it may, it is clear that the "quantitative" behavior theorist must carefully balance the "level" of his quantitative intentions against the demand for empirical generality of functions.

It will, of course, be seen that the problem of arriving at the specification of function forms is essentially the problem of *postulate construction,* for the postulates are the "primitive" statements which assert functional relationships among the theoretical variables. Against the background of such problems as have been limned in above, the quantitatively oriented behavior theorist must make a set of difficult decisions about how best to arrive at his postulates. The language for talking about "techniques" of empirical postulate construction is as vague as current knowledge about such "methodology." Two extremes on what is perhaps a continuum of possible approaches are roughly characterized as the "rational" (the theorist's "enlightened, best guess" as to the equation describing a relationship among the theoretical variables) and the "empirical" (the application of curve-fitting techniques to obtained values of an experimental dependent variable as a function of an experimental independent variable, both such variables being regarded as "realizations" of the *theoretical* variables whose relationship is under determination). If the approach be rational, the resulting function must stand or fall via tests of its deductive empirical consequences. If the approach be empirical, it is important for the theorist to perceive, provided his function is to have a generality greater than the locus of its discovery, that the equation-fitting procedure must only be taken to *suggest* the relationship between the *theoretical* variables under consideration. Thus, the resulting empirical function must stand or fall by precisely the same criterion as the rational equation—empirical test of its consequences. It is, of course, more than unlikely that an empirical equation will prove satisfactory without some degree of modification on a "rational" basis. It is, perhaps, even less likely that a "rational" equation will prove satisfactory without further modification in the light of its empirical consequences.

A final point—which applies with peculiar force to Hull—is this. Should the theorist employ intervening variables, and should he assert the option of using "empirical" curve-fitting methods in order to "discover" relations among them (or relations connecting intervenings with *systematic* independents and dependents), it becomes particularly important that the intervening variables not be crudely *identified* with their "realizations" in terms of the specific *experimental* independent and dependent variables used to *suggest* their functional relations. In other words, in the case of intervening variables, it becomes especially unwise to transfer the obtained relationships from the experimental variables of curve-fitting experiments *directly* to the "corresponding" intervening variables. For the *intervening variable functions*,[14] (if the use of intervening variables is to serve any purpose) must express relationships of great generality. Such functions must, by definition, be far fewer in number than the total set of direct functional relationships between the systematic independent and dependent variables which could be presumed capable of generating the same set of deductive consequences. Intervening variable functions, therefore, must be gotten at by *indirect means*, if they can be "gotten at" at all. This means that a generous component of the "rational" must figure in the construction of "successful" intervening variable functions. And this necessitates, in turn, an enormous component of luck.

With these considerations in mind, we may now proceed to the discussion of (a) Hull's *techniques for the measurement of independent and dependent variables,* and (b) Hull's *methods for the construction of "quantitative" functions.*

a. Techniques for measurement of independent and dependent variables. There is no question but that Hull's intentions with respect to "level of quantification" of intervening variable functions were extremely bold. Although, in *Pr.B.*, he was content to hold himself to the identification of equation types, both his stated aims and subsequent efforts (cf. Part II) make it quite clear that his sights were set on the specification of equation type together with estimates of parameters. This being the case, it was essential that the independent and dependent variables of

---

[14] An "intervening variable function" is any functional relationship involving an intervening variable as *at least one* of its terms, i.e., a relation between independent and intervening variables, *or* intervening and intervening variables, *or* intervening and dependent variables.

the theory be susceptible to as close an approximation of *fundamental measurement* as possible.

Hull nowhere gives explicit consideration to the mensurational status of his independent and dependent variables. It is clear, though, that Hull supposed his *mode of identifying* independent and dependent variables to be such as to insure, automatically, a "high" level of mensurability. For Hull represented his independent and dependent variables as *being, or being reducible to, variables which have a well-defined mensurational status in physical science*. This would mean that most of the empirical variables of *Pr.B.* could be regarded as ordered to "fundamental" or "derived" mensurational scales.

That the preceding assumptions are wishful in the extreme requires no further documentation. We have seen, in the consideration of *Independent and Dependent Variables* (pp. 25-46, this report), the manifold deficiencies in their definitions. We already know that the independent and dependent variables as *explicitly* discriminated within the theory language are *not*, in general, the same variables as they function in data language reductions (S, R, W, w, and d are cases in point). We know, too, that *within the theory language* the same independent and dependent variable terms are often differently defined in verbal as against mathematical formulations of postulates, the glossary, and the text (e.g., G, w, A). We know that certain variables (notably, G) require further sub-specification into a collection of variables of different empirical significance and theoretical function. We know also that certain key empirical variables (e.g., R) have no unequivocal definition at all, quite independently of any of the complications mentioned above.

It is, therefore, clear that, far from attaining mensurability of its empirical variables by "fundamental" or "derived" physical scales, the "theory" of *Pr.B.* has not succeeded even in *identifying* its empirical variables in a manner adequate to the theoretical objectives. Since, however, previous discussions of the status and mode of definition of independent and dependent variables have not been explicitly organized around the problem of conformity to physical measuring scales *as such*, it may be useful to consider the matter briefly at this place.

No matter how charitably we adjust our interpretation of the confusing definitions of empirical variables to the theorist's intention, and to the programmatic status of the theory, analysis will show that only a small subset of these variables can be regarded as measurable by physical scales. In general, we can distinguish:

(*a*) Empirical variables which seem legitimately measurable in terms of physical scales.

(*b*) Empirical variables which are *apparently* measurable in terms of such scales, but which do not function, as so measured, within the theory.

(*c*) Empirical variables which are not, in principle, measurable in terms of extant physical scales.

We restrict discussion to the presentation of a few instances of each class.

(1) *Physically measurable variables.* Perhaps the only variables which claim this status are the group of *time* variables distinguished in various postulates, namely:

t —"the duration of the delay in reinforcement" (p. 407).

t' —"degree of asynchronism . . . of $\dot{S}$ and R when both are of brief duration" (p. 178).

t'' —"duration . . . of the continuous action of $\dot{S}$ on the receptor when R begins" (p. 178).

t'''—"the duration in minutes following a sequence of unreinforced evocations of R during which neither reinforced nor unreinforced evocations of R have occurred" (p. 408).

If the assignment of numbers to physically discrete events belonging to a given class ("enumeration") is regarded as a type of physical measurement, then the independent variable N, "the number of reinforcements," and dependent variable n, "the number of unreinforced reactions required to produce . . . extinction," may also be regarded as physically measurable.

(2) *Apparently physically measurable variables.* We have seen that S is identified as physical "stimulus energy," but that S does not necessarily function in this way in data language reductions. As the "energy of sound, light, or heat waves, pressure, etc.," S is, of course, measurable in terms of standard physical scales. Let us assume, however, that the discrepancy between the identification of S as physical energy, and its data language usage did not exist. Would *S, as physically measurable, now* function in a way which is adequate to the demands of the theory? The answer still seems to be, "No." Postulate 1 links S to s with relative determinacy (if not correctness). Postulate 2, however, does not link s to $\bar{s}$ with sufficient specificity to get to $\bar{s}$ from S. But, by assumption of the theory, it is always $\bar{s}$ which is the immediate "determiner" of behavior. Thus, S may be physically measurable, but the *physical measurement* of S functions (with respect to the theory) only as an indicator of the variable $\bar{s}$. Since the function relating S as indicator to $\bar{s}$ is not adequately specified, the fact that the "basic" independent variable S is susceptible to physical measurement is not sufficient for the "secure anchorage" to the theory for which Hull aims. Since *every* independent variable of the theory is linked to a corresponding intervening variable, and since all of the relevant functions can be shown to be insufficiently specified or programmatic, a similar difficulty would hold for the other independent variables, *even assuming that the variables, per se, were physically measurable.* Should this consideration be pressed, even the

time variables would have to be classified under this heading (i.e., they would be "apparently physically measurable," but *not* as they function within the theory).

The basic dependent variable R is presumably physically measurable as "muscular, glandular, electrical" (p. 406) phenomena. And the four indices or "measures" of R (p, $_st_R$, n and A) are given in terms amenable to physical mensuration. Let us neglect the fact that data language applications of R are not consistent with its definition as "muscular" movement, or "glandular" or "electrical" activity. Observe, though, that p, $_st_R$, n and A are scaled in different and non-intertranslatable units which, whatever their status in physics, cannot function as R *measures* in any consistent way. Observe, further, that aside from any other limitation, these "measures" must remain apparent until adequate criteria for the delimitation of the R's of which they are allegedly "measures" are provided.

As a final example, we may cite the case of independent variable w, or "the magnitude of a reinforcing agent" (p. 408). *Illustratively*, Hull has equated this with the weight of food reinforcement. Illustratively, this is all very well. Recall, however, that w must represent quantitatively the composite influence of the complex of factors associated with "quantity" and "quality" of reward. What the mensurational technique for determining *this* might be, Hull does not suggest.

All of the dependent variables, and the vast majority of the independent variables, of *Pr.B.* seem to fall into the present category, on one ground or another.

(3) *Variables not physically measurable, in principle.* It is entirely possible that, should the *actual* independent and dependent variables, *as these function within the theory of Pr.B.*, be reconstructed from data language applications, and from definitions in use based on all relevant formulations in *Pr.B.*, most of the variables would turn out to be not physically measurable, *in principle*. Be this as it may, the theory contains one variable which is explicitly constituted as a variable not orderable to a *physical* scale. This is "d" which is introduced in the principle of stimulus generalization (postulate 5), and defined as "the number of j.n.d.'s lying between the two stimulus aggregates $\dot{S}$ and S" (p. 403). Quite aside from the limitations in the adequacy of the suggested mensurational procedure to the role of this variable in the theory, we should note that d is a *psychophysically scaled*, not a physically scaled, variable.

b. Quantitative function specifications and the technique of their construction. From the preceding discussion, it should be obvious that the "level of mensurability" of Hull's independent and dependent variables is not such as to justify the attempt to achieve any high level of specificity in the mathematical description of function forms. Yet, we already know that Hull's intention in *Pr.B.* was to achieve a level of quantification so demanding as the specification of equation type, and that even this was conceived as but the preliminary step to actual estimates of parameters. We know also, both from Hull's metatheoretical statements and from the form of the postulates, that the theory of *Pr.B.* is intended as a theory of *unrestricted generality* offered as potentially adequate to the major phenomena of organismic behavior. In constructing the functions asserted by the postulates of *Pr.B.*, Hull was therefore setting himself the inordinately difficult task of combining a high degree of specificity with "maximal" empirical *generality*. Such an effort, of course, is necessarily doomed to failure in the present phase of psychology, and whether these objectives will ever become feasible is an open question. That Hull *did* fall enormously short of these objectives is shown in detail by our consideration of the "structure of the theory," and, indeed, by the entire trend of the preceding discussions. At this place, we will be concerned primarily with Hull's *methods for constructing quantitative functions* in order to exploit Hull's experience with such problems for any further insight this may yield with respect to general issues concerning the quantification of behavioral relationships. Before we proceed to this topic, it may be well to summarize from scattered discussions the *status of the function "quantifications" actually attained in Pr.B.*

(1) *Summary of the status of the function quantifications.* A widespread impression that the theory of *Pr.B.* provides "mathematical" statements for all postulates is incorrect. For three postulates (1, 2, and 3) no "mathematical statement" is given. Of these, postulates 1 and 2 (introducing the afferent impulse and afferent interaction, respectively) would demand quantitative specification of the functions, if the theory were to become truly quantitative (at any level). For two postulates (11 and 16) the so-called "mathematical statement" represents a translation of the verbal formulation into symbolic logic. Postulate 11 (on the reaction threshold) does not necessarily demand further mathematization. Postulate 16 (on incompatible reaction potentials) is admittedly a simplification in its present form, and would demand quantitative specification, if the theory were to become adequately quantitative. Thus five postulates in all are not given quantitative specification.

The remaining eleven postulated "mathematical statements" are equations specifying various function forms. The most frequently occurring function forms are *linear* and *exponential* (of the positive and negative "growth" type). No values are specified for the "empirical constant" terms which occur in these equations. There is no discussion of the significance of such "constants," their intended generality, etc., nor is there any attempt to specify general procedures for obtaining the values which must be substituted for these constants, if the equations are to be solvable.

All intervening variable symbols which occur in these equations designate constructs ordered to purely programmatic scales, having no empirical significance. Thus, no empirically meaningful values can be substituted for *these* variables.

If we recall the manifold definitional and mensurational inadequacies of the systematic independent and dependent variables, it becomes evident that significant substitutions cannot be made for *these* classes of variables, either.

Taking all the above circumstances together, it is obvious that the "quantification" of *Pr.B.* is, in every discriminable respect, programmatic and empirically empty. At best, the postulates of this theory can permit only qualitative, "more or less" derivations. Any manipulation of *numbers* according to these rules must be an indeterminate manipulation of empirically meaningless numbers for illustrative purposes.

(2) *Methods for constructing "quantitative" functions.* We have already seen that, in general, Hull relies on empirical curve-fitting techniques in the construction of the function forms which enter the postulates. The data used for such purposes derive from (*a*) already available experiments selected by Hull as the inductive source for a given postulate (and often subjected to various transformations in order to make the data suitable for curve-fitting), and (*b*) "curve-fitting" experiments specifically designed by Hull in order to supply relevant material for quantification. Mere recognition of Hull's reliance on empirical equation-fitting techniques, however, tells us little about his response to the manifold problems of function quantification. In the following discussion, we must inquire into the detailed role of Hull's empirical equation-fitting procedures within the total context of his methods of working towards a *quantitative theory of high generality, adhering to the independent, intervening, dependent variable paradigm.*

We noted that, if one seeks a theoretical function of high empirical *generality,* this entails (*a*) that the theoretical variables related by the function be linked to a "rich" *plurality* of reductive symptoms (i.e., potential *experimental* variables), and (*b*) that the function factually hold over a wide range of empirical conditions presumed to be independent of the variables related by the function. A purely "positivistic" theory would proceed to identify a set of systematic independent and dependent variables and investigate the laws of their relationship. Such laws could conceivably vary greatly in "generality," depending on the range of *reductive* implications (empirical "richness") of the variables, and the range of empirical conditions for which the function holds, as previously indicated. Thus, even the "positivistic" theorist, if he were to construct his laws by equation-fitting techniques, could not merely proceed to transfer a function form fitted to any *single* experimental "realization" of his theoretical variables, to the theoretical variables themselves, and at the same time *count* on any useful degree of generality in the resulting law. It is obvious that "generality" could be claimed only to the extent that the function were subsequently verified in a variety of experimental "realizations." The positivistic theorist, however, may *presuppose* a close parallelism between the function forms exhibited by any given empirical "realizations" of theoretical variables whose relation is under scrutiny, and the *theoretical* function form. This being the case the results of empirical curve-fitting may be used in a relatively *direct* way, either for suggesting a theoretical function form, or for testing a theoretical equation which was rationally assumed.

A problem of a *very different order* arises for a theorist who wishes to attain the degree of "generality" made possible, at least in principle, by the use of intervening variables. Such variables are, by definition, indirectly "inferred" constructs, the use of which is calculated to minimize the number of postulated functions necessary to generate a given set of empirical consequences. Presumably, a *markedly greater* number of positivistic (independent-dependent variable functions) would be necessary to mediate the same range of empirical consequences. *By definition* then, there can be no direct parallelism between a theoretical function containing an intervening variable as (at least) one of its terms, and *any* experimental "realization" of that function. One way of explicating the rationale for this may be as follows.

A positivistic law asserts a relationship between variables, the reductive "symptoms" of which *are* sets of experimental independent and dependent variables. The variables of a "positivistic law" can be placed in correspondence to *experimental* independent and dependent variables in simple one to one fashion. Intervening variable functions are related to experimental relationships in another way. They are "elements" in a *function chain* which links systematic independent variables initially to intervenings, and then to dependent variables. The *entire chain* is presumably capable of generating *consequences* which may be placed in correspondence with *experimental* independent and dependent variables. But no single function in the chain can be ordered to a given experimental relationship. There is no variable in the experiment that *could correspond* to the inferred construct that is the intervening variable.

From the above considerations, it is evident that intervening variable functions *cannot* be constructed via any *purely* "empirical" method of function fitting. The construction of intervening variable functions must then depend on a set of *rational* best guesses. Such guesses must, to be sure, be *guided* by the theorist's estimate of the possibilities that the given function taken together with the others in the theory will be capable of generating consequences which agree with available empirical evidence, but these "guesses" *cannot*, in the nature of the case, be *uniquely deter-*

mined by the available evidence. The "invention" or "intuition" of successful intervening variable functions is, of course, a central context in which theoretical creativity may be manifested. The great creative theoretical insights in the history of science consist precisely in such felicitous "perceptions" of the "intervening variable functions" which can unify an extensive range of empirical relationships. These considerations have not always been recognized by psychologists who advocate theories which employ intervening variables.[15]

It is to Hull's credit that he recognized the difficulties of inferring intervening variable functions from empirical relationships, even if he did not achieve a methodology capable of resolving these difficulties. In *Pr.B.*, the response to these difficulties was faltering—incorporating joint elements of arbitrariness, inconsistency and programmaticity. We will see, in Part II of the report, that the attempt to grapple with these intricate issues in a determinate way was central in the final phase of Hull's career.

An empirical theory which employs intervening variables must, of course, contain *three classes* of intervening variable functions. These are functions relating (a) independent and intervening variables, (b) intervening and intervening variables, and (c) intervening and dependent variables. In order to reconstruct the methodology of function construction of *Pr.B.*, it will be instructive to examine Hull's procedure in arriving at the critical independent-intervening variable relation of the theory—the relation of $_sH_R$ to "the number of reinforcements," N.

Hull begins with the observation that "habit strength cannot be determined by direct observation, since it exists as an organization as yet largely unknown, hidden within the complex structure of the nervous system" (p. 102). He points to the difficulty in determining the functional relationship between variables, when one of the variables "under investigation is a logical construct, and so is neither observable nor directly measurable" (p. 113). The "strength of a receptor-effector connection can," therefore, "be determined . . . only indirectly" (p. 102). "There are," however, "two groups of such observable phenomena associated with habit: (1) the antecedent conditions which lead to habit formation, and (2) the behavior which is the after-effect or consequence of these antecedent conditions" (p. 102).

Hull then cites four studies which he deems relevant to the relationship of habit strength and number of reinforcements. Each of these studies presumably explores this relationship in terms of different manifestations of habit strength. They are:

(a) *Amplitude.* Hovland's (25) determination of amplitude of conditioned *G.S.R.* as a function of the number of reinforcements.

---

[15] Tolman, for instance, has consistently overlooked these problems both in general discussions of intervening variables, and in his own theoretical constructions.

(b) *Latency.* Simley's (112) determination of syllable reaction latencies (to nonsense characters) as a function of trials of practice.

(c) *Resistance to extinction.* Williams' and Perin's (103, 142) data
for the number of extinction reactions as a function of number of
reinforcements.

(d) *Probability (percentage of correct response evocations).* B. I.
Hull's determination of percentage of occurrence of correct bar
responses (directional movements of a pivoted Skinner box manipulandum which can be moved in four directions) as a function
of "successive hundreds of responses."

In cases (a), (b) and (c), fitted curves are presented, (a) and (c)
being "growth functions," and (b) the reciprocal of a growth function.
No equation is presented for the data of (d).

Taking his "point of departure from extensive observations in the
field of habit formation typified by the experiments which yielded" the
data of (a), (b), (c) and (d), Hull concludes that:

1. Habit strength is an increasing function of the number of reinforcements.
2. This function increases up to some sort of physiological limit beyond which
no more increase is possible.
3. As habit strength approaches this physiological limit with continued reinforcements the increment ($\Delta\ _sH_R$) resulting from each additional reinforcement decreases progressively in magnitude (pp. 113-114).

Hull continues:

Now, there are numerous algebraic expressions which yield results conforming
to the above specifications. One of these, however, has a rather special promise
because it is known to approximate closely a very large number of observable
empirical relationships in all sorts of biological situations involving growth and
decay. Indeed, Figures 21, 22, and 23 are all cases in point. [The reference here
is to the figures presenting the data for (a) (b) and (c) above.] The basic
principle of the simple positive growth function . . . is that the amount of
growth resulting from each unit of growth opportunity will increase the amount
of whatever is growing by a constant fraction of the growth potentiality as yet
unrealized (p. 114; brackets mine).

The above constitutes Hull's *rationale* for assuming the growth hypothesis as to the relation of $_sH_R$ and N. Note that Hull begins with
explicit recognition of the difficulties involved in the indirect inference
of the functions linking "unobservables" (i.e., intervening variables) to
their "observable" determinants (i.e., systematic independent variables).
He then proceeds to take four selected examples of functional relationships between the "directly measurable" antecedent (N) and consequents
(A, $_st_R$, n, p) of his inferred intervening variable ($_sH_R$). To three of
these relationships, curves are fitted which turn out to be *growth
functions*. From these empirical materials, Hull goes on to hypothesize
the conditions which the *theoretical function* linking $_sH_R$ to N would

have to satisfy in order to generate the *observed* relationships. These specifications turn out to represent a set of conditions compatible with the properties of "numerous algebraic expressions." "One of these, however, has a rather special promise" because of its approximation to empirical growth and decay relationships "in all sorts of biological situations." And so we come out with a *growth relationship*. From the empirical data on which a growth relationship is imposed, we make our "indirect" inferences about the function defining our "unobservable" intervening variable, and, by a curious circularity we come out with what?—a *growth* function.

Be this as it may, Hull, on the basis of the above analysis, advances his theoretical equation for $_sH_R$ as a function of N (p. 119):

$$_S^N H_R = M - Me^{-iN}$$

where $M = 100$, N is the number of reinforcement repetitions, e is 10, and

$$i = \log \frac{1}{1 - F}$$

where F is the reduction constant. . . .

Since the fitted equations for (*a*) (amplitude) and (*c*) (number of extinction responses) are growth functions, this procedure results in *linear* relationships as between $_sH_R$ and the two response variables. In the case of (*b*) (latency), the empirical "equation represents the reciprocal of a slightly complicated positive growth function" (p. 121). In this case, therefore, the relation between $_sH_R$ and $_st_R$, on the assumption of the *theoretical* (non-complicated) growth relation between $_sH_R$ and N, turns out to deviate from linearity in the direction of slight negative acceleration (cf. pp. 336-337).

Whatever the ambiguities in Hull's discussion of the $_sH_R$-N function, two things can be said with confidence: (1) Hull was distinctly aware of the illegitimacy of directly transferring functions fitted to *experimental* independent and dependent variables, to an intervening variable function relating a systematic independent and *an intervening variable;* (2) he develops a confusingly mixed argument, based *both on rational and empirical considerations,* for assuming an intervening variable function which *does* mirror the characteristics of the empirical function used as the induction base.

At bottom, this inconsistency probably derives from the fact that Hull recognized the difficulties involved in the construction of intervening variable functions for a comprehensive theory, and yet wished somehow to push on to such a theory despite these difficulties. If the recognition that only a primarily *rational* approach could mediate the construction of intervening variable functions were *implemented*, this would entail resignation to the fact that a comprehensive behavior theory can only be worked towards very modestly, if at all; that, indeed, a *general* theory of behavior of the "intervening variable" variety is enormously out of reach. Hitting on "fruitful" intervening variable functions, even with respect to the systematization of narrowly delimited empirical domains, must in the present phase of psychology involve an immense element of luck, and "luck" of this order cannot be expected to emerge without an immense sequence of "rational" hypothesis formation and adjustment in the light of indirect empirical consequences.

It would clearly be much to the interest of a theorist with Hull's ambitious intentions, if intervening variable functions could, nevertheless, be located in a relatively immediate way from empirical data. Thus, Hull's response to this intolerable dilemma seems to have been to look for (or create) *rational* grounds for legitimating the assumption of a close correspondence between theoretical construct relations and the variables in curve-fitting experiments. Such grounds could be provided, if certain very simple relations were assumed to hold between the intervening variables and certain of the dependent variables (i.e., response measures) of the theory. For, if these relations are sufficiently straightforward, then the results of appropriate curve-fitting experiments, designed in terms relevant to the theoretical dependent variables, could be used to suggest construct interrelations in a relatively direct way. The simplest expedient would be to develop *rational* grounds for assuming that the basic intervening variable of the theory ($_sH_R$), and the intervening variable chain related to it, were connected to the independent variable N by a function having the same form as the *empirical* learning curves relating N to at least a subset of the *dependent variables* of the theory. If this assumption were made, then a *linear* relationship would obtain between $_sH_R$ (and thus the terminal intervening variable of the chain, $_s\bar{E}_R$) and the dependent variable measures in question. This is precisely what Hull seems to have done in positing that $_sH_R$ is related to N, according to a function having the same form (growth) as that relating A to N and n to N.[16]

At this point in the argument, it perhaps looks as if the basis for Hull's choice of the growth relation between $_sH_R$ and N was empirical, rather than rational. But now an additional consideration must be introduced. No one, including Hull, would argue that *all empirical learning curves* conform to a growth function. Nor is it necessarily the case that any given set of extant learning data, including the data chosen by Hull, is best fitted by a growth function. There is always an element of arbitrariness in curve-fitting procedures, and, as we will later have oc-

---

[16] It is significant to note that most of the experiments *specifically designed* by Hull (and collaborators) to suggest construct relations for the theory of *Pr.B.* utilized the two dependent variable measures—n and A—which presumably have this *linear* relationship with $_sH_R$.

casion to note, the arbitrariness is rather pronounced in many of Hull's "fits." It seems fairly definitely the case that Hull assumed, on the basis of *rational* considerations similar to those adduced in the passages quoted above, that the growth relation is the type of function best geared to the *conceptual* requirements of a construct like $_sH_R$ (and other "learning" variables). Our point, then, is that Hull did not assume the growth relation between $_sH_R$ and N because this was the function that best fitted the Hovland and Perin-Williams data, but rather that the design of these studies and the mathematical treatment of the data reflected the prior growth function assumption. Thus, the most reasonable interpretation of the $_sH_R$-N function is that it is primarily "rational" in origin.

A corollary to the above analysis is that, once the growth relation between $_sH_R$ and N enters the theory as a rational component, it becomes "permissible" to construct all other "mathematical" intervening variable functions, with the exception of the terminal linkages between $_s\bar{E}_R$ and the dependent variables, by the direct transposition of function forms fitted to experimental data. In other words, the single "rational" component of the theory is so chosen as to permit a reliance on *empirical* procedures of function induction with respect to most of the remaining components of the theory.[17] In line with this, it is significant to note that in discussing the rationale for *all further* "quantitative" intervening variable functions preceding the dependent variable linkages Hull does not, *on a single occasion*, question the practice of directly transforming empirically fitted curves into relationships among "unobservables." The uniform procedure becomes that of selecting or designing an experiment, the independent variable of which is presumed to correspond to the antecedent theoretical variable under consideration, and the dependent variable of which corresponds to the consequent theoretical variable. To the experimental data is fitted an equation, and the *form* of the resulting equation is then transposed (minus parametric values) to the intervening variable function under construction.

A case in point is provided by the very next intervening variable function that Hull considers after the introduction of $_sH_R$ as a function of N. This is, "Habit Strength as a Function of the Nature and Amount of the Reinforcing Agent" (w) (Chapter IX, pp. 124-134). It may be instructive to summarize the high spots in the discussion.

---

[17] When the $_sH_R$-N function is referred to as the *"single* rational component of the theory," the reference is to the *mathematical* intervening variable functions, for which "equations" are asserted. As already indicated, there are several postulates in the set—e.g., postulate 2 on "neural interaction," postulate 3 on $_sU_R$, postulate 11 on the "reaction threshold"—which are given only verbal, "qualitative" formulation. In some broad sense of the term, these postulates may be said to be based on "rational" considerations, but not in the sense in which a distinction is made between "rational" versus "empirical" *equations*.

a) The data chosen as induction basis for this relationship derives from Grindley's experiment (16) on the speed of runway traversal of five groups of chicks rewarded with 0, 1, 2, 4, and 6 grains of boiled rice, respectively. Grindley plotted learning curves for the five groups in terms of 100 *x* the reciprocal of the running time. From *measurements* made on Grindley's published graphs, Hull computed the "mean score at the last 5 of 7 trials" (p. 126) for each group. To these data, Hull fitted a *growth function*. This, despite the fact that the plots for the four groups which received reward seem arrayed in a perfect straight line (cf. Fig. 28, p. 126).

b) Hull then decides, on grounds which seem thoroughly arbitrary, that the amount of the reinforcing agent influences the *asymptote* of the $_sH_R$ curve, rather than the magnitude of the growth constant (F) (pp. 127-128).

c) The hypothesis about the influence of "quantity of the reinforcing agent" on $_sH_R$ is then extended to the influence of *quality* of reward, with only a bare and question-begging attempt to indicate the grounds for this extension (pp. 128-129).

From such considerations, it is concluded that (p. 128):

. . . the limit (M') of habit strength . . . attainable with unlimited number of reinforcements is a positive growth function of the magnitude of the agent employed in the reinforcement process.

The "magnitude of the agent" here refers *both* to "quantity" and "quality." To be entirely fair, Hull indicates that the hypothesis "is based on admittedly inadequate grounds" (p. 128). Yet this function enters into the critical principle of reinforcement as one of the four basic sub-functions constitutive of $_sH_R$. Note, though, that *in this case*, Hull transfers a function "fitted to experimental data" (and a very crass fit to very questionable data) *directly* to an intervening variable function *without considering at all the legitimacy of such an identification*.

It would be boresome to spell out further examples of this practice of constructing intervening variable functions directly from empirical materials. A characteristic example of the intervening-intervening variable type is provided by the construction of postulate 7 from the Perin-Williams data. As we already have seen (cf. pp. 22-24, this report), the procedure here was to set the experimental variables, "number of Skinner box reinforcements" and "number of hours of food privation," into correspondence with $_sH_R$ and D, respectively, while "number of extinction responses" was ordered to $_sE_R$. An equation was then fitted to the joint functional relationships between the two antecedent experimental variables and the experimental dependent variables. The form of the resulting function was then transposed to the theoretical constitution of $_sE_R$ by $_sH_R$ and D.

When Hull arrives at the ostensibly difficult task of relating the terminal intervening variables ($_s\bar{E}_R$ and $_s\dot{\bar{E}}_R$) of the theory to the systematic *dependent* variables, he is able to make capital from the fact that these functions were already, as it were, "built in" to the theory via the nature of the original $_sH_R\text{-}N$ assumption. The critical supposition mediating the construction of the four functions relating reaction potential to p, $_st_R$, n and A (postulates 12-15, p. 344) is as follows:

> Since reaction potential is a joint multiplicative function of habit strength and drive . . . , it follows that so long as drive remains constant, reaction potential will also closely approximate a simple growth function of the number of reinforcements (p. 326).

It thus becomes possible to analyze equations fitted to empirical learning curves into two components, one a growth function relating reaction potential ($_s\bar{E}_R$ or $_s\dot{\bar{E}}_R$) to N, and the other the residual function relating reaction potential to each of the response "measures," in precisely the same way that the learning curves cited in connection with the $_sH_R\text{-}N$ function (pp. 120-122) were analyzed. As a matter of fact, for three of the functions—those relating $_sE_R$ and $_st_R$, n, and A, respectively—the *same* learning data as those used in the $_sH_R$ discussion are analyzed. The relationship of reaction potential to p (probability of reaction evocation) is derived, not from an empirical curve, but from a *theoretical* curve (quasi-ogival in form) built up by combining the growth hypothesis of $_sE_R$ as a function of N with the Gaussian $_sO_R$ function (postulate 10), together with the assumption of the existence of the reaction threshold ($_sL_R$). In the first three cases, the procedure in deriving the dependent variable linkages is simple, consisting essentially in the substitution of $_sE_R$ for the growth expressions which are present in the empirical equations fitted to the learning data in question. Since the fitted equations contain a number of empirical constants which are independent of the growth expressions, these are retained as parameters of the resulting equations linking $_sE_R$ to the various response measures. In the case of the $_sE_R\text{-}p$ function, no problem arises in making it give forth precisely what was put into it. The theoretical curve (p. 331) is a synthetic composite of a growth function (for $_sE_R$) with a normal probability function (for $_sO_R$), to represent dispersions of $_sE_R$, at different N values, above the reaction threshold ($_sL_R$). From this, it is an easy matter to derive that p "is a normal probability (ogival) function of the extent to which the effective reaction potential ($_s\bar{E}_R$) exceeds the reaction threshold ($_sL_R$)" (p. 344).

The trend of the preceding discussion has been to suggest that Hull's approach to the demanding problem of "inferring" intervening variable functions was: (*a*) to recognize that such functions could only be constructed by "indirect" rational means, and (*b*) to develop a pat, arbitrary and over-schematic "rational" basis (the $N\text{-}_sH_R\text{-}response\ variables$ analysis) which, nevertheless, "legitimated" direct reliance on *empirical* procedures for the construction of the majority of functions in the theory.

Remember that the basic objective behind the entire problem was to attain a set of laws approximating "maximal" empirical generality and quantitative specificity, for a comprehensive theory of behavior. We already know that, no matter *what* the adequacy of Hull's methods of function construction, such an objective was entirely out of reach. Not the least of the reasons for this derives from the manifold definitional and mensurational inadequacies of the systematic independent and dependent variables previously noted. It is now clear that Hull's actual method of function construction—which in effect equates intervening variables (and *systematic* independents and dependents) with *experimental* variables—further curtails any remote possibility that quantitative laws of wide generality could be attained. Nevertheless, *suppose for the sake of argument*, that Hull's use of empirical curve-fitting procedures *was* an entirely acceptable route to the specification of intervening variable functions. It then becomes necessary to enquire into the adequacy both of the curve-fitting procedures, and the experimental data to which they are applied. Accordingly, we conclude the present section with a few summary remarks about (*a*) the characteristics of the data used for equation-fitting, and (*b*) goodness of fit.

a) There is much evidence to suggest that the data chosen for curve-fitting are highly "selected" (cf. 81, 92, 105, 108). Relevant experiments seem chosen largely in terms of coincidence with prior assumption, or amenability to some kind of curve-fitting determination. Contrary findings (e.g., "intermittent reinforcement," "latent learning") are often ignored. Restricted subsets of the data of a given experiment are sometimes chosen. For instance, the Simley rote learning data employed in the construction of the $_sH_R$-N function, derived from one subject. Sometimes, as in the case of the Grindley data, use is made of measurements taken from crude curves rather than reported measurements. On occasion, data derived from subjects under different experimental conditions, and of questionable comparability, are combined in the same averages. For instance, the data to which the S-R asynchronism function (for the "delay" case) is fitted, consists of the combined per cent CR values taken from two animals trained under *different* conditions in the Kappauf-Schlosberg experiment (82). In this case, too, the measurements were determined from published graphs. Again, it is not generally recognized that the four groups of animals of the Williams study (142), and the eight groups trained by Perin (103), which *together* comprise the basis of the very important Perin-Hull equations (postulate 7), were subjected to distinctly different experimental routines. Over and above these limitations in the data used for curve-fitting, is Hull's consistent failure to give adequate concern to the *generalization ranges* within which the empirical findings may rationally be expected to hold.

b) It is hardly necessary to mention Hull's widely recognized tendency to fit equations projectively rather than objectively. The number of data plots is often dangerously small. It is rare that more than four or five data plots are used for the determination of a given function. The Mowrer-Jones curve for the number of extinction responses as a function of grams of lever pressure (p. 280), which provides the basis for one of the major assumptions relevant to inhibition (I_R as a function of W), contains only *three* data plots. Further, the data points, whether they be many or few, are not always judiciously distributed over the range of the function. In particular, sometimes limiting or extreme values are omitted, at the risk of highly misleading extrapolations (e.g., Perin's extrapolated resistance to extinction values for "zero" food privation, cf. 87, p. 109). Finally, a cursory running of the eye over the many graphs of fitted functions in *Pr.B.* will provide a crude but revealing index of the extent to which the equations actually generate values which conform to the plotted data points, such as they are.

3. Techniques of Derivation

Taking Hull's theoretical efforts as a whole, it can unquestionably be said that he has made the most intensive and persistent attempt of any learning theorist to achieve rigorous and explicit derivation. Nevertheless, as in the case of the discussion of "explicitness of axiomatization," it is necessary that we conduct our inquiry on a less relative scale.

There is, of course, a direct tie between explicitness of axiomatization and explicitness of the derivations which the "axioms" can mediate. Thus, our discussion of Hull's "explicitness of axiomatization," together with the manifold preceding considerations concerning the "axiomatic" structure of the theory of *Pr.B.*, should provide a voluminous definition of the *limits* within which "derivations" are feasible. In this section, we will supplement these considerations with (1) a brief resumé of the *characteristics of the "derivations" in formulations preceding Pr.B.*, and (2) the *derivational procedures of Pr.B.*

a. Derivations in Pre-*Pr.B.* formulations. Hull's early theoretical articles are notable for clarity of exposition, and the detail in which the attempt is made to indicate the consequences of the assumptions being explored. The exploration, however, is conducted *informally*. No claim is made that "deductions" have been carried out with a full exhibition of mediating steps or that all of the assumptions have been made explicit. Rather, "deductions" are put forward as the "kind of thing" that *would* follow—given the major assumptions under exploration—under such and such conditions. The "conditions," in turn, may be exemplary or hypothetical, or they may be conditions actually realized in previously performed experiments, or realizable in experiments to be performed. Assumptions are stated qualitatively, and "deductions" are also qualitative. *Ad hoc* quasi-mathematical assumptions are often, but overtly, made in operating with the hypotheses being explored.

In the case of such "miniature systems" as the 1935 system on rote learning (39) and the 1937 "adaptive behavior" development (42), an attempt is made to spell out the main steps of the derivations. In these cases, too, postulates and derivations are *qualitative*. Formal, verbal definitions are given for the major terms. Step by step derivations are aided by diagrammatic and arbitrary pseudo-mathematical illustrative devices. "Degree of formality" (rigor, explicitness) of derivations falls far short of what would be requisite in a formalized system, but is far in excess of the expository procedures of other learning theorists.

The derivations in the 1940 rote learning systematization (51) show perhaps the greatest degree of rigor and explicitness of any formulation in psychology. The possibility of achieving this level of explicitness and detail appears to result from the restriction of the theory to a limited empirical domain, and one in which the variables are highly controllable and manipulable.

b. The derivational procedures of *Pr.B.* We have developed many considerations which must imply that "derivation" in any *strict* sense is impossible within the theory of *Pr.B.* Among them are: the ambiguities in the independent and dependent variable identifications, the vagueness in the postulate formulations, the relational lacunae and indeterminacies in construct inter-connections, the programmaticity of the intervening variable "units," and the mensurational deficiencies of the systematic empirical variables. Any attempt to "solve" the equations represented by the postulates, for any given set of empirical conditions, must depend on a series of "as if" assumptions about the necessary substitutions for systematic independent variables, empirical constants and prior intervening variables, which can have only *illustrative* significance. The absence of *formal* explicit and operational definition, and of rules of inference, would *alone* preclude explicit logical derivations, while the programmaticity and incompleteness of the quantification would certainly prohibit rigorous mathematical derivations.

It is fair to note, however (as we did once before), that the *intention* of *Pr.B.* is not to carry out any marked number of derivations, or even to provide all necessary conceptual tools for strict logico-mathematical derivation, but to concentrate on the formulation and explication of a tentative postulate set for a comprehensive theory of behavior. Nevertheless, considering the postulate set of *Pr.B.* even as a *tentative* axiomatic component (minus formal explicit and operational definitions) of a *potential* formal theory, there still remains good reason to believe that derivations of a high degree of determinacy could not be achieved, if the potential theory reflected many characteristics of the actual one.

The above comments are not intended to suggest that the theory of *Pr.B.* is any the worse off with respect to potential derivational rigor than are alternate behavior theories. But, as in the case of so many other issues having to do with hypothetico-deductive status, it is necessary to separate Hull's metatheoretical statements about the status and objectives of the theory from the actual status of the theory.

Despite the concentration on the discussion of postulates, *Pr.B.* includes a "random sampling of some fifty or so secondary principles (corollaries) . . . given chiefly for purposes of illustrating the meaning of the primary principles" (p. 398). These represent Hull's estimates of certain of the more direct and/or important consequences of the postulates of *Pr.B.* Certain of these "corollaries" represent sequences of consequences mediated primarily by key postulate "clusters" of the theory (e.g., the twenty-two corollaries of the inhibition assumptions in Chapter XVI, the twelve corollaries of the "primary motivation" postulates in Chapter XIV), while other corollary sequences represent attempts to mobilize all relevant postulates of the theory on key empirical problem areas (e.g., the eight corollaries on stimulus "patterning" in Chapter XIX). It may be useful to consider summarily the status of these corollaries.

In general, nothing approaching formal or even highly explicit informal derivation is attempted. The procedure, in most instances, involves a verbal indication of what should follow when certain postulates are taken in conjunction with hypothetical sets of empirical conditions, or empirical conditions corresponding to previously reported experiments. It is important to recognize that the corollaries can be no more "genuinely" *quantitative* than the postulates which are believed to generate them. Many of the corollaries are "qualitative" consequences which follow, for given conditions, from the general function forms assumed by the postulates (taken singly or in combination). Others, however, are "derived" via sheerly arbitrary settings of the empirically empty variables in the postulated equations, and as such cannot be regarded as generated by any explicit part of the theory. Usually, when this is done, the values substituted in the equation, are chosen in such a way as to fit the requirements of the hypothetical or known empirical phenomena under analysis. It must be emphasized that most of the more conspicuous *"tours de force"* among the "corollaries" of *Pr.B.*, such as the sequence on stimulus patterning (pp. 358-372) are "derived" in this *ad hoc* fashion. Indeed, in the theory of *Pr.B.*, the line of demarcation between "derivation" (at any level) and *illustration* is somewhat blurred.

A special class of *ad hoc* "derivations" within the theory of *Pr.B.* seems to stem from the occasional covert use of the empirical constants present in empirical equations used to *suggest* construct interrelations. It will be recalled that Hull meticulously avoids the insertion of such parametric values into *postulates*. Corollaries which presuppose such empirical constants, then, cannot be regarded as consequences of the *theory*, but only as implications of empirical equations which are *outside the theory*. For instance, corollary II in the analysis of "primary motivation and reaction potential" (p. 247) states that:

When primary drive strength (D) is zero, reaction-evocation potential $(_sE_R)$ has an appreciable but relatively low positive value which is a positive growth function of the number of reinforcements.

This corollary could not conceivably follow from postulate 7 (p. 254) which asserts merely that:

$$_sE_R = f(_s\bar{H}_R) \times f(D).$$

It *can*, however, follow from the concrete details of the equation fitted to the Perin-Williams data (p. 255), or from a set of assumptions—the "quantitative derivation of $_sE_R$ from $_sH_R$ and D" (cf. pp. 242-247)— arbitrarily adjusted to the content of this equation.[18] The presence in the theory of *Pr.B.* of such "corollaries" adds another dimension of ambiguity to what the "postulates" of *Pr.B.* assert.

It should be added that the complexity and detail of the formulations at certain points can tend to obscure soft area in alleged "derivations." For instance, the "quantitative derivation of $_sE_R$ from $_sH_R$ and D" alluded to above, represents an elaborate *ad hoc* attempt to reproduce the details of the Perin equation from a combination of the prior assumptions of the theory (postulates 4, 5, and "major corollary" 1) together with postulate 7. From arbitrary mathematical settings of these assumptions, a table is constructed purporting to represent theoretical values, at various N's, for: (1) the habit strength mobilized by the drive stimulus, (2) the habit strength mobilized by non-drive components of the stimulus complex, and (3) the multiplicative effects of certain drive strengths on the physiological summation of (1) and (2). All this is very impressive, but an entire column of values in this table (Col. 4, Table 5, p. 243) presents substantial positive values for the habit strength loadings of an *absent* (zero drive strength) drive *stimulus* at all numbers of reinforcements greater than zero.

Despite difficulties of the sort mentioned above, and the gap between the "derivations" of *Pr.B.* and strict formal derivation, it would be unjust not to underline in this section the great distance between Hull's efforts in the exploration of theoretical consequences and conventional practice among recent theorists. After all, "derivations" can be no more explicit than the theories which generate them, and theories can rarely be as full or explicit as the desires of the theorists who generate *them*. Perhaps the most impressive and consistent quality in Hull's work may be seen in the ingenuity and range of the attempts to explore the consequences

---

[18] Consult (88) for a detailed discussion of related issues.

of his hypotheses. In the early stages of the development of a theory, such explorations of the deductive potentialities of incompletely determinate initial hypotheses, even when the "deductions" involve *ad hoc* supplementation, is essential. Hull demonstrated great brilliance in this regard in his early theoretical articles. In the ambitious rote learning system (51), he was able to demonstrate perhaps the closest approximation to explicit derivations yet attained in a non-natural science theory. In *Pr.B.*, the imaginative brilliance in the *informal* calculation of consequences which was evident in the early articles is somewhat submerged by the preoccupation with the explication of primary principles. Further, the status of "derivations" is confused by the nonfunctional quantitative trim and definitional vagaries of the postulates. Yet, even in *Pr.B.*, the *attempts* to bring the principles to bear in a relatively detailed way on experimental issues still offer a refreshing contrast to the practice of many other recent theorists.

D. EMPIRICAL CONTENT AND ADEQUACY

So far in this report, we have concentrated on the stated objective of determining the systematic status of the theory of *Pr.B.* At many points, our inquiries into theoretical structure and methodology have involved necessary reference to matters of *empirical content*. And, at all points, our considerations of "formal" issues have had obvious implications for the evaluation of *empirical adequacy*. Any full or authoritative evaluation of the empirical adequacy of all hypotheses embedded in the formulations of *Pr.B.*, or the fruits of Hull's theoretical thinking generally, is not within the scope of this report. The function of the present, brief section is to bring together under a set of rubrics relevant to over-all questions of empirical adequacy certain clear implications of the previous analyses. In Part II, which carries the concern with Hull's theoretical methodology into the later phase of his career, further consideration of matters of empirical adequacy will arise as we pursue the fate of the theory of *Pr.B.* The concluding remarks of Part III will also raise, at least superficially, issues having to do with the empirical fruitfulness of Hull's contributions in general.

In the following discussion, we will consider these characteristics of the theory of *Pr.B.*: (1) *the range of data covered*, (2) *degree of confirmation*, (3) *flexibility* (in practice) *with respect to empirical evidence*, and (4) *special virtues* which may prove useful outside the context of the theory, as specified.

1. Range of Data Covered

By *intention*, *Pr.B.* is a tentative postulate set designed to account for the major phenomena of organismic behavior. The postulates are presumed to represent the primary principles of a comprehensive theory, conceived as a theoretical basis for "all the social sciences" (p. 398). A faint conception of the ambitiousness of Hull's objectives may be derived from the following statements:

The main concern of this work has been to isolate and present the primary or basic principles or laws of behavior as they appear in the current state of behavioral knowledge; at present there have been isolated sixteen such principles. In so far as these principles or postulates are sound and sufficient, it should be possible to deduce from them an extensive logical hierarchy of secondary principles which will exactly parallel all of the objectively observable phenomena of the behavior of higher organisms; such a hierarchy would constitute a systematic theory of all the social sciences. Considerable progress has been made in this direction [here there appear 28 bibliographical citations], though because of the limitations in available space only a random sampling of some fifty or so secondary principles (corollaries) is included in the present volume; these are given chiefly for purposes of illustrating the meaning of the primary principles (p. 398; brackets mine).

It is to be hoped that as the years go by, systematic treatises on the different aspects of the behavior sciences will appear. One of the first of these would naturally present a general theory of individual behavior; another, a general theory of social behavior. In the elaboration of various subdivisions and combinations of these volumes there would develop a systematic series of theoretical works dealing with different specialized aspects of mammalian behavior, particularly the behavior of human organisms. Such a development would include volumes devoted to the theory of skills and their acquisition; of communicational symbolism or language (semantics); of the use of symbolism in individual problem solution involving thought and reasoning; of social or ritualistic symbolism; of economic values and valuation; of moral values and valuation; of aesthetic values and valuation; of familial behavior; of individual adaptive efficiency (intelligence); of the formal educative processes; of psychogenic disorders; of social control and delinquency; of character and personality; of culture and acculturation; of magic and religious practices; of custom, law, and jurisprudence; of politics and government; and of many other specialized behavior fields (p. 399).

An index to the *claimed deductive accomplishments* of the theory of *Pr.B.* is suggested by Hull's statement above that "considerable progress has been made in this direction," the direction being the deduction of "an extensive logical hierarchy of secondary principles which will exactly parallel all of the objectively observable phenomena of the behavior of higher organisms." As testimony to this "progress" Hull cites, in the first passage quoted above, twenty-eight references. These include eleven of Hull's pre-*Pr.B.* theoretical articles (28, 29, 30, 32, 34, 35, 38, 42, 44, 48, 53), several bound volumes of *seminar memoranda* (46, 52, 58), *Mathematico-Deductive Theory of Rote Learning* (51), six of Spence's articles on discrimination learning (116, 117, 118, 119, 121, 123), Miller and Dollard's *Social Learning and Imitation* (96), John Whiting's *Becoming a Kwoma* (140) and other miscellaneous items.[19] There can,

---

[19] Among these, there appear, somewhat gratuitously it would seem, Guthrie's *The Psychology of Learning* (19) and *The Psychology of Human Conflict* (20).

of course, be no question about the range and ingenuity of the theoretical applications and analyses in the indicated sources. Whether, when taken together, they constitute *"considerable progress"* towards the deduction of "all the objectively observable . . . behavior of higher organisms" is distinctly another question.

We already know that, *strictly speaking,* no derivations of concrete empirical theorems are possible within the theory of *Pr.B.* This is because the indeterminacies of the postulates, incompleteness of the formal structure, and the empirical hollowness of many of the variables are such that no *full* set of premises are available to mediate *all* steps in the derivation of any given empirically meaningful consequence. The theory can be made to generate empirical consequences for stated sets of empirical conditions *only* in the sense that various of its components can function as premises, *along with* other premises of an *ad hoc* type imported for purposes of the "deduction" at hand. This state of affairs is, of course, inevitable in any incompletely specified or "young" theoretical formulation, and assessments of the fruitfulness of preliminary theoretical hypotheses in terms of such a maneuver is indeed desirable. But such *ad hoc, quasi-systemic*[20] derivations should not be confused with derivations which are fully determined by a theory (i.e., with *systemic derivations*).

The entire range of "deductions" represented by Hull as following from the *theory of Pr.B.* must be regarded as "quasi-systemic derivations" which are not uniquely determined by elements within the theory. This, of course, means that, strictly speaking, the ascertained or ascertainable probability value of the theorems has no determinate relationship to the probability value of the theory. The question of greatest importance in connection with quasi-systemic derivations is the *extent* to which their premises are determined by the theory; this obviously may vary over a wide range. If the degree of determination by the theory turns out to be high, this leads to the expectation that suitable development and further specification of the theory will make possible "genuine" systemic derivation of the theorem in question. It cannot be our purpose in this report to evaluate degree of systemic determination for each of the extensive group of "derivations" claimed by Hull, or each major class of such. We can, however, hazard a few general statements about such questions.

We must note that the wide and heterogenous class of "deductions"

---

[20] A term is badly needed in methodological discussion to designate "derivations" of theorems from a set of premises which contain *both* legitimate primitive or derived components of the theory *and* assumptions extrinsic to the theory. In such a case an entirely legitimate derivation is being made, but it is not a *derivation from the theory* which contains the theoretical subset of the premises. Derivations of this order we will call "quasi-systemic derivations," while derivations *all* premises of which are uniquely determined by a theory, we will call "systemic derivations."

defined by Hull's cited references, are, in general, not derivations (at any level) *from the theory of Pr.B.* Those contained in the nine pre-*Pr.B.* theoretical articles were "derived" from varied sets of principles, considered either independently or in groupings relevant to some problem area (e.g., "simple trial-and-error learning," "stimulus equivalence," etc.), *and these principles do not necessarily correspond to the postulates of Pr.B.* Indeed, there are marked differences between whatever theory was implicit in the pre-*Pr.B.* articles taken together, and the theory of *Pr.B.* There were also frequent assumptional changes at various points *during* the pre-*Pr.B.* period, as Hull's theoretical thinking evolved. Again, there are *marked* differences between the postulate set of *Mathematico-Deductive Theory of Rote Learning* and that of *Pr.B.* And, of course, the differences from the postulates of *Pr.B.* of the assumptions used by such of the cited authors as Miller and Dollard, and Spence are even more marked. Spence, for instance, in his theory of discrimination learning (116), assumes an entirely different relation between $_sE_R$ (there was no $_sH_R$ at the time) and N, than does the theory of *Pr.B.* It must be emphasized that these considerations affect by far the largest number of "derivations" cited by Hull, including the majority of the more interesting and suggestive theoretical analyses that he has put forward.

The only "derivations" unequivocally related (at some level) to the *theory of Pr.B.* are the "random sampling of some fifty or so secondary principles (corollaries) . . . included in the present volume" (p. 398). That these must be regarded as "quasi-systemic derivations" we already know. That the *degree of systematic determination* of these quasi-systemic derivations must be regarded as *severely limited* is implied by the entire trend of the present report.[21]

The far ranging group of "derivations" alluded to by Hull cannot be regarded as ordered to any determinate comprehensive theory of behavior, or even any set of *determinate* narrow-scope theories. These quasi-systemic derivations must be regarded as explorations of the *potential* fertility of a large number of *preliminary* theoretical hypotheses, some of which are given a certain coherence by their relation to a common set of orienting attitudes. Such "pre-theoretical" hypotheses represent "guesses" about possible explanatory mechanisms considered rele-

---

[21] There is in *Pr.B.*, and elsewhere in Hull's writings, a class of "theorems" (potential or, in some cases, explicitly given) for which degree of systemic determination is sufficiently high to merit designation as "systemic derivations." These consist of relatively "immediate" implications of postulates and definitions mediated by simple rules of logic or mathematics (not necessarily stated) which do not involve any "substitutions" for, or "applications" of, theoretical variables in accordance with concrete empirical conditions, or classes of such. A large number of derivations of this sort are, of course, possible within the theory of *Pr.B.* and others of Hull's formulations. Such derivations are trivial, however, except insofar as they function as steps in the derivation of further theorems which are meant to have concrete empirical reference.

vant to various empirical problem clusters, *not* the components of a mature, or adequately specified theoretical structure. They are guesses *towards* theory, not theory. As explorations of the explanatory possibilities of such hypotheses, many of the quasi-systemic derivations put forward in one context or another by Hull take on a very great importance. Among them are to be found the brilliant and detailed explorations of the adequacy, to a wide range of empirical phenomena, of various "peripheralistic" explanatory mechanisms, which constitute the best fruits of Hull's thinking. Since *Pr.B.* involves only slight reference to many of these ideas, any evaluation of the fruitfulness of Hull's over-all contribution based *exclusively* on *Pr.B.* must do him a great injustice.

It may be instructive to provide some impression of the *range* of "theorems" and "theorem sequences" put forward in one source or another by Hull. Even a random list would include "deductions" relevant to: detailed selective and trial-and-error learning phenomena (e.g., 28, 32, 45, 48, 65, 66, 78); detailed empirical relations arising from CR research (e.g., 3, 26, 37, 47, 56); human rote learning phenomena (39, 40, 51); stimulus and response equivalence (34, 35, 47, 56, 67, 78); stimulus "patterning" (50, 56, 60); many phenomena concerning empirical relations among learning and motivational variables (33, 42, 56, 75, 78); complex adaptive behavior phenomena such as factors associated with "purpose," "knowledge," "foresight," "behavioral short-circuiting," conflict, various forms of complex "transfer" phenomena, certain forms of "insightful" problem solution, and "reasoning" (e.g., 29, 30, 34, 35, 38, 44, 78). In a series of seminar memoranda, and in a little-known article (49), provisional rendering of a number of psychoanalytic relationships and psychopathological phenomena within the terms of the "theory" has been attempted. Two articles (57, 61) inquire into the possibilities of dealing with empirical phenomena of "value" within the concepts of the theory. And, of course, there are the many derivations—relevant to all of these topics and others—represented in work done by students and collaborators which, to one extent or the other, bear the imprint of Hull's theoretical ideas (e.g., 1, 11, 12, 14, 22, 84, 96, 97, 99, 102, 116, 131, 140, 144, 148).

Among the most interesting of these "derivations" are the attempts to apply a number of potential explanatory principles to behavioral relationships of great complexity and subtlety (e.g., "reasoning and insight," the role of "guiding ideas," complex forms of "transfer," etc.). These, for the most part, involve constructs the lawful properties of which are considered by Hull to represent *secondary principles*. Important examples would be the principles connected with: "the fractional anticipatory goal response" (r_G and its associated stimulus s_G) (e.g., 30, 32, 34, 35, 38, 42, 44, 78); various functional roles of proprioceptive stimulation such as s as a function of "the pure stimulus act" (e.g., 29); and "the habit family hierarchy" (e.g., 34, 35, 38, 44). Such mechanisms, because they were regarded as corresponding to *secondary* principles, were not considered in *Pr.B., despite the fact that they are among Hull's most valuable contributions.* No theorist has pushed the evaluation of the explanatory potentialities of possible peripheral mechanisms further than has Hull, and no theorist has been more ingenious in "constructing" such mechanisms. It is likely that no future attempt to develop theoretical formulations of behavior—whether within the framework of what is currently regarded as a "purely" *S-R* approach, or outside of it—can afford to neglect the role of such factors.

Other "derivational" accomplishments of Hull which are impressive, though hardly as fruitful for the future of our science as those just considered, should be mentioned. Among them are the many theorems pertaining to detailed aspects of human rote learning derived within *Mathematico-Deductive Theory of Rote Learning* (51). These are perhaps the only empirically significant theorems among all of Hull's derivations which have the status of *systemic* rather than *quasi-systemic* derivations. But it must be emphasized that these derivations are systemic only with respect to the *rote learning theory.* With respect to the theory of *Pr.B.,* they—like all other cited "derivations"—must be regarded as quasi-systemic. Finally, we should note that Hull's concern with attempts to derive as *theorems* principles assumed by other theorists as *primary,* led, on occasion, to interesting if *ad hoc* analyses, such as the consideration of "patterning" (pp. 349-380) in *Pr.B.*

2. Degree of Confirmation

There are two "levels" at which evaluation of the evidence supporting the theory of *Pr.B.* might be carried out:

(1) The first would have to do with the detailed evidence on which each of the postulates is based, and the evidence for the *consequences* of these postulates taken singly or in combination as they apply to determinate sets of empirical conditions within their range.

(2) The second "level" would proceed on the assumption that *Pr.B.* defines an *approach* to a certain *kind of theory.* Such an evaluation would proceed by first isolating those assumptions which seem most crucial to the delimitation of the approach ("core" assumptions), and appraising the empirical evidence for these core assumptions.

The purpose here is merely to consider these two "levels" of evaluation in a cursory and general way. Level (2), when properly interpreted, represents an important line of activity which can only be carried out by the efforts of many workers, and preferably in the context of Hull's theoretical contributions in general, rather than as exclusively related to *Pr.B.*

a. Evidence for the detailed content of *Pr.B.*, as formulated. The implications of the entire preceding analysis of *Pr.B.* are such as to justify conclusions of some determinacy, at this level of evaluation. We have already adduced many grounds to show that both in mode of formulation, and mode of construction, the postulates of *Pr.B.* are such that they cannot possibly be empirically valid over the very general (indeed universal) range of reference for which they are asserted. Since these postulates are in effect based directly on curve-fitting determinations, their detailed empirical validity, for any finite sub-part of the intended range of application, can best be evaluated in terms of the experiments on which they are based, and the accuracy with which the experimental data are described by the fitted function forms.

With regard to certain of the experiments which serve as inductive base for postulates of *Pr.B.*, we have had occasion to note these things:

(*a*) They are selected or designed with little prior concern for their "representativeness" as instances of the reductive symptoms of the theoretical variables to which they are ordered.

(*b*) The data are often—by virtue of "selectedness," size of statistical *N*, laxity or inappropriateness of experimental conditions, paucity and injudicious distribution of the obtained values over the range of the function—entirely unsuitable for quantitative specification.

(*c*) Fits of the data by the empirical equations often seem far from precise.

It would be boresome and superfluous to spell out such points for all experiments on which the postulates of *Pr.B.* are based. A substantial quantity of such commentary is already available in the critical literature on Hull (e.g., 21, 91, 92, 108, 109, 114). Adding to such literature would, in any case, constitute a revival of dead issues, for Hull in his later formulations abandoned many of the experiments which comprise the induction basis of *Pr.B.*, and substituted new ones. In Part II, we will have much to say about the content and adequacy of these newer studies.

Hull and many of his followers have often tended to place primary emphasis on evaluating the empirical validity of postulates in terms of their *consequences*, rather than via relatively direct examination of the evidence on which postulates are based. What seems involved here is a legitimate, but misapplied, point in scientific method. The establishment of empirical validity of a *postulate* is, to be sure, logically independent of the considerations (inductive or otherwise) which have suggested the assumption. By *definition*, a postulate can only be verified in terms of its consequences. But when an empirical postulate is constructed by direct curve-fitting procedures of the sort Hull employs, *then* the experimental relationship to which the equation has been fitted must become a *very immediate "consequence"* of the postulate. Since, as we already know, a theory of the form of *Pr.B.* can generate only *quasi-systemic derivations*, no "consequences" more remote than the fitted data can be expected to possess a comparable degree of systemic determination.

This appeal of Hullians to "consequences" for the empirical validation of such postulates as those of *Pr.B.* is apparently prompted by the very large range of experimental and observational phenomena which are made to appear "in line" with the theory by Hull's quasi-systemic derivations. Though a good number of these "derivations" may justly strengthen our confidence in *something* within the theory of *Pr.B.*, it is difficult to determine in *what*. Since the derivations *are* quasi-systemic, certainly this "something" cannot be the specific details of the theory of *Pr.B.*, *as formulated*. The determination of *what* these "somethings" are is a fruitful direction in which the future exploitation of Hull's contributions might go.

b. Evaluation of "core" assumptions. Suppose that empirical evaluation of the detailed content of the theory (level 1) leads to the conclusion that the evidence level for all or most of the postulates is not acceptable. The option now arises of interpreting the "theory" of *Pr.B.* as a prematurely over-detailed *program* towards theory, which happens to be wrong in most of its details. A question which may now become dominant is: "How good is the program?" Does, in other words, *Pr.B.* limn in the contours of a fruitful approach within which an empirically adequate theory may ultimately be constructed? One direction of inquiry established by this question is towards isolating those assumptions which *critically* determine the contours of this approach, and examining the evidence for such "core" assumptions.

This latter direction has in fact been taken in much experimental work and conceptual discussion in recent years. The motive, however, has not uniformly been one of dispassionate analysis. More often such efforts have represented (*a*) polemical attempts to "refute" the entire superstructure of the theory by presumably "critical" tests of foundation assumptions, or (*b*) equally polemical attempts to establish the plausibility of the entire structure by the verification of foundation assumptions. In both cases, the value of the work has been mitigated by failure to explore the *concrete relations* between the "foundation" assumptions under test and the theory, or theoretical program, presumably founded on these assumptions. Agreement has been general that the core assumptions on whose empirical validity the entire "theory" or program must stand or fall is some form of the principle of reinforcement (postulate 4), and possibly the principle of primary stimulus generalization (postulate 5). Furthermore, a consensus seems established, on both sides, that the core assumptions under test need not be postulates 4 or 5 *as formulated,* but more fairly some irreducible residue of these principles beyond which they cease being Hull.

What seems to have been considered not at all is the possibility that no single postulate or group of postulates of *Pr.B.* can be considered as containing empirically testable core assumptions *on which some integrated framework of theory logically depends.* The trend of this report is to suggest that the formulations of *Pr.B.* are of a type which do not permit the identification of "core" assumptions *in this sense.* The indeterminacies in all classes of definition of all classes of variables, and in the statements of postulated linkages are such as to preclude (*a*) determinate isolation of empirically significant core assumptions, and (*b*) determinate tests of *apparent* core assumptions, once isolated.

The preceding observations are borne out, in part, by the difficulties in arriving at unequivocal specification of what is under dispute in such issues as the "latent learning" (132) and "continuity-noncontinuity" (90, 106, 119) controversies. At best, the object of dispute might be localized (in terms of relevance to Hull's theory) in some such way as: "Any statement which links $_sH_R$, via some kind of increasing functional relationship, to the number of reinforcements." But—merely to take one difficulty—matters get very fuzzy indeed when the attempt is made to specify the empirical meaning of "reinforcement" in a sense *necessarily* constituted by *Pr.B.* If we add to this the fact that Hull's theory of 1949 includes a revised formulation of the "law of habit formation" which seems entirely compatible with the phenomena of "latent learning" (cf. Part II), the situation becomes more equivocal than ever. There is no doubt that in such experimental controversies as the "latent learning" issue and the question of continuity versus noncontinuity interpretations of learning, problems of considerable importance relevant to the conditions governing "learning" are under dispute, but their bearing on the empirical content of Hull's "theory" or theoretical program must remain as indeterminate as the structure of that theory or program.[22]

Another group of findings which have been represented as embarrassing to the principle of reinforcement of *Pr.B.* are the observations of Skinner (113, 115) and others (79, 80, 81) on "intermittent reinforcement." These findings indeed point to certain empirical variables (associated with "pattern" and distribution of "reinforcements") omitted in any of Hull's specifications of the conditions constitutive of $_sH_R$. As such, they have a definite bearing on any empirical interpretation which can be made of postulate 4. They do not, however, "overthrow" the "core" of Hull's approach, because we have seen that it is meaningless

---

[22] Let us not forget that this statement applies with equal or greater force to the "cognitive" and "field" theories whose "consequences" are also allegedly under test in these disputes.

to identify any interpretation of any postulate of *Pr.B.* as a "core" of anything, other than the postulate in question.

Similarly, the rationale behind the analysis of generalization has been interpreted as a core component of *Pr.B.*, notably by Lashley (91). There is no question but that the quantitative form of this principle (postulate 5), deriving as it does from Hovland's two experiments (23, 24) concerned with a single sensory modality, must be regarded as only tenuously established. Nor can it be denied that the Hullian conception of $_sH_R$ as a connection between a "zone" of "stimuli" (or afferent impulses), varying in "similarity" on a "stimulus dimension," and a reaction (or "zone" of similar R's or r's), contains grave difficulties. Not the least of these, is the ambiguity in the definition of "similarity" (the d variable), and the inadequacy of extending the notion of a simple stimulus-attribute continuum like frequency or intensity to *stimulus object "continua"* (e.g., Hull's example of the rotated die, p. 33). And the inconsistency with known physiological limiting conditions, of the behavioral (*sic*) assumption that association occurs between afferent impulse *zones* and reaction or reaction-zones, is not entirely irrelevant. Nevertheless, any contention that such difficulties must lead to a denial of the "validity of the entire structure" of Hull's theory (91) assumes that this structure is sufficiently determined to be unsettled by the inadequacy of a single principle.

If our analysis of the condition of the theory of *Pr.B.* is correct, it becomes *meaningless* to look for "core" assumptions in the sense in which this has been customary in the experimental polemics surrounding Hull's theory. It is realized that this is a radical statement which will perhaps be accepted less readily than the analysis of *Pr.B.* by which it is implied. It is important that what we assert be understood. We do *not* say that it is valueless to test possible empirical *interpretations* of the assumptions of *Pr.B.* We do not say that such experiments have no inferential bearing on the plausibility of *these interpretations*, and that the interpretations have no bearing on the relevant principles of *Pr.B.* We say only that the *postulates of Pr.B.*, considered either as defining a theory or the framework of theory, are not of sufficient determinacy to permit isolation of *core* dimensions of Hull's theoretical program. To make this point specific, we should note that many of the types of "consequences" which Hull has represented as "following," say, from the principle of reinforcement, continue to "follow" to the same extent, even if we substitute a principle of contiguity (or, in general, the same "consequences" follow from a wide range of alternate interpretations of various components of the principle). Again, many of the "derivations" involving the principle of generalization remain "derivable" to the same extent, from alternate principles which include no reference to stimulus "zones" or "continua." The belief that empirical core assumptions can be found in a sense in which investigators have sought them is premised on the belief that Hull's formulations are far more *advanced* towards theory than they are.

There *is* a sense in which it is fruitful to look for core components of Hull's *approach* to theory. But this is not in the direction of *postulates*. It is in the direction of his orienting attitudes, and the various guiding ideas, explanatory mechanisms, scattered hypotheses which *look towards* theory, that function in some way in the many "derivations" and pre-theoretical analyses he has put forward. The evaluation of which of the orienting attitudes of a theorist like Hull are both feasible and fruitful is a matter of great moment for the future development of the field. Also of great importance would be the isolation and further development of those pre-theoretical hypotheses which, in one context or another, appear to contain promising explanatory potential. In this connection, it must be remembered that the fertility of such mechanisms as r_G, certain applications of S_D, various of the concrete roles imputed to proprioceptive stimulation, mechanisms such as *secondary* and *indirect* generalization, the habit family hierarchy, etc., is independent of their "derivability" from the postulates of *Pr.B.*, or any alternate set that Hull has put forward. Their possible fertility is also independent of any commitment to *exclusively* peripheral or *S-R* variables for the analysis of behavior. It is likely that such materials are much closer to anything that may be considered the *core* of Hull's *approach* than are the postulates of *Pr.B.* It is also clear that a search for core components of this order can go only a short way via any analysis restricted to *Pr.B.*, but rather must be based on the entire range of Hull's writings.

As a final point in this section, we should add that the several research clusters developed largely in the attempt to test Hullian "core" assumptions may be interpreted as having quite another utility. Although it is outside the scope of this report to discuss the details of these experiments, what seems most instructive about the results is the extent to which they underscore our present distance from any confident *general identification of the conditions under which learning may be expected to occur*. Recognition of that distance could lend a note of sobriety to the evaluation of the currently feasible in the field of learning theory.

3. Empirical Flexibility in Practice

Hull has argued in many contexts that only through the explicit use of hypothetico-deductive procedure can a determinate relationship be established between theoretical principles and empirical evidence. Thus, "openness" to modification and refinement in accordance with empirical evidence has often been represented as a virtue of Hull's theory. We have already given sufficient attention to the fact that the hypothetico-deductive explicitness attained in *Pr.B.* by Hull was more a matter of appearance than reality, and thus that only "quasi-systemic" derivations of empirical theorems was possible. Nevertheless, the "degree" of systematic determination of theorems, particularly as regards relatively immediate consequences of the postulates, is certainly greater in principle than in most presumably general "theories" of behavior.

Since what has been called "theory" in recent psychology is largely a system of the *theorist's behavior*, it may be of interest to evaluate briefly the extent to which the theorist of *Pr.B.* showed a disposition to adjust the principles of the theory to apparently conflicting empirical outcomes. Nothing would be gained by a detailed tracing through of "cases," but in general we can say these things:

(*a*) There is certainly evidence that Hull showed a tendency to neglect contrary empirical data (sometimes at least as adequate as the data selected) in the *initial formulation* of the postulates of *Pr.B.* (92). Analysts may disagree on the *extent* to which such selectiveness is inevitable and legitimate, but they cannot disagree on the fact of selectiveness.

(*b*) Both before and after the publication of *Pr.B.*, Hull showed an imperviousness to the apparently "embarrassing" data of "latent learning" and "intermittent reinforcement." Other workers within the Hullian framework can certainly not be accused of such neglect (10, 120, 124, 128), but Hull himself remained aloof from this material.

(*c*) During the years between 1943 and 1949, Hull showed a tendency not to acknowledge the bearing on his theory of apparently contrary findings deriving from certain other experiments specifically designed to test details of his assumptions (e.g., 87, 109).

Despite the above points, it is not true that Hull held fixedly to some "frozen" formulation of his principles over any long interval of his career. In the pre-*Pr.B.* days, revisions and further specifications of formulations on the basis of empirical evidence were frequent. In general, though, these changes tended to rely on experiments carried out at Yale in connection with Hull's research program, and only rarely reflected responsiveness to findings from other laboratories. As we will see in Part II, almost immediately after the publication of *Pr.B.*, Hull embarked on a methodologico-experimental program calculated to remove many of the quantitative deficiencies of that work. This effort culminated in the postulate sets of 1949-1951 which define a radically new "theory" of behavior. The many changes, as against the postulates of *Pr.B.*, produce an initial impression of marked responsiveness to the empirical evidence which had accumulated over the intervening years. Closer analysis will show, however, that virtually all changes register a far reaching response to the demands of the new quantificational methodology, and not to empirical evidence.

It would be futile to compute coefficients of empirical flexibility for the theoretical behavior of Hull's rivals during the past few decades. We may sharply doubt, however, that competing systematists have yielded more gallantly to the encroachments of fact. The main purpose served by the preceding brief discussion is to suggest that the responsiveness of a set of hypotheses to evidence is not an automatic by-product of the "degree of systemic determination" of their consequences. The fact that Hull's formulations were modeled more closely on a hypothetico-deductive pattern than has been the rule in psychology, provided no guarantee that any given degree of empirical "sensitivity" would prevail.

4. "Special Virtues" of the Formulations of Pr.B.

From everything we have said, it is evident that the chief "virtues" of the "theory" of Pr.B. are not to be found in the detailed postulational content, or in any reasonably concrete framework for a *future* theory of behavior. The fruitful components of Pr.B. represent various orienting attitudes, preliminary variable identifications, and "pre-theoretical" hypotheses, some combination of which may prove useful in the slow approach towards future theoretical analyses of behavior. For the most part, such potentially valuable components of Pr.B. are apparent only to the extent that they reflect emphases and ideas developed by Hull in the wider context of his theoretical writings generally. Thus, many of the "virtues" of Pr.B. can best be gotten at only through consideration of the fruits of Hull's over-all effort, and this we propose briefly to do in Part III. In the present section, we restrict attention to a few advances in Hull's theoretical thinking which were defined (in published form) for the first time in Pr.B.

Pr.B. introduced a large number of changes as against earlier formulations of Hull's theory. In retrospect, certain of these, such as the introduction of s (the afferent impulse) and r (the efferent discharge), and the principle of "neural interaction," do not seem entirely judicious. The attempt to approximate a greater degree of "quantitativeness" than in earlier formulations has certainly not proven judicious. It would be difficult to regard the inhibition assumptions (postulates 8 and 9) in the form in which they appear in Pr.B. as an improvement over anything. One set of modifications, however, stands out as a major advance. This has to do not with the detailed content of any postulate, but rather with the general arrangement of the variables discriminated within Pr.B.

In pre-Pr.B. formulations of his system, Hull had represented behavior as directly derivable from "excitatory potential" (or "excitatory tendencies") which was conceived to be directly established by reinforcement or "conditioning." No distinction comparable to that between $_sH_R$ and $_sE_R$ was in existence. Thus, in pre-1943 presentations, no systematic distinction was made between variables (and principles) constitutive of *habit acquisition* ("learning") and variables or principles governing *habit functioning* ("performance"). It has become more or less a convention to note this feature of *Pr.B.* as an advance in Hull's theoretical thinking, but it is rare that the importance of this apparently modest stride is fully appreciated.

The distinction between "learning" and "performance" had been available in the field for some years (89, 136), and had been much stressed by a certain group of theorists. Nevertheless, this distinction had been "exploited" in only two senses: (*a*) to emphasize the obvious methodological point that, *if* "learning" be conceptualized as a set of relatively permanent intra-organismic modifications, *then* the (intervening) variables which represent learning "structures" cannot be *identified* with the observable changes in behavior from which they are inferred; and (*b*) to point to the "existence" of empirical phenomena which imply that changes in learning variables may take place *independently* of concurrently observable changes in behavior (i.e., "latent learning").[23] The learning-performance distinction seems simple enough, but it has important consequences for the structure of any ("non-positivistic") theoretical approach to the analysis of behavior, and correspondingly important implications for the experimental analysis of behavior. It implies that any attempt to conceptualize behavior which deals with "training-effects" in terms of relatively permanent changes in value and/or state of a special class of intervening variables (e.g., habit, "expectancy," trace), must contain *two* cleanly discriminated sets of principles. One set of principles must relate relevant empirical characteristics of the training situation to the original "formation" or "acquisition" of such learning "structures." An independent set of principles must bring to bear, on another class of intervening variables ("performance" variables), the effects of relatively transient empirical conditions, *other than* those of original training, which may influence behavior at any given time. Such a conceptualization would then consider *momentary* behavior to be some joint function of the learning variables, as calculated from the conditions of original training, and the performance variables representing conditions concurrent with the momentary behavior.

It would be unfair to say that *no* "theory" preceding *Pr.B.* had made provision for such a distinction in the arrangement of its variables. Certainly Lewin had realized in his formulations some such distinction, although the identification and the relevance of learning variables had

---

[23] The additional implication that such changes may take place under conditions which preclude the operation of certain versions of the principle of reinforcement need concern us *here* no more than it did Hull. Unfortunately, the psychologists who stressed the distinction between "learning" and "performance" placed almost exclusive emphasis on this presumptive implication of certain experimental findings, and tended to forget that the distinction has important heuristic implications for the detailed experimental analysis of behavior.

remained vague in the extreme. Tolman, too, had "arranged" some of his variables in rough accordance with this distinction. Neither, however, had implemented the distinction with any experimental program designed to unscramble detailed "learning" and "performance" relationships. It is to Hull's credit that the "theory" of $Pr.B.$ showed the most consistent and comprehensive recognition of the need for independent sets of principles relevant to habit acquisition as against habit functioning of *any* prior formulation, and, *at the same time,* suggested an experimental methodology capable of differentially exploring such relationships in more than a token way.

It will be recalled that in $Pr.B.$ Hull consistently distinguishes $\dot{S}$ and $\dot{s}$ (the stimulus or afferent impulse of original "conditioning") from S and s (the stimulus or afferent impulse of "action-evocation"), and similarly that $\dot{R}$ is consistently discriminated from R. Postulate 4 introduces the basic "learning" variable $_sH_R$ as a function of the presumably relevant empirical conditions of the training situation. *Final* behavior is mediated by $_s\dot{\bar{E}}_R$ as the terminal intervening variable of the formulation. Between $_sH_R$ and $_s\dot{\bar{E}}_R$ is a chain of intervening variables calculated (with the possible exception of $_sI_R$) to represent various *momentary* behavior-production factors. Thus, $_s\bar{H}_R$ is designed to bring differences in the current stimulating situation (from that of original learning) into the causal analysis; $_sE_R$ introduces the role of *current* drive conditions; $\dot{I}_R$, the momentary conditions of inhibition; and $_sO_R$, the effect of various nonpredictable sources of momentary variability in $_s\bar{E}_R$.

Perhaps more important than this merely formal arrangement of variables, is the appearance in connection with the formulations of $Pr.B.$ of one of the first experiments to embody a design which implements the learning-performance distinction in other than a demonstrational or casual sense. This is the Perin experiment (103) which, *despite* its shortcomings as the exclusive basis for a quantitative and general "postulate" on primary motivation, is the first experiment in the literature to attempt dissociation of the effects of variation in drive "strength" on performance as contaminated by concurrent training, from its effects on performance *in combination with* controlled degrees of previous training. The simple multi-variable design of the Perin experiment may not appear to be a contribution of cosmic importance; nevertheless, it constitutes one of the few clear-cut forward steps in mode of question formulation in several decades of research on interrelations among "learning" and "motivational" variables.

In line with the clear distinction between learning and performance variables, and the considerations giving rise to the Perin experiment, Hull in 1943 extended his analysis of primary motivation in a fruitful direction. The former attempt to deal with the behavioral elaborations of motivational factors exclusively in terms of S_D is now supplemented by the direct "sensitizing" or "energizing" effects of drives on the habit structures mediating response evocation. This addition, while hardly bringing Hull close to a "complete" analysis of motivation, makes possible suggestive preliminary treatment of a far wider range of motivational phenomena than was possible when drive was *equated* with a conditionable, persisting stimulus.

Though these "advances" may appear somewhat modest as against the intentions of *Pr.B.*, or the wishes of those who consider such intentions feasible, they are genuine. Their apparent magnitude may serve as an index to where we stand *vis à vis* theory in the heroic mode.

Part II. The 1949-1951 Postulate Sets [24]

As already indicated (p. 2), the substance of this report has been devoted primarily to the form of Hull's theory set forth in *Pr.B.*, in the belief that this will remain the most influential of Hull's general formulations. It is largely the business of the following consideration of the new postulate sets to justify this belief. Since the new postulates are the terminal consequences of the same theoretical objectives that produced the theory of *Pr.B.*, detailed consideration of those postulates should give additional insight into the significance of the earlier formulation, and of Hull's theoretical efforts generally.

The 1949-1951 postulate sets pose special difficulties for the analyst. In the case of *Pr.B.*, whatever its shortcomings in regard to explicit formal procedure, there is at least sufficient *informal* elucidation and application of the concepts in the textual "embedding material," the notes and the glossary, to give the analyst something to work with in a reasonably determinate way. The four nearly identical postulate sets of 1949-1951, however, are given with very little explanatory material of any kind. The first three of these consist of bare statements of postulates and corollaries "in an unbroken sequence." The situation is only

---

[24] The designation "1949-1951 postulate sets" refers to four separate but highly similar collections of postulates which were issued during that interval. The first two of these were put forward as mimeographed *memoranda concerning behavior theory* (68, 69) under dates of October 4, 1949, and November, 1949. The third appeared as an article (70) in the May, 1950 issue of the *Psychological Review*, while the final collection is contained in the 1951 book, *Essentials of Behavior* (75). The second postulate set departs only slightly from the first. The third departs even more slightly from the second, and the fourth is practically identical with the third. Since most discussions of the final form of Hull's theory are likely to be based on the 1951 book, it was felt desirable to record the fact that this terminal form of the theory dates from 1949, in the title of the present discussion. A portion of the present analysis had been written before the appearance of *Essentials of Behavior,* having been based on the 1950 set. This part of the discussion has been revised in the light of the elucidative material in *Essentials of Behavior,* while the remainder has been directly based on that volume. *Essentials of Behavior* will be abbreviated to *Essentials* throughout the text.

slightly improved in the small 1951 volume, *Essentials of Behavior* (75), which provides brief textual elucidation with each of the postulates.[25] For these reasons, much reading between lines becomes necessary, and much of the content and rationale of the theory must be reconstructed by collation of the new postulates with the "memoranda" and journal articles of the post-*Pr.B.* period. Thus, the analyst must face a greater than ordinary risk of being proven injudicious, and is almost certain to be construed as unfair.

The examination of the new postulates proceeds in terms of a detailed comparison with the 1943 version of the theory. It was not considered desirable to do this in terms of the set of analytic rubrics which determined the organization of our account of the earlier theory. This would have eventuated in much overlapping, and would in any case represent a mode of analysis unsuited to the skeletal condition of Hull's recent formulations.

Background considerations. The publication of *Pr.B.* in 1943 had widespread repercussions on the experimental and theoretical activity in "fundamental" behavioral psychology. It is a tribute to Hull that from 1943 to the present his conceptions have literally dominated the scene within "learning theory," either as foci of controversy, or as sources of hypotheses for further experimental elaboration or evaluation. During the interval 1943-1949, many experiments designed to test specific consequences of Hull's theory were performed, and many experiments not motivated by this intention yielded relevant data. In addition, the interminable "latent learning" (132) and "continuity-noncontinuity" (90, 106, 119) controversies raged on, at both conceptual and experimental levels. Despite the accumulation of much incompatible experimental data and conceptual criticism (e.g., 81, 87, 91, 92, 94, 101, 105, 108, 109, 114, 137), Hull seemed to cling, during most of this period, to his 1943 formulations with a tenacity unbecoming to a hypothetico-deductive theorist. The pendulum swung dramatically in the opposite direction with the new postulate sets. These sets are not only replete

---

[25] *Essentials* was apparently a stop-gap publication intended by Hull to provide sufficient elucidation of the 1949-1950 postulates to render them intelligible, in some degree, to the psychological public, until the time when fuller exposition could be provided in a more extensive book. Hull completed this book, in which the new postulates are used "in making concrete deductions of the systematic details of individual (non-social) behavior" (70, p. 174), shortly before his death. During the writing of the present report, the author did not know whether this final book of Hull's would be published posthumously. Actually, the book here referred to—*A Behavior System* (78)—was published shortly before the manuscript for this report was sent to the editor. It was therefore possible to give this volume brief consideration in the Appendix to the present analysis (cf. pp. 167-169, this report). It may be interesting to note, at this place, that *A Behavior System* does not carry the elucidation of the new postulates much beyond the point of *Essentials,* but concentrates instead on the relatively "informal" derivation of theorem-sequences pertaining to a large number of empirical problem-clusters.

with modifications in the detail of many of the assumptions; they represent a *major realignment of the entire theoretical framework*—a realignment so radical as to include, as only one of its features, *something very close to a total abrogation of the reinforcement principle*. Only the barest index to the magnitude of the alterations is given by Hull's statement (70, p. 174) that:

. . . the mathematical aspects of many of the postulates have been formulated, or reformulated, and the verbal formulation of nearly all has been modified by a certain extent. One postulate . . . [the reference is to postulate 10 of *Pr.B.* on $_sO_R$] has been dropped in part as empirically erroneous, some postulates have been divided, and others have been combined; several new postulates have been added, and a number of the original postulates have been derived from others of the present set and now appear as corollaries. The net result is an increase of from sixteen to eighteen postulates, with twelve corollaries (brackets mine).

In actuality, the scope of the changes is such as to produce what must be considered an essentially *new theory*, related to the theory of *Pr.B.* in terms of the orienting attitudes which govern its construction and the general identification of variables, but differing in the content of almost every assumption. No meaningful perspective on the significance of Hull's contributions can be achieved without careful inquiry into the grounds for these changes. Hull's death makes it all the more important to arrive at an understanding of the factors responsible for the terminal status of his theory.

Plan of discussion. We begin the analysis with an indication of (A) the *major changes of emphasis* which the 1949-1951 postulate sets introduce. We continue with consideration of (B) *the new technique of quantification and postulate construction*, and its impact on the 1949-1951 theory, and (C) *a sampling of further changes* with regard to certain key hypotheses and concepts. A brief set of *concluding considerations* (D) considers the import of the new theory for the evaluation of Hull's long-range theoretical effort.

A. MAJOR CHANGES OF EMPHASIS

One of these is a glaring modification of "core" assumptions which we will refer to as attenuation of the reinforcement principle." The second is a more subtle affair which seems to betoken an increased sensitivity on Hull's part to the difficulties occasioned by the unrestricted generality of his previous formulations. This we discuss under the heading: "increased localism of the theory language."

1. Attenuation of the Reinforcement Principle

The change likely to produce maximum amazement, even to the casual reader of the 1949-1951 postulate sets, is the marked shift in the identification of the conditions which govern *habit functioning* or "performance" ($_sE_R$), as against habit acquisition or "learning" ($_sH_R$). In 1943, the crucial principle of the theory, postulate 4 on reinforcement, defined habit strength as a mathematical function of four empirical variables: (1) number of reinforcements (N), (2) magnitude of need reduction (w), (3) delay of reinforcement (t), and (4) degree of S-R asynchronism (t' and t''). In the 1949 postulate set, *only one of these variables—N* (now written $\dot{N}$)—is retained as a determinant of habit strength. Two of the others—w (albeit redefined with great specificity as "weight of food given as reinforcement") and the delay of reinforcement (t)—are now functionally related to *reaction potential* rather than *habit strength*. S-R asynchronism is eliminated as a determinant of anything, its systematic burden now apparently being carried by the new V or *stimulus intensity dynamism* factor in conjunction with other principles of the theory (such as the new postulate II on "molar stimulus traces").

More concretely, the present arrangement, in comparison to the past, is this: Corresponding in function to the old principle of reinforcement (postulate 4) are the two "new" postulates, III ("Primary Reinforcement") and IV ("The Law of Habit Formation"). Postulate III states that (75, p. 20):

Whenever an effector activity (R) is closely associated with a stimulus afferent impulse or trace (s) and the conjunction is closely associated with the rapid diminution in the motivational stimulus (S_D or s_G) there will result an increment to a tendency for that stimulus to evoke that response.

Postulate IV reads (75, p. 32):

If reinforcements follow each other at evenly distributed intervals, everything else constant, the resulting habit will increase in strength as a positive growth function of the number of trials, according to the equation,

$$_sH_R = 1 - 10^{-a\dot{N}}.$$

Notice that in addition to dropping the three other variables which in 1943 determined $_sH_R$, the event which follows the stimulus process—response process conjunction is now no longer the "*diminution of a need*," but rather "*the rapid diminution in the motivational stimulus*." [26]

---

[26] It may be of interest to note that in the statement of postulate III in the *1950* set (70), the phrase "diminution in the receptor discharge characteristic of a need" occurred in place of "rapid diminution in the motivational stimulus (S_D or s_G)." This is one of the very few changes as between the 1950 and the 1951 postulate sets. The insertion of "rapid" may register some concern on Hull's part over the flagrantly non-differentiating implications of "diminution" *per se* as the mark of reinforcement, but we are not told what "rapid" means in this connection. The change from "receptor discharge characteristic of a need" to "motivational stimulus" may betoken nothing more than a vagrant desire to avoid physiological-sounding language in this place, but it is possible also that Hull was no longer comfortable about referring to "receptor discharges" or even "stimuli" as a *property* of drives. There are evidences in *Essentials* to the effect that Hull had reverted to

Also, the principle of secondary reinforcement, which in 1943 was embedded in the primitive reinforcement assumption, is now a derived principle, appearing as corollary ii under postulate III.

It will be recalled that old postulates 6 and 7 introduce the concepts of D and S_D (postulate 6), and assert the well known multiplicative constitution of $_sE_R$ by $_sH_R$ and D (postulate 7). Analogous in function to these, are new postulate V on *primary motivation or drive*, and new IX along with contributory postulates VI, VII and VIII. Postulate VI on *stimulus intensity dynamism* introduces the new intervening variable V as a function of stimulus intensity. Postulate VII introduces the *incentive motivation* variable K as a function of w. A delay in reinforcement variable J is introduced by postulate VIII as a function of t. Postulate IX can then assert that (p. 59):

$$_sE_R = D \times V_2 \times K \times J \times _s\dot{H}_R,$$

where

$$_s\dot{H}_R = {}_sH_R \times V_1$$

and where V_1 is that [i.e., the stimulus intensity dynamism] involved in the original learning" (brackets mine).[27]

It is clear that these changes alone make the 1949 postulate set a very different system than the theory of *Pr.B*. There are already signs that even one of Hull's staunchest defenders is not entirely comfortable about them.[28] That the "theory" must now generate a wide variety of conse-

---

his pre-1943 view which *equated* all functional effects of drives with stimulation. The *direct* "sensitizing" or "energizing" attributes with which Hull had enriched (in the opinion of many) his theory of primary motivation in 1943 seem to have been lopped off in 1951. Instead, Hull had come to a view similar to his pre-1943 formulation in that drive seems equated with stimulation, but different in that the emphasis is rather more in the Neal Miller (96) direction of *strong* stimulation than in the early Hullian direction of *persisting* stimulation.

[27] The variables, V_1 and $_s\dot{H}_R$ (as distinct from V_2 and $_sH_R$) make a rather sudden appearance in postulate IX. In effect, this partly undoes what the preceding postulates had been asserting. They had been saying that habit strength ($_sH_R$) is a unique function of N. With postulate IX we find the first formal indication that actually another determinant of habit strength had been intended all along, this being "the stimulus intensity during the learning process," as mediated by the stimulus intensity dynamism variable V_1. An interesting implication of this addition to the constitution of habit strength is that, since Hull regards strength of drive to be essentially a matter of *drive stimulus intensity*, differential drive intensity during learning *now* should lead to differential rates of habit acquisition. In 1943, differential drive intensity was not considered as a possible variable determining $_sH_R$. Here a historical paradox is worthy of note: in 1943 the drive intensity variable was not in the theory as a determinant of $_sH_R$, *despite* the presence of another determinant—"magnitude of need reduction"—which seems logically to require the inclusion of drive intensity. In 1951, drive intensity seems clearly to be a determinant of $_sH_R$, *despite* the fact that the magnitude of need reduction variable is *now* abandoned.

[28] After a brief summary of the changes discussed above, Spence (129, p. 253) adds, "In changing his formulation of these factors from that in *Principles of Behavior* to the above form, Hull has revealed an admirable readiness to be influenced

quences which markedly differ from those of the earlier theory is obvious.

Perhaps most striking among the altered deductive potentialities of the new Hullian framework is the *apparent increase in facility with which many of the so-called "latent learning" data* can be handled.[29] The acquisition of habit strength ("learning structures") is still held to be a function of the number of *reinforced* repetitions of an *S-R* coincidence, but the word "reinforced" no longer has reference to *amount of need reduction* or to the *delay of need reduction*, or even to *need reduction*. It has reference to the *"rapid diminution in the motivational stimulus,"* and "diminution" apparently means *diminution per se*, not *amount* of diminution. This, in turn, means that, everything else constant, a habit strength increment will be the same habit strength increment, whether the "reward" be great or infinitesimal, and independently of *when* the reward arrives within the indeterminate interval designated by "closely associated." This means, in short, that all "latent learning" and other data which previously seemed to "strain" the theory because of its commitment to the dependence of the *size* of the increment of habit strength on the *amount* and the *delay* of need reduction can now be derived with easy abandon. After all, it is always possible to find a drive whose "stimulus" is reduced to some unspecified extent at the termination of any *S-R* sequence, the reinforcement of which is demanded by theoretical exigency.

Most of the above points have already been clearly perceived and stated by Seward (110). Seward, however, goes on to an elaborate search for some way of reconstituting the concept of "reinforcement" in order to square it with Hull's current theory. Now, the semantics of "reinforcement" has had a curious and involved history. But, if Hull was once a reinforcement theorist in the sense that his basic acquisition postulate demanded a *quantitative* dependence of learning increments on amount of need reduction, he is no longer a reinforcement theorist *in that sense*. If he was once a reinforcement theorist in the sense of holding *need reduc-*

---

by the experimental findings. However, the evidence with respect to the role of some of these variables is not as yet clear cut." Spence's uneasiness is further indicated by the fact that he is constrained to provide a "presentation of Hull's reformulation of his theory . . . not strictly in accord with the version presented by Hull . . . , but [one which] represents a somewhat simplified treatment that the present writer favors" (129, p. 251).

[29] In an earlier draft of this section, prepared before the appearance of *Essentials*, it was suggested that the change in the status of "amount of need reduction" from that of a *learning* to a *performance* variable (i.e., determinant of $_sH_R$ to determinant of $_sE_R$) was perhaps *motivated* by an intention to do justice to certain refractory instances of "latent learning" data. The writer now believes that this was not the case. Indeed, *Essentials* contains much evidence to suggest that the general reshuffling of learning and performance variables in the new postulate set was not motivated by any empirical data at all. Instead, it seems probable that these and many other changes in the new theory were forced by Hull's attempt to achieve a genuine quantification of his major intervening variables. This interpretation will be argued in a later part of the report.

tion to be a necessary condition of learning, he is no longer a reinforcement theorist in precisely *that* sense. He *may be*, at present, a reinforcement theorist in the sense of holding S_D diminution to be a necessary condition of learning, but notice that this makes the reinforcement principle even more tenuous and "nondifferentiating" than it has ever been in Hull's hands. Drive stimulus diminution, as an all or none occurrence, is a flagrantly untestable event, an event which may be postulated with much greater imaginative impunity than the occurrence of a given magnitude of drive reduction sufficient to mediate such and such an increment in habit strength. Considerations of this sort make it highly likely that, *in practice,* Hull's current principle of reinforcement would generate consequences in no way distinguishable from those mediated by an unadorned association by contiguity principle. The possibility of retranslating S_D diminution as an "emphasizer" or some kind of confirming event (cf. Tolman chapter) should not go unnoticed.

In some highly attenuated and residual sense of his earlier use of the term, Hull may still be characterized as a reinforcement theorist. But there is reason to doubt that the *current* principle of reinforcement will function in concrete derivations in any way differently than alternate non-reinforcement estimates of the conditions of acquisition.

2. *Increased Localism of the Theory Language*

By explicit statement of intention (cf. p. 87), and by the "tone" of his theory language, Hull had always given the impression that he was presenting a *comprehensive* theory of behavior, having an unrestricted range of application. This view has, at times, not been shared by certain of his advocates who have argued that Hull's theory was meant to hold essentially for certain aspects of the behavior of the white rat. Perhaps even those who regard Hull's system as a restricted theory *will be surprised to find evidences in his current theory language of a retreat to specificity that far transcends the preceding characterization of his theoretical aims.* On the other hand, there is no explicit indication of an intention to narrow down the domain of the theory, and much of the theory language is characterized by the same unrestricted generality of reference as before.

The net result is an essential ambiguity. Does Hull offer his new formulation as a *"limited"* or *"narrow-scope"* theory, or as a *general* theory of behavior? The third possibility, of course, is that he offers it as both of these, thus leaving open the opportunity to shift from one interpretation to the other, in accordance with polemical exigency.

In the following paragraphs, we will assemble at random some of the many instances of "localism" in the language of the 1949-1951 theory.

Postulate 6 on *primary motivation* in *Pr.B.* was a perfectly general statement linking drive and the drive stimulus. The failure of this assumption to connect D and S_D to any independent variable has already been noted. The *primary motivation* assumption of the *new* theory, postulate V, corrects certain of the deficiencies of the old postulate; it links D and S_D to C_D. *But it does this only for one drive condition—"food privation."* The language of this postulate is a curious admixture of specificity and generality. Part A leads off with the phrase: "Primary motivation (D), at least that resulting from food privation, consists of two multiplicative components" (75, p. 38). Part B defines the "functional relationship of drive (D) to one drive condition (food privation)," the relationship turning out to be a highly detailed paraphrase of the specific results derived in an experiment by Yamaguchi (147). Part C (75, p. 39) is completely general in formulation, assigning the "old" monotonic increasing function to the relation between "each drive condition" (not D as formerly) and S_D. Part D, finally, achieves an intermediate degree of generality (or specificity) with the statement that (p. 40):

At least some drive conditions tend partially to motivate into action habits which have been set up on the basis of different drive conditions (ital. mine).

A marked increase in localism is apparent in the treatment of *independent variables* in the new postulate set. This is particularly striking in the case of the w variable which formerly was a determinant of $_sH_R$, but now contributes to $_sE_R$ via K. In the old theory, w was treated (at least part of the time) as "magnitude of need reduction." In the new formulation, w has become simply "the weight of food given as reinforcement." W, one of the independent variables constitutive of $\dot{I}_R$, was referred to in postulate 8 of the 1943 theory (56, p. 300) as "the work . . . involved in the execution of the response." In the three occurrences of this variable in the present postulate set (75, postulate X.E., p. 81; corollary ix, p. 84; corollary x, p. 85), W is uniformly identified as "the work . . . involved in operating the manipulandum." The reference is presumably to the gadget moved by the rats in the Skinner boxes of the two studies on which the current assumptions relating W to $\dot{I}_R$ are based.

On the *dependent variable* side, a most remarkable increase of localism occurs in the redefinition of A. In *Pr.B.*, this variable was variously identified as "the amplitude (A) of responses mediated by the autonomic nervous system" (p. 344), "amplitude, magnitude, or intensity of a reaction" (p. 403). *Now*, it is cautiously referred to in the new postulate XVI as "the Tarchanoff galvanic skin reaction amplitude" (75, p. 179).

As a final example[30] of some kind of extreme in the field of theoretical

---

[30] At first blush, another apparently glaring example of theoretical localism seems to be the indeterminate restriction imposed on the basic law of reinforcement (postulate IV) by the antecedent clause, "If reinforcements follow each other at evenly distributed intervals." In the pre-*Essentials* draft of this section, the writer interpreted this as a concession to the phenomena of intermittent reinforcement (81). Such a concession would have registered an admirable sensitivity to empirical findings, but it would have reduced the generality of the basic learning assumption

"localisms," we cite Hull's "preliminary suggestion" in *Essentials* for a definition of the wat, the unit for measuring reaction potential (75, p. 100):

The wat is the mean standard deviation of the momentary reaction potential $(_s\dot{\bar{E}}_R)$ of standard albino rats, 90 days of age, learning a simple manipulative act requiring a 10 gram pressure by 24-hour distributed trials under 23 hours' hunger, water available, with reward in the form of a 2.5-gram pellet of the usual dry dog food, the mean being taken from all the reinforcement trials producing the habit strength from .75 to .85 habs inclusive.

Since, as we shall see, the wat is the basic quantitative unit on which all variable interrelations in the present system are premised, one is almost caused to wonder whether the scope of the new theory is to be literally restricted to the manipulandum-pushing behavior of the 59 rats whose latencies provide the sole empirical basis (13) for the quantification of reaction potential.

These evidences of localism impose some delicate conditions on any evaluation of Hull's theoretical efforts. If Hull intended the new postulate set as some kind of limited theory whose empirical domain is no broader than certain aspects of Skinner box behavior, or perhaps certain limited aspects of the behavior associated with the learning of instrumental responses in the white rat, this *could* be interpreted as an encouraging development. It could mean that Hull perceived the futility of comprehensive theorizing in the present phase of psychology, that he acknowledged the limited inductive base, the relational lacunae, the arbitrariness of quantification of his own previous attempts at such theory. Advocates of limited theory would have reason for satisfaction. But note that, if this *was* Hull's intention, *he has made his own evaluation* of his past theoretical efforts. Note also that, if the theory is currently a limited one, there has been no explicit indication of *what it is limited to*.

The matter, however, is complicated by the fact that the evidences of localism are present in only *part of the theory*. Certain postulates and sub-parts of postulates are stated with the same unbridled generality as before. If the postulate set of 1949 *is* interpreted as a general theory, it must be evaluated by the same yardstick as was the earlier formula-

---

to only one indeterminate special case of the temporal conditions and "pattern" of reinforcements. The explanatory material made available by *Essentials*, however, makes it entirely clear that the clause merely has reference to the fact that the latency data on which the law is indirectly based were gathered under conditions of a 24-hour spacing of the individual trials. Such a distribution was employed in order to minimize the conditions which would presumably result in the accumulation of I_R, thereby yielding an approximation to "pure" $_sE_R$ and thus "pure" $_sH_R$. The antecedent clause, then, indicates that the specific form of the law given in the rest of the postulate holds for cases where I_R is at a minimum. Presumably, the cases in which I_R is present in some determinate degree could be derived as theorems from postulate IV together with the inhibition assumptions (postulate X, corollaries ix and x) and other principles of the system.

tion. The question of most immediate concern then becomes: is the 1949 version of the theory a closer approximation to an adequate general theory than the 1943 version? This question has, we think, been partly answered by the theoretical indeterminacies already alluded to in the above discussions. Within the limitations imposed by the paucity of elucidative material given with the 1949-1951 postulates, the question will be pursued further in the following sections.

B. THE NEW TECHNIQUE OF QUANTIFICATION AND POSTULATE CONSTRUCTION

The key to virtually all of the changes in Hull's 1949-1951 theory, as against the theory of Pr.B., is to be found in his attempt to approximate genuine quantification. This statement holds both for the major changes of emphasis and for the greater part of the many less striking changes of detail.

From the period of his earliest theoretical articles, Hull had been looking towards the mathematization of the principles of his behavior theory. In *Pr.B.*, Hull had attempted to presage this goal by putting forward an entirely programmatic set of mathematical "equations" for his major postulates, and a group of pseudo-mensurational units for his principal intervening variables. Although there were admissions of programmaticity thinly scattered through the pages of *Pr.B.*, there is little doubt that the net effect of the presentation was to create an impression of quantitative determinacy far in excess of the actual state of affairs. That Hull himself had a fully realistic appraisal of what this state of affairs was is indicated by the fact that, immediately after the publication of *Pr.B.*, he set himself the explicit task of formulating a "quantificational methodology" for defining his major intervening variable units, and for translating his programmatic "equations" into actual ones. Already in July and December of 1943, Hull issued two *memoranda* (58) announcing a program for achieving quantification. By 1945, it was possible for Hull to circulate a revision of these statements—*Research Memorandum Concerning the Quantitative Empirical Determination of Certain Basic Behavioral Constants and Their Functional Interrelationships* (62).[31] This lengthy memorandum puts forward the substance of the quantification program which eventuated in the five articles, published by Hull and others between 1947 and 1950 (13, 15, 64, 141, 145), that deal with the

---

[31] In the 1943 memoranda, Hull had suggested that the basic empirical data for the quantification procedure be derived from the Cowless-Pennington technique of conditioning the squeak of the rat by shocking its tail. Hull indicates in the 1945 memorandum that, during 1943-1944, exploratory work demonstrated the infeasibility of this technique. During 1944-1945, the technique of obtaining response latencies in a modified Skinner-Ellson box was developed. The program defined by the 1945 memorandum is based on this latter procedure, and this procedure was retained for the subsequent quantificational work.

quantification of reaction potential and related matters. The quantificational methods and findings reported in these articles are, in turn, reflected in the 1949-1951 postulate set.

Exactly how pressing a task Hull felt this matter of quantification to
be is revealed in the first article of the quantification series—*Reaction
Latency ($_st_R$) as a Function of the Number of Reinforcements (N)*. He
says (13, p. 214):

> In the writing of the volume *Principles of behavior* . . . , the author found
> it almost an expository necessity to have available at least the formal charac-
> teristics of a number of important mathematical behavioral principles or molar
> laws. These were accordingly postulated even though elaborated evidence was
> at the time largely lacking. Moreover, the expository need of giving specific
> examples of the working of the general theoretical approach necessitated the
> assumption of numerous quantitative constants which are essential characteristics
> of the equations necessarily involved. Finally, also for expository reasons, a
> number of behavioral measurement units (the wat, the hab, the mote and the
> pav) were employed, for which satisfactory quantitative definitions and genuine
> values had not been worked out. In short, a considerable part of the systematic
> structure in question was programmatic. . . .
> *That such a state of affairs should continue longer than circumstances make
> necessary is intolerable.* Accordingly, early in 1943 definite efforts to perform
> these quantitative determinations were begun . . . , and since that time work
> has continued without interruption (ital. mine).

It is interesting to observe that nowhere in the literature is there a
clearer or stronger statement of the programmaticity of *Pr.B.*, and of
the purely illustrative character of the quantitative material therein
contained. It is regrettable that a comparably emphatic statement to
this effect had not appeared in *Pr.B.* itself. Be this as it may, the quotation leaves little doubt as to the importance attributed by Hull to the
quantificational program in his post-*Pr.B.* career.

The passage just quoted is almost an exact replica of the initial paragraphs of the 1945 research memorandum on the quantificational program (62) alluded to above. *There,* however, after noting the intolera-
bility of the state of affairs represented by *Pr.B.*, Hull adds (p. 1):

> Needless to say a considerable number of changes, possibly radical ones, in
> the postulates of the system are expected to result from the carrying out of this
> series of investigations. Such changes must be recognized as normal in the evo-
> lution of a scientific theoretical system; indeed, this is one of the chief dis-
> tinctions between scientific theory and metaphysics.

With this anticipation of the theme of the present section in Hull's own
words, we will proceed to its documentation. We begin with a brief summary of (1) the *objectives and nature of Hull's quantificational methodology;* we then discuss certain of the (2) *relations between the results
of the quantification and the new postulate set,* and we conclude with
(3) an *evaluation of the quantificational program.*

1. Objectives and Nature of the Quantificational Methodology

The objectives of Hull's new quantificational program may best be seen in contrast to the quantitative procedures, insofar as they exist, which are implicit in *Pr.B.* A detailed reconstruction of Hull's typical procedure in arriving at "equational" function specifications has been presented earlier in this report (pp. 70-82). In crudest outline, the situation seems to have been as follows:

Hull recognized the complex problem of inferring relationships between intervening and empirical variables ("unobservables" and "observables") *as a problem*. The desideratum was to express a set of lawful quantitative relations which would interconnect systematic independent, intervening and dependent variables. But the "realizations" of the *intervening* variables provided by any experimental data used to suggest such quantitative interrelations (i.e., used for curve-fitting purposes) have the status only of crude *indicators* of the "unknown" intervening variable values to which they are presumably related.[32] Should it be assumed that the indicators "mirror" the correlative intervening variable "values," there would result as many intervening variable "continua" as there are indicator continua, and the intervening variables might then as well be abandoned for their generalizing properties would be lost.

Hull's tentative solution to this problem incorporated joint elements of arbitrariness, inconsistency and programmaticity. One assumption in the theory—the growth relation between sH_R and N—seems based on rational[33] considerations. In the case of most of the other assumptions of the theory, however, the typical procedure is to select or design an experiment, the independent variable of which is presumed to correspond to the antecedent

---

[32] A somewhat analogous problem exists with regard to the relations between *systematic* independent and dependent variables and their "realizations" in terms of the *experimental* independent or dependent variables of a given study. A systematic independent variable like C_D, for instance, cannot be *equated* with the number of hours' hunger under such and such a maintenance routine in such and such an experiment. As any analysis of "operational" or empirical definition which approximates adequacy will show, this would involve the *identification* of an empirical construct with only one member of the (possibly very extensive) class of its "reductive symptoms." Indeed such classes of "reductive symptoms" are rarely uniquely determined, because the growth of empirical knowledge may make it possible to add new reduction sentences (or reduction chains) to the empirical definition of a given concept (cf. 85). Yet, as we have seen (p. 26, this report), Hull has consistently tended to identify his *systematic* empirical variables with "direct observables." Thus the problem of constructing quantitative relationships between intervening and *systematic* empirical (independent or dependent) variables is as much a "problem" on the empirical variable side, as it is on the intervening variable side. For Hull, however, this aspect of the problem does not exist.

[33] As we have already tried to argue (pp. 74-78), the presentation in *Pr.B.* was unclear as to whether Hull intended the growth relation of sH_R to N as a "rational" or an "empirical" assumption. Hull seems to want it both ways, but the trend of the argument of Chapter VII (56, pp. 102-123) seems to demand that the assumption be regarded as "rational," however mixed Hull's actual intention.

theoretical variable under consideration, and the dependent variable of which corresponds to the consequent theoretical variable. To the experimental data is fitted an equation, and the *form* of the resulting equation is then *directly transferred* to the relationship between the theoretical variables under consideration. In these cases no question is raised about the legitimacy of *identifying* a relationship between indicators with a relationship between theoretical (e.g., intervening-intervening or independent-intervening) variables. Nevertheless, programmatic measuring units (the hab, mote, wat, and pav), ordered to a nonexistent "centigrade scale," are assigned to the chief intervening variables in order to exhibit the virtues which *would* obtain, if these units could be linked with quantitative consistency to the indeterminate collection of indicators with which each is related. To round out the picture, it should be added that in the "quantification" of the relations between the terminal intervening variables of $Pr.B.$ ($_s\bar{E}_R$ and $_s\dot{\bar{E}}_R$) and the four dependent variable "measures" (p, n, $_st_r$, and A), the procedure is to fit equations to "typical" curves of each of these measures as a function of N, and (1) assuming that $_s\bar{E}_r$, other things constant, must be a growth function of N, and (2) finding an explicit growth expression in each equation, it becomes possible to utilize "the method of residues . . . to determine the functional relationship of $_s\bar{E}_R$ to the particular behavior phenomena employed" (p. 395).

As the 1945 memorandum on quantification makes clear, the over-all objectives of Hull's new quantificational procedures are to remedy all of the deficiencies of the earlier methodology implicit in the above account. In Hull's estimation, the pivot on which the whole operation could be made to turn was the quantification of $_sE_R$, because this is the construct which, of all intervening variables in the theory, is most immediately related to performance indicators. Once $_sE_R$ is scaled, Hull reasoned (62), it should become feasible to derive other intervening variable measures (habs, motes, pavs) by a combined rational and empirical maneuver. Since, for instance, it is rationally assumed that

$$_sE_R = {}_sH_R \times D,$$

and that

$$_sH_R = f(N),$$

the availability of a set of "genuine" scale values for $_sE_R$ as a function of N, might yield an equation containing two multiplicative components which could be identified as corresponding to $_sH_R$ and D. The law of $_sH_R$ as a function of N would then take the same form as the original equation with the D term omitted, and $_sH_R$ could thus be indirectly scaled in terms of $_sE_R$. Similarly, D might now be indirectly scaled via an elaborate experimental program which would determine $_sE_R$ values as a function of a relevant independent variable condition of D (C_D), $_sH_R$ remaining constant. From the fitted equation, one could presumably derive the law representing D as a function of C_D.[34] The *immediate objective of the program thus becomes the quantification of $_sE_R$.*

Hull devotes relatively little attention to the *formal properties* of the type of mensurational scale he is trying to achieve. It is evident, however, that he is after something with the properties of at least an *interval*, and preferably a *ratio*, scale. In the second article of the quantification sequence (64), Hull is entirely clear about the desiderata at which a satisfactory quantification of $_sE_R$ would aim. He recognizes that the "objective manifestations" of $_sE_R$ "take . . . many different forms." Furthermore (64, pp. 237-238):

These manifestations, while measurable, are usually measured in different units and rarely or never, even when measured in the same units, yield results which are comparable. Moreover, in some cases, e.g., muscular contraction, several different aspects of the response, such as latency, amplitude, and force, can be employed as indicators of what at bottom is presumably the same thing.

After presenting a "tabular summary" of twelve indicators of $_sE_R$, Hull specifies the following requirement (64, pp. 238-239):

. . . all quantifications of reaction potential, however empirically manifested, should be expressible on the same scale and in terms of the same unit.

At the end of this article, there is a detailed statement of "criteria of quantificational validity" which serves further to define the requirements of the mensurational program:

---

[34] We have referred to the scaling of other intervening variable "measures" in terms of the scaling of $_sE_R$ as a combined rational and empirical maneuver. We think that Hull would have had to agree with this description, but it must be remembered that the *content* of many of the assumptions that function as rational components of the present procedure (e.g., the assumption that $_sE_R$ is a multiplicative function of D and $_sH_R$) *had been represented in Pr.B. as based on empirically determined relationships.* In *Essentials,* Hull still speaks as if many such assumptions are based on empirical evidence. To the extent that Hull took this position, it should be noted that he was still tacitly assuming that *equations fitted to "indicator" values yielded relationships having the same form as equations fitted to genuine measures.* Such an assumption would seem to make the elaborate quantificational procedure in large part unnecessary, except perhaps for the determination of empirical constants.

The simplest way out of this dilemma is to admit that formal construct interrelations of the sort under discussion are pure "rational" guesses. The validity of such guesses could then only be determined by the *fruits* of the quantificational procedure—e.g., the extent to which quantitative derivations were checked by further experimental evidence. As shall be shown later, such a determination of validity had not been made in a single case. In *Essentials,* Hull apparently assumes that such rational guesses find empirical validation, if analysis of the equations fitted to "quantified" data discloses expressions within the equations which exhibit the formal relations rationally assumed. But there are many evidences which suggest that the curve-fitting procedures were often extremely loose, Hull in one place even admitting that a growth expression was chosen despite the fact that a different function gave a better fit. In other words, it is probable that the "rational" construct interrelations were *projected* into the equations which presumably verify them.

As Bergmann and Spence remark . . . , "The actual excellence of physical measurement is entirely a matter of fact." These excellences have been found in the facts of quantitative consistency of the results of measurement with related phenomena and the great extent to which they have facilitated the simplified systematic organization of the field in which the quantifications have been employed. *Similarly, the present and all other proposed methods of behavioral quantification must depend for their validation, at least in part, upon the quantitative consistencies and systematizations to which they give rise* (64, p. 252, ital. mine).

Hull then goes on to present two "specific examples of such . . . possibilities in the present field. . . ." The first is that "a closely related [quantificational] method based on reaction thresholds in the case of conditioned winking of the type reported by Reynolds" (107) should yield a curve of learning having the same form as the rat latency curve emerging from the initial quantificational study. In Hull's own words, the second example is as follows:

It is probable that some forms of learning can be found which yield two or more . . . objective indications of the *very same* habit strength acquisition, each one of which could be used independently. . . . It would seem that such curves of learning even though secured from quite different data should agree as to the type of best fitting equation and also, within the limits of the data sampled, as to the various constants. Such a determination may very well prove to be a critical test of the methodology (64, p. 252).

How does Hull actually proceed to the quantification of $_sE_R$? Faced with the most critical methodological problem at the frontier of current behavior theory—the boot-strap lifting operation of climbing from *indicators* to *measures*—Hull turns to the resources of classical psychophysics. He comes up with an *ad hoc* adaptation of the method of paired comparisons, as rationalized by Thurstone (133, 134, 135). On the assumption that an indicator like *latency* has "an inverse monotonic functional relationship" to reaction potential, Hull proposes to apply the paired comparisons technique to latency data secured from a group of rats during the learning of a simple instrumental response tendency. In this way, a series of quantified $_sE_R$ values for the various trials of training would be derived, and the "law" of $_sE_R$ as a function of N would become available.

A basic "calibration" experiment (13) was therefore designed having the following characteristics: Fifty-nine rats were trained in a modified Skinner-Ellson box to move a small brass tube 1/16 of an inch to the left, in order to secure a pellet of food. The behavior compartment was equipped with a "shutter" (door) which separated the rat from the panel containing the manipulandum, and which was always closed when the animal was inserted. Latencies were defined as the time between the raising of this door and the animals' response to the manipulandum. Appropriate operation of the manipulandum always caused an automatic retraction (disappearance) of the manipulandum, and was always reinforced by the immediate appearance of a standard pellet of food. Animals were trained, on a one trial per day basis, and under twenty-two hours of hunger, until they attained a stable latency asymptote. The extreme distribution of trials was used in order to minimize contamination of the latencies as a measure of reaction potential, due to inhibitory and other effects. *This single experiment, as we shall later see, provides the principal basis for the quantification of $_sE_R$, and the far reaching changes in the entire Hullian theory thereby mediated.*

Hull's assessment of the *differences* between his application of the paired comparisons technique to these data, and its conventional application to judgmental data in psychophysics is instructive. They are (64, pp. 241-242) as follows.

1) In psychophysics, judgments are based on "a comparison of stimulations which are systematically varied," habit strength being constant. In Hull's application the stimulation is constant, "while the relevant habit strength which mediates the reaction is the critical difference." [35]

2) In psychophysics, "the two things compared are ordinarily" simultaneous "or in close succession," whereas in this situation the "states under comparison cannot possibly exist simultaneously." Rather, permanent records of the latencies are taken, and the judgments of relative magnitude are later made by an investigator.

3) Only "one significant comparison can ever be secured from any two habit strengths of a given organism." This differs from the ordinary psychophysical situation where the same comparison-pair of stimuli may recur on many occasions. Thus to get "adequate numbers of comparisons of what corresponds to the same habit strength, many different organisms are placed in a comparable learning sequence so that all acquire corresponding habits, it being assumed that the increments of habit strength at the successive reinforcements are in some sense comparable, though hardly equal because of individual differences in learning capacity. For this reason the latencies of a given organism are here only compared with each other, never with those of other organisms."

With these differences in the conditions of application, Thurstone's Case III form of the immensely laborious paired comparisons methodology (133, 134, 135) is applied to the latency data of the calibration experiment for a "judicious sampling of twenty-five trials distributed

---

[35] For some reason, Hull entitled the article on which this discussion is based, *A Proposed Quantification of Habit Strength* (64), and the presentation, towards the beginning of the article, is couched in terms of "habit strength" rather than "reaction potential." The rationale given for this is the familiar assumption, $_sE_R = {_sH_R} \times D$, plus the fact that the D term in the quantification is constant. Nevertheless, it is clear that what is being *directly* quantified is reaction potential, and in the later part of the article Hull lapses into consistent reference to reaction potential rather than habit strength.

over the entire range of sixty" (64, p. 243) available trials. This procedure presumably yields scale values which are based on reaction potential differences "between the central tendency of the many [reaction potentials] of the group of organisms as a whole at two different numbers of reinforcements, in terms of the standard deviation of the pooled reaction potential variabilities of the same group of organisms as a whole."

The paired comparisons method (and similar techniques of psychophysical or "psychological" scaling) is, of course, based on the characteristics of the normal curve. Empirically, the technique involves the comparison of each of the "stimuli" to be scaled with every other, with respect to the relative magnitude of a specified property. It is assumed, in the language of Thurstone, that on each occurrence, a given stimulus gives rise to a "discriminal process" within a psychological continuum, that chance factors will result in a variation in the magnitude of the discriminal process produced by the same stimulus on different occasions, and that such a distribution of discriminal processes (the "discriminal dispersion") is normal. This being assumed, it can also be assumed that the *differences* between the discriminal processes of two discriminal dispersions associated with two different stimuli ($R_b - R_a$) will also form a normal distribution. The mean of such a difference distribution would give the scale separation ($S_b - S_a$) between the two stimuli in question. The scale separation can therefore be expressed in terms of the deviate on the abscissa of the distribution of differences (X_{ba}). The unit of this distribution is, of course, its standard deviation. Thus the scale separation $S_b - S_a$ is $X_{ba\sigma diff}$. The basic *empirical* datum from which this value is computed is the proportion of cases in which stimulus R_b has the relation ">" to stimulus R_a ($p_{b>a}$). Such data may be transformed into scale difference values by virtue of Thurstone's "law of comparative judgment" (134).[36]

The equation for the law of comparative judgment cannot be solved directly, because it assumes, among other things, that the standard deviations of the discriminal dispersions of R_b and R_a are known. Thurstone thus distinguishes five cases which, when given sets of assumptions are made, it is possible to derive an estimated solution (18, pp. 220-221).

_____

[36] The equation for this law, in Guilford's notation (18, pp. 219-220), is.

$$S_b - S_a = X_{ba} \sqrt{\sigma_b^2 + \sigma_a^2 - 2r\sigma_b\sigma_a}$$

where S_b and S_a = the scale values for two stimuli R_b and R_a, respectively.

X_{ba} = the deviate corresponding to the proportion of judgments $R_b > R_a$.

σ_b and σ_a = the standard deviation of the dispersions made by R_b and R_a on the psychological continuum.

r = the correlation between the discriminal deviations of R_b and R_a during the same judgments.

The above account of the paired comparisons method is derived from Guilford's (18, pp. 217-243) presentation.

Hull chooses Case III as the most suitable form of the method for his purposes.

This *precis* of the Thurstone rationalization should serve to indicate how tenuous and assumption-laden the method is even within the field of its original and appropriate application (psychophysics and "psychological" scaling). It also helps to define certain of the gratuitous assumptions that Hull was forced to make in his unique application of this method. Among the major of these, is the necessary assumption that: "*the spontaneous variability in the momentary reaction potential ($_s\dot{E}_R$) approximates the normal form of distribution . . . , $_sE_R$ remaining constant*" (64, p. 240, ital. mine). This, of course, also means that the distributions of $_s\dot{E}_R$ differences must also be normal in form. In *A Proposed Quantification of Habit Strength*, Hull was especially sensitized to these points, even going so far as to say (64, p. 242):

As Thurstone has pointed out, this pooling of the variability of numerous somewhat different organisms introduces an *additional uncertainty* regarding the normality of the distribution of differences the σ of which is here used as the preliminary measuring unit of the quantification of reaction potential. Sooner or later, of course, the characteristics of this pooling of many variability distributions must be objectively determined if possible (ital. mine).

2. Relations Between the Results of the Quantification and the New Postulate Set

The application of the methods just described to the data of his single defining experiment put Hull in possession of twenty-five "quantified" reaction potential values, corresponding to the "judicious sampling" of twenty-five of the training trials of the fifty-nine animal experimental group. This thin mensurational bridgehead being gained, Hull tried to proceed to the conversion of his entire pseudo-quantitative system into "genuine" quantitative form. The general strategy for such an operation, as laid down in the 1945 memorandum on quantification, has already been summarized in our discussion of "objectives." The *results* of this general strategy as well as the *tactics* of its application are revealed in the 1949-1951 postulate sets. These reflect the "considerable number of changes, possibly radical ones," which Hull had anticipated in the memorandum of 1945.

The tactics employed in building up the basic assumptions of the new theory, as exhibited in *Essentials*, are clearly *in line* with the *general* strategy formulated in the 1945 memorandum. This memorandum, however, had called for an ambitious series of experiments, which *in the case of each major assumption* would provide *scaled* data, based ultimately on the $_sE_R$ scaling technique, for purposes of defining the particular construct interrelations under scrutiny. Until the formulation of the 1949-1951 postulate sets, only the $_sE_R$ calibration experiment, and two additional "scaled" studies (141, 146), both quite inadequate for their purposes, had been completed. Thus, the methods employed in the construction of the 1949-1951 postulates reveal the 1945 strategy only as watered down by many makeshifts and compromises of the most gratuitous sort.

The critical difference in the technique of postulate construction from the procedure of *Pr.B. is the now consistent convention of regarding all empirical curves and equations as* $_sE_R$ *(i.e., performance) functions.* This practice is apparently forced by two interrelated considerations: (1) Hull's desire to rectify the faulty logic of directly transferring the obtained relations among *empirical indicator variables* to *quantitative theoretical variables*, (2) the fact that the only "scaled" values available are those for $_sE_R$.

The clearest indication of how these procedural assumptions are now translated into practice may be found in the construction of the theoretical relationships which, in the new theory, generate $_sE_R$. The steps are essentially these.

1) The calibration experiment already described gives Hull the opportunity to fit an equation to the twenty-five *"scaled"* reaction potentials as a function of the number of reinforcements $(\dot{N})$. It is (75, equation 4, p. 31):

$$_sE_R = 3.55\ (1 - 10^{-.0305\dot{N}}).\text{[37]}$$

This is the basic equation of the entire new theory.

2) Possession of this equation presumably makes it possible to derive the law of $_sH_R$ as a function of $\dot{N}$—not the old, "programmatic" $_sH_R$, but $_sH_R$ as *scaled* in terms of the quantified $_sE_R$. Such a maneuver is accomplished quite directly by adhering, as formerly, to the *rational* assumption that $_sH_R$ is a positive growth function of $\dot{N}$. On the basis of this, the parenthesized exponential expression in equation 4 is identified as corresponding to $_sH_R$, while the coefficient "3.55" is held to represent the D conditions prevalent in the calibration experiment, in much the same way as the earlier analysis (56, pp. 254-255) of the Perin-Williams *indicator* equations was made.

3) Hull now suggests that the law of D as a function of relevant independent variables (C_D), such as hunger, could be determined by an elaborate experiment designed to yield a family of scaled $_sE_R$ curves as a

---

[37] In the new theory, $\dot{N}$ stands for the "number of reinforcements from [the] beginning of learning, i.e., from [the] absolute zero (Z)" of reaction potential (75, p. 129). It is distinguished from N, the "number of superthreshold reinforcements," and N, "number of reinforcements in general." Equation 4 is a transformation of a prior equation which was fitted to $_sE_R$ as a function of N. The case for $\dot{N}$ was derived on the assumption that Z lies two reinforcements below the threshold. This latter assumption is purportedly justified by the empirical results of the calibration experiment which indicate that a median of two reinforcements were required before the initial conditioned reaction evocation (cf. 15, pp. 512-515).

function of $\dot{N}$, the C_D being systematically varied. This would be expected to provide a sufficient number of coefficients analogous to the "3.55" in equation IV to permit fitting equations to the *coefficients*. The results would give the law of D as a function of C_D in terms of parameters based ultimately on $_sE_R$, and would be, *ipso facto*, susceptible to "genuine" scaling. In this connection, Hull cites the Yamaguchi (147) experiment which was designed with some such purpose in view. This is one of the three studies in the entire theory which employs the $_sE_R$ scaling technique, and it is used as the main empirical basis for the present postulate V on *primary motivation*.

4) *A precisely analogous method to that described in items 1 to 3 above, is now used for the isolation of the three additional "constituents" of $_sE_R$—V (stimulus intensity dynamism), K (incentive motivation), and J (delay of reinforcement).* In each case, Hull begins with a family of equations, presumably for $_sE_R$ as a function of $\dot{N}$, each equation of the "family" corresponding to a different setting of the independent variable (e.g., weight of food) associated with the intervening variable (e.g., K) whose law is under scrutiny. In each case, the discovery is made that: (*a*) the right hand member of each equation of a family contains a growth expression multiplied by a coefficient; (*b*) the coefficients for a given family vary in an orderly way; and (*c*) the growth constants presumably show no significant change. The growth expressions, of course, are uniformly held to represent $_sH_R$. In accordance with the principle that "the parts of the equations which are nearly alike are so because . . . the empirical conditions . . . are alike, and . . . the parts . . . which are different are so because of the empirical conditions which are different" (75, p. 35), Hull assumes, in each case, that the variation of coefficients reflects the effect of the independent variable in question, and the law for the relation of this empirical variable to its appropriate intervening variable can now be derived by fitting an equation to the coefficients.

At this point, it is important to recall that the most startling set of changes in the new theory is the "attenuation" of the reinforcement principle, and the shifting of the "magnitude of need reduction" (w) and "delay of reinforcement" (t) variables from the determination of $_sH_R$ to $_sE_R$. Hull's *claimed* rationale for this is that the habit strength expressions which appear in the families of learning curves which are fitted to $_sE_R$ as a function of N data, for different settings of w and t, show no change in the values of their constants, whereas the coefficients in these equations show a systematic variation. Forgetting, for the present, the slim range and tenuous nature of the experimental data used, and the fact that the $_sE_R$ values in these cases are uniformly makeshift *indicator* values and not of the *scaled* variety, this claim is simply not justified. For instance, in the consideration of the delay in reinforcement variable, Perin's latency data (104) are used. Four separate equations are fitted to estimated values of $_sE_R$ as a function of N for different delay groups. In these equations, *both* the coefficients *and* the exponential constants vary over a wide range. Indeed, Hull points out that (75, p. 54):

> . . . the steepness of the rise of the learning curves as shown by the magnitude of the exponential constants . . . obviously is not constant. Instead it appears to be a consistently decreasing function of the amount of delay in reinforcement. This suggests that the exponent may ultimately also be expressed as a function of the delay in reinforcement. If this tendency is verified it will evidently complicate the interpretation now to be made.

The "interpretation . . . to be made" is, of course, that a curve fitted to the four coefficients (asymptotes of the $_sE_R$ learning curves) yields the law relating t to $_sE_R$, as mediated by J, and the fact that the "evidence" indicates a dependence of $_sH_R$ on J, quite as much as a dependence of $_sE_R$ on the same variable, is promptly forgotten.[38]

It is not likely, in the light of the foregoing, that the claimed rationale for the transfer of the former habit variables to $_sE_R$ is the true rationale. *Indeed, it is unlikely that any new evidence, or novel considerations with respect to deductive fertility, were responsible for these far-reaching changes.* Rather, the changes seem forced by blindly following the directives of the new quantificational program. The only directly "quantified" element available was equation 4 for $_sE_R$ as a function of $\dot{N}$. If other major intervening variables must be (even programmatically) derived from this thin "quantitative" wedge, the obvious and immediate thing to do is lift out $_sH_R$ in accordance with the formal relations assumed in the old theory ($_sE_R = D \times _sH_R$, and $_sH_R$ is a positive growth function of N). This being accomplished, how determine the relations between $_sH_R$ *and other determining variables of the sort formerly assumed to be relevant?* Only, of course, by fitting equations to empirical curves in which some performance indicator is assumed to represent $_sH_R$ as a function of the relevant variable. *But the new quantificational method entails the convention that all performance indicators (or preferably measures) must be uniformly interpreted as $_sE_R$.* In accordance with this, the simplest and happiest possibility is that all other variables which formerly were believed to determine $_sH_R$ (or which, on rational grounds, might be *believed* to determine $_sH_R$) directly determine $_sE_R$. Thus, the way is open to the series of equational analyses of $_sE_R$ functions which, as we have seen, is the characteristic tactic of *Essentials.*

Once this tactical approach is adopted, many, if not most, of the *other* innovations in the 1949-1951 postulate sets directly or indirectly follow. *Every* postulate of the new theory contains departures from the 1943 formulations, major or minor. The changes may involve the identification

---

[38] This circumstance is not entirely forgotten, though, because in a note at the end of the volume (75, p. 121) Hull refers to it as "a special reason for the uncertainty in regard to J." He refers to other sources of uncertainty as well.

of variables, construct interrelations, mathematical function forms, or any combination of these. At this point, we supplement the preceding account of the redistribution of $_sH_R$ and $_sE_R$ variables with some additional conspicuous examples of how the new procedures ramify upon the content of the 1949-1951 postulates. In a later section, we will itemize a sample of further changes in order to suggest the scope of the recent modifications.

In the succeeding paragraphs, we exhibit the connection between the new procedures and the current treatment of (a) *stimulus intensity dynamism* (V), (b) *behavioral oscillation,* and (c) *the postulates* (XV to XVII) *which relate $_sE_R$ to the dependent variable indicators of the theory.*

a. Stimulus intensity dynamism (V). In 1943, Hull indicated that "other important factors" probably "enter into the determination of habit strength" (56, p. 181), in addition to those explicitly incorporated in the reinforcement postulate (postulate 4). One such factor explicitly pointed to was stimulus intensity. In the 1949-1951 sets, an intervening variable representing the dynamic effects of stimulus intensity on behavior appears for the first time as a formal part of the theory. In accordance with the methods already discussed, this variable is built up from an $_sE_R$ equation fitted to a set of highly indirect calculations based on some ancient psychophysical data of Cattell's (7). This presumably makes possible the formulation of a logarithmic relation between S and the stimulus intensity component (V) of reaction potential, and thus we are provided with another determinant of $_sE_R$ (not $_sH_R$ as conceived in 1943).

Towards the end of the brief discussion of V in *Essentials,* we are suddenly informed (p. 45):

At this stage of our exposition we must point out that stimulus intensity dynamism has an important influence on habit formation of a multiplicative nature. This is expressed in the following equation:

$$_s\dot{H}_R = {_sH_R} \times V_1,$$

where V_1 represents the stimulus intensity involved in the original learning.

This V_1 of original learning is apparently to be distinguished from the V of action evocation which directly enters $_sE_R$ and which later is designated as V_2. What is especially curious here is that V_1 represents a second factor which apparently determines $_sH_R$ (in addition to N) but this fact is not registered in "the law of habit formation" (postulate IV) or any related law. At first blush, this seems like an oversight. A little speculation will show, however, that this assumption cannot possibly find a place within the postulate set as a *direct* determinant of $_sH_R$ on the basis of the present technique of postulate construction. The equational analysis of $_sE_R$ curves can only reveal V_2, not V_1. V_1 could be rationally assumed (as it has been), and possibly verified in terms of its indirect consequences, but it could not be represented as a direct determinant of $_sH_R$ within the law of habit formation, where it seems to belong, without becoming a glaring example of departure from the "quantitative" methodology. It therefore becomes a glaring example of a construct which is at once in the theory and out of it.[39]

b. Behavioral oscillation. In 1943, Hull had assumed that (56, p. 319)

Associated with every reaction potential $(_sE_R)$ there exists an inhibitory potentiality $(_sO_R)$ which oscillates in amount from instant to instant according to the normal "law" of chance, and whose range, maximum, and minimum, are constant.

It will be recalled that the recognition of this variable involves the introduction of the construct "momentary effective reaction potential" $(_s\dot{\bar{E}}_R)$, which is defined in terms of the difference between effective reaction potential $(_s\bar{E}_R)$ and the "oscillatory force." In the 1949-1951 postulate sets, the variable $_sO_R$ assumes a special significance for the obvious reason that the new quantificational program is based on the scaling of $_sE_R$, and the *unit* of quantification is the dispersion of the momentary effective reaction potential $(_s\dot{\bar{E}}_R)$. This, by definition, makes the unit of $_sE_R$ tantamount to the dispersion of $_sO_R$ (i.e., the dispersion of $_s\dot{\bar{E}}_R$ and $_sO_R$ are identical). Recall, further, that the *normality* of the distribution of $_s\dot{\bar{E}}_R$ and $_s\dot{\bar{E}}_R$ *differences* is a basic presupposition of Hull's paired comparisons scaling technique.

It was naturally very important for Hull to explore the legitimacy of this latter assumption. The "calibration" experiment for $_sE_R$ previously described presumably gives some slim basis for the evaluation of the normality assumption. Accordingly, Hull et al. (145) plotted a frequency distribution for five thousand "corrected" $_s\dot{\bar{E}}_R$ scale value differences derived from the latencies of this experiment. In order to get a large sample of values from a given stage of training, latencies at the performance asymptote, of which twenty were available for each of the fifty-nine animals, were used. The individual latencies were converted into "scaled" $_s\dot{\bar{E}}_R$ values via a modified form (145, equation 5, p. 218) of an equation for $_sE_R$ as a function of latency (145, equation 1, p. 217) which had been fitted to the original scaled values of the quantification study.

The resulting distribution turned out to be leptokurtic rather than normal, Pearson's β_2 giving a value of 3.9873. This rather unhappy finding set Hull off on an elaborate search for a method of correcting $_sE_R$

---

[39] V_1, as a multiplier of $_sH_R$ to form $_s\bar{H}_R$, is originally introduced as a brute assumption (without *any* explication) in connection with the discussion of stimulus dynamism (75, p. 45). It ultimately gets into the *formal* postulate set only by the back door, *via* postulate IX which reads (75, p. 59):

$$\text{``}_sE_R = D \times V_2 \times K \times J \times _s\bar{H}_R,$$

where

$$_s\bar{H}_R = _sH_R \times V_1,$$

and where V_1 is that involved in the original learning."

values, scaled on the *assumption* of normality, for the *fact* of leptokurto-sis. We will have occasion to refer to this enterprise later (pp. 129-131), but it is not relevant to the immediate purpose. What *is* immediately rele-vant is that this particular consequence of the new quantificational method must, to the extent that it is taken seriously, now force a revision in the $_sO_R$ assumption of 1943. In consequence, the $_sO_R$ postulate (XIII) of the 1949-1951 theory begins as follows (75, p. 97):

A. Reaction potential ($_sE_R$) oscillates from moment to moment, the distribu-tion of $_sO_R$ deviating slightly from the Gaussian probability form in being leptokurtic with β_2 at about 4.0. . . .

In *Pr.B.*, the "range, maximum, and minimum" of $_sO_R$ had been assumed to be constant. The possession of the equation, referred to above, for scaled $_sE_R$ as a function of latency, now makes it possible to derive the standard deviations of $_s\dot{\bar{E}}_R$ differences between successive trials of training, over the range of the sixty training trials of the quantification experiment. A plot of these values (145, p. 233; 75, p. 98) shows a marked and apparently un-systematic variability of the sigmas over the various trials of training. In this way, another major change is introduced into the theory as a direct consequence of the new quantificational method. The change is recorded in part B of postulate XIII (75, p. 99)—which represents a rather loose paraphrase of the phenomenal properties of the graph for the $_s\dot{\bar{E}}_R$ differ-ence sigmas as a function of the training trials. It reads:

The oscillation of $_sE_R$ begins with a dispersion of approximately zero at the absolute zero (Z) of $_sH_R$, this at first rising as a positive growth function of the number of superthreshold reinforcements (N) to an unsteady maximum, after which it remains relatively constant though with increasing variability.[40]

---

[40] Although an attempt has been made in the presentation of the new quantifica-tional methods to reserve evaluative comments for a subsequent section, it is difficult to abide by that rule at this place. Two opposed aspects of postulate XIII. *B.* should be noted: (1) The extreme literalness with which *general* signifi-cance is imputed to highly indirect, assumption-laden calculations based on part of the data from one learning experiment, and (2) the extreme imaginativeness shown in rendering the general trends and quantitative implications of these already questionable data. Why, for instance, should the oscillation of $_sE_R$ begin "with a dispersion of approximately zero at the absolute zero (Z) of $_sH_R$?" Hull cites as his only ground for this the fact that "the first seven superthreshold trials . . . show a very rapid rise in dispersion. If a curve should be drawn through these values and projected backward it is evident that it would cut the base-line at around two trials less than the conventional zero. Now it happens that this is the number of the trials marking the true zero" (75, p. 99). Again, what is the evidence for the dispersion of $_sE_R$ "at first rising as a positive growth function of the number of . . . reinforcements?" It is apparently the fact that the first seven of the sixty plotted trials *show some* kind of increase in the $_sE_R$ dispersion measure. There is no indication even that an equation was fitted to these values, if the fitting of a growth function constitutes evidence. Indeed, in 1948 (145, p. 233), Hull had described the same values as merely conforming "to a simple increasing function of N." These joint characteristics of almost fantastic over-generalization from a limited induction-basis *and* a loose rendering of the empirical findings within the content of the generalization, are present in almost every component of the 1949-

c. The dependent variable postulates. The impact of the new quantificational program on the content of the theory is nowhere shown more strikingly than in the case of the assumptions which tie the theory to empirical states of affairs on the *dependent variable* side. These are the postulates (XV through XVII) which relate $_sE_R$ to the systematic dependent variables of the new theory.

In 1943, postulates 12 through 15 (56, p. 344) tied $_s\bar{E}_R$ and $_s\dot{\bar{E}}_R$ to four reaction indicators—probability of response evocation (p), latency ($_st_R$), number of extinction reactions (n), and amplitude of responses mediated by the autonomic nervous system (A). The function forms imputed to these relationships were derived by a procedure (already described) of *assuming* that $_sH_R$ is a growth function of N, and then analyzing characteristic learning curves, for each of the four indicators, into components in accordance with this assumption.

In the 1949-1951 theory, the reaction potential—dependent variable relations are constructed, of course, in terms of the new methodology. The procedure now becomes quite direct, at least in general principle. Since it is now assumed that $_sE_R$ is in some sense quantified, all that must be done is to determine the relation between $_sE_R$ and corresponding values of the dependent variable indicator in question.

The problem of the relation of $_sE_R$ to reaction *latency* is automatically solved by virtue of the fact that the $_sE_R$ values of the original quantification experiment were derived from latency data. Indeed, we have already had occasion to refer to the fact that the quantification study had yielded, by highly indirect means, an equation for $_sE_R$ as a function of latency ($_st_R$). In consequence this equation provides the content for postulate XV which reads (75, p. 107):

Reaction potential ($_sE_R$) is a negatively accelerated decreasing function of the median reaction latency ($_st_R$), i.e.,

$$_sE_R = a_s t_R{}^{-b}.$$

Remarkably enough, this is one of the few elements of the **1949-1951** theory which remains in about the same form as the corresponding assumption (postulate 13, p. 344) in *Pr.B.*, *despite the fact that the former assumption was constructed without benefit of "quantified" data.*

Going on to the relation of $_sE_R$ to amplitude, we run into a predictable difficulty. No "scaled" $_sE_R$ values for amplitude happen to exist. As Hull points out (75, p. 108), the "methodology for doing this seems now available, though it has not been utilized." In rigid accordance with the new methodology, however, Hull proceeds to make "the best temporary shift possible," to wit (75, pp. 108-109):

1951 sets. Although such tendencies were evident enough in 1943, they have become even more conspicuous in the new theory.

Hovland . . . utilized four groups of 32 human subjects each in setting up the galvanic skin reaction to a tone with 8, 16, 24, and 48 reinforcements respectively. Substituting these N values in a learning equation obtained from 59 albino rats whose . . . reaction potentials had been quantified by means of the paired-comparisons technique based on reaction latencies . . . , we obtain the corresponding $_sE_R$ values.[41]

The operation can now be completed by fitting an equation to these $_sE_R$'s as a function of the corresponding obtained galvanic skin response amplitudes, and we thereby get the content of postulate XVI (75, p. 109):

Reaction potential . . . is an increasing linear function of the Tarchanoff galvanic skin reaction amplitude (A), i.e.,

$$_sE_R = cA - b.$$

For a second time, we are confronted with one of the rare cases of a correspondence with a function form assumed in *Pr.B.* (postulate 15, p. 344).

Continuing to the relationship of reaction potential to n, the number of extinction responses (75, postulate XVII), it still remains necessary to use a makeshift technique to estimate $_sE_R$'s. Hull deems it necessary to determine two cases of this law, the first (A) for "reaction potentials . . . acquired by massed reinforcements" (p. 112) and the second (B) for "reaction potentials . . . acquired by quasi-distributed reinforcements" (p. 114). The utility of this is not quite clear, since the basic "law of habit formation" (postulate IV) is stated only for the *second* of these conditions.

In any event, $_sE_R$'s for case A are derived in a manner analogous to the amplitude function, by combining certain of the Perin-Williams data (103) with the basic $_sE_R$ as a function of N equation. Estimated reaction potentials for case B are indirectly derived from a part of the Yamaguchi motivation study (75, pp. 112-113). Equations fitted to these two sets of $_sE_R$ values as a function of n yield the two parts of postulate XVII (75, XVII.A., p. 112; XVII.B., p. 114). It turns out that the functions for parts A and B are markedly different, and that both differ from the corresponding principle (postulate 14, p. 344) of *Pr.B.* In this case, therefore, the new quantificational method leads to a substantial change in the theory.

At this point, we must note another substantial change with regard to dependent variables. Probability of reaction evocation (p), which was linked to $_s\bar{E}_R$ by postulate 12 in 1943 (56, p. 344), *is nowhere to be found.* This, after all, is not a minor omission, because what a theory can talk about (i.e., make predictions about) is restricted to the referents of its dependent variables, and probability of response occurrence would seem

---

[41] We have felt it worthwhile to quote Hull's account of this "makeshift," because a similar procedure is used repeatedly in arriving at other assumptions in the theory. The few scaled $_sE_R$ values in existence must obviously carry a great load.

to be one of the things that any S-R theory of learning would have to talk about, if it were to have applicational utility.

The reason for the elimination of p is hidden in a note at the end of *Essentials* (pp. 125-126). There Hull indicates:

It has been pointed out above . . . that $_sO_R$ probably begins with a zero dispersion when $_sE_R$ stands at zero and increases as a growth function, at least through the first eight or nine reinforcements. This is very different from the hypothesis earlier utilized . . . which was that the dispersion of $_sO_R$ is invariable. . . .

This changed assumption naturally greatly reduces the amount of variability in the probability (p) of reaction evocation in simple reaction situations as the threshold is being crossed by $_sE_R$ during the learning process. Felsinger's empirical results [the reference is to the ubiquitous calibration experiment] indicate . . . once the response had risen above the reaction threshold and had been reinforced, it relatively infrequently failed to do so during the continuing learning process, which is what would be expected by the present revised hypothesis regarding $_sO_R$ dispersions (brackets mine).

In other words, pursuit of the new quantificational program leads, by a route we have already mapped, to the "discovery" that the dispersion of $_sO_R$ (or $_s\dot{\bar{E}}_R$) is very slight in the area of the reaction threshold. This would imply that, immediately after the threshold is crossed, the likelihood of a fluctuation of $_s\dot{\bar{E}}_R$ sufficient to depress the reaction below the threshold is very small. Therefore, any assumption which implies a very *gradual* increase in reaction probability as the initial reinforcements accumulate (as did the 1943 postulate 12 which assumed an ogival relationship between $_s\bar{E}_R$ and p) must be abandoned. *Therefore, p as a primitive dependent variable of the theory must be abandoned.*[42]

Once more, then, the new quantificational method forces a major change in the theory. It might perhaps be argued that in *this* particular case it is not the new quantitative commitments *per se*, but these in conjunction with the evidence of the Felsinger experiment, which force the change. However, examination of the details of this study (13, pp. 216-217) will show that the procedure was such as to *insure* a p of close to unity after

---

[42] In all fairness to Hull, it should be acknowledged that he recognized that the high stability of the response after the first "superthreshold" reinforcement in the calibration experiment "contrasts sharply with . . . the very slow increases in p observed in the case of conditioned blinking . . . and in rote learning" (75, p. 126). He hypothesized that "these latter forms of learning are in reality cases of simple trial-and-error learning, and that what was formerly supposed to be the reaction threshold was a strong competing reaction." Thus, it is evident that he hoped to deal with certain of the relations between $_sE_R$ and p in terms of a sequence of theorems relevant to simple trial-and-error learning. It is even possible that this elimination of p from the postulates of the theory, recognizing as it does the situation-bound character of quantitative behavioral relationships, may be a happy alteration of the system. But, from this point of view, Hull might as well have abandoned *all of the postulated relations between $_sE_R$ and the dependent variables, as indeed every other "quantitative" postulate of the theory.*

the occurrence of the first superthreshold reinforcement. And this aspect of the procedure was such, because the quantificational program which motivated the study demanded that it be such.

By way of summary, then, in *all* of the dependent variable postulates of the new theory,[43] and indeed in all of the examples considered in this section, the dominating factor is the new quantificational program. No matter how slight the *realized* portion of this program may be, no matter how tenuous, remote or arbitrary is its application in a given case, the dictates of the new method are followed. When, as in the case of postulates XV and XVI, pursuit of this method yields results which agree, through some distant coincidence, with earlier assumptions, they are retained. When, as in the case of new postulate XVII, and the dropping of *p*, the method yields findings at gross variance with earlier assumptions, it is *these* findings which determine the content of the new theory. In no case do the changes seem related to a careful assessment of experimental evidence, or a rational calculation of theoretical plausibility. In this way does the new theory, which superficially seems by virtue of the magnitude of the changes to register marked empirical sensitivity, register only the consequences of a premature attempt to achieve quantification. The only "evidence" underlying, at one inferential distance or another, most of the changes are the twenty-five pooled $_sE_R$ values for the fifty-nine rats of the calibration experiment.

3. Evaluation of the Quantificational Program

In the preceding presentation of the objectives, nature and consequences of the new quantificational program, an effort has been made to hold evaluative analysis to the minimum. This has seemed desirable in order to reveal the rather complex strategy and intricate tactics of the program in an unencumbered way. Since, in the limited explanatory material connected with the 1949-1951 postulate sets, Hull had been far from clear-cut about the relations between the quantification of $_sE_R$ and the new theory, the tracing out of these relations seemed to merit undivided attention. It has also seemed desirable to let the new quantificational program speak for itself, because in a sense it is *self-evaluating*. The methods (and their results) contain at every point so many gratuitous assumptions, remote extrapolations, arbitrary mathematical transformations of data, autistic anticipations of empirical outcomes, that it becomes almost meaningless to fix on any given set of inadequacies to the exclusion of

---

[43] As an addendum to the above discussion of the dependent variable postulates, it should be noted that there is still no evidence of any more satisfactory constitution of the response class than there was in 1943. Thus, the present dependent variable indicators are just as ambiguous with respect to what it is that they indicate (i.e., response) as were the dependent variables of *Pr.B.* (cf. p. 44, this report).

others. Such inadequacies should be conspicuous enough from any close reading of the foregoing account, but it must be emphasized that any selective account of this material can only impart a remote flavor of the actual state of affairs.

In this section, we will present only a *small sample* of the evaluative points that might be brought to bear on the quantificational method and its consequences. Generally speaking, we will confine the discussion to issues which may provide additional insight into the characteristics of the quantificational program and the new theory which it has produced. In the following discussion, then, we present evaluative analyses of (a) *the scaling of reaction potential,* and (b) *the associated procedure of postulate construction which determined the content of the new theory.*

a. Evaluation of the $_sE_R$ scaling technique. The most effective way to evaluate Hull's "quantificational methodology" for the scaling of $_sE_R,$ is *in terms of his own stated objectives.* One could devote time to questioning the logic of transferring a scaling method, the properties of which are ambiguous even within the original psychophysical setting for which it was developed, to a radically different situation. Again, assuming that the Hullian modification of the procedure is entirely legitimate, and its application to the data of the calibration experiment impeccable, one could still raise a number of severe questions about the *a priori* theoretical utility of the resulting scale values. One might, for instance, question the *a priori* assumption that Hull must make to the effect that the different empirical *indicators* of $_sE_R$ are ordinally correlated to a sufficiently high degree, to permit predictions, from $_sE_R$ values based on the scaling of a given indicator (e.g., latency), of the corresponding ordinal values of some *other* indicator (e.g., amplitude). The direct way to proceed, however, and the one most likely to give further insight into the terminal status of Hull's theory, is to test the methodology in terms of the explicitly stated objectives.

We will recall that the basic requirement demanded by Hull was that "all quantifications of reaction potential, however empirically manifested, should be expressible on the same scale and in terms of the same unit" (64, pp. 238-239). *There is ample evidence that the methodology did not meet this requirement.*

Evidence which plainly shows the untenability of assuming that the $_sE_R$ values arising from the calibration experiment have comparable significance in any context outside that of initial determination, has already been alluded to in the discussion of behavioral oscillation. It will be recalled that in the attempt to test the normality assumption with respect to the dispersion of $_s\dot{\bar{E}}_R$ differences (145), Hull plotted the distribution of a large number of calculated $_s\dot{\bar{E}}_R$ differences at the latency asymptote for the fifty-nine animals of the calibration experiment. The resulting distribution was symmetrical but leptokurtic. This, of course, posed for Hull the critical problem of how the scale values were affected by such a departure from the presuppositions underlying their construction.[44]

Since the scale values of the calibration experiment are based upon standard tables of ordinates and areas of the normal probability integral, Hull proceeded to construct analogous tables based on the empirical characteristics of the obtained leptokurtic distribution. These tables clearly (and predictably) imply that scale-separation values constructed on the assumption of a Gaussian distribution, must be substantially distorted when a distribution is actually leptokurtic. From the empirical leptokurtic distribution, Hull is then able to compute new scale values corresponding to the twenty-five scaled $_sE_R$ values of the original study. These *corrected* $_sE_R$ values are shown by tests of internal consistency to contain significantly less scale-separation distortion than the original values, and Hull is *presumably* out of his dilemma. Indeed, after all this laborious work, the dilemma seems spontaneously to evaporate, for Hull maintains that a fit of the *corrected* $_sE_R$ values gives almost an identical equation to the one fitted to the original values, except for a 10.6 per cent reduction in the coefficient determining the asymptote. This, despite the fact that there are marked apparent differences in many of the scale-separation values.

In this way does Hull extricate the "quantificational methodology" from the impasse created by a failure to confirm the normality assumption. But at this point it is necessary to raise an unhappy question. Does not the entire rationale of the paired comparisons and similar scaling techniques depend on the assumption of a *canonical* distribution of scale value differences, i.e., a distribution having certain invariant mathematical properties? The fact that the "5000 calculated momentary reaction potential $(_s\dot{E}_R)$ differences of fifty-nine albino rats at the limit of latency reduction due to training" (145, p. 220) yields a leptokurtic distribution with a β_2, of exactly 3.9873 does not mean that precisely the same amount of leptokurtosis will be present in the next study, or indeed a repetition of the same study.[45]

---

[44] The rather tortured character of the article (145) in which these considerations are reported is perhaps an indication of Hull's concern over the resulting challenge to his quantificational method. Hull's disturbance can perhaps be inferred from the fact that he felt it necessary to devote considerable space (pp. 227-228; pp. 234-236) to an analysis of three early studies of Thurstone, with the intention of demonstrating that there are indications in these studies, as well as his own, of "scale separation distortion produced by the application of a Gaussian probability table to a leptokurtic distribution of paired-comparison data" (p. 229). Indeed, he goes so far as to suggest in a footnote (p. 237) that "leptokurtosis may be the true basis of individual psychophysics and individual behavior theory generally, as well as of the pooled results by the Thurstone type of procedure."

[45] Hull indicates (145, p. 221): "In the case of β_2, the statistical indication is that the .9873 deviation beyond 3.00 has a ratio of 1.352 to its probable error, which corresponds to a probability of about 1 in 5 that it is due to the chance of sampling."

A c matter of fact, there is no particular reason to expect leptokurtosis at all in the next study, or symmetry, or indeed anything, but we are trying to remain within the framework of Hull's argument.

That Hull was concerned about such considerations is revealed in a footnote (145, p. 236):

In case the degree of leptokurtosis varies from one project to another this will present a practical difficulty. However, with modern calculating devices it should not be too laborious to compute several leptokurtic tables covering the range over which data vary. . . . As a beginning, tables could perhaps be made which are based on β_2's of 3.75, 4.00, and 4.50. Meanwhile we may be able to establish a dependable rule which will enable us to estimate rather closely in advance which table will be required. If not it will be fairly easy to apply our test for scale-separation distortion, or some improved version of it, to the Thurstone Case III procedure and try the suitability of one table after another to the paired-comparison data until one is found which will yield a zero or near-zero degree of distortion.

The above statement makes it clear that, if the difficulty is a "practical" one, it is certainly a cumbersome practical difficulty, to say the least. But is the difficulty merely a *practical* one? "All quantifications of reaction potential" must be "expressible on the same scale and in terms of the same unit." Hull grants the possibility of the degree of leptokurtosis varying from project to project. This means that the resulting scale values will be on different scales (and in different units) in different projects. A possible reply to this is that so long as both scale values and β_2's for the different projects are specified, the values should be intertranslatable. But, at this point, an *additional* complication must be introduced. If Hull grants that degree of leptokurtosis may vary from project to project, he must also grant that it may vary for the distributions of $_s\dot{E}_R$ at different stages of learning *within the same project*. The assumption that such $_s\dot{E}_R$ differences at different stages of learning will have precisely the same β_2's is more than a little demanding on reality. We have already seen that Hull's plot of the *standard deviations* of the $_s\dot{E}_R$ differences for successive trials of the rats of the calibration study, at the different stages of learning, shows *marked variability*. What reason is there to assume that the various distributions show any *less* variability with respect to other characteristics, including β_2? This would obviously mean that, *even within a given study, $_sE_R$ scale value differences are not "in terms of the same unit,"* and indeed no *unambiguous scale can arise.*

Hull's requirement that all quantifications of reaction potential be on the same scale and in the same units is a rudimentary requirement dictated by the logic of measurement. There is, however, a position gaining ground among psychological methodologists (e.g., 4, 18) to the effect that, since all mensurational scales are essentially approximations to the conditions demanded by the logic of measurement, the critical test of a mensurational technique should be its *fruits* in mediating quantitative consistencies among lawful empirical relations. When a mensurational procedure deviates from the formal requirements of measurement to the *extent* that Hull's "quantification" of sE_R does, it becomes autistic to believe that such a procedure could conceivably lead to empirically fruitful consequences. Nevertheless, it is clear that Hull intended such considerations to serve as the *critical* test of his methodology.

Hull is very explicit about this in the foundation article of the quantification sequence (64)—*A Proposed Quantification of Habit Strength.* We will recall that after their pointing out that the "excellences" of physical measurement "have been found in the facts of quantitative consistency of the results of measurement with related phenomena and the . . . extent to which they have facilitated the simplified systematic organization of the field," Hull goes on to say (64, p. 252): "Similarly, the present and all other proposed methods of behavioral quantification must depend for their validation, at least in part, upon the quantitative consistencies and systematizations to which they give rise." Recall, further, that Hull cites two *concrete examples* of the possibilities for making an initial evaluation of the capacity of the sE_R scaling technique to mediate "quantitative consistencies" with "related phenomena." The first of these requires that an sE_R learning curve of the same form as that resulting from the initial calibration experiment should emerge from the application of a similar scaling method to "reaction thresholds in the case of conditioned winking of the type reported by Reynolds." The second example, and one represented as a possible "critical test of the methodology," demands that a fit of equations to scaled values based on two independent indicators of the same habit acquisition should result in expressions which agree both in form and in the values of their constants. Although the above suggestions for a test of the methodology were published in 1947, *there is no evidence that these or any comparable determinations of validity were ever carried out.* Indeed, *there is not a single instance, in any subsequent publication, of an attempt to assess the consistency of the results of the scaling procedure in terms of its application to two independent sets of data.* In one of the two published studies, other than the calibration experiment, which employs the scaling procedure (141), Hull found *internal* evidence which led him to conclude that (p. 199) it "is quite possible . . . that this unit [sE_R in sigmas] could vary from one situation to another and especially from one type of behavioral process . . . to another. . . ." Despite these circumstances, and despite the wide and obvious departure of the method from the *formal* requirements of measurement, the quantificational results of the calibration experiment (and the study just cited) are allowed to ramify into every part of the new theory.

In publications subsequent to *A Proposed Quantification of Habit Strength,* the demand that the methodology be validated in terms of the quantitative consistency of its results with related phenomena undergoes a subtle reinterpretation. To take but one example, the next article in the quantification sequence—*Some Functional Relationships of Reaction Potential ($_sE_R$) and Related Phenomena* (15)—gives promise, in terms of its title, of carrying out precisely the type of validity determination mentioned above. Actually, what Hull does in this article is to put forward some twelve equations, all of them deriving, in one way or another, from the basic scaled (and unscaled) data of the calibration experiment.

For example, equation 1 (15, p. 513) is the foundation equation for $_sE_R$ as a function of the number of *superthreshold reinforcements* (N). Equation 2 (15, p. 514) is merely the definitional assumption that the "absolute zero" (Z) of reaction potential lies two reinforcements below the threshold. Equation 3 (15, p. 514) gives the scale value for Z as derived by the substitution of "-2" for N in equation 1. Thus, we now have a number for the scale distance separating the absolute zero of reaction potential from the threshold ($Z = -.426$). From this and equation 1, it is now possible to write equation 4 (15, p. 515) which specifies $_sE_R$ as a function of $\dot{N}$ (number of reinforcements from absolute zero). Other equations in the sequence are of the order of the equation for $_sH_R$ as a function of $\dot{N}$ (equation 8, p. 516) which, as we already know, is essentially equation 1 with its coefficient omitted, and equation 9 (15, p. 518) which is the fitted equation for $_sE_R$, as a function of the median latencies of the calibration experiment.

In the final paragraph of this article, Hull remarks (15, p. 526):

And, finally, attention may be called to the fact that the method of quantifying reaction potential upon which the most of the conclusions listed above are based has satisfied the pragmatic test of fertility in the following respect: the methodology for quantifying reaction potential taken jointly with its theoretical setting has yielded a number of equations, several of which may be considered as first approximations to potential primary molar behavior laws, the determination of parameters involved in such laws, or both.

The "pragmatic test of fertility" that Hull is referring to here has plainly nothing to do with the pragmatic test of validation in terms of "quantitative consistencies" of the sort referred to in the previous article. In that article the "consistencies" involve the agreement of *independent* applications of the methodology to related empirical phenomena. In the present connection, the *entire analysis remains within the framework of the original quantificational study*. The only "fertility" in evidence is the demonstration that, given the initial equation 1, and making a number of arbitrary theoretical and definitional assumptions, it becomes possible to write a number of relatively simple transformations (e.g., equations 4, 8, etc.). In not one case does a transformation test the empirical validity or plausibility of either the quantificational methodology, or the resulting $_sE_R$ learning curve, or any of the other assumptions which mediate the equation sequence. We may add that in *every other* instance in which Hull discusses the "fertility" of the quantificational method, the attempted demonstration discloses only an illusory fertility of the sort just considered.

Before closing this section, it should be recorded that there is reason to believe that Hull, himself, had grave doubts about the feasibility of his quantificational procedure. Although much of the time he succeeded in suppressing these doubts, there are many evidences in the tone of his final publications of a degree of tentativeness far in excess of his earlier writings. We have already indicated that in the second of the published experiments which employ the scaling method, Hull was forced by the evidence to admit the possible failure of the technique. This study by Wilcoxen, Hayes and Hull will be discussed in detail in a later consideration of the inhibition postulate. Towards the end of *Essentials*, Hull makes a statement that again goes further than a protestation of tentativeness. This arises in connection with the presentation of the finding, mentioned above, that the σ's of $_s\mathring{E}_R$ (and thus $_sO_R$) dispersions, vary for different trials of training. He says (pp. 99-100):

> Since the dispersion of $_sO_R$ is the unit of quantification of $_sE_R$ in the present system, the variability . . . suggests a serious problem. It is true that in a certain sense the Case III methodology devised by Thurstone, with its σ_K, largely equalizes the $_sO_R$ units actually utilized in any particular quantification. One trouble with the quantifications employed to date is that in our experience the various portions of the learning process are unequally sampled by this procedure . . . , so that in effect a more or less different unit is used in each study. This means that within any given quantification the unit is approximately constant—namely, the σ_K, though different quantifications are not exactly comparable with one another.[46]

This admission of "serious difficulties" is left hanging in mid-air in *Essentials*. Quite aside from the possible implications of such difficulties with regard to the bankruptcy of the entire quantificational method, it is evident that they represent critical deficiencies in the specific quantitative findings which have so far resulted from *application* of the method.

---

[46] The difficulties that Hull alludes to here, while severe, are not as final in their implications for the method as are certain of the ones already considered in the text. Thurstone's σ_K—which presumably yields a correction for variability in the sigmas of the difference dispersions at different points on the scale—yields only an *approximate* correction, and Hull seems to acknowledge this. As for the fact that different studies unequally sample different portions of the learning process, this is merely a reflection of the circumstance that Hull selectively scaled $_sE_R$'s for only 25 of the 60 or more trials of the original study, while other *unscaled* studies, the findings of which are in various places combined with the $_sE_R$ equation, were obviously not so treated. *What is of interest about this statement is Hull's admission that difficulties with the initial quantificational findings, sufficiently severe to call into question whatever part of the new theory is based on their application, exist*

It is these findings which have determined the *content* of many of the assumptions advanced in *Essentials*. Thus we have here a kind of implicit disclaimer, *on Hull's part*, of much of the new theory.

In summary, the argument of this section is that evaluation of the $_sE_R$ scaling method in terms of Hull's stated criteria discloses a failure to satisfy these criteria, in every case.

b. Evaluation of the procedure of postulate construction. We have already tried to show that the procedure of postulate construction employed in the new theory was largely determined by the nature and results of the method for scaling $_sE_R$. Thus, evaluation of the scaling technique is in many respects tantamount to an evaluation of the method of postulate construction. Nevertheless, brief consideration of a number of issues in this connection will enable us to arrive at a fuller characterization of the status of the 1949-1951 theory as against the theory of *Pr.B*. Accordingly, in this section we evaluate Hull's new technique of postulate construction with respect to: (1) *the problem of inferring intervening variable functions from empirical functions*, and (2) *adequacy of the induction-basis*.

(1) *The problem of inferring intervening variable functions from empirical functions.* By an "intervening variable function," we will mean a statement having the form of an empirical law which relates (*a*) two or more intervening variables, or (*b*) one or more empirical variable(s)[47] with one or more intervening variable(s).

By an "empirical function," we mean a statement having the form of an empirical law which relates two or more empirical variables. The problem involved in constructing "intervening variable functions" from "empirical functions" is often rather inexactly referred to in some such way as the problem of inferring *learning* relationships or "processes" from performance data.

We have seen, at a number of points, that Hull recognized the problem of constructing intervening variable functions from empirical ones as a critical problem. We will recall that the solution of *Pr.B*. was an inconsistent one, eventuating in the *direct transfer* of the empirical variable function forms to the postulated intervening variable function forms, in

---

[47] The "empirical" variables in the cases we will consider correspond to the *systematic* independent and dependent variables of Hull's theory. Hull considers such variables as direct "observables" and, in practice, *equates* them with what we have termed the *experimental* independent and dependent variables of given studies. Actually, the problem of the construction of *systematic* independent and dependent variables from relevant classes of *experimental* independent and dependent variables is a theoretical problem of great complexity (related, of course, to the problem of satisfactory "operational" or empirical definition) which Hull and most other theorists largely neglect. In this discussion, as in all preceding discussions of similar issues, we are forced to follow along with Hull and speak *as if systematic* independent and dependent variables = experimental independent and dependent variables = *empirical* variables. This is a very gratuitous "as if."

the case of most of the assumptions in the theory. It will also be recalled that Hull apparently felt he could avoid this difficulty in terms of the new quantificational procedure. The rationale behind this might, once more, be retraced in the following terms.

The *dependent* variables of all empirical functions are, by definition, $_sE_R$ ("performance") indicators. If a scaling technique exists for transforming $_sE_R$ indicators into "genuine" quantitative measures of $_sE_R$, then a bridge exists between all *empirical* dependent variables and at least one key intervening variable ($_sE_R$). If now a number of rational assumptions are made which (1) identify other intervening variables of which $_sE_R$ is a function and (2) posit certain very general formal relations as holding among these variables, *then* a mathematical analysis of the components of quantified $_sE_R$ functions *may* reveal the detailed quantitative relationships between the other intervening variables and $_sE_R$. In this way, one can presumably get (*a*) from any given empirical function to a corresponding intervening variable function in terms of $_sE_R$, and (*b*) from the intervening variable $_sE_R$ function in question to other intervening variable functions which are constitutive of $_sE_R$.

We have already tried to show how Hull applied this methodology to the construction of the postulates which determine the *primitive* constitution of $_sE_R$ (postulate III through IX). Here it should be added that the same logic is used in the construction of all other intervening variable functions in the theory; e.g., in the case of the inhibitory assumptions, by analyzing equations based on empirical functions whose independent variable conditions presumably legitimate the phrasing of the dependent variable of the equation as $_s\bar{E}_R$, rather than $_sE_R$.

Our previous account, however, was restricted to a presentation of the program for quantification and postulate construction in its relation to the *content* of the new theory. But we already know too well that the only extant *scaled* $_sE_R$ values derived from the foundational latency study (13), and to a lesser extent from the two remaining studies (141, 146) which employ the scaling method. Thus, the only presumptive $_sE_R$ equations having the status of intervening variable functions (by Hull's criterion), and thus legitimately available for the construction of postulates, were the ones deriving from these three studies. It follows that the construction of most of the postulates in the theory must proceed from the analysis of empirical functions in which the dependent variable is *not* scaled $_sE_R$, but an $_sE_R$ indicator. In this very real sense, Hull in the 1949-1951 theory is doing precisely what he did in *Pr.B.*: he is directly imputing to intervening variable functions the characteristics of empirical functions. The entire quantificational program calculated to avoid this practice remains a *program*, and the practice continues.

Hull indirectly acknowledges this practice early in *Essentials*, when he is citing the Perin-Williams equations to demonstrate that their coefficients vary as a function of D, while the exponential constants do not. He says (p. 34):

> In reporting their studies these authors utilized the number of unreinforced re-action evocations (n) instead of $_sE_R$, because these values are quantitatively somewhat similar to $_sE_R$ and the true $_sE_R$ determination was not available at the time. As an expository device, we accordingly used the symbol $_sE'_R$ instead of either.

From this point on, virtually every equation in the book, the analysis of which is used for purposes of postulate construction, is in terms of $_sE'_R$, not $_sE_R$.

(2) *Adequacy of the induction basis.* Since the "quantitative" equations deriving from the calibration experiment comprise either the full or partial basis for the construction of virtually every postulate, an over-all evaluation of the adequacy of the induction basis need not detain us for long. The pooled reaction latencies of fifty-nine rats provide a slim empirical basis for *any* theory of behavior, independently of what interpretation is made of the scope of the 1949-1951 theory. If Hull intended this theory as a completely general one, so much the worse; the situation improves only slightly, however, if the theory be interpreted as a rat theory, or a rat manipulandum-operation learning theory, or indeed even a theory of rat manipulandum-reaction-latency in a modified Skinner box.

Assuming that the scaling technique were entirely satisfactory, there would still remain reason to believe that the data of the *foundation experiment per se* are inadequately described by the equations that represent them. For instance, Hull admits, at one point (15, pp. 520-522), that of "three different equational forms" which "were originally considered as possibilities for the representation of $_sE_R = f(N)$," the one which gave the best fit was a log function. Yet, because "the simple learning process should approach a genuine maximal asymptote" (p. 522), one of the other equations, the growth function which ultimately entered the theory of 1949-1951 as its basic equation, was chosen. Again, Hull admits (15, p. 522) that "there is . . . an extremely obvious defect in the learning data from which the quantifications of $_sE_R$ were made." This is "the fact that latency records of animals of quite different rates of learning are pooled." Hull then indicates that, in the original study, sets of $_sE_R$ values had been calculated *both* for Vincentized and non-Vincentized data, but that in "Thurstone's linearity of slope tests for the normality of the dispersions . . . the Vincentized data did not show up nearly so well as did the ordinary raw data" (pp. 522-523).[48] The *non-Vincentized*

---

[48] Later in the same article, Hull presents a set of calculations (15, p. 524) designed to show that the *actual* effect of pooling the data of fast and slow learners produces a distortion confined mainly to the earlier trials, but one "so slight" as not to justify the labor of the Vincent procedure. He suggests that, in general, the Vincentizing of learning data may be unnecessary.

results were accordingly used. Nevertheless, in an earlier article (13) concerned with deriving the law of *reaction latency as a function of the number of reinforcements* from the *same* data, Hull reports alternate equations which are based respectively on the Vincentized and non-Vincentized latencies. In *this* case, he concludes that "the one based on the Vincentized latency values is believed to be distinctly the more significant of the two" (13, p. 228). Consequently, the equation for the Vincentized latencies is represented as "the best approximation of the quantitative molar law relating $_st_R$ to N."

In this latter study, there are further clues as to how well the fitted equations can represent the empirical findings of the basic latency study. It is made clear that the data showed great variability and skewness, both with respect to the successive post-asymptotic trials of individual animals, and with respect to individual differences among average post-asymptotic latencies for the fifty-nine animals. So great was the spread between *mean* and *median* latency values for the various trials of training, that Hull felt impelled to "fit" equations to both sets of values. Thus four equations in all—one each for the mean and median values of the Vincentized and non-Vincentized latencies, respectively—eventuate from the data of this study.[49] Needless to say, equations for the means and medians turn out to contain markedly different constants. Since there is also substantial disagreement between the pairs of equations for the Vincentized as against the non-Vincentized data, it becomes anyone's guess as to which equation best describes the data. If we add to this fact that (p. 224) "the explorational nature of the present investigation does not warrant the great labor involved in the complete least squares fitting techniques" (a short-cut method of estimation being used), it becomes something of a guess as to whether *any* of the equations bear an accurate relationship to the data.

Insofar as Hull uses studies *other* than the calibration experiment as the inductive basis for various elements of the 1949-1951 theory, the treatment accorded these empirical materials is even more cavalier. This is evident in the extreme selectedness of the data chosen to suggest construct interrelations; the tendency to twist data gathered for quite

---

[49] Hull "believed" the "medians . . . to yield the more significant measures" (13, p. 228). Accordingly, the equation finally selected as the best representation of the law for $_st_R$ as a function of N, was the one based on the *median Vincentized latencies*. The difficulties and restrictions stemming from high variability in the data taken as induction basis for postulates are not new to Hull. Most of the earlier work done with the Yale modification of the Skinner box (e.g., 103) yields data distributions characterized by high variability, and the convention at Yale of treating such data in terms of medians is an old one. Thus, many of the equations given in *Pr.B.* are for medians. I. J. Saltzman and the present writer (109, pp. 364-368) have argued that so great is the variability in the distributions of extinction measures deriving from the Yale-Skinner box, as to make the data unfit for purposes of formulating quantitative behavior laws.

different purposes to the demands of the theory; the practice of fitting equations to data which are inappropriate for quantification; the casual attitude towards the number of data points and the goodness of fit; and the willingness to make remote inferences by *combining* arbitrary calculations deriving from unrelated sources of data. In short, most of the canons of inductive "logic" are in some way violated. These tendencies were only too obvious in the theory of *Pr.B.*; yet they are incalculably compounded in the 1949-1951 postulate set.

At various stages in the preceding discussion, reference has been made to a number of empirical studies (in addition to the $_sE_R$ quantification experiment) which have figured in the construction of postulates. Itemization of a few of these, together with a number of studies which have not thus far been mentioned, should provide an adequate sample of the inductive materials on which the new theory is based. We will neglect in the following considerations the fact that most of the equations in *Essentials* are in terms of $_sE'_R$ rather than $_sE_R$.

1) We have already noted that the logarithmic *stimulus intensity dynamism* (V) function is based on indirect reaction potential calculations imposed on the data of a visual reaction time experiment (7) done by Cattell in 1886. The "reaction latencies for Cattell's two subjects" are averaged and then converted into equivalent reaction potentials by means of the modified form of an equation which recently became available" (75, p. 44). The equation referred to is, of course, the equation for $_sE_R$ as a function of latency which was derived from the calibration experiment.

2) The very important *incentive motivation* (K) function is based on an experiment by Crespi (8, 9), the data of which hardly justify quantitative treatment. The mathematical transformations to which Hull subjects these data are characteristically gratuitous. Equations are fitted, respectively, to three of six highly irregular learning curves given by Crespi for rate of runway locomotion as a function of training trials, under varying amounts of food reward. The resulting equations presumably show that "the coefficient representing the fitted asymptotes varies systematically with variation in the incentive magnitude (w)" (75, p. 49). However, the "available data . . . are inadequate since only three of the . . . learning curves were adequate for equation fitting" (75, p. 49). Thus, in order to determine the incentive motivation function, Hull fits an equation to five of the *empirical* "asymptote values presented in Crespi's published data." Nevertheless, he notes that the "three highest data points correspond to the coefficients" of the three equations fitted in the first instance, "except that all have considerably smaller values" (p. 49). But this would seem to imply that the original three fits were poor. And if these fits are poor what credence can be placed in the substance of what these equations are claimed to demon-

strate: namely, that "the numerical constants in the three exponents are about the same" (pp. 48-49), but that the coefficients vary.

It should be added that the same Crespi data, as represented by postulate VII (the incentive motivation function), are further utilized, and even more gratuitously elaborated, in the analysis of "The Problem of the Behavioral Summation . . . of Incentive Substances" (75, pp. 70-72) that produces corollary vii of the new theory.

3) The findings of the Mowrer-Jones study (100) on resistance to extinction as a function of work are heavily leaned upon for the construction of an important part of the inhibition postulate (postulate X.E. 75, p. 81), and for the formulation of corollary ix (p. 84), another element in the present analysis of inhibition. Yet it will be recalled that these investigators employed but *three* different settings of their independent variable (grams required to depress the Skinner box lever). This yielded *three* data plots for the fitting of a function which has played an important role in both the 1943 and the present theories.

4) In like manner, several of the other studies which had only a questionable value for the purely "programmatic" quantification in *Pr.B.* are still used in the *altered* quantitative context of the new theory. For instance, the thin strand of evidence provided by the Hovland experiments (23, 24) on pitch and intensity generalization for the construction of the 1943 form of the stimulus generalization postulate, still figures prominently in the current analysis of generalization (75, pp. 86-92).

The Perin-Williams study (103), which in 1943 defined the role of D in the determination of $_sE_R$, is currently used, in supplementation of the "scaled" Yamaguchi (147) study, for the same purpose. Its systematic burden, however, has been markedly increased. It now is used, in combination with the Mowrer-Jones experiment, to provide the basis for a tenuous set of calculations designed to yield information about the joint relations of "the total number of unreinforced reaction evocations" (n) and the amount of work (W) to net inhibitory potential ($\dot{I}_R$) (75, pp. 80-85). This supplies the basis for corollaries ix (p. 84) and x (p. 85). Finally, the Perin-Williams study is used to provide the foundation for part A of postulate XVII (p. 112) on the reaction potentials acquired by *massed* reinforcements, as a function of the median number of extinction reactions. Whether the highly variable data of the Perin-Williams experiment are suitable even for the fitting of the original descriptive functions is open to question (109, pp. 364-368). The situation approaches absurdity, however, when these data are operated upon in accordance with the remote and arbitrary chain of assumptions of the foregoing applications.

As a final point in this section, it should be emphasized that underlying the use of *all* data in the 1949-1951 theory, as in the theory of *Pr.B.*, and as in Hull's theoretical thinking generally, is the tacit assumption that fundamental behavior laws of unspecified generality can be derived from single "curve-fitting" experiments, *independently of any analysis of the generalization ranges within which the findings can be expected to hold.* The limits within which a finding may be bound by the special empirical conditions of a study is a question that never seems to bother Hull. Quite aside from any deficiencies in the logical and mathematical inferences made from data, every empirical study used as the basis of Hull's theory, in any of its variants, is open to suspicion from this point of view.

C. A SAMPLING OF FURTHER CHANGES

In the coming years, the impact of Hull's work will be defined by certain of the general hypotheses that he has contributed or elaborated. Thus, it is desirable that we examine the fate, as between 1943 and 1949-1951, of a number of the Hullian conceptions which have not so far been considered in our discussion of the new theory. In the following paragraphs, then, we itemize a sample of additional changes and innovations which register the terminal status of Hull's thinking on a number of key issues. We discuss, in turn: (1) *secondary reinforcement and secondary motivation,* (2) *the inhibition assumptions,* (3) *the stimulus trace assumptions,* and (4) *the problem of constants in behavior laws.*

1. Secondary Reinforcement and Secondary Motivation

In *Pr.B.,* the major assumption made available for the analysis of the phenomena of secondary motivation was the "principle" of secondary reinforcement.[50] This assumption was embedded in the formulation of the primitive principle of reinforcement (postulate 4, p. 178), and so represented a postulated element of the theory. As there stated, the assumption simply maintains that an increment of habit strength will result not only when an *s-r* coincidence is followed by "the diminution of a need" (primary reinforcement), *but also* when followed by "a stimulus which has been closely and consistently associated with the diminution of a need." Despite the fact that "secondary reinforcement" had the formal status of a *postulate,* Hull showed much concern over finding a rationale that might make this arbitrary assumption intelligible. He

[50] This is not, of course, to imply that the principle of secondary reinforcement performs no other systemic function. In 1943, this assumption figured importantly in the derivation of the extended "goal gradient" from the short gradient of "primary" reinforcement found by Perin (56, pp. 142-146). Hull's analysis of secondary reinforcement in *Essentials* gives indirect reason to believe that he had subsequently taken over, at least in part, Spence's (125) explanation of the *primary* gradient of reinforcement in terms of *immediate* secondary reinforcement. It must be remembered, of course, that in the 1949-1951 theory—whatever the interpretation of the reinforcement gradient—it is no longer regarded as associated with the constitution of $_sH_R$, but rather $_sE_R$ as mediated by the delay in reinforcement variable J.

seemed inclined towards the view that (56, p. 100) both forms of reinforcement "are at bottom, i.e., physiologically, the same" and put forward
the hypothesis that a "secondary reinforcing stimulus acquires its
power . . . by virtue of having conditioned to it some fractional component of the need reduction process."

Aside from the purely conjectural nature of the foregoing hypothesis,
we should note that "secondary reinforcement" contained grave limitations as an account of the phenomena of secondary motivation. It could
deal (at some level) with the circumstances under which "learned *rewards*" were built up, but it could not, except in an incorrigibly *ad hoc*
fashion, deal with the conditions under which acquired *drives* were
formed. The principle provided no mechanism which could characterize
that (the drive, motivational system, what not) which was being secondarily rewarded. Miller and Dollard (96), however, had already before
the appearance of *Pr.B.*, put forward their now well-known acquired
drive hypothesis—which seeks, within the framework of a reinforcement
theory, to account for the genesis of learned drives in terms of the
association between a neutral stimulus and the "strong" internal responses characteristic of a primary need. It seemed curious, during the
years after the publication of *Pr.B.*, that some similar hypothesis was
not added to Hull's theory in order to supplement the principle of
secondary reinforcement in the treatment of acquired motivational
phenomena.

In the 1949-1951 theory, precisely this latter has been done. The theory
now contains *both* an acquired drive hypothesis and a secondary reinforcement hypothesis: corollary i on "secondary motivation" (75, p. 25),
and corollary ii on "secondary reinforcement" (75, p. 28).

Notice that secondary reinforcement is now offered as a "corollary,"
not a postulate. The ground for this change is apparently a further specification of the tentative suggestion of 1943 to the effect that the secondary reinforcing stimulus acquires its potency through association with
"some fractional component of the need reduction process." It is now
held (75, pp. 27-28), in accordance with an analysis recently advanced
by Miller (99), that primary reinforcement brings about a relaxation
of the "autonomic activity" associated with the presence of the primary
drive. This "relaxation process" presumably becomes attached to the
"stimuli active at the time, together with the traces of earlier stimuli,"
including the proprioceptive stimulation resulting from earlier activity.
The relaxation—which is identified as giving "rise to conditioned inhibitions"—"generalizes forward on those traces" and has the effect of reducing proprioceptive stimulus intensity which, in turn, "reduces the drive
stimulus wherever it occurs." But "a reduction in drive stimulus constitutes the condition of reinforcement. It follows that any stimulus consistently associated with a reinforcement situation will through that

association acquire the power of evoking the conditioned inhibition, i.e., a reduction in stimulus intensity, and so of itself producing the resulting reinforcement" (75, pp. 27-28).

Whether this new account of secondary reinforcement is really a scientific hypothesis, or a play upon words, is hard to determine from Hull's brief discussion. Note, however, that the concept of "conditioned inhibition" is here used in a sense which is given the term nowhere else in the current (or former) theory. Note also that, insofar as this analysis can be given meaning, it seems inappropriate to many cases in which the primary drive is of an approach (e.g., hunger) rather than an avoidance (e.g., fear) character, and in which reinforcements reduce the drive by small decrements. Under these circumstances we can expect very little of the "autonomic relaxation" which apparently is the basis of the present hypothesis. Note further that, if the implications of this analysis are followed through, it would have the effect of making the amount of *secondary* reinforcement dependent on magnitude of the reduction in the drive stimulus, while according to the present law of habit formation (postulate IV), the accumulation of $_sH_R$ in relation to *primary* reinforcement is not so dependent.[51] In this manner, does the *general* extrasystemic conjecture about the basis of secondary reinforcement put forward in 1943, become translated into a detailed component of the 1949-1951 theory. If the original conjecture was a remote theoretical possibility, its further specification in the new theory converts it into a downright impossibility.

2. The Inhibition Assumptions

In our discussion of *Pr.B.*, a detailed analysis of the inhibition postulates (postulates 8 and 9, p. 300) was presented. The analysis was calculated to show that these assumptions were among the most inadequate, both in mode of formulation and empirical support, in the entire theory. Despite the presence of many changes of detail in the inhibition assumptions of the *present* theory, most of the major deficiencies are still in evidence. We record the principal changes in the 1949-1951 assumptions, as against those of *Pr.B.*, in the following paragraphs.

1) The two compound postulates of 1943 (8 and 9), each consisting of a number of sub-parts, are now reduced to one postulate (X; 75, pp. 74-81) containing five sub-assumptions. One of the 1943 postulates (9) served to introduce the concept of conditioned inhibition ($_sI_R$), asserting that "conditioned inhibitions . . . summate physiologically with reactive

---

[51] The only way out of this dilemma is to assume that secondary reinforcement is effective only in influencing $_sE_R$ (performance) and not $_sH_R$ (learning). It is doubtful that Hull would have wished to accept the systematic consequences of this position. In any event, secondary reinforcement is nowhere specified in the theory as one of the direct determinants of $_sE_R$, and so this alternative must be ruled out.

inhibition (I_R)" thereby prcducing net inhibition $(\dot{I}_R)$. In *Pr.B.*, Hull had hinted at the possibility of deriving conditioned inhibition "from other principles of the system." In the new theory this apparently has been done, as is indicated by the fact that $_sI_R$ is introduced and implicitly defined in a *corollary* (corollary viii, p. 75). So far as can be inferred, the "derivation" is made on precisely the same basis as it *could* have been made in 1943.[52]

2) As we saw in detail, in 1943 the central ambiguity in the inhibitory assumptions derived from the failure to specify the extent to which the independent variables given for the determination of *net inhibition* $(\dot{I}_R)$ *differentially* affect the summative components of $\dot{I}_R$—reactive inhibition (I_R) and conditioned inhibition $(_sI_R)$ (cf. pp. 37-39, this report). This circumstance seemed peculiarly hamstringing, since a specific quantitative relationship was asserted as linking I_R and $_sI_R$ in the production of $\dot{I}_R$ ("physiological summation" as defined by part (a) of the mathematical statement of postulate 9, 56, p. 300),[53] yet no functions were available which would permit—even programmatically—the independent calculation of I_R and $_sI_R$.

In *Essentials*, there is evidence of a recognition of the preceding set of difficulties. Part C of postulate X (75, pp. 75-76) states that I_R "summate[s] with $_sI_R$ to make up an inhibitory aggregate $(\dot{I}_R)$, i.e.,

$$\dot{I}_R = I_R \dotplus {}_sI_R."$$

But (75, p. 75) "unfortunately we do not have precise evidence as to the quantitative law of these summations." Thus, in 1951, we at least get a relatively clear-cut indication that the inhibition assumptions are incompletely specified; that, aside from any other empirical or quantitative inadequacies, "postulate X" is not a postulate, but a program for a postulate.

Despite this honest recognition of ambiguity, the essential ambiguities of 1943 are still present in 1951. Part A of postulate X introduces the

---

[52] The "derivation," however, involves an ambiguity in the concept of $_sI_R$ which was already present in 1943, but is even more pronounced in the new theory. It is assumed that $_sI_R$ arises by virtue of the conditioning of I_R "to any stimuli or stimulus traces accompanying or shortly preceding" response termination (p. 75), the reinforcing event causing this being the reduction of I_R due to the cessation of response. But the conditioning of "stimuli or stimulus traces" to I_R (reactive inhibition) must imply that I_R has the characteristics of a *response*. Nevertheless, I_R is identified as "a primary negative drive" (p. 74). If Hull's words are taken literally, this would mean that he is here introducing a mechanism which depends on the association of a stimulus and a *drive*. Since, in the 1951 theory, it is probable that Hull *equates* drive with the *drive stimulus* (S_D), the mechanism seems ultimately to involve an association between *one stimulus and another*. Such an associative connection is obviously at variance with the rest of the system. These considerations make $_sI_R$ a peculiarly indeterminate concept.

[53] This is a variant of the Perkins-Day equation (56, p. 200; p. 223) the original purpose of which was to define the law of habit strength summation.

notion of reactive inhibition in much the same way as part (a) of postulate 8 (1943). Part B of postulate X assumes that reactive inhibition "spontaneously dissipates" according to the same decay function of time that was assumed in part (d) of postulate 8. Part C of postulate X presupposes the construct of $_sI_R$—which is defined in corollary ix (1951) in much the same way as it was originally identified in postulate 9 (1943)— and is mainly devoted to the assertion (given above) that $_sI_R$ summates with I_R to produce $\dot{I}_R$ according to an unspecified function. Parts D and E of postulates X are analogous in significance to (b) and (c) of postulate 8. Parts D of X and (b) of 8 link *net inhibition* $(\dot{I}_R)$ to the independent variable, "number of reaction evocations" (formerly designated n; now $\dot{n}$). Parts E of X and (c) of 8 both link the independent variable "work" to *net inhibition*, E doing this in a considerably more indirect manner than (b).[54] Nevertheless, just as was the case in 1943, *the new theory does not specify how $\dot{n}$ and W differentially influence I_R as against $_sI_R$*, but deals only with the relations of both to $\dot{I}_R$. In 1943, this difficulty lurked behind the muddy formulations of postulates 8 and 9, but seemed not to be recognized by Hull. In 1951, the difficulty is obliquely, but clearly, pointed up by Hull's admission that the relation between I_R and $_sI_R$ in the determination of $\dot{I}_R$ cannot, as yet, be specified. But the difficulty remains.

3) Another set of changes is registered by the specification of *altered function forms* in certain of the inhibitory assumptions. This occurs in connection with the functions attributed in *Pr.B.* to the relations between net inhibition and the two independent variables just considered—"number of reactions" and "work." We discuss these, in turn.

Part (b) of postulate 8 asserted that $\dot{I}_R$ is a "simple linear increasing function of the number of evocations." The analogous part D of new postulate X assumes that "the $\dot{I}_R$ present . . . after the successive reaction evocations is a positive growth function of the order of those responses $(\dot{n})$" (75, p. 80).[55] This change is of particular interest be-

---

[54] Sub-assumption (b) of postulate 8 supposed simply that $\dot{I}_R$ was "a positively accelerated increasing function of W" (56, p. 300). Part E of new postulate X links W to the "number of unreinforced responses (n) producible by massed extinction," for "constant values of superthreshold reaction potential" (75, p. 81). From part E, together with a tenuous set of calculations based on the joint use of the Mowrer-Jones and a portion of the Perin experiment, Hull tries to derive two corollaries. The first of these (ix, p. 84) expresses *net inhibition* as a function of W, for a constant value of the number of extinction responses. The second (x, p. 86) states *net inhibition* as a function of the number of reactions required to produce extinction, for a constant value of W. It is clear, then, that part E of X, different in formulation as it is from (c) of 8, *mediates* the linkage of net inhibition to W (through corollary ix), though it does not directly do so.

[55] It will immediately be noticed that this change serves to eliminate a possible internal contradiction pointed to in an earlier part of this report (p. 62): namely, the apparent incompatibility of assuming that $_sH_R$ accumulates as an asymptotic (growth) function of n, while the $\dot{I}_R$ is concurrently accumulating as a non-asymp-

cause it represents the only modification of the inhibition assumptions which is based on *new* experimental evidence, and the experiment in question is one of the three extant studies employing the paired comparisons quantification methodology.

This study involved the determination by Wilcoxen, Hayes and Hull (141) of *effective* reaction potential ($_s\bar{E}_R$) as a function of "the ordinal number of Vincentized extinction reactions." Thirty-six rats were trained to traverse a distance of eight inches and push open a door to a food compartment. They were given one hundred such training trials (the last sixty of which were under differing conditions for various subgroups), and then subjected to a massed extinction procedure until a five-minute criterion of no response.[56] Since extinction occurred at differing time intervals after training for the various animals, "each animal was given some retraining before his extinction trials began" (p. 196). Latencies, defined as the time between the opening of a start compartment "shutter" and the time at which the animal raised the food compartment door a distance of one inch, were recorded throughout training and extinction.

In accordance with the conventions of the quantification procedure, the raw latencies were regarded as reaction potential indicators. Since, however, the latencies *here* were for reactions occurring during *extinction*, they were regarded as indicators of *effective* reaction potential ($_s\bar{E}_R$), i.e., reaction potential *minus* the net inhibitory potential produced by the number of extinction responses preceding any given extinction response. The "considerable variability in the number of trials required by the different animals to meet the . . . extinction criterion" (141, p. 196) was indicated by a range of from 4 to 242 trials, the median being 44. Accordingly, "the record of each of the animals was converted to a comparable Vincent series of 44 intervals" (p. 196). The paired comparisons scaling technique was then applied "to 26 strategically located sets of these Vincentized latencies" (75, p. 78). To the scaled $_s\bar{E}_R$ values a decay function was fitted, via the same short-cut procedure of "successive approximations" previously employed (13) for the determination of latency as a function of the number of reinforcements.

It is this latter equation which Hull uses as the basis of part D, postu-

---

totic ("simple, linear, increasing") function. In the light of the analysis subsequently to be presented in the text, it is unlikely that this consideration was responsible for the change, or that it increases the plausibility of the new assumptions.

[56] In *Essentials*, Hull states that the animals "each received 40 reinforcements in walking eight inches and pushing under a light, sloping door to secure food" (75, p. 78). The article (141) reporting this experiment, however, makes clear that each animal received one hundred reinforcements, the "final sixty" of which "were given under slightly different conditions for three subgroups of the 36 animals." The "differences involved having different stimulus cards attached to the response door . . . and were instituted for the purpose of investigating a problem not dealt with in the present article" (141, p. 195).

late X. On the assumption that the reciprocal of $_s\bar{E}_R$, during *extinction*, must be a direct registration of $\dot{I}_R$, Hull simply rewrites the negative growth function obtained for $_s\bar{E}_R$ as a positive growth function for $\dot{I}_R$. This, of course, yields the substance of what is asserted in X.D.

The results of the Wilcoxen, Hayes, Hull study are worthy of further scrutiny because it is one of the very few studies which has employed the new scaling technique. The casual procedural details of the experiment are apparent in the above summary. What is not so far apparent—nor is it made so in *Essentials*, where the results of the study are unqualifiedly injected into the theory—are the implications of certain of the findings for the entire quantificational program. In particular, the investigators report (p. 198) a "relatively narrow range in $_s\bar{E}_R$ values" (1.84σ units) as resulting from the fitted equation. But the first 40 of the *training* trials, it develops, had *also* been scaled, "and the value for $_s\bar{E}_R$ at the asymptote of latency amounted to slightly over 4σ units." Since extinction would seem to demand the neutralization of precisely this latter amount of $_s\bar{E}_R$, the authors conduct a search for the missing 2.16 + σ units.[57] After an explanation for a part of the discrepancy is hypothesized, the search terminates in these words (141, pp. 198-199):

> The most likely possible explanation of the remaining discrepancy appears to be that the unit of measurement in the learning scale is different from that in the extinction scale. Since the unit of these scales is based on the variability in performance of the group of organisms used as subjects . . . , there is excellent reason to expect that the unit itself will vary in magnitude between situations in which there is different variability among the subjects. It is quite possible, therefore, that this unit could vary from one situation to another and especially from one type of behavioral process (learning) to another (extinction).

It would be difficult to formulate a more definite admission of the failure of the entire quantificational method.

Aside from the deficiencies in the evidence on which X.D. is based, it is of interest to note that the use of the new technique of postulate construction in part D of this postulate, but not in preceding parts, confers a peculiar "methodologically mixed" status on the entire assumption. Part B, which asserts that I_R "spontaneously dissipates" according to a decay function is based on the same *unscaled* data (12) as was the original counterpart of this assumption in 1943. Thus, within the *same* postulate, Hull is at different points perpetuating his earlier practice of directly attributing the characteristics of what we have called *empirical functions* to *intervening variable functions*, and trying to avoid this.

The second change in function form has to do with the relationship between W (work) and I_R. In 1943, it was simply assumed (on the basis

---

[57] A factor which Hull, for some reason, does not take into account is the very real possibility that extinction to a five-minute criterion of failure to respond does not result in *complete* extinction. We are not, of course, suggesting that the study would have been placed on firmer ground, if Hull *had* considered this possibility.

of the Mowrer-Jones study) that the "amount of net inhibition . . . generated by a sequence of reaction evocations . . . is a positively accelerated increasing function of the work . . . involved in the execution of the response" (56, p. 300). *Now* it is assumed (75, p. 84) that:

For a constant value of n [total number of reactions required to produce extinction], the inhibitory potential . . . generated by the total massed extinction of reaction potentials set up by massed practice begins as a positively accelerated increasing function of the work . . . involved in operating the manipulandum, which gradually changes to a negative acceleration at around 80 grams, finally becoming asymptotic at around 110 grams (brackets mine).

The above is the substance of corollary ix. Although the marked increase in the "localism" of the formulation may *suggest* a corresponding increase of empirical cautiousness on Hull's part, the very indirect route by which this assumption is derived shows that this is not entirely the case. Let us retrace this route briefly:

The new inhibitory postulate no longer contains a *direct* linkage of W to I_R. Rather, part E of X links W to n for cases such that the "values of superthreshold reaction potential" are constant. It is assumed, in accordance with an altered form of the equation originally fitted to the Mowrer-Jones data, that (75, p. 81) n is a "linear decreasing function of the magnitude of the work . . . involved in operating the manipulanda, i.e.,

$$n = A \ (a - bW)."$$

The next step is to seek the law for n as a function of superthreshold reaction potential ($_sE_R$). This is done by turning to the much exploited Perin-Williams (103) data, choosing five of the groups of that experiment which had been extinguished under the same conditions but after receiving differing numbers of reinforcements during training, and computing "reaction potentials . . . from these five N's together with an N of zero, which represents an approximation to the reaction threshold . . . or zero n" (75, p. 81).[58] An equation is now fitted to these $_sE_R$'s as a function of the obtained n (the total number of extinction responses). The resulting growth expression is then transformed into an equation for n as a function of $_sE_R$, to wit (equation 34; 75, p. 81):

$$n = -87.7 \log (1 - .25 \ _sE_R).$$

Now, the altered Mowrer-Jones equation, as adapted to the conditions of the Perin experiment in which a 15-gram pressure was required to activate the bar, is (equation 33; 75, p. 81):

$$n = 325 \ (1.1476 - .00984 \ W).$$

---

[58] We are not told *how* these reaction potentials were computed. Since the equation fitted to them is represented in terms of $_sE_R$ rather than $_sE'_R$, the *implication* is that the "basic" equation of the calibration study, for $_sE_R$ as a function of N, was used.

It is assumed that the value of the n in equation 34 "corresponds approximately" to the "325" in equation 33. The two equations are therefore combined into a single one (equation 35; 75, p. 82) which expresses n as a joint function of $_sE_R$ and W. It is assumed by definition, however, that superthreshold reaction potential ($_sE_R$) is equivalent to the amount of superthreshold net inhibitory potential ($\dot{I}_R$) required to neutralize it. Thus we can substitute $\dot{I}_R$ for $_sE_R$ in equation 35, and we come out with (equation 36; 75, p. 82):

$$n = [-87.7 \log (1 - .25\ \dot{I}_R)] (1.1476 - .00984\ W).$$

The mission of linking n and W to $\dot{I}_R$ is now, in some sense, accomplished. The relation of $\dot{I}_R$ as dependent on W, for a constant n, is calculated by arbitrarily setting n at 30, and then solving equation 36 for a series of W values (ranging from 0 to 100 grams). The resulting $\dot{I}_R$ values are plotted as a function of W (in grams), and the substance of corollary ix becomes a paraphrase of the characteristics of the plotted "theoretical" curve.[59] In this way is the function relating inhibition and W asserted in postulate 8 of $Pr.B.$ revised in the new theory.

Further comment on this "derivation" of corollary ix (or x, for that matter) is hardly necessary. In this instance, not only do we find a looseness in the use of empirical materials characteristic of the new theory, but the "deduction" hinges on combining into a *single* equation sets of indirectly calculated values based on two entirely unrelated studies. We must add to this that the calculation of certain of these values (the reaction potentials computed for the Perin-Williams data) presupposes the details of a third study (the "calibration experiment," 13) performed under a still different set of conditions.

3. *The Stimulus Trace Assumptions*

There is evidence in *Essentials* of a far reaching set of changes in the treatment of the "stimulus trace" and "afferent impulse" concepts, although precisely what these changes are is very difficult to infer from the presentation.

It will be recalled that postulate 1 of $Pr.B.$ (p. 47) links the independent variable S ("stimulus energy") to the initial intervening variable of the theory, s, which is described as "an afferent neural impulse . . . propagated along connected fibrous branches of nerve cells in the general direction of the effector organs, via the brain." The postulated character of the relationship between S and s is, in part, a paraphase of more or less standard neurophysiological findings. It is assumed that "During the continued action" of S, the s, "after a short latency, rises quickly to

---

[59] Corollary x, which has already been referred to as relating $\dot{I}_R$ and n for a constant value of W is also, of course, "derived" by substituting appropriate values in equation 36.

a maximum of intensity, following which it gradually falls to a relatively low value as a simple decay function of the maximum." However, Hull points out in the text (p. 41) that certain "molar behavioral observations" make it probable "that the after-effects of receptor stimulation continue to reverberate in the nervous system for a period measurable in seconds, and even minutes," and he finds the basis of such "stimulus traces" (p. 42) in the demonstration by Lorente de Nó of the "existence of nerve-cell organizations which might conceivably serve as a locus for a continuous circular self-excitation process." Accordingly, it is assumed in postulate 1 that *after* "the termination of the action of the stimulus energy . . . on the receptor, the afferent impulse (*s*) continues its activity in the central nervous tissue for some seconds, gradually diminishing to zero" according to a "simple decay function." Thus, in 1943, *the stimulus trace is equated with the afferent impulse, or at least the post-stimulational segment of the afferent impulse.*

It should also be recalled that the stimulus-response *asynchronism* assumptions, which are among the determinants of $_sH_R$ in *Pr.B.*, are represented in an elaborate analysis by Hull (pp. 167-169) as ultimately derivable from the "neurological" characteristics of the "receptor discharge, or the intensity of the resulting afferent impulse" (p. 168). In their actual formulation in postulate 4 (p. 178), however, the asynchronism assumptions (both for the case of "brief" and "continuous" stimuli) are treated on a *behavioral* basis in terms of the time relations between *S* and *R*, and *not* in terms of the afferent impulse (*s*) and the efferent discharge (*r*). It is clear, nevertheless, that Hull regarded the behavioral phenomena of trace and delayed conditioning as potentially derivable from the characteristics of *s*.

A third point that must be recalled is the uneven and inconsistent usage of *s*, throughout *Pr.B.* Although the *intention* of the theory is clearly to phrase all lawful relationships in terms of *s* and *r*, we saw that (*a*) this was far from uniformly the case in the formulation of postulates, and (*b*) practically never the case in applications, derivations, or illustrations.

In *Essentials*, the treatment of *s* in its relation to the "stimulus trace" markedly changes. "Stimulus trace" gives way to "molar stimulus trace (*s'*) and a definite but indeterminately specified distinction is now intended as between the afferent impulse (*s*) and the molar stimulus trace (*s'*). As before, the afferent impulse "during the action of *S* on the receptor" rises in intensity "from zero very rapidly to a maximum after which it gradually falls to an unspecified level" (p. 7).

However, there is also reason to believe that *s* may not directly become reinforced to responses, but does so indirectly through some additional molar process of unknown physiological nature. The main evidence for this is that the submolar impulse (s) from the receptor seems to reach its maximum sooner than the corresponding molar impulse (s') appears to do so. Our knowledge of this molar afferent impulse is essentially indirect. This naturally produces great difficulty in our determination of its quantitative characteristics, and at the same time lays us open to special danger of making errors in so doing (75, pp. 7-8).

This is the only explication of s' to be found in the new postulate sets. Clearly, the "great difficulty" encountered in the determination of the quantitative properties of the molar stimulus trace is paralleled by an even greater difficulty in specifying its *qualitative* characteristics. Nowhere in Hull's earlier work is there a more dramatic example of the tendency to employ concepts which straddle physiology and behavior theory in a systematically ambiguous way.

Whatever the nature of this molar stimulus trace, it is evident that its "molarity" derives, at least in part, from the fact that Hull proposes to infer its properties from the *behavioral* facts of trace and delayed conditioning, rather than those of receptor-nerve fiber function. Indeed (p. 8), "it will be more convenient to deal with the intensities of these molar afferent impulses in the form of their *equivalent functional* stimulus intensities" (S'). The construction of postulate II concerning the stimulus trace (s'), therefore, becomes a search for the law relating equivalent functional stimulus intensities (S') of the molar stimulus trace and the time (t) since the beginning of the stimulus.

In *Pr.B.*, when confronted with a similar problem in connection with the construction of the asynchronism relations, Hull had turned to the delayed conditioning study of Kappauf and Schlosberg (82), and the trace conditioning work of Wolfle (143). In the interim, two new experiments had become available, the trace conditioning study of Reynolds (107), and one on delayed conditioning by Kimble (83). Both studies employed a conditioned eye-blink technique, Reynolds' trace data giving determinations for four intervals after an .050″ *auditory* stimulus, ranging from .250″ to 2.25″, and Kimble's delay data giving six values, for durations of a continuous *visual C.S.*, ranging from .100″ to .400″. Noting (75, p. 8) that much "evidence indicates that molar stimulus traces . . . have a brief *recruitment phase* ($\acute{S}'$, $\acute{s}'$)," and a "protracted . . . *subsident phase* (S', s')," and observing that (p. 8) "there does not appear to be much difference between the molar after-effects of a continuous stimulus and . . . a very brief stimulus," Hull feels justified in combining these data in seeking postulate II. Accordingly, the following steps are taken:

1) Reaction potential values are calculated for the obtained response percentages, at the various intervals, for the two sets of data. The technique for computing these $_sE_R$'s is not mentioned in *Essentials* but is given in two "memoranda" (73, 74) under dates of February 7 and March 6, 1950, on the quantification of the stimulus trace. There it may

be seen that the method employed must have an entirely different significance than the latency techniques already described.

2) From the calculated reaction potential values, approximations of the equivalent S''s were derived. In *Essentials*, there is no indication of how this is done. The memoranda just cited show that the procedure involves a conversion of each $_sE_R$ value into V values by an arbitrary series of "solutions" of the equation on the constitution of $_sE_R$ (postulate IX). These V values are then substituted in the very fanciful equation for V as a function of stimulus intensity, which had been fitted to the Cattell data (equation 10, 75, p. 44), and the equation is solved for S.

3) Equations are now fitted to the calculated S' values, the values from Kimble's experiment being regarded as corresponding to the *recruitment* phase of s', and those from Reynolds' experiment as corresponding to the *subsident* phase of the trace.

These latter equations, both of which turn out to represent S' as power functions of time, comprise the substance of parts A and B, postulate II (75, p. 11). A final part of postulate II (C) assumes (on undisclosed grounds, but presumably in accordance with equation 10 for V) that the "intensity of the molar stimulus trace (s') is a logarithmic function of the molar stimulus equivalent of the trace" (S').

It is evident from the preceding account, that Hull's exposition is such as to render evaluation of the significance of the changes in the trace assumptions exceedingly difficult. Nevertheless, at least the following points seem warranted:

In 1943, the *intention* was to derive the properties of the stimulus trace from the characteristics of the afferent impulse (s) as such. However, postulate 1, which implicitly defines s for the theory, and thus presumably the trace, is *supplemented* by the asynchronism assumptions in the law of reinforcement. These latter assumptions link the temporal relations between S and R (not s and r) to $_sH_R$ (according to a "negative growth function" for both the "brief duration" and the "continuous" case), and *in effect it is these assumptions* which mediate most of the "derivations" within the theory of *Pr.B.* involving "quantitative" characteristics of the stimulus trace.

As always, the basis for the changes in 1950, seems to be the new quantitative techniques. Hull is, of course, no longer prepared to make inferences from any data other than performance-based $_sE_R$ indicators; thus the attempt to treat the trace in terms of the afferent impulse (s) as such, must go. More importantly, the new quantification has led to a redistribution of variables such that $_sH_R$ (in the guise of $_s\dot{H}_R$) is a function of V_1, and $_sE_R$ a function, among other things, of V_2. A place must therefore be found within the new theory to carry the systematic burden of the former asynchronism assumptions, i.e., to deal within the new theory with cases such that the V_1 or the V_2 at the time of response corresponds not to the *objective* stimulus intensity,[60] but to the after-effect of a stimulus which has ceased, or the functional effects of a given duration of continuous stimulation. Postulate II is therefore constructed, in accordance with the new methods, to fill this requirement.

In general, though, the confused treatment of the trace in 1943, gives way to an even more confusing one in 1951. In *Pr.B.* the intention to build up all theoretical relationships in terms of *s*, never gets very far, the postulational statements shifting indifferently from *s* to *S*. Neverthe-less, what gets *directly* reinforced is clearly identified (at least initially) as *s*. In the new theory (p. 7), there "is reason to believe that *s* may not directly become reinforced to responses, but does so indirectly through some additional molar process"—the molar stimulus trace (*s'*). Postulate II of *Essentials*, therefore, introduces *s'* (and *S'*) and defines its charac-teristics. *But no other postulate in the present theory is stated in terms of s' or S'*. The very next postulate, for instance (postulate III, p. 20), which defines the conditions of reinforcement, identifies *s* as what directly becomes reinforced" to response. And similarly all other postulates are formulated in terms of *S* or *s*, never *S'* or *s'*. Furthermore, the tendency for formulations to fluctuate indifferently as between *S* and *s* is as con-spicuous in the new theory as in the old. Thus, the two-pronged ambiguity of the former theory is supplanted by a three-pronged ambiguity in the current one.

4. The Problem of Constants in Behavior Laws

As noted in the analysis of Hull's earlier work, Hull had given little consideration to the significance of the empirical *constants* which ap-peared in many of the quantitative behavior principles he put forward. This was a serious omission because, *without some assessment of the range of conditions over which these constants can be expected to hold, it is impossible to evaluate the potential fruitfulness of Hull's technique of theory construction, in any of its several variants*.

To be sure, in *Pr.B.* Hull had assiduously avoided the insertion of values for the empirical constants in the *formal* statement of postulates, but certain of the "derivations" of corollaries in that work seem to pre-suppose such parameters. In the new theory, a similar situation prevails. But, in the new theory, great pains have been taken to determine critical constants in terms of the new quantificational procedure, and the re-sulting values play an essential role not only in the derivation of corol-laries but even in the indirect construction of certain of the postulates.

Towards the close of *Essentials*, Hull breaks his silence on the question

---

[60] In principle, of course, the theory demands that the *V* *always* correspond to some segment of the molar stimulus trace, and never directly to the objective intensity. Nevertheless, the law for *V* as a function of the stimulus intensity is given in terms of *S*, not *S'* or *s'*.

of constants for the first time in any systematic context.[61] His position
(p. 116) is surprisingly conservative, to say the least:

It is important to observe that the "constant" values . . . in the equations
expressing natural laws are not necessarily constant. . . . Similarly, but much
more markedly, the "constants" appearing in the laws of molar behavior are not
constant. Presumably if a group of organisms strictly comparable in all other
respects to those from which this equation $[_sH_R = 1 - 10.^{.0305\ \dot{N}}]$ was secured
were tested on the *same behavior form*, a value within the sampling range of
.0305 would be again secured. But if older or younger or diseased organisms
were used, or if a different genetic strain or a different species, and particularly
if single individuals were used, presumably rather different exponential values
would result (ital. and brackets mine).

Hull had previously (59) indicated the intention to deal with "innate
individual and species differences" in terms of differing values of the
constants in behavior equations. In the above passage, however, the
range of the factors expected to produce variability in these parameters
has been enlarged. There may be a certain ambiguity in the phrase
"same behavior form," but it is an ambiguity which seems studied, because it leaves open the possibility that the "constants" may be specific
to extremely "local" characteristics of the habit mechanisms being dealt
with. Indeed, it leaves open the possibility that a constant deriving from
data based on the "behavior form" of pushing a manipulandum 1/16th
of an inch to the left is a constant containing predictive implications
unique to that particular activity.

In accordance with such considerations, Hull introduces postulate
XVIII (75, p. 117) into the new theory. It is worthy of quotation in full:

The "constant" numerical values appearing in equations representing primary
molar behavioral laws vary from species to species, from individual to individual,
and from some physiological states to others in the same individual at different
times, all quite apart from the factor of behavioral oscillation $(_sO_R)$.

When we add to this blank-form postulate, the possibility that the
"primary molar behavior laws" in question may hold only for a narrowly
delimited "behavior form," an immense restriction seems imposed on the
theory. Even if *every other* postulate had a probability approaching
unity, the theory could mediate only a very limited range of predictions.

The restrictions conferred by postulate XVIII, and related considerations, on the 1949-1951 postulate set, may constitute an honest recognition of the primitive status of the theory. Such restrictions may indeed
have to be imposed on any quantitative behavior formulations attempted
in the present phase of psychology. Nevertheless, these reservations can
hardly increase confidence in the *fertility* of the specific quantitative
functions that Hull has advanced, and the techniques on which these

---

[61] The matter had been considered with regard to the question of innate individual
and species differences in a 1945 article (59).

functions are based. Moreover, with such reservations now explicitly within the theory, the question of whether Hull's theory is of unlimited or any wide degree of generality, becomes no longer a matter of interpretation.

In concluding this section, it may be said with confidence that with respect to most of the issues considered—*secondary reinforcement and secondary motivation*, the *analysis of inhibition*, the *stimulus trace notion*—there has been no evidence of constructive advance since 1943. In one case—the *problem of "constants"*—there has perhaps been an advance in the sense of a more determinate specification of the restrictedness of the theory. *Extensive changes* there have been, but most of these, like the many alterations previously discussed, have been enforced by the relentless demands of an infeasible and prematurely over-elaborated quantificational methodology.

Other important Hullian hypotheses, such as "stimulus generalization" and "afferent interaction" have been altered, but much less radically than those chosen for discussion. In these cases, too, the changes have been imposed by the consequences of the new methodology. There is little evidence that *any* of the changes in the new theory have been motivated by a careful assessment of theoretical or empirical plausibility, other than conformity with the new quantificational commitments.

D. CONCLUDING CONSIDERATIONS

We have seen in the foregoing that the 1949-1951 postulate sets define a radically new theory. This theory is genetically related to the old in terms of underlying orientative attitudes and the *general* identifications of variables, but it differs in the relational and "quantitative" linkages interconnecting virtually every theoretical variable. Certain new variables, both independent (e.g., stimulus intensity) and intervening (e.g., s', $_sH_R$, V, J, K), have made an appearance. Certain of the former, 1943 variables (e.g., t'', p) have been dropped, and some have been sub-specified (e.g., the acretion to N of $\dot{N}$ and $\underline{N}$).

Thus, the *implicit* or *postulational* definition of almost every construct in the theory has changed. Many of the *explicit* definitions, insofar as they are given or are inferable from use, have been altered. Similarly, a large proportion of the *operational* or *empirical* definitions, so far as they exist, are either modified or completely new.

We have seen that among the most fundamental altered characteristics of this new theory are:

1) *An attenuation of the reinforcement principle* to such an extent that its consequences are, in *effect*, indistinguishable from an association by contiguity assumption. Corollary to this is the far-reaching redefinition of the conditions of habit-acquisition ($_sH_R$) and those of habit-functioning ($_sE_R$, $_s\bar{E}_R$, etc.).

2) *A conspicuous, but uneven, increase in what has been termed "localism" of the theory language,* to an extent that makes it difficult to assess the intended and actual range of application of the theory.

3) *Most fundamental of all, a new technique of postulate construction which is based, in turn, on a program for achieving the "genuine" quantification of major intervening variables.*

We have seen that it is ultimately this new quantificational program which has enforced the major changes. The magnitude of the alterations made in the short interval between the publication of *Pr.B.* and the new theory creates the *initial* impression of an hypothetico-deductive system giving way, generously and constructively, to empirical evidence. *In reality,* the system has responded to a demonstrably infeasible technique for achieving the quantification of behavioral laws. So rigidly are the demands of this quantificational program followed that major changes and innovations are often introduced into the theory without regard to their empirical plausibility or deductive consequences.

In this examination of the new theory, we have pursued the contextual analysis of written scientific materials, the sentences that define Hull's theory. But under certain circumstances, the *results* of contextual analysis must force analysis outside of its immediate linguistic context. The inadequacies of Hull's terminal formulations, and the technique of theory construction on which they are based, are so comprehensive and patent that one is forced to look for an explanation.

Much evidence has been cited throughout the present report which entitles us to conclude that Hull's dominant orientative attitude from the inception of his theoretical program was the desire to achieve "truly" quantitative behavior laws. The new quantificational program is no accident; it is the culmination of the entire trend of Hull's theoretical work from the period of the earliest systematic articles through the verbal miniatures systems, the elaborate rote learning theory, and *Pr.B.* What *was* an accident, in the literal scholastic sense of the term, was the fact that Hull was driven by illness during the final years of his life to prosecute this program at a rate and in a manner which was entirely injudicious.

Extrapolating from Hull's earlier work, there is much to suggest that under ordinary circumstances the tendency to proceed with almost complete disregard for theoretical and empirical plausibility, to leap to sweeping generalizations from a minute induction basis, to remain under the total domination of a quantificational program which had hardly begun, would not have been so strongly in evidence. Alterations of basic assumptions would at least have been made in a more conservative and considered way; the quantificational program would have been supplemented with a wider range of perhaps more careful experimental work.

Nevertheless, the trend of the present analysis has been to indicate that all of the tendencies evident in the new theory were presaged in the theory of Pr.B., and in Hull's earlier work generally. The new theory is not Hull at his best or in his most finished form, but its major deficiencies can be traced to Hull's long-range theoretical aims, orientative attitudes and methods.

Side by side with the evidence of domination by these aims, however, there are evidences of another sort. There are strong indications that in the final phase of his career Hull was arriving at an honest recognition of the prematurity of certain of his theoretical objectives. We have had occasion to note many examples of a heightened tentativeness, a stronger recognition of programmaticity, an increased willingness to admit difficulties and limitations, in Hull's recent publications. The articles of the quantification sequence are replete with reservations and qualifications. Indeed, we have seen that at one place (141, pp. 198-199) Hull so much as admitted the failure of the new quantificational methodology. Another case in point is the new postulate XVIII on "individual differences."

Perhaps the most forceful indication of a change in Hull's conception of the limits on the theoretically feasible in present psychology comes from an aspect of the new theory which at first may seem puzzling. *This is the frequent occurrence of the highly specific expressions and "situational" references in presumably general behavior postulates, which we have designated "localisms" of the theory language.* Such compromise formulations are precisely what one would expect from a theorist who has perceived the prematurity of attempts at *comprehensive* theories of behavior, yet whose entire career has been premised on that objective.

Whatever the degree of retrenchment in Hull's final estimate of the feasibility of comprehensive or highly quantified theory, there are evidences of great insecurity with regard to the most fundamental assumptions of the 1949-1951 theory. One of the most significant phrases in all of *Essentials* is inconspicuously embedded in the verbal formulation of postulate IX, the basic law of the constitution of reaction potential. We italicize this phrase in the following quotation of the law (75, p. 59):

The reaction potential ($_sE_R$) of a bit of learned behavior at any given stage of learning, *where conditions are constant throughout learning and response evocation,* is determined (1) by the drive (D) operating during the learning process multiplied (2) by the stimulus-intensity dynamism of the signaling stimulus in response evocation (V_2), (3) by the incentive reinforcement (K), (4) by the gradient of delay in reinforcement (J), and (5) by the habit strength ($_sH_R$). . . .

The qualification introduced by this phrase is amplified further in a footnote that Hull adds to the initial statement of the equation defining the constitution of $_sE_R$. It reads (75, p. 58):

This equation assumes that D, V, K, and J remain constant during learning and response evocation. It is not general enough to cover cases where changes are made in these factors during the experiment.

Examination of the nearly identical postulate set of 1950 (70), will show that neither the qualifying phrase, nor the footnote, appeared in the theory at that time.

These changes, as between 1950 and 1951, impose so great a restriction upon the theory as virtually to legislate it out of existence. If the theory cannot mediate predictions for any situations in which either the stimulus intensity conditions (thus V), or the drive conditions (thus D), or the incentive magnitude conditions (thus K), or the delay of reward conditions (thus J) vary, *then for what sets of conditions can it mediate predictions?* The theory would be limited to predicting the form of a standard learning curve.

What this qualification seems to mean is that Hull was prepared to reject the new $_sE_R$ assumption, was sorry that he ever made it. It is entirely possible that the assumption was introduced into the theory before *any attempt* was made to calculate its consequences for changes in D, or V, or K, or J. It may or may not be significant that Seward (110) had pointed in 1950 to the altered potentialities, given the theory by this assumption, to mediate "latent learning" phenomena, and Spence (129) had raised questions about the altered consequences for such conditions as changes in J, early in 1951, *before* this footnote appeared in *Essentials*.

That Hull was nostalgic about the state of affairs represented by *Pr.B.* seems confirmed by the following note which appears at the end of *Essentials* (p. 122):

AN EARLIER ACCOUNT OF THE CONSTITUTION
OF REACTION POTENTIAL

The original published account of the constitution of reaction potential [here there appears a reference to *Pr.B.*, p. 178, equation 16] was not clear owing partly to the expository difficulty of treating $_sE_R$, as distinguished from $_sH_R$, before the principle of primary motivation had been presented. In current symbolism, the $_sH_R$ of the original equation, #16, should be changed to $_sE_R$, and the M, to D. The present account agrees in the general multiplicative relationship assumed at that time. It has one new factor (V) and omits one factor, that of the temporal asynchronism of the conditioned to the unconditioned stimulus in conditioned-reaction formation. . . . (Brackets mine.)

On the surface, this note seems to be trying to justify the theory of *Pr.B.* by purportedly showing that it had foreshadowed the new $_sE_R$ postulate. We are inclined to believe it more likely that Hull was trying to gain reassurance about this new postulate by establishing some kind of continuity with the theory of *Pr.B.*

Part III. General Conclusions

A. TREND OF THE PRESENT ANALYSIS

In the preceding part of this report, we have done what may be construed as a nasty thing. We have proceeded on a literal interpretation of some such proposition as: "Hull has put forward a hypothetico-deductive theory of behavior." It can be fairly maintained, when a twentieth-century psychologist claims he has a "general" theory of behavior, or when someone claims this of the theory, that the word "general" is necessarily meant with reservation and that "theory" is a metaphor. Indeed, much evidence may be found, in the writings of a theorist like Hull, to support the contention that he was cognizant of programmaticity, evidence which we have not suppressed. In the present state of our ignorance, no one can *seriously* believe that a comprehensive, quantitative, hypothetico-deductive theory of behavior is possible. Yet, in the present state of our ignorance, many people *want* to believe this.

The present analysis has gone on the assumption that there is a certain utility in exploring the dimensions of a metaphor. It is one thing to detect the presence of a metaphor; quite another to derive its meaning. We must determine to what *extent* the more ambitious theories of the recent past are metaphors, in what specific *senses* they are metaphors, and why they are metaphors, if we are to derive from them whatever instruction they contain for the future of psychology.

Unfortunately, the only way to measure the "dimensions" of the metaphor is to proceed from a *literal* interpretation of what the metaphor asserts. Accordingly, our analysis of Hull's formulations has measured them against the *literal* criteria of hypothetico-deductive and quantitative method, and against a *literal* interpretation of Hull's stated objectives.

We have raised, in some form, most of the types of questions that can be asked in characterizing the status of a scientific theory. We have inquired into the adequacy of all classes of definition of all classes of the theoretical variables. We have inquired into the postulated interconnections among all classes of variables. We have looked into the methods of postulate construction, of quantification, of derivation. We have examined the induction basis, and the general state of the evidence, for certain of the assumptions. Under close scrutiny, not a single member of a single class of such theoretical components satisfied the requirements for rigorous scientific theory of the sort envisaged within the theorist's explicit objectives. More importantly, many of the detailed solutions embodied in the theory of major problems in the methodology of psychological theory construction—e.g., the techniques employed for the "measurement" of independent and dependent variables, the techniques for the construction of quantitative, or even qualitative function forms—proved to have little merit within their concrete theoretical context, however suggestive certain of them may be in defining the problems that behavior theorists must face.

The preceding points may, perhaps, register more vividly, if we bring the findings of this report to bear on Hull's explicitly stated precautions against theoretical indeterminacy. One of these is that intervening variables must be "securely anchored on both sides to observable and measurable conditions or events" (56, p. 22). A related caution states the need for "a grim and inflexible insistence that all deductions take place according to the explicitly formulated rules stating the functional relationships of A to X and X to B" (56, p. 24), A and B, of course, being independent and dependent variables respectively, and X being the intervening variable or chain of such. In other words, Hull quite properly demands that explicit and univocal linkages interconnect independent, intervening and dependent variables, and that the independent and dependent variables be "securely anchored" to their reductive (operational) symptoms.

This report makes it fair to say that:

(1) Secure anchorage, either in a quantitative or a qualitative sense, does not hold in a single case for the relations of systematic independent and dependent variables to their intended range of reductive symptoms.

(2) No given intervening variable is securely and univocally anchored to its relevant systematic independent and/or dependent variables, either quantitatively or qualitatively.

(3) No given intervening variable is related to any other intervening variable in the chain with sufficient determinacy to permit quantitative passage from one to the other,[62] nor are certain of the variables, and the relations connecting them, defined with sufficient precision to permit "qualitative" passage.

In general, any "grim and inflexible insistence that all deductions take place according to the explicitly formulated rules stating the relations of A to X and X to B," must, *for any A in the theory*, be thwarted at precisely that point.

This analysis has not been intended to destroy Hull's reputation, or minimize his very great contributions. It has seemed a necessary job because of the paramount importance of making explicit the limits within which it is feasible to aim for theory in the current phase of psychology. The belief that Hull's theory—right or wrong—is a realized (or approxi-

---

[62] A trivial possible exception to this statement would be such purely definitional, arithmetic linkages as:

$$_S\bar{E}_R = {_S}E_R - I_R.$$

mately realized) wide-scope, hypothetico-deductive system is a belief that such an objective is currently feasible, and the belief that such an objective is currently feasible can well block what chances we have of moving towards adequate theoretical formulations of behavior.

The cumbrous detail of this analytic study would hardly be justified, if the intention were merely to establish the thesis that Hull had not realized his theoretical objectives. We have gone on the assumption that an essay towards theory so ambitious and influential as Hull's, might provide a strategic vehicle for the exhibition, in a concrete context, of a wide range of methodological problems which stand between the desire for theory and its achievement. That Hull fell short of theory is not particularly instructive; *that Hull fell short of theory in such-and-such specific ways could well be as instructive as anything that our generation needs to learn.* No recent theoretical formulation can be more instructive in this sense than Hull's, because none has been modeled on so explicit and, in some ways, sophisticated a conception of theory, nor has any competing formulation been pressed towards its goal in a comparably detailed and ambitious way.

In this report, we have therefore tried to locate specific sources for Hull's inevitable failures, as he faced the manifold problems of building theory. We have tried to show that he failed not *merely* because he aimed at comprehensive theory, or because relevant empirical knowledge is too painfully slim to justify even far more limited attempts. We have tried to show that he failed because he did not adequately meet concrete problems of *empirical definition,* of *measurement,* of *quantification,* of *intervening variable function construction,* and various sub-specifications of all of these. He could not meet these problems because no one else had met them, or currently can meet them. And this is the case because such problems have as yet received only the vaguest definition, while anything approaching useful resolution is still far out of sight. Nor can these problems be legislated out of existence by some over-simplifying proposal like the demand that we restrict ourselves to narrow-scope theory. Such a proposal may be eminently rational, so far as it goes. But it must be recognized that all major unresolved problems in the methodology of behavior theory remain equally unresolved for "theories" of all sizes; the scope of such problems does not automatically scale down to the scope of the theorist's intentions.

B. HULL'S CONTRIBUTIONS

Hull's influence on the field has already been profound. His future influence, while it will probably be less direct than he might have wished, can be expected to remain far-reaching. How salutary this influence will be depends more on what the future does with his formulations, than on the formulations *per se.* Though this report has plainly not dwelled on

Hull's positive contributions, there has been allusion to many of them at various places. It is fitting that we here recapitulate, and more generally state, what we believe to be Hull's major contributions. At the same time, we may hint at the general directions within which they may best be exploited in the future development of the science.

1. Impact on Theoretical Practice and Attitudes Towards Theory

It is fashionable to regard Hull's missionary zeal in holding before psychology the procedural model of high order, natural science theory as having had a highly beneficial impact on the field. There seems every reason to believe that the *net* effect of Hull's continuous educational efforts with respect to such matters as hypothetico-deductive procedure *has* been salutary. Any tendency among psychological theorists to confuse the methods and values of science with the methods and values of literature, has certainly been curtailed as a result of Hull's effort. Yet, one must be careful to distinguish the senses in which Hull's methodological manifesto to the future is usable, and the senses in which it is not. The entire present report may be regarded as an essay towards this task.

Recent history does not easily fall into perspective, but it must be remembered that when Hull began his theory, the dominant temper of theoretical psychology was still philosophical, belletristic and casual. During the immediately preceding decades, there had been a steady and rapid advance in those disciplines which converge on the study of scientific method—e.g., philosophy of science, foundations of mathematics, symbolic logic, semantics, linguistics, foundations of physics, etc. The codification of the resulting findings by logical empiricists, and other methodologists of science, led to a more coherent account of the nature of scientific theory than had before been available. Hull was one of the first psychological theorists to import these insights into our field, and to attempt their implementation.

That Hull held up to psychology such values as those associated with careful axiomatic procedure was, and will remain, of the first importance. But his significance is lost, if we do not appreciate him as a transitional figure. Hull's attempt to implement these values of rigorous systematic procedure could not but fail to be contaminated by certain residual values deriving from the literary, "system-building" tradition to which he reacted. Not the least of these was the assumption that "theory" has no boundaries smaller than the entire science; this, after all, is characteristic of the grandiosity and diffuseness of purpose traditional to the "philosophical" system builder.

There is another sense in which Hull's significance is transitional. The very model of scientific theory which he emulated was itself a transitional model. It was based mainly on the characteristics of only a few of the systematic formulations in the single science of physics, and even these were criterion achievements like Newtonian mechanics and relativity theory. It has become increasingly apparent that the extent to which other systematic formulations in science may be expected to conform to such a model, or even approximate any specified subset of its properties, is an open question, requiring patient and imaginative exploration in each case. Hull's trend was to prejudge such questions. Does the model demand postulational form, wide empirical generality, quantitative specificity, etc? "Good," says Hull, in effect, "I will give you a behavior theory with precisely these properties." Nothing could have more forcefully established the need for re-examining the representativeness of the model, and its detailed applicability to psychology, than the very shortcomings of the resulting attempt.

2. Recognition of Complexity

Hull's impact on the field will by no means be restricted to the sensitization of psychologists to matters of theoretical methodology. Not only will many concrete components of his formulations have continuing value, but certain of his orienting attitudes, and certain features of the style and direction of his thinking, are worthy of emulation. Conspicuous among the latter is his respect for the phenomenal complexity of behavior.

In the discussion of Hull's orientative attitudes (pp. 4-17, this report), we saw that it was Hull's firm intention to assume intellectual responsibility for developing the orienting commitments of earlier behaviorism into detailed explanatory theory. In this, he was setting himself an impossible goal. But he showed no disposition to bring this goal more easily within reach by closing his eyes to the complexities and subtleties of behavior. Hull was the first S-R theorist who made a dedicated attempt to avoid cutting down problems to the size of his concepts.

As we have seen, from 1929 on, the attempt to do justice to complex facts of behavior, and to empirical phenomena stressed by other groups of theorists, was impressive. Indeed, in this attempt, Hull showed remarkable theoretical flexibility, even to the extent of significantly departing from a "pure" S-R groove (cf. pp. 8-9, his report). Although certain of the conceptual elements introduced in the effort to make the theory applicable to complex behavioral phenomena previously neglected by S-R theorists (e.g., "neural interaction," s, r) were perhaps not entirely successful, it was in the course of dealing with such complex problems in behavioral dynamics as "insight," "reasoning," and the role of "guiding ideas" that Hull developed some of his most valuable hypotheses.

3. Fruitful Hypotheses

At this moment in the history of psychology, there is naturally much interest in whether Hull's formulations can or will be perpetuated as a coherent systematic approach to the analysis of behavior. Very few would argue—least of all the author of the present report—that any of the postulate sets that Hull left behind can be retained in any form substantially resembling its initial formulation. There is still, however, a widespread belief that if Hull's theory will not survive in substantially unaltered form, there are good prospects for working towards a more adequate theory within the "Hullian framework." It has not been an explicit intention of this analysis to pre-judge the prospects for Hullian revisionism or "neo-Hullian" formulations. It is desirable that the several extant attempts in this direction be pressed as far forward as they can, and that they be evaluated in their own right, rather than in terms of their genetic antecedents. But the results of the present analysis *do* point up the need for emphasizing the semantic trickiness of such phrases as "the Hullian framework." In Part I, we were forced to consider the radical possibility that no single postulate, or group of postulates, of *Pr.B.* can be considered as containing empirically testable core assumptions, on which some integrated framework of theory depends. If such a statement has even modest plausibility for the theory of *Pr.B.*, it must have overwhelming cogency for the theory of *Essentials*.

To imply that the behavioral theory of the future may not be an elaboration of the Hullian postulates, or even written within the Hullian idiom, is not to suggest that Hull's formulations do not contain many specific hypotheses which either have proved or will prove sufficiently fruitful to survive in one form or another. It will require much future effort on the part of many workers to isolate all of the valuable explanatory hypotheses, or ideas towards hypotheses, embedded in the massive bulk of Hull's formulations, to test them, restate or further specify them in a maximally effective way, and more fully explore their consequences. Among the potentially most useful items in Hull's bequest to the future are the many ingenious "peripheral" mechanisms which were elaborated, in the first instance, in his earlier theoretical articles. These we have referred to as "pre-theoretical" hypotheses, in the sense that they were stated and explored in a relatively informal way, and also that their validity seems largely independent of the truth value of the specific postulates put forward in any of Hull's sustained theoretical formulations. Included in this group would be such mechanisms as:

(1) The proprioceptive stimulus (s), and its role in sequential and internally maintained behavior (e.g., 29, 30, 51, 65, 66, 78).

(2) The functional potentialities of the "stimulus trace," as a conditionable element in behavior situations (e.g., 39, 42, 51, 75, 78).

(3) The mechanism of S_D, and its concrete roles in the dynamics of motivation (e.g., 29, 30, 33, 56, 78).

(4) The sensitizing effects of current "drive" states on "habit" structures (e.g., 56).

(5) R_G and the associated S_G, and the elaboration of their theoretical

potentialities for the phenomena of purpose, expectation, transfer and reasoning (e.g., 29, 30, 32, 38, 78).

(6) The habit family hierarchy, its role in the dynamics of trial and error behavior, and its potentialities for the explanation of complex transfer phenomena (e.g., 34, 35, 44).

(7) "Indirect" and "secondary" stimulus generalization (e.g., 47, 56).

It is likely that concepts of this order point to factors which must ultimately be taken into account by any theory of behavior, even theories which assign greater importance to "central" variables.

A second class of hypotheses may be distinguished which perhaps have more limited chances of ultimate survival, yet which represent distinct contributions to the field. If some of these turn out to be blind alleys, Hull's excursion into them will have at least speeded the discovery that they lie off the true path. Conspicuously within this group are such hypotheses as: the drive reduction treatment of reinforcement, the principle of secondary reinforcement, the principle of primary stimulus generalization, and a two-component analysis of "inhibition" (or extinction phenomena). We have adduced many grounds to show that none of these hypotheses can survive in any of the concrete formulations in which Hull cast them. And in the case of some, it is not easy to find an empirically testable interpretation which can be confidently presumed to reflect the intention of Hull's theory. But *some* testable interpretation of each of these is possible, and in each case it is well that the resulting hypotheses continue to be evaluated and further refined.

4. Useful Experiments and Impact on Experimental Practice

Whatever the definitional inaccuracies of the independent and dependent variables discriminated by Hull's theory, they are all related to specifiable (if not adequately *specified*) dimensions of variation in empirical behavior situations. Should satisfactory, theoretically neutral definitions be reconstructed for them, they would be seen to correspond to manipulable and observable features of behavior situations whose causal inter-relations it would be useful to explore in the approach to any systematic formulation of behavior. As a matter of fact, most, if not all, of Hull's empirical variables (e.g., number of rewarded practice trials, time relations between CS and US, "similarity" between training and test S, hours of hunger, etc., on the independent variable side; probability, latency, amplitude, resistance to extinction, on the dependent variable side) had already been discriminated, and investigated, in a variety of situations, by previous workers. In pushing forward his ambitious, quantitatively oriented theory, Hull has been responsible for a greater advance in our knowledge of the empirical relations among such variables than perhaps any other worker during the past two decades.

Despite the fact that Hull's theoretical intentions led to an uncritical, and often autistic, *systematic* use of the experiments that he performed or stimulated, the very same intentions led, paradoxically, to a marked improvement in the quality of the experimental designs used in such work, and perhaps in the general standards of experimental craftsmanship. Where earlier investigators were content with (say) showing a difference between two contrast groups with respect to a given variable, Hull's quantitative intentions forced a fuller determination of the trend of the function. To note, as we already have in the present report, that Hull's experimental designs were, in general, not adequate to his quantitative intentions, is not to say that his quantitative intentions did not have a favorable influence on his experimental designs.

The demands of Hull's systematic thinking led also to the utilization of pre-existing experimental techniques in fresh ways (e.g., the use of the modified Skinner-box and other simple trial and error situations for studying relationships suggested by classical *CR* work), the exploration of novel situations (e.g., speed of locomotion gradients in the straight runway, the Arnold (1) apparatus for the study of reaction chains), and the invention of experimental designs calculated to tease out subtle behavioral relationships. Most impressive in this last category, was the systematic variation of both training and test conditions embodied in the design of experiments—like Perin's—which were calculated to partial out "learning" and "performance" relationships.

A very large part of whatever small advance has been made in recent decades with respect to empirical knowledge of basic "learning" and motivational relationships, must be attributed to experiments conducted by Hull and his collaborators, or by others in the attempt to evaluate or extend his formulations. This can be said with confidence, even though no one can yet delineate the resulting knowledge with precision. For this, we must return to the experiments and determine what they say when theoretically neutralized.

5. The Heritage of Hull's Failures

With this category of Hull's contributions, we return to the theme of which this report has been the interminable documentation. We can profit by Hull's mistakes more determinately than in the case of any recent theorist. This is only partly because Hull aimed at greater explicitness than others; we have seen the extent to which Hull's formal procedures camouflaged ambiguity. It is mainly because of the tenacity, detail, often brilliance with which he translated his orienting attitudes into action.

These commitments towards action were determined in part by the behaviorist prolegomenon towards theory, and in part by Hull's intense desire to jump from an era of prolegomenizing to an era of mature and rigorous theory. They demanded that *in content* the theory be "objective," "peripheralistic," "S-Rish," while *in form* it be hypothetico-deductive, highly quantitative and completely general. To some, these will seem admirable attitudes; those who dislike certain of them will at least admit that it was historically desirable that they be entertained in a responsible way. No one has entertained them more responsibly—thus instructively—than has Hull.

If he has not "put the behavioristic house in order" (47, p. 29), he has at least thrown light on where it is in disorder. It will remain in disorder until the concepts of *S* and *R*, and other independent and dependent variables, are adequately defined. It will remain in disorder until its theory language is put into a more satisfactory relation with its data language. It will remain in disorder until its explanatory concepts and principles are put in order, and to put these in order—if they can be—will require much more detailed empirical knowledge about the conditions of behavior than we now have.

If Hull has not given us a comprehensive theory, he has added a note of reality to our estimate of how general a theory it is rational to look towards. If he has not given us strict hypothetico-deductive rigor, he has pointed up the fact that in *empirical* systems determinacy must necessarily be limited by the determinacy of current knowledge.

He has not given us satisfactory intervening variables, but his persistent, tortured, grappling with problems in the logic of constructing intervening variable functions has defined the complexity of the issues, and revealed the superficiality of accepted methodological cant.

Nor has Hull given us what he most wanted, and all of us most want: "genuine" quantification of behavioral relationships. But his twenty years of striving has done more than any previous effort in psychology to put this enterprise on a realistic basis—for those who will read the lessons.

Appendix

TERMINAL NOTE ON "A BEHAVIOR SYSTEM"

Hull's posthumous book, *A Behavior System* (78), came into the writer's hands too late for consideration in the present report. It should at least be recorded that in this work Hull seems to have come explicitly to the same evaluation of the trend of his theoretical effort that has been made in this report. Our analysis of *Essentials*, and the articles of the quantification sequence, led us to conclude that "in the final phase of his career Hull was arriving at an honest recognition of the prematurity of certain of his theoretical objectives" (cf. Concluding Considerations, Part II). Such a retrenchment seemed implicit in the tone of Hull's 1949-1951 theory language, and in scattered reservations made in *Essentials* and the articles on the quantification of reaction potential. At some point before February, 1952, when the manuscript for *A Behavior System* was sent to the publisher, Hull was prepared to substitute direct statement for nuance. The following quotations speak for themselves:

They who know the history of theoretical psychology will understand that the present system *is merely the most recent of a series of miniature systems* evolved by the present writer. The coming generation of scientists will, it is hoped, present other theoretical systems, each succeeding one of a progressively more precise and quantitative nature (78, p. 353; ital. mine).

In the following pages I have made a serious attempt to give a quantitative, systematic account of some of the more important forms of non-social behavior. I make no pretense of having said the last word on any of them. *I trust that the quantitative methodology employed will readily make apparent to all serious students the errors which presumably have eluded our scrutiny and insight; hidden fallacies may seriously delay the advancement of a young science* (78, p. vii; ital. mine).

. . . All scientific systems of importance must be quantitative; quantification requires units, and systematic quantification requires a most meticulous definition of the units in their various relationships. . . . This will be an exacting task, probably extending over a very long time. *The small and tentative beginning made in the present system (σ) will serve mainly to call attention in a concrete manner to the problem.*

The behavioral units employed are closely related to the matter of the quantitative equations representing the relation of the various behavior functions, such as $_sH_R$, $_sE_R$, D, $_sI_R$, and so on, in the present system, to the number of reinforcements (N), the length or amount of food privation (h), the number of extinction trials (n), and so on. In the midst of these problems is the critical series concerned with the numerical values of the constants or parameters which enter into these equations. The history of the physical sciences indicates that this presumably will be accomplished by a series of approximations, but that even though the problem is urgent it will be a very long time before a final stage is reached. *Small beginnings have been made in this by the rough postulation of various constants in the present system; this, again, will serve mainly to call attention to the problem* (78, p. 354; ital. mine).

Strictly speaking, the body of a scientific system consists of the mathematical derivations of the theorems which correspond to the empirical facts of the science. The deductions presented in this volume are all of a relatively simple concrete form, and are mostly quite informal. At one time a few of us worked out for a limited range of behavior a strict system to explore its possibilities [*Mathematico-Deductive Theory of Rote Learning*]. *It is probably too early to do this on a large scale*, though the rare persons qualified for such a task should before very long attempt to do it at least for the field covered by the present volume (78, p. 3; ital. and bracketed insert mine).

We must note that this set of postulates and corollaries differs in some respects from any previously put forward. For example, the delay-in-reinforcement principle (J) is changed from a postulate to a major corollary (*iii*). *Also, where the substance of a principle is expressible as a provisional numerical equation, the latter is now given as the best available approximation* (78, p. 4; ital. mine).

As an addition to the above excerpts, we might even cite the title of the book in which they appear: *A Behavior System*. Contrast this with the 1943 title, *Principles of Behavior*, or the 1951 *Essentials of Behavior*.

A Behavior System is concerned with the application of a very slightly altered form of the 1951 postulates "to the deduction of the simpler phenomena characterizing the behavior of single organisms" (78, p. VII). Hull thus returns to the task—held more or less in abeyance in all extended publications since 1940—of tracing out secondary consequences of his assumptions. In the process of considering the "178 formal theoretical propositions" exhibited in the volume, Hull returns to many of the themes dealt with in the early theoretical articles. Thus there are chapters containing "theorem" sequences on "Simple Trial-and-Error Learning," "Behavior and the Molar Stimulus Trace," "Fractional Antedating Goal Reactions," "Simple Behavior Chains," "Behavior in Relation to Objects in Space," "Multidirectional Maze Learning," and "The Problem-Solving Assembly of Behavior Segments." There is also an analysis of "Discrimination Learning," "Learning Within the Individual Behavior Link" and of "Value, Valuation, and Behavior Theory."

It is significant to note that many of the "theorems" presented as following from the present postulate set are either identical with or similar to consequences which had earlier been derived from markedly different versions of the theory. Indeed, the new volume lends dramatic support to the belief that many of the secondary explanatory "mechanisms" which Hull has elaborated are independent of the specific details of the principles from which they presumably "derive."

The drawing together, in one place, of a large number of the "deductions" previously scattered in a variety of sources (plus the exhibition of many new "derivations") offers a useful convenience to future analysts of Hull interested in extricating fruitful hypotheses and "pre-theoretical" ideas. At the same time, the use of the curiously formulated, and speciously "quantified," *1951* postulates to mediate derivations already made from alternate postulate sets, may tend further to muddy the contours of the genuinely fruitful components of Hull's formulations.

Bibliography

(This list includes all of Hull's publications relating to his theory of behavior with the exception of reviews and abstracts. Mimeographed "seminar memoranda" and "memoranda concerning behavior theory" are included only to the extent that they are cited in the textual discussion. The bibliography does not include Hull's writings in other fields such as applied psychology, aptitude testing and hypnosis.)

1. ARNOLD, W. J. Simple reaction chains and their integration. I. Homogeneous chaining with terminal reinforcement. *J. comp. and physiol. Psychol.*, 1947, 40, 349-363

2. BAERNSTEIN, H. D., & HULL, C. L. A mechanical model of the conditioned reflex. *J. gen. Psychol.*, 1931, 5, 99-106.

3. BASS, M. J., & HULL, C. L. The irradiation of a tactile conditioned reflex in man. *J. comp. Psychol.*, 1934, 17, 46-65.

4. BERGMANN, G., & SPENCE, K. W. The logic of psychological measurement. *Psychol. Rev.*, 1944, 51, 1-24.

5. BIRCH, H. G., & BITTERMANN, M. E. Reinforcement and learning: The process of sensory integration. *Psychol. Rev.*, 1949, 56, 292-308.

6. CARNAP, R. Testability and Meaning. *Phil. Sci.*, 1936, 3, 420-471; 1937, 4, 1-40.

7. CATTELL, J. McK. The influence of the intensity of the stimulus on the length of the reaction time. *Brain*, 1886, 8, 512-515.

8. CRESPI, L. P. Quantitative variation of incentive and performance in the white rat. *Amer. J. Psychol.*, 1942, 55, 467-517.

9. ———. Amount of reinforcement and level of performance. *Psychol. Rev.*, 1944, 51, 341-357.

10. DENNY, M. R. The role of secondary reinforcement in a partial reinforcement learning situation. *J. exp. Psychol.*, 1946, 36, 373-389.

11. DOLLARD, J., & MILLER, N. E. *Personality and psychotherapy; an analysis in terms of learning, thinking and culture.* New York: McGraw-Hill, 1950.

12. ELLSON, D. G. Quantitative studies of the interaction of simple habits. I. Recovery from specific and generalized effects of extinction. *J. exp. Psychol.*, 1938, 23, 339-358.

13. FELSINGER, J. M., GLADSTONE, A. I., YAMAGUCHI, H. G., & HULL, C. L. Reaction latency (str) as a function of the number of reinforcements (N). *J. exp. Psychol.*, 1947, 37, 214-228.

14. GIBSON, E. J. A systematic application of the concepts of generalization and differentiation to verbal learning. *Psychol. Rev.*, 1940, 47, 196-229.

15. GLADSTONE, A. I., YAMAGUCHI, H. G., HULL, C. L., & FELSINGER, J. M. Some functional relationships of reaction potential ($_sE_R$) and related phenomena. *J. exp. Psychol.*, 1947, 37, 510-526.

16. GRINDLEY, G. C. Experiments on the influence of the amount of reward on learning in young chickens. *Brit. J. Psychol.*, 1929, 20, 173-180.

17. GUILFORD, J. P. *Psychometric Methods.* New York: McGraw-Hill, 1936.

18. ———, & COMREY, A. L. Measurement in psychology. In H. Helson (Ed.), *Theoretical foundations of psychology.* New York: Van Nostrand, 1951.

19. GUTHRIE, E. R. *The psychology of learning.* New York: Harper, 1935.

20. ———. *The psychology of human conflict.* New York: Harper, 1938.

21. HILGARD, E. R. *Theories of Learning.* New York: Appleton-Century-Crofts, 1948.

22. HILL, C. H. Goal gradient, anticipation, and perseveration in compound trial-and-error learning. *J. exp. Psychol.*, 1930, 25, 566-585.

23. HOVLAND, C. I. The generalization of conditioned responses: I. The sensory generalization of conditioned responses with varying frequencies of tone. *J. gen. Psychol.*, 1937, 17, 125-148.

24. ———. The generalization of conditioned responses: II. The sensory generalization of conditioned responses with varying intensities of tone. *J. genet. Psychol.*, 1937, 51, 279-291.

25. ———. The generalization of conditioned responses. IV. The effects of varying amounts of reinforcement upon the degree of generalization of conditional responses. *J. exp. Psychol.*, 1937, 21, 261-276.

26. HULL, C. L. A functional interpretation of the conditioned reflex. *Psychol. Rev.*, 1929, 36, 498-511.

27. ——, & BAERNSTEIN, H. D. A mechanical parallel to the conditioned reflex. *Science*, 1929, 70, 14-15.

28. HULL, C. L. Simple trial-and-error learning: a study in psychological theory. *Psychol. Rev.*, 1930, 37, 241-256.

29. ——. Knowledge and purpose as habit mechanisms. *Psychol. Rev.*, 1930, 37, 511-525.

30. ——. Goal attraction and directing ideas conceived as habit phenomena. *Psychol. Rev.*, 1931, 38, 487-506.

31. ——, & KRUEGER, R. C. An electro-chemical parallel to the conditioned reflex. *J. gen. Psychol.*, 1931, 5, 262-269.

32. ——. The goal gradient hypothesis and maze learning. *Psychol. Rev.*, 1932, 39, 25-43.

33. ——. Differential habituation to internal stimuli in the albino rat. *J. comp. Psychol.*, 1933, 16, 255-274.

34. ——. The concept of the habit-family hierarchy, and maze learning. Part I. *Psychol. Rev.*, 1934, 41, 33-54.

35. ——. The concept of the habit-family hierarchy, and maze learning. Part II. *Psychol. Rev.*, 1934, 41, 134-152.

36. ——. The rat's speed of locomotion gradient in the approach to food. *J. comp. Psychol.*, 1934, 17, 393-422.

37. ——. Learning: II. The factor of the conditioned reflex. In C. Murchison (Ed.), *A Handbook of General Experimental Psychology*. Worcester, Mass.: Clark Univ. Press, 1934.

38. ——. The mechanism of the assembly of behavior segments in novel combinations suitable for problem solution. *Psychol. Rev.*, 1935, 42, 219-245.

39. ——. The conflicting psychologies of learning—a way out. *Psychol. Rev.*, 1935, 42, 491-516.

40. ——. The influence of caffeine and other factors on certain phenomena of rote learning. *J. gen. Psychol.*, 1935, 13, 249-274.

41. ——. Special review: Thorndike's *Fundamentals of learning*. *Psychol. Bull.*, 1935, 32, 807-823.

42. ——. Mind, mechanism and adaptive behavior. *Psychol. Rev.*, 1937, 44, 1-32.

43. ——. A comment on Dr. Adams' note on method. *Psychol. Rev.*, 1937, 44, 219-221.

44. ——. The goal-gradient hypothesis applied to some "field-force" problems in the behavior of young children. *Psychol. Rev.*, 1938, 45, 271-300.

45. ——, & SPENCE, K. W. "Correction" vs. "non-correction" method of trial-and-error learning in rats. *J. comp. Psychol.*, 1938, 25, 127-145.

46. HULL, C. L., & MOWRER, O. H. *Hull's psychological seminars, 1936-38. Notices and abstracts of proceedings.* Bound mimeographed material on file in the libraries of the University of Chicago, University of North Carolina, and Yale University.

47. HULL, C. L. The problem of stimulus equivalence in behavior theory. *Psychol. Rev.*, 1939, 46, 9-30.

48. ——. Simple trial-and-error learning—an empirical investigation. *J. comp. Psychol.*, 1939, 27, 233-258.

49. ——. Modern behaviorism and psychoanalysis. *Trans. N. Y. Acad. Sci.*, 1939, *I*. Ser. II, 78-82.

50. HULL, C. L. Explorations in the patterning of stimuli conditioned to the G.S.R. *J. exp. Psychol.*, 1940, 27, 95-110.

51. ———, HOVLAND, C. I., ROSS, R. T., HALL, M., PERKINS, D. T., & FITCH, F. B. *Mathematico-deductive theory of rote learning: a study in scientific methodology.* New Haven: Yale Univ. Press, 1940.

52. HULL, C. L. *Psychological seminar memoranda, 1939-1940.* Bound mimeographed manuscript on file in the libraries of Yale Univ., Univ. of Iowa, and Oberlin College.

53. ———. Conditioning: outline of a systematic theory of learning. *Yearb. nat. Soc. Stud. Educ.*, 1942, 41, Part 2, 61-95. Chicago: Univ. of Chicago Press, 1942.

54. ———. The problem of intervening variables in molar behavior theory. *Psychol. Rev.*, 1943, 50, 273-291.

55. ———. A postscript concerning intervening variables. *Psychol. Rev.*, 1943, 50, 540.

56. ———. *Principles of behavior: an introduction to behavior theory.* New York: Appleton-Century-Crofts, 1943.

57. ———. Value, valuation, and natural science methodology. *Phil. Sci.*, 1944, 11, 125-141.

58. ———. *Psychological memoranda, 1940-1944.* Bound mimeographed manuscript on file in the libraries of Yale Univ., Univ. of Iowa, and Univ. of North Carolina.

59. ———. The place of innate individual and species differences in a natural-science theory of behavior. *Psychol. Rev.*, 1945, 52, 55-60.

60. ———. The discrimination of stimulus configurations and the hypothesis of afferent neural interaction. *Psychol. Rev.*, 1945, 52, 133-142.

61. ———. Moral values, behaviorism, and the world crisis. *Trans. N. Y. Acad. Sci.*, 1945, 7, 90-94.

62. ———. Research memorandum concerning the quantitative empirical determination of certain basic behavioral constants and their functional relationships. May 29, 1945 (mimeographed manuscript on file in Yale Library).

63. ———. The problem of primary stimulus generalization. *Psychol. Rev.*, 1947, 54, 120-134.

64. ———, FELSINGER, J. M., GLADSTONE, A. I., & YAMAGUCHI, H. G. A proposed quantification of habit strength. *Psychol. Rev.*, 1947, 54, 237-254.

65. HULL, C. L. Reactively heterogeneous compound trial-and-error learning with distributed trials and terminal reinforcement. *J. exp. Psychol.*, 1947, 37, 118-135.

66. ———. Reactively heterogeneous compound trial-and-error learning with distributed trials and serial reinforcement. *J. exp. Psychol.*, 1948, 38, 17-28.

67. ———. Stimulus intensity dynamism (V) and stimulus generalization. *Psychol. Rev.*, 1949, 56, 67-76.

68. ———. Memorandum on behavior theory. Oct. 4, 1949 (mimeographed manuscript on file in Yale Library).

69. ———. Behavior postulates and corollaries. November 12, 1949 (mimeographed memorandum on file in Yale Library).

70. ———. Behavior postulates and corollaries—1949. *Psychol. Rev.*, 1950, 57, 173-180.

71. ———. Simple qualitative discrimination learning. *Psychol. Rev.*, 1950, 57, 303-313.

72. ———. A primary social science law. *Sci. Mon.*, N. Y. 1950, 71, 221-228.

73. HULL, C. L. Memorandum concerning behavior theory. February 7, 1950. (mimeographed manuscript on file in Yale Library).

74. ———. Memorandum concerning behavior theory. March 6, 1950 (mimeographed manuscript on file in Yale Library).

75. ———. *Essentials of behavior.* New Haven: Yale Univ. Press, 1951.

76. ———, JOHNSTON, R. L., ROUSE, R. O., & BARKER, A. H. True, sham, and esophageal feeding as reinforcements. *J. comp. Physiol. Psychol.,* 1951, 44, 236-245.

77. HULL, C. L. Clark L. Hull. In Boring, E. G., Langfeld, H. S., Werner, H., and Yerkes, R. M. (Eds.), *A history of psychology in autobiography— Volume IV.* Worcester: Clark University Press, 1952.

78. ———. *A Behavior System.* New Haven: Yale University Press, 1952.

79. HUMPHREYS, L. G. The effect of random alternation of reinforcement on the acquisition and extinction of conditioned eyelid reactions. *J. exp. Psychol.,* 1939, 25, 141-158.

80. ———. Generalization as a function of method of reinforcement. *J. exp. Psychol.,* 1939, 25, 361-372.

81. JENKINS, W. O., & STANLEY, J. C. Partial reinforcement: a review and critique. *Psychol. Bull.,* 1950, 47, 193-234.

82. KAPPAUF, W. E., & SCHLOSBERG, H. Conditioned responses in the white rat. III. Conditioning as a function of the length of the period of delay. *J. genet. Psychol.,* 1937, 50, 27-45.

83. KIMBLE, G. A. Conditioning as a function of the time between conditioned and unconditioned stimuli. *J. exp. Psychol.,* 1947, 37, 1-15.

84. ———. An experimental test of a two-factor theory of inhibition. *J. exp. Psychol.,* 1949, 39, 15-23.

85. KOCH, S. The logical character of the motivation concept. I. *Psychol. Rev.,* 1941, 48, 15-38.

86. ———. Review of Hull's Principles of behavior. *Psychol. Bull.,* 1944, 41, 269-286.

87. ———, & DANIEL, W. J. The effect of satiation on the behavior mediated by a habit of maximum strength. *J. exp. Psychol.,* 1945, 35, 167-187.

88. ———. Form and content in hypothetico-deductive systems: a reply to Woodbury. *J. Psychol.,* 1947, 24, 237-246.

89. LASHLEY, K. S. Learning: I. Nervous-mechanisms of learning. In C. Murchison (Ed.), *The Foundations of Experimental Psychology.* Worcester, Mass.: Clark Univ. Press, 1929.

90. ———. An examination of the "continuity theory" as applied to discriminative learning. *J. gen. Psychol.,* 1942, 26, 241-265.

91. ———, & WADE, M. The Pavlovian theory of generalization. *Psychol. Rev.,* 1946, 53, 72-87.

92. LEEPER, R. Dr. Hull's Principles of Behavior. *J. genet. Psychol.,* 1944, 65, 3-52.

93. MACCORQUODALE, K., & MEEHL, P. E. On a distinction between hypothetical constructs and intervening variables. *Psychol. Rev.,* 1948, 55, 95-107.

94. MEEHL, P. E. An examination of the treatment of stimulus patterning in Professor Hull's *Principles of Behavior. Psychol. Rev.,* 1945, 52, 324-332.

95. ———. On the circularity of the law of effect. *Psychol. Bull.,* 1950, 47, 52-75.

96. MILLER, N. E., & DOLLARD, J. *Social learning and imitation.* New Haven: Yale University Press, 1941.

97. MILLER, N. E. Experimental studies of conflict. In Hunt, J. McV. (Ed.), *Personality and the behavior disorders.* New York: Ronald Press, 1944.

98. MILLER, N. E. Studies of fear as an acquirable drive: I. Fear as motivation and fear-reduction as reinforcement in the learning of new responses. *J. exp. Psychol.*, 1948, 38, 89-101.

99. ———. Learnable drives and rewards. In Stevens, S. S. (Ed.), *Handbook of experimental psychology.* New York: Wiley, 1951.

100. MOWRER, O. H., & JONES, H. M. Extinction and behavior variability as functions of effortfulness of task. *J. exp. Psychol.*, 1943, 33, 369-386.

101. MOWRER, O. H. On the dual nature of learning—a reinterpretation of "conditioning" and "problem-solving." *Harvard Educ. Rev.*, 1947, 17, 102-148.

102. ———. *Learning theory and personality dynamics.* New York: Ronald Press, 1950.

103. PERIN, C. T. Behavior potentiality as a joint function of the amount of training and the degree of hunger at the time of extinction. *J. exp. Psychol.*, 1942, 30, 93-113.

104. ———. A quantitative investigation of the delay-of-reinforcement gradient. *J. exp. Psychol.*, 1943, 32, 37-51.

105. POSTMAN, L. The history and present status of the law of effect. *Psychol. Bull.*, 1947, 44, 489-563.

106. PRENTICE, W. C. H. Continuity in human learning. *J. exp. Psychol.*, 1949, 39, 187-194.

107. REYNOLDS, B. The acquisition of a trace conditioned response as a function of the magnitude of the stimulus trace. *J. exp. Psychol.*, 1945, 35, 15-30.

108. RITCHIE, B. F. Hull's treatment of learning. *Psychol. Bull.*, 1944, 41, 640-652.

109. SALTZMAN, I., & KOCH, S. The effect of low intensities of hunger on the behavior mediated by a habit of maximum strength. *J. exp. Psychol.*, 1948, 38, 347-370.

110. SEWARD, J. P. Secondary reinforcement as tertiary motivation: A revision of Hull's revision. *Psychol. Rev.*, 1950, 57, 362-374.

111. SHEFFIELD, F. D., & ROBY, T. B. Reward value of a non-nutritive sweet taste. *J. comp. physiol. Psychol.*, 1950, 43, 471-481.

112. SIMLEY, O. A. The relation of subliminal to supraliminal learning. *Arch. of Psychol.*, 1933, No. 146.

113. SKINNER, B. F. *The behavior of organisms.* New York: Appleton-Century-Crofts, 1938.

114. ———. Review of Hull's Principles of behavior. *Amer. J. Psychol.*, 1944, 57, 276-281.

115. ———. Are theories of learning necessary? *Psychol. Rev.*, 1950, 57, 193-216.

116. SPENCE, K. W. The nature of discrimination learning in animals. *Psychol. Rev.*, 1936, 43, 427-449.

117. ———. Analysis of the formation of visual discrimination habits in the chimpanzee. *J. comp. Psychol.*, 1937, 23, 77-100.

118. ———. The differential response in animals to stimuli varying within a single dimension. *Psychol. Rev.*, 1937, 44, 430-444.

119. ———. Continuous versus non-continuous interpretations of discrimination learning. *Psychol. Rev.*, 1940, 47, 271-288.

120. ———, and LIPPITT, R. O. "Latent" learning of a simple maze problem with relevant needs satiated. *Psychol. Bull.*, 1940, 37, 429.

121. SPENCE, K. W. Failure of transposition in size discrimination of chimpanzees. *Amer. J. Psychol.*, 1941, 54, 223-229.

122. ———. Theories of learning. In F. A. Moss (Ed.), *Comparative Psychology* (Rev. ed.). New York: Prentice-Hall, Inc., 1942.

123. ————. The basis of solution by chimpanzees of the intermediate size problem. *J. exp. Psychol.*, 1942, 31, 257-271.

124. ————, & LIPPITT, R. O. An experimental test of the sign-gestalt theory of trial and error learning. *J. exp. Psychol.*, 1946, 36, 491-502.

125. SPENCE, K. W. The role of secondary reinforcement in delayed reward learning. *Psychol. Rev.*, 1947, 54, 1-8.

126. ————. The postulates and methods of "behaviorism." *Psychol. Rev.*, 1948, 55, 67-78.

127. ————. Cognitive versus stimulus-response theories of learning. *Psychol. Rev.*, 1950, 57, 159-172.

128. ————, BERGMANN, G., & LIPPITT, R. O. A study of simple learning under irrelevant motivational-reward conditions. *J. exp. Psychol.*, 1950, 40, 539-551.

129. SPENCE, K. W. Theoretical interpretations of learning. In C. P. Stone (Ed.) *Comparative Psychology* (3rd ed.). New York: Prentice-Hall, Inc., 1951.

130. ————. Theoretical interpretations of learning. In Stevens, S. S. (Ed.) *Handbook of experimental psychology.* New York: Wiley, 1951.

131. SPROW, A. J. Reactively homogeneous compound trial-and-error learning with distributed trials and terminal reinforcement. *J. exp. Psychol.*, 1947, 37, 197-213.

132. THISTLETHWAITE, D. A critical review of latent learning and related experiments. *Psychol. Bull.*, 1951, 48, 97-129.

133. Thurstone, L. L. Psychophysical analysis. *Amer. J. Psychol.*, 1927, 38, 368-389.

134. ————. A law of comparative judgment. *Psychol. Rev.*, 1927, 34, 273-286.

135. ————. Stimulus dispersions in the method of constant stimuli. *J. exp. Psychol.*, 1932, 15, 284-297.

136. TOLMAN, E. C. *Purposive behavior in animals and men.* New York: Appleton-Century, 1932. Also reprinted: Berkeley: Univ. of California Press, 1949.

137. ————. Operational behaviorism and current trends in psychology. In *Proc. 25th Anniv. Celebr. Inaug. Grad. Stud.*, Univ. So. Calif., 1936, 89-103.

138. ————. The determiners of behavior at a choice point. *Psychol. Rev.*, 1938, 45, 1-41.

139. ————. Cognitive maps in rats and men. *Psychol. Rev.*, 1948, 55, 189-208.

140. WHITING, J. W. M. *Becoming a Kwoma: teaching and learning in a New Guinea tribe.* New Haven: Yale Univ. Press, 1941.

141. WILCOXEN, H. C., HAYS, R., & HULL, C. L. A preliminary determination of the functional relationship of effective reaction potential ($_sE_R$) to the ordinal number of Vincentized extinction reactions ($\dot{n}$). *J. exp. Psychol.*, 1950, 40, 194-199.

142. WILLIAMS, S. B. Resistance to extinction as a function of the number of reinforcements. *J. exp. Psychol.*, 1938, 23, 506-522.

143. WOLFLE, H. M. Time factors in conditioning finger-withdrawal. *J. gen. Psychol.*, 1930, 4, 372-378.

144. WOODBURY, C. B. The learning of stimulus patterns by dogs. *J. comp. Psychol.*, 1943, 35, 29-40.

145. YAMAGUCHI, H. G., HULL, C. L., FELSINGER, J. M., & GLADSTONE, A. I. Characteristics of dispersions based on the pooled momentary reaction potentials ($_sE_R$) of a group. *Psychol. Rev.*, 1948, 55, 216-238.

146. YAMAGUCHI, H. G. Superthreshold reaction potential ($_sE_R$) as a function of experimental extinction (n). *J. exp. Psychol.*, 1951, 41, 391-400.

147. YAMAGUCHI, H. G. Drive (D) as a function of hours of hunger (h). *J. exp. Psychol.*, 1951, 42, 108-117.
148. YOUTZ, R. E. P. The weakening of one Thorndikian response following the extinction of another. *J. exp. Psychol.*, 1939, 24, 294-304.

SECTION 2

Edward C. Tolman

KENNETH MacCORQUODALE
and PAUL E. MEEHL

I. INTRODUCTION

THE PRESENT DISCUSSION of Tolman's theory is based upon his statements of it as they have appeared beginning with 1932 when *Purposive Behavior in Animals and Men* (128) was published; the most recent statement we have considered is the 1949 article: "There is more than one kind of learning" (151). We have not included in our bibliography or in our discussion Tolman's more recent views on the conceptualization of social behavior; neither have we considered the several constructive commentaries and interpretations authored by others, such as White (185). Our reasons for not treating Tolman's most recent writings stem in part from our understanding that he is currently engaged, with Postman, in a major restatement of his views. We are speaking in this section, then, of Tolman as he has been understood for the past twenty years. Whether our criticisms will still be up-to-date after publication of his new book depends upon whether he proposes a conceptually new statement or a restatement of the present concepts with greater felicity of expression, and remains to be seen.

Our aim has been two-fold: first, to display and critically examine Tolman's system as it is; secondly, to state a set of more formal "laws" which introduce those concepts we consider to be most central to Tolman's views and which are intended to preserve the flavor while increasing the formalization of an expectancy theory.

The system will be considered according, generally, to the outline described in Chapter I. Considerable emphasis will be given to the aspects

Tolman's theory which differentiate it from the other theories con-
ed in this volume, and for this reason it is important to stress that
much of the content of his 1920 to 1932 publications, and even of *Purposive Behavior in Animals and Men,* is in substantial agreement with
the views of *S-R* and *S-R* reinforcement theorists. To mention one obvious example, most psychologists trained since the early thirties, whether
Tolmanites or not, find it so natural to think in terms of "reinforcements," "rewards" or "goal-objects" when speaking of instrumental
learning, that we easily forget the importance of Tolman's work in reducing the plausibility of the variant of pure frequency-recency connectionism which was held by many prior to around 1930. There are
some characterizations of Tolman's theory, often said to differentiate
him from other theorists, which will not be emphasized here at all. An
example is the frequent reference to Tolman as a Gestalt or field theorist.
The justification for our omission of this emphasis will be made in a later
part of the discussion.

In several places we will point out a difficulty and include a comment
to the effect that "this problem is not peculiar to Tolman." Such indications of common difficulties, which appear especially in Part IV, are not
to be interpreted as mere *tu quoque* or as denials of problems. Needless
to say, we have not pretended to suggest directions of solution for all
problems; and since our subject is Tolman, we have devoted particular
attention to those questions which arise from the special orientation that
distinguishes him as a systematist. This seemed to us the more necessary
because Tolman is sometimes criticized for lacks or ambiguities which
seem to be peculiar to him, but on careful examination are found to be
present, although obscured, in competing systems.

II. THE STRUCTURE OF TOLMAN'S THEORY

Data Language

Considering first Tolman's use of a data language, the first chapter of
Purposive Behavior in Animals and Men contains statements which appear to attempt to make such words as "purpose" and "cognition" a part
of the data language. For example: "Behavior qua behavior has descriptive properties of its own . . . getting-to or getting-from" (p. 10);
"These purposes and cognitions are of its immediate descriptive warp and
woof . . . behavior reeks of purpose and of cognition" (p. 12). However,
these may be understood as devices used by a theorist in an introductory
chapter of a theoretical work, proposing a behaviorism in which such
apparently non-behavioral words as "purpose" and "cognition" will
appear with behavioral definitions. That he intends to define such words
as "purpose" in terms of certain features of behavior seems clear.

When actual experiments are being discussed, a relatively clean, neutral data language seems to be maintained (although when theoretical derivations are being performed, there are some confusions, as will be seen below). As an example of an unequivocal description of experimental events, the following appears in *Purposive Behavior in Animals and Men* (p. 48):

In this maze he [Blodgett] ran three groups of hungry rats. Each group had one trial per day. The *control group* (Group I) was allowed to eat in the usual manner for three minutes in the food-box at the end of the maze. They were then immediately fed the remainder of their day's ration in another cage (not the home cage). The *first experimental group* (Group II) ran the maze for the first six days, without immediate reward. That is, at the end of the maze they were confined in the exit-box without food for two minutes and obtained their day's ration only one hour, or more, afterwards in another cage (not the home cage). After six days of such running, this group, on the seventh day, suddenly found food in the exit-box, and continued so to find it on all subsequent days. A *second experimental group* (Group III) ran the maze without food at the exit-box for two days. For these two days they, like Group II, obtained their day's ration only one hour or more afterwards in another cage. On the third day, however, food was given them in the exit-box and they continued to find it there on all subsequent days.

In the above, the word "hungry," though not further defined here, has become a frequently used and accepted ellipsis; the word "suddenly" is perhaps extravagant, but seems to carry no illicit descriptive connotations here.

In general, Tolman's departures from explicitness in the data language are those which can either be easily filled in (e.g., "hungry") or are permissible as being defined in another discipline (e.g., "sunflower seeds" from botany, or "gravitational" from physics).

Operational Definitions

Tolman's use of operational reduction is seen most explicitly in the article "Studies in Spatial Learning I. Orientation and the short-cut" (173). The following is the definition of an expectancy "revised to better express the original intent of the senior author" (p. 15):

When we assert that a rat expects food at *L*, what we assert is that *if* (1) he is deprived of food, (2) he has been trained on path *P*, (3) he is now put on path *P*, (4) path *P* is now blocked, and (5) there are other paths which lead away from path *P*, one of which points directly to location *L*, *then* he will run down the path which points directly to location *L*.

When we assert that he does *not* expect food at location *L*, what we assert is that, under the same conditions, he will *not* run down the path which points directly to location *L*.

Restated as a conditioned definition, this becomes:

If x is deprived of food and *x* has been trained on path *P* and *x* is now put on path *P* and path *P* is now blocked and there are other paths which lead away from path P, one of which points directly to location L, *then* (x runs down the path which points directly to location $L \equiv x$ expected food at location L).

Three comments on this formulation may be offered. First, as a reduction sentence it is incomplete in several respects. It fails to specify, for example, what else may have been in the rat's history, and what restrictions are placed on path P's stimulus properties in contrast to other paths. In the case, not excluded by this definition, in which path P is white and it is blocked, and there is among the "other" paths one white path (among non-white paths) which leads to location L, *then* if the rat takes "the path which leads to location L" are we prepared to assert that he "expects food at L"?

Secondly, the significance of the negative case is somewhat puzzling by this definition; it would seem, as stated in the singular, that the rat which *fails* to turn down path P does *not* expect food there. Does an expectancy theorist really mean to assert this? Along the same lines, the statement of the operational reduction in terms of the behavior of the individual rat suggests a disturbing statistical consideration: If 12 out of 100 rats run down path P from among 8 paths, shall we assume that these 12 had expectancies and the remainder did not? Now, it might be objected that these criticisms are petty, that *of course* it is intended that the paths should not be different in other than spatial respects, and *of course* ordinary statistical significance is demanded. Since, however, the intent in the use of operational definitions is to make explicit the complete set of relevant characteristics of an event, the above definitions must be considered incomplete.

Our third comment refers less to the adequacy of this definition as an example of the operational method, than to the rationale of its appearance in a theoretical structure such as Tolman's. He says: ". . . I do not hold, as do most behaviorists, that all learning is, as such, the attachment of responses to stimuli. Cathexes, equivalence beliefs, field expectancies, field-cognition modes and drive discriminations are not, as I define them, stimulus-response connections. They are central phenomena, each of which may be expressed by a variety of responses" (151, p. 146). By giving a directly operational definition of a central state, such as an expectancy, in terms of a locomotion, Tolman is in danger of losing precisely that advantage which a centralism has over a peripheralism. In Hull's 1943 *Principles of Behavior* (38, p. 383) the basic learning construct, $_sH_R$, is four steps removed in the intervening variable chain from his "operational" measures of actual momentary response strength. Speaking loosely for the moment, one might suppose that one of the advantages of a more centralist approach is in the matter of some such *causal distance* of the hypothetical cognitive unit from the effector-activity. The kind of means-to-ends appropriateness shown by behavior occurring in altered environmental circumstances which has traditionally intrigued the expectancy theorist is, from a methodological viewpoint, an argument for increasing this causal distance, and for getting, so to speak, more "play" into the system. See, for instance, Tolman's quotation from Gilhousen on the character of crayfish learning (128, p. 18). The question of an alternative mode of definition of such central states will be considered later in the discussion of Tolman's principal constructs and their appearance in derivation of experimental results.

Dependent and Independent Variables

In his presidential address to the American Psychological Association in 1937 (141), Tolman has formally listed the dependent and independent variables with which he proposes to deal. The following are the independent variables listed with briefer definitions of the symbols:

ΣOBO : The sum of the preceding occasions on which stimulus complex O_x has been followed by behavior B_x, which has been followed by stimulus complex O_y.

M : Maintenance schedule.

G : Appropriateness of the goal object.

S : Types and modes of stimuli provided.

R : Types of motor response required.

P : Pattern of preceding and succeeding maze units.

There is also a class of Individual Differences variables on the independent variable side:

H : Heredity.

A : Age.

T : Training.

E : Endocrine, drug and vitamin conditions.

There are several noteworthy characteristics of the above "independent" variables. G, the appropriateness of the goal-object, depends upon an adequate definition of "appropriateness" if it is to be firmly anchored in the data language. Although it is not so anchored by Tolman, it appears as a general term for such characteristics of an incentive as its relation to the drive state (or maintenance schedule), its hardness, bigness, saltiness, etc.; in brief, to characteristics which are expressible in a data language. May we not say that Hull would presumably encounter a similar difficulty in defining his "(amount and) quality of the reinforcing agent" variable, and left the *quality* dimension largely undefined?

More striking is the fact that several variables which are ordinarily characterized as being intervening or dependent have, in this list, found their way to the independent variable side of the causal system. Thus "R, the types of motor response required," which refers to whatever class of topographies the experimenter rewards, is an independent variable only in this sense: that the experimenter can manipulate it by progressively altering its frequency of occurrence through the learning itself. This variable must occur, or at least recur, as a dependent variable. Moreover, it is difficult to discriminate among the three variables referring to the effects of past training, which, as *state* variables are doubtfully appropriate for this list. These are ΣOBO, T and P. Insofar as P, the pattern of preceding and succeeding maze units can affect behavior at a choice point only in consequence of previous OBO's in those units and in the given maze, while T refers to previous OBO's in other mazes and might be referred to as transfer effects, these three variables are not discrete.

For the choice point example, Tolman specifies the *behavior ratio* as the dependent variable. The behavior ratio is defined as

$$\frac{\text{frequency of turn into alley } L}{\text{total frequency of turns into alleys } L \And R}.$$

It will be noted that in practice, it is difficult or impossible actually to compute the behavior ratio for *a* rat at *a* choice point, since one rat cannot, during the course of learning, be made to choose repeatedly at the same choice point at the same response strength. This is one of the several defects of the maze as an instrument, as Skinner has pointed out. For this reason, the literal definition of the behavior ratio is rarely applied, and for it is substituted a count of the number of entries into all culs by a rat (his "score"), when there are several culs involved. When the "behavior ratio" needs to be determined for a specified choice point, determinations of left and right choices for *groups* of rats may be made, but this gives no direct indication of the strengths for individual organisms. The mathematical relationship of the choice ratio to the strengths of the two competing responses is not indicated.

Relation Between Empirical Area Covered and Orientative Attitudes

The dependent and independent variables listed above are specifically appropriate for the discussion of the maze running case, and this is the empirical area to which Tolman has largely restricted himself. It should be pointed out, however, that in Part V of *Purposive Behavior in Animals and Men* Tolman has systematically considered conditioned reflex and trial-and-error learning (as these were understood in 1932), and tried to show that his vocabulary can be applied to them. He has recently discussed psychoanalytic mechanisms such as fixation, regression and displacement (150) and social behavior (153). In neither case, however, has he specifically derived social or psychoanalytic phenomena as formal consequences of his theory.

Hypothetical Constructs

Tolman's definitions of the kinds of constructions which he intends to use indicate that he wished (1932) to avoid hypothetical constructs in the sense proposed by MacCorquodale and Meehl (56), in which a construct acquires attributes which exceed its original defining operations.[1] He proposed instead (134, 135, 141) to define his intervening variables by an inductive breaking down of the function f_1 (relating the dependent and independent variables) into intervening variables a,b,c, with a set of f_2 functions to connect these with the independent variables on the one hand and a set of f_3 functions to connect them with the dependent variables on the other. Tolman has felt it important to emphasize that his usage of such intervening terms as "expectancy" and "cognition" is to be understood in terms of the establishing operations, since these words have such extensive lay connotations; however, as will be pointed out below, the power of these concepts for Tolman in the derivation of experimental results is severely lessened by their exclusively "intervening variable" character. Some of the empirical support Tolman adduces for his constructs

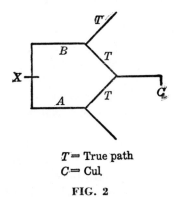

$T =$ True path
$C =$ Cul

FIG. 2

appears to be support only because the common-sense kind of surplus meaning is informally attached to these theoretically "neutralized" terms.

To test the actual reducibility of these construct-terms to the physical or data language two approaches will be taken here: first, one can find *concrete* instances of the use of a term and test the adequacy of its reduction in the context of its occurrence; second, it is interesting to study how concept words as defined in the glossary of *Purposive Behavior in Animals and Men* are *there reduced* to the data language.

As an example of the first kind, refer to *Purposive Behavior in Animals and Men*, Chapter XI: "Inference—the means-end-field," p. 175. In an experiment by Buel, two groups of rats ran the same maze made up of several similar units (Fig. 2) with the difference that for one group, barrier X was present so that the culs A and B constituted separate blinds; for the other group, the barrier X was removed so that culs A and B were continuous, or "constituted the reverse ends of one and the same detour."

---

[1] He has, however, recently (152) expressed a preference for hypothetical constructs as defined by us.

The rats of the second group made fewer entrances into B than did the rats of the first group. "In other words, whereas B has to be learned as a separate independent blind for the animals of Group I, for Group II it can be *recognized as but the other end of A, already entered.*" If we are interested in the definitions of the terms in the italicized part of the sentence (not italicized in the original) we discover that *recognize* is not defined here, nor does it appear in the glossary or index; and surely it is not a word in the data language. *The other end of A* is a phrase ordinarily in the data language, but *used* thus only when it describes facts about the maze. In this sentence, however, it occurs in a clause following the word *as*, where the whole sentence of which it is a part says something, not about the maze, but about the *rat's state* (of recognition). *Already entered* could be considered data language only by virtue of its antecedent, *A*, a place-term. Suppose, to take an example Tolman is fond of himself, the rats were "deceived" by the use of mirrors, or by making the "true" path resemble the other end of a detour. The rats should then avoid it, according to the hypothesis. In characterizing, for such a "deception case," either the animal's expectancy, or his actual response (i.e., avoidance) there would be no difference from similar characterizations in the Buel case; in terms of either the *behavior* or hypothesized "inner events," the psychological situation would be identical with that in which the rat is confronting an actual detour. Hence, as a psychologist, Tolman must say the same thing about the rat's state in both situations. But this shows that ". . . already entered" cannot here be data language referring either to (1) the maze, or (2) the animal's previous reaction, for this phrase indicates (in the Buel experiment) a fact, and in the deception case, a falsehood.

Consider a sentence of the form, "As the rat pauses at choice point 4, he expects [clause or phrase consisting of words denoting maze parts, incentives, pathways, etc.—all individually being data words]." This is intended to characterize the rat's state at the moment of making choice 4. Now, in case E has in fact removed or destroyed the remainder of the maze (maintaining adequate experimental control of sensory cues) the rat's state must be presumed to be as yet wholly unaffected by this fact. Hence the complex sentence (which is "about" the state of the rat) is not dependent for its correctness upon the correctness of its subordinate clauses which themselves assert (or, as in the above case of a past participle, directly imply) something about the maze or the rat's previous history. As the logicians would say, Tolman's complex cognition-statements are not themselves truth-functions of their components.

In this connection, it is interesting to note a "philosophical" point about Tolman's system which some of its opponents have perhaps dimly perceived. Tolman himself explicitly disavows any dualistic reference for his "freshly defined" words, and has for over thirty years insisted upon his consistent behaviorism. We do not mean even to suggest that he is anything else, either consciously or unconsciously. Nevertheless, there is a peculiar sense in which his formulation has, willy-nilly, a certain affinity with the dualistic or, as he prefers to call it, "mentalistic" scheme. This arises from the feature we have just treated. For many thinkers of both past and present (e.g., Brentano), it is *intentionality* that ultimately defines the realm of "mind." Those cases of psychological description which require the use of subordinate clauses, following words like "believe," "know," "expect," such that the complex sentence is not a truth-function of its component propositions, are still a source of difficulty for philosophers basically sympathetic to the behaviorist program (cf. 11, 83). When we commit ourselves to speaking of the rat's "expectancies" rather than his "habits," we are likely to find ourselves involved in the problem of *reference, intention,* or *aboutness* (as in the above example) whether we like it or not. We do not suggest, of course, that such involvements are a necessary consequence of *all* formulations of cognitive theory; the sketch of formalization below seems to us free of it. But the danger is greater than in a system which is couched wholly in response language. "Learning *to* . . ." is intrinsically less referential in its stress than is "learning *that.* . . ." The reluctance of some more suspicious psychologists to take Tolman's behaviorist protestations at face value may be subtly related to this linguistic fact.

In discussing Tolman, one needs a special terminology for this situation. We have a phrase whose components (words) ordinarily occur in the data language and there refer to parts, aspects, or relations of the environment; if this phrase sometimes occurs in a grammatical context following behavior-words such as "know," "expect," "infer" (with the connective *that*), we shall say the phrase is in the "quasi-data language" when so used. We conclude from the analysis of the Buel example that the clause "that it can be recognized as but the other end of *A,* already entered" must, for a consistent behaviorism, be treated *as a whole;* that is, the sub-divisions such as "end of *A,* already entered" cannot be considered satisfactorily defined *in this context* just because they contain data words and thus *appear* to designate objects (maze parts) and events (movements). Such a phrase must be behaviorally defined. If such definitions cannot be found in Tolman, the entire phrase remains unclear in spite of the fact that all of its *elements* also occur in the data language or are readily reducible to it.

An example of the second approach to testing reducibility is found in the definition of *Inference* as given in Tolman's glossary, viz:

Inference. One of the three moods of sign-gestalt-expectation (see expectation). The other two moods are perception (*q.v.*) and mnemonization (*q.v.*). In inference commerce with the sign-object only has ever occurred before. Nevertheless (perhaps because of past experience with "relatively similar" situations, or because of pure creativity), the organism is led to invent the sort of signified object and sort of direction-distance relations to this signified object which will result from commerce with the given sign-object.

The action of such inferential sign-gestalt-expectations is probably the fundamental feature in inventive learning (*q.v.*).

Inventive ideation (*q.v.*) is to be conceived as a special, sophisticated, and recondite form of inference as just defined (p. 446).

The negative part of this definition is clear ("commerce with the sign-object only has ever occurred before") but we doubt it is an exact rendition of Tolman's intent. The rat may have had contact with *both* the sign and significate. For example (see Fig. 3), a rat is allowed to run repeatedly from A to B_1 and also from A to B_2; subsequently he is run from B_2 to B' which contains a demanded object. If his demand for that object is now raised and he now goes to B_2 from A, Tolman would presumably

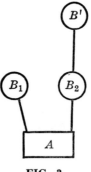

FIG. 3

consider it an "inference," although the rat has had commerce with all significates, only not in the inference-revealing *sequence*.

As for the positive identification of *inference* in the Glossary, note the clause ". . . the organism is led to *invent* the sort of signified object. . . ." The word *invent* does not appear as a defined term in the Glossary, but "inventive ideation" does. (Note: No verb forms appear in the Glossary; the rules for the use of verb forms, given the noun, are not indicated.)

Inventive ideation. The type of ideation (*q.v.*) called "inventive" is that in which the ideational "runnings-back-and-forth" involve, in addition to the alternative and succedent routes of a given means-end-field which the organism has already actually overtly been over, new routes or features, never as such actually experienced by the organism. In inventive ideation these new routes are ideationally extrapolated. Such extrapolation is to be conceived as brought about by behavior adjustments (*q.v.*) to those portions of the field which are already grasped perceptually or mnemonically plus the presence in the organism of a certain amount of creative instability.

The key phrase "ideationally extrapolated" suffers because "extrapolated" is not given in the Glossary. Ideation is:

Ideation. The more recondite form of conscious awareness (*q.v.*), in which the sampling of alternative or succedent means-end-possibilities occurs by virtue of mere behavior-adjustments (*q.v.*) to runnings-back-and-forth.

"Recondite" is not in the Glossary, although the dictionary definition is possibly sufficient; "conscious awareness" reduces to "the process of sampling by running-back-and-forth in front of environmental object."

Thus, if we wish to reduce this statement: *The rat infers that path P leads to food,* with the aid of the Glossary, we arrive at the following statement:

"The rat extrapolates by a more recondite form of running-back-and-forth in which the running-back-and-forth is done by a non-overtly-observable surrogate for running-back-and-forth and relative to environmental objects not then and there sensorially present, these objects being food and the path *P* leading to it."

If we use the device of substituting a symbol for words or phrases that are neither in the data language nor in (theoretically neutral) words of ordinary English, we get:

"The rat (Ψ) by a more (Φ) form of running-back-and-forth in which the running-back-and-forth is done by a non-overtly-observable (Π) for running-back-and-forth (Δ) environmental objects not then and there sensorially present, these objects being food and the path *P* leading to it." It is unclear whether a modifier such as "non-overtly-observable" retains any utility however precisely defined, when it refers to an unknown. We have substituted symbols for several words which do have, ordinarily, clear enough meaning, but whose meaning in this context is certainly not clear. Thus, "relative to" is reasonably unambiguous if actual running-back-and-forth is its referent, but since the running-back-and-forth referred to as "ideational" is metaphorical only, the phrase "relative to" loses the usual spatial or directional referents which give it definite meaning.

It is instructive to refer to the Glossary for the reduction of sentences which contain the word "expect." Thus, to know what the sentence: *The rat expects food at the end of path P,* means, we start by looking for "expect" in the Glossary. "Expect" is not given in the Glossary; however, we do find:

Expectation. An expectation is an immanent cognitive determinant aroused by actually presented stimuli. An expectation probably always actually occurs as the expectation of a total sign-gestalt (*q.v.*). But for purposes of analytical discourse there may be abstracted out for separate consideration, within such a total sign-gestalt-expectation, discriminanda expectations, manipulanda expectations—as to the sign-object (*q.v.*), i.e., means object (*q.v.*); as to the signified-object (*q.v.*); i.e., goal-object (*q.v.*); and as to the means-end-relations (*q.v.*), i.e., direction-distance correlations (*q.v.*) between the former and the latter.

There are three fundamental moods of expectation, viz., perception (*q.v.*), mnemonization (*q.v.*), and inference (*q.v.*).

There are no indications of behaviors in this definition. However, the definition does refer us "upward" in the definitional hierarchy to:

Cognition (cognitive). A generic term for one of the two classes of immanent determinants (*q.v.*) of behavior. A cognition (a means-end-readiness (*q.v.*) or an expectation (*q.v.*)) is present in a behavior insofar as the continued going-off of that behavior is contingent upon environmental entities (i.e., types of discriminanda, manipulanda, or means-end-relations) proving to be "so and so." And such a contingency will be testified to whenever, if these environmental entities do not prove to be so and so, the given behavior will exhibit disruption (*q.v.*) and be followed by learning.

Thus, an expectation occurs as the expectation of a total sign-gestalt, that is, discriminanda- and manipulanda-expectations *as to* the sign-object, i.e., means object and signified object, and the means-end-relations (direction-distance correlations) between these two. But in the definition of an *expectation* taken literally, all references are to the stimuli involved, and these references involve a serious ambiguity because, although we generally consider references to stimuli as being in (or easily reducible to) the data language, the "stimuli" referred to in this definition of an expectancy are not the "stimuli" of the data language at all, but rather the object of the expectation itself (intentionality again!). Insofar as this basic ambiguity exists, and conduces to an unjustified feeling of security in the acceptance and use of such a definition, we feel that this usage of "stimuli" should be understood to belong outside the data language, and in what we called above the "quasi-data language."

A related example, pointing out the easily overlooked failure of these concepts *in use* to conform to their formal, Glossary definitions, may be found in Tolman's discussion (128, p. 71) of the Elliott study. Water-deprived rats had run a maze to water, and error reduction was considerable. Deprivation and incentive were then shifted to food, and on the day of the shift there are increases in the time and error curves, with rapid recovery on subsequent days. The bump is explained as due to the "old cognitive expectation of water" (p. 72). A superficial and sympathetic reading leaves this explanation seeming very plausible. But we have just seen that the "operational definition" of an expectation of water amounts to saying that if the rat does *not* find water, the behavior breaks down; the "content" of a cognition is that state of the environment the *failure of which* produces a disruption of behavior. Since here it is instead the demand variable which is manipulated to produce the disruption, there is no rigorous basis for the use of the disruption criterion to establish the "cognition." The explanation in terms of the *expectation* of a non-demanded goal object has a certain common-sense appeal; but it requires common-usage connotations, exceeding those of Tolman's formal definition, to do the explaining job it is given here.

Although these constructs have been given unsatisfactory formal definitions, it is not correct to infer that the constructs themselves have no definitions or lack all utility. They do lack definitional precision. In such a case, definition is intimately tied to the theoretical use made of the concepts in derivation. A further discussion of the definition problem appears below, in the context of our treatment of derivation.

Principal Constructs

In any listing of the principal intervening variables which Tolman has set forth, one encounters the difficulty that he has renamed some of these variables from time to time as he felt it appropriate in the context of discussion, more felicity of expression, etc. It seems safe to say, however, that if we ignore the *names* and observe the part played in the theory by the several variables, there has been little change since the publication of *Purposive Behavior in Animals and Men.* The following list is a collation of intervening variables mentioned there, and in the articles "Determiners of behavior at a choice point" (1938) (141) and "There is more than one kind of learning" (1949) (151). In each case, the anchoring variables on the independent variable side are noted wherever Tolman has himself stated them.

Demand. Functionally related to the independent variable M (Maintenance Schedule).

Cathexis (1949) or appetite (1938). A joint function of demand and certain properties of the object cathected, the goal-object.

Expectancy (1932; 1949) or hypothesis 1938). Functionally related to ΣOBO, a frequency notion, but most recently related also to motivation (1949) though *not* necessarily, he says, to need-reduction. There are three moods (or, variously, *modes*) of expectancy: perception, inference and mnemonization.

Means-end-readiness (1932). This variable is not clearly anchored; however, there seem to be two classes: a means-end-readiness may be an innately given tendency to make certain responses in given environments under various demands; in addition, it may refer to ("field-cognition modes"; 1949) a second-order disposition to acquire such first-order dispositions (3, pp. 472-481) as perceptions, mnemonizations and inferences.

Differentiation (1938). Functionally related to stimuli; the reference is to experimental facts more generally called *discrimination.* The concept seems not to warrant separate status; it is an instance in which a parameter of a function describing another intervening variable, the drawing apart of expectancies, has been given separate status as though it were another "variable."

Motor skill (1938) or motor patterns (1949). A dispositional concept relating to the organism's motor potentialities.

Biases (1938). Functionally related to P, the pattern of preceding and succeeding maze units. As stated previously in the discussion of the independent variable P, the utility of giving these separate status from expectancies (as a function of ΣOBO) is not clear.

Equivalence beliefs (1949). These differ from cathexes in that the object of a cathexis is actually ingested, copulated with, etc., while the object of an equivalence belief is a sort of "foyer," anteroom, or place where cathected objects are found. They would seem to play a role somewhat comparable to that of "secondary reinforcers" in S-R-reinforcement theories.

Drive discrimination (1949). These would seem, on the independent variable side, to be anchored to the same variables as are cathexes; on the dependent variable side they seem to be undifferentiable from them. Thus, to say that a rat "knows that he is thirsty rather than hungry" presumably means among other things, that he will go wherever water is, engage in consummatory behavior with respect to water, etc. The category of equivalence beliefs means that water jars and nozzles will be cathected by him; together these would seem to cover all of the *data* that are covered by "drive discrimination." The drive-discrimination variable specifies a qualification on the cathexis statement by asserting that all demands do not indiscriminately affect all cathexes.

Relations Assumed Among Constructs

These constructs, as enumerated above, have not been formally related to one another; if they had been, the occasional difficulties in discriminating the differences between them might vanish either through the additional definition which the relating itself would provide, or through a redefinition by Tolman himself if the relating reveals that some of the variables are functionally indistinguishable.

There is available (128, p. 407) what appears to be a mixed causal-functional chain of variables leading to a final response occurrence. The diagram is incomplete for the present purpose, since it does not include all the proposed intervening variables. This chain runs as follows:

(1) Starting with Stimulus Variables, these *lead to* discriminanda and manipulanda-expectations, related to the organism's capacities (capacity variables: discriminanda and manipulanda capacities) which function here as parameter values;

(2) The discriminanda-manipulanda-expectations thus established lead to a Sign-Gestalt-Expectation, depending parametrically on the organism's means-ends-capacities (that is, capacities for perception, mnemonization and inference). It is not clear here whether the Sign-Gestalt-Expectation is supposed also to depend on the means-end-*readinesses,*

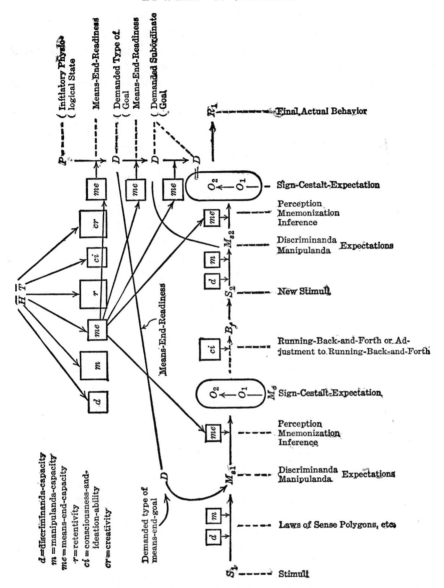

FIG. 4. From E. C. Tolman, *Purposive Behavior in Animals and Men.* New York: Appleton-Century, 1932. P. 407.

which include not only the "endowment" (capacity) but also the past-training values of perception, mnemonization and inference, but presumably it does.

(3) This Sign-Gestalt-Expectation leads to "Running back-and-forth or adjustment to Running-back-and-forth" (an earlier form of *VTE?*)

depending parametrically on the O's consciousness-and-ideation-ability.

(4) As a result of this Running-back-and-forth (VTE) the O provides himself with S_2 (new stimuli, presumably both exteroceptive and interoceptive) which lead to new manipulanda-discriminanda expectations, thence to new sign-gestalt expectations, with the same parameters affecting these linkages.

(5) Throughout the chain, the Demand variable has been present; "These depending demands control the whole line of the $S \to R$ process" (p. 407). An initial physiological state leads to a "Demanded Type of Goal" (presumably this means *demand for a given* type of goal) depending on means-end-readinesses, innate and acquired, and also demand for subordinate (equivalence belief) goals.

(6) The all-important linkage to response is handled rather casually as follows (p. 407): "[These demands lead the organism] to respond to the given S as presenting an appropriate means-object."

It has been repeatedly pointed out by Tolman's critics that this sort of diagram is really not a *system* or a proposed set of laws, but rather a framework *for* laws, in which we are told *what is related to what* in the construct system but not much (if anything) about the character of the relations.

Methodological Characteristics

Explicitness of formulation. Until the publication, in 1949, of the article, "There is more than one kind of learning" (151), the explicitness of Tolman's system was limited to a statement of the *kinds* of variables and kinds of axioms that he intends to use (see *Purposive Behavior in Animals and Men*, pp. 372-374, for his list of "modified and new laws" for conditioned response, trial and error, and inventive learning). The 1949 article discusses the laws of acquisition, de-acquisition and forgetting of cathexes, equivalence beliefs and (field) expectancies. The explicitness of these laws may be estimated by a consideration of them separately.

For *cathexes*, acquisition depends upon the adequacy of the object for physiological need reduction, and it is guessed that "numbers of repetitions and amounts of need reduction per repetition would, no doubt, turn out to be the two major causal variables and that the curves would undoubtedly be exponential in form" (151, p. 147). For de-acquisition, if need reduction following, say, the ingestion of food could be prevented, the cathexis for such food would weaken. Cathexes are not, however, forgotten with the mere passage of time.

For *equivalence beliefs*, primacy, frequency and intensity of need-reductions, as well as early traumatic experiences, are tentatively suggested as the principal causal factors in acquisition. There is no guess as to the condition of de-acquisition (although this is recognized as a major clinical problem; the neurotic may be thought of as having erroneous equivalence beliefs). As for forgetting, Tolman admits that the evidence is small, but postulates that equivalence beliefs are not forgotten but have to be unlearned. It can be seen here that, within the limits of the tentativity of these "axioms," an additional differentiation between cathexes and equivalence beliefs is suggested in the clear difference in their laws; cathexes weaken if need-reduction is withheld, but the hall-mark of the equivalence belief is the substitute acceptability of a *means* for an *end*. and hence the continued strength of an equivalence belief without need-reduction. This seems to put Tolman with Allport in the matter of functional autonomy.

For *field expectancies* (the older sign-gestalt-expectations and the newer cognitive maps), the factors of acquisition are frequency and motivation. "But this does not mean that I hold that such learning consists in the stamping in of *S-R* habits by reinforcement . . . [a goal] . . . probably does give a special vividness to that locus in the total field expectancy" (151, p. 151). To these must be added the perceptual, mnemonic and inference *abilities* of the organism. De-acquisition occurs when, and only when, the environment changes so that the previous expectancy is unsuitable; hence de-acquisition is an "interference" at the cognitive level. As to forgetting of expectancies, true forgetting with the passage of time does occur; particulars may be lost, in the Bartlett-Gestalt sense of simplifying and sharpening.

For *motor patterns*, Tolman points out (151, p. 146) that these "have to be included by me, since I do not hold, as do most behaviorists, that all learning is, as such, the attachment of responses to stimuli." To include them, Tolman expresses a willingness to agree with Guthrie that *movements* are learned rather than *acts*, and the Guthrian formulation of conditioning by contiguity is accepted with a protest that movements which are learned are "embedded in a larger goal-directed activity." These movements, when learned, are available to the organism for trying out in new situations. Great caution would seem to be required in the interpretation of these assertions; if they are taken quite literally, a good case could be made that these "laws" of movement acquisition involve a striking concession, if not an essential capitulation, to the peripheral (as opposed to the central) entailments of an *S-R* or *S-R*-reinforcement theory. Unfortunately, Tolman has not been very explicit as to the limits of this agreement with Guthrie. If, however, we attend to other very clear statements as to the central character of a learned expectancy, and to the spirit of the system, we note: "Cathexes, equivalence beliefs, field expectancies, field-cognition modes and drive discriminations are not, as I define them, stimulus-response connections. They are central phenomena, each of which may be expressed by a variety of responses. The actual nature of these responses is, however, also determined by the character of the motor patterns at the organism's command" (151). Perhaps an acceptable translation would be: *given* the final field expectancy, the *form* of the responses may be a motor habit. The problem of getting to the response has always been considered to be a special problem for Tolman. Part IV of this section will consider this "problem of getting to the response" and offer one kind of suggestion for its solution.

Tolman has only recently offered the above axioms; they are seen to be very tentative and imprecise. These are not, of course, sufficient grounds for criticism; the sense in which they are criticizable will be noted in the section in this chapter dealing with our own suggestions toward axiomatization.

Quantitativeness. Tolman's system would seem to be so constituted as to permit quantification, but the step has never been taken. Hilgard (37) has stated:

> In spite of a clear outline of what a systematic theory ought to be, Tolman has nowhere attempted quantitative predictions paralleling those of Hull, so that his conjectures have not, in that sense, been put to the test. This does not mean that his experiments are unrelated to his theory. There are, in fact, many predictions, but they assert that one path will be preferred to another, that under one set of circumstances the problem will be easier than another set, and so on. The dimensional analysis that completes the function is not provided (p. 265).

It is difficult to make an assessment of the degree of quantification of this or any other theory. See Part IV, this section, for a possible "scale of quantification," with remarks as to Tolman's position on it.

Consistency and independence of the postulate set. In order really to evaluate the consistency of Tolman's system, explicit formalization is a necessary first step. Since this has not been taken, the evaluation is impossible. Similarly, since to show that the postulates are independent would involve showing that none can be derived from the others as theorems, the proof of independence would presuppose an explicitness of axiomatization not present in Tolman. Formal treatments of the question of independence are hardly necessary at this stage of behavior theory.

Models. Tolman has not used models in his system-making up to 1949.

Techniques of derivation. The derivation of experimental results from Tolman's system is, due to the informal axiomatization which characterizes it, exclusively informal. To illustrate this informality, it is an interesting exercise to note in a recent paper by Tolman ". . . the actual experiments . . . out of many which I have selected to report . . . which seem especially important in reinforcing the theoretical position I have been presenting" (150, p. 193), and to examine critically his method of relating these *to* the theory. He treats of five classes of experiments:

(1) *Latent learning.* In discussing the results of the Blodgett experiment, Tolman says:

It will be observed that the experimental groups as long as they were not finding food did not appear to learn much. (Their error curves did not drop.) But on the days immediately succeeding their first finding of the food their error curves did drop astoundingly. It appeared, in short, that during the non-rewarded trials these animals had been learning much more than they had exhibited. This learning . . . Blodgett called "latent learning." Interpreting these results anthropomorphically, we would say that as long as the animals were not getting any food at the end of the maze they continued to take their time in going through it—they continued to enter many blinds. Once, however, they knew they were to get food, they demonstrated that during these preceding non-rewarded trials they had learned where many of the blinds were. They had been building up a "map," and could utilize the latter as soon as they were motivated to do so (pp. 194-195).

Aside from the fact that it is not quite correct to say that the error curve of the latent group did not drop in the latent phase, one could note that the actual "derivation" of latent learning phenomena *from* Tolman's theory here is simply not given. The tie-up is made only by pointing to it as a presumed instance. His earlier negative use of Blodgett's results, as a criticism of the law of effect, was clearer (128, p. 343).

(2) *Vicarious trial and error, or VTE:*

But what, now, is the final significance of all this *VTE*ing? . . . My answer is that these facts lend further support to the doctrine of a building up of maps. *VTE*ing, as I see it, is evidence that in the critical stages—whether in the first picking up of the instructions or in the later making sure of which stimulus is which—the animal's activity is not just one of responding passively to discrete stimuli, but rather one of the active selecting and comparing of stimuli (p. 200).

Here derivation is pursued by the device of opposing such vague, un-defined terms as "passively" and "discrete stimuli" to such phrases as "active selecting and comparing of stimuli." It is hardly possible to view this as acceptable deduction of experimental consequences, even within an avowedly incomplete theoretical structure.

To get from the axiom: *Organisms form maps,* to the theorem: *VTE occurs,* it is not sufficient, or even clearly relevant, to refer thus loosely to the contrasted *S-R* formulation. However, since it *is* referred to, one may question the incompatibility between the statements:

(a) Jumping to a white card is strengthened by a reinforcing consequence; jumping to a black card is weakened by its absence; and
(b) Animals look at the stimuli several times before they jump.

As a matter of fact, Spence (95) has shown how "non-passivity," or "paying systematic attention to the relevant stimuli," may be derived as a consequence of reinforcement theory. We are not concerned here, of course, to defend Spence's derivation. Even if it were rejected, the point is that Tolman seems to take as somehow obvious the relation between his (or Spence's) theory and the facts, letting such words as "passively" and "significant" serve as substitutes for an actual derivation. It may be that statements (*a*) and (*b*) above *are* incompatible in some way not clear to us; but surely their incompatibility needs to be exhibited by some line of argument.

(3) *Searching for the stimulus.* The experiment referred to is an unpublished one by Hudson in which rats failed to exhibit an avoidance response to a stimulus which disappeared coincidently with the administration of an electric shock. In commenting on this, Tolman says:

> I feel that this experiment reinforces the notion of the largely active selective character in the rat's building up of his cognitive map. He often has to look actively for the significant stimuli in order to form his map and does not merely passively receive and react to all the stimuli which are physically present (p. 201).

The alleged inference seems to hang chiefly on the vague and emotionally connotative word *passively*. The impossibility of deriving this "searching" on *S-R* principles also needs to be shown; and there is no move made toward showing it.

(4) *The "hypothesis" experiments.* Reference is made to the non-random response sequences exhibited by Krechevsky's rats when he presented them with an unsolvable problem in maze running. Again, Tolman does not relate this phenomenon to the theory.

(5) *The spatial orientation experiments.* None of these is explicitly derived in the article. However, the point of the spatial orientation series in supplying an evidential basis for a cognitive map view (and against *S-R* views) is somewhat obscure because of the failure of theorists on both sides to define clearly what they intend by "a response." This will be discussed at length below.

Two things may be said in respect to these five classes of experiments as supports for the cognitive map point of view: First, those which are offered as embarrassments of law-of-effect or contiguity formulations cannot be considered as arguments *for* the cognitive map formulation unless the competing systems are shown to be mutually exclusive *and* exhaustive. Secondly, there is no evidence of formal derivation in Tolman's discussion of them. It does seem as if these results might flow as consequences from "some such theory," and the failure to be able to show whether they would do so is due to the method of definition of concepts and the informality of the axiomatization.

It is appropriate now to refer back to the question of the definitions of the concepts, whose clarity has not increased much by noting their use in derivation. The argument might be made that, for example, the terms for which the Greek letters were substituted above are *implicitly* defined. Thus, when a critic asks for a definition of a certain term or expression which occurs in a scientific theory he may be answered simply by exhibiting all of the sentences of the theory. The "meaning" of a construct is disclosed by seeing it's role in the system. Philosophical workers in the field of logical analysis are increasingly aware of serious and involved problems in this area (9, 34, 82). To the extent that words occurring in the theorems have empirical coordinating definitions, and if the theorems really do follow from the axioms, then all of the words in the axioms are, so to speak, "given empirical meaning." Therefore, in an admittedly incomplete system the *truth* of the axioms is not only doubtful, but even the *meaning* of the terms partakes of a certain vagueness. Such a set of terms is said by Hempel to be "partially interpreted." There are many difficulties and unsolved problems here, and psychologists cannot afford to be dogmatic when the methodologists are in such doubt.

Recognizing this unsettled condition of the general issue, it seems admitted that the meanings of such implicitly defined terms, are, so to speak, nailed down by piling up the theorems derived from them. When a word, e.g., *hunger*, is found in several contexts, it is possible to "take a fix" on it, to carry out what Feigl has called "triangulation in logical space." The defining of terms by exhibiting their formal roles presupposes, however, a formal role to exhibit; hence, discussion of implicit definitions in Tolman's system has necessarily been delayed. The Greek letters in our expansion of the "Inference" construct might be justified as introduced by implicit definitions via the system as a whole, were it explicitly axiomatized. But, as has been shown, these derivations are "informal," when they are not simply absent! In such a system it is hardly possible to speak of implicit definitions since the formal role of a construct cannot very well be exhibited informally. We conclude that Tolman's formulations do not permit any satisfactory implicit definitions for the "operational" ones he officially advocates.

Empirical Content and Adequacy

Range of data purported covered. Tolman's is obviously intended to be a "complete" psychology of "docile" behavior. In all fairness, it must be said that he is under no illusion that he has, indeed, completed it. It has been noted previously that rats in mazes have nearly exclusively been his source of empirical support, so that at least he could be considered as intending to develop a fairly complete theory of maze behavior. Whether the laws of learning as "laid bare" in, or by, the rat, will ever constitute a complete psychology in a broader sense is a question that cannot be answered until its own laws are reasonably complete; but this is applicable to any theory and is hardly uniquely remarkable of Tolman.

Specificity of prediction demonstrated. Insofar as Tolman's is not a highly quantified system, predictions from it have been, perhaps exclusively, of a *presence or absence, right or left, more or less, faster or slower* sort. Insofar as the axioms and derivations are informally stated, it is not always clear whether the predictions that have been made follow from the theory or whether they are, as some are admittedly, guesses made anthropomorphically or on the basis of common sense.

Obvious failure to handle facts. Since the derivation of experimental results has been characterized by extreme informality, gaps in the theory are difficult to detect. There is, at least, a vocabulary with which to discuss most of the data of learning, although the quantitative vocabulary is lacking as the theory now stands. The inadequacies of definition of the principal constructs (as pointed out earlier) suggest that more complete operational definition of the concepts would make them unsuitable for some of the explanatory sentences in which they now stand. A more flexible method, and one more likely to preserve the connotations of the constructs as Tolman now uses them, would be to define these terms implicitly, in which case a test of the adequacy of the theory with respect to the data would depend upon the explicitness of the axiomatization. But as neither of these steps has been taken, the range of applicability of the theory is nearly impossible to assess. The temptation to over-estimate the utility of the concepts is heightened by the non-technical connotations that accrue to such words as "expect" and "infer."

There are certain guarantees built into the system which may be used to account for failures of prediction. Thus, *emphasis,* as a relatively undefined property associated with motivation, may be used to account for the failure of the rats in one type of latent learning study (called Type 4 below) to learn where a non-valenced goal-object is to be found; or "fixation" of responses by overlearning, or emotion, may be used to account for failures of place-learning. We do not mean to suggest that these concepts are intrinsically without merit; but until they have been more carefully defined and quantified, there is no clear restraint on their *ad hoc* usage.

Programmaticity

The most serious obstacle to an evaluation of the cognitive learning theory of Tolman is the unspecificity of its axiom set. Tolman has shown a tendency to restate the system by revising its vocabulary (i.e., "sign-gestalt-expectations" become "cognitive maps") and by recounting illustrative experiments (often mainly because they are disquieting to the law of effect theorist, though only thus deviously related to the affirmative side of the cognition theorist's argument). The programmatic nature of this system is most clearly suggested by noting that in 1932 *Purposive Behavior in Animals and Men* lists (pp. 372-374) only the *kinds* of laws that will be needed in a purposive behaviorism; and in 1949 he says, "And although, as usual, I have been merely programmatic and have not attempted to set up, at this date, any precise systems of postulates and deduced theorems, I *have* made some specific suggestions . . ." (151, p. 154).

III. ABILITY OF TOLMAN'S THEORY TO ACCOUNT
FOR FACTS NOT PREDICTABLE FROM
COMPETING THEORIES

If we ignore the question of whether such facts are accounted for by Tolman's theory as it stands, we can note that the data of the *latent learning* studies are the kind which Tolman intends to account for, and for which he believes S-R and S-R-reinforcement theories are inadequate. The experimental designs which are used to test for latent learning are very diversified; Thistlethwaite has reviewed this literature (106). In general, latent learning is revealed in an abrupt, or somehow discontinuous, change in response tendency when drive and incentive are first irrelevantly matched (the latent learning period) and then relevantly matched (the test period or trial) in a given experimental setting. "Relevant" and "irrelevant" are definable in terms of maintenance schedule operations, behavior of the organism in the presence of the incentive, etc. "Abruptness" may be given statistical definition, as a significant shift from the random or systematic response tendencies before the drive-incentive matching experience (as in the T-maze studies, the behavior of the rat running the maze hungry for the first time after previous exposure to a food incentive in the maze while satiated for food; or as in the Blodgett design, the reduction in cul-entries when rats first find food in the maze after having run the maze while hungry but without food in the goal-box).

Part of the question with respect to the latent learning studies is the extent to which they do reveal inadequacies in the S-R-reinforcement formulations. From this standpoint, certain of the designs seem to us not to be determinate, as will be seen below. In this regard, it may be noted that the reinforcement theorist's use of the r_G construct, at least its use according to a broad definition in which no peripheral event is entailed, can apparently mediate any outcome which a cognition theorist would call an "expectancy." The r_G construct *with* a peripheral event entailed is equally powerful (although severely strained for the Blodgett and free maze exploration types), but then the burden of proof of the peripheral activity presumably falls on the user of the concept.

Five categories of latent learning studies are noted:

1. *The Blodgett type.* Drive is strong and unmanipulated (by maintenance schedule) throughout; the incentive is introduced later in a series of maze runs. Latent learning is revealed by the error record on the trial subsequent to the first feeding in the maze if the drop in errors is larger than the first, or the largest single, drop in the error curve of a control group which has been fed from the first run, or by a steeper drop in errors from the same level on the ordinate. There have been nine such studies reported; of these, seven have been interpreted as positive [Blodgett (2),

Elliott (23), Herb (35), Simmons (89), Tolman and Honzik (162), Wallace, Blackwell and Jenkins (184), and Williams (186)]. Two are negative [Meehl and MacCorquodale (65), Reynolds (76)]. The "latent" groups in both these studies showed considerably more error reduction during the latent phase than Blodgett's did.

The Blodgett experiment is extensively cited as *the case* for which S-R-reinforcement theory is inadequate, and it is often used to display the difference between S-R-reinforcement and cognition theories. Hence it is important to examine its design and the results it provides to determine whether it is, indeed, an *experimentum crucis* in any respect.

The core of the argument from the Blodgett design concerns the drop in errors following a reinforcement introduced after a series of less strongly rewarded maze runs. It is not the fact of, but the size of, this error reduction that is crucial. S-R-reinforcement theory predicts a drop in errors following the first rewarded run; but cognition theorists assert that this drop is actually greater than reinforcement principles can account for, and thus that in the pre-reinforcement runs "learning that didn't show" was taking place. As an estimate of the magnitude of error reduction to be predicted from one reinforcement, the cognition theorist points to the error drop occurring after the first reinforcement of a *control* group, which is fed on its first run. The comparison may also be made against the largest single drop in errors shown by the control group, or against the drop made by the controls from the same point on the ordinate. The third of these comparisons has the most methodological soundness in terms of learning curves, and we shall confine our discussion to it as an example of the difficulties met in interpreting the findings of the Blodgett experiment. The important question to answer here is whether the reinforcement operation by being performed not on the first, but on, say, the seventh run would actually be presumed by the S-R-reinforcement theorist to have the same effect on error scores. By his theory the effects of a given reinforcement upon the habit strengths of the two groups may be equal, but the drop in the error scores ($_sE_R$) may still be unequal if other variables which affect the *utilization* of habit strengths are unequal at the times involved in the comparison.

Two major variables specified by S-R-reinforcement theory as affecting the probability of response when habit strength is constant are (1) drive and (2) competing $_sE_R$'s. If in the Blodgett experiment reductions in errors following a reinforcement are to be used to measure the resulting shifts in *habit strength* (not $_sE_R$) the structure of the experiment should be inspected for its guarantee that the conditions of drive and competing $_sE_R$'s are equal for the two groups at the times of the comparisons. "Guarantee" means showing that conditions for the two groups should theoretically be equal, except for the random factors which enter the error term of the significance test.

The burden of this proof of equality rests with the user of this design if he intends to demonstrate the inadequacy of reinforcement theory to account for *as much* learning as is observed. The S-R-reinforcement theorist need not, actually, show that these other factors are *in fact* unequal in this design, if he can show from findings in other experimental settings that the different histories of the two groups *might have* produced systematic differences in either drive or competing response tendencies by the times the comparisons are made, and that these differences would be in the direction which favors a larger drop in errors by the experimental group. If this can be done, the cognition theorist's argument that these histories have produced differences unaccounted for by reinforcement principles is vitiated. Only to the extent that in the Blodgett design "equal errors" implies "equal habit strength" is the cognition theorist's argument *from* the Blodgett design valid; to the extent this equivalence does not hold, the argument is invalid. The Blodgett type of experiment is cited by cognition theorists as inexplicable by S-R-reinforcement theory. In such an argument, one must obviously allow the S-R-reinforcement theorist *all* of his theory when he is asked to account for the results. Consequently the burden of proof upon the cognition theorist includes a showing that the conditions for any comparison within the framework of S-R-reinforcement theory have been met by the experimental design.

It seems doubtful that he can do so. When the comparison in the Blodgett design is between the Experimentals' post-reward drop and the drop in the Control's curve from the same point on the ordinate which characterized the Experimentals on their first rewarded run, what should be the S-R-reinforcement prediction? S-R theory predicts that the effects of reinforcement would be equal for the two groups only if the two groups are shown to be equal in *three* additional respects: (1) the initial $_sH_R$'s must be the same; (2) the increment to $_sH_R$ must be the same; (3) following the reward with the resulting and still equal $_sH_R$'s, drive and competing $_sE_R$'s must be the same so that the equal $_sH_R$'s will yield equal post-reward error scores, hence equal drops in the error curve. Let us examine these three required assumptions.

Consider first the assumption of equality of the $_sH_R$'s at the point of comparison. In the cognition argument this is claimed from the equal height of the ordinates just *before* the experimental group is reinforced. But equal performance implies equal $_sH_R$'s only, again, if (1) the drive states of the two groups are equal, and (2) competing responses are equal. There is some reason to doubt that in the Blodgett experiment the drive states of the two groups were equal at the times the "corresponding" reinforcements were given. If the comparison made is with reference to an ordinate reached by the controls at any time subsequent to their first maze run, S-R-reinforcement theory implies some degree of drive inequality favoring the controls, on the basis of conditioned motivation.

Exteroceptive maze cues should become elicitors for some of the components of hunger-drive as a result of the feeding experiences in the maze situation, so that after one or more food-rewarded runs the controls should be psychologically "hungrier" than the experimentals on the same maintenance schedule who have not, however, been getting fed in the maze. This concept of conditioned drive was explicitly set forth in Hull's 1949 postulate set (39, Postulate III, Corollary i, p. 175) and appears in his posthumous book (40, Postulate III, Corollary i, p. 6). Earlier (1941) but less formally, the notion was developed and extensively utilized by Miller and Dollard in their application of S-R-reinforcement theory to the human social case (68, Chap. IV and *passim*). Once the idea that there are stimulus and response components of drive is admitted, the occurrence of drive-conditioning flows readily as a consequence of the postulates proposed by Hull in his 1943 book (38). Several experimental approaches to this concept are possible, one of which we have taken in an experiment modified from Blodgett's (67). We showed that a feeding experience in a maze-like situation, *not* following a maze run and *not* at the goal-box end (or in its direction), produced a significant drop in errors and faster running, with no further maze exposure to yield an increment in habit strengths (or cognitions, for that matter). This finding would seem to support a suspicion that Blodgett's experimentals must have lacked some of the evocative drive of the controls, due to the lack of opportunity for acquiring such conditioned motivation. In a series of studies utilizing a different experimental setting, Seward, Datel, and Levy (86) attempted to test our hypothesis, with equivocal results. *If* the experimentals, on their last pre-food-reward day, are less motivated than the controls on their comparison day, a matching of ordinates (reaction potentials) implies a systematic *unmatching* of habit strengths. That is, at a comparable level of performance the experimentals (being less motivated) must have more habit strength favoring the correct path than the controls. The food-reward given for the first time at the *end* of this run makes available, on the following day, a heightened drive factor. According to Hullian theory, this increment acts mathematically as a *multiplier* of any habit-strength differences between true path and culs, and (under a suitably chosen range of parametric assumptions) should produce a steeper drop than that given by the habit-strength increment at some post-initial stage of the acquisition process.

During the latent phase, the experimentals are accumulating $_sH_R$ favoring the true path. Two replications of the Blodgett experiment (65, 76) show considerable error reduction before the first feeding of the experimentals; Tolman and Honzik's curves show the beginning of such a reduction. It must, of course, not be forgotten that this first rewarded run *also* contributes an increment to habit strength. On our assumption that the experimentals' "unmanifested" habit strength exceeds that of the controls when the latter's ordinate was comparable to that of the experimentals immediately pre-reward, the $_sH_R$ increment yielded by one food-reward should be less for the experimentals (due to the decelerated form of the $_sH_R$-acquisition function). This complication operates in opposition to the effect just discussed. Whether it would be sufficient in amount to obscure the hypothesized effect entirely involves several rather complex quantitative questions, not readily (if at all) answerable within the Blodgett design itself. Avoiding rash assumptions about these matters, it seems legitimate to argue that the drive-conditioning hypothesis must be given serious consideration as one of the contributors to the Blodgett effect; and that, in the light of our present ignorance of the parameter questions involved, it cannot be excluded as a possible S-R-reinforcement explanation of the phenomenon.

But even this does not exhaust the complications which the design generates within a Hull-type theory, and, presumably, for any form of S-R-reinforcement theory made sufficiently explicit to predict for the maze case. In the preceding discussion we have treated the habit strength and drive multiplier as if they were associated with some abstract, "generalized" choice-point; so that the quantitative arguments relating changes in these variables to the observed datum (total errors per maze run) would hold strictly only if the relative effects of conditioned motivation and $_sH_R$ increment were not different over the several maze units. And this is surely not the case. Having been given food-rewards in the goal-box, the controls (when manifesting any given level of "performance" defined as total errors) can be assumed on the basis of other maze studies to show a start-to-goal error gradient, although Blodgett does not present an error breakdown by units. This gradient should be less distinct for the experimentals, who (when at a comparable total-error performance level) have been operating on the basis of non-alimentary incentives and for whom the goal-box as such must be presumed to be less rewarding. In other words, the "total correct choices" for the experimentals on their last pre-food-reward day is very probably distributed *more equally over the six units* than is the same quantity for the controls. This situation creates a further asymmetry in the relation of the two sorts of strengthening operations being compared (drive-conditioning versus $_sH_R$-increment due to the reward); and the asymmetry favors a Blodgett effect. For when the drive-conditioning factor is already present (control group), the increment in $_sH_R$ given by one additional food-reward *cannot* be assumed to be equal over all six units, and in fact, in the case of units in which an error was made during the run in question, the impact of the terminating goal-box reward is a very delicate question. It might conceivably even be negative at such early stages of learning as the second or third day, before secondary reinforcement has moved back far enough to create a series of supporting sub-goals. One would, therefore, expect the $_sH_R$ increments yielded by a single food-reward for the controls to be unequally distributed over the six units, varying considerably from rat to rat depending upon just what he did (and the all-important temporal factors of his doing it!) on the run in question; but, statistically speaking, being progressively feebler as we consider units more remote from the goal.

For the experimentals, with a more equalized $_sH_R$ difference from unit to unit, the drive-conditioning operation should theoretically exert a more massive effect, since it operates mathematically as a *multiplier applied to all six units at once.* A little computation with plausible quantitative examples will convince the reader that this asymmetry between the reward as an $_sH_R$-increaser and the reward as a drive-conditioner can, within a considerable range of parametric assumptions, make a marked difference in the performance error-drop. A fairly direct test of the above reasoning would probably require a longer maze and large numbers of animals, since the Blodgett maze is very highly patterned as to error-frequencies and the sixth unit is so quickly eliminated (even by non-fed animals) as to yield an essentially five-unit maze after very little exposure.

Consider next the third necessary assumption, that of the equality of competing response tendencies. The chief competing response tendencies involved in maze running may be subsumed under the general rubric "exploratory disposition." Whether it is appropriate to speak of the exploratory disposition as a *drive* or not we need not discuss here. It does seem to have at least some drive properties, such as dependence upon a maintenance schedule and an energizing effect upon behavior capable of overcoming opposing incentives such as shock. Whether we speak of it as a drive or not, the fundamental operation known to weaken exploratory behavior is repeated exposure (18, 19, 20, 58, 69, 70, 71, 187) and this has been permitted to the animals in Blodgett's experimental group to the extent that their first food-rewarded run is delayed until later in the series of maze exposures. No one who has observed rats during their early exposures to a maze could dismiss the exploratory disposition as of negligible strength. Not to mention the specific experimental quantification of this "need" in the Columbia obstruction-box studies, one thinks of such informal (but common) observations as the long latency in eating shown by 24-hour hungry rats in a novel situation, and the frequent interruptions of this overlearned consummatory behavior by the competing "investigatory" responses. We have unpublished data showing that if hungry rats have been run and rewarded in the Blodgett maze with culs blocked off, the number of trials being more than sufficient to yield errorless runs as this maze is ordinarily used, unblocking the blind alleys leads nearly every rat into every cul. We have also shown (58) that the tendency to enter a cul is an inverse function of the "total past penetration" into it, quite apart from any reward associated with getting to the maze end.

These considerations show that what is customarily designated as a "learning curve" in multiple-unit maze studies is *not* a pure learning curve (either in the sense of habits or cognitions), but is a composite curve—the resultant of interaction between the underlying course of learning and the reduction ("satiation" or "negative adaptation") in the exploratory tendency. The usual maze experiment presumably gives us a very obscured indication of the building up of habits or cognitions; we do not know what the form and parameters of the acquisition function would be like for an "ideal rat," constructed so as to be a pure $_sH_R$-accumulator (*or* knowledge-acquirer). We suggest, however, that the kind of performance curve exhibited by Blodgett's experimentals, once their food-reward is introduced, is a better approximation to the idealized case of a learning process uncontaminated by emotional and investigatory interferences—a better mirror of the underlying acquisition function—than is the usual "maze-learning" curve as represented by the controls. Regardless of the stand one takes on this question, it seems fair to say that matching performance ordinates is *not*, prima facie, matching the underlying $_sH_R$'s, but rather is systematically unmatching them. Here, however, the presumed (correct-path) $_sH_R$ favors the controls, since their ordinate is a resultant of the influence of the true-path $_sE_R$'s and an opposed "exploratory" $_sE_R$ which is stronger than that of the experimentals (on a later day). The impact upon $_sH_R$ of a food-reward is thus greater for the experimentals, making the usual Hullian assumption of deceleration for the $_sH_R$-acquisition function. Hence the decline in errors following this reward should be steeper than that for the controls starting from an equated performance level.

But there are still additional complications. Whatever the impact of the single food-reward upon the habit strengths, what of the competing exploratory $_sE_R$'s on the *next* trial? We have suggested that the effect of the first food-reward upon the next day's choices for the experimentals may be looked upon as the "pure, unadulterated" consequence of reinforcement, now unimpeded by the interference of exploratory responses. Whether this factor works "for" or "against" the Blodgett effect depends upon further quantitative issues. If one thinks of the effective $_sE_R$ for true path as a linear resultant of the exploratory $_sE_R$'s for cul (*and* true path!) together with the new $_sE_R$ contributed by food-reward, the *form* of the exploratory-satiation function becomes all-important. If it is markedly decelerated, this summative process works counter to a Blodgett effect; since the decrement in cul-$_sE_R$ between two early trials (control group) should exceed that between two late trials (experimentals). If it is approximately linear over the interval concerned, this complication can be ignored, and the above development predicts ₹

Blodgett effect. If, finally, it is ogival, and the flex point lies somewhere between the abscissas determined by the equating of performance ordinates, whether a Blodgett effect were favored or not would depend upon the slopes at the two points of the ogive.

The preceding discussion treats the exploratory disposition as if its only contribution to the situation lay in its role as an $_sE_R$ for cul entry, competing with the "correct" $_sE_R$'s. Again, even superficial familiarity with the actual character of a "naive" rat's early maze behavior shows that this is a gross oversimplification. In terms of S-R-reinforcement reconstructions of maze-learning, the greater strength *and variability* of such concurrent investigatory responses as halting, reversal, standing up, sniffing in corners, freezing, sudden spurts and the like, so characteristic of the less adapted rat, should theoretically reduce the efficiency of the various mediating mechanisms (e.g., chaining effects, secondary reinforcement, "pure stimulus acts," drive conditioning) and hence attenuate the impact of a reward given at the termination of a run.

It must be emphasized that the entire preceding discussion of the probable role of competing $_sE_R$'s contains lacunae at several critical stages due to our experimental ignorance of certain quantitative matters; and that some of the possibilities work in directions antithetical to others, although to an unknown extent. None of the behavioral tendencies invoked are purely *ad hoc*, however, being here carried over from empirical findings in other setups. Some of them have received reasonably direct support within the Blodgett situation itself. At the least, it seems fair to say that the required assumption of equality of competing $_sE_R$'s is not prima facie justified, but, if anything, rather unlikely. The core difficulty seems to be that any experimental procedure which allows a rat an opportunity to establish *either* cognitions or habits in a maze will also, unavoidably, permit him to adapt emotionally and "satiate" his exploratory drive. To the extent that he has, S-R-reinforcement theory predicts that the effect of one reinforcement will be, if not an exactly specifiable amount, at least greater than that for an unadapted, unsatiated animal.

A final complicating factor in the Blodgett design is that we are unable to state definitely that the two groups are equal in unconditioned drive strength. The crucial reinforcements are given at times when the two groups have been on the feeding cycle for different periods. In Blodgett's experiment a pre-experimental feeding cycle was in effect only three days; thus the control group was first reinforced on the fourth day, while one experimental group was first reinforced as late as the tenth day after inception of the cycle. We attempted (65) to reduce the relative discrepancy necessarily involved here by extending the pre-experimental feeding cycle to *seven* days. It is surely possible that by the time of its first feeding, the experimental group, with its longer history of deprivation periods, has an accumulated deficit which makes it hungrier. It would be difficult to do, but the design would seem to require that a prolonged pre-experimental feeding cycle be used, to ensure that both groups are at the asymptote of (unconditioned) drive strength for the deprivation period used (22 hours) and the amount of food given. It seems unlikely that such stability could be achieved unless the amount of food given were carefully calibrated so as to ensure day-to-day equality of drive strength for "22-hour hungry rats." The literature on the effect on $_sH_R$ of deprivation at the time of reinforcement is ambiguous (6, 29, 44, 60, 77, 103); the functions seem not to be linear or even monotonic, but the evidence does not preclude drive level's acting as a parameter in the acquisition function. If there is a range over which this relationship is positive, and if the Blodgett design is operating within it, the influence for the experimental group opposes the action of conditioned drive, presumed (as we have seen) to be *less* for the experimentals before and at the time of its first reinforcement. But on the other hand, it suggests that the $_sH_R$ for the experimentals must *have been* lower than that of the controls on the matched run, and, therefore, that the $_sH_R$-increment yielded by the terminal reinforcement should be larger for the experimentals due to the deceleration of the $_sH_R$-acquisition function. Hence this possible inequality in unconditioned drive works at two points in the intervening variable chain in favor of a Blodgett effect, and at one point in opposition.

Whatever its effect at the time of reinforcement, drive strength is clearly at issue as a relevant variable on the first post-reinforcement run, when the $_sH_R$'s created earlier are "activated." In predicting the size of the drops for the two groups, the possibility of this difference and its direction must be taken into account—conjointly, of course, with the differences between the $_sH_R$'s and competing response tendencies of the two groups just previously discussed.

We seem to have a plethora of contradictory hypotheses to account, reinforcement-wise, for various Blodgett-design phenomena. The fact that there are so many and some subsets of them are contradictory shouldn't reflect on them, nor does it unsettle us: the point is that the Blodgett design *presupposes* the availability of a valid estimate of the experimentals' error drop. Our welter of hypotheses shows that making this estimate is just not feasible.

Since this is a chapter on Tolman, not Hull, we have not commented upon the derivation of the Blodgett effect which appeared with Hull's last book (40, pp. 140-148). Hull's analysis has not, at this writing, been the subject of discussion by Tolman's school. It invokes the new factor of incentive motivation, or K, in a manner mathematically analogous to our use of drive-conditioning. For a commentary on the K-component in Hull's revised (1949) postulate set (39) see the section by Koch in this volume. Our analysis into S-R-reinforcement terms uses the pre-1949 variant of the theory in which these problems have most commonly been discussed before.

It might be argued that this set of methodological considerations reveals a defect in S-R-reinforcement theory: the several variables affecting the dependent variable are not experimentally separable. But this is the case only in this setting; each of them can be shown in other experimental settings, and, as such, may be supposed by the usual processes of induction to be operating, even though their lack of quantification does not permit prediction beyond direction of sub-effects, in this more complex case.

2. *The free-exploration type.* In these studies, as in the Blodgett type, the manipulated variable is the incentive. Rats explore a maze freely, usually under conditions of increasing deprivation of food and water. The "test" condition involves feeding the now-hungry rats either following a run or directly in the goal-box. The criterion of latent learning is met if the exploration group make fewer than chance errors, or fewer errors than are made by a naive group on their first run. An experiment in which the first feeding occurs directly in the goal-box, not preceded by a run through the maze, does not give us any estimate of the effects of the free maze exploration alone. There is one such study [Buxton (5)]; this study was positive. The effects of free maze exploration uncomplicated by any feeding in the maze can be tested in the second type by noting the error scores for the first run on which the rats are fed. Where the data are reported [Daub (18), Haney (33)] it can be seen (although these authors do not point it out) that these rats, *even before reinforcement is ever encountered,* have developed dispositions to stay out of the culs during their free-exploration period. Four such studies are reported, all showing "positive" results [Daub (7), Haney (33), Karn and Porter (42), Lashley (51)]. MacCorquodale and Meehl (58) have shown that within a 15-minute period of free exploration of a multiple T-maze, rats will significantly reduce their tendencies to enter culs, and will on a subsequent day exhibit striking tendencies to choose "correctly" on a test run. In this latter experiment no food-reward, and indeed no reward of any kind, even mere return to the home cage, had been associated with "getting to the goal-box." Looking at the animals on their test run, it would be easy to project goal-seeking into their behavior, especially if a food-reward had been somehow paired with the goal-box.

The above data serve to substantiate some of the hypotheses, discussed above, that a Hullian could use to account for the Blodgett effect. Insofar as the free maze exploration design is a variant of the Blodgett design in which the latent period experience is free access to the maze rather than successive runs from start to end-box, some of the considerations that show the Blodgett design to be inappropriate in the role of *experi-*

mentum crucis show the free exploration design to be similarly inappropriate.

The next two types of latent learning study differ from the above in that the rats, during the latent phase, encounter an incentive for which they are operationally satiated. They may or may not be irrelevantly motivated and reinforced, and presumably some rewards are operating even in the satiated case, e.g., removal from the restraint of the maze, return to the home cage, etc. On the "test" trial the rats are run, after a period of deprivation, for the previously encountered but unwanted incentive.

3. *Incentive present with no competing strong drive.* Rats operationally satiated for food and water are given a series of runs in a T-maze (except that Szymanski used a multiple-unit T-maze) with the incentives present in opposite arms of the maze, or in one case, with both food and water present in the same arm [MacCorquodale and Meehl (57)]. Seven positive studies using this design have been performed [Meehl and MacCorquodale (64), MacCorquodale and Meehl (57), Spence and Lippitt (100), Spence, Bergmann and Lippitt (98), Seward, Levy and Handlon (87), Szymanski (104) and Thistlethwaite (107)]. There are two negative studies [Kendler (45) and Maltzman (61)]. It is interesting to note that in both of the studies in which it was tried [Spence and Lippitt (100), Meehl and MacCorquodale (64)] the rats were, after a successful "test" under conditions of deprivation for one of the incentives, unable to shift their responses when the deprivation conditions were shifted to the alternative incentive, and, at least in the Meehl and MacCorquodale study, the first, successful test response had not been reinforced.

This design is considerably freer from methodological defects than either the Blodgett or free-exploration designs. A positive result using it (and the percentage is higher than for most other designs) is more embarrassing to the S-R-reinforcement theorist. He can deduce a molar-descriptive "cognition" by positing the secondary reinforcement of fractional antedating responses to the goal-objects during the latent phase. To the extent that the drive inducing operation prior to the test run also strengthens antedating responses appropriate to the deficit, it may mediate correct turnings on the test (64). The difficulty with this explanation is the general vagueness of the r_G construct as to the conditions of its strengthening, its role as *elicitor*, and, finally, its specification as to locus. (See below for a discussion of the r_G concept in its relation to "cognition.") The implications of one such attempted derivation of descriptive cognition by use of the r_G concept (64) have been experimentally tested by Thistlethwaite (107) with results adverse to the S-R-reinforcement analysis.

4. *Incentive present with strong irrelevant (competing) drives.* Of

eighteen such studies, seven are positive [Bendig (1), Christie (14), Diesenroth and Spence (22), Strange (102), Thistlethwaite (108), Walker (182), and Walker, Knotter and DeValois (183)]; and eleven are negative [Christie (13), Fehrer (28), Gleitman (31), Grice (32), Kendler (46), Kendler and Mencher (49), Kendler and Kanner (48), Littman (54), Spence and Lippitt (101), Shaw and Waters (88) and Walker (180)]. The difficulties in accounting for the discrepancies between these studies are enormous. If one draws up a master table comparing the possibly relevant details between the positive and negative studies of this group, and with the generally positive studies of the previous (non-competing drive) group, he finds he can make only the broadest generalizations, to each of which exceptions can be found.

The only systematic difference between Types 3 and 4 seem to be the basis on which they were classified: whether the irrelevant incentive was encountered with or without a strong competing drive. In general, this design, in which the animal is tested for his cognitions of goal-objects encountered while he was strongly motivated for a different goal-object, takes too little account of other, explicitly stated, aspects of the cognition view to be a wholly adequate, or even fair, test of it. The "emphasis" value of an incentive is small when the organism is satiated for that incentive; it is less, or even frustrating, when he is motivated for another incentive, which he has encountered in this situation before. A further, and related, difference between these is that when the organism is motivated for one incentive during training he must be forced to the side of the T-maze containing the irrelevant incentive (except in those cases where the relevant incentive is placed in both arms of the maze); forcing is suggested as conducing to negative emotional conditioning to the side of the test incentive.

We have been unable to detect any clear-cut differences in method between the positive and negative studies within Type 4, incentive learning with strong competing drive. Although the drive *present* during the latent period has usually been thirst, these are about equally divided between the positive and negative, and of two studies in which the training drive was hunger, one is positive, one negative.

There is some evidence to suggest that irrelevant incentive learning is more likely if the relevant incentive during the latent period is symmetrically located in the maze, i.e., rats motivated for water find water on one side, food *and* water on the other. The necessity of forcing the animals to the side containing the irrelevant incentive is reduced by this method, and studies in which forcing is absent or minimal (involving a small percentage of runs) tend to give positive evidence of irrelevant incentive learning more often than studies in which forcing characterizes half or more of all trials [see Walker, Knotter and DeValois (183) for direct evidence on this variable].

The attempt to favor discriminability of the two arms of the T-maze by painting them black vs. white, by using a marked illumination difference in the two sides, or by using different coarseness of screening on the floors of the two sides, seems to be ineffective if not somewhat contrary to the aim; this is apparently due to the fact that such discriminative cues conduce to position habits. Most studies in which black vs. white alleys are used show a strong avoidance response to the white alley. Walker, Knotter and DeValois (183) have shown that rats who have developed strong position habits during the latent learning period are less likely to respond appropriately on the test trial, after motivation is shifted.

Training in drive discrimination, or at least experience in deprivation of the test incentive to match that for the training incentive, might favor irrelevant incentive learning (13). It would be profitable also to investigate the effect of providing additional alleys on the test trial, to discover whether those rats which shift performance on the test trial are *avoiding* the previously preferred alley (in which event they would choose equally among alternatives) or are indeed responding on the basis of earlier encounters with the incentive for which they are now motivated (in which case the alternative, "neutral" alleys should also be avoided).

The last latent learning design, Type 5, involves a first phase in which animals are run in or permitted to explore T-mazes whose goal-boxes are tactually or visually discriminable, usually hungry but without incentives present. The rats are subsequently fed *directly* in one goal-box, i.e., they are placed directly in the goal-box, or run through a straightway to it. The test of the learning of maze characteristics is made by reintroducing the rat to the entry box of the maze and observing his tendency to choose the side which leads to the goal-box in which he was fed. Tolman and Gleitman, after a training phase in which the rats were fed in both goal-boxes, shocked them in one end-box (withholding the usual food) and fed them (as usual) in the other—these experiences not following an actual run. The criterion measured was subsequent avoidance of the shock side of the maze. Four positive studies of this design have been reported [Tolman and Gleitman (159), Iwahara and Marx (41), Gilchrist (30), Seward (85)]; three are negative [Leeper (52), Denny and Davis (21), Seward, Datel and Levy (86—two of three replications, the third was positive)].

This design appears to be most like Type 3 in constituting, when the results are positive, an embarrassment to the S-R-reinforcement theorist. Here the r_G concept seems to us to be even more strained in use; the r_G's acquired during the latent phase are unrelated to the goal object and minimally reinforced. The "reinforcement" in the goal-box not following a run might strengthen the r_G's peculiar to that goal-box and thus the turn leading to it on the next run. But here, again, the lack of independent verification of the r_G event and its non-quantitative status reduce its utility.

We have four general comments to make upon this extensive and rather puzzling experimental literature. First, and of greatest importance, is the necessity for sufficient replication using each of the five designs to justify confidence that a describable design does consistently yield a certain (positive or negative) result. There is no satisfactory classification of experimental setups, even using multiple criteria, which permits a clear sorting into "positive" and "negative" outcomes, although Thistlethwaite's review (106) is a valuable contribution in that direction. One can only conclude that there is something wrong with our controls or with our standards for what constitutes an adequate description of them. It cannot be too strongly emphasized that there is little point in disputing about the causal interpretation of an experimental effect when we have not yet apparently described the conditions sufficient for obtaining it.

Secondly, even if finer sub-classes of designs can be finally made replicable, one must beware of assuming that because they are all called "latent learning," they must be explainable in the same, or even a similar, way. It is perfectly possible, for example, that the Blodgett effect is based upon satiation of exploratory drive in the experimentals, and is further enhanced by the drive-conditioning mechanism we hypothesized above; and yet that the positive findings which preponderate in Types 3 and 5 will ultimately find *their* explanation in cognition-theory terms.

Thirdly, cognition theory must be developed beyond the point where its proponents' main use of latent learning studies is in the form of criticizing "the opposition." The demand "How do you explain *that* one?" is, to be sure, not wholly obscurantist, since any finding clearly adverse to a theory is, indirectly, favorable to its competitors—provided they already have some inductive support of their own. But it seems legitimate to insist that failures to get "latent learning" pose a serious explanatory problem for cognition theorists, just as positive results do for the S-R-reinforcement view. Cognition theorists are not entitled to take the position that any positive design gives them their case, in spite of the negatives. Thistlethwaite has argued very insistently that ". . . it must be possible to demonstrate for *each* instance of latent learning or of irrelevant-incentive learning (1) that some source of reinforcement was operative in the experimental setup . . ." (106, p. 120). The word *demonstrate* in this quotation needs scrutiny. In any developed science, when we attempt to understand the complex case, we recognize that there may be great difficulties in experimental separation of the determining variables. Actually, most scientific experiments presuppose (i.e., do not attempt to prove, independently) a whole network of causal laws, including those relating hypothetical constructs, that have been confirmed in other research. Even the use of complex measuring apparatus would be impossible if this sort of inductive extrapolation were forbidden. So, we can accept Thistle-thwaite's desideratum only if a rather weak meaning is given to his word "demonstrate," somewhat like "render probable on the basis that factors present in the design have been shown in other designs to act as re-inforcers." If this weakened demand cannot be met, grave doubt is surely cast upon S-R-reinforcement theory. Whether such doubt gives *strong* support to cognition theory depends upon the difficulties of the latter, *and* upon the plausibility of still other causal models (e.g., S-R-theories not stressing reinforcement). Intermediate types, such as Seward's (84, 85) and the theory we shall present below, must also be considered. One can imagine an accumulation of experimental evidence on latent learning alone which would render both S-R-reinforcement theory and cognition theory thoroughly untenable, neither being capable of generating correct predictions as to the pattern of positive and negative results.

Finally, definitive interpretation of the experiments is rendered difficult by a terrible lack of data regarding certain quantitative matters, both in theory and at the descriptive level. It is customary for Tolman's critics to attack his formulations on these grounds, but it is not sufficiently ap-preciated how vulnerable we all are in this respect. For example, S-R-reinforcement reconstructions of "positive" latent learning designs char-acteristically invoke r_G, and require suitable quantitative assumptions about such matters as the "similarity" of the afferent consequences pro-duced by fractional eating and fractional drinking. It would be an inter-esting exercise to bring together all of the applications of this device with an eye to the question, whether the quantitative assumptions required by S-R-reinforcement theory to "deduce" experimental outcomes in the vari-ous settings are compatible. It is refreshing to reflect upon the discon-certing consequences of a direct experimental attack upon the hunger-thirst "stimuli," such as Heron's (36), for such theorizing. We have never seen an empirical curve for the generalization gradient of any "pure stimulus act" in the rat, nor even any rigorous theoretical treatment of it. It hardly seems quite proper for S-R-reinforcement theorists to attack Tolman on this front, when they themselves have frequent recourse to such an elastic explanatory construct as r_G.

In spite of the preceding difficulties of interpretation, it seems safe to say that the current state of the evidence is at least encouraging to the theorist oriented to some form of expectancy theory. We were, frankly, somewhat more impressed by the overall trend of the evidence than we had expected to be. This reaction led us to attempt a somewhat greater degree of formalization of the expectancy position, which we present in the following section.

IV. SOME TENTATIVE PROPOSALS AS TO FORMALIZATION

The commonest criticism of Tolman is that he has failed to make his theory "explicit" and "rigorous," the critical emphasis often being on "quantification." The matter of explicitness and rigor has been treated in Part II, and this criticism seems, in the main, to be valid. As for quantification, the most casual reading convinces one that Tolman either is not strongly interested in it or feels it to be premature. In a recent article he says:

> Curves could be fitted. Equations for these curves could be mathematically determined and the magnitudes of the constants could be found. In fact, all the precise techniques of quantitative method could be elegantly carried out . . . and bring about closure for all those psychologists who are probably at heart mere physicists or perhaps mathematicians gone wrong (151, p. 147).

And in the same paper we find the following:

> And although, as usual, I have been merely programmatic and have not attempted to set up, at this date, any precise systems of postulates and deduced theorems, I *have* made some specific suggestions. . . . I feel that once we have thought of really good defining experiments . . . we can then hypothesize equations, fit empirical curves, and dream up constructs to our hearts' content (151, p. 154).

If we ignore the touch of sarcasm, and the suggestion that physicists are somehow more entitled to an interest in quantifying than are psychologists, what can we see in these quotations? The description of himself as ". . . as usual . . . merely programmatic" suggests that Tolman believes in the *ideal* of a quantified science. Indeed, it would be difficult to doubt this in a writer who for many years has presented us with "functions" of "variables," albeit in the most general form possible as "f_1," "f_3," etc.

It is perhaps worthwhile to pause a moment and consider the degrees of quantification a behavior theory may attempt. Without claiming any sort of exact scale for degrees of quantification let us present a crude ordering system for convenient reference. At the lowest level, we have (1) statements as to *which* variables determine the dependent variables. This already has an element of quantification since it claims a non-zero value for certain partial derivatives and assigns a zero value to all others. Such a list of "relevant variables" almost always includes a further degree of quantification, (2) a statement of the sign of the first derivative. This latter may include a statement of the range over which this direction of influence holds (e.g., "monotonically increasing" if it holds throughout). Frequently, but by no means always, we are given (3) statements of signs of higher derivatives, e.g., "monotonically increasing decelerated function." Without specifying numerical values, we may be told (4) the *order* of sizes of the various first partial derivatives. Thus, "x_1 affects y more than x_2 does." It is often difficult, in the case of dimensions differing qualitatively, to say just what this latter kind of statement means even when nothing but order is claimed. Still further, we may have (5) various degrees of specification of the function *form*, as "a decay function," "a second-degree polynomial," and so on. Finally, we come to (6) estimates of the parameters in these functions.

No one can prophesy whether making an effort to attain one of these levels of quantification will be fruitful at any given stage of knowledge. Certain of Hull's later efforts, both experimental and postulational, seem to indicate that he believed work at level (6) to be in order, and quite obviously he had been for some years thinking at level (5). It is important to see that there are intermediate degrees of quantification, so that a theorist may be very cautious about levels (5) and especially (6), but still may attempt more than Tolman has to date. One does not need to be "anti-quantitative" to raise the question whether the painstaking determination of parameters arising from the study of a particular species, drive, response and apparatus is not somewhat premature. On the other hand, there is a degree of quantification which is necessary for any *important* sort of "explicitness." That is, one may set his sights lower than levels (5) or (6), but he can hardly attempt a usable (prediction-generating) set of postulates if he stops, say, at level (1) or (2). Unfortunately, Tolman seems to have done just this. It is questionable whether we can even proceed with the search for the "really good defining experiments" of which he speaks in the second quotation, until some efforts have been made at quantification levels beyond (2).

There is no important "system" at present which does not use hypothetical constructs or incompletely reduced intervening variables, such as some form of the learning-performance distinction. When Tolman speaks of "defining experiments" for each of his "types of learning," we have to remember that such defining experiments will in each case involve an inference *from* facts about response strength *to* values of the hypothetical entity or process. Thus, we cannot study the acquisition of an equivalence belief without having some notions about asymptotes of the cathexes being utilized in such an experiment. Again, we will be utilizing some instrumental act, so our discussion will be bound up with assumptions about the animal's field-expectancies. If we were to interest ourselves, say, in such a curve-fitting question as: "In what way does the rate of acquisition of an equivalence-belief depend upon the cathexis of the final goal?" we would need to have *some* quantification of final goal-object cathexes for the abscissa, and it is evident that cathexis is not a word in the data language. We know the kind of experiment Tolman uses for this preliminary problem—it appears in Chapters III and IV of *Purposive Behavior in Animals and Men*. But such experiments, while they are the obviously appropriate beginning, can only establish an ordinal series of cathexes, which is insufficient for purposes of a defining experiment on equivalence-beliefs unless it is to deal with order only. The point is that *somewhere* in the system of assumptions there must appear a minimal degree of hypothesized quantification in order to get a foot in the door prior to an empirical determination via a defining experiment of any of the theoretical quantities.

This is, of course, only one of the several forms in which the same fundamental dilemma recurs in all theory construction. We are constantly in the position of leaning upon *some* poorly confirmed "laws" as we try by experimentation to tease out others. So long as we are aware of this and see clearly the mutual support aspect of the components of a theory, there need be nothing disturbing in the situation. Such free play, with limitations, has to be expected in any ongoing inductive enterprise.

The chief aim of the Dartmouth Conference was analytic and critical rather than synthetic-constructive. However, the great stress usually laid upon lack of explicitness in the criticism of Tolman impelled us to tentative efforts toward developing his views in this respect. We cannot emphasize too strongly that what follows could most appropriately be given some such Teutonic title as "Prolegomena to an introduction to proposals for the skeleton of an incomplete postulate set generating a modified expectancy theory." In order to avoid repetitive apologizing, we shall use the unqualified terms "axiomatization" and "formalization" to designate our procedure. But we hope we are under no illusions as to the appropriateness of these designations. There are, in particular, two misinterpretations of our intentions which we wish the reader to guard against.

1. We do not propose the following as a sufficient set of "postulates" for the derivation of all or even most empirical behavior-laws. Nor have we made a formal effort to investigate them as to independence or consistency. The reader should look upon them as "programmatic," but less so than Tolman as he stands.

2. They attempt to explicate not so much "Tolman" as "an expectancy theory." While we have tried to be oriented by Tolman's emphasis and have not knowingly contradicted him, it would be absurd to expect that Tolman himself would accept all of the following as falling within the range of his own broader hunches. We will begin with a few general remarks to clarify our orienting attitudes toward an expectancy theory. As a first approximation to be elaborated as we proceed, we could express our notion of an "expectancy-type" of theory as follows: An expectancy-type of theory is a learning theory in which the fundamental learning construct, the "what-is-learned," is notationally specified by explicit reference to the stimulus-event which has commonly terminated a stimulus-response sequence in an organism's history (the "expectan-

dum"), in addition to making the usual reference to the eliciting stimulus and the (strengthened) response. A correlated feature, without which this notational practice would be sterile, is that the activation postulate which relates this learning construct to a behavior-disposition makes explicit reference to this third element; whereas in non-expectancy theories the "usual terminator" (e.g., reinforcer) of an S-R sequence plays only a historical role, in the sense that it occurs as an experimental factor in the acquisition postulates but is not "part of" the learning construct itself nor, therefore, available for use in the activation postulate.

It is our belief that a phrase such as "field-cognition" or "field-expectancy" is confusing, since it links together two words the emphases of which, while perhaps not wholly independent, are at least distinguishable (cf. Spence, 96). The term "field" makes a reference to the Gestalt and perceptual emphases in Tolman, while (in our opinion) the term "expectancy" indicates a quite different aspect of the system. It is the latter, "expectancy" aspect which we have taken as definitive of the system, since we are not persuaded that there is any very intimate connection between acceptance of the Gestalt laws of stimulus organization and acceptance of either an S-R-contiguity, an S-R-reinforcement, or a (so-called) S-S theory of acquisition. The problems of stimulus equivalence, and of the physical statement of configural properties on the stimulus side which will yield stimulus-equivalence or various degrees of generalization, *will recur in any form of behavior psychology;* and it is a historical accident that the leading expectancy theorist has Gestalt-emphasizing leanings. Thus, Skinner, clearly an S-R-reinforcement non-expectancy theorist, would find it unnatural to connect configural emphasis in any *essential* way with the matter of acquisition laws. If experimentation shows, e.g., physical triangularity of the visual stimulus to be a basis for strong generalization effects, so be it. The specification of relations among the apices of such a "physical triangle" which yield such-and-such degrees of generalization can be achieved if desired (62).

If one speaks in terms of the raw data that give rise to a science of psychology, all behavior-data theories are "S-R" theories, in the broad sense. The empirical variables are movements of the organism and environmental events which occur in certain temporal relations to them. That his system is an out-and-out behaviorism is one of the things on which Tolman has been most explicit. There is, to be sure, a more restricted and less innocuous sense of the phrase "S-R theory" which does *not* apply to Tolman, as we shall develop below. But the point here is that, at the data-language level, Tolman is the same as Guthrie, Skinner, or Hull, and he intends to be.

Since all of the theories considered by us make the learning-performance distinction in some form, the mere making of this distinction cannot differentiate an expectancy theory from the others. Once the organism has acquired *whatever* sort of bond or knowledge the theories respectively specify, all of them allow for a manipulation of overt behavior strength by means of control of drive, fatigue, emotion, or competing responses. This means that having learned, and not having yet unlearned, an animal may still fail to exhibit the behavior. Guthrie, Hull, and Skinner all make their various places for this fact. If it was ever an adequate rendition of the Tolman position's uniqueness to say that "The organism learns certain things but may exhibit this learning in different ways depending upon . . . ," it is no longer. The distinguishing feature of an expectancy approach is not as simple as this, nor is it easy to state in any short characterization.

V. EXCURSUS: THE RESPONSE CONCEPT

Since Tolman's system is a behaviorism, its dependent variable necessarily reduces to some aspects of the organism's activity. Therefore, the problem of "defining the unit of response" exists for Tolman as it does for all behavior theorists. From *Purposive Behavior* through the series of experiments on "spatial learning" (78, 79, 80, 81, 160, 173, 174, 175, 176) to his recent theoretical papers (150, 151), Tolman has obviously felt that the definition of the unit, the specification of "what is learned," was one of the major differentiators of his position. In an earlier paper, we stated our own opinion as follows:

We early concluded that certain views which have been linked historically to Tolman's formulation are logically unrelated to the "core" concepts of an expectancy theory. Other views seemed related to Tolman's formulation until preliminary efforts to formalize them indicated their independent status as well. We shall merely list those dogmatically as "properties *not* definitive of an expectancy theory":

1. Gestalt-configural stress.
2. Perceptual field stress.
3. Pure contiguity as a sufficient condition.
4. Specification of reaction-class by reference to position, direction, or locomotion (rather than by effector-properties).
5. Discontinuity view of discrimination learning.
6. Insistence upon the learning-performance distinction (66, p. 230).

In a personal communication, Professor Tolman states his agreement with us that four of these emphases are not crucial to his position, but he feels that two of them, the "Gestalt-configural stress" and the "specification of the reaction-class" are basic points on which he differs from *S-R* theorists. Consequently, we feel it necessary to digress for a somewhat more extended treatment of the response question before proceeding with our own formalization proposals.

To begin with, in denying the cruciality of the response-definition as a mark of expectancy theory, we do not mean to suggest that there is no problem here, or that Tolman tries to solve it no differently from others. But we do think it incorrect for a Tolmanite to assume that *S-R* theory necessarily means an *R*-term specified by muscle-twitches, and that experiments indicating the utility of a more "molar" *R*-term are, prima facie, embarrassing to non-expectancy theories. The distinction is not that simple, witness the fact that one major *S-R*-reinforcement theorist (Skinner, 90) wrote a whole book in which the reports of raw data tell us, strictly speaking, *nothing* about the actual activity of effectors. A glance at the experimental reports of Hullian and neo-Hullian workers shows the same thing. Levers are pressed and maze "choices" are made, and the observations are narrated in these terms, for the contemporary *S-R* theorist operates with a "molar" (in the sense of levels: 55) defini-tion of response and in practice worries very little about this aspect of his methodology. It is interesting to note that Hull (38, 40) devotes no discussion to the question of what are "admissible" modes of specifying *R*. The Glossary of his posthumous book defines response thus: "*R* = response; an act of some kind" (40, p. 358). However, it seems unlikely that all formulable *R*-terms would be equally acceptable to Hullians (e.g., the "act of some kind" being strengthened is *"getting to the goal-box"*). One meets clinical psychologists who are suspicious of the learning-theory approach to psychotherapy because they perceive *S-R* formulations as "atomistic," as attempting to analyze personality into "discrete responses" rather than treating the "whole person." These obscurantist attitudes spring at least in part from the inadequate atten-tion usually given to the methodological questions devolving about the response concept.

Any effort to clarify the response problem must begin by explicit recognition that, for all learning theorists and all experimenters, the "re-sponse" is a *class*. This follows directly from a definition and a fact. Learning is defined as a change in an organism which is reflected by a change in the strength of some specified way of acting; and it is a fact that no two (numerically distinct) intervals in the flux of an organism's activity are absolutely identical in all of their properties. Hence, any experimenter who talks about learning's having taken place must be classifying two or more occurrences as "instances" of this way of acting, in spite of their detectable differences. This is simple and obvious, but it is one of those simple things which is easily forgotten and very clarifying when remembered. As an example of the resolving power of this class-concept, consider the objections one sometimes hears that a bit of *S-R* analysis "abstracts from the total activity," and hence somehow distorts in describing. The obvious reply is that *all* description which names an activity and identifies its recurrence is already abstracting. Two "in-stances" of any kind of behavior, classified at any level of molarity, are unavoidably abstractions, in the sense that they select certain features of the flux for attention and ignore others. So when a critic voices this sort of objection to a given formulation, he must be made to see that all conceivable formulations would be subject to the same complaint, and that a claim to be telling *nothing but* the truth about an event is never a claim to be telling the *whole* truth about that event. The individual, dated behavior-event is "unique"; the very concept of learning presupposes that we are willing to group these dated events under one class-name by virtue of certain common properties and neglect those other properties or quantitative variations with respect to which the class-members differ among themselves.

This leads directly to another important point in connection with the question of "what is learned." It is evident that a given interval of the flux can be classified in more than one way, and that conjunctions and disjunctions of classes can be set up for study. This shows that, at the purely *descriptive* level, there may be alternative and seemingly quite different ways of narrating the flux, *all equally "valid."* Some implications of this for the learning controversy will be developed in the course of our discussion. Tolman emphasized in *Purposive Behavior in Animals and Men* that his concentration on the lawful features of goal-seeking behavior "at its own level" was perfectly compatible with the usual assumption that the efficient causes of these behaviors lie in the physiology. We must not assume that there are no intermediate levels of analysis between these two extremes, which would exhibit a lawfulness of their own. Whether there is always some one "optimal" degree of specification of the response properties which will generate maximum orderliness as suggested by Skinner (90, p. 38) is a complex problem which cannot be discussed here. But it is an obvious mathematical possibility to obtain a very smooth curve of responding when the behavior is classified at a more "molar" level, this curve being a resultant of the several curves which would be generated by counting responses further subclassified at a *less* "molar" level. These latter curves, perhaps equally "smooth" as the original, might individually share its form or instead exhibit other orderly (e.g., cyclical) properties. The idea of smoothness or orderliness invoked by Skinner in this connection seems to require some clarification before it can be rigorously applied to the problem of defining the response.

We begin with the complete stream of activity as it runs off in the time sequence, the rich, raw, unclassified *flux* of behavior. Any arbitrary *interval* of the flux can be demarcated by time-points and examined for the presence of certain properties. The operational specification of a *descriptive property* of an interval permits the use of words referring to the animal's visible anatomy, the descriptive words of the physical thing-language, and special words which we define explicitly in terms of these.

Observation-sentences are formulated in these words, and must not involve even implicit reference to any other intervals of the flux. There does not seem to be any cogent objection to the inclusion of words referring to *contact* with environmental objects ("The rat put his paws on the lever"), or to *orientation* ("The rat turned his head toward the light"), or to *locomotion* ("The rat approached the tray"), so long as these environmental objects and the organism's relation to them are describable by explicitly defined words or phrases referring solely to the interval under consideration. If a rat is oriented so that his nose is pointing to a lighted circular disk, "locomotion forward in a straight line" is a legitimate descriptive property of the ensuing ten seconds of the flux, and such a specification of R would presumably be just as available to Spence as to Ritchie.

It is perhaps noteworthy that more "complex" flux-properties are introducible without going beyond pure description. For example, the "if . . . then" (which is the "not . . . unless") relation in the sense of material implication (105, pp. 23-28) is definable in terms of the (intuitively simpler) logical constants "not" and "or" or "not" and "and." Hence, complex properties such as "Lifting the paw, whenever he has in the preceding five seconds wiggled the whiskers, provided that . . ." etc., are clearly still descriptive. Sequence specifications, with or without a metric time-property, are also admissible.

On the other hand, non-extensional connectives such as "in order that . . ." or "necessitates that . . ." are clearly forbidden as going beyond the descriptive properties of the interval. If they occur, they must occur as theoretical discourse, not as pure description.

In practice, we do not begin by slicing up the flux into a huge (theoretically infinite) set of intervals and then by examining each one for the presence of the desired property. There are certain "striking" features of the flux which, in addition to our theories and our anthropomorphic identifications, help us direct our attention to some intervals and, for that matter, to certain properties. That theory and anthropomorphism are among the *causal* sources of our experimental attention is of course quite irrelevant to the question as to whether what we emerge with in our narration is itself purely descriptive.

Some of the more obvious features of the flux which make our trial-and-error not arbitrary but rapidly convergent on the relevant properties and intervals may be briefly mentioned. Suppose a non-anthropomorphic and non-theoretical experimenter blindly plotted time-lines of numerous distances and angles in the flux (e.g., angle at elbow-joint, distance of chin from floor). How would he "notice" promising regions of the flux, avoiding the trying out of tentative R-classes which would be theoretically and predictively useless?

1. *Inception and termination of contact with an environmental object.* The rat touches the lever and his pressing of it is usually followed by a breaking of this contact.

2. *"Phasic" property:* Most extreme excursions of any effector-position measure are followed shortly by an undoing. Rarely does rat or human lift the head high or greatly reduce the angle at a joint without shortly reversing the change. The blindly plotted time-lines would thus exhibit a tendency for cycles and overshootings in returning from an extreme excursion.

3. *Segmental:* An obvious possibility is to examine all intervals in which the flux shows changes of a considerable magnitude in the measures on a given limb or other anatomical region.

4. *Multimodal distribution:* Distribution of excursions may be multimodal. Thus, the distance of a rat's nose from the ceiling can take on all intermediate values within a certain range. But the plot of this distance for numerous intervals would show a small mode near the upper extreme—these being chiefly occurrences of the exploratory reaction "standing up, sniffing ceiling."

5. *Intrabehavioral covariation:* Families of the arbitrary time-lines would show concurrent variations of activity; e.g., "speech" involves a burst of excursions and cycles of reference points and lines on lips, jaws, tongue, diaphragm, glottis. Such a highly configurated pattern as a "shrug" might be isolated and recognizable after only one occurrence of it.

6. *"Achievement":* This very common, if not commonest, criterion raises such difficult problems that it will be separately treated below.

Having found an interval I in the flux which is identified by its possession of a simple or complex property P, what is "the reaction" $(= R)$? It does not consist of the whole interval, because we want to be able to speak at times of several "concurrent reactions" all of which take place *in* the interval or an interval I' which overlaps I. If the property P includes a specification of a certain body segment or effector-system, the reaction R may be defined as the movement of the relevant part(s). If P has been defined as a disjunction of alternative parts or movements, the reaction consists of those which verify the occurrence of P in the given instance. Thus, if "touching lever with paw or paws" is P, the reaction R is the touching by right paw when that happens, but if instead both paws had been used, the movement and touching by both would constitute the reaction. Note that we cannot speak of *instances* of the reaction R. The reaction R is dated, a unique, unrepeatable *event* in the flux. It has "parts" but it has no "instances." Any parts of the reaction are in the relation of part-to-whole to it, and link-in-chain to one another; but not in the relation of class-membership to it. The *R-class* has instances, each of which is a reaction. Elsewhere herein we shall use the term "response" as a synonym for "R-class," the family of reactions identifiable by their common possession of some property P.

We have now to consider the common procedure of defining an R-class in terms of *achievement*. This practice ranges from the usually non-controversial case in which the achievement is a simple, concrete manipulandum-event ("Rat pressed the lever") to very complex and debatable instances such as occur in describing human social behavior. ("He kept at it until he had put Smith in his place!") It is in this type of R-class specification that the line between pure description and covert theorizing becomes difficult to draw. It is here also that the lines of battle are likely to be drawn between Tolmanites and others insofar as the response becomes an issue between them.

First of all, one must distinguish between what the experimenter bothers to narrate (or is ingenious enough to discern) and what he can be confident is objectively the case. In point of fact, any R-class specified by achievement is a truth-function of a finite set of R-classes specified by non-achievement flux-descriptions. There is more than one way to get a lever down, but there is not an infinite number of ways. (A "way" here is a sub-class defined by fairly restricted effector topography, but necessarily allowing for certain quantitative variations over its own instances.) Whether we as experimenters have the skill or make the effort to state what they are, there is some finite disjunction of effector-event-classes matched to any manipulation- (or locomotion-) attainment class. Presumably, this is why workers of varying theoretical persuasions seem equally comfortable with describing the two most commonly studied types of rat-behavior in achievement language. The data emerging from Skinner-box work are obviously of that sort. As for the maze, the word "turn" may perhaps be construed as an effector-event word. But the use of "choice" as a common synonym, or electrical recording or opal-flash glass where we cannot see the rat, suggests that "turn" is, like "press," ordinarily an achievement-word.

The most hard-headed operationist can afford to be relaxed about this use of achievement-words in description because studying the quantitative laws of such achievement-classes need not (in fact cannot) commit him immediately to any particular theory about the learning process. To the extent that docility with respect to a goal or sub-goal is *really* immanent in behavior, *really* part of behavior's "immediate descriptive warp and woof" (128, p. 12), all theoretical issues remain to be settled after such behavioral descriptions have been given. It is important to see that the lawfulness exhibited by attainment-specified R-classes does *not* imply, or even suggest, that the coordinated flux-disjuncts are not lawful. Nor does a finding that attainments show lawful changes tend to show that attainments, *rather than* the coordinated flux-disjuncts, are "what is really being learned." From the fact that a rat presses the lever now with left paw, now with right, sometimes with teeth, we cannot infer anything about "what is learned," but must undertake further behavioral analysis to tease out the conditions for occurrence of each of these topographies. After all, if a rat "learns to press with chin" and "learns to press with paw," it is a logically trivial consequence of these statements that he "learns to press."

An achievement-learning *may* be interpreted as more than purely descriptive, of course. This ambiguity is impossible if the achievement-statement is applied to a single interval, since "At 12:07 the rat depressed the lever to the point that an electrical contact was made" is pure description. It is not in terms of effectors, and it is very incomplete ("abstracted") as a characterization of the interval. But it is pure description nonetheless. However, if I say "Over the hour the rat learned to press the lever," it is not clear how much I intend. I may still intend pure description, which expands to something like "Over the hour there was a significant increase in the rate of occurrence of effector-events which had the mechanical effect of depressing the lever." This amounts to "Over the hour there was a significant increase in the rate of occurrence of [foot *or* teeth *or* jaw] contacts which. . . ." This is all quite innocent of theory, and the variations are matters of dividing the classes into finer classes, depending upon one's desire for detail in narration.

The interesting question is, what else can the original assertion be taken to mean, which would *not* be purely descriptive? The alternatives are not so easy to list, but they vary from a slight inductive extrapolation, such as "If the rate of R_1-disjunct declines, some other one R_x of the whole family of effector-event-classes coordinated to the attainment-class R_L will increase in strength enough to maintain the R_L level (Cf. 91, pp. 211-212)" to a layman's anthropomorphism that the rat "knows the idea is to get the lever down and would tell us as much if he could talk." Even the simple inductive extrapolation about a compensatory increase in one effector-event-class is often used as a counterfactual conditional, "If we *had* prevented R_i, then R_j *would have* been employed to do the job." This asserts a lawful relation not immediately established by the flux and is not a truth-function of the observation-sentences.

This is one disadvantage of the achievement type of description: it is capable of being over-interpreted. However, ambiguous achievement-statements can always be explicated upon demand, in order to see whether their maker does intend more than description. Why, then, are there any arguments about this? Leaving aside some real disagreements as to the reproducibility of certain factual outcomes, there may be differing inductive extrapolations on the near-descriptive level, and differing theoretical interpretations based upon these.

In a recent methodological paper (47), Kendler rejects the question "what is learned" as being an unsuitable question for the learning theorist. We would prefer to take as a provisional hypothesis that arguments over "what is learned" *are* about something, and try to tease out what this something is. We would see "what is learned" as what Carnap calls an explicandum (8, pp. 513, 517-521, 531-532), the task being the formulation of some more precise explicata as alternatives. There is no cut-and-dried way to do this; but for any proffered explication of the initially vague question we try to see how the experiments usually cited in controversy and how the words used in associated discussion would fit. In the end we will have formulated somewhat more exact questions even if they are rejected as not being "adequate" explications by the original protagonists.

Proceeding thus, we may ask, "What sorts of causal analysis of an achievement-statement would be rejected by those theorists who like to stress that the rat 'Learns to press the lever'?" Consider the classical experiments of Muenzinger (72, 73) on the lever-pressing behavior of the guinea pig, which Tolman cites (128, p. 171; cf. also p. 18) as evidence for behavior's "multiple trackness": the use of alternative paths to attain a given end (achievement). Muenzinger studied the variations in the effector-pattern of a simple lever-pressing response through 1000 reinforced occurrences, long after there was no further possibility of "improvement" insofar as latency, speed, or elimination of competing responses were concerned. He classified the pressings into nine topographies—three emphasizing left foot, three right, and one each with both feet, teeth, and "head" (lower jaw). Working thus at the asymptote of the achievement-class, he found what Tolman views as substitutability of means—a rise and decline of strength among the competing effector-classes, this competition persisting throughout the course of the experiment. Muenzinger himself believed that the habit should have become "mechanized" in the sense that one specific effector-pattern should steadily increase until all others are excluded, according to the law of effect; and he argued for an interpretation in terms of the "meanings" assumed by environmental objects. But how much does such an experiment actually show? Examination of Muenzinger's tables shows that the subclasses themselves are by no means chaotic in their temporal changes, but exhibit a certain lawfulness. What is to prevent the S-R theorist from saying that, after hundreds of trials, *all* of the topographies were at fairly high strength, so that whenever one fell momentarily behind there was always a competing one available to "replace" it? (Cf. 25, 91.) The point is that all nine effector-disjuncts *did* get the lever down, hence were all repeatedly reinforced. At the time Muenzinger wrote, the laws of frequency and effect were stated more crudely than they are in any current S-R-reinforcement theory, so Muenzinger may have been quite right in supposing that his experiment was adverse to them. But does a more sophisticated and elaborate effect-and-frequency theory have any obvious trouble here? Suppose we view the "lever-pressing" as the environmental outcome mechanically coordinated to a set of nine effector-event-classes. Members of any of these nine "succeed," i.e., are reinforced. If R_1 and R_2 designate two of these classes, does S-R-reinforcement theory imply that the "initially stronger" must come to dominate to the exclusion of the others? Consider just a few of the possible complications which interfere with any such easy inference:

1. R_1 may be stronger than R_2 initially but may have a lower asymptote.
2. R_1 and R_2 may have different growth rates. Nor is there any assurance that higher growth rates will be associated with higher asymptotes, and of course "accidents of history" might reverse the order of either or both of the above in relation to initial strength.
3. The evidence (92) indicates that some R-classes are "harder," i.e., mechanically difficult, requiring more work, or are even painful, so that their strength may decline faster either with or without reinforcement. So R_1 might have an initial edge in strength but fatigue sooner than R_2.
4. The number of responses put out per reinforcement ("extinction ratio") varies from R_1 to R_2. Hence, a given reinforcement-probability for an R_1 which is not 100 per cent mechanically effective may maintain it at a stable rate which is lower than that of an R_2 about equal in effectiveness.
5. Since mechanical or emotional prevention of an R_1 results in a "bottling up" effect, so that the momentary rate when the constraint is removed is much in excess of the previous rate (24) (27) (43, p. 71) (90, pp. 345-350), it may be that a similar effect occurs when a run of competing instrumental responses R_2 prevents emission. In that case any of numerous factors capable of transitorily decreasing the competitor may lead to a burst of R_1.
6. Extinction is accompanied by irregularities, which Skinner considers chiefly "emotional" in character.
7. R_1 may be effectively on a lower schedule of reinforcement than R_2, giving it less strength but in the extreme case greater resistance to extinction. If later in the series fatigue or a decline in drive begins to alter the R-forms slightly so that their mechanical efficacy is lessened, the weaker may catch up again.
8. Spontaneous recovery occurs and the parameters are not the same for all R's.
9. It is not known whether induction between responses is quantitatively symmetrical. Possibly the increment in strength given to R_1

due to a reinforcement of R_2 is not the same as that in the other direction.

10. In the earlier stages of learning, the increment in strength given by a reinforcement to an R of the less probable class will exceed that given to an R of the more probable class (other things being equal) due to the negative acceleration of the acquisition function, the ordinal number of a given reinforcement being higher for the initially more probable R.

The interaction of all these factors, with suitable values of the numerous parameters involved, could lead to a very long series of cyclical fluctuations in response dominance of the sort Muenzinger describes. What looks in achievement-terms as one homogeneous mass of interchangeable "means-to-ends" may in fact be the resultant of a very complex series of changes composed of fatigue, rest, extinction, spontaneous recovery, reconditioning, emotional upset, stimulus discrimination, decline in drive, induction (43), response differentiation, and the like. But after a long reinforcement history for a fairly "easy" response, there are always enough effector-classes at high strength to keep the achievement-R stable, the whole system being restricted only by the mechanical constraints of the apparatus and the drive-level of the animal.

Where would an experimenter preferring the achievement-language stand on such an analysis? If he finds it acceptable, it indicates that his use of the achievement-language was purely descriptive; if he rejects it, we assume his use of the achievement-language springs from a theoretical preference. The proposed analysis seems to require no learning construct referring notationally to the "achievement" as such—no intervening variable tied somehow to the situation "lever-down." Its learning-theoretical elements refer only to the several effector-classes, and the relation of the disjunction of these *to* "getting the lever down" is merely a matter of causal laws in the science of mechanics, requiring no behavioral counterpart or representative.

Consider another case. Suppose a rat has always used his teeth, never his paws, in the course of an experiment. We muzzle him, find he presses promptly and at a high rate with his paws. Even if we give no further reinforcement, the paw-pressing continues to develop a nice extinction curve. Under certain conditions, this would not be of any special relevance in the "what-is-learned" controversy. For example, if this rat has been accustomed in the living-cage to operate a food-dispenser by means of a lever and is known to have used teeth and paws in that setting, the S-R theorist would argue that R_{paw} to the experimental lever gets induced and generalized strength from R'_{paw} to the home-cage dispenser, and is emitted as soon as the stronger member of the experimental hierarchy (R_{teeth}) is prevented from competing with it. In general, an observed "multiple trackness," "substitutability," or "interchangeability of means" is not theoretically exciting when it can be shown that the substituted R is (1) already in the repertory and (2) under control of a discriminative stimulus sufficiently similar to the present stimulation to allow for easy stimulus generalization. "Sufficiently similar" is necessarily vague, but the principle seems clear.

A second uninteresting case is response induction. If we know for the species that whenever R_1 is strong R_2 is strong also (unless it has been differentiated), the occurrence of R_2 as a surrogate for R_1 in attainment-mediation is not likely to be invoked as an argument against an S-R interpretation.

What other cases can arise? It might seem at first impossible to imagine any, for if the stimulus field resembles previously experienced fields which have acquired response control, the S-R theorist can invoke generalization; and if it is so unlike the past to be "wholly new," does any theorist predict substitution will be exhibited? Let us look more closely at the lever-pressing situation alluded to above.

S_h: Home cage stimulus field (cup, dispensing bar, etc.)
S_1: Experimental stimulus field (tray, lever)
R_p: Operating dispenser with paws
R_t: Operating dispenser with teeth
R'_p: Pressing experimental lever with paws
R'_t: Pressing experimental lever with teeth

Assume that $S_h \cdot R_p$ and $S_1 \cdot R_t$ have never become strong in the home cage, because they were rarely or never reinforced with food. Both, however, have nevertheless *occurred* a large number of times in the pre-experimental history. The pre-reinforcement strengths of $S_1 \cdot R'_p$ and $S_1 \cdot R'_t$ in the experimental box are also very low. Now we strengthen $S_1 \cdot R'_p$ by reinforcing in the box. Suppose that $S_1 \cdot R'_t$ does not occur in the box. This latter is an ambiguous fact, since we cannot tell whether its failure to occur (once we have begun reinforcing "lever pressing") is due to low strength or to the ascendancy of the reinforced competitor $S_1 \cdot R'_p$. But suppose we now prevent R'_p. If R'_t occurs more than for a suitable control, yielding a large extinction curve, how do we "explain" it? We cannot invoke stimulus generalization from $S_h \cdot R_t$ to $S_1 \cdot R'_t$, because we know that $S_h \cdot R_t$ is weak and if generalized to the box as $S_1 \cdot R'_t$ it should be even weaker. On the response side, can we simply invoke induction from $S_1 \cdot R'_p$ to $S_1 \cdot R'_t$? In a crude operational sense of "induction," this *is* the answer. If the rat behaves as described, we have "by definition" succeeded in inducing strength in $S_1 \cdot R'_t$ by first strengthening $S_1 \cdot R'_p$. What is there to disagree about?

Here again, as in the case of the statement "He learns to press the lever," we have to decide between response induction as a *descriptive* or as an *explanatory* concept. As description, there could be no argument if the facts were as we have imagined. But, of course, this broad descriptive use of the concept *induction* says almost nothing. Any experiment—"insight," problem-solving, concept-formation, maze-learning, complex verbal task—in which one response topography is strengthened indirectly by virtue of an operation we have performed on another, may in such a usage be dismissed as a case of "response induction." All cases are covered in a rather empty and useless sense, and such a use would not be theoretically powerful because we cannot predict or control via it unless some rules for conditions which will yield such induction are stated. If a rat behaved very "rationally and insightfully" in choosing a new route when it was made available, any theorist could shrug off the problem thus posed as merely a case of induction! It seems obvious that we ordinarily have some narrower meaning of the term in mind. To help us get a lead on this narrower meaning, let us consider a series of cases of such indirect response strengthening, asking which ones would make Tolmanites happy and not, prima facie, gratify Hullians?

- *a.* Soft pressing $\longrightarrow$ Harder pressing. Once the class-character of all R-terms is clear to disputants, this case loses its theoretical interest.
- *b.* Pressing down $\longrightarrow$ Pressing sidewise. This one is a little more interesting, but still would not cause much concern in the S-R camp.
- *c.* Pressing with right paw $\longrightarrow$ Pressing with left paw. This case is more doubtful still.
- *d.* Paw press $\longrightarrow$ Teeth press. We suspect most psychologists would rule this out as not a fair case of response induction. Why?

Inspection of this series suggests that it is mostly a matter of topography. We feel most comfortable speaking of induction when the related R-classes involve the same effectors and a fairly "similar" pattern of use of them, differing mainly in matters of force, distance, speed, duration, etc. It is as if we have in mind some *primary induction*, comparable to primary generalization on the stimulus side, and based fairly directly upon the biology of the species. Without an extreme degree of experimental control and a very detailed, continuous record of the entire history of the organism, such a primary induction would be hard to separate from any more complex or "high-level" basis for an indirect strengthening effect. In principle, if we know that R_2 has never occurred, and find that when we strengthen R_1, R_2 receives strength and can maintain itself for a time without further reinforcement, we would infer a primary response induction. In practice, psychologists examine topography as a substitute for any such detailed record of the history, apparently assuming that if the topographies are too dissimilar, the primary induction would be negligible.

Now if primary induction could be claimed from R_p to R_t, the hypothetical experiment would again lose most of its theoretical interest. A Tolmanite might prefer to think of the process in achievement terms, but the more "atomistic" analysis is no longer immediately threatened by the mere fact of substitutability of teeth for paws. Suppose, however, that we know enough about the species to be confident that primary induction, at least to the quantitative extent required, does *not* hold between R_t and R_p. What, then, are the theoretical possibilities? One may flirt with the idea of S-R theory's adding a new postulate, dealing with "secondary response induction." It might take some such form as the following: "If S_1R_1 and S_1R_2 are both > 0 (on the basis of separate histories of reinforcement), the strengthening of a new habit S_iR_1 will induce strength in S_iR_2, beyond any primary induction obtaining between R_1 and R_2 as related topographies." I.e., two responses acquire an inductive *relation* whenever they have been conditioned to a common stimulus. This strikes us as a rather odd sort of postulate for an S-R theory, but oddity is hardly an objection to it. The issue between an S-R theory thus augmented and an expectancy theory would then not be decidable on the basis of experiments concerning "multiple trackness" such as the one described. If it turned out that *other* types of experiments supported an expectancy framework, perhaps the job done by this special postulate in dealing with multiple trackness could be done by a derivable *theorem* in expectancy theory, in which case the latter theory would, *ceteris paribus*, be preferred. Whether multiple trackness can be derived without special auxiliary assumptions from the type of expectancy theory here proposed must be considered after we have presented the postulates.

A special use of the achievement language occurs in the description of certain "choice"-problem experiments. The behavior of Nissen's chimpanzees (74) seems to him best characterized as "approaching the white stimulus card," where the approach is not a locomotion but a "selection" of the white card in preference to the black. During the training period, there are two (compatible!) ways of describing the behavior changes. One can say that the response-disposition $S_{WB} \rightarrow R_{\text{Left}}$ and $S_{BW} \rightarrow R_{\text{Right}}$ are increasing in strength; he can also say that the response R_W ("selecting white card") is increasing in strength while R_B ("selecting black card") is not. Nissen shows that excellent transfer occurs when the spatial arrangement of the presented stimuli is up-down rather than left-right. If we have chosen the first sort of description, the prediction of the experimental result would seem to involve problems similar to those raised in the preceding discussion of multiple trackness in lever-pressing. The second type of description is free of these difficulties, but it requires *an explicit reference to the stimulus side in its characterization of the response*. It is, therefore, a clear case of the achievement language, and one which does not seem so easily reformulated in non-achievement language as is the case of gross locomotion toward a light. Some of the theoretical difficulties likely to be encountered in such a reformulation are treated in Nissen's thought-provoking article.

We conclude this lengthy but unavoidable digression on the response concept by emphasizing the complexity of the problems and the fact that some of them still await analytic or experimental solution. For our own purposes in what follows, we shall use the symbol R in a fairly broad sense. Locomotion, orientation, and the kind of "achievement" class that can be specified by wholly descriptive language (including language describing manipulandum-events) and which refers wholly to the currently occurring behavior, are admissible sorts of R-class. Language which refers even implicitly to the properties of other intervals or to stimulation *not present to the organism at the time the response is being emitted*, is excluded. We do not believe that these rules are either so narrow or so wide as to prejudge any significant theoretical issue.

The reader who is accustomed to having his non-expectancy theories served up with such verbal adornments as "mechanical," "blind," "helter-skelter," or "meaningless" will be disappointed. Making psychology "like physics" is very probably an overly ambitious aim, but one easily available way for us to work at it is to dispense with these obfuscators. Thus, if we want to distinguish in what follows between an *expectancy* and a *stimulus-response connection*, we shall not find it necessary to label the latter a *"mere* stimulus-response" connection. We would not take Tolman's approach as a serious scientific one unless we assumed that its spirit could be caught by the postulate proposals themselves, without bolstering it with any such verbalisms.

We have concluded that the usual distinction "*S-S*" versus "*S-R*" should be sought in the more complex relations *among* constructs, i.e., their role in the whole system of laws, rather than in any differences in how the empirical variables are defined. Thus, we shall argue that the concept *expectancy* is more conveniently introduced by implicit definition than by any such direct "operational" reduction-sentence as that employed by Tolman, Ritchie, and Kalish (173). Even if the supposed "operational definition" were an acceptable one, which we have argued above it is not, it does not seem to us a step in the fruitful direction. Is there nothing in common between an "expectancy" in the spatial learning problem and an "expectancy" in the Skinner box? If not, this definition of expectancy would be tied to a certain design, in a way which can hardly be the intention of a general theory. Of course, another reduction-sentence can be written for the Skinner box, and the same word used. But is this really what Tolman has in mind? Presumably some *general* laws *about* expectancies are envisaged. Why not, then, make the concept general from the first?

The history of experimentation, particularly in the latent learning area discussed in the section preceding, strongly suggests that it is unrealistic to search for an *experimentum crucis* which will strictly force a decision between an expectancy theory and others. Probably many experimenters designing latent learning studies have had some "crucial" intentions, but with over 49 such studies at the time of this writing, the controversy continues and new experimental designs continue to appear. It seems that we can only hope to proceed by partial formulations which entail, in an "other-things-equal" sense, certain rather broadly specified consequences, and the gradual accumulation of confirmed or disconfirmed consequences will progressively support or disconfirm the theory. Whether or not one agrees with most of his arguments, Thistlethwaite's review (106) points up the complex character of our inductive problem. We are in relative ignorance of many factual matters, of which the following seem to us among the more important: hunger-thirst interaction, the arousers and satiators of the "exploratory" drive, alternation effects, emotional consequences of frustration, dependence of "behavioral oscillation" parameters upon overall drive level, the safest methods of guaranteeing "satiation," effects of past experience upon the goal-character of objects, relative value of primary and secondary reinforcers as rewards, potency and discriminability of the proprioceptive input (particularly as it arises from damped consummatory responses) as a source of either reinforcement or discriminative control, and so on and on. New experimental data on any one of these may necessitate large revisions of our thinking about whole families of experiments. A possible example would be Christie's work on pre-experimental experiences with the incentives (12, 13, 14). *No available theory*, it seems to us, says enough "in advance" about *all* of these and similar questions, to rule out all possibility of recourse to various *ad hoc* explanations after the fact. To be sure, any such auxiliary hypotheses must themselves have further factual implications if they are not to be rejected as *purely ad hoc*. Even so, when we set up experiments to test the implications of these special hypotheses, we find the same problem recurring afresh. No one can be "blamed" for this, for the interdependence of theoretical constructs is in the nature of science. Over 20 years ago such logical empiricists as Schlick were pointing out that there is *a sense* in which any single experiment, even though conceived with reference to a specific hypothesis, can be regarded as an indirect test of the entire causal framework within which the scientist operates. The physicist "takes for granted" the accurate working of his ammeters while he is engaged in studying something other than instrumentation problems; but a complete explication of how a pointer-reading is *able* to confirm a statement concerning mesons would, of course, have to "unpack" the internal physics of the ammeter. Hence, his successful prediction of the experimental outcome furnishes a small increment to the inductive support for the latter.

One difficulty with contemporary learning theory is that our ammeter-reading is an animal's "response-strength"; the behavioral analogue to the physics of the ammeter (or, better, of the whole experimental circuit) would, strictly speaking, have to include the answers to all the questions in the above list; and in the present state of our factual knowledge it simply does not.

It is easy, for example, to write an "operational reduction" of, say, "expectancy." We may take a Carnap reduction pair (7) as our model, and treat "this rat is hungry" analogously to "this sugar-lump is soluble." But this is too easy. Carnap could get by with it because (1) it takes very little to specify the conditions, and (2) the specified conditions are readily realizable. When Carnap says "If put in water, then, 'It is soluble' is equivalent to 'It will dissolve,'" no one needs to be told that, e.g., the solvent used as a test-substance must not already be a super-saturated sugar-solution! This kind of example presupposes a whole set of "obvious" and "unstated" test-conditions. But the point is that they *can* be stated, and *their own* test-conditions given by additional reductions, upon request. We, unfortunately, are not in comparable circumstances. In order to make "This rat is expecting food at L" equivalent to "He locomotes to L," we have to include such statements as "This rat is not frightened" and "This rat is not angry" and "This rat's exploratory-drive with respect to M and N is near-zero" *among the realizable test-conditions*. To the extent that the law-structure defining *them* is incompletely worked out, this task cannot be immediately carried through. Of course, one can take a super-conventionalist line and flatly claim that he offers the reduction-pair as his introduction of the notion "expectancy." No one can quarrel with such a definition, since (at least if it is a bilateral reduction-sentence) it makes no truth-claim. But within the context of discovery, we like to know that a proposed formalization catches the *intent* of the initially vague explicandum, because as a matter of scientific history, if it does not, it may have lost in conceptual fruitfulness what it gained in precision. Philosophers of science of different basic persuasions are still agreed that it is easier to write *merely* operational definitions than to work up operational definitions that lead to the possibility of powerful laws and theories in virtue of the fact that, while in a sense "conventional" or "arbitrary," they still select out for mention the causally relevant aspects of the world—that they "slice the cake rightly" or "carve Nature at its joints." It seems, for example, unlikely that any reduction-sentences for such constructs as "expectancy," "habit," or "hunger" will in the long run lead to a predictively powerful theoretical structure if they are framed so as to ignore such nuisance variables as "fear," "fatigue," or "strength of competing exploratory response R_2."

We have gone into this question in considerable detail, because this is the methodological orientation which leads us to prefer an implicit definition approach, via a whole system of postulates, to the more "direct operational reduction" attempted by Tolman, Ritchie and Kalish. It will be evident that the incomplete formalization which follows does *not* attempt to include guesses as to the causal laws defining such constructs as "exploratory drive" and "frustration." Experiments aimed at testing the proffered system can, at best, claim to have (1) eliminated or (2) randomized, these unreduced factors. If any particular "test" experiment (pro or con) is then criticized as not having actually achieved the necessary elimination or randomization, such an *ad hoc* claim must then be itself formulated so as to permit an experimental test, new postulates being added for the purpose of defining the hypothesized nuisance factors in the given setting (and, if possible, more generally). We suggest that the present approach via implicit definition allows for these accretions with less violence to the basic theoretical structure than is the case with allegedly "direct, operational" definitions of the core constructs of the theory.

There seems to be no justification for leaping from Tolman's near-zero degree of quantification to specific guesses at high levels of quantification. We have tried to carry him to around level (3) as a starter.

In considering an informal system such as Tolman's, one must try to catch the flavor, get the kernel, isolate the *kind* of thing that seems to be stressed, and then say it in a reasonably specific confirmable form. In doing so, we must be prepared for the objection that "But that isn't *quite* what Tolman means." It is not easy to state precisely what Tolman means, and in many cases he has not intended to express an opinion on points which an axiomatization must ultimately say something about. After all, it would be presumptuous to offer a formulation of somebody if he had already formulated himself. On the other hand, it would be surprising if an informal system of proposals, offered as a basis for a specified set of theorems, could be seen as in exact isomorphism with a more formalized set which actually did the job.

Anthropomorphic, intuitive, or common-sense content may be used freely at first, in arriving at formulations. This is especially true in working with Tolman's ideas since he himself proceeds thus in the context of discovery. Furthermore, the "naturalness" of a Tolman type of formulation for the layman, who usually finds its closer to his introspective notions than is the case with other theories, suggests that we might attend more closely to our common, naive view of behavior while trying to get a firmer grasp upon whatever theoretical truth lies in the expectancy approach. Such crutches are not, of course, part of the formulation arrived at, and are not to be considered relevant in evaluating the theory.

As the word *expect* is ordinarily used, it may be seen as involving three elements. When one says "I expect to find food in the refrigerator," he is referring implicitly to

(1) What he sees, initially: "The refrigerator."
(2) What he does when he sees it: "Open it."
(3) What he sees after doing that: "Food."

In the vernacular, these three components are not equally stressed. Thus, in the example, the reference to behavior is suppressed or barely indicated by the verb "find." Verbalization of expectations concerning *loci* are especially likely to suppress the reference to behavior, confining themselves to a statement as to where something is. Verbalization of other types of expectancies are more likely to include a reference to behavior. Thus, "If I reach toward a (seen) pencil, I expect to feel it," "When you insult people they get angry at you," "You have to turn the knob before it will open," "That rat expects food when he presses the lever." It is possible that Tolman's almost complete dependence upon the maze as an instrument of discovery has led him to carry over this easy suppression of the response term, and thus given him the difficulty in "getting to" behavior indicated by Guthrie's well-known gibe that Tolman leaves the rat buried in thought. If this mistake (as we see it) is avoided, the getting-to-behavior need not present a problem any more acute for Tolman than for a non-expectancy theorist, as we shall try to show. The exclusive concern with the "learning a locus" kind of problem, where the stimuli are characteristic of *places* and the responses studied are *locomotions*, makes it easy to formulate an expectancy theory as "S-S," a decision which generates endless difficulties in the ensuing development.

So when we characterize an organism's expectancy, we have to indicate *what* he expects under *what* circumstances when he does *what*. The "basic theoretical element" in an expectancy theory differs from such an element as $_sH_R$ in that the expectancy involves somehow a *reference to what is expected*. In Hull, this expected thing is involved only "historically," in the sense that it appears in the laws which state how $_sH_R$ *grows* (i.e., it is involved as the reinforcer of a specified $_sH_R$). But it is not involved in the characterization of $_sH_R$ itself, wherefore to identify the habit we need only two subscripts, not three. On the other hand, the basic theoretical element introduced below in our reformulation of Tolman does involve a reference to R. The problem of how to get to the response is solved by putting R in at the beginning, as in non-expectancy theories.

In what "language" are these three components to be characterized? Let us call them, the *elicitor*, the *response*, and the *expectandum* (from Latin gerundive ". . . to be expected"). Thus:

Elicitor	Response	Expectandum
S_1: Choice-point stimulation	R_1: Right turn	S_2: Food-box

Obvious simplifications occur here, of course. "Turning right" is a reaction-class of variable members. The elicitor is a proximal stimulus field bearing complex statistical relations to the physical situation. However, neither of these simplifications seems clearly more characteristic of Tolman's than of any other theory. A probabilizing treatment of "stimulus-elements" [such as Estes (26)] could be carried out within an expectancy frame as well.

The *expectandum* is also really a class of proximal stimulus fields, the members of which are dated occurrences. If one says loosely "an occurrence of *the* expectandum," he means the occurrence of a member of this class of proximal stimulus-fields which the organism realizes by entering into a certain physical relation to the named external object. Strictly, of course, this external relation also has a class-character. Often, as is also true of the elicitor, the expectandum will be alluded to in terms of physical objects. But this is always understood to be elliptical, and in any case where it makes a difference the term should mean a proximal stimulus class.

An *expectant* is a unique, dated occurrence of a sequence in which S_1 (elicitor) occurs and arouses a central state (r_1s_2). The aspect, "component" or phase of the central state designated by s_2, is an *expectate* (thus, also a unique, dated occurrence).

A disposition to have expectants of a certain sort (i.e., characterized by components S_1,R_1,S_2) is an *expectancy*. It must be understood that these remarks are in the nature of preliminary explications, since they are manifestly not "operational definitions" in behaviorese. Such concepts as these are finally to be defined by the whole system of postulates in which they occur. Therefore, in the present volume they *remain* very incompletely defined.

S_1 (the elicitor) is obviously to be characterized in the usual stimulus language, and R_1 in the response language. While S_2 (expectandum) is a stimulus, in what language is its central representative (s_2, the expectate) to be characterized? Four "languages" are available:

(1) Physical stimulus language.
(2) Response language.
(3) Physiological language.
(4) Phenomenal language.

All but (1) are quickly eliminated as candidates. There is serious doubt as to whether there exists a (4) which is not really (1) with the subject reporting under special instructions; and in any case the rat hasn't told us his. Language (2) would miss the point by turning us back to a response theory (cf. role of r_G in non-expectancy formulations). Language (3) will be fine when we get it, although probably even then not the most useful for behavioral purposes. This leaves (1), which is what commonsense suggests anyway. "*What* do you expect around the corner?" calls for a description of the *objects* and *events* that will be there. It is also

convenient to have the expectate in stimulus language since at some stage
of the matter of "confirming expectancies" it will come up for quantification ("how *well* did the environment confirm the expectant?"), and it
will be desirable if the same qualities and dimensions are available in
discussing both the expectate and the confirming (or disappointing) environment.

Thus, to characterize the components of an expectancy we will ultimately require three sets of properties:

S_1—Properties characterizing the elicitor.
R_1—Properties characterizing the reaction-class ($=$ response).
S_2—Properties characterizing the expectandum.

The entire central state aroused by the elicitor S_1 is the "expectant"
($s_1 r_1 s_2$). While the denotatum of s_2 is a neural event, *in its role as a hypothetical construct it is characterized by a set of stimulus-numbers;* just
as the dimensions needed to identify the subscript R in $_s H_R$ are *movement* dimensions, although $_s H_R$ as a hypothetical construct itself is a
central state or, as Brown and Farber would view it, a "calculational
device" (4, p. 467). This sort of oddity seems to be the fate of a molar
behaviorism and all one can do is try to get accustomed to it. There seems
to be nothing methodologically wrong with it, since the presence and the
quantification of a particular expectancy is inferred from the strength of
a disposition to emit R_1 in the presence of S_1 provided the terminating
stimulus S_2 is currently valenced. That is, the central construct ($S_1 R_1 S_2$)
is tied to certain sets of data sentences about S_1, R_1, and S_2. When these
three symbols occur conjoined *in the brackets,* they (jointly!) denote an
expectancy; which latter is a theoretical construct and hence *not* in data
language. But when we want to know *"which* expectancy" is being talked
about we need a notation which links us up to the ultimate coordinating
definitions in data language. The expectandum, a proximal stimulus class,
has stimulus dimensions; when the same capital letter occurs in the
brackets, it does not—*could* not, for within the brackets it has no independent designating function at all.

The following skeletal set of "postulates," with accompanying brief
comments, illustrates how the expectancy-concept might be introduced.
We have kept fairly close to Tolman's language to avoid yet another new
vocabulary. Each "law" contains sub-principles of varying independence.
The term *monotonic* is to be understood throughout when functions are
mentioned.

1. *Mnemonization.*—The occurrence of the sequence $S_1 \rightarrow R_1 \rightarrow S_2$
(the adjacent members being in close temporal contiguity) results in an
increment in the strength of an expectancy ($S_1 R_1 S_2$). The strength increases as a decelerated function of the number of occurrences of the
sequence. The growth rate is an increasing function of the absolute value

of the valence of S_2. If the termination by S_2 of the sequence $S_1 \rightarrow R_1$ is random with respect to non-defining properties of S_1, the asymptote of strength is $\leqq$ the relative frequency P of S_2 following $S_1 \rightarrow R_1$ (i.e., a pure number). How far this asymptote is below P is a decelerated function of the delay between the inception of R_1 and the occurrence of S_2.

Comment: This is one of the "basic acquisition postulates" for an expectancy theory, playing a role similar to Postulate 4 in Hull's 1943 set. We have taken as a first guess the assumption that the valence of the expectandum affects *rate* of acquisition only, not asymptote. In common-sense terms, if an animal confirms an expectancy often enough he will become "certain" of it whether it is valenced or not although, if it is not highly valenced, this process may take a very long time. The "absolute value" refers to the supposition that strong negative valences also yield rapid growth of expectancies, although presumably this will ultimately have to be greatly qualified by additional postulates concerning emotional "disrupting" effects.

Professor Tolman (personal communication) raises the question whether the third sentence, referring to the dependence of growth rate upon expectandum valence, is meant to imply that *zero* valence of S_2 would mean zero growth. If so, he states that he would be in disagreement with it. We have left this question open deliberately in our phrasing of the postulate, to emphasize our own view that the necessity of reinforcement in the acquisition of "whatever is learned" is *not* the defining property of an S-R theory, nor is a denial of the necessity of reinforcement for learning the feature which defines an expectancy theory. We agree with Spence (97) that the issue "S-R versus expectancy theory" is logically distinct from the issue "reinforcement versus contiguity-as-sufficient," and we are taking the first issue as crucial in what follows. Confining the discussion entirely to instrumental learning, it seems that four possibilities can be sketched *a priori* for the forms of learning theory, thus:

Reinforcement issue

		Reward necessary for the acquisition	Reward not necessary for the acquisition
Issue as to form of basic learning construct ("what is learned")	*Habits: S-R connections*	Hull Miller Skinner (Type R)	Guthrie
	Expectancies: SRS connections	?	Tolman

If the parameters of the mnemonization function $(SRS) = f(n)$ are so chosen that $\dfrac{df}{dn} = 0$ when $|\mathbf{V}| = 0$, we would have a theory to fill the lower left box. If $\dfrac{df}{dn} > 0$ when $|V| = 0$, we have Tolman. The very fact that one can adopt the entire set of postulates and then make his guesses about this question *within* the expectancy frame seems to us the more reason for rejecting the "necessity of reward" as defining a major theoretical issue. The acquisition postulate might be, say, of the form $(SRS) = M [1 - e^{-(a+bV)n}]$ and it is hard to see the argument between "map" theories and "response" theories as somehow concealed in the question whether the constant a is exactly zero or instead is near zero. It is an interesting question why, historically, the above table has an empty cell.

The matter of asynchronism between S_1 and R_1 has been ignored except insofar as "close temporal contiguity" is required, since we are here dealing with instrumental (operant) learning only. The reference to the valence of S_2 attempts to do some justice to the insistence of Leeper (53, p. 105) and Tolman (151, p. 150) that the animal's cognizing of an expectandum depends to some extent upon the latter's "importance" to the need-state, without prejudging the exact quantitative question just discussed. It will appear later that this is *not*, as a superficial analysis might suggest, tantamount to admitting the truth of some non-expectancy theory. Note also that the present form includes a reference to confirmation-frequencies < 1, since such cases are by far the commonest in "real life." Such less-than-invariable successions generate expectancies of lower strengths, which in turn lead (via the activation postulate below) to lower instantaneous strengths of response. Of course, if the probability of S_2 is *non-random* with respect to some property of S_1, we are in effect setting up a discrimination between two elicitor subclasses S_1' and S_1'', and hence must reformulate the problem in terms of two expectancies. There must also be the possibility of a time-reference in the elicitor-term, to take care of those temporal discriminations reflected in curves obtained under periodic reinforcement. Similarly, if there are non-defining properties of R with respect to which the S_2 probability is not invariant, we deal then with a problem in response differentiation, i.e., these properties *become* defining properties for two new reaction-classes R_1' and R_1'' and again we must begin speaking of two expectancies. In both cases the single postulate leads to a gradual drawing apart in strength. We have called the whole a principle of *mnemonization* following Tolman's distinction (1932) between this process and the other two cognition forms (perception and inference).

We have considered a radical addition to this postulate which would make the rate of expectancy-growth depend not merely on the valence of S_2 but on the valences of all the approximately simultaneous stimuli; and such an addition may be found unavoidable. But after the *first* occurrence of a sequence $S_1 \rightarrow R_1 \rightarrow (S_2 S^*)$ where the star superscript indicates that S^* is valenced, the expectandum S_2 will have an induced cathexis (see 6: Secondary Cathexis below); and the response will, in addition, be receiving strength from the expectancy $(S_1R_1S^*)$. Hence experimental evidence for the suggested addition would be hard to get, requiring either a very sensitive operant or large numbers of animals.

2. *Extinction.*—The occurrence of a sequence $S_1 \rightarrow R_1$, if not terminated by S_2, produces a decrement in the expectancy if the objective S_2-probability has been 1.00, and the magnitude of this decrement is an increasing function of the valence of S_2 and the current strength of $(S_1R_1S_2)$. Such a failure of S_2 when P has been $\doteq 1$ is a *disconfirmation* provided $(S_1R_1S_2)$ was non-zero. For cases where the S_2-probability has been < 1.00, if this objective probability P shifts to a lower P', and remains stable there, the expectancy strength will approach some value $\leqq P'$ asymptotically.

Comment: This principle is in particularly poor shape, and we would perhaps do better to over-simplify by ignoring anything but expectancies near 1.00 at this stage. The principle is qualitatively analogous to the usual extinction principle in non-expectancy theories. The notions of inhibition and energy-expenditure are not, however, introduced. To do so in this context would depart too much from the spirit of an expectancy theory. We are not primarily "tiring out" *responses,* we are instead "learning *that* S_2 no longer follows unfailingly." The undoubted relevance of the work-parameters and the whole problem of spontaneous recovery must somehow be dealt with by an expectancy theory, but will better be fitted in somewhere else than here. Three different components of this question may be tentatively distinguished. First, we will have (as in this postulate) the reduction of the "cognitive" strength of the expectancy by a failure of the usual terminator. Secondly, we may assume that there are some work-related consequences of movement similar to Hull's I_R, which depress effective reaction-potential without altering expectancies (just as it does not alter $_sH_R$ in Hull). Thirdly, there is a possibility of an effort-dependent *parameter* being required in the equation for $_sE_R$, quite apart from any question of "accumulating consequences" of work. Such a parameter would not be confined to extinction effects but would also enter into the ordinary determination of a rate of responding, whether the schedule of reinforcement were periodic, aperiodic, or continuous (cf. 91, p. 202).

If we had enough leads on "anxiety" to anchor it more adequately on the dependent variable side, we would be tempted to insert here some kind of "Law of Disappointment: The occurrence of a disconfirmation of $(S_1R_1S_2)$ if S_2 has positive valence arouses anxiety, the amount of anxiety being an increasing function of the valence of the expectandum S_2."

When the initial $P < 1$, the decline from P to P' presents special problems. In the case of a schedule of periodic reinforcement we have the option of (a) speaking of a family of expectancies, the elicitor of each being made to include time, rate, or serial position as a "stimulus" variable (cf. 90, pp. 263-265) ; or (b) speaking of some sort of generalization gradient from the strongest value of a single expectancy. But on an aperiodic schedule these possibilities are not available, at least in any obvious way. Common sense would say, "If the rat gets a pellet every time, a disconfirmation will be noticed. Similarly, although with a slight vagueness because he cannot differentiate time precisely, the rat notices a failure to deliver at the end of four minutes. But if the administration of S_2 has been random, he must be kept on the new schedule for a time before he lowers his anticipations." These problems remain to be taken up constructively, but the skimpy state of present evidence hardly justifies an attempt as yet.

Another interesting possibility is that of inducing negative cathexes via the disconfirmation operation. There might be some principle to the effect that "Disconfirmation of an expectancy $(S_1R_1S_2)$ by terminating the sequence $S_1 \rightarrow R_1$ by a non-valenced stimulus (or, less-valenced) S_k instead of S_2 induces a negative cathexis in S_k provided that the expectandum S_2 had a positive valence at the time of the disconfirmation. The increment given to this negative cathexis (or, more generally, the decrement given to this cathexis) is an increasing function of the valence of S_2, and the negative *valence* given S_k by this negative cathexis will covary with subsequent change in the need which gave S_2 its valence." Such a principle might be used to deal with the Kendler-Mencher data (49), where each sight of food in the "wrong" cup meant disappointment of the water-expectancy. One thinks also of the oft-cited "disappointment" of Tinklepaugh's (109) monkeys, or Crespi's work on shifting to smaller maze rewards (15, 16). As stated in the postulate, the idea is that the *single* disconfirmation produces a decline in a near-unity expectancy. It also produces a decline in a weaker expectancy which is, however, approaching unity as an asymptote under a continuous schedule $(P_2 \rightleftharpoons 1.00)$. But in this second case the absolute decrement is less. In both cases the decrement also depends on the valence of S_2. If we have a $P_2 < 1.00$ to start with, the single "disconfirmation" cannot play such a role, as we have just discussed.

3. *Primary stimulus generalization.*—When an expectancy $(S_1R_1S_2)$ is raised to some strength, expectancies sharing the R and S_2 terms and resembling it on the elicitor side will receive some strength, this generalization strength being a function of the similarity of their elicitors to S_1. The same is true of extinction of $(S_1R_1S_2)$.

Comment: This again plays a role similar to that which generalization plays in a non-expectancy system. It seems repugnant to common sense in one way, namely, that we do not seem to expect S_2 when S_1' is "similar," in certain cases when we can "tell it apart from" S_1. But this common-sense objection seems to be mainly true of our expectations regarding *places*. Perhaps some additional assumptions as to long-term breaking down of generalization tendencies, i.e., a reduction in the parameters themselves, may be needed.

The use of the non-committal term *similarity* instead of a reference to units on a particular stimulus continuum is deliberate. The postulate is intended to cover a host of specific perceptual laws, each to be separately investigated. No reference to the acceleration of the generalization function is here appropriate; the many sorts of abscissa-variables which will occur in these gradients of "similarity," and a certain arbitrariness in their quantification, make untimely a reference to the sign of the second derivative of such gradients.

Tolman has been accused of referring vaguely to "laws of perception" when the problems of generalization and stimulus equivalence come up. To be sure, this is what he does; but it is not clear just who is in a position to criticize him for it. There is a serious question as to whether anyone else does more than this (validly) for any but the simple, one-dimensional case. For this simple case, a decay function against abscissa stimulus values (whether in absolute units or j.n.d.'s) may be substituted in the above postulate by the reader who wishes to do so.

4. *Inference.*—The occurrence of a temporal contiguity $S_2 S^*$ when $(S_1 R_1 S_2)$ has non-zero strength, produces an increment in the strength of a new expectancy $(S_1 R_1 S^*)$. The induced strength increases as a decelerated function of the number of such contiguities. The asymptote is the strength of $(S_1 R_1 S_2)$ and the growth rate is an increasing decelerated function of the absolute valence of S^*. The presentation of S_2 without S^* weakens such an induced expectancy $S_1 R_1 S^*$. The decrement is greater if the failure of S^* occurs at the termination of the sequence $S_1 \rightarrow R_1 \rightarrow S_2$ than if it occurs as a result of presentation of S_2 without S^* but not following an occurrence of the sequence.

Comment: We believe that this is the sort of postulate whose presence contributes heavily to the identification of an expectancy theory as such. The term "expectancy," while it occurs in the Law of Mnemonization, cannot immediately be distinguished in its empirical consequences by its role there, from the alternative "habit" or "S-R bond." From reading the law of mnemonization one could see no good reason for including S_2 as part of the "expectancy." For if the valence of S_2 depends jointly on *need* and *cathexis*, and the latter is not being experimentally manipulated, then the only really relevant use of the valence of S_2 is in the acquisition postulate, where we can often make S_2 play the role of the "reinforcer" and drop any reference to it in characterizing *that which* is being thus strengthened.

In such a case we would have reduced $(S_1 R_1 S_2)$ to $_S H_R$. But the role an expectancy takes on by virtue of the occurrence of S_2 in the Inference Postulate, *and by the kind of strengthening operation this makes possi-*

ble, permits it to behave in the entire system in a new way. This new way makes the "basic bond" $(S_1R_1S_2)$ correspond in its properties more to what Tolman (and the layman) seem to mean by an "expectation," and less to the usual psychological definition of a "habit."

The common sense of the situation is obvious. If one has learned to expect that he can bring about a certain situation by doing so-and-so; and then (subsequently) he finds that a new element is to be found in that situation; he "infers" that he will be able to bring about the presence of this new element by doing so-and-so. It may be objected that this differs from the idea of secondary reinforcement of an $_sH_R$ only in the time-order of the two acquisition procedures. In the usual case covered by the "secondary reinforcement" concept, we first pair a known reinforcer S^* with a neutral S_2; this pairing is said, by the principle of secondary reinforcement (a postulate?), to confer the "reinforcing property" upon S_2. When we now terminate the sequence $S_1 \rightarrow R_1$ by presenting S_2, the basic principle of reinforcement can then be invoked to derive the consequent strengthening of $_{s_1}H_{R_1}$. Expectancy theory proceeds almost identically by use of the principle of secondary cathexis. In the other time order, we first run off the sequence $S_1 \rightarrow R_1 \rightarrow S_2$ repeatedly (observing no increase in the tendency of S_1 to elicit R_1). Following this, we pair S_2 with the valenced S^*, but not following runnings-off of the sequence. This pairing confers the "reinforcing property" upon S_2; but there is no principle which we can now apply retroactively to strengthen the bond between S_1 and R_1. "Only" the time-order is what makes the big difference. *One* order is easy for both expectancy and non-expectancy formulations, given a postulate or corollary of secondary reinforcement. The *other* order is practically impossible for non-expectancy theories except by an introduction of additional responses as mediators. After all, there is a sense in which time-relations are the *essence* of all learning theories, since they all make use of the basic relations of contiguity and temporal succession. For instance, if an association of topographically unrelated elements took place on the basis of a "contiguity" involving a five-year interval, all theorists would be equally stupefied. The time-relations are the crux of learning situations, so an objection that the difference is "merely one of time-order" cannot be sustained.

We have ignored here the generalization problem. It must be supposed that contiguities of S^* and some fourth stimulus S_2' will induce strength in $S_1R_1S^*$ provided that S_2 and S_2' are sufficiently similar. Perhaps a Law of Primary Generalization should be stated for expectanda as well, as follows:

5. *Generalized inference.*—The occurrence of a temporal contiguity S_2S^* produces an increment in the strength of an expectancy $S_1R_1S^*$ provided that an expectancy $S_1R_1S_2'$ was at some strength and the expectan-

dum S_2' is similar to S_2. The induced strength increases as a decelerated function of the number of such contiguities. The asymptote is a function of the strength of $S_1R_1S_2'$ and the difference between S_2 and S_2'. The growth rate to this asymptote is an increasing decelerated function of the absolute valence of S^*.

6. *Secondary cathexis.*—The contiguity of S_2 and S^* when S^* has valence $|V|$ produces an increment in the absolute cathexis of S_2. The derived cathexis is an increasing decelerated function of the number of contiguities and the asymptote is an increasing decelerated function of $|V|$ during the contiguities, and has the same sign as the V of S^*. The presentation of S_2 without S^*, or with S^* having had its absolute valence decreased, will produce a decrement in the induced cathexis of S_2.

Comments: This is "secondary reinforcement," and in Tolman's 1950 language some mixture of the learning of cathexes and equivalence-beliefs. Since we have been unable to distinguish these two to our satisfaction, we have put them into one principle. They also appear somehow fused in the principle of Elicitor-Cathexis below.

The induced cathexis presumably cannot be said to approach an asymptote which depends only upon the *cathexis* of the primary stimulus S^*, since under low drive we would expect that contiguity to confer less induced value upon S_2. Hence, we have made this asymptote hinge upon the *valence* (cathexis-need combination) of S^*. But the reasoning here is not so evident as is sometimes thought. A more daring guess would be to rephrase the asymptote reference and say ". . . and the asymptote is that of the inducing cathexis," (*not* valence). This would mean that if a neutral stimulus is repeatedly paired with a strongly cathected goal-object but under low need, a subsequent rise in need should give the (now) secondarily cathected stimulus the same large valence it would have had if the pairing had taken place under high need.

7. *Induced elicitor-cathexis.*—The acquisition of valence by an expectandum S_2 belonging to an existing expectancy $(S_1R_1S_2)$ induces a cathexis in the elicitor S_1, the strength of the induced cathexis being a decelerated increasing function of the strength of the expectancy and the absolute valence of S_2.

8. *Confirmed elicitor-cathexis.*—The confirmation of an expectancy $(S_1R_1S_2)$, i.e., the occurrence of the sequence $S_1 \rightarrow R_1 \rightarrow S_2$ when $(S_1R_1S_2)$ is of non-zero strength, when S_2 has a positive valence, produces an increment in the cathexis of the elicitor S_1.

This increment in the elicitor-cathexis by *confirmation* is greater than the increment which would be *induced* by producing a valence in S_2 when the expectancy is at the same strength as that reached by the present confirmation.

Comment: Some such postulate seems in order considering the reinforcing properties acquired by discriminative stimuli (cf. 90, pp. 245-253;

43, p. 236). The distinction between induced and confirmed means that, e.g., choice-point stimuli acquire more cathexis when hungry rats run the T-maze to food, than such stimuli would acquire if rats are made hungry after a large number of satiated runs, even if enough of the latter have occurred to bring the expectancies themselves to a level comparable to those acquired in the first case.

9. *Valence.*—The valence of a stimulus S^* is a multiplicative function of the correlated *need D* and the *cathexis C^** attached to S^*. (Applies only to cases of positive cathexis.)

Comment: Such a principle is empirically useless without the whole mass of imbedding material required to elucidate the relation of cathexes and needs. The need-concept may be introduced solely by reference to the two basic facts of (a) strengthening responses by manipulation of their stimulus-consequences, and (b) experimental relevance of maintenance schedule with respect to the stimuli used. If such a "non-physiological" approach is followed there are, strictly speaking, as many "needs" as there are goal-object-classes found to be not completely interchangeable and which can be shown to be related to a maintenance-schedule (cf. 63). If this procedure is followed, we have two other principles to go on, once a class of stimulus-situations has been identified as a goal-situation and the strength of the associated need defined by its maintenance schedule.

10. *Need strength.*—The need (D) for a cathected situation is an increasing function of the time-interval since satiation for it.

Upon present evidence, even basic questions of monotonousness and acceleration are unsettled for the alimentary drives of the rat, let alone other drives and other species. There is no very cogent evidence that all or most needs rise as a function of time since satiation, although this seems frequently assumed. The notion of satiation itself, even in connection with "simple" alimentary drives, presents great difficulties.

11. *Cathexis.*—The cathexis of a stimulus situation S^* is an increasing decelerated function of the number of contiguities between it and the occurrences of the consummatory response. The asymptote is an increasing function of the need strength present during these contiguities. (There may, however, be some innately determined cathexes.)

Comment: Such a principle would seem to be required unless we assume more biologically given cathexes for exteroceptive stimuli than seems plausible. If correct, it makes necessary an ample opportunity to acquire the cathexes in pre-experimental exposures, before an experiment on latent learning is begun (cf. 13, 14).

Perhaps any special effort to introduce postulates concerning goal-objects should be avoided, and the whole problem handled by implicit definition in which the consummatory response is itself merely treated as the response-term of an expectancy. This final expectancy has, e.g., food as the elicitor, eating as the response, and immediate gustatory and proprioceptive consequences as expectanda. These latter are highly cathected, the confirmation is immediate and invariable, and the number of confirmations is tremendous. The primary cathexis is then assumed to lie in the feel, taste, and smell of the food in the mouth, and the proprioceptive consequences of chewing and swallowing. By the principle of Elicitor-Cathexis, the sight, smell, or touch of food not yet ingested ought to acquire a strength of cathexis very close to the primary. Here, of course, one must make a guess as to how far back is "primary," and whether what is primary in the Law of Effect is stimulation, cessation of stimulation, the necessary behavior-supports to *respond* in a certain way, the alteration of a central state via the bloodstream, or some composite of these. Tolman has referred to certain "to-be-got-at physiological quiescences," with respect to which all other goal properties are ultimately docile. In the absence of any clear evidence, we have formulated the expectancy principles in terms of a *stimulus*-reinforcement view. That is, food has been treated as rewarding by being seen, smelled, or touched. We spoke of S^* and S_2 being contiguous, and made no mention of a consummatory response. Beliefs may differ as to the reinforcing value of the consummatory response itself. However, whether the *act* of chewing (as an efferent event) or the immediate sensory consequences of the act, is what gives it its reward-value, makes little difference for the present task. Since the two are (barring surgical tricks) necessary and sufficient conditions for each other, we can refer merely to the "consummatory response" and get to all anterior (and presumably derived) cathexes from there.

12. *Activation.*—The reaction-potential $_sE_R$ of a response R_1 in the presence of S_1 is a multiplicative function of the strength of the expectancy $(S_1R_1S_2)$ and the valence (retaining sign) of the expectandum. There are momentary oscillations of reaction-potential about this value $_sE_R$, the frequency distribution being at least unimodal in form. The oscillations of two different $_sE_R$'s are treated as independent, and the response which is momentarily "ahead" is assumed to be emitted.

Comment: From here on in the intervening variable chain there need be little or no difference between expectancy and non-expectancy theories. As in the case of non-expectancy theories (cf. Postulate VIII, Corollary v in 40, p. 8), a problem arises in connection with multiple expectancies having the same response term. We have made no attempt to consider the formalization of the overlapping case. One sense in which the "field" emphasis might seem intimately connected with the expectancy view (contrary to our separation of these issues) involves this question. For one might set up (conceptually) as many separate expectancies as there are stimuli in the goal-box. That is, there is an expectancy of wood, of white color, of sawdust, of a food-cup, and so on. A disturbing arbitrariness arises here, since by "cutting it fine" we could find ourselves considering indefinitely large numbers of expectancies, each coordinated to some describable aspect of the physical situation terminating $S_1 \rightarrow R_1$. It might be inferred from this that some substituting of the "field" as expectandum will avoid the difficulty, and hence that the "field approach" *is* more intimately related to an expectancy theory than to *S-R* formulations. However, the same appearance of arbitrariness occurs on the elicitor side, and hence for non-expectancy theories. Why are there not as many *habits* being conditioned in the T-maze as there are physically describable "stimuli" at the choice point? And, since the rat does not always sample all of the available (external) stimulus energies on every trial, these habits must be presumed to be growing at different rates; presumably they also have different asymptotes because of the different modalities and stimulus intensity dynamisms involved. We do not mean to underestimate the difficulties merely by pointing to their occurrence elsewhere, of course. But the present interest is not in those difficult problems which are shared by expectancy and non-expectancy theories. What is actually done in most contemporary experimental speaking about S_1 is to characterize the apparatus and let it go at that. Skinner's emphasis on the generic nature of stimulus and response stems from his awareness of the problem. Interest is centered on actual stimulus components of the starting-box or choice-point only when they are playing a discriminative role—in which case we would talk similarly about *two* expectancies (with different elicitors) in the present formulation also.

A law of threshold of $_sE_R$ to produce response, laws relating response measures (amplitude, latency, response-probability), and a more detailed law of oscillation might be similar to or identical with Hullian principles.

Some principle of chaining may be in order, beyond what is yielded by, e.g., the elicitor-cathexis principle. But the statement of a chained-expectancy postulate is pointless until some activation-postulate for chains is also stated. We might, for example, choose to concern ourselves only with how to calculate the strength of the initial member since, as soon as it occurs, the problem is re-presented. (We ignore the "prediction" of any $_sE_R$ until we are in the presence of *its* elicitor.) But the problem is to formulate a law regarding the manner of summation of the valences attached to expectanda later in the chain. Looking at Tolman's fused balloons on page 147 of the *Purposive Behavior in Animals and Men*, one feels the need for some postulate which will attach the subsequent expectanda of a chain to the response term of each member expectancy. Presumably this strength depends on the strengths of the links (perhaps not stronger than the weakest), and is greater when the chain has been formed by the running off of the chain *sequence* than when it is only induced by the separate confirmation of its elements. But obviously all of this is the sheerest speculation and we have not even sketched a postulate.

For a few sample derivations from these principles for the T-maze case, the reader is referred to (59). Here let us return briefly to the possibility of deriving "multiple trackness" for the lever-pressing case considered above in connection with the response problem. The expectancy $(S_h R_t S_{\bar{h}})$ where the bar over h or l means home-cage or experimental lever *down*, has been strengthened by the pre-experimental history in the home-cage (Postulate 1, Mnemonization). Since the home-cage bar for operating food-dispenser and the lever in the experimental box are similar, the expectancy $(S_l R_t S_{\bar{h}})$ is strong by Postulate 3, Primary Generalization. In the box, repeated pairings of "lever down" $(S_{\bar{l}})$ with food-pellet presentation $(S_f{}^*)$ generate an expectancy $(S_l R_t S_f{}^*)$, by Postulate 5 (Generalized Inference), since $S_{\bar{l}}$ resembles $S_{\bar{h}}$. Any topographic difference between teeth-pressing in the home-cage and that in the box is assumed to be well within the inductive range of the class R. If this were not assumed, the substitution of $(S_l R_t{}' S_{\bar{l}})$ for $(S_l R_t S_{\bar{l}})$ would, of course, require an additional postulate of response induction. The important point here is that the derivation is mediated by the inference postulate, and hence involves a learning construct which notationally refers not only to the elicitor and the response but to a third element, the expectandum, as well. It is via the reference to $S_{\bar{l}}$, "lever down," that the derivation can be carried through. The formal structure here mirrors our informal notions of an expectation, and would be paraphrased roughly thus: "In the home-cage, the rat has learned that when he sees a lever-like object, he can get it down with his teeth; in the box he learns that when the lever is down he gets food. He infers that he can get food by using his teeth." An alternative derivation would invoke Postulate 6, Secondary Cathexis, proceeding via the acquisition by $S_{\bar{l}}$ of a cathexis. These two are not, of course, opposed in their outcome or in any way incompatible. It is perhaps worth noting that, as is often the case, not *all* of the "common-sense" notion of the situation appears in the more formal deductions. The derivation actually makes no use of the cage-expectancy $S_h R_p S_{\bar{h}}$, and its resemblance to $S_l R_p S_{\bar{h}}$. The occurrence of the sequence $S_l \rightarrow R_p \rightarrow S_{\bar{l}}$ serves only to bring about the juxtapositions $S_{\bar{l}} S_f{}^*$ needed for the generalized inference postulate. The anthromorphic linkage between "there are two ways to get a lever down" and "the first way gets food" to "then so also will the second way" finds no place in the formal reconstruction. Whether this would turn out to be the case for all instances of multiple trackness, or even whether all experimental instances of the latter could be derived from the present postulates, we shall not consider here.

VI. APOLOGY TO TOLMANITES AND OTHERS

We are aware that certain objections can be made to the foregoing as even a partial formalization of Tolman's proposals. As was pointed out in the preceding, the question "Does such-and-such a formulation say what Tolman had in mind?" is, strictly speaking, unanswerable, since answering it involves the comparison of a semi-definite set of proposals with an even less definite set. Perhaps an informal consideration of the spirit of Tolman's approach is the most we can offer beyond what has been said. Obviously what follows can make no claims to rigor, but we hope that certain intuitively based or common-sense resistances to such a formalization will be somewhat reduced.

The most striking departure from Tolman's general line is probably our stress on the *response*. The basic theoretical element, the whatever-it-is that receives an increment from the occurrence of the sequence $S_1 \rightarrow R_1 \rightarrow S_2$, while called an *expectancy*, nevertheless has a response reference in it from the first. We are prepared to admit that this is a radical departure from the current form of Tolman's thought, although not so much from that of the 1932 book. (Cf. 128, pp. 10-12, 82.) However, in other places, e.g., p. 136, the explicit reference to *behavior* has almost vanished except for the phrase "commerce with." It is difficult to judge the book on this point because of Tolman's constant use of "means-end-relation," a phrase which does not clearly exclude or include a response-reference. The Glossary does not help (p. 451), since the word "direction" appears in the definition and the definition of this term (p. 441) is similarly interpretable in both ways. On the whole, the *map* emphasis and the failure to include a specific response-reference is already detectable in 1932. But we are not persuaded that this aspect is as definitive of Tolman as, say, the kind of acquisition assumption involved in our Inference Postulate, or the kind of energizing assumption involved in our Activation Postulate.

Now one of the basic difficulties with Tolman's system, admitted at times by Tolman himself and stressed by his critics, is the difficulty of getting from "knowledge" to "action." His tentative concession to Guthrie as to how a motor pattern gets acquired (151, pp. 153-154) is not, insofar as we understand it, fitted into his general cognitive framework with any great care. Taken literally, it almost seems incompatible with the rest. Tolman seems to be agreeing with Guthrie that "Any response (i.e., any movement) which goes off will . . . get conditioned on a single trial to whatever stimuli were then present" (p. 153). At face value such a remark concedes the case to the S-R-contiguity theorist. Although this cannot, of course, be Tolman's intention, he can hardly be said to have resolved the conflict by such a general remark as ". . . such a learning of motor patterns is of necessity always imbedded in a larger goal-directed activity . . ." (p. 154). "Imbedded in" is not a precise methodological expression and as here used bridges some very serious axiomatic gaps.

Roughly speaking, there are two approaches to the response-cognition problem. One is to formulate the hypothetical cognition without reference

to a response term or dimension, so that the characterization of an animal's cognition takes the form of some sort of quasi-propositional event
occurring within the animal. The elements of such an inner event are
alluded to by quasi-data words, i.e., words which (out of the psychological context) would denote environmental objects and their relations, as
discussed above. This approach is indicated by the use of such metaphors
as "map," and the increasing use of this metaphor by Tolmanites we
interpret to mean that they favor such an "environment-referential" approach. The phrase "to learn the location of" stresses the same thing, in
contrast to the phrase "to learn what response leads to." Now it appears
to us that what we may call the "environmental" kind of expectancy
theory would present great difficulties in behavior linkage *even if the
axiomatization of the cognition-acquisition process were well-developed.*
Presumably a rat must have some additional expectancies regarding
"what locomotions take me to S_2" or "what manipulations by me in the
presence of S_1 will produce S_2." Otherwise, his purely *map*-expectancies
regarding the "objective" relations of S_2 to other S's would remain, so
to say, behaviorally irrelevant. Tolman has not addressed himself
seriously to this question, but has left it at a rather common-sense level.
If the rat, as a reasonable being, knew what led to what, he would do
so-and-so. But if we try to anticipate the difficulties, it seems likely that
an expectancy formula which *does* contain the response as an integral
part of the strengthened element will have ultimately to be inserted as a
sort of subtheory in order to get from an "environmental" expectancy to
the behavior. If we are right in this, the obvious suggestion would be to
start afresh and put R in somehow at the beginning. If this means "water-
ing down the difference between Tolman and Hull," so much the better
for it. Of course, the complicated problems of response-equivalence and
the specification of the reaction-class R_1 are still with us, shared with the
competitor theories.

This "response" form of expectancy theory may retain a good deal of
the (non-metaphorical) properties suggested by the map-metaphor. But
the map-properties will have to emerge as derivative properties, the basic
elements still involving response reference. This remark must, of course,
not be taken to mean that responses in the sense of effector-activity-
classes are the "building-blocks," links, or units out of which expectancies
are *physically* constituted—that the elicitation of an expectancy always
involves the occurrence of an effector response, however minimal. That
would be S-R theory again, of course. We mean merely that the characterization of a complex cognitive map will involve a reference to its con-
stituent expectancies, and these expectancies are themselves characterized
notationally by response *reference*. Such a statement is quite different
from any statement that reduces cognitions to implicit movements (cf. 59,
p. 56).

The experimental use of even relatively simple space-and-locomotion set-ups may already involve too great complications for the present primitive state of expectancy theory. In the absence of carefully controlled studies of the effect of early, non-experimental space-traversing experience in the rat, we must not neglect the possibility that appropriate behavior in direction- and locus-learning set-ups is itself a high-level, derivative phenomenon, actually unsuitable for the elucidation of the primary laws of expectancy in spite of its apparent simplicity (to human beings with very similar spatial-locomotor histories!). In order to give some concreteness to our suggestion that the map-properties might be viewed as high-level, derivative consequences of primary response-referring expectancies, the following skeleton analysis of a "simple" spatial inference is offered. Needless to say we do not offer the "postulate" as even a guess at the truth, but only as illustrative. In what follows, reference to an expectancy merely designates its terms, so that it may in fact be of zero strength. If an expectancy has been strengthened by the occurrence of the sequence, it is confirmed, otherwise induced. The class relationships are thus:

$$\text{Expectancies}\begin{cases} \text{Zero} \\ \text{Non-zero}\begin{cases} \text{? "Primary" or "native"} \\ \text{Confirmed (e.g., by mnemonization)} \\ \text{Induced (e.g., by inference)} \end{cases}\end{cases}$$

Before we can even state the single postulate, we need a rather cumbersome set of definitions:

1. A set of k expectancies, $(k\text{-}1)$ of which belong to a chain and the kth one has elicitor and expectandum terms stimulus-equivalent with the elicitor and expectandum of the chain, is a *circular set*. The chain and its alternate expectancy are *equivalent*.
2. If both the chain and the equivalent of the circular set have been confirmed, we have a *confirmed circular set*.
3. Two circular sets in which
    (a) The number of expectancies is the same
    (b) The response-terms in corresponding positions in the two sets are so similar in topography that near-perfect primary induction would occur between them (or: that the amount of primary induction between a member of R_j belonging to the first circular set *and* a member of R_j' homologous to it in the other set, is as great as that between two randomly chosen members of R_j, on the average)
    are *isomorphic circular sets*.
4. Two or more isomorphic circular sets which are confirmed belong to a *confirmed subfamily* of circular sets.

5. The class of all isomorphic circular sets some of which are a confirmed subfamily is a *confirmation-family*.

6. The *diversity* of a confirmation-family is some increasing function of the differences between stimuli which are in homologous positions in the circular sets of the confirmed subfamily. (The term "difference" here is not question-begging, since the differences of these stimuli will have been investigated directly, outside of this context, through studies of primary stimulus generalization and equivalence.)

With all this vocabulary we can now state a "postulate":

Postulate 1001: The strengthening of a chained expectancy which belongs to a circular set will induce strength in the equivalent expectancy of the set, provided that the circular set belongs to a confirmation-family. The amount of induced strength is an increasing function of the chain strength, of the strengths of the expectancies in the confirmed subfamily, and of the number and diversity of the confirmed subfamily. It is a decreasing function of the variability of strengths over the confirmed family.

Let us illustrate this ponderous business by something concrete. A rat has had the following set of expectancies very consistently confirmed in his home cage:

I.
$\begin{cases} H_1 & S_1: \text{distant metal tag. } R_1: \text{forward.} \\ & S_2: \text{close tag, cage wall.} \qquad\qquad\qquad\quad \text{Confirmed} \\ H_2 & S_2: \text{close tag, cage wall. } R_2: \text{left turn.} \\ & S_3: \text{water nozzle.} \qquad\qquad\qquad\qquad\quad\;\; \text{Confirmed} \\ H_3 & S_1: \text{distant metal tag. } R_3: 45° \text{ left turn.} \\ & S_3: \text{water nozzle.} \qquad\qquad\qquad\qquad\quad\;\; \text{Confirmed} \end{cases}$

H_1, H_2, H_3 are a confirmed circular set. H_1H_2 is a chain, and H_3 is its equivalent.

Now suppose during a test breaking phase this rat has the following circular set confirmed (equally consistently, although with a lower total frequency) while exploring a table-top:

II.
$\begin{cases} H_{13} & S_{13}: \text{north wall. } R_1': \text{forward.} \\ & S_{14}: \text{edge of table.} \qquad\qquad\qquad\qquad\;\; \text{Confirmed} \\ H_{14} & S_{14}: \text{edge of table. } R_2': \text{left turn.} \\ & S_{15}: \text{cup at NW corner.} \qquad\qquad\qquad\; \text{Confirmed} \\ H_{15} & S_{13}: \text{north wall. } R_3': 45° \text{ left turn.} \\ & S_{15}: \text{cup at NW corner.} \qquad\qquad\qquad\; \text{Confirmed} \end{cases}$

H_{13}, H_{14}, H_{15} are a confirmed circular set. $H_{13}H_{14}$ is a chain and H_{15} is its equivalent.

I and II are each confirmed circular sets. Since the responses in corresponding positions are similar (R_1 to R_1', R_2 to R_2', and R_3 to R_3')

they are isomorphic circular sets. Since each is confirmed, they define a confirmed subfamily. Actually, of course, not two but a considerable number of such sets are confirmed by any normal organism in the course of its non-experimental history, even in a rather restricted environment.

Now we put a rat in a "new" situation, teaching him two expectancies:

H_{49} S_{49}: wood floor. R_1'': forward.
       S_{50}: iron cross-piece.   Confirmed
H_{50} S_{50}: iron cross-piece. R_2'': left turn.
       S_{51}: goal-box.   Confirmed

Now consider an expectancy

H_{51} S_{49}: wood floor. R_3'': 45° left turn.
       S_{51}: goal-box.   Unconfirmed

H_{49}, H_{50}, H_{51} are a circular set, and they belong to a confirmation family. Hence, by the postulate, H_{51} will have induced strength. Since the family is well-confirmed and the diversity is great (the homologous elicitors and expectanda being very different), the induced strength should be high. The rat should "expect" goal-box 45° to the left, even though he has never made such a response to get it. The important thing to see is that the "inference" is mediated by a somewhat complex relational fact involving both response-resemblance and a confirmation-history, rather than any straightforward, simple stimulus generalization or response induction.

One may be struck by the cumbersomeness of this schematizing, but we have been unable to reduce it. Actually the formulation is grossly over-simplified and elliptical at several points, e.g., in a reference to the "strength of the chain," where variation among the several link strengths would presumably make a difference. This "simple" kind of appropriate behavior will almost certainly require a *more* rather than a *less* complicated mediation than the present one. If the reader is inclined to react (as we were) by saying, "All that, to say that if a rat learns to take an oblique angle as a short-cut, he'll try it in new situations," that is *precisely* the point of our example. Anyone attempting a development of this "obvious good sense" shown by the rat, reducing the number of definitions needed to frame a postulate and yet aiming at some reasonable approximation to rigor, will be convinced, we think, that we are not here straining at a gnat. And it seems to us that, *if* such a postulate were to be made the basis for a rat's "inference" and his resulting $_sE_R$ at 45°, the scientifically important components of the map-metaphor would be contained therein. It should be unnecessary to add that such a postulate would hardly be confined to the "map" case. The term *response* occurs in the postulate without restriction, and presumably such a high-order sort of generalization effect, if postulated, would apply to *social* and *manipula-*

tive as well as *locomotor* behavior. One thinks of Harlow's "learning sets," and of Lashley's famous monkey shifting to the other hand, or his rat running over the maze top "toward the goal."

This development may be expected to arouse criticism from non-expectancy theorists, and one which it is easy to make against the whole formulation suggested in the foregoing pages. One gets the feeling that too much of what we "know" at the ordinary, common-sense level is being put into the basic principles. Since our own bias is mainly on the non-expectancy side, we have had that feeling almost constantly. However, Tolman's system *is* somehow closer to lay thought, and this in itself is surely no basis of rejection. Everyone would be interested in knowing more about intermediate steps, but what if the postulates were "correct" and the intermediate steps were in the central nervous system? When one feels the urge to request the "mediating processes" underlying an expectancy-formation or (especially) the inference postulate, he should ask himself: Do I require this because my *S-R* orientation gives me a conviction that any such gross-behavior law really involves a chain of effector-events mediating it? If the answer to this question is affirmative, it means that the postulate is not being taken as it is offered in an expectancy theory. If the answer is negative, the critic must presumably be demanding a reduction to the neurophysiology.

It is in this sense that the Tolman-Hull controversy involves a centralism-peripheralism issue (cf. 66). In one rather trivial use of the words, any behavioral system is both a "centralism" and a "peripheralism." The confirmation-basis is sentences about an organism's movements, and movements are the data which the science is *about*. Hence, Tolman is a peripheralist, because he is a behaviorist. On the other hand, hypothetical constructs utilized to mediate the stimulus-response laws are universally assumed to have their physical locus in the animal's brain, so that in this respect a Hullian is necessarily a centralist. This locus is admitted by psychologists who have no scientific interest in it. But we cannot agree with the view that the centralism-peripheralism distinction is irrelevant. It is not, however, to be exhibited in a difference of data language, nor in the theorist's mere admission that the brain is somehow involved in the mediation of behavior! The difference lies in the physical locus assigned to *certain specified events characterized by the postulates*. And if a theorist makes assertions assigning such a locus, these assertions are just as much a part of the "real theory" as any of his other assertions. A methodological proposal has been made (e.g., 47) to define behavioral theory very restrictively, as by confining the *content* of theory to the mathematical equations that occur in it. This is well and good as an expression of an interest, but somewhat arbitrary when used as a basis of exclusion against all other theoretical interests. At the very least, the theoretical meaning of learning constructs has to be given by a certain amount of nonmathematical context—we have at least to be informed that one of Hull's growth-functions refers to the change in habit strength rather than the growth of forelimbs. So far as the logic of science is concerned, we are surely not forbidden to introduce assertions of physical locus, or membership of an occurrence in a class specifiable in the language of another science, or actual identity of constructs inferred from originally unrelated empirical studies. If a theorist asserts, say, "The physical locus of the event designated r_G in theory T is in the periphery: that is, r_G is an effector-activity," Kendler's proposal seems to us tantamount to informing the theorist that this utterance is not part of his *real* theory. This is as if one were to inform the author of a genetics text that he had better delete all propositions identifying his statistical genetic constructs with certain physical loci on the visible rods called chromosomes, because this identification is not part of "real theory." Isn't this a rather arbitrary definition of what the theory consists of? Certainly it cannot be derived from any tenets of the general logical empiricism shared by all of us as scientists. The plain fact is that a scientist's theory concerning a specified empirical domain consists of the entire set of empirically meaningful sentences he asserts regarding it. One may not think it was clever of him to assert some of them; one may have little or no interest in some of them, such as those which identify constructs with those of allied sciences; one may accept most of the theory but reject or suspend judgment regarding the locus- or identity-assertions. All these attitudes are available to a critic such as Kendler; but what is *not* available to him is any sort of rule which will *exclude* from the theory some of the empirically meaningful propositions found in it. Nor are we here indulging in any confusion between Reichenbach's two contexts of discovery and justification (75, pp. 6-7). It is not a question of whether the personal imagery of Hull or Tolman during their creative hours constitutes part of the theory. Of course it does not. But if what finally emerges is a set of significant sentences, they are all part of the theory whether some of us are interested in them or not.

Suppose, for example, that an inference postulate is not needed, but is derived as a theorem by some use of, say, r_G. The obvious Tolman retort is, "Very good. Capital. Only, I don't believe it." Now, just what is it the Tolmanite doesn't believe? One might say that, having admitted the derivability of the inference postulate from postulates not of that form, but which involve throughout the strengthening of S-R bonds, there is nothing left to be "denied." We cannot admit this. The rat is a physical mechanism, with parts whose structure and function are the subject-matter of several non-behavior sciences. There is, therefore, nothing "metaphysical" or "transcendent" about the question, "are the expectancies of the inference-postulates in fact mediated by chains of habits, the response terms of which are effector-event-classes?" The degree of confirmation of such a hypothesis *by behavior studies alone* cannot, perhaps, be very high. But this merely shows that a dogged "molar behaviorist" can ask more intelligible questions than he can easily answer by relying wholly upon his preferred behavioral methods. One need not be interested in Tolman's question; it is quite likely that such a question is currently not a profitable one. But neither of these is tantamount to a denial of its empirical meaningfulness.

So, our Tolmanite doesn't believe that the inference occurs via any such effector event as, say, r_G. He points to experimental data that seem to necessitate an inference postulate (assuming for the present discussion that he can do this and make it stick). The non-expectancy theorist grants him the postulate at the "first level" below behavior laws, but derives it as a theorem. The terms which occur in this derivation include not only the stimulus and response classes designated in the postulate, but certain other constructs such as r_G. In a concrete use of the postulate (theorem), this means the invocation of chewing-movements, sense-organ-adjustments and the like. One can spend considerable time trying to invent experimental designs which will raise or lower the confirmation of such concrete applications of the "implicit response" type of construct, but the task is not easy. This is partly because, for all of the emphasis on quantification by non-expectancy theorists and especially by Hullians, the fractional goal response is at present almost wholly unquantified, so that it can be applied to almost any experimental outcome as an "out" with about as much abandon as Tolman can invoke attention, emphasis or the map's "strip-width" when the going gets hard. There are, however, some designs which, if they yielded positive results would render a peripheral mediator so unlikely that a centralist would be justified in requesting more direct (physiological) confirmation.

Another complaint a neo-Tolmanite would make is the total neglect of "perceptual organization" in our formulation. We have spoken of the *elicitor* as what gives rise to the *expectant;* whereas many centralists would say that in so doing we had skipped over what is the first, big step in learning—the transition from the elicitor to some central state consequent upon proximal stimulation, the configural properties of which are causally antecedent to the arousal of an expectant. We have avoided some aspects of this problem by emphasizing (*a*) the class-character of the elicitor and (*b*) the unlimited possibilities for configural specification of the (physical) stimulus side. But we are aware that a staunch centralist with perceptual interests will not feel these are sufficient. This problem was not discussed at any length at the Dartmouth Conference, chiefly because of the conferees' stronger interests in other issues. What little discussion of the topic took place in our sessions indicated considerable disagreement among us as to the importance and even as to the meaningfulness of certain perceptual distinctions. Consequently, we have nothing to say here except that we are fully aware of the omission of such considerations from our formalization proposals. The interposition of another intervening state, say, the *elicitant*, would not necessarily require profound alterations in the remaining axioms. As we have chosen a quasi-stimulus language to characterize the expectate, so a quasi-stimulus language could be chosen for the elicitant's characterization. Postulates would then be needed to indicate the lawful relationships assumed to hold between the proximal elicitor and the (central) elicitant. Even if the remaining axioms remained unchanged, except for the substitution of *elicitant* for *elicitor* in referring to the sequence $S_1 \rightarrow R_1 \rightarrow S_2$, such a change would obviously have a considerable effect on the laws relating observables. Thus, number of exposures, even if the experimental procedure guaranteed adequate proximal representation of the elicitor, would take on a new meaning in the working of the whole theoretical system. If genuine discontinuities in the acquisition-function for *elicitants* were allowed for (e.g., sudden alterations in figure-ground relationships) the form of many derivative laws would be radically altered. It is our belief that the initial efforts at confirmation of expectancy assumptions ought *not* to be complicated by the use of experimental designs rich in perceptual-reorganizing possibilities. We do not think this reflects merely a bias for the response side, although it may in part. But there is present, regardless of one's bias, a peculiar asymmetry in the confirmation-relations of perceptual and expectancy postulates. The changes which occur in the animal's perceptual field as a function of exposures to the stimulus situation are inferred (or, constructed) from behavior-changes. Unless it is assumed that no quantitatively important changes are concurrently taking place in his expectancies (of which the perception is elicitant), we have two processes occurring at once, and their effect on the behavior is serial and cumulative. The components $(y_1, y_2, \ldots y_m)$ characterizing the perceptual field are related via some functions $g_1, g_2, \ldots g_m$ to the components of the stimulus side; and the behavior in turn is functionally dependent $f(y_1, y_2, \ldots y_m)$ upon the perceptions. In the case of human verbal reports made during perception experiments, we ordinarily operate on the plausible assumption that the values of the f-functions are very near their asymptotes (i.e., saying "red" when one *perceives* red has been thoroughly overlearned in the pre-experimental history). Hence, we can determine the form of the g-functions by studying the relation between verbal responses and the stimulus variables. But the corresponding inference from response to perceptual field is obviously much more dangerous in the case of infra-human organisms.

The other horn of the dilemma is much less serious. As Spence has emphasized in his papers on the discontinuity controversy (93, 94, 95), we ought to choose stimuli of such a nature that the g-functions are of negligible importance. We can, of course, never be sure of this either, but we can usually be surer of it than we can of the expectancy (or habit) strengths. If an experimenter employs a goal-box, the floor and all walls of which are white, it is hard to doubt that the rat "perceives" its whiteness provided he has his eyes open. The curve of acquisition of an expectancy having this as the expectandum can then be investigated with some assurance, despite a possible lack of "complete psychological correlation" between the perception and the proximal stimulus. Once having such a law, we can investigate expectanda which are "perceptually" more interesting.

If, on the other hand, we should try to confirm the expectancy-acquisition postulates by utilizing—e.g., form discrimination—a negative result, or a quantitative outcome of a certain order would be contaminated in indeterminate ways and amounts by the well-known slowness of rats in making discriminations on the basis of form. If the "appropriate" behavior failed to appear following a latent learning procedure, it might merely indicate that the rat "had barely started to distinguish the triangle *as such*," and hence prove nothing as to the expectancy postulates proper. Such interpretive ambiguities are in principle inevitable in the early stages of experimentation upon multivariable systems, as we pointed out in our preliminary discussion of quantification. But there is little justification for inviting them by one's choice of design and apparatus.

SUMMARY AND CONCLUSIONS

We find it hard to bring together the preceding in a summary fashion. In its main outlines, we have seen no reason to criticize Tolman's approach as a *kind* of behavioral theory. Like its other critics, we wonder at its lack of even a minimal amount of formalization over the 20 years of controversy and experiment. It is hard to say to what extent this informality accounts for its viability under some very determined attacks. The question of its "factual adequacy" is a difficult one for this very reason, but we have concluded that within the limits imposed by its predictive vagueness, it cannot be said to stand refuted by the body of experimental evidence most clearly relevant—the latent learning studies. These findings seemed sufficiently encouraging to lead us to a preliminary attempt at formalization. The essential feature of that formalization is the *expectancy*, a cognitive unit sharing with *S-R* theory the explicit notational reference to response, but differing from *S-R* theory in its equally explicit reference to the expected consequences of responding. It is proposed that development of expectancy theory in this direction will be more fruitful than in the direction of "maps" and "perceptions" currently favored by Tolman himself.

At the risk of triviality, we cannot close without mentioning the contribution of the theory in generating informative experiments. Even if

S-R theory should turn out to be, ultimately, the "whole truth" of the matter, no one would deny that the form of such an *S-R* theory will have been profoundly molded by the character of the opposition and the facts of learning discovered because of it. In closing, we would like to remind the reader of the words penned by R. M. Elliott in his editorial introduction to *Purposive Behavior in Animals and Men:*

Professor Tolman's argument may be ignored in some quarters; it will certainly be amplified by himself and others as new and crucial research data come to light; it will not, I think, be radically revised, that is "disproved"; and it will never be discredited, that is, shown to be either fictitious or unnecessary. Behaviorism of this sort has come of age (128, pp. viii-ix).

Bibliography

1. BENDIG, A. W. Latent learning in a water maze. *J. exp. Psychol.*, 1952, 43, 134-137.
2. BLODGETT, H. C. The effect of the introduction of reward upon the maze performance of rats. *Univ. Calif. publ. Psychol.*, 1929, 4, 113-134.
3. BROAD, C. D. The "nature" of a continuant. In H. Feigl and W. Sellars (Eds.), *Readings in philosophical analysis.* New York: Appleton-Century-Crofts, 1949. Pp. 472-481.
4. BROWN, J. S., and FARBER, I. E. Emotions conceptualized as intervening variables—with suggestions toward a theory of frustration. *Psychol. Bull.*, 1951, 48, 465-495.
5. BUXTON, C. E. Latent learning and the goal gradient hypothesis. *Contr. psychol. Theor.*, 1940, 2, #2.
6 CARLIN, Jean E. Drive stimulus generalization. Unpublished M.A. thesis, University of Minnesota, 1952.
7. CARNAP, R. Testability and meaning. *Phil. Sci.*, 1937, 4, 1-40.
8. ——. The two concepts of probability. *Phil. phenomenol. Res.*, 1945, 5, 513-532.
9. ——. Empiricism, semantics, and ontology. *Rev. int. de Phil.*, 1950, 4, 20-40.
10. CARR, H. Teaching and learning. *J. genet. Psychol.*, 1930, 37, 189-218.
11. CHISHOLM, R. M. Intentionality and the theory of signs. *Phil. Stud.*, 1952, 3, 56-63.
12. CHRISTIE, R. Experimental naïveté and experiential naïveté. *Psychol. Bull.*, 1951, 48, 327-339.
13. ——. The role of drive discrimination in learning under irrelevant motivation. *J. exp. Psychol.*, 1951, 42, 13-19.
14. ——. The effect of some early experiences in the latent learning of adult rats. *J. comp. physiol. Psychol.*, 1952, 43, 281-288.
15. CRESPI, L. P. Quantitative variation of incentive and performance in the white rat. *Amer. J. Psychol.*, 1942, 55, 467-517.
16. ——. Amount of reinforcement and level of reinforcement. *Psychol. Rev.*, 1944, 51, 341-357.
17. DAUB, C. T. The effect of doors on latent learning. *J. comp. Psychol*, 1933, 15, 49-58.
18. DENNIS, W. A comparison of the rat's first and second explorations of a maze unit. *Amer. J. Psychol.*, 1935, 47, 488-490.

19. DENNIS, W. Spontaneous alternation in rats as an indicator of the persistence of stimulus effects. *J. comp. Psychol.*, 1939, 28, 305-312.

20. ——, and SOLLENBERGER, R. T. Negative adaption in the maze exploration of albino rats. *J. comp. Psychol.*, 1934, 18, 197-206.

21. DENNY, M. R., and DAVIS, R. H. A test of latent learning for a non-goal significate. *J. comp. physiol. Psychol.*, 1951, 44, 590-595.

22. DIESENROTH, C. F., and SPENCE, K. W. An investigation of latent learning in the white rat. *Psychol. Bull.*, 1941, 38, 706. (Abstract)

23. ELLIOTT, M. H. The effect of appropriateness of rewards and of complex incentives on maze performance. *Univ. Calif. publ. Psychol.*, 1929, 4, 91-98.

24. ESTES, W. K. An experimental study of punishment. *Psychol. Monogr.*, 1944, 57, No. 3 (Whole No. 263).

25. ——. Effects of competing reactions on the conditioning curve for bar-pressing. *J. exp. Psychol.*, 1950, 40, 200-205.

26. ——. Toward a statistical theory of learning. *Psychol. Rev.*, 1950, 57, 94-107.

27. ——, and SKINNER, B. F. Some quantitative properties of anxiety. *J. exp. Psychol.*, 1941, 29, 390-400.

28. FEHRER, Elizabeth. Latent learning in the sophisticated rat. *J. exp. Psychol.*, 1951, 42, 409-416.

29. FINAN, J. L. Quantitative studies in motivation. I. Strength of conditioning in rats under varying degrees of hunger. *J. comp. Psychol.*, 1940, 29, 119-134.

30. GILCHRIST, J. C. Characteristics of latent and reinforcement learning as a function of time. *J. comp. physiol. Psychol.*, 1952, 45, 198-203.

31. GLEITMAN, H. Studies in motivation and learning: II. Thirsty rats trained in maze with food but not water; then run hungry. *J. exp. Psychol.*, 1950, 40, 169-174.

32. GRICE, G. R. An experimental test of the expectation theory of learning. *J. comp. physiol. Psychol.*, 1940, 41, 137-143.

33. HANEY, G. W., The effect of familiarity on maze performance of albino rats. *Univ. Calif. publ. Psychol.*, 1931, 4, 319-333.

34. HEMPEL, C. G. Problems and changes in the empiricist criterion of meaning. *Rev. int. de Phil.*, 1950, 4, 41-63.

35. HERB, F. H. Latent learning—non-reward followed by food in blinds. *J. comp. Psychol.*, 1940, 29, 247-255.

36. HERON, W. T. Internal stimuli and learning. *J. comp. physiol. Psychol.*, 1949, 42, 486-492.

37. HILGARD, E. R. *Theories of learning.* New York: Appleton-Century-Crofts, 1948.

38. HULL, C. L. *Principles of behavior.* New York: Appleton-Century-Crofts, 1943.

39. ——. Behavior postulates and corollaries—1949. *Psychol. Rev.*, 1950, 57, 173-180.

40. ——. *A behavior system.* New Haven: Yale University Press, 1952.

41. IWAHARA, S., and MARX, M. Cognitive transfer in discrimination learning. *Amer. Psychologist*, 1950, 5, 479. (Reported by title only.)

42. KARN, H. W., and PORTER, H. M., Jr. The effects of certain pre-training procedures upon maze performance and their significance for the concept of latent learning. *J. exp. Psychol.*, 1946, 36, 461-469.

43. KELLER, F. S., and SCHOENFELD, W. N. *Principles of Psychology.* New York: Appleton-Century-Crofts, 1950.

44. KENDLER, H. H. Drive interaction: II. Experimental analysis of the role of drive in learning theory. *J. exp. Psychol.*, 1945, 35, 188-198.

45. ———. A comparison of learning under motivated and satiated conditions in the white rat. *J. exp. Psychol.*, 1947, 37, 545-549.

46. ———. An investigation of latent learning in a T-maze. *J. comp. physiol. Psychol.*, 1947, 40, 265-270.

47. ———. "What is learned?"—a theoretical blind alley. *Psychol. Rev.*, 1952, 59, 269-277.

48. ———, and KANNER, J. H. A further test of the ability of rats to learn the location of food when motivated by thirst. *J. exp. Psychol.*, 1950, 40, 762-765.

49. KENDLER, H. H., and MENCHER, H. C. The ability of rats to learn the location of food when motivated by thirst—an experimental reply to Leeper. *J. exp. Psychol.*, 1948, 38, 82-88.

50. KRECHEVSKY, I. "Hypotheses" versus "chance" in the presolution period in sensory discrimination-learning. *Univ. Calif. publ. Psychol.*, 1932, 6, 27-44.

51. LASHLEY, K. S. A simple maze: with data on the relation of the distribution of practice to rate of learning. *Psychobiol.*, 1918, 1, 353-367.

52. LEEPER, R. W. The role of motivation in learning: a study of the phenomenon of differential motivational control of the utilization of habits. *J. genet. Psychol.*, 1935, 46, 3-40.

53. ———. The experiments by Spence and Lippitt and by Kendler on the sign-gestalt theory of learning. *J. exp. Psychol.*, 1948, 38, 102-106.

54. LITTMAN, R. A. Latent learning in a T-maze after two degrees of training. *J. comp. physiol. Psychol.*, 1950, 43, 135-147.

55. ———, and ROSEN, E. Molar and molecular. *Psychol. Rev.*, 1950, 57, 58-65.

56. MacCORQUODALE, K., and MEEHL, P. E. On a distinction between hypothetical constructs and intervening variables. *Psychol. Rev.*, 1948, 55, 95-107.

57. ———. "Cognitive" learning in the absence of competition of incentives. *J. comp. physiol. Psychol.*, 1949, 42, 383-390.

58. ———. On the elimination of cul-entries without obvious reinforcement. *J. comp. physiol. Psychol.*, 1951, 44, 367-371.

59. ———. Preliminary suggestions as to a formalization of expectancy theory. *Psychol. Rev.*, 1953, 60, 55-63.

60. MacDUFF, Mary A. The effect on retention of varying degrees of motivation during learning in rats. *J. comp. physiol. Psychol.*, 1943, 33, 369-386.

61. MALTZMAN, I. M. An experimental study of learning under an irrelevant need. *J. exp. Psychol.*, 1950, 40, 788-793.

62. MEEHL, P. E. An examination of the treatment of stimulus patterning in Prof. Hull's *Principles of Behavior*. *Psychol. Rev.*, 1945, 52, 324-332.

63. ———. On the circularity of the law of effect. *Psychol. Bull.*, 1950, 47, 52-75.

64. ———, and MacCORQUODALE, K. A further study of latent learning in the T-maze. *J. comp. physiol. Psychol.*, 1948, 41, 372-396.

65. ———. A failure to find the Blodgett effect, and some secondary observations on drive conditioning. *J. comp. physiol. Psychol.*, 1951, 44, 178-183.

66. ———. Some methodological comments concerning expectancy theory. *Psychol. Rev.*, 1951, 58, 230-233.

67. ———. Drive conditioning as a factor in latent learning. *J. exp. Psychol.*, 1953, 43, 20-24.

68. MILLER, N., and DOLLARD, J. *Social learning and imitation*. New Haven: Yale University Press. 1941.

69. MONTGOMERY, K. C. "Spontaneous alternation" as a function of time between trials and amount of work. *J. exp. Psychol.*, 1951, 42, 82-93.

70. ———. The relation between exploratory behavior and spontaneous alternation in the white rat. *J. comp. physiol. Psychol.*, 1951, 44, 582-589.

71. ———. Exploratory behavior and its relation to spontaneous alternation in a series of maze exposures. *J. comp. physiol. Psychol.*, 1952, 45, 50-57.

72. MUENZINGER, K. F. Plasticity and mechanization of the problem box habit in guinea pigs. *J. comp. Psychol.*, 1928, 8, 45-69.

73. ———, KOERNER, L., and IREY, E. Variability of an habitual movement in guinea pigs. *J. comp. Psychol.*, 1929, 9, 425-436.

74. NISSEN, H. W. Description of the learned response in discrimination behavior. *Psychol. Rev.*, 1950, 57, 121-131.

75. REICHENBACH, H. *Experience and prediction.* Chicago: Univ. Chicago Press, 1938.

76. REYNOLDS, B. A repetition of the Blodgett experiment on "latent learning." *J. exp. Psychol.*, 1945, 35, 504-516.

77. ———. The relationship between the strength of a habit and the degree of drive present during acquisition. *J. exp. Psychol.*, 1949, 39, 296-305.

78. RITCHIE, B. F. Studies in spatial learning. III. Two paths to the same location and two paths to two different locations. *J. exp. Psychol.*, 1947, 37, 25-38.

79. ———. Studies in spatial learning. VI. Place orientation and direction orientation. *J. exp. Psychol.*, 1948, 38, 659-669.

80. ———, AESCHLIMAN, B., and PEIRCE, P. Studies in spatial learning. VIII. Place performance and the acquisition of place dispositions. *J. comp. physiol. Psychol.*, 1950, 43, 73-85.

81. RITCHIE, B. F., HAY, Alice, and HARE, Rachel. Studies in spatial learning: IX. A dispositional analysis of response performance. *J. comp. physiol. Psychol.*, 1951, 44, 442-449.

82. SELLARS, W. S. Concepts as involving laws and inconceivable without them. *Phil. of Sci.*, 1948, 15, 287-315.

83. ———. Mind, meaning, and behavior. *Philos. Studies*, 1952, 3, 83-95.

84. SEWARD, J. P. A theoretical derivation of latent learning. *Psychol. Rev.*, 1947, 54, 83-98.

85. ———. An experimental analysis of latent learning. *J. exp. Psychol.*, 1949, 39, 177-186.

86. ———, DATEL, W. E., and LEVY, N. Tests of two hypotheses of latent learning. *J. exp. Psychol.*, 1952, 43, 274-280.

87. SEWARD, J. P., LEVY, N., and HANDLON, J. P., Jr. Incidental learning in the rat. *J. comp. physiol. Psychol.*, 1950, 43, 240-251.

88. SHAW, M. E., and WATERS, R. H. An experimental test of latent learning in a relatively free-choice situation. *J. genet. Psychol.*, 1950, 77, 283-292.

89. SIMMONS, Rietta. The relative effectiveness of certain incentives in animal learning. *Comp. Psychol. Monogr.*, 1924, 2, 1-79.

90. SKINNER, B. F. *The behavior of organisms.* New York: Appleton-Century-Crofts, 1938.

91. ———. Are theories of learning necessary? *Psychol. Rev.*, 1950, 57, 193-216.

92. SOLOMON, R. L. The influence of work on behavior. *Psychol. Bull.*, 1948, 55, 1-40.

93. SPENCE, K. W. The differential response in animals to stimuli varying within a single dimension. *Psychol. Rev.*, 1937, 44, 430-444.

94. ———. Continuous versus non-continuous interpretations of discrimination learning. *Psychol. Rev.*, 1940, 47, 271-288.

95. SPENCE, K. W. An experimental test of the continuity and non-continuity theories of discrimination learning. *J. exp. Psychol.*, 1945, 35, 253-266.

96. ———.The methods and postulates of "behaviorism." *Psychol. Rev.*, 1948, 55, 67-78.

97. ———. Theoretical interpretations of learning. In S. S. Stevens (Ed.), *Handbook of Experimental Psychology.* New York: John Wiley and Sons, 1951.

98. ———, BERGMANN, G., and LIPPITT, R. A study of simple learning under irrelevant motivational-reward conditions. *J. exp. Psychol.*, 1950, 40, 539-551.

99. SPENCE, K. W., and KENDLER, H. H. The speculations of Leeper with respect to the Iowa tests of the sign-gestalt theory of learning. *J. exp. Psychol.*, 1948, 38, 106-109.

100. SPENCE, K. W., and LIPPITT, R. "Latent" learning of a simple maze problem with relevant needs satiated. *Psychol. Bull.*, 1940, 37, 429. (Abstract)

101. ———. An experimental test of the sign-gestalt theory of trial and error learning. *J. exp. Psychol.*, 1946, 36, 491-502.

102. STRANGE, J. R. Latent learning under conditions of high motivation. *J. comp. physiol. Psychol.*, 1950, 43, 194-197.

103. STRASSBURGER, R. C. Resistance to extinction of a conditioned operant as related to drive level at reinforcement. *J. exp. Psychol.*, 1950, 40, 473-487.

104. SZYMANSKI, J. S. Versuch über die Wirkung der Faktoren, die als Antrieb zum Erlernen einer Handlung dienen Können. *Pflüg. arch. ges. Physiol.*, 1918, 171, 374-385.

105. TARSKI, A. *Introduction to logic.* New York: Oxford University Press, 1941.

106. THISTLETHWAITE, D. L. A critical review of latent learning and related experiments. *Psychol. Bull.*, 1951, 48, 97-129.

107. ———. An experimental test of a reinforcement interpretation of latent learning. *J. comp. physiol. Psychol.*, 1951, 44, 431-441.

108. ———. Conditions of irrelevant incentive learning. *J. comp. physiol. Psychol.*, 1952, 45, 517-525.

109. TINKLEPAUGH, O. L. An experimental study of representative factors in monkeys. *J. comp. Psychol.*, 1928, 8, 197-236.

110. TOLMAN, E. C. More concerning the temporal relations of meaning and imagery. *Psychol. Rev.*, 1917, 24, 114-138.

111. ———. Retroactive inhibition as affected by conditions of learning. *Psychol. Monogr.*, 1918, 25, No. 107, 50 pp.

112. ———. Nerve process and cognition. *Psychol. Rev.*, 1918, 25, 423-442.

113. ———. Instinct and purpose. *Psychol. Rev.*, 1920, 27, 217-233.

114. ———. A new formula for behaviorism. *Psychol. Rev.*, 1922, 29, 44-53.

115. ———. Can instincts be given up in psychology? *J. abn. Psychol.*, 1922, 17, 139-152.

116. ———. The nature of instinct. *Psychol. Bull.*, 1923, 20, 200-216.

117. ———. A behavioristic account of the emotions. *Psychol. Rev.*, 1923, 30, 217-227.

118. ———. The effects of underlearning upon long- and short-time retentions. *J. exp. Psychol.*, 1923, 6, 466-474.

119. ———. The inheritance of maze-learning ability in rats. *J. comp. Psychol.*, 1924, 4, 1-18.

120. ———. Behaviorism and purpose. *J. Phil.*, 1925, 22, 36-41.

121. ———. Purpose and cognition: the determiners of animal learning. *Psychol. Rev.*, 1925, 32, 285-297.

122. TOLMAN, E. C. The nature of the fundamental drives. *J. abn. soc. Psychol.*, 1926, 20, 349-358.

123. ———. A behavioristic theory of ideas. *Psychol. Rev.*, 1926, 33, 352-369.

124. ———. Habit formation and higher mental processes in animals. *Psychol. Bull.*, 1927, 24, 1-35; 1928, 25, 24-53.

125. ———. A behaviorist's definition of consciousness. *Psychol. Rev.*, 1927, 34, 433-439.

126. ———. Purposive behavior. *Psychol. Rev.*, 1928, 35, 524-530.

127. ———. Maze performance a function of motivation and of reward as well as of knowledge of the maze paths. *J. gen. Psychol.*, 1930, 4, 338-342.

128. ———. *Purposive behavior in animals and men.* New York: Appleton-Century, 1932.

129. ———. Lewin's concept of vectors. *J. gen. Psychol.*, 1932, 7, 3-15.

130. ———. Sign-gestalt or conditioned reflex? *Psychol. Rev.* 1933, 40, 246-255.

131. ———. The law of effect. A reply to Dr. Goodenough. *J. exp. Psychol.*, 1933, 16, 463-470.

132. ———. Backward elimination of errors in two successive discrimination habits. *Univ. Calif. publ. Psychol.*, 1934, 6, 145-152.

133. ———. Theories of learning. In F. A. Moss, *Comparative Psychology.* New York: Prentice-Hall, 1934. Pp. 367-408.

134. ———. Psychology versus immediate experience. *Philos. Science*, 1935, 2, 356-380.

135. ———. Operational behaviorism and current trends in psychology. *Proc. 25th Anniv. Inauguration Graduate Studies.* Los Angeles: University of Southern California, 1936, 89-103.

136. ———. Connectionism: wants, interests, and attitudes. *Character and Personality*, 1936, 4, 245-253.

137. ———. Operational behaviorism and current trends in psychology. *Proc. 25th Anniv. Inauguration Graduate Studies.* Los Angeles: University of Southern California, 1936, 89-103.

138. ———. Demands and conflicts. *Psychol. Rev.*, 1937, 44, 158-169.

139. ———. The acquisition of string-pulling by rats—conditioned response or sign-gestalt? *Psychol. Rev.*, 1937, 44, 195-211.

140. ———. An operational analysis of "Demands." *Erkenntnis*, 1937, 6, 383-392.

141. ———. The determiners of behavior at a choice point. *Psychol. Rev.*, 1938, 45, 1-41.

142. ———. A reply to Professor Guthrie. *Psychol. Rev.*, 1938, 45, 163-164.

143. ———. The law of effect. *Psychol. Rev.*, 1938, 45, 200-203.

144. ———. Prediction of vicarious trial and error by means of the schematic sowbug. *Psychol. Rev.*, 1939, 46, 318-336.

145. ———. Spatial angle and vicarious trial and error. *J. comp. Psychol.*, 1940, 30, 129-135.

146. ———. Motivation, learning, and adjustment. *Proc. Amer. Philos. Soc.*, 1941, 84, 543-563.

147. ———. Discrimination vs. learning and the schematic sowbug. *Psychol. Rev.*, 1941, 48, 367-382.

148. ———. A drive-conversion diagram. *Psychol. Rev.*, 1943, 50, 503-513.

149. ———. A stimulus-expectancy need-cathexis psychology. *Science*, 1945, 101, 160-166.

150. ———. Cognitive maps in rats and men. *Psychol. Rev.*, 1948, 55, 189-208.

151. ———. There is more than one kind of learning. *Psychol. Rev.*, 1949, 56, 144-155.

152. TOLMAN, E. C. Discussion: Interrelationships between perception and personality. *J. Personal.*, 1949, 18, 48-50.
153. ———. The psychology of social learning. *J. soc. Issues*, 1949, 5, Supplement No. 3, 5-18.
154. ———. The nature and functioning of wants. *Psychol. Rev.*, 1949, 56, 357-369.
155. ———, and BRUNSWIK, E. The organism and the causal texture of the environment. *Psychol. Rev.*, 1935, 42, 43-77.
156. TOLMAN, E. C., and DAVIS, F. C. A note on the correlations between two mazes. *J. comp. Psychol.*, 1924, 4, 125-135.
157. TOLMAN, E. C., and GEIER, F. M. Goal distance and restless activity. I: The goal gradient of restless activity. *J. comp. Psychol.*, 1943, 35, 197-204.
158. ———, and LEVIN, M. Individual differences in emotionality, hypothesis formation, vicarious trial and error, and visual discrimination learning in rats. *Comp. psychol. Monogr.*, 1941, 17, No. 3. 20 pp.
159. TOLMAN, E. C., and GLEITMAN, H. Studies in learning and motivation: I. Equal reinforcements in both end-boxes, followed by shock in one end-box. *J. exp. Psychol.*, 1949, 39, 810-819.
160. ———. Studies in spatial learning: VII. Place and response learning under different degrees of motivation. *J. exp. Psychol.*, 1949, 39, 653-659.
161. TOLMAN, E. C., HALL, C. S., and BRETNALL, E. P. A disproof of the law of effect and a substitution of the laws of emphasis, motivation, and disruption. *J. exp. Psychol.*, 1932, 15, 601-614.
162. TOLMAN, E. C., and HONZIK, C. H. Introduction and removal of reward, and maze performance of rats. *Univ. Calif. publ. Psychol.*, 1930, 4, 257-275.
163. ———. The perception of spatial relations by the rat: a type of response not easily explained by conditioning. *J. comp. Psychol.*, 1936, 22, 287-318.
164. ———. The action of punishment in accelerating learning. *J. comp. Psychol.*, 1938, 26, 187-200.
165. ———. "Insight" in rats. *Univ. Calif. publ. Psychol.*, 1930, 4, 215-232.
166. ———. Degrees of hunger, reward and non-reward, and maze learning in rats. *Univ. Calif. publ. Psychol.*, 1930, 4, 241-257.
167. ———. Introduction and removal of reward, and maze performance in rats. *Univ. Calif. publ. Psychol.*, 1930, 4, 257-275.
168. ———, and ROBINSON, E. W. The effect of degrees of hunger upon the order of elimination of long and short blinds. *Univ. Calif. publ. Psychol.*, 1930, 4, 189-202.
169. TOLMAN, E. C., and HOROWITZ, J. A reply to Mr. Koffka. *Psychol. Bull.*, 1933, 30, 459-465.
170. TOLMAN, E. C., and KRECHEVSKY, I. Means-end-readiness and hypothesis. A contribution to comparative psychology. *Psychol. Rev.*, 1933, 40, 60-70.
171. TOLMAN, E. C., and MINIUM, E. VTE in rats: Overlearning and difficulty of discrimination. *J. comp. Psychol.*, 1942, 34, 301-306.
172. TOLMAN, E. C., and RITCHIE, B. F. Correlation between VTE's on a maze and on a visual discrimination apparatus. *J. comp. Psychol.*, 1943, 36, 91-98.
173. ———, and KALISH, D. Studies in spatial learning. I. Orientation and the short-cut. *J. exp. Psychol.*, 1946, 36, 13-24.
174. ———. Studies in spatial learning. II. Place learning vs. response learning. *J. exp. Psychol.*, 1946, 36, 221-229.
175. ———. Studies in spatial learning. IV. The transfer of place learning to other starting paths. *J. exp. Psychol.*, 1947, 37, 39-47.

176. TOLMAN, E. C., RITCHIE, B. F., and KALISH, D. Studies in spatial learning. V. Response learning vs. place learning by the non-correction method. *J. exp. Psychol.*, 1947, 37, 285-292.

177. TOLMAN, E. C., and SAMS, C. F. Time discrimination in white rats. *J. comp. Psychol.*, 1925, 5, 255-263.

178. TOLMAN, E. C., and WHITE, A. E. A note on the elimination of short and long blind alleys. *J. comp. Psychol.*, 1923, 3, 327-332.

179. WALKER, E. L. The acquisition of a response to food under conditions of food satiation. *Amer. Psychologist*, 1948, 3, 239. (Reported by title only.)

180. ———. Drive specificity and learning. *J. exp. Psychol.*, 1948, 38, 39-49.

181. ———. The demonstration of learning acquired under a strong irrelevant drive previously masked by a primarily reinforced response. *Amer. Psychologist*, 1950, 5, 479. (Reported by title only.)

182. ———. Drive specificity and learning: Demonstration of a response tendency acquired under a strong irrelevant drive. *J. comp. physiol. Psychol.*, 1951, 44, 596-603.

183. ———, KNOTTER, M. C., and DeVALOIS, R. L. Drive specificity and learning: The acquisition of a spatial response to food under conditions of water deprivation and food satiation. *J. exp. Psychol.*, 1950, 40, 161-168.

184. WALLACE, S. R., Jr., BLACKWELL, M. G., Jr., and JENKINS, G. Pre-reward and post-reward performance in the "latent learning" of an elevated maze. *Psychol. Bull.*, 1941, 38, 694. (Abstract)

185. WHITE, R. K. The case for the Tolman-Lewin interpretation of learning. *Psychol. Rev.*, 1943, 50, 157-186.

186. WILLIAMS, K. A. The reward value of a conditioned stimulus. *Univ. Calif. publ. Psychol.*, 1929, 4, 31-55.

187. WINGFIELD, R. C., and DENNIS, W. The dependence of the white rat's choice of pathways upon the length of the daily trial series. *J. comp. Psychol.*, 1934, 18, 135-148.

SECTION 3

Burrhus F. Skinner

WILLIAM S. VERPLANCK

"A PURELY DESCRIPTIVE SYSTEM IS NEVER POPULAR"

So FAR AS scientific method is concerned, the system set up . . . may be characterized as follows. It is positivistic. It confines itself to description rather than explanation. Its concepts are defined in terms of immediate observations and are not given local or physiological properties. A reflex is not an arc, a drive is not the state of a center, extinction is not the exhaustion of a physiological substance or state. Terms of this sort are used merely to bring together groups of observations, to state uniformities, and to express properties of behavior which transcend single instances. They are not hypotheses, in the sense of things to be proved or disproved, but convenient representations of things already known. As to hypotheses, the system does not require them—at least in the usual sense.

It is often objected that a positivistic system offers no incentive to experimentation. The hypothesis, even the bad hypothesis, is said to be justified by its effect in producing research . . . and it is held or implied that some such device is usually needed. This is an historical question about the motivation of human behavior. There are doubtless many men whose curiosity about nature is less than their curiosity about the accuracy of their guesses, but it may be noted that science does in fact progress without the aid of this kind of explanatory prophecy. Much can be claimed for the greater efficiency of the descriptive system, when it is once motivated.

Granted, however, that such a system does possess the requisite moving force, it may still be insisted that a merely descriptive science must be lacking in direction. A fact is a fact; and the positivistic system does not seem to prefer one to another. Hypotheses are declared to solve this problem by directing the choice of facts (what directs the choice of hypotheses is not often discussed), and without them a distinction between the useful and the useless fact is said to be impossible. This is a narrow view of a descriptive science. The mere accumulation of uniformities is not a science at all. It is necessary to organize facts in such a way that a simple and convenient description can be given, and

for this purpose a structure or system is required. The exigencies of a satisfactory system provide all the direction in the acquisition of facts that can be
desired. Although natural history has set the pattern for the collection of
isolated bits of curious behavior, there is no danger that a science of behavior
will reach that level.

—B. F. SKINNER, *The Behavior of Organisms*, pp. 44-45

I. THE SYSTEM

In dealing with Skinner, we are concerned with a theorist who now
espouses no theory, a systematist whose system is still developing, and a
constructive thinker some of whose most important contributions have
been those of a critic.

In the course of his writings, Skinner has presented the results of a
comprehensive experimental program, and elaborated a theory of behavior based upon it. Since its publication in comprehensive form in *The
Behavior of Organisms*, he has, one may infer from more recent writings,
modified it greatly by eliminating several central concepts without substituting others. These publications are not sufficient to enable us to
analyze the system in its current status, so that we will restrict ourselves
to its earlier form.

From an examination of this theory, we may learn something of the
reasons for its alteration, and perhaps reveal some relationships between
the adequacy of the theory as it was stated and the procedures which
were followed in its construction. That portions of the theory as it was
presented in 1938 no longer find complete acceptance is not relevant to
our purpose; much may be learned from autopsies.

The revision of Skinner's theoretical views has not extended downward
to his basic assumptions with respect to the nature of psychological
theory, nor to the elementary statements of much of his data language
and of the basic laws of behavior. The systematic position is unchanged.
It is largely at the level at which complex concepts are introduced that
revisions have been made.

General Systematic Position

Skinner sees as the problem of modern psychology the development of
a comprehensive system, or theory of behavior (44, 57) designed to
predict and control (and hence to explain) the ongoing activities, motor
and verbal, of living organisms. The system must grow from the raw data
of behavior, without bias from preconceptions based on self-observation,
on ill-defined concepts with theological connotations and capricious
properties, or on the limited physiological knowledge of our day. Such a
theory must be *objective*, in that it must take as its subject matter inter-
subjective events, *descriptive* and *positivistic*, in that it must be purely
empirical, and it must refrain from elaborating mediating concepts borrowed from unrelated fields. It must be *analytic*, isolating significant and

lawful relationships between behavioral dependent and environmental independent variables. Ultimately, it will be statable *quantitatively*, and consist in a set of empirical mathematical laws. Its vocabulary will include terms referring to the basic data, i.e., to the analytic units which are teased out experimentally and their relations to one another. The theory will have, as Skinner states at one place, "nothing to do with the presence or absence of experimental confirmation. . . . [Theories] are statements about organizations of facts. . . . They are all statements about facts, and with proper operational care they need be nothing more than that" (57, p. 28). To speak of verifiability of theories, according to this view, is meaningless, since a theory will contain no statement which was not verified before it was placed, in conjunction with others, in the theory.

The unique characteristics of the system may be found implicit in this pre-systematic orientation. The emphasis on positivistic[1] description is reflected in a definite rejection of formal theory with its explicitly stated postulates, axioms or hypotheses, and subsequent formal derivation of logical consequences which may be verified by experimental test.

Some logicians argue that the hypothetico-deductive is the unique method of science. They do so on the basis of their own analysis. But that is not what Skinner finds that most scientists do—they experiment on the basis of "intuition" or "hunch," elaborated from daily experience in and out of the laboratory. They arrive inductively at general laws and put these together into systems. The general laws come *after* the experimental facts are in (61). The great majority do not formally postulate, deduce, test—only the minority who have studied the logicians. There need be no formal check of a system for consistency and independence of its laws, for these are empirical assertions, and need not meet the requirements, at any given time, of a logic-tight system. The Maxwells and the Bohrs follow the Faradays and the Rutherfords. Laws are subject to modification or rejection as new experimental data come in, not with demonstrations of logical inadequacy. Experimental failure tells.

The positivistic position is interpreted as one that deals with behavior at its own level. The lawfulness, the orderliness to be found in observation of an organism interacting with its environment is statable without reference to events primarily dealt with by other sciences. To be sure, physiological, chemical, and physical events may uniquely correlate with that behavior, but statements about these, however lawful, however well worked out, add nothing to the basic data and laws with which the psychologist must concern himself. They are interesting, to be sure, and certainly the psychologist will not wish to formulate laws or to develop concepts which will be in any obvious conflict with those laws, but that is

---

[1] It is apparent that Skinner's positivism is closer to that of Mach and Pearson than to that of the more recent logical positivists and scientific empiricists.

all. The psychologist, in dealing with his subject matter, may (and should) keep half an eye on the contents of the physiological journals; he should not feel it necessary to bind his own investigations and concepts to information found there. Presumably a comprehensive set of physiological correlates of behavior may be found, but there is nothing in behavioral data which renders this logically necessary or even possible. Psychologists, concerned with the investigation of behavior, lose time when they engage in physiological diversions.

The psychologist should equally be careful to refrain from the use of concepts derived from his "common-sense" thinking about his own activities, for the vernacular is deeply contaminated with older, usually animistic, systems and theories of the causation of behavior. The task of the psychologist is to relate behavior to the environment within which it occurs, and the laws of behavior will be reducible to statements of relationships between the two. Although it may be convenient for the present to make inferences with respect to "non-behavioral" intervening concepts (e.g., drive), these should be developed only when they are completely necessary, and they must then be assumed to be completely lawful, that is, never to act capriciously. They must, moreover, be stated only in terms of explicit behavioral operations. Formulations involving mental states, whether termed ideas, beliefs, or expectancies, or derived from colloquial verbal behavior with respect to "minds" cannot be readily freed, however redefined, from an element of capriciousness and subjectivity.

Skinner's views on other current theories of behavior may be summarized—"A science of behavior must eventually deal with behavior in its relation to certain manipulable variables" (61). It will *not* be developed so long as theories are constituted of "explanation[s] of . . . observed fact[s] which appeal to events taking place somewhere else, at some other level of observation, described in different terms, and measured, if at all, in different dimensions . . ." (61). Such theories serve only to create a false sense of security and to produce research which is essentially wasteful. Skinner's positivism looks for no models, whether in physiology, physics, or in the social behavior of little men housed in the cranium.

How can one pass from the laws derived from a restricted set of data to laws adequate to the whole area with which they purport to deal? For some theorists, there is no problem. A theory is set up to deal with a restricted set of data, and that alone; no attempt is made to extend the theory. Such miniature theories are readily exemplified. But Skinner's specified area of interest is all the (lawful) behavior of all organisms in all environment. The inductive basis of the system is limited to rather restricted performances of members of a few species. When formal theory is lacking, one may expect that a mechanism for orderly extrapolation, as distinguished from analogizing, will be absent as well. And, indeed, it is. A basic terminology for behavior, derived from studies of the dog and of the white rat, is applied to the activities of other organisms, and so too, are certain experimental procedures. When this terminology and these laws are established, and when similar variables may be identified in more complex instances of behavior, extrapolation follows directly. But the statement of precise laws, and the detailed application of high-order concepts must await, for Skinner, the labor of experimentation in each new field. Such experimentation, it is assumed, will verify the extrapolation by analogy that must serve in the interim.

For Skinner, then, the work of the behavioral theorist is largely performing experiments, of the functional rather than the correlational type. Theory grows concomitantly in three explicit steps.[2] One must *identify* the *data* which are dealt with and develop a consistent terminology for dealing with them, *state laws* relating classes of data to one another, and, when the number and precision of laws justify it, *develop* high-order integrative *concepts* which summarize the laws on a broad basis.

The implications of this position are too often overlooked. It is, in a sense, nihilistic. It proposes that all the conventional modes of thought in psychology, phenomenalistic, mentalistic, physiological, be rejected. It insists that psychologists begin their labors over again, that they develop their concepts from the ground up, and base them on the characteristics of the data themselves, and not on the language habits and intellectual biases of the theoretician. Earlier data may, where they meet the criteria of experimental control and orderliness of result, be salvaged, but earlier concepts may not.

The Theory

General. The system, or, as we shall see, theory, of behavior developed by Skinner finds its intellectual forebears in the experimental tradition of the physiological investigation of the reflex, and its immediate empirical basis in the behavior of dogs in the Pavlovian stock, of rats (and, latterly, pigeons) in the Skinner-box,[3] and of humans in their use of words and in guessing. Its theoretical constructs are remarkably free of the products of other trends in psychological thought, and the data accepted for treatment include no maze studies, no jumping-stand discriminations—indeed, the work of few psychologists working outside the framework of the system. Skinner is not interested in the experimental problems with which most learning theorists concern themselves, unless they are formulated as he might have done. The reasons for this parochialism are perhaps many, but two can be recognized as most important. Many psychological ex-

---

[2] These steps, described by Skinner in 1947 (57, pp. 34-38), parallel closely his own procedure, experimental and theoretical.

[3] Skinner did not so name this instrument.

periments are unsystematic and complex, that is, they involve scattered values of too many parameters of behavior, with the result that the relative control exerted by each cannot be evaluated. Second, they make use of measures of behavior that are considered limited in significance and treacherous to interpret.

The Skinner-box, which permits precise control of the environment, sharply limits the variety of behavior which can be manifested, and easily provides measures of *rate of response,* was designed early (23) in the course of the system's development. It proved to be especially apt for the determination of behavioral laws not already found in the work of Sherrington (19) and Pavlov (17). The only other apparatus employed to any extent in the experimental phase of the program has been the activity wheel, used in certain studies of drive (26, 44). To be sure, Skinner has occasionally employed other kinds of apparatus, but these have been turned to the demonstration of the efficacy of the system's concepts in their application to the control of behavior engineering-wise,[4] and not to scientific research.

The system of behavior which has developed from these bases is essentially a simple one that has shown itself sensitive to the demands of new empirical data. The "finished" or relatively complete form of the theory has been fully presented in the book, *The Behavior of Organisms* (44).[5] The changes which have been made since that time are not generally familiar to the psychological profession, for they are largely unpublished, and were not at all considered (although they were available) in a recent summary of learning theories (14) widely considered authoritative. The earlier form is that with which we are concerned, and it will be briefly outlined to serve as a point of departure for an analysis of behavioral theory construction as it is currently practiced.

Specific treatments. The basic products of analysis of the flow of behavior ("what [an organism] is observed by another organism to be doing") (p. 6)[6] in a changing environment are *stimulus* and *response,* defined, respectively, as "a part, or a modification of a part, of the envi-

---

[4] And very effectively, too. Those who have observed work with animal behavior in different laboratories are often struck by the remarkable degree of control which the experimental technique of Skinner and his students enables them to exert over rats, pigeons, pigs and people (e.g., 2). While it may be argued that the group has avoided problems or situations yielding poorer control, it must be pointed out that many who have tried to duplicate the procedures cannot always do so until they have had an opportunity to observe them in action. These experimental skills should not be mistaken for tests of the adequacy of the theory.

[5] Later references to this work will give *only* page citations.

[6] Also, "that part of the functioning of an organism which is engaged in acting upon, or having commerce with the outside world" (*ibid.*), and "the movement of an organism or of its parts, in a frame of reference provided by the organism itself or by various external objects or fields of force . . . it is often desirable to deal with an effect rather than with the movement itself, as in the case of the production of sounds" (*ibid.*).

ronment" (p. 9) and a part of behavior. A second product of the analysis of the environment may also be distinguished (although it is not explicitly stated as such in the system). This is the class of events called *operations* (e.g., deprivation and reinforcement): manipulations of the environment of the organism according to specified rules. The laws of behavior state orderly dependent relationships between properties of stimuli and of responses, and of operations and of responses. Two classes of reflexes, relationships between stimulus and response, are distinguished, according to the laws, static and dynamic, that pertain.

The kind of behavior that is correlated with specific eliciting stimuli may be called *respondent* behavior, and a given correlation *a respondent*. . . . Such behavior as is not under this kind of control I shall call *operant* and any specific example an *operant*. . . . The term reflex will be used to include both respondent and operant even though in its original meaning it applied to respondents only. A single term for both is convenient because both are topographical units of behavior and because an operant may and usually does acquire a relation to prior stimulation (pp. 20-21).

A respondent, then, *regarded as a correlation of a stimulus and a response and an operant regarded as a functional part of behavior are defined at levels of specification marked by the orderliness of dynamic [vide infra] changes* (p. 40).[7]

Neither stimulus nor response, then, may be defined independently of each other and both are classes of events, whose defining properties must be determined by experiment. Thus the identification of stimulus, response, and reflex require more than that the experimenter, on the one hand, present an object to the organism or otherwise produce a change in the environment, and that he observe, on the other, a correlated movement or act. He must demonstrate the repeatability of the observation, and he must also show by a series of experiments that this stimulus-response, or operation-response relationship behaves as do others already shown to obey the laws of the respondents and operants. These usages of the terms "stimulus" and "response" do not correspond to those of physiologists.[8]

---

[7] This definition, taken with the tenth and the twelfth of the laws of behavior, implies that both operants and respondents can be *conditioned*, i.e., that they are "docile." The first of these two quotations further clearly suggests, then, that *all* behavior obeys one or the other of two sets of laws, and hence can be conditioned.

[8] The restrictions placed on the use of the terms "stimulus" and "response" in Skinner's system are often overlooked; most writers consider that Skinner's responses are "acts," i.e., effects upon the environment produced by the organism and not the simple, reproducible movements which are the reflex response of the physiologists. As Skinner has defined his terms, a response may be of either sort; it is the organism's behavior that determines whether an "act" or a "muscle-twitch" is a response. Similarly, whether stimuli are "mazes of a particular pattern," "chairs," "bars," or a "light of a specified wave-length, intensity, size and duration, emitted by a patch of such and such size, pattern, and distance from the organism," will depend on the organism's behavior, rather than the predilection of the theorist. The cant terms "molar" and "molecular" cannot be applied in an intelligible way to this construction.

Given this analysis of behavior and environment, Skinner has developed a series of laws, in part restated from Sherrington's reflex physiology, in part from Pavlovian conditioning ("conditioning of type S"), and the remainder derived from his own researches. It is with these latter that we are concerned, since Skinner has not expanded a treatment, theoretical or experimental, of respondents. The system developed in *The Behavior of Organisms*, then, deals principally with *operant* behavior.

Although it appears that operant behavior includes all behavior that is not elicited by specific stimuli, in detailed treatment only those responses are termed "operants" that can be brought under experimental control through the operation of "reinforcement" (so that their rate of occurrence becomes high, and changes in an orderly and predictable way as a function of schedules of reinforcement, of "drive," and, in some cases, of the presence of specific "discriminative stimuli"). They are spoken of as "emitted" rather than elicited since their first occurrence is neither predictable nor controllable except to a crude approximation; that is to say, it is "spontaneous" (p. 20).

The presentation of a reinforcing stimulus following the occurrence of an operant response is found to have two effects: first, that of increasing the strength of the response (as measured by its rate of occurrence), and secondly, of increasing the "reflex reserve," a store of potential responses that may occur without further reinforcement and that show themselves in extinction. Thus if reinforcing stimuli are withdrawn, the animal continues to respond, at a declining rate, "until the reserve is emptied," at which time the response reaches its initial strength and is no more predictable or controllable than it was before reinforcement was introduced.

Two quantifiable variables, aspects of the identified response, underlie these concepts: the *rate* at which the response occurs in the situation, and the *total number of times* the response is given after reinforcement is withdrawn. Both are typically obtained from response curves generated by the organism in the Skinner-box, which show the course of changes in rate and total number of responses, and hence in strength and reserve, and whose form approximates an "envelope," a smooth and ideal extinction curve.

Skinner's earlier laws relate these two dependent variables, through their set of correlated constructs, "reflex strength" and "reflex reserve," to environmental variables. Additional concepts, some closely related to these (e.g., strength/reserve ratio, immediate reserve) and others, correlated with complexes of operations (drive, emotion) enter. Further sets of operations permit the operant response to come under the control of discriminative stimuli whose presence "set the occasion" for (p. 22) the emission of (n.b., they do *not* elicit) a response. In these terms, Skinner is able to handle almost all the conventional data-set problems of conditioning and learning. This treatment may be briefly stated.

Conditioning. The acquisition of an operant *C.R.* is shown by an increase in the rate of response following reinforcement. "A *C.R.* is said to be conditioned in the sense of being dependent for its existence or state upon the occurrence of a certain kind of event, having to do with the presentation of a reinforcing stimulus" (33).

[It] may be identified as such by showing . . . that it did not exist until the operation of reinforcement had been performed. It may also be distinguished by showing that through elicitation without reinforcement it is removed from the repertoire of the organism (p. 61). "The change in strength called conditioning is distinguished . . . by the specific operation that brings it about (p. 62).

One reinforcement (the presentation of a reinforcing stimulus) in the absence of complicating variables such as emotional stimuli, raises the (momentary) *strength* of the response to a maximum. As the number of reinforcements increases beyond one, the size of the reflex reserve increases, but the strength does not change. The reflex reserve has the "dimension" of a *number of responses,* which will occur without reinforcement. Reinforcing stimuli, such as food and water, must be presented immediately following the response if conditioning is to occur. As the presentation of a reinforcing stimulus is delayed, its effectiveness in changing response strength and in increasing the reflex reserve is decreased.

Stimuli that regularly produce behavior that has been reinforced by food (23) become reinforcing stimuli themselves.[9]

Extinction. As responses are made without reinforcement, the reflex reserve is depleted until it is emptied. The strength of response is a function of the size of the remaining reserve (the number of responses available to be made after extinction is complete), so that the rate of response drops off gradually to its unconditioned value ("operant level"). The process reverses the process of conditioning (24). It is dependent upon the occurrence of the response extinguished: "In a chain of reflexes not ultimately reinforced only the members actually elicited undergo extinction" (30).

Stimulus generalization (or equivalence). The strength acquired by an operant response through reinforcement is a function of the stimuli present at the time of acquisition, and will vary as a function of the degree of similarity of the stimuli present at the time it is emitted to those under which it was conditioned. The size of the reserve, however, is independent of these stimuli. This behavioral phenomenon is called "induction."

Response equivalence. If two parts of behavior, however different topographically, may be interchanged without altering the form of func-

---

[9] Skinner states it, "The sound of the magazine now acquires reinforcing power. . . ." (p. 53); and again, "the sound of the magazine thus becomes the *S* [reinforcing stimulus] of the second formula for conditioning" (23).

tions obtained when both may and do in fact occur, they fall into the same response class; i.e., they are both instances of the same response. Thus, a movement of either the right or left paw may constitute a "bar-press." Further analysis may be left to the physiologist; this is not the psychologist's immediate concern.

Discrimination. "The strength acquired by an operant through reinforcement is not independent of the stimuli affecting the organism at the moment, and two operants having the same form of response may be given widely different strengths through differential reinforcement with respect to such stimuli" (p. 228).

Response decrement (not associated with fatigue). Other learning theorists deal with problems developing from experiments where the spacing of trials is varied in terms of concepts such as "reactive inhibition." In the Skinner-box, when rate of response is the dependent variable, such effects cannot occur, and correspondingly, Skinner gives no treatment of this and allied problems.

Drive. "[Drive] presents itself simply as a class of dynamic changes in strength" (p. 23). Certain operations (withholding food from the animal) define "states" of the organism, of which the proportionality between response strength and reflex reserve is a function. These do not affect the size of the reserve. The learning-performance distinction is handled in terms of this ratio. It should be noted that reinforcing stimuli are most effective in conditioning when they are "appropriate" to the drive (p. 376). Thus: "Whenever we present a state of affairs which is known to be reinforcing at a given drive, we must suppose that conditioning takes place" (59), and "the reinforcing effect of a pellet of food varies linearly with the amount previously eaten" (38), and "the reconditioning effect of a single reinforcement is a function of the drive" (p. 402). Again, "in a conditioned operant, the drive governing the strength is determined by the reinforcement" (p. 372). No theoretical account of this relationship between reinforcement and drive is given. Drive reduction theory is avoided as follows: "behavior that is strengthened during the heightened state of a drive usually leads to an operation affecting that drive" (p. 373).

Higher mental processes. No full accounts are given of the "higher mental processes," which presumably include such behavior as matching, choosing, and so on. It is proposed, however, that they may be fully understood in terms of simple modes of behavior: "The data in the field of the higher mental processes transcend single responses or simple S-R relationships. But they appear to be susceptible to formulation in terms of the differentiation of concurrent responses, the discrimination of stimuli, the establishment of various sequences of responses, and so on. There seems to be no *a priori* reason why a complete account is not possible without appeal to theoretical processes in other dimensional systems"

(61).[10] Thus of choosing it is said, "choosing (like discriminating, matching, etc.) is not a particular piece of behavior. It is not a response, or an act with specified topography. The term characterizes a larger segment of behavior in relation to other variables or events" (61).

Such, briefly stated, is Skinner's theory of behavior as it was outlined in 1938. We may note that no quantitative laws have been stated. There are a few equations which may have this status, one of which relates the number of responses made during the extinction to the time since reinforcing stimuli were withdrawn $(N = k \log t)$ (p. 88). Time, it should be noted, is the independent variable given in almost all of Skinner's data; the other independent variables appear as parameters.

Since 1938, several changes have been made in the formulations presented in *The Behavior of Organisms*. In one case, an explicit change in the statement of the properties of a higher-order concept (reflex reserve) is made (48); thereafter the concept is termed "not particularly useful" and presumably dropped (61). In others, new concepts and terms are introduced in the place of those used earlier; these are formulated without the rigor needed to make it possible to restate the system. They are, however, explicit enough to indicate that certain older concepts are no longer advocated. Thus, "novelty" (61) of the environment displaces the concepts of reflex-reserve and reflex-strength in some contexts, and the notion of "probability of response" (61)[11] in others.

It may be inferred that, since the publication of *The Behavior of Organisms*, both new results and the inadequacies of the system presented here have led Skinner to give up for the time being attempts to systematize the experimental data as extensively as in that book, and to devote himself to the gathering of experimental data that may serve to suggest further concepts, equally positivistic, to replace or extend the old (61).

Since this seems to be the case, there is little point in attempting to bring Skinner's more recent work into the scope of the present critique.

II. A STRUCTURAL ANALYSIS OF THE SYSTEM

The structure of Skinner's theory, its special usages and systematic conceptions prove to be determined in many respects by the pre-theoretical point of view of its writer. Certain difficulties in the derivation of concepts, and in the relating of laws and primitive terms to their experimental bases appear. Similarities in terminology often obscure gross dif-

---

[10] Skinner uses the term "dimensions" in the sense of sets of independent and dependent variables associated together at a given level of observation.

[11] This term is not well-defined in Skinner's usage; it cannot easily be interpreted in terms of its usual mathematical meaning. It might be defined as "the distribution of responses in time," which is not very different from the previously employed rate of response.

ferences between this theory and some others; these exhibit themselves
when the structure of the theory is extracted from its experimental and
polemic context.

Data Language

Among behavior theorists, Skinner has been concerned most explicitly
with the problem of the general terminology and data language of psychology, a language whose function is unequivocal communication between individuals on the subject matter of the science, whose referents
are the intersubjectively observable, and whose terms are the undefined
primitives of theory.

The data language which Skinner employs is composed of several parts.
The first is ordinary English, that is, the vernacular, with the very important restriction that all terms or grammatical constructions that
imply conceptual schemes be barred. As Skinner puts it: "The sole criterion for the rejection of a popular term is the implication of a system
or of a formulation extending beyond immediate observations" (p. 7).
Thus, "hear," "feel," "try," "need," "in order to," and "intention" cannot
be included in the data language of a science of behavior, although in
many cases it might be possible, by a Watsonian process of translation
or by the recently fashionable and perhaps over-worked "operational
definition," [12] to give these terms a sharply restricted meaning within the
data language, and so to introduce them into it.

Data language. In this first component, Skinner is in excellent agreement with other behavior theorists, and his usage meets all the criteria
for an adequate data language for a science of behavior. Examples of this
data language may be found in Chapter II, "Scope and Method," of *The
Behavior of Organisms,* e.g.:

The principal precaution that must be taken is in the handling of the animals
at the beginning of an experiment. The effects of handling may be minimized
by confining the rat behind a release door when it is put into the experimental
box and allowing it to remain there for a minute or two after the box is closed
and before the experiment proper begins. The release door should be reasonably
silent in operation and out of reach of the rat when open. The drawing in
Figure 1 shows such a door in place. It is operated by a projection of the shaft
upon which it is mounted and is held against the ceiling when open (p. 57).

The entire behavior of lifting up the forepart of the body, pressing and releas-
ing the lever, reaching into the tray, seizing the pellet of food, withdrawing
from the tray, and eating the pellet is, of course, an extremely complex act (p.
51).

The movement of the lever is recorded electrically as a graph of the total number
of responses plotted against time. The required apparatus consists of a slow
kymograph and a vertically moving writing point. At each response the point
is moved a uniform distance by an electrically operated ratchet. A step-like

---

[12] Or, more often, operational redefinition.

line is obtained, the slope of which is proportional to the rate of responding. The speed of the kymograph and the height of the step are chosen to give a convenient slope at the more frequent rates of responding. In Figure 2, some representative slopes are given for the coordinate values used in the greater part of the following account. The step-like character is not shown in the figure. [The movement of the lever operates the recorder by closing a mercury switch on the other side of the panel bearing the lever. In the first experiments with this method a needle attached to the lever-arm dipped into a small cup of mercury. When the lever was moved slowly there was a tendency for the contact to chatter, and this was corrected by inserting into the circuit to the recorder a device which made it impossible for a second contact to be recorded within, say, one second. It has been found that a commercial mercury tube switch does not require this precaution.] (Pp. 59-60.)

Doubtful data language. A second component of Skinner's data language is in quite different status. Terms that function as data terms are introduced into the system without definition. Theoretical concepts are derived from them, but not in such a way that the derivations can be said to constitute implicit definition. These words do not meet one very important criterion for data language. Specifically, they are *not* such that agreement upon usage can be obtained from workers in the field regardless of theoretical biases and which are free of any reference to theory (that is, to the theory for which the set of terms in question functions as data language).[13] Since these terms often appear in conjunction with theoretical concepts, and in the statement of quasi-empirical laws, they introduce serious problems to the analyst. A simple example is the following:

A few special aspects of the records may be noted. The last horizontal line in each case might have been extended considerably to the right, for with the last recorded pellet the rat ceased eating altogether. The curves, therefore, end abruptly. This is typical of records obtained with either procedure. An example of another characteristic, which has already been discussed, is offered by Figure 3. At about the fiftieth piece of food the rat stops eating for a short period and consequently falls slightly behind the schedule set by the equation. The delay is followed, however, by a sharp acceleration, which brings the curve back to its proper position. After the first step, which is exceptional, the recovery curve is convex upward and remarkably uniform in its curvature. Note that its initial rate is greater than that of the beginning of the main record (23).

More difficult terms appear in further statements about cumulative response curves, and they are used to derive several higher-order constructs such as the "immediate reserve." They include the following: "scallops" on the curves, "compensatory increase," "grain," "wave-like character," "nearly maximal value," "depressions," and, especially, "en-

---

[13] We should perhaps entertain the suggestion that if one were to work with Skinner, and read his records with him, he would find himself able to make the same discriminations as does Skinner and hence eventually give some of them at least data-language status.

velop." It is impractical to assemble an exhaustive list. We shall, however, analyze one such term in its context.

"Envelop" is introduced in this wise:

> In Figure 8 we may inspect more easily the theoretical curves that have been fitted to the data. They are logarithmic and are drawn as envelops, upon the assumption that the deviations are depressions (p. 77).

And again:

> A logarithmic envelop may be drawn above the curve (the broken line is for the equation $N = K \log t$, where N is the number of responses at time t and K is a constant), although the actual contacts with the experimental curve are no justification for such a form in this particular case (p. 88).

The difficulty is this: the "envelop" refers to a line drawn above empirical curves. These lines seem to have been drawn so that they touch a number of points on the curve where the rate of response drops off sharply for a time, and so that they are approximately logarithmic. When equations are given for them, as in the example in the preceding paragraph, they are referred to as theoretical. Irregularities, departures from orderliness in empirical extinction curves are thus taken to be deviations *below* a "real" curve. Thus the term envelop is introduced into and used as part of the data language, drawn, perhaps, from mathematical English. It is not, however, used in the mathematicians' sense, and it communicates little to the reader.

This use of the term disturbs the theory-analyst, since it plays a large role in the "explanation" of data and in the definition of the higher-order constructs already mentioned. Such data-language usage of the term envelop, with its consequent ambiguities, could be avoided if the writer had included among his defining laws one stating a specific form for the "extinction curve." If this had been done, the family of concepts based on the envelop would have an explicit basis. One is, in fact, forced to conclude that just such a defining law (postulate) is involved in the theorist's use of "envelop" but that it has been suppressed.

The third class of data language. Members of the third class of data-language terms are perhaps the most difficult to evaluate. As we shall see later, the theory incorporates a set of concepts that are defined in terms of the primitive laws and concepts of the theory. These concepts are reducible to the data language, through the chain of laws, formal definitions, and the usual paraphernalia of theory. These concepts are also linked to the data through a second series of steps. Such a dual linkage of concepts to data is not unusual: since the concepts are thus able to integrate *two* sets of laws, one might prefer them. Indeed, some would consider it essential to a concept that such explicit duality be demonstrable.

In the present instance, however, the second series of reduction chains are not clearly stated as such. The chain is omitted, and the theoretical terms are endowed with data-language status. An equivocation occurs. The analyst, interpreting what has been done after the presentation, may state that the theorist is giving the experimental symptoms of the concept introduced. Skinner, however, often writes as if he were making assertions in the data language about observable events. Examples of these usages which are pertinent to the present discussion include the following:

> So defined a reflex is not, of course, a theory. It is a fact. It is an analytical unit, which makes an investigation of behavior possible (p. 9).
> The reflex as an analytical unit is actually obtained *in practice*. The unit is a fact, and its validity, and the validity of the laws . . . do not depend upon the correctness of the analytical assumptions or the possibility of a later synthesis of more complex behavior (p. 29).

As we shall see later, a "reflex" is indeed a term that is formally defined, and is only eventually coordinated with statements in the data language.

These words do not have data-language status, but the theorist seems to be stating that they do. Not everyone can identify a reflex.

The data language employed, then, is basically sound, but it is contaminated by data-language usage of two other sets of terms. Tolman, we shall see in the section of this book dealing with his theory, also employs such a quasi-data language. The difficulties Skinner encounters in his data language are quite different from Tolman's; they come from an uncritical introduction into the data language of terms that cannot be successfully used by many others, and from a tendency to treat the names of higher-order concepts as if they had data-language status, that is, as if they referred to events directly observable and atheoretical.

Basic Concepts and Laws

The technique followed by Skinner in introducing the primitive terms of the theory is straightforward. When the embedding material is stripped away, his procedure is this: the primitive terms, such as "stimulus," "response," "reflex," "operant," "respondent," and "reflex strength" are implicitly defined in a set of formally stated laws. At this stage, the terms have *no* empirical content, and are not subject to any kind of independent definition. When the laws serving as rules for the use of the terms within the system have been stated, definitions coordinating these terms with data-language statements, and hence asserting an empirical status for the laws, are explicitly given. The whole operation, then, serves to define the subject matter of the theory and to make explicit those kinds of events with which the system deals. Given this system, still further laws are stated, which have been arrived at inductively through experimental procedures. It is necessary, then, to consider the status of these laws, and of the primitive concepts together.

The formal laws.[14] The first twenty laws, which include five "Static Laws," eight "Dynamic Laws," and seven "Laws of Interaction," are purely formal and are those that yield the definitions referred to above. "We are [however] in a position to demonstrate [them]" (p. 12).[15] The balance have the character of empirical laws, since they have been established independently of both the other laws and of the definitional system, although once stated they play a formal role as well. Each of these formal laws involves a statement relating a dependent variable to an independent variable. These variables are specified as some property of the terms "stimulus," "response," "reflex," "strength of a reflex"; they are brought into relationships with one another through the medium of a verbal structure which has the character of data language, descriptive of some manipulation. The defining laws are approximations to empirical laws in that they are statements based upon classical experimentation on the spinal reflex, and the salivary conditioned reflex. They are not empirical laws in the absence of independent definition, formal and coordinating, of the terms that appear in their statement.

The terms appearing in the laws are next brought into relationship with one another formally, in further statements:

Such a part, or modification of a part, of the environment is traditionally called a *stimulus* and the correlated part of the behavior a *response*. Neither term may be defined as to its essential properties without the other. For the observed relation between them I shall use the term *reflex*. . . . Only one property of the relation is usually invoked in the use of the term—the close coincidence of occurrence of stimulus and response—but there are other important properties to be noted shortly (p. 9).

A respondent [reflex], then, regarded as a correlation of a stimulus and a response and an operant regarded as functional part of behavior are defined at levels of specification marked by the orderliness of dynamic changes [i.e., obedience to the dynamic laws]" (p. 40).

In these formal terms, full definitions within the system of "operant" and "respondent" behavior are achieved, as well as of "reflex strength." When this self-contained system is complete, then and only then are coordinating definitions that relate these terms to data-language statements and that assert empirical relationships, achieved. This resolution proceeds in an orderly way, beginning with the word "response," which is coordinated, in *The Behavior of Organisms*, with "pressing a bar." "Reflex strength" is coordinated with the frequency of occurrence of closures of a bar-operated relay. "Reflex strength," incidentally, acts as both a primitive concept, and a higher-order concept, as we shall see later.

The empirical laws. Many empirical laws are formally stated; these

---

[14] These laws are given in the appendix to this section.

[15] This is perhaps another instance of Skinner's use of a third class of data language.

appear in the appendix of this chapter. Others are not, and their generality remains questionable. For example, consider: "it may be concluded from the high frequency of occurrence of the instantaneous change that a single reinforcement is capable of raising the strength of the operant to essentially a maximal value" (p. 69). The informal statement suggests that this is not a very important generalization; the phrase "is capable," that it is a tentative statement. But the next few pages of the text give five reasons that account for observed *failures* of the law. These are treated in some detail. The status of this law, like that of many others, is doubtful.

Basic Constructs

Stimulus. The specification of those parts of the environment which are coordinated with the term "stimulus" is determined empirically. "Stimulus" refers to any part of the environment that is related to some specified operant or respondent according to the laws of the system. Thus, *any* specifiable part of change in a part of the environment may prove to be identifiable as a stimulus. *Doors* and *bars* may be stimuli, *lights, buzzers,* may be stimuli, and further specification need not be given. Any physical event or object, however, produced by and controlled by the experimenter is not a stimulus; it must be shown empirically to play a role in the lawful relationships that have been stated.

Stimuli are not, then, independent variables in the strict sense of the term, although once they have been identified they can perhaps be manipulated as such. The result is that, within the system, stimuli cannot be identified or specified in advance of an investigation. They must be discovered in the course of it. Parts of the environment may be manipulated by an experimenter as if they were stimuli, but it falls upon the experimenter to demonstrate that they do indeed control the dependent variable, frequency, or rate of a *specified* operant or magnitude or strength of a *specified* respondent according to the laws. It may prove impossible to specify stimuli verbally other than in such terms as "the bar," "the lower right angle of a triangle," and even "anything red."

This treatment of "stimulus" is extended to human verbal behavior. *Words* are "stimuli" *only* if they act as such in lawful behavior. In an experiment in which abstract words were manipulated as stimuli, response distributions deviated from those obtained with other words, whose status as "stimuli" was unequivocal. In Skinner's words, "This may mean, not that the relation is invalid, but that words of this sort are not properly to be regarded as simple units in the dynamics of verbal behavior" (42a).

The specified independent variables of behavior—stimuli—are then, in fact, "chosen by the organism," i.e., they are inferred from the organism's behavior just as are Lewin's "behavior fields." Once identified, however, they may be manipulated independently of it. In practice, it should be noted that this restriction of the word stimulus is overlooked, and "stimulus" is used much as others use it. If Skinner's experimental interest in "stimuli" were greater and the use of the term in describing behavior more rigorous, the difference might be more evident. But so far, experiments concerned with determining the defining properties of a stimulus class[16] are seldom encountered, and the striking difference between Skinner's concept of "stimulus" and Hull's is submerged.

Some remarks on "stimulus." If one looks into the various definitions and usages of the word "stimulus" by psychologists, one finds at least four different ways in which the term is used.

The first usage, which we shall call "Stimulus I," places "stimulus" unequivocally in the data language, and corresponds closely to the verbal definition given by Skinner: a part, or a change in a part of environment. This simple definition is often amplified by the inclusion of statements about states or changes in states, of physical energy. In ordinary use, this amplification is not made, either because it is considered unnecessary or because it is not feasible. Stimulus I appears in the experimental learning literature as a data-language term (e.g., "the positive stimulus was a single white circle eight inches in diameter"), in psychophysiological experimentation ("the intensity of the stimuli presented varied in steps of .10 log units over a range of 1.40 log units, which made it possible to obtain the complete frequency of seeing function"), and is perhaps implicit in Hull's position. The most explicit treatment of this use of the term is that of Bergmann and Spence (1).

"Stimulus II" corresponds with the concept of stimulus found in dictionaries of psychology, in physiology, and in textbooks. Both Harriman's definition (9), "any form of energy which elicits a response," and Warren's (64), "an energy external to a receptor, which excites the receptor," accept the basic definition of Stimulus I, but they limit the kinds of environmental events that will be termed stimuli to those classes that have been found empirically to produce some kind of response (unspecified) in some kind of organism (unspecified) under some kind of conditions (again, unspecified). Thus, a tone of 40,000 *cps* is now a stimulus if we are talking of bats, but not if we are concerned with men, and an illuminated area of specified physical characteristics whose brightness is 3.50 log micro-micro-lamberts is a stimulus for Doakes, who is normal, but not for Oakes, who is night-blind. This definition places a limitation on the use of the term which is perhaps based on the fact that there is

---

[16] Despite the exhaustive and powerful theoretical treatment of the word "stimulus," Skinner may not have completely clarified the meaning of the term to himself. Thus the failure of an animal to increase his rate of response maximally after one reinforcement (one-trial conditioning) is attributed in one paper to conditioning of the response to "elements of the stimulus" (23) in Guthrian fashion. This statement is meaningless within the systematic treatment given to "stimulus" in other places (32, 44).

seldom any occasion, in psychology, to speak of energy changes to which no known organism ever responds (and hence which appear in no law). It leads to a shift of stress in the specification of environmental independent variables to the *organism*. This may have rather peculiar consequences; for example, one becomes rather uneasy in speaking of "sub-threshold stimuli." It is no wonder that this definition of stimulus, supposed by many to be employed by all psychologists, is more honored in the breach than in the observance.

A third usage, Stimulus III, is that followed by Skinner. Here, "stimulus" refers to a class of environmental events that cannot be identified independently of observations of a specified activity of the organism and that must control that activity according to a specified set of laws. A red triangle of specified physical characteristics may not be termed a stimulus when it is repeatedly presented in association with food to, say, a dog, until the dog comes to salivate regularly in response to it according to the laws of behavior. Thereafter, it need be specified only insofar as it can be seen to control the *specified* behavior systematically. But if we find, upon further experimentation, that *any* red object controls the response, according to precisely the same laws, and also that triangles that are *not* red do not, then, by this usage, the red triangle can no longer be termed the stimulus, and something else, presumably "anything red," is the stimulus. And so, although we may empirically identify manipulable objects and events that we may call stimuli, we do this on the basis of a construct, in Skinner's case, the reflex—and the term stimulus is stripped of all data-language status. It is a quasi-independent variable, and when the term is used rigorously must be carefully stated as a stimulus-for-knee-jerk, stimulus-for-bar-press, and so on. A parallel concept of stimulation, the "releaser" is found in the work of the ethological school of students of instinctive behavior (62).

The fourth common usage of the term in psychology corresponds to the second usage, with the very important modification that hypothetical or inferential classes of physical events (usually intraorganismic) are also referred to as stimuli. This important extension of the concept "stimulus" is based upon physiological laws. Given these laws, and the observation of some of the events the physiological laws describe, the occurrence of appropriate stimuli is assumed. Stimulus IV, then, refers to purely hypothetical events, inferred from the behavior of the organism, much as Skinner's "stimulus" is a logical construct derived from the observation of orderly behavior. Thus, Guthrie (8) speaks of "movement-produced-stimuli," and Miller (16) of "response-produced-stimuli." There is a difference between these two, however, since Guthrie uses the word indifferently and Miller seems to restrict himself to the use of stimulus for the hypothetical concept, and to use the word "cue" for what we have termed Stimulus I.

In neither of these last two usages, however, can the word "stimulus" be considered as referring to an experimentally manipulable environmental variable.

It is unfortunate that a single term is employed for such different concepts; theoretical difficulties will necessarily ensue, as they have for Skinner. By his indifferent use of the term—data-language-wise, and construct-wise, he produces a store of future difficulties for the system, although they are not immediately apparent in *The Behavior of Organisms* itself. In this work both usages I and III of the term are applied to the same environmental events, and the inconsistency seldom becomes apparent. In large part the superficial success of the ambiguity is an artifact of the particular experimental problems with which Skinner has concerned himself, and with his lack of interest in the stimulus control of behavior as such. If he had studied problems such as transposition in discrimination learning, the equivocation would quickly be evident[17] and perhaps a solution found.

In Skinner's system, then, the term stimulus does not refer to an entirely independent variable of behavior. Stimuli are not identifiable, except on the basis of the organism's behavior; they are not manipulable,[18] except by inference through the laws of the reflex.

This use of a term ordinarily employed in referring to the classical independent variable of behavior is a significant one. The restricted range of experiments on which the theory is based, and the extreme positivistic point of view both seem to have facilitated the easy intrusion of an equivocation and the evasion of its consequences, experimental and theoretical. The difficulty suggests, for all learning theorists, the need for a terminology that will not permit such an ambiguity to arise in the first place.

Such inference-backward to quasi-independent variables in behavior seems to be characteristic of the work of many behavior theorists. Guthrie, we have noted, speaks of "movement-produced-stimuli," Lewin of behavior fields and forces, and others of perceptions. Quasi-variables are almost characteristic of psychological theory. It is not impertinent to ask whether, since this is so regularly the case, it will ever be possible to develop a science of behavior in which laws relating data-language-

---

[17] In Skinner's most recent publication (61) the difficulty *does* arise. In this, an account of the shape of the extinction curve obtained under specified conditions is given in terms of "novelty"—presumably alterations in the stimulus field which affect the organism during extinction. But the physical environment is not varied in these experiments.

[18] Skinner is not entirely clear on the question whether stimuli, once identified, can be manipulated except in the sense of being presented or not to the organism. In the latter sense, they are indeed manipulable. But any radical changes in responding associated with changes in, say, the intensity of a buzzer sounded as a discriminative stimulus could force the conclusion that the loud buzzer was not a stimulus. In this sense, stimuli are not manipulable.

stimuli to data-language-responses can be found. Is it necessarily the case that "stimuli" become response-inferred concepts, bearing no necessary relationship to what is put in front of the organism?

One possible solution to this problem can be found in psychophysics. In dealing with the response to electromagnetic radiation, a parallel problem was encountered. The solution achieved required considerable experimental work, and was not easily arrived at. But by the introduction of a hypothetical construct—"retinal sensitivity to wave length" on the basis of empirical functions (the visibility curves), which were systematically related, on the one hand to the physical dimensions of the stimulus, and on the other to a simple response—a system has been constructed which provides for the rescaling of physical energies for convenient prediction of response, such that the manipulation of electromagnetic energy as a relatively simple independent variable, and the elaboration of laws relating various values of this variable to behavior become possible.

Few behavior psychologists have recognized the existence of this problem, and where they have (as Tolman may have, 63), the labors of developing the necessary constructs have perhaps led them to hold in abeyance work on this critical problem.

Response. The term response presents analogous difficulties, which remain unresolved within the theory. It is used indifferently in referring to a broad concept, the class of responses that produce the cumulative curves, which is "generically" defined (32), and to the single observed event. In the latter instance the term is used as if it were part of the data language. Operant responses are typically defined in terms of the "response," and yet it is possible, it appears, to refer to "two operants with the same form of response," (the 23d law, page 313 of this article, even before "two" operants have been distinguished on the basis of differences in discriminative stimuli.

The testability of the laws of behavior. It is clear from the foregoing that it is impossible to choose responses, or to specify stimuli or reflexes, as one wishes. The procedures for relating the terms of the theory to the data language require that in each new case where it is desired to use the terms, empirical investigations first show that the specific coordination leads to another verification of the laws of behavior. If it does not, then the behavioral and environmental variables were not "responses" and "stimuli." Thus many of Skinner's laws of behavior are exhibited as untestable. Those twenty that define "stimulus" and "response" are formal, definitional laws, which are not subject to disproof. They state the conventions for the application of the terms stimulus and response. They serve, in empirical application, to define that segment of the activities of an organism, those parts of his environment with which the theory will deal. Thus the theory only deals with that part of the activities of organisms that obeys its laws; this is behavior (cf. p. 273 above). Anything else that the organism is observed to do is presumably not behavior, for it is asserted that operants and respondents together include all behavior. To test the empirical content of this last statement is difficult. It is not at all impossible, or improbable, that much of what others call behavior may lie quite outside Skinner's system. This is especially interesting when we consider the concept "reinforcement." If a change in behavior which acts like conditioning can be shown to occur without the administration of "reinforcing stimuli," then it simply does not fall within the scope of Skinner's system. "Reinforcing stimuli" might have to be hypothesized if this were the case, even though they were unobservable. They might be termed "unidentifiable," or "unspecifiable," as is the case with the stimulus components presumed for operant reflexes before they are conditioned.

This state of affairs does not lead to difficulties as serious as it might, since in practice the defining laws can be restated if they prove to exclude too much of an organism's activities from consideration. In effect, they can be treated as if they were verifiable.

The "operant-respondent" distinction. The system, it will be remembered, distinguishes between two broad classes of reflexes, "respondent" and "operant," which are distinguished on the basis of the reflex laws which each follows. Respondents are defined as those reflexes which obey the "static" laws of the reflex; operants are those that do not.

Respondent behavior includes all responses elicited by stimuli. Operant behavior is "spontaneous," in that its "originating forces . . . are not located in the environment. . . . It might be said to be emitted" (p. 20).[19] "An operant is an identifiable part of behavior of which it may be said, not that no stimulus can be found that will elicit it (there may be a respondent the response of which has the same topography), but that no correlated stimulus can be detected upon occasions when it is observed to occur" (p. 21). The application of the term *reflex* to both "operant" and "respondent" behavior necessarily ensues from the preliminary formal development of the reflex concept.

[But] the term reflex [is] used to include both respondent and operant even though in its original meaning it applied to respondent only. A single term for both is convenient because both are topographical units of behavior and because an operant may and usually does acquire a relation to prior stimulation (pp. 20-21).

Respondent behavior varies as a function of stimulus intensity; operant does not. Operant behavior varies as a function of drive manipulation; respondent behavior, in most cases, does not. The latencies, magnitudes, and duration of respondents are significant dependent variables; only

---

[19] At a later date, and in other treatments, these are indeed located in the environment but are considered unidentifiable or unspecifiable.

rate of response and total number of responses in extinction are legitimate measures of operant behavior. These differences follow from the differing sets of laws[20] entering into their definitions. No attempt is made to reduce this differentiation experimentally. On the contrary, there is an insistence on maintaining it. Although many experiments (e.g., 7) have shown that behavior which Skinner terms "operant" obeys the same laws as the static laws which define "respondents" when the appropriate experimental conditions (control of presentation of the stimuli, discrete trials, and so forth) are introduced, these are rejected because measures deemed inappropriate to operant behavior are introduced. Such experiments define their observables outside Skinner's system. For reasons that are not clear to many psychologists concerned with learning theories, only "rate of response" is an acceptable measure of behavior.

The independent and dependent variables of the system. At the conceptual level the primary independent variables are stimuli, and the dependent variables responses, or properties of them. But this is only as it seems. In practice, and indeed in theory, the independent variables are quite otherwise. Consider the case of operant behavior.

The dependent variables measured in operant behavior are two. The first is rate of response, and the second is cumulative number of responses. Both of these measures of behavior are directly related to theoretical concepts: *strength* and *reflex reserve,* respectively. Both are significant only after the "response" has been quantitatively defined. Typically, both are measured by the use of the cumulative response curves obtained from the operation of the Skinner-box. The whole curve is often reproduced, and numerical values are not taken from the records.

The independent variables are more complex and provide new theoretical problems. Presumably the basic independent variables of behavior are *stimuli*. But we have already seen that, as Skinner develops this concept, *stimuli* are not independently specifiable, as independent variables ordinarily are, nor do they appear in the experimental procedures of the program as independent variables. Rather, stimuli (together with time and the animal's behavior) appear in the specification of operations, and it is these operations that act as the independent variables of the system. But even operations do not appear very often as independent variables in experimental work. They are the experimental parameters of particular experiments, and the actual independent variable is *time:* time in the box, time since beginning of extinction, and so on. In a given experiment nothing is varied, but time passes with the stated operations remaining constant as the data accrue.

---

[20] It is possible to introduce several other classes of behavior at this level of analysis; defining operations can be stated for avoidance and escape conditioning that clearly distinguish them from "operant" and "respondent" conditioning.

Taken as a parameter of an experiment (and hence, after rearrangement of the data treated as an independent variable), an operation may lead to theoretical and practical difficulties.

Consider the most important of the operations, *reinforcement:* "the presentation of a certain kind of stimulus in a temporal relation with either a stimulus or a response" (p. 62). For operants, the "certain kind of stimulus," or "reinforcing stimulus," is any that has been shown, experimentally, to produce an increase in the strength of a response that it has followed at some time in the past. When a stimulus has been shown to have this property under a given drive, it is henceforth referred to as reinforcing. It is not the *reinforcing stimulus*[21] that causes trouble, but the "temporal relation with . . . a response," into which it may enter. The experimenter may manipulate the interval between response and reinforcement. He may select the number of unreinforced responses preceding a reinforced one (fixed-ratio). He may reinforce a response, on the average, every thirty seconds (a periodic reinforcement). But in all these cases, it is the responding animal that determines the delivery of the reinforcement, and hence that determines the values of many temporal parameters of reinforcement. In a very literal sense, the independent variables of Skinner's system are under the direct control of the subject of the experiment, and not of the experimenter.[22] Much the same difficulties, of course, can arise in other treatments of behavior.

This ambiguity of experimental control serves to reveal new and orderly phenomena of behavior. That all these phenomena will lend themselves easily to quantitative theoretical treatment is questioned, since it does not seem possible to specify accurately all the experimental conditions under which they appear. What is perhaps a more serious difficulty is that this self-imposed limitation on experimental control and the restriction of measurement to rates of response and to total numbers of responses given over stated periods of time automatically prevent those working within the system from finding certain behavioral effects. These effects occur when the temporal interval between successive presentations of given environmental changes (either "discriminative" or "reinforcing" stimuli) is varied. They have led to Hull's concept of "reactive inhibition," among many others. Although such laws do have a place in re-

---

[21] The reinforcing stimulus usually encountered in the experimental program is the food pellet—certainly relatively easy to specify. We have already noted that Skinner has made no attempt to relate this function of stimuli to the concept of drive theoretically, except as follows: "In a conditioned operant the drive governing the strength is determined by the reinforcement" (p. 372).

[22] At Columbia University, undergraduates are well aware of the Skinner-box. It was the *Columbia Jester* in which a cartoon appeared that showed two rats at the bar of a Skinner-box. Said one rat to the other: "Oh boy, have I got this guy conditioned. Every time I press the bar, he gives me a pellet. . . ."

spondent behavior, they cannot be found in operant behavior by the methods described in *The Behavior of Organisms*.

Higher-order constructs and relations among them. Tastes differ considerably in the specification of higher-order concepts. Variables related in a central construct by some differ from those related by others. From time to time, a particular theorist rearranges his order, seeking simpler and more effective schemata.

There are many constructs in Skinner's system. They differ widely in the empirical laws that they relate to one another, in the rigor of their definition and treatment, and in the range of data that they integrate. It is neither possible, nor necessary, to treat with all of them exhaustively, to track down each usage to which each construct is put, or indeed, to specify all of them. Our present purpose, critical evaluation, can be adequately served by indicating, with some examples, the procedures followed in the formulation of several of Skinner's higher-order constructs.

Skinner's system incorporates two identifiable types of construct. The first type includes such concepts as "reflex strength," "reflex reserve," and "immediate reserve." The first two of these are in part defined explicitly in the laws of the reflex; their definition is extended in a series of statements that may be found largely in the opening chapters of *The Behavior of Organisms*. All three are constructs that relate in a complex way the dependent variables of behavior (latency, rate and magnitude of response for respondents, and rate of response and number of responses to extinction for operants) as a function of independent variables (number of reinforcements and number of elicitations for respondents, and preceding rate and number of responses for operants). Although, as we have already noted, these are clearly constructs that integrate empirical laws, they are considered by Skinner to be "very near to being directly treated experimentally" (p. 26). They are treated as if they were basics of the system and not conceptualizations pulling together many properties of behavior not directly observable.

The second class of constructs includes those that relate various operations to changes in reflex strength, reflex reserve, and other members of the first class. They include "drive" and "emotion."

Reflex strength. This term is most interesting analytically. Indeed, one term refers to two quite different concepts, one for respondents, and the other for operants. Respondent reflex strength is understood to "describe the state of the reflex with respect to all its static properties [i.e., with respect to the static laws] at once. . . . The value of the strength of a reflex is arbitrarily assigned to it from the values of the static properties and is never measured directly. . . . [It] is not to be confused with the magnitude of the response" (p. 15). This concept is an intervening variable, defined in terms of a number of operations, and measured in terms of a number of measures of response. In practice, no attempt is made to develop the concept of respondent reflex strength beyond these statements.

Operant strength is defined otherwise. Since the operant is distinguished on the basis, among other things, of the failure of the static laws to apply, the former definition cannot be applied. We find that operant strength is defined as "proportional to its [a response's] frequency of occurrence" (p. 21), and that "the dynamic laws describe the changes in the rate of occurrence that are brought about by various operations performed upon the organism" (p. 21). Thus where respondent strength is quite clearly given the status of a higher-order construct, operant strength is at once directly coordinated with the primary dependent variable of the experimental program, although, at the same time, it is treated as an intervening state variable in relationship to the concept of "reflex reserve."

Reflex reserve. We have already indicated that this concept is a construct, which is occasionally spoken of as if it were a data-language term. Its hypothetical status is clear. It is defined as *"available activity, which is exhausted during the process of repeated elicitation of which the strength of the reflex is at any moment a function"* (p. 26). For respondents, the reflex reserve is assigned the property of constantly being restored spontaneously when it is not already at maximum. It is, then, related to the experimental facts of recovery from fatigue and adaptation for the respondent.

For the operant, the reserve is defined in direct relationship to the previously defined concept of strength, and also to the total number of responses given in extinction. Thus:

> Since the strength of a reflex is proportional to its reserve, it may be altered in two ways. Either the size of the reserve or the proportionality between it and the strength may be changed. All operations that involve elicitation affect the reserve directly, either to increase or to decrease it. Conditioning increases it; extinction and fatigue decrease it. The other operations [which are not unique in their action and affect groups of reflexes] change the proportionality between the reserve and the strength. Facilitation and certain kinds of emotion increase the strength, while inhibition and certain other kinds of emotion decrease it without modifying the reserve. The operations that control the drive also affect the proportionality factor. Without altering the total number of available responses, a change in drive may alter the rate of elicitation of an operant from a minimal to a maximal value. Several demonstrations of the distinction between altering the reserve and altering the proportionality will appear later (p. 27).

The *immediate reserve* is a subordinate concept, which does not receive extensive theoretical treatment. The concept is introduced in this way:

> The phenomenon of compensation, like that of recovery, requires the notion of an *immediate* reserve distinct from the total reserve which determines the

rate in the absence of interruption. The process is catenary. The rate is proportional to the immediate reserve, which is contributed to from the total reserve. When elicitation is continuous, the total reserve controls the process. When elicitation is interrupted, the immediate reserve is built up; and a period of increased activity is made possible when responding is resumed, until the total reserve again becomes the controlling factor. The period of time during which responding may be suspended without making the original envelop inaccessible will depend upon the size of the immediate reserve (p. 85).

The "immediate reserve" is inferred from the phenomena of spontaneous recovery and from sets of data where a "depression" is followed by "compensation." It is nowhere related systematically to another concept, based upon the opposite effect—where a high rate of response is followed by a low rate—which is called *"strain on the reflex reserve."* [23]

The concept of "strain on the reserve" is not developed, experimentally or otherwise, although a set of statements such as the following may be assembled: ". . . we may assume that the effect of the accumulation of S_{PR}^D is to strain the reserve by bringing out responses which under normal discriminative stimulation would have remained within the reserve for some time" (p. 296) and "the recovery of the reserve from the strain imposed by the preceding run of responses" (p. 293). An attempt to tease out a set of rigorously stated relationships among these concepts meets with little success. Suffice it to say that both "immediate reserve" and "strain" are derived from the "envelop," and hence from the suppressed postulate with respect to the form of the extinction curve which has been mentioned already. Both are used in the *a posteriori* explanation of results, but neither is formulated so that it can be manipulated directly or through control of the environment. They suggest that some kind of a model is involved.

Drive. Skinner's concept of drive is perhaps one of the best specified and "purest" examples of what have been termed "intervening variables" that can be found in psychological theory. It is defined in terms of sets of operations and of response changes. For the drive "hunger," the operations relate to various procedures involving food deprivation, and the response changes are alteration in the rate of occurrence of a variety of response (those that have to do with the ingestion of food). Drive is also related, through a series of laws, to the concept of the reflex reserve: the reserve/strength ratio is a function of drive strength. Similarly drive is related to the effectiveness of certain stimuli in reinforcing behavior. If food is reinforcing, then the animal is hungry. If an animal can become conditioned and shows extinction with the use of water as a reinforcing stimulus after a period of water deprivation, then it may be stated that thirst is a drive (32). The technique followed in conceptually developing a state variable in terms of a set of antecedent inducing operations, and

---

[23] This concept may be related by some analysts to "reactive inhibition."

a correlated set of related consequences is impeccable. But it is not quantitative.

Emotion. Emotion is also given the status of a concept of the "intervening variable" class, analogous to drive in that it must be defined in terms of a set of operations and correlated changes in reflex strength. "The important thing is the recognition of a change in strength as a primary datum and the determination of the functional relationship between the strength and some operation" (p. 409). The operations, in the case of emotion, remain only vaguely specified. One seems to be the withholding of reinforcing stimuli (extinction), and the other the presentation of emotional stimuli, which are not independently defined. Unfortunately, the concept of emotion appears frequently in the role of a *deus ex machina,* in that it is used to account for changes in strength which are observed when the conceptual system, taken with the experimental procedures, would otherwise lead to the expectation (but not prediction) that no change in strength would occur. Thus "when the lever has not been present prior to the day of conditioning, its movement may have an emotional effect, one result of which is a depression in rate" (p. 70).

A final set of higher-order constructs that has not been extensively treated includes those relating to human behavior. These represent analyses, followed by redefinition in the terminology of the system, of terms used commonly in the description of behavior. In most instances, the effect of this redefinition is to sharpen the content of the concept considerably. An example is this: "A simple way to state the fact of perseveration is in terms of the covariation in strength of groups of related responses" (40). Again, "Anticipation must be defined as a reaction to a current stimulus S_1 which arises from the fact that S_1 has in the past been followed by S_2, where the reaction is not necessarily that which was originally made to S_2" (6). "Guessing is a special kind of (usually verbal) behavior in which two or more responses are about equally likely to be emitted" (51). Not very much has been done with such concepts, either in the direction of redefining the whole vocabulary of psychology, or of pursuing the experimental and theoretical implications of the redefinitions proposed.

Unclassifiable concepts. A few concepts employed in the system are not easily analyzed from the viewpoint of theory construction. Each is used in explanation. Two, at least, bear names that suggest that they are related to the laws of the reflex and hence that they represent no more than the application of these laws to the explanation of behavior. When the statement of the laws is examined, however, this hypothesis proves to be untenable. Another is unrelated to anything else in the system; it seems a purely *ad hoc* explanatory device.

An example of the first sort is "adaptation." In some contexts the term is used as might be expected. In others, it is applied where the strength of an operant fails to reach its maximum after one reinforcement. Thus one reads that such failure may occur because ". . . administration of any stimulus to which adaptation has not taken place will normally depress the rate of eating" (24). This depression in rate is elsewhere referred to as an "emotional effect" (pp. 70, 80). Unfortunately, adaptation is undefined with respect to the concept of emotion.

A more interesting case is this: In the course of his writings, Skinner has developed a powerful case against a concept of "inhibition" (cf. p. 290 above). All instances where such a process is inferred by others are shown to fit descriptively into a system that uses no such concept. In one experiment (42), however, benzedrine was shown to have the effect predicted by inhibition theorists. The concept of "total energy-output" was then introduced to account for the data. This concept finally appears as a "state of general excitability in which a response characteristic of the situation is emitted at a high rate" (p. 415). It is otherwise undefined, and is used only with reference to the one experiment.

Of the principal higher-order constructs of the system, then, some are defined in terms of the laws, and sometimes are given the status of being "directly observable." Some are conceptually undeveloped and are introduced unsystematically on the basis of independent definition (envelop) or of as yet unspecified operations (emotions). A final one, drive, is clearly defined, and is employed in explanation in a way quite in accord with its definition.

General Remarks

Our analysis has been made, and it becomes possible to characterize the theory in fairly general terms. First, it is a highly formal, but not a highly formalized, theory. Its formal structure, so far as it goes, contrasts with its "empirical," "inductive," "descriptive," "non-postulational" intentions. Rather than being a set of empirical laws embodying statements that represent inductive generalizations based on a set of terms initially defined in a data language, it is a set of formally defined terms, and defining laws, which are only coordinated with data-language statements after they have been fully stated. Stimuli and responses cannot be identified independently of the theory; they are defined by the theory for the theory. Similarly, the central variable of the system, with which the experimental program has been preoccupied, the operation "reinforcement," rather than being inductively achieved as a central principle for the explanation of behavior, turns out to be a principle that serves, with some others, to define the area with which the theory deals. The actual independent variables of the system are different both from those of other systems and from those stated for the system.

The interesting result of this procedure, with its expository stress on empiricism and its structural stress on formality, is that despite very great differences in the meanings of many terms used in the theory from meanings of the same terms as used by other people, very few psychologists seem to be aware of the divergence. In fact, most *SR* psychologists, if not students of learning in general, find its tenets familiar, and customarily employ many of its data-language usages. This is doubtless a tribute to the broad empirical program associated with the system and suggests that most behavior can indeed be successfully classified as operant or respondent. In practice, the terms seem theoretically neutral, and not only Skinner, but such divergent theorists and experimentalists as Schiller (18) and Graham (7) can refer to "operant responses" without introducing possible confusion or indicating the kind of theory they are suggesting. Indeed, an examination of recent publication reveals that Skinner's data language and primitive concepts are in practice almost identical with those used by experimental followers of Tolman, Hull, and Spence, even though these men do not seem to have sought explicitly to develop or use a single data language. The careful empiricism of the coordinating definitions must account for these agreements on usage in the face of very real differences in the underlying concepts.

III. GENERAL METHODOLOGICAL SUMMARY

On the basis of a survey of the mode in which Skinner's systematic treatment of behavior works out in practice and of a careful analysis of such explicit statements as may be found, it is possible to examine the position taken by Skinner on certain broad methodological issues that have become generally accepted as critical, if not crucial, in the evaluation of such systems and to indicate how the position is reflected in the structure of the theory.

Quantification

The system of behavior expounded by Skinner in *The Behavior of Organisms* is explicitly a *quantitative* one. It has been developed with the intent of deriving empirical quantitative laws, presumably stated mathematically; the basic experimental procedures encountered are selected so as to yield physically quantifiable measures of behavior. Both the dependent and independent variables of behavior are defined in terms that should render easy the ultimate development of a fully quantitative system.

Yet in practice, in the actual gathering and analysis of data, quantification, i.e., measurement, the assignment of number, plays a small role. The data presented are, in almost all cases, *quantifiable*. The reader may extract from the data presented (which are largely copies of cumulative response curves) relatively precise measures of rates of response, of numbers of responses to extinction or to satiation and so on. Yet, these quantities, determinable though they may be, are not evaluated and play little or no role in the procedure by which general propositions are derived from the data. In practice Skinner is satisfied with statements of the type "more than," "equal to," and "less than." He is more interested in statements of the sort "The retardation has been greatly reduced by the procedure. . . ." than in statements such as "Operation X reduces rate of response from 20 per minute at $t = 0$, to 5 per minute at $t = 10$ minutes." In graph after graph, the independent variable is specified as "time in minutes," "daily period," or "days," with no numerical scale. The intent toward quantification is not everywhere reflected in action.

Much the same gap between intent and execution is encountered in the statement of quantitative laws. On the one hand, it is possible to find verbal laws stated precisely enough to permit their translation into straightforward and unequivocal mathematical terms, but the statement is not made. On the other hand, quantitative laws are sometimes stated [in some contexts referred to as "empirical" (p. 189), and in others as "theoretical" (p. 88)] as relating variables within the system, when analysis shows that the mathematical statements are not in accord with the observations they are intended to describe.

The most interesting example of verbal laws stated in such a way that they may be translated into mathematical terms is found in the series of statements relating to extinction curves and the reflex reserve collected by Ellson (5). Ellson summarized these statements in the equation

$$(1) \qquad r = R\,(1 - e^{-ct})$$

where r is the number of responses at time t, R is the asymptotic number of responses (which has been defined as the *reflex reserve*), t is the time since the first response in extinction, and c is a constant. Although this equation does not itself appear in Skinner's writings, Ellson states:

This is apparently the form used by Skinner to plot his theoretical curves; it permitted the duplication of the curves which he presents graphically within the limits of error of measurement.

In any event, this expression may be directly derived from explicit statements with respect to the proportionality obtaining between the magnitude of the reflex reserve, and the rate of response at any time. Experimental tests of this function led Ellson to conclude that the concept of the reflex reserve required rather drastic modification (a view which Skinner later adopted on the basis of his own experimental work); the function did not fit any large set of data. The empirical concept, "reflex reserve," proved to be not empirical, but theoretical.

The second type of difficulty with the statement of quantitative laws is found in another law (p. 88), which describes the relationship of the number of responses to the time since the beginning of the extinction operation. This is of the form

$$(2) \qquad N = k \log t,$$

where N is the number of responses in extinction (the reserve), t the time since the beginning of extinction, and k a constant. This function, of course, does not reach an asymptote, and N will increase logarithmically with t throughout the animal's life in the Skinner-box, a result which is an implication contrary to the verbal statement of the concept of the reflex reserve and is unsupported by data. Again, the function describing "the rate at which a white rat eats a daily ration of a standard food" (20, 22),

$$(3) \qquad N = kt^n$$

where N is the amount of food eaten in unit time, t is the time since the beginning of eating, and n and k are empirical constants, is not well adapted to describing the cyclical free-eating behavior of the rat and is especially incompatible with the phenomenon of satiation.

Skinner is quite explicit, however, in giving the reasons for his rather casual treatment of quantification. Two quotations will seem to clarify this:

> The need for quantification in the study of behavior is fairly widely understood, but it has frequently led to a sort of opportunism. The experimenter takes his measures where he can find them and is satisfied if they are quantitative, even if they are trivial or irrelevant (p. 58). . . . there are many relevant variables, and until their importance has been experimentally determined, an equation that allows for them will have so many arbitrary constants that a good fit will be a matter of course and a cause for very little satisfaction (61).

And elsewhere, the science of behavior is characterized as not ready for formal representations of the data reduced to a minimal number of terms (61).

Other theorists have argued, of course, that quantification serves quite different purposes from those implicit in Skinner's statements—e.g., that it makes it possible to test the adequacy of general laws that have been stated verbally, and hence that it facilitates the progressive growth of both experimental data and theoretical constructions based on them. Ellson's analysis is an interesting case in point, for the failure of the reserve concept exhibited by him foreshadows Skinner's own rejection of it, on much the same grounds, but at a later date. The rigorous statement of the reserve in quantitative terms exhibited its emptiness.

There is another role in which numbers may appear in a science.

Statistics is a class of mathematics that may play a role in a theoretical system, and it represents a type of quantification that Skinner rejects. He is willing (pp. 442-443) that the system be termed "statistical," if by statistical we mean correlational, and if by correlational we mean the explication of relations between dependent and independent variables.[24] He distinguishes, however, two other usages of the term. One relates to the *number* of measurements made. It is assumed by some experimenters that only through the use of large numbers can smooth and orderly functions be obtained. The other concerns the relatively imprecise and unrefined measures obtained in some classes of experiment where statistics is emphasized. In these senses, the system is characterized as *not* a statistical one, and indeed it is not.

There are two other usages of "statistical" that we might examine. One relates to the use of probability theory models for the development of a theory of behavior. No such model appears in our basic reference, although more recent publications suggest that future formulations will rely in part upon some such formulation. The exact use to which the concept "probability" will be put remains unclear.

The last usage of the term which must be examined is perhaps the most common. Statistics is a field of mathematics which has provided many of the sciences with a method of relating conclusions, general statements and laws, to the data on which they are based. It embodies "rules of inference" which permit one to state whether the changing values of supposed independent variables do indeed relate to changing values of a supposed dependent variable. In the sense that a system or set of data is "statistical" if these rules of inference are used, the present system is not a statistical one. Small groups of animals are used, and orderly results are obtained. But it is left to the reader's discretion whether he is to agree with the interpretations given and conclusions drawn. He is offered no statistical props, no mean values, no indices of variability, or tests of significance to lean upon.[25] The argument is everywhere based upon the smooth and reproducible data presented. Statistics, like other forms of mathematics, is never employed for the verification of generalizations.

Reasons for this failure to use statistics in the manner typical of psychologists are given. With adequate experimental techniques, and proper measures of behavior, statistical procedures are obviated; exact rather than statistical laws, exact rather than approximate predictions, may be made of the behavior of individuals rather than populations of them.

We may summarize Skinner's treatment of the problem of quantification in the following way: the system accepts implicitly the desirability

---

[24] Elsewhere (57) Skinner elaborates on his views towards the "correlational" approach (used in the Pearsonian sense) and suggests that it is one of the means by which applied psychology may be distinguished from experimental.

[25] An especially interesting case (37) gives conclusions based on four groups of three rats each; no means, no measures of variability, are given, although conclusions are based upon inter-group differences.

and inevitability of quantitative laws in psychology; the data are quantifiable, and in some cases quantified. But quantification within the
system is not achieved.

Degree of Axiomatization, Consistency, and Independence of Axioms

A scientist, in building a systematic treatment of his subject matter,
necessarily accepts certain axioms with respect to his observations which
are acceptable to all scientists; nature is orderly, and empirical science
can reveal that order. The game is worth the candle. Skinner differs not
at all from other scientists with respect to these axioms; he accepts them.
A second class of axioms includes postulates of the explicitly stated type
most characteristic of Hull (and perhaps essential to the writing of a
finished scientific theory). Skinner has expressed himself clearly on the
status of such axioms. A third set of axioms are assumptions peculiar to
the general approach of a given systematist. They are seldom explicitly
recognized. It is possible to find, implicit in Skinner's writings, many
unstated assumptions upon which much of his systematic thinking seems
to be based.

The second class of axioms, the "postulates" of Hull's system, have
the character of general laws of behavior, which have been derived inductively. At the same time, they are treated as statements appearing
from "nowhere" that constitute the skeletal structure of a theory. If we
are to follow most analyses of theory construction, such axioms need not
be derivable by any formal procedure of inference from an empirical
foundation. It is asked of them only that they generate verifiable
theorems. This characteristic seems typical of the application of mathematical theory to the data of the physicist.

Skinner, on the contrary, is preoccupied with the problem of arriving
at empirical laws, by induction, from the data. He explicitly rejects
theory construction by the axiomatic method.[26] To quote, "For the man
whose curiosity about nature is not equal to his interest in the accuracy
of his guesses, the hypothesis is the very life-blood of science" (p. 426).
The fundamental variables of a system must be experimentally isolated:
there are too many alternatives that might be set up hypothetically, too
many possible consequences to make it probable for an experimental scientist to use a hypothetico-deductive procedure fruitfully.

Deduction and the testing of hypotheses are actually subordinate processes in
a descriptive science, which proceeds largely or wholly without hypotheses to
the quantitative determination of the properties of behavior and through induction to the establishment of laws (p. 437).

Hull, he states, has "failed to set up a system of behavior as distinct
from a method of verification" (p. 436).

---

[26] Cf. Kantor's striction on "imposing theories on the data" (15).

In developing a system, Skinner has, however, inadvertently written a theory and has formulated as empirical law statements of the sort that serve as the postulates of a system. These have been presented at some length elsewhere in this section. Such laws presumably have many of the properties of the axioms of a hypothetico-deductive system.

With his basic assumption that behavior is orderly, Skinner accepts the view that his laws must have logical *consequences* that are presumably not distinguishable from theorems. These consequences should be experimentally verifiable, else the inductive law is not adequately stated. They must, by the same argument, *also* be internally consistent. To quote Skinner,

The virtue of Hull's work lies in an insistence upon the experimental validation of statements about behavior and upon the necessity of confining oneself to statements that are internally consistent and may be experimentally verified (p. 436).

The rejection of postulational technique is, then, not an unqualified one: many "postulates," or "assumptions" are acceptable for a scientific system. Thus we read ". . . these 'assumptions' are actually nothing but descriptive statements. . . ." and ". . . it is possible that any example of postulational method in the empirical sciences may be interpreted in the same way and that 'predicting' a fact from a set of assumptions is never intended to mean more than describing it. But if this is the case, the pretense of deduction should be abandoned, at least by those who are interested in a descriptive science of thought and who wish, therefore, to see the number of thought processes reduced to a minimum" (51).

It is not, then, unfair to inquire whether the laws of Skinner's theory are consistent, independent, and verifiable. The evidence shows that many of them are not verifiable, but definitional. Whether or not they are independent cannot be determined in their present statement. Inconsistencies, it is submitted, have already been shown in the statements that define the principal constructs of the system. This is our finding, and not that of Skinner, for he has made little or no effort to examine either the logical status of his theory or the verifiability of the laws found therein.

Where Hull's technique has led him and his followers to explore in detail the experimental status of many theorems derived from one or two postulates and to make a more or less conscientious effort to avoid inconsistencies within the system and between theory and data, Skinner's approach has led him from generalization to generalization. Having arrived at a general law experimentally, he has not preoccupied himself with exploring its every implication, or with demonstrating that it is *not* inconsistent with some earlier law. He has rather gone ahead, to manipulate further variables in a search for further laws. The experimental consequences are evident. Skinner spends no time studying "latent learning."

Skinner has uncovered a wide new range of phenomena, involving variables not at all considered by others and has obtained results beyond the scope of other theorist-experimenters. He has done so by foregoing careful tests of many of the implications of his system. If, in the course of experimentation not *designed* to test hypotheses, one of the implications of a law fails of verification, then modification occurs. Thus the experimental data that led to the abandonment of the concept of the reflex reserve as it was originally formulated were not obtained in an experiment designed to test the law, but rather in an experiment on drive, in which the magnitudes of reflex reserves were relatively incidental measurements. "Rectification" occurs in Skinner's system, but not by the mechanism of explicit effort to test the theory nor by any formal procedure.

No attempt is made to demonstrate that the laws are consistent with one another. That they are is inferred only from their empirical status and the orderliness of nature.

Similarly, we cannot find any activity by Skinner calculated to test the independence of his laws. By his procedure, he needs not do so, since he does not propose them as independent postulates, even though he may use them as such. In any event, it is clear from other chapters in this book that the process of axiomatization, or postulation, is not necessarily an efficient or even foolproof method of avoiding inconsistencies in the statement of laws.

The third class of axioms that Skinner accepts are different from those we have just discussed. They are nowhere clearly stated as such. These axioms have the nature of prescriptive and proscriptive statements; they have served to mold the system in a variety of ways and to give it some of the special flavor which distinguishes it sharply from other systems. They are not easily teased out of the system. They are not stated explicitly, but lie embedded at the foundation of the whole approach to the problem of behavior. Nor can it be said how many of them there are. It is possible, however, to exhibit certain of the more important ones and to demonstrate their status as axioms from which both theoretical constructions and experimental procedures are developed.

The first of these is this: The behavior of an organism may be fruitfully analyzed into correlations of stimulus and response. Overt events, physicalistically described,[27] are the sole object matter of the system. The apparent converse of this axiom, however, is not stated. Skinner does

---

[27] That is to say, stated in the same language as that which serves as the substratum of physical theory (3, 10). No implication should be drawn as to the reducibility of behavioral events to statement in terms of physical concepts.

not axiomatically rule out of the reach of science "psychic" or "internal events"; they are simply not included in his subject matter.

A second such axiom may be stated this way: "A science of behavior which will permit the adduction of laws permitting the prediction and control of behavior can be developed without reference to the internal physiological events which may accompany behavior." This statement has probably led to more misunderstanding of Skinner than any other feature of his systematic structure. It is not a denial of the occurrence of events that are systematically correlated with behavior. It is not a statement that laws of behavior cannot be developed from such events. It is not a statement prohibiting the statement of laws relating behavior to such events. It is, above all, not a dictum prohibiting psychophysiological investigation to the student of behavior, although it has been interpreted by one or another psychologist as any or all of these. It is a simple axiom which permits Skinner to proceed with his experimental investigations and system-building without reference to the physiology of the organism or to the structure and function of the neuro-skeletal system. The absence of physiological constructions and laws is attributable, not to the axiom in question, but to the quite different consideration that, strategically, it is more expedient to work at the behavioral level, since the science of physiology, where it is itself not based upon behavioral data, is not sufficiently well developed to permit its useful application to behavioral problems.

"Adequate experimental control of the independent variables of behavior and appropriate measurement of the dependent variables are achieved when orderly changes in the dependent variable occur, i.e., when smooth and reproducible curves appear on the recording paper. . . ." (p. 442) is an axiom that has not attracted the critical evaluation that it unquestionably deserves. Yet the definitions of the terms "stimulus," "response," and "reflex" derive from it. It has determined the level of specification at which these terms are coordinated with the subject matter, as well as the mechanical features of the recording apparatus. In both cases, the uncharitable have not hesitated to point out that the orderliness found in Skinner-box data is in part attributable to the use of crude cumulative measures of behavior. This same axiom is related to the rejection, in deriving general laws, of the use of any of the statistical tests that most psychologists find necessary to apply to their data before stating their conclusions. The smooth and orderly function is enough. Lastly, the axiom has produced, as corollaries, the concept of the "envelop of the extinction curve" (a smooth and orderly function from which the experimental data present departures), and several other terms and concepts developed for such departures. These have been discussed elsewhere, and we need not go over them again. Here is the suppressed axiom noted earlier.

When the statement of this axiom of orderliness is examined, the more extraordinary it becomes that it is taken as axiomatic and the more questionable the experimental and theoretical practices that have derived from it. It is not evident that adequate control and measurement necessarily yield "smooth and reproducible curves" (p. 442), nor that such smooth curves, such "orderliness of dynamic changes" (p. 40), can be obtained *only* by adequate "uniquely determined" (*ibid.*) control and measurement, nor that they mark a "unique point in the progressive restriction of a preparation" (p. 40). Neither statement is true in the physical sciences [and Skinner's system seems modeled after physical chemistry (p. 434)], nor need they be true in the behavioral sciences. Without denying the esthetic merits of smooth curves, whether they appear in treatises on analytical geometry or on the recording paper of a Skinner-box, one can argue that smoothness is an inadequate criterion for determining the care with which an experimenter will control his variables and for rejecting the statistical procedures for arriving at inductive generalizations that have earned wide acceptance in all the sciences.

Many scientific laws embody gross discontinuities. The "triple point" of water is a case in point. The occurrence of discontinuities in empirical data is not taken to be a problem for more or less careful experimentation, but rather as a problem for the theorist, who finds himself forced to talk about "states," and to bring in new hypotheses, new principles which may account for the discontinuities. Since it is not Skinner's goal to present, at this time, such a theory, it would seem incumbent upon him to accept discontinuities as something other than the inevitable and undesirable consequences of either too careless or too careful experimentation.

On the other hand, it *is* possible to get smooth and orderly functions where experimental manipulations are inadequate, although it is not necessarily easy to do so. Fortuitous combinations of variables and crude techniques of measurement by no means assure that the data will display discontinuities or that they will be unreproducible. For reproducibility all we need is to reproduce the same combination of variables. Let us take an example in psychology. We bring a subject into the laboratory for an hour a day and measure his reaction time, now to auditory, now to cutaneous, now to visual stimuli, both with and without ready signals. Let us measure, on any one day, the reaction time of anywhere from 200 to 2000 responses to such stimuli. On some days, our subject is fresh, on others fatigued, on some days hungry, on others stuffed from overeating. Let us use Marietta, Standard Electric, Hipp, and Dunlap, chronoscopes, all uncalibrated. Let us, furthermore, continue this procedure until 40,000 reaction times have been taken, and present the data in the form of a curve, in which "cumulative reaction time" is plotted as the function of "time in the laboratory" or "number of stimulations." We will get a smooth curve for one subject that "looks like" a curve obtained by the same means from another subject. To be sure, if we introduce the obvious controls (derived from experiments where data are accepted as variable and necessitate the calculation of means and statistical tests of significance), the curves will be "smoother." But how smooth is smooth enough? Given this axiom, on what criterion, except the *perception of smoothness,* are we to conclude that the curve we have obtained reveals, or does not reveal, inadequate control of stimulation, or adequate measurement of behavior? There is none, and our axiom is a dubious one indeed.

It can be asserted then, that something more than "smooth and reproducible" curves must serve as the basis for a definitive system of behavior, even though, within limits, this criterion may prove temporarily useful in some instances.

We shall not take time here to present an exhaustive set of inexplicit axioms such as, "There is no set of data adequate to define a concept 'inhibition.'" There seem to be many, that vary widely in content. We shall rest with having pointed out that such a class of axioms can be distinguished in Skinner's system.

The Use of Models

"Model" is a fashionable term, but of variable referent. If we restrict ourselves to the use of the term as it appears in the physical sciences (e.g., Riemannian space or the Newtonian mechanics of perfectly elastic spherules of the older gas theory), no models appear in Skinner's system, nor could there be any in such a nonpostulational system.

If we use the term loosely, in the fashion of psychologists, we *could* defend the position that the spinal-reflex is taken as the model of *all* behavior but that the reflex reserve is based on a cash register, water-bucket,[28] or reservoir, model, into which we may place determinate quantities of response-stuff and withdraw it in rather different units but with the total "stuff" available invariant. We will *not* defend it; "models," in this sense, are insignificant analogies. It would be otherwise, of course, if these "models" were employed hypothetico-deductively.

Techniques of Derivation

It is evident that Skinner's technique of derivation is entirely informal. Data are presented and graphs displayed. Statements describing them in the data language and the primitive terms of the system are added. The final description, in these terms, has the status of a law. After a number of such statements have accrued within a section dealing with a defined set of variables, a summarizing statement is found which states a law broadly embedded in collateral textual material.

---

[28] Skinner acknowledges this model in a recent writing (61).

In other cases, where general laws are presented, their formulation and presentation may be more formal. Thus, "The Law of the Discrimination of the Stimulus in Type S" is stated after a preliminary treatment which states the problem of discrimination in the terms of the system, and which is largely concerned with the rejection of alternative treatments.

GENERAL EVALUATION

Our analysis has been relatively detailed. It has been based on a well-established view of the role of theory in the development of science and of the structural characteristics of useful theory. Such analyses almost inevitably develop into listings of the sins of omission and commission of particular theorists, especially when one treats with a theorist whose views on theory diverge from the analyst's.

Hull, Tolman, and even Guthrie and Lewin share with us much of our view of theory. It is, then, appropriate to point out gaps between many of their stated objectives and their performances. But it is not clear that Skinner is dealing with the same subject matter as these others. He often seems to be developing a system that not only differs from the others in particulars of theoretical detail, but also represents a re-orientation towards the science.

We have indicated certain shortcomings in the theoretical and systematic developments offered by Skinner. Many of his proponents will sharply dispute these judgments. Criteria highly suited to the examination of such highly axiomatized and deductive systems as Hull's may be irrelevant to Skinner's, since he has explicitly disavowed any intention of writing such a theory, and as we have seen, has used formal laws solely to define his subject matter. In its constructional aspects, however, Skinner's work falls within the scope of the term "theory," and can be so examined. Skinner *has* written a theory. On the other hand, it remains necessary to examine the status of the structure as a "system."

Skinner states that he is concerned with the setting forth of *a system*. A system "consists of an aggregation of related variables, singled out for the sake of convenient investigation and description from all the various phenomena presented by a given subject matter. In the case of behavior, a system in this sense can be arrived at only through the kind of experimental analysis to which this book is devoted, in which the parts or aspects of behavior which undergo orderly changes are identified and their mutual relations established" (pp. 434-435).

Skinner, then, since he has defined his subject matter, considers that his work is solely one of empirical investigation, the assembling of an orderly body of experimentally established facts of the sort that must exist before a succinctly stated group of lawful relationships can summarize varied sets of experimental data within the area. The area is formally defined; only afterwards is the procedure empirical, descriptive, inductive, nonpostulational. A system, in this view, is not so much a "theory" as it is a *Weltanschauung*.

How successful has Skinner been in setting forth such a system? Certainly, the body of experimental fact is there and secure. Certainly, the most important variables that are manipulated, and the dependent ones that are measured, are established. The experimental substrate of a system has been developed. Much of the vocabulary and definitional system needed to handle the results of the program is given within the system. But what is available is not entirely adequate to define the kind of system Skinner is concerned with, and we must turn to the embedding material, what the systematist has to say about what he is doing, rather than to the formal statements themselves, for further illumination. When we do so, we find that the kind of system conceived is quite different from what the hasty reader thinks is there, and that it is indeed based on premises with respect to the nature of things which will not be universally accepted.

That Skinner's concepts have often been misunderstood and misinterpreted probably stems from his choice of a set of terms. Implicative and associational values turn up frequently in the selection of a theorist's terminology. To the "Tolmanite," conditioned responses are *mere*, or *mechanical*. To the "Hullian," *expectancy* and *cognition* carry the suggestion of the capricious intervention of entities extraneous to behavior. Skinner has attempted to avoid such considerations, and to eliminate the preconceptions (about what organisms ought or ought not to do) that may flow from the use of terms with extensive connotations. He wishes to find out how animals behave and seeks a vocabulary that will let him talk about how they behave. Because of the existence in Sherrington and Pavlov of sets of data of the kind he believes are needed, he has adopted many of their terms and applied some of their laws in defining his area. As a consequence, he has been misinterpreted. In his choice of terminology, Skinner has assured that his works and those of his fellows will be read easily by the followers of Hull and Guthrie and only with emotion, if not with difficulty, by those who have selected the organismic-field-Gestalt-force family of words to work with. Skinner's conditioned responses seem to many readers just as *mere* as those of Pavlov or Hull, with the extraordinary result that he has been classed with Hull rather than with Tolman, with Guthrie rather than with Lewin, in his general position. Skinner's work has, in fact, very little in common with that of any of these men. Controversies, such as those over "latent learning," and "continuity" and "discontinuity" interpretations are pointless within the Skinnerian framework.

Skinner, as we have shown, does not endow his concept of stimulus with the physical-energy specification given to the word by Hull; nor "drive." Hull uses the terms in rough correspondence with the usages of physiology, and they are stated in a physically reduced way. He employs them, not physicalistically, but physically. Skinner, on the contrary, does not attempt to write a set of statements about behavior which may be readily related to statements about protons, molecules, quanta, nerve impulses, or brain structures. Such a treatment, by its analytical omissions, produces disparities between physical world and psychological world, and so leads to a necessity for phenomenological investigations such as those of the Gestalt psychologist, that seek to put the "two" back together again. These problems are meaningful only when we accept as basic data for a point of departure the analytic *products* of other sciences. It may ultimately become desirable to incorporate reductive statements of some sort, as a more and more complete description of behavior develops. But it is not clear that this procedure is logically necessary or pragmatically desirable for a science of behavior that aims to predict and describe. The experimental analyses forced by an acceptance of reductionism often displaces scientific inquiries into behavior from the observation and quantification of the organism's activities, to the elaboration of detail on relatively insignificant phenomena.

Skinner's approach, then, bears no more than a terminological resemblance to Hull's or to Pavlov's, but it is at least first cousin to Kantor's system (15), which explicitly rather than implicitly accepts a metaphysical position, naive realism, and rejects even the logical possibility of a reductionism. His approach has affinities to Tolman's. Tolman postulates that the so-called laws of perception, derived from phenomenological studies, apply to the rat; Skinner does what amounts to the same thing implicitly, by starting with what comes to him, to all the other experimenters, and until proven otherwise, to the experimental animal. Hull, on the contrary, seems to wish (where he does not evade the issue by speaking of "stimulus interactions") to derive "perceptual" laws on the basis of his reductively stated postulates. Skinner wants to start with a point-at-able world, with point-at-able operations, and to carry on from there. He accepts as his point of departure the world of things and activities and leaves to others, who start reductively, the fields of "perception" and "sensation." It is often with surprise that persons most familiar with earlier frames of references in psychology recognize that this is true of other current behaviorists. Physiological elementarism, in the style of Watson, is not a necessary characteristic of today's behaviorists.

As a systematist, then, Skinner attempts a clean break with much of traditional psychology, a fact that has escaped many psychologists.

How does Skinner's work stand if it is evaluated in terms of its own stated objectives? One must say that it survives examination more successfully than when it is viewed as just another theory. Its very faults seem to accent its fundamental merit; they come from the fact that, even with the best of intentions, Skinner has not been able to eschew theory as he wished. Theoretical constructs have appeared within the system, and have been assigned properties that do not appear in the data. Data-language terms have accrued surplus meanings. Statements incorporating operationally defined terms assert relations that have not yet been experimentally demonstrated. If Skinner had followed the critical analysis of theory construction that we have expounded, and if the highly formal nature of much of the system had been recognized, perhaps some of these difficulties might have been circumvented. Skinner, too, would object to the very things to which we have objected.

The experimental program, on the other hand, has developed in a satisfactory manner. The experimental data that have accumulated over the years do not show the result of a preoccupation with "critical" (and complex) experiments, whose outcome becomes a matter of indifference to all, as soon as the theoretical point to which they were addressed is re-evaluated. In any event, as a system, Skinner's is still growing, and data-gathering has outstripped theory.

We may finally test the system against those evaluative criteria that were proposed in an earlier section of this monograph.

Clarification of events. Does the system "clarify the description of the world which is possible in ordinary language?" There is little doubt that in eliminating, in an explicit way, terms of loose referent and vague connotation, Skinner has enabled many theorists to find for themselves suppressed premises in their thinking. Beyond this consideration, the terms employed in the system are such that many phenomena may be restated to reveal relationships that might otherwise be overlooked. These results, in turn, necessarily lead to experimental investigation. The same terms, we have noted, however, have led to confusion about the content of the system.

Summarization of existing data. How effectively does the system summarize existing knowledge? Skinner has sharply delineated the classes of existing scientific knowledge that he is willing to incorporate within his system. While doubtless accepting as highly defensible the proposition that any set of scientific psychological data may be interpreted in terms of his variables, he explicitly refuses to admit, as a basis for scientific induction, the results of most psychological experiments. The reason for this is that the selection, manipulation, and control of the independent variables is so erratic and incomplete that significant sets of data are lacking. Further, the measures of behavior that have been used are meaningless. Many experimental designs are, finally, too complex for fruitful analysis. To a remarkable degree, the theory is applied only to behavioral experimentation in its defined area, so that it "fails" to handle many data for the simple reason that it does not attempt to do so.

For the same reasons that most existing psychological data are ignored in developing the system, the system is not responsive to data currently obtained in non-Skinnerian experiments. Only when the variables have been adequately selected and manipulated according to the standards of the system, and when appropriate measures of behavior have been made does the system take account of experimental data. Then it shows itself highly sensitive to experimental results. Concepts well established in the system such as "reflex reserve" [29] have been abandoned since their original statement on the basis of experimental results (48) without any particular attempt to reformulate them or otherwise to salvage them. Systematic problems are likewise faced, and new hypothetical constructs have been, or are being, developed to account for new classes of data. The experimental program proceeds, and no particular attempt is made to "tidy up" the theorizing that goes with it. In short, the system is highly sensitive to data deemed appropriate. Almost no effort is made to reinterpret, in terms of the system, data gathered in other experimental contexts or in any other way to make use of them or to synthesize them within the system. The data may be valid (i.e., reproducible), but they are taken as inappropriate for the systematic science of behavior toward which Skinner is striving. The system, then, summarizes such knowledge as has been obtained by the specified experimental techniques.

Prediction. Does the system mediate the application of knowledge to new situations? Does it predict?

Some systems or theories of behavior lay great stress on their ability to predict the outcome of planned experiments—often taken to be *experimenta crucis*. It is not surprising, however, that a theory of restricted empirical basis, "informally stated," and "inductively" developed does not generate rigorous predictions about the behavior to be observed in novel situations. In fact, such statements as these must be qualified. Several aspects of Skinner's view of the problem of prediction and extrapolation must be treated individually. Although one of our more conservative theorists when he is making statements *about* prediction, Skinner is more willing than most to extrapolate his concepts from the situations in which they have been developed to some of the more intricate cases of human behavior. This willingness is clearly indicated in the title of the treatise, *The Behavior of Organisms*, which deals with the white rat in the Skinner-box.

Two situations may be distinguished in which a systematist may wish to make predictions. The first is that in which a logical or operational analysis shows that the "same" variables that have already been isolated and studied in the laboratory are operative elsewhere in the "same"

---

[29] This is now (61) characterized as "not a particularly useful concept, nor does [it] . . . add much to the observed fact that extinction curves are curved in a certain way." It is "a defensible description at the level of behavior," and not "a theory, . . . not assigned to a different dimensional system. . . ." It "could be operationally defined as a predicted extinction-curve, even though, linguistically, it makes a statement about the momentary condition of a response."

relationships that have been investigated. The data are in, and the theorist simply asserts the genotypicality of the situation, applies his theory, and "predicts" the course of events. In the other situation, familiar variables may be encountered, but in novel configurations, and the theorist is required to generate statements that go beyond those he has already made. Or, again, new variables may be encountered, and, again, prediction may be called for. While Skinner will predict, or rather extrapolate freely where a logical analysis reveals familiar variables acting in familiar ways, he will not predict at all under other circumstances. As a consequence, it is possible to find no predictions at all of the behavior of rats, or of pigeons, when novel combinations of stimuli are presented to them in the Skinner-box, and many predictions among Skinner's writings with respect to human behavior in a social environment. The great difficulty is that these predictions are usually unverifiable, because of the complexity of the situation and the consequent impossibility of meaningful experimental test. Prediction, then, is represented by extrapolation, by analogy; its use for the generation of propositions that may be put to experimental test is avoided.

Does the system lead to fruitful lines of experimental inquiry? There can be no doubt that the theory has been associated with a very active experimental program. There can be no doubt that its atheoretical orientation dictates that experimentation shall proceed at all times, with full exploration of the behavioral consequences of varying the many experimental variables that the system discovers and treats. Many experimenters have argued that such parametric approaches to experimentation are fruitless, and that only experimentation directed toward particular theoretical points have the merit of fertility. If anything, the development of the Skinnerian system argues against this view. The theory does not predict, and experimentation is not designed to check, theoretical statements. Yet the experimental program has been an exceedingly productive one. The experimental pages of *The Behavior of Organisms* speak for themselves. Most particularly, the area of research on schedules of reinforcement was first explored and developed within the system. This set of results was not anticipated in other theoretical frameworks and still represents a difficulty for them. It constitutes a body of data that very likely will have considerable influence on theory for years to come. The experimental stress of the theory has freed the experimental program from restrictions forced by respect for the integrity of theoretical constructs. It is difficult to find a match in either quantity or variety in the works of other theorists with whom we have been concerned for the experimental program associated with this system. That this reflects much with respect to the *system* may be doubted. It is certainly a tribute to the systematist, and it demonstrates the force of his strongly empirical position.

Appendix

THE FORMALIZED LAWS OF BEHAVIOR
(*The Behavior of Organisms*)

Static Laws

1. *The Law of Threshold.* The intensity of the stimulus must reach or exceed a certain critical value (called the threshold) in order to elicit a response.

2. *The Law of Latency.* An interval of time (called the latency) elapses between the beginning of the stimulus and the beginning of the response.

3. *The Law of the Magnitude of the Response.* The magnitude of the response is a function of the intensity of the stimulus.

4. *The Law of After-Discharge.* The response may persist for some time after the cessation of the stimulus.

5. *The Law of Temporal Summation.* Prolongation of a stimulus or repetitive presentation within certain limiting rates has the same effect as increasing the intensity.

Dynamic Laws

6. *The Law of the Refractory Phase.* Immediately after elicitation the strength of some reflexes exists at a low, perhaps zero, value. It returns to its former state during subsequent inactivity.

7. *The Law of Reflex Fatigue.* The strength of a reflex declines during repeated elicitation and returns to its former value during subsequent inactivity.

8. *The Law of Facilitation.* The strength of a reflex may be increased through presentation of a second stimulus which does not itself elicit the response.

9. *The Law of Inhibition.* The strength of a reflex may be decreased through presentation of a second stimulus which has no other relation to the effector involved.

10. *The Law of Conditioning of Type S.* The approximately simultaneous presentation of two stimuli, one of which (the "reinforcing" stimulus) belongs to a reflex existing at the moment at some strength, may produce an increase in the strength of a third reflex composed of the response of the reinforcing reflex and the other stimulus.

11. *The Law of Extinction of Type S.* If the reflex strengthened through conditioning of Type S is elicited without presentation of the reinforcing stimulus, its strength decreases.

12. *The Law of Conditioning of Type R.* If the occurrence of an operant

is followed by presentation of a reinforcing stimulus, the strength is increased.

13. *The Law of Extinction of Type R.* If the occurrence of an operant already strengthened through conditioning is not followed by the reinforcing stimulus, the strength is decreased.

Laws of Interaction

14. *The Law of Compatibility.* Two or more responses which do not overlap topographically may occur simultaneously without interference.

15. *The Law of Prepotency.* When two reflexes overlap topographically and the responses are incompatible, one response may occur to the exclusion of the other.

16. *The Law of Algebraic Summation.* The simultaneous elicitation of two responses utilizing the same effectors but in opposite directions produces a response the extent of which is an algebraic resultant.

17. *The Law of Blending.* Two responses showing some topographical overlap may be elicited together but in necessarily modified forms.

18. *The Law of Spatial Summation.* When two reflexes have the same form of response, the response to both stimuli in combination has a greater magnitude and a shorter latency.

19. *The Law of Chaining.* The response of one reflex may constitute or produce the eliciting or discriminative stimulus of another.

20. *The Law of Induction.* A dynamic change in the strength of a reflex may be accompanied by a similar but not so extensive change in a related reflex, where the relation is due to the possession of common properties of stimulus or response.

21. *The Law of the Extinction of Chained Reflexes.* In a chain of reflexes not ultimately reinforced only the members actually elicited undergo extinction.

22. *The Law of the Discrimination of the Stimulus in Type S.* A reflex strengthened by induction from the reinforcement of a reflex possessing a similar but not identical stimulus may be separately extinguished if the difference in stimuli is supraliminal for the organism.

23. *The Law of the Discrimination of the Stimulus in Type R.* The strength acquired by an operant through reinforcement is not independent of the stimuli affecting the organism at the moment, and two operants having the same form of response may be given widely different strengths through differential reinforcement with respect to such stimuli.

24. *The Law of the Operant Reserve.* The reinforcement of an operant creates a single reserve, the size of which is independent of the stimulating field but which is differentially accessible under different fields.

Bibliography

1. BERGMANN, G., & SPENCE, K. W. The logic of psychophysical measurements. *Psychol. Rev.*, 1944, 51, 1-24.
2. BRELAND, Keller, & BRELAND, Marion. A field of applied animal psychology. *Amer. Psychol.*, 1951, 6, 202-204.
3. CARNAP, R. Logical foundations of the unity of science. In H. Feigl & W. Sellars. *Readings in philosophical analysis*. New York: Appleton-Century-Crofts, 1949. Pp. 408-423.
4. COOK, S. W., & SKINNER, B. F. Some factors influencing the distribution of associated words. *Psychol. Rec.*, 1939, 3, 178-184.
5. ELLSON, Douglas G. The concept of reflex reserve. *Psychol. Rev.*, 1939, 46, 566-575.
6. ESTES, W. K., & SKINNER, B. F. Some quantitative properties of anxiety. *J. Exper. Psychol.*, 1941, 29, 390-400.
7. GRAHAM, C. H., & GAGNÉ, R. M. The acquisition, extinction, and spontaneous recovery of a conditioned operant response. *J. Exper. Psychol.*, 1940, 26, 251-280.
8. GUTHRIE, E. R. *The psychology of learning*. New York: Harpers, 1935.
9. HARRIMAN, P. L. *The new dictionary of psychology*. New York: Philosophical Library, 1947.
10. HEMPEL, C. G. The logical analysis of psychology. In H. Feigl & W. Sellars. *Readings in philosophical analysis*. New York: Appleton-Century-Crofts, 1949. Pp. 373-384.
11. HERON, W. T., & SKINNER, B. F. Changes in hunger during starvation. *Psychol. Rec.*, 1947, 1, 51-60.
12. ———. The rate of extinction in maze-bright and maze-dull rats. *Psychol. Bull.*, 1939, 36, 520. (Abstr.)
13. ———. The rate of extinction in maze-bright and maze-dull rats. *Psychol. Rec.*, 1940, 4, 11-18.
14. HILGARD, E. R. *Theories of learning*. New York: Appleon-Century-Crofts, 1948.
15. KANTOR, J. R. *Principles of psychology*. New York: Knopf, 1924.
16. MILLER, N. E. Studies of fear as an acquirable drive: I. Fear as motivation and fear-reduction as reinforcment in the learning of new responses. *J. Exper. Psychol.*, 1948, 38, 89-101.
17. PAVLOV, I. P. Conditioned reflexes. London: Oxford Univ. Press, 1927. (Transl. G. V. Anrep.)
18. SCHILLER, P. S. Analysis of detour behavior. I. Learning of round-about pathways in fish. *J. Comp. Physiol. Psychol.*, 1949, 42, 463-475.
19. SHERRINGTON, C. S. *The integrative action of the nervous system*. New York: Scribner, 1906.
20. SKINNER, B. F. On the conditions of elicitation of certain eating reflexes. *Proc. Nat. Acad. Sci.*, 1930, 16, 433-438.
21. ———. The concept of the reflex in the description of behavior. *J. Gen. Psychol.*, 1931, 5, 427-458.
22. ———. Drive and reflex strength. *J. Gen. Psychol.*, 1932, 6, 22-37.
23. ———. Drive and reflex strength: II. *J. Gen. Psychol.*, 1932, 6, 38-48.
24. ———. On the rate of formation of a conditioned reflex. *J. Gen. Psychol.*, 1932, 7, 274-286.

25. SKINNER, B. F. On the rate of extinction of a conditioned reflex. *J. Gen. Psychol.*, 1933, 8, 114-129.

26. ———. The measurement of "spontaneous activity," *J. Gen. Psychol.*, 1933, 9, 3-23.

27. ———. The rate of establishment of a discrimination. *J. Gen. Psychol.*, 1933, 9, 302-350.

28. ———. "Resistance to extinction" in the process of conditioning. *J. Gen. Psychol.*, 1933, 9, 420-429.

29. ———. The abolishment of a discrimination. *Proc. Nat. Acad. Sci.*, 1933, 19, 825-828.

30. ———. The extinction of chained reflexes. *Proc. Nat. Acad. Sci.*, 1934, 20, 234-237.

31. ———. A discrimination without previous conditioning. *Proc. Nat. Acad. Sci.*, 1934, 20, 532-536.

32. ———. The generic nature of the concepts of stimulus and response. *J. Gen. Psychol.*, 1935, 12, 40-65.

33. ———. Two types of conditioned reflex and a pseudotype. *J. Gen. Psychol.*, 1935, 12, 66-77.

34. ———. A discrimination based upon a change in the properties of a stimulus. *J. Gen. Psychol.*, 1935, 12, 313-336.

35. ———. A failure to obtain "disinhibition." *J. Gen. Psychol.*, 1936, 14, 127-135.

36. ———. The reinforcing effect of a differentiating stimulus. *J. Gen. Psychol.*, 1936, 14, 263-278.

37. ———. The effect of the amount of conditioning of an interval of time before reinforcement. *J. Gen. Psychol.*, 1936, 14, 279-295.

38. ———. Conditioning and extinction and their relation to drive. *J. Gen. Psychol.*, 1936, 14, 296-317.

39. ———. Thirst as an arbitrary drive. *J. Gen. Psychol.*, 1936, 15, 205-210.

40. ———. The verbal summator and a method for the study of latent speech. *J. Psychol.*, 1936, 2, 71-107.

41. ———. The extinction ratio and its modification by a temporal discrimination. *Psychol. Bull.*, 1936, 33, 784. (Abstr.)

42. ———, & HERON, W. T. Effects of caffeine and benzedrine upon conditioning and extinction. *Psychol. Rec.*, 1937, 1, 340-346.

42a. SKINNER, B. F. The distribution of associated words. *Psychol. Rec.*, 1937, 1, 71-76.

43. ———. Two types of conditioned reflex: a reply to Konorski and Miller. *J. Gen. Psychol.*, 1937, 16, 272-279.

44. ———. *The behavior of organisms: an experimental analysis.* New York: Appleton-Century-Crofts, 1938.

45. ———. The frequencies of occurrences of associated words. *Psychol. Bull.*, 1938, 35, 675. (Abstr.)

46. ———. The alliteration in Shakespeare's sonnets: a study of literary behavior. *Psychol. Rec.*, 1939, 3, 186-192.

47. ———. A method of maintaining an arbitrary degree of hunger. *J. Comp. Psychol.*, 1940, 30, 139-145.

48. ———. The nature of the operant reserve. *Psychol. Bull.*, 1940, 37, 423. (Abstr.)

49. ———. A quantitative estimate of certain types of sound patterning in poetry. *Amer. J. Psychol.*, 1941, 54, 64-79.

50. SKINNER, B. F. Some quantitative properties of anxiety. *Psychol. Bull.*, 1941, 38, 539. (Abstr.)
51. ———. The processes involved in the repeated guessing of alternatives. *J. Exper. Psychol.*, 1942, 30, 495-503.
52. ———. Reply to Dr. Yacorzynsky. *J. Exper. Psychol.*, 1943, 32, 93-94.
53. ———. Review of Hull's principles of behavior. *Amer. J. Psychol.*, 1944, 57, 276-281.
54. ———. The operational analysis of psychological terms. *Psychol. Rev.*, 1945, 52, 270-277.
55. ———. Differential reinforcement with respect to time. *Amer. Psychol.*, 1946, 1, 274-275. (Abstr.)
56. ———. The effect of the difficulty of a response upon its rate of emission. *Amer. Psychol.*, 1946, 1, 462. (Abstr.)
57. ———. Experimental psychology. In W. Dennis (ed.), *Current trends in psychology*. Pittsburgh: Univ. of Pittsburgh Press, 1947.
58. ———. "Superstition" in the pigeon. *Amer. Psychol.*, 1947, 2, 426. (Abstr.)
59. ———. "Superstition" in the pigeon. *J. Exper. Psychol.*, 1948, 38, 168-172.
60. ———. Concurrent operants. *Amer. Psychol.*, 1948, 3, 359. (Abstr.)
61. ———. Are theories of learning necessary? *Psychol. Rev.*, 1950, 57, 193-216.
62. TINBERGEN, N. The hierarchical organization of nervous mechanisms underlying instinctive behaviour. In *Physiological mechanisms in animal behavior*. New York: Academic Press, 1950.
63. TOLMAN, E. C. *Purposive behavior in animals and men*. New York: Appleton-Century-Crofts, 1932.
64. WARREN, H. C. *Dictionary of psychology*. New York: Houghton-Mifflin, 1934.

Kurt Lewin

⇶⇶⇶⫷⫷⫷

WILLIAM K. ESTES

INTRODUCTION

DURING recent years reviewers and text writers, if not theorists themselves, have come to characterize, or dramatize, the psychology of learning in terms of a conflict between two camps, the one commonly called
stimulus-response or stimulus-response-reinforcement theory and the
other gestalt, cognitive or, most generally, field theory. The lines of
demarcation are not entirely distinct. The *S-R* label covers at least Hull,
Guthrie, Skinner, and a large number of associates and students of these
men; the field label covers the gestalt theorists Koffka and Köhler, Lewin,
and sometimes others with viewpoints as divergent as Maier and Wheeler.
Tolman has usually been classified in the latter group, although it is
by no means clear upon detailed examination of his work that the
classification is entirely accurate (or judging from recent writings, that
he is entirely happy with it). For brevity in the following discussion
we shall refer to the former line of development simply as learning theory
and the latter as field theory.

By learning theory we shall mean, then, the rather loosely defined
class of psychological systems which has grown out of the American
functionalist-behaviorist tradition and which is associated historically
with the names of Pavlov, Thorndike, Loeb, Jennings, Watson, and
Carr, and contemporarily with the names of Hull, Guthrie, and Skinner.
Although learning theory, so defined, includes several rather disparate
theoretical programs, they all have much in common. The underlying
philosophy is strongly marked by the influence of logical positivism and
operationism. The point of view is characterized by an assumption of

continuity with physiology and physics and a tendency to take the experimental and theoretical methods of the physical sciences as a starting point for approaching the problems of behavior. All are committed to the view that the concepts of a science of learning must be confirmable in terms of prediction of observable behaviors. In the early stages of theorizing, at least, they proceed by analyzing learning situations into behavioral and environmental components and developing empirical generalizations that describe relations among classes of behavioral and environmental variables. The concepts of learning theory have for the most part grown out of experimental facts in a rather straightforward fashion. This point of view has assumed a dominant role in relation to research on learning in this country. The vast majority of studies of learning reported in the experimental journals in recent years are formulated in terms of S-R theory. This fact is in great measure responsible for the emphasis given S-R learning theory in the work of the Dartmouth conference.

There is no reason to expect that direct comparison of learning theory and field theory will be easy, for the empirical sources of the two theoretical enterprises are quite different. Whereas the concepts of learning theory have grown out of a fairly well defined set of experimental data, the inductive source of field theory seems to be compounded of informal observation of various sorts of human behavior, usually in social contexts; introspective reports from human subjects; experimentation on human behavior, mostly concerned with conflict, perceptual phenomena, and group interactions; and a small amount of animal experimentation, mostly involving complex activities in the higher organisms, problem solving, etc. In so far as we expect a theory to grow out of facts, we should be prepared to find many differences between field theories and conventional learning theories. Despite these considerations, the proponents of field theories are frequently found to hold that their formulations are superior to learning theory in handling the empirical domain with which the latter has been especially concerned. There are several specific ways in which this might be accomplished. On the one hand the laws of learning theory might prove to be derivable as theorems or special cases of field-theoretical laws. Another possibility is that the field theory might interpret the same data quite differently, so that while field theory and learning theory would not, then, literally handle the same facts, nevertheless, field theory might prove to be the superior instrument for mediating the prediction and control of behavior in learning situations. The former possibility we can hope to evaluate in reasonably objective fashion; the latter may well prove indeterminate.

Now we may ask what are the distinguishing characteristics of the enterprises which claim or at least permit the appellation field theory? It should be noted first of all that most of the attributes claimed by field theorists and sympathetic reviewers tend to vanish or at least become non-differentiating upon critical scrutiny. It is not clear to the present writer in what technical sense the term field theory is especially applicable to the systems of Lewin (11, 12), Koffka (7), Köhler (8), or Tolman (18). The term field has been taken over from physics, but it is not easy to find a basis for the presumed analogy between field theories of physics and the so-called field theories of psychology. In any physical theory the system of events under consideration is characterized by a set of state variables (e.g., in mechanics one may take as a system a material particle and characterize the state of the system at any moment by the mass, position, and velocity); the theory predicts the behavior of the system by means of laws relating these state variables to one or more independent variables. In non-field theories—e.g., classical mechanics—time is the only independent variable. In field theories spatial as well as temporal coordinates take on the role of independent variables and the laws are expressed as partial differential equations. It is not obvious, however, that this mode of differentiation between field and non-field theories makes much sense in the context of contemporary psychology. Certainly the so-called field theories of psychology have not made great use of partial differential equations; even the commoner and less formidable methods of quantitative analysis have generally been less prominent in these systems than arguments in favor of "treating the organism as a whole."

The field theorists of psychology criticize over-mechanistic views of causality and emphasize multiple determination, but it is mainly the stimulus-response learning theorists who have proceeded to formulate laws relating behavior changes to multiple independent variables (as, for example, in the joint determination of momentary action tendency by reinforcement history, drive, and stimulus properties in the theories of Hull (5) and Skinner (16). Some of the field theorists, especially Lewin (14), emphasize the role of "the present situation" and claim that science can go no farther toward the explanation of a phenomenon than to provide a conceptual representation of the situation in which it occurs; this view will be examined in detail below.

One of the rallying points of the field theorists has been the claim of being more dynamic than stimulus-response or association theorists (13). Again we seem to have a term taken over from physical theory with no obvious basis for its analogical use in psychology. In physics dynamical laws are those which express rates of change of processes while statical laws deal with conditions of equilibrium. Clearly the use of "dynamic" in characterizing psychological field theories does not refer to this distinction. Evidently dynamical terms are borrowed by the psychologist for the glamor and prestige of their connotations. One of the uses of "dynamic" in psychology reflects an animistic view of scientific explanation according to which a satisfactory account of an observed phenomenon must involve words connoting force or energy. Thus we find (10) association theory criticized for failing to provide a source of energy for mental processes, and field theories such as Lewin's given credit for handling the problem of motivation simply because the word force is used to label one of the theoretical concepts. It is our view that progress in psychology depends upon achieving freedom from this sort of "dynamic" theorizing and rising above the primitive stage of theoretical development where the demand for explanation can be satisfied only by animistic or analogical forces, faculties, energies which reside in or behind observed phenomena. Among field theorists Lewin has been an outspoken critic of animistic views of causation and yet has not been able to resist the temptation to assign to his theoretical concepts attributes of direction, attraction, repulsion, etc., thus remaining effectively in bondage to the mechanical models of classical physics. It seems to be not the field theories but the more sophisticated S-R theories, notably that of Skinner (16), which are beginning to achieve freedom from the animistic theories implicit in everyday language and to reflect the methodological developments of physical theory.

A detailed comparison of field and learning theories reveals a number of fairly clear-cut differences. First of all, the field theories are characteristically much broader in scope. They take their origins in everyday problems or in complex laboratory situations involving perceptual and inferential processes, formulate theoretical concepts reflecting the grossly observable "directional," "organizational," "meaningful," aspects of behavior, then at a later stage try to show that the results of learning experiments can be verbalized in the same terms. To a great extent the field and learning theories simply do not deal with the same problems. The learning theorist typically begins with the restricted laboratory situation, develops a conceptual model which will mediate detailed predictions in a narrowly defined area, then wanders afield to see what light his model may shed upon extra-laboratory problems (but ready to retire sheepishly if caught off his inductive base by other theorists). Differences in interest and in methodological assumptions make comparisons between field and S-R points of view always difficult and frequently unrewarding. Because of differences in the data languages which are taken as the bases of definition, it is rarely possible to compare field and S-R theories with respect to efficacy in handling a given phenomenon.

Learning theorists tend to accept the desirability of proceeding so that theoretical concepts can be defined, either explicitly or by some sort of reduction, in terms of a common pre-theoretical language in which all statements are confirmable by observation.

A set of concepts defined entirely in terms of one another constitutes a purely formal system. A formal system may be of great interest in its own right (e.g., projective geometry), but it has no necessary reference to empirical events. The concepts of a *scientific* theory must, in order to go beyond this sort of circularity, be reducible to a set of terms which are taken as undefined within the theory but which can be set in correspondence with observables; we shall refer to this set of terms as the data language of a given theory. The status of this language should be clearly understood. The terms are not necessarily simple in the sense of being familiar to everyone or of being self-evident. A portion of the data language comes from everyday English and includes the terminology needed for the description of observations and operations. In psychology the chief function of the data language is the description of behaviors and of the situations in which they occur. The terms used in description must be limited to those for which agreement upon usage can be obtained from workers in the field regardless of theoretical biases and which are free of any reference to theory (that is, to the theory for which the set of terms in question functions as data language). Terms from related disciplines are usually included in the data language. All or nearly all psychological theories accept the language of physics as undefined, and usually part of the language of physiology. Borrowing from physiology has to be done with care since much physiological doctrine is as much in question as are psychological concepts that incorporate them. Many physiological terms would be generally accepted by psychological theorists as suitable elements of the data language (e.g., isometric contraction, action potential, nerve impulse, refractory period of a nerve fiber) ; others clearly would not (e.g., decrease in synaptic resistance, central inhibitory state, equipotentiality).

It is difficult to formulate any simple general rules for ascertaining precisely what portion of a scientific work belongs to the data language (except in the case of highly formalized theories such as the "hypothetico-deductive theory of rote learning" (4) which present the set of primitive terms explicitly). In general the terms belonging to the data language will be susceptible to ostensive definition. Sentences formulated in the data language refer to observable events or operations. And in so far as a theory is intended to be communicable and susceptible of general acceptance among researchers, it is necessary that the data language be limited to terms for which agreement upon usage can be obtained among qualified investigators regardless of theoretical orientation. As Skinner (16) has pointed out, some terms from ordinary English are appropriate for inclusion in the data language of a science of behavior; others are not. In the description of animal behavior, for instance, agreement can be reached upon the use of terms referring to movements of the animal or its parts (e.g., walk, run, forelimb flexion), but not upon terms with hidden theoretical implications (e.g., attempt, belief, search).

Different theories purporting to deal with the same subject matter can be compared for critical purposes only in so far as they are reducible to the same data language. The reviews of current theories in the present volume have been influenced by this fact. It will be seen, for example, that the theoretical concepts of such otherwise diverse systematists as Guthrie, Hull, Skinner, and Tolman assume essentially the same data language. The works of these men are directly comparable in many respects, and theories or fragments of theory growing out of their work may be regarded as sometimes competitive, sometimes complementary formulations of a common subject matter. Certain other theories, those of Köhler and Koffka, for example, which might appear superficially to be alternative formulations to those mentioned above, prove upon analysis to assume different data languages and therefore to present quite different tasks to the critical analyst.

Lewin's theory has seemed to us the most suitable of the field theories to select for detailed consideration. It has been elaborated in great detail and applied to many concrete situations. Methodological assumptions are given explicitly, so that by giving adequate consideration to these assumptions it should be possible to avoid one of the common errors of the critic—criticizing a theory upon irrelevant grounds. Further, Lewin's thinking falls within the natural science tradition, and his views as to the mode of verification of theory and definition of concepts have seemed close enough to those characteristic of learning theorists so that we felt able both to come to grips with his theory and to compare it in certain respects with learning theory.

A critical or comparative analysis of any intellectual undertaking must be carried out within a given framework, with reference to which comparisons and evaluations have meaning. Our reviews must be understood with reference to the scheme of analysis set forth in the introduction to this monograph. We have had to limit ourselves to certain theories which assume the same language system and accept the same means of confirming theoretical statements that we do. These comments will explain the complete omission of certain gestalt theories from our discussions and the selection of Lewin's work to represent the so-called field approach.

The present critique will be subject to certain strict limitations. The view will be taken that a psychological theory is one which attempts to account for the observable activities of organisms. The test of a theory is prediction. This does not mean that detailed prediction is the main goal of a theory. Probably not. In fact most laymen can provide better predictions of behavior for certain individual organisms than any available theory. Nevertheless, a body of concepts constitutes a theory only insofar as it entails statements which are confirmable by observation. In psychology these observation statements relate observable behaviors of organisms either to other aspects of behavior or to observable environmental events. It is likely that Lewin's view of the nature of psychological theory does not agree entirely with that of the present reviewer. Consequently it may seem to workers in the Lewinian tradition that the review has missed the point of some of the Lewinian theoretical developments. This may quite well be true. In any case the purpose of the following analysis is not to decide whether Lewin's theory is good or bad, regarded as a social institution, but to determine how it stands with respect to a particular set of standards.

Even from this point of view, it is entirely likely that we will not be able to do complete justice to Lewin's views. It will be necessary to extract some of his theoretical concepts from context in order to exhibit the structure of his theory in terms of our analytical outline. There seems, however, to be ample evidence in Lewin's writings that analysis of his work in our terms is not unreasonable. He has expressed views concerning the relation of theory and fact very similar to our own. For example:

The task of psychology is that of conceptually representing and deriving psychological processes. Oddly enough such derivations (or, as one might say, explanations) are not possible if one attempts to link directly with other observable facts (B_2, B_3) the behavior (B) which has to be explained. It is becoming increasingly clear that it is necessary to introduce between these groups of directly observable facts a number of concepts or "constructs" which one can call "intervening concepts" . . . or "conditional genetic concepts" . . . or, briefly, "dynamic concepts" (12, p. 11).

And again:

The sole purpose of constructs is that of deriving scientifically the observable processes which one might want to explain or predict. . . . Such a scientific derivation is possible only if (1) the conceptual properties of the dynamical facts are clearly defined (i.e., if the logical-mathematical properties of these constructs are clear), (2) an empirical process or operation is defined which permits one to determine whether or not, in a concrete case, the dynamical fact exists.

The growing interest in "operational" definitions in psychology . . . has helped to emphasize the necessity of introducing concepts (constructs) beyond the level of directly observable phenomena, and has helped emphasize the necessity of linking these constructs in a definite way to concrete manipulations (12, p. 13).

It would appear, then, that our plan of analysis in terms of observable variables, constructs, and rules of correspondence between theory and data language is not prima facie an unreasonable program given Lewin's stated views on scientific methodology.

Lewin has not developed a learning theory in the same sense as Hull or Guthrie. Like other field theorists, Lewin and his followers have not carried through any intensive or sustained investigations into problems of learning and have not formulated a set of concepts especially for the interpretation of learning phenomena. Nevertheless, Lewin and others sympathetic with his views, as Leeper (9) and Hilgard (3), have indicated frequently that Lewin's broader field theory can handle problems of learning incidentally. Since field theories are rather widely regarded as alternatives or competitors to learning theory it may be instructive to take Lewin's as the most explicitly formulated of the field theories and investigate the extent to which it has been possible to handle problems of learning within this framework.

I. METHODOLOGICAL CONSIDERATIONS

We shall discuss first Lewin's general point of view and methodological assumptions, then the more detailed structure of his topological and vector psychology, and finally applications of this system to learning phenomena.

Lewin's program represents one of the first serious attempts in psychology to interpret an existing formal system in terms of an empirical domain. This theoretical procedure has had a number of spectacular successes in other sciences, as in the application of non-Euclidean geometry to relativity physics. (For a discussion of some of the methodological problems involved, with particular reference to the theoretical enterprises of Lewin and Hull, see Koch (6).) Even in physics this kind of theoretical blitzkrieg has been successful only upon certain occasions when favorable circumstances have enabled a convergence of previously separate lines of thought. The stage has been set by extensive study and systematization of the empirical subject matter, leading to the establishment of low level empirical laws or limited theories, each well established within restricted empirical areas but not satisfactorily interrelated within any broader framework. It is under these conditions that coordination of experimentally defined concepts to terms in a deductive formal system has proved extraordinarily fruitful.

Lewin has attempted to apply a similar strategy to psychological system building by interpreting mathematical topology in terms of psychological concepts, and where topology has not proved suitable, going on to invent a new geometry, hodology, with properties which seemed to be needed for the representation of psychological situations. We shall review this enterprise in some detail in the following pages. It should be pointed out at the outset, however, that a detailed evaluation of Lewin's theory is complicated greatly by the status of the empirical domain which he took for his starting point. Unlike the situation in physics at the time of Einstein's contributions, current psychology does not offer a generally accepted preliminary systematization of its subject matter or any well established limited theories. Consequently, in order to carry out his ambitious undertaking Lewin has had to take as his empirical base a hodge podge of terms taken over from classical psychological literature and from the vernacular, and then proceed to coordinate these terms to terms in the mathematical system. In evaluating Lewin's program it is necessary to consider both the methodological problems in a vector-topological representation of psychological concepts and also the status of the psychological concepts themselves. To the extent that the latter are ambiguous or ill-defined the entire theory will be untestable. One of the chief tasks of the critic must be to ascertain the extent to which statements in the theory are confirmable by observation and experiment. In Lewin's writings we find a curious sort of contradiction on this issue. On the one hand, Lewin recognized as clearly as any theoretical writer in psychology the importance of coordinating conceptual and empirical terms and providing means for empirical confirmation of theoretical statements. Take, for example, the following very explicit statement of his position:

> The fact that we have to deal with mathematics in the empirical sciences means that the question of which mathematical concepts we have to use for the representation depends in each case upon the characteristics of the special empirical facts. We are not dealing with questions of pure mathematics. Our task is to represent certain empirical data adequately. . . . The problem of coordination is essentially an empirical problem in that its task is to demonstrate the nature of certain empirical facts, in our case facts of psychological dynamics, and to coordinate to them mathematical concepts which represent the logical structure of these empirical relationships adequately. . . . In actual research, problems of coordination and purely mathematical problems are so closely connected that it is not always easy to distinguish between them. Nevertheless, as the history of physics shows, the greatest possible accuracy in this respect is important for the progress of science (11, pp. 59-60).

On the other hand, Lewin has not given the same critical attention to the "empirical facts" which he has attempted to interpret. In one sense his work has been entirely consistent with his theoretical position. He has been scrupulous in providing coordinating definitions linking his mathematical concepts with empirical, in this case psychological, terms. But he has not proceeded to examine the psychological concepts in turn for operational meaning. This is a remarkable omission, for surely no one of Lewin's theoretical sophistication would maintain that any proposition that can be formulated in the conventional psychological vocabulary can be assumed uncritically to be confirmable by observation. He proceeds in practice, and at times writes (see the next to last sentence of the quotation above) as though psychological facts are immediately given and thus not in need of the same critical attention given mathematical concepts. It is our view that the facts themselves are constructions representing the efforts of scientific investigators to systematize their observations and continually modified with the progressive refinement of both experimental techniques and theoretical concepts.

By fact we mean the result of a particular experiment, or somewhat more generally, a relationship between observables established for some well-defined situation. We accept an observed relationship as a fact only if we believe it to be reproducible, but it may have no generality beyond the situation for which it is established. In the most primitive stages of a science, commonly accepted bits of everyday observation may be taken as facts, in later stages only the results of controlled observation and experiment. Even among facts derived from experiment perfect democracy cannot be claimed. Always some facts are more heavily weighted than others by the theorist. In psychology at the present time many investigators, including the present writers, favor the results of relatively simple experiments as the principal inductive base for learning theory. This preference is not due to any naive belief that all of the principles which may eventually be needed to account for complex behaviors can be derived from these experiments, but rather to a conviction that only in these experiments can we have confidence that the effects of different variables have been isolated. Like Lewin and his followers we feel the urgent need for a learning theory which can aid in the solution of human problems, but we can see no grounds for believing that the beginnings of an adequate theory can take root from anything but the patient analysis of experimentally isolated situations.

The coordination of mathematical with psychological concepts does not in itself provide an adequate link with reality. The psychological concepts themselves, whether arising in the pre-theoretical stage of the science or borrowed from other systems, need to be coordinated just as scrupulously with non-theoretical terms which refer directly to observable events and for which common usage can be obtained among all scientific investigators. A principal task in reviewing Lewin's theory is to determine whether the linkage can be completed between his formal concepts and empirical events.

II. PRELIMINARY CHARACTERIZATION
OF THE THEORY

In order to make the following critique intelligible let us begin by sketching briefly the main features of Lewin's system as we understand it, where possible comparing his conceptions with those of learning theory.

First, let us compare the starting points, the immediate inductive sources, of these two varieties of theory. Learning theory takes as its sole method of verification the prediction of behavior in specific situations. It has grown out of a body of fact drawn from laboratory experiments, usually with animal subjects, which provide functional relations between aspects of behavior and controlled antecedent conditions. Its low level concepts are typically rather straightforward generalizations of these observed relationships. Theoretical concepts are usually linked explicitly to the observable variables which enter into the low empirical generalizations. For example, Hull attempts to anchor the concepts *habit strength* and *excitatory potential* via explicit links to experimental operations such as reinforcement on the one hand and measures of behavior on the other; Tolman gives us operational definitions of expectancies and demands in terms of observable behavioral and environmental events; etc. In contrast Lewin begins his theorizing by noting certain very general characteristics of psychological events, or perhaps more accurately characteristic ways of describing psychological events. He points out, for example, that behavior can nearly always be described as having *direction*, toward or away from some aspect of the environment. Like other field-gestalt writers he emphasizes the fact that an organism may respond quite differently to the same physical situation upon different occasions, and describes this observation in terms of the organism's responding to the "environment as perceived" or to a "psychological environment" rather than to a "physical environment." Lewin proceeds from this point by setting up a formal system designed to handle the general characteristics of psychological activity, the terms and relations in the formal system being either borrowed from mathematics or physics or invented as needed. Then the formal concepts are given coordinating definitions in terms of psychological concepts in order to give the theory empirical content. Unlike the learning theorist he does not usually link formal concepts explicitly to directly observable characteristics of behavior or environment, but coordinates them to concepts drawn from various branches of psychology (e.g., need, perceive, etc.) or from the vocabulary used by the layman to deal with introspection and immediate experience. To take a concrete example, the important formal concept *tension* is coordinated to the psychological concept *need* but the latter is not in turn defined in terms of observable behavioral or environmental events within Lewin's system.

Whereas learning theory has been for the most part a gradual and cautious outgrowth of physics and biology, Lewin's psychological theory does not exhibit the same obvious continuity with other lines of theoretical development. Lewin has, in fact, tried to place his theory upon an entirely independent footing by defining a psychological space with a geometry especially developed for the representation of psychological events and no obvious relations to the space of physics. The conception of psychological space, or life space, is one which many readers have great difficulty in coming to grips with since it is not defined in terms of physical space and regions of the life space do not necessarily have any specific physical locus.

The life space is, first of all, the space in which Lewin's theoretical concepts may be represented. It is not necessary to be able to visualize this space, or even to feel intuitively at home with the concept in order to understand Lewin's theory. Speaking of a psychological space with a special geometry may be taken as merely another way of saying that a certain set of axioms and rules of inference is to be used in carrying out derivations within the theory. Regions in the life space are carriers of positive and negative valences; these in turn represent fields of psychological forces which influence the individual. Leeper (9) has suggested that regions in the life space should be identified with actual or potential activities of the individual, but Lewin does not seem to have accepted this limitation. It is our impression that one will not go far wrong in identifying the regions of the life space with the totality of situations in which the individual may find himself. By "situation" we mean to include both the activity of the individual and also whatever portions of the environment influence the activities. Then the behavior, or other psychological activity, involved in transforming one situation into another is coordinated with the term locomotion. Locomotion may refer either to overt behavior or to "cognitive restructuring" of the environment, that is, coming to perceive the environment differently. Forces are the determiners of locomotion. Any locomotion is coordinated with the resultant of the forces acting at the time. Presumably in applying the theory to behavioral situations we should use knowledge of the surroundings and of the history of the organism to measure the psychological forces affecting him. The forces acting upon an individual at any time depend upon (1) the cognitive structure of his environment, and (2) tensions in the individual. The first component includes the positive or negative valences which available regions of the environment have for the individual and also the psychological distance between the individual and those regions (psychological distance between regions A and B may be thought of as the number of situations or activities which would have to be traversed in proceeding from A to B); the second component is coordinated to the concept need, as we have indicated above.

In some respects Lewin's system is rather similar in structure to conventional learning theory, despite the strange terminology. In general the behavior of an individual is determined by his surroundings and by the effects of past experience. Certain concepts in the theory can be fairly closely coordinated to relevant environmental variables. In practice, although not by formal definition, positive and negative valences are identified with the conventional concepts of reward and punishment and are handled in much the same way as those terms. Effects of more remote environmental and physiological determiners are represented in the concept of tension, which has obvious similarities to the conventional concept of motivation. Past experience modifies present behavior by changing the way in which the individual structures (perceives or interprets) his environment; but here Lewin's theory diverges from learning theory in including no concept explicitly referring to the characteristic of the individual responsible for the way in which he structures the environment and in failing otherwise to summarize or conceptualize changes in modes of

structuring in relation to relevant features of past experience. The concepts of associative strength or habit strength have no clear analogue in
Lewin's theory. It is assumed, however, that experience modifies the
mode of structuring the environment, including the valences of various
regions of the life space. (We do not mean to imply that valences are
solely a matter of cognitive structure; they are held also to be functions
of tensions in the individual.) It will be seen that it is quite conceivable,
on logical grounds alone, that Lewin's theory might turn out to handle
the same facts as learning theory. In order to ascertain whether this is
the case it will be necessary to examine certain features of Lewin's theory
in more detail with a view to answering such questions as (1) how are
locomotions and cognitive restructurings linked to observable characteristics of behavior, (2) does the system include laws which will enable us
to predict how an individual will structure a given environment, (3) how
are force fields and planes of reality linked to experimental variables?
Only to the extent that these questions can be answered will it be possible
to evaluate Lewin's attempt to handle problems of learning and motivation.

III. STRUCTURE OF THE THEORY

A. *Data Language*

As we have indicated above we are inclined to emphasize the role of
what we have called the data language of any scientific discipline. This
language is regarded as literally the foundation of a theory—serving both
as a linkage between a theoretical construction and the physical world
and as a basis of communication between scientists. The terms used in a
theory must be given meaning by some form of definition, and in
general this can be done in only two ways: (1) relating the terms to be
defined to other words and (2) relating the terms directly to objects or
events by a behavioral act such as pointing. Of course, the former procedure alone will not suffice to define a scientific concept—at some point
the chain of words must be related to observations. Procedure (2), actual
ostensive definition, is ordinarily impractical for scientific purposes, and
in practice is short-circuited by the use of the data language.

In view of his many erudite discussions of methodological issues, the
lack of any explicit consideration of the data language appears as a rather
striking omission from Lewin's works. And corresponding to this apparent blind spot in his methodological writings is a crucial weakness in
the structure of Lewin's psychological system. He has neither defined nor
used a data language which, to our way of thinking, could provide an
adequate basis for definition or communication. In going through one of
Lewin's systematic treatises for definitions or elucidations of theoretical
concepts, one finds them reduced to such terms as mental event, psycho-

logical existence, consciousness, belief, expectation, perceptual field, and so on (these examples are from *Principles of Topological Psychology* (11)). But one cannot, surely, assume that uniform usage of these terms exists among psychologists of diverse theoretical viewpoints. Statements formulated in the theory cannot be reduced to statements directly confirmable by observation so long as these terms are taken as undefined.

Let us illustrate the difficulties that arise by considering a specific example. A central theoretical term in Lewin's topological psychology is cognitive structure. The definition of this "dynamic concept" given is, "structure of the life space corresponding to the knowledge of the person" (11, p. 218). This definition puts us in a position to coordinate cognitive structure (of the life space) to observables provided that we understand the term knowledge. "Knowledge" is not defined, however, either explicitly or, so far as we can determine, by usage. The latter sort of definition might be claimed if the system specified some unambiguous method of determining an individual's knowledge at a given time or some laws enabling the prediction of an individual's current knowledge from antecedent conditions; but our study of Lewin's works reveals neither. How then is the impression given that statements involving the term cognitive structure have factual content? The answer is to be found in a procedure which seems decidedly out of harmony with the formality of Lewin's conceptualizations. Throughout his works countless "concrete situations" are interpreted in terms of the theoretical concepts. These situations are drawn from literature, from various anecdotal sources, and from experiments. In all cases the theoretician writes from the standpoint of an omniscient being who is in a position to evaluate cognitive structures, valences, tensions, etc., for the individuals involved in these situations without revealing how this information could be obtained in any concrete case. Take, for example, a discussion of maze learning in rats.

A rat may have found the food for the first time in a new maze. It is brought back to the starting point. It then "knows" that it is possible to get from its place to the food, but it does not yet know the path. . . . The rat "knows" the path as soon as it is able to decide at each branching . . . which of the adjacent regions "leads to" the food and which does not. In other words the rat is able to find its way as soon as it knows the topological relationships of the regions well enough to make the correct decision at each critical point . . . (11, pp. 133-134).

The latent learning variation is handled in the same vein.

If one puts a rat into the maze without food, he gets a chance to "orient" himself, which means that what is first an unstructured field becomes structured. Insofar as this process of structurization tends to be complete, the animal will know at any point the relation to the adjacent regions and perhaps also to the more distant ones (11, p. 134).

The discussion reads plausibly enough, but there are no constraints upon the interpreter. In "explaining" or "deriving" the results of any given maze experiment one is free to assign to the subject at each stage of the experiment whatever knowledge is needed to make the results fit the theory. The status of cognitive structure in Lewin's theory is quite different from, say, habit strength in Hull's or reflex strength in Skinner's. No attempt is made in the case of cognitive structure either to link the term with behavioral phenomena or to incorporate it in laws which would make it predictable from antecedent conditions. Neither do we find that the concept cognitive structure taken together with other terms in the theory generates confirmable statements. There is no way in which the mode of application of cognitive structure can be confirmed or refuted in any concrete instance. In general, the relation between this concept (and the same holds for other dynamic concepts in Lewin's theory) and empirical situations may be characterized as follows. The results of any conceivable psychological experiment can be translated into the terms of the theory; it seems to be always possible in any situation to assign knowledge, needs, degrees of reality, etc., in such a fashion as to yield a plausible representation of the situation. But on the other hand, no predictions can be derived from the theory; this is not to say that they cannot be made, often successfully, by the theorist on the basis of his knowledge and experience. In summary, it is our conclusion that cognitive structure is a "free floating" concept in that no statement involving the term is refutable by experience. We do not mean to say, however, that the term is entirely meaningless. It is quite possible that certain uniformities in usage of this term have developed among those who have worked closely with Lewin; that possibility can have no bearing upon our criticism of Lewin's formal theory unless such uniformities can be codified and incorporated into the system.

B. Dependent and Independent Variables

We have been able to obtain from Lewin's works only a very rough characterization of the empirical domain that his system is supposed to handle. Unlike recent learning theorists he does not set the stage for his theoretical enterprise with a detailed analysis or categorization of observable variables. The term "behavior" is frequently used to denote that which is being predicted or explained by the theory. But "behavior" does not have the meaning here that is customary in American psychological writing. "Behavior" is defined by Lewin as "any change in the life space," including not only observable activities of the organism but also psychological processes such as knowing, realizing, perceiving, expecting, structuring, which are not defined in terms of observable activities.

Similarly, there seems to be no explicit statement available concerning the independent variables of Lewin's system. Behavior is considered to be a function of "person and environment," but the latter term refers, not to the physical world, but to the environment as "structured" by the organism. The set of definitions and postulates presented in Lewin's works is not reducible, so far as we can ascertain, to laws relating psychological activities to independently manipulable variables. For this reason we have not found it possible to derive rigorously any empirical predictions from the theory. In practice, Lewin and his followers circumvent this deficiency in the theory by tacitly setting certain aspects of the theory in correspondence with common experimental operations. Thus as we have noted above the experimental procedure of presenting rewards or punishments to an organism is treated, in discussing concrete situations, as the empirical counterpart of affixing positive or negative valences to regions of the life space. This informal development of coordinating definitions in use enables the theorist to give plausible accounts of concrete situations, but with no possibility of having the theory refuted by the outcome of the behavioral situation, since the correspondence between theoretical and empirical terms is adjusted in accordance with the empirical findings and is never formally incorporated into the system. Flexibility is obtained at the cost of testability.

C. Hypothetical Constructs

1. Mathematical concepts. The labelling of Lewin's system as "topological psychology" together with the extensive discussions of geometrical concepts in Lewin's works (11, 12) tend to give a somewhat misleading impression of the role of mathematics in Lewin's theory. One finds that students commonly receive the impression that mathematical disciplines are a part of Lewin's theory in a sense which is not true of other theories. This point should be clarified. It is merely a matter of convention whether the mathematical and logical apparatus used for derivation is considered as part of a given scientific theory or simply as an auxiliary device, or tool, used in operating with the theory, but for clarity one view or the other should be followed consistently. Whichever view is adopted, no essential difference will be found between the role certain geometrical concepts could be expected to play in Lewin's theory, and, say, symbolic logic in Hull's (4) or algebra in Spence's (17). In applying topology, Lewin is simply attempting to utilize a set of formal rules of inference and calculation in operating with his theory. One source of confusion for the reader of Lewin's works is the common practice of using the same word to designate corresponding mathematical and psychological concepts. Thus "region" is (1) a geometrical concept, presumably subject to the rules of topology, and (2) a portion of the life space of an individual.

A second source of confusion lies in Lewin's manner of applying topology. His application seems in brief to consist in coordinating certain concepts of topology to psychological concepts, and then utilizing topological principles as guides for the drawing of diagrams "representing" psychological situations. We cannot find that he has proceeded anywhere to utilize topology as deductive machinery for the derivation of theorems which would predict new psychological relationships. His mode of representing situations seems to have always, and we should judge necessarily in the present state of his system, the character of a post hoc reconstruction. Suppose, for example, we want to construct a "topological" representation of a situation involving an individual at an arbitrary point of an unfamiliar maze. Since we assume the maze to be unfamiliar, the individual does not know the location of the goal, $G;$ so the individual at the point C and the goal at G are represented (12, p. 59) by unconnected regions. Parts of the maze between (physically) C and G are represented by an unstructured region which is connected with neither. (We must of course assume that the individual knows that there is a goal somewhere in the maze.) Now we ask whether a blind alley, L, available to the individual at C should be represented as lying in the same psychological direction as G. The discussion in the text makes clear the point that the answer will depend upon the individual's experience in the maze. If he has not yet explored L, it must be represented as part of the cognitively unstructured region lying between C and G. Now suppose the individual enters the alley L once and finds that it does not contain the goal; should we now change the diagram to specify the psychological direction of L with respect to G? The answer is indeterminate. If the trial sufficed to change the individual's cognitive structure, then the diagram should be changed. But we can ascertain whether his cognitive structure was actually changed in a permanent fashion only by observing further trials. There is no rule which would enable us to specify the likelihood that the trial in question will change the cognitive structure. And once the situation at time t is adequately represented (diagramed) the role of topology is completed. Ordinarily in science, when one symbolizes aspects of a situation in terms of some mathematical discipline, it is with the purpose of utilizing the mathematical machinery for derivation of the outcome of the situation. This purpose is not served by Lewin's procedure, however, for one must observe the outcome of the situation before the symbolization can be completed.

We shall not proceed here to present Lewin's mathematical concepts in detail. A summary of the principal mathematical concepts used in the system has been made available by Leeper (9) and the uses and misuses of topology involved have been criticized in detail by London (15). It is our conclusion that the geometrical features of Lewin's theory amount in practice to an elaborate set of procedures for diagraming selected features of psychological situations. The possible fruitfulness of mathematical topology as a deductive tool in the development of psychological theory has not been tested by Lewin's applications.

2. **Concepts mainly concerned with observable facts (11, p. 215).**

The concepts given under this heading fall into two main categories.

a. Psychological concepts which are the counterparts of mathematical concepts—e.g., life space, psychological region, structure of a region, boundary.

b. Concepts which are apparently intended to provide a close link between the theory and the empirical domain—behavior, environment, locomotion, person, situation. Close inspection of these terms reveals the appearance of explicit empirical reference to be illusory.

Behavior is defined as "any change in the life space"; life space as "the totality of facts which determine the behavior (B) of an individual at a certain moment"; environment as "everything in which, toward which, or away from which the person can perform locomotions"; locomotion as change of position (in the life space) or change of structure (of the life space) ; person as "a differentiated region of the life space"; and so on. In no case do we find anything even roughly approximating an operational definition.

3. Dynamic concepts. The dynamic concepts are in general one step further removed from observables than those considered under 2. These concepts are not supposed to be explicitly definable in terms of data words but should be coordinated to other concepts in such a way that statements involving them can be confirmed by observation.

It will be impractical for us to review all of the dynamic concepts explicitly. Even a complete list is formidable; examples are force, tension, valence, barrier, rigidity, reality, weight, friction, elasticity, fluidity, plasticity, accessibility, communication. Many of these terms are taken over from physics by presumed analogy between physical and psychological situations and are not developed in detail in Lewin's works. Certain others—e.g., reality—carry meaning by connotation or metaphor and are used in such a flexible and literary fashion that the present writer has great difficulty in coming to grips with them. We shall select for detailed examination a small number of the dynamic concepts, those which are most used in illustrative derivations in Lewin's works and which are most familiar to the general reader—force, valence, and tension. These concepts seem to have an importance in Lewin's theory comparable to reaction potential, reinforcement, and need in Hull's or purpose, goal, and cognition in Tolman's. In order to clarify the methodological status and the functions of dynamic concepts in Lewin's system, it will be necessary to examine the definitions and the formal interrelations of these concepts and to evaluate the possibility of confirming statements of psychological fact derived from postulates in which the concepts appear.

Lewin has noted frequently (e.g., 12, p. 82) that a definition of a construct must contain "(*a*) the conceptual properties of the construct and (*b*) its coordinating definition." Let us examine the definitions of the three concepts under consideration.

Force is assigned the following conceptual properties: direction, strength, and point of application (12, p. 83). The coordinating definition is:

Definition: If the resultant of psychological forces acting on a region is greater than zero, there will be locomotion in the direction of the resultant force, or the structure of the situation will change so that the change is equivalent to such a locomotion (12, p. 85).

Valence is defined (12, p. 88) as a region in the life space of an individual which attracts or repulses this individual. If a region has a positive or negative valence, then the resultant force acting on the individual has a direction toward or away from that region respectively. A valence may thus be coordinated to a "force field" and this in turn to locomotion.

Tension refers (12, p. 98) to the state of a system (region?) of an individual which tries to change in the direction of equality to surrounding systems and always involves forces at the boundary of the system in tension. We infer that "system" is synonymous with "region" since only regions have boundaries. Tension is coordinated to the psychological concept of need,

As the *coordinating* definition of tension one can use the following statement . . . Hypothesis: Whenever a psychological need exists, a system in a state of tension exists within the individual (12, p. 99).

It is specified that the empirical facts to which the definition refers are

those acts or behaviors which are generally recognized as a syndrome indicating a need (12, p. 99).

It is added that the concept of need will have to be replaced eventually by some "more precise behavioral symptoms for tension" (12, p. 99).

These coordinating definitions contain the key to one of the enervating deficiencies of Lewin's theory. In every one of these cases, and the same is true for the other dynamic concepts, the concept is coordinated to a psychological concept which refers to some aspect of behavior, never to independently manipulable variables or independently observable events. This means that in any situation the dynamic concepts involved in an instance of behavior can be evaluated only after the behavior has occurred. For example, a locomotion will occur in the direction of a resultant of forces, but one can ascertain the magnitude and direction of a resultant of forces only by observing the locomotion.

D. Relations Among Constructs

At least two types of relations may be distinguished among the dynamic concepts: (1) logical relations—those which follow from the definitions, and (2) relations postulated by the theorist, presumably in accordance with empirical facts.

Examples of the first type are the relations between force and valence

$$f_{P,G} = F(Va(G)/e_{P,G})$$

where f is the force impelling the individual toward G; F is some function; $Va(G)$ is valence of G; $e_{P,G}$ is the psychological distance between the person, P, and the goal, G; and the relation between force and tension which is said (12, p. 222) to hold "aside from other factors."

$$t = F(f)$$

t being the tension, F some function, and f the force.

An example of the second type is the relation between valence and tension

$$Va(G) = F(t,G).$$

To illustrate Lewin's use of these concepts in a learning context, let us consider his handling of the Skinner type conditioning situation as a method for measuring strength of drive.

Topology of consumption.—With rats as subjects, Skinner (1937) investigated the following situation: Every tapping of a lever produces a small amount of food. Skinner found that the frequency with which a rat taps the lever within a time unit decreases as the animal approaches satiation.

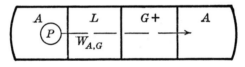

FIG. 44

The topology of the situation is given in Fig. 44. The animal starts from the region A which represents its present state of activity. It might tap the lever L and reach the food G. The amount of food is small. Therefore, after consuming G the animal will find itself in a state which is approximately the same as that before tapping the lever. In other words, it will be again in a region A.

After several days of experience the cognitive structure of the situation will have somewhat changed. . . . The animal knows that tapping the lever will produce food. Therefore, after consuming the food G^1 reached by the first tapping of the lever (L^1), the animal finds itself in A but can proceed immediately to the second tapping of the lever L^2, from there to G^2, A, L^3, G^3, and so on. (It might be appropriate to eliminate the regions A in the representation of at least a certain period of the experiment.) The driving force in this situation is probably determined by the valence $Va(G)$ of the total amount of food the animal expects ($G = G^1 + G^2 + G^3 + \ldots$). This amount is not limited. Therefore the amount G ahead of the animal can be considered as practically the same during the whole experiment. Also the distance ($e_{P,G}$) to the next food and to the rest of the food ahead can be considered as being constant. According to (21) is

$$f_{P,G} = F\left(\frac{Va(G)}{e_{P,G}}\right)$$

In our case is $e_{P,G} =$ constant. Therefore, the driving force $f_{P,G}$ can be considered to be a direct function of the valence of $G(f_{P,G} = F(Va(G)))$ which decreases during satiation.

Indeed Skinner found that the frequency of tapping the lever within a time unit decreases with the decrease in hunger (t). One can consider the frequency of tapping the lever in a time unit as the velocity $v_{A,L^n,G}n$ with which the animal passes through one group of regions A,L^n,G^n. Skinner's observation can then be expressed by the formula:

$$\text{(Ex. 24)} \quad v_{A,L^n,G}n = F(t)$$

The velocity $v_{A,L^n,G}n$ refers to the total time which the animal needed for: "tapping the lever once, consuming the food received, getting ready to tap the lever the next time." The time necessary for actually tapping the lever is probably rather short and relatively constant. Therefore the difference of velocity is probably mainly a difference in consumption and getting ready for the next tapping of the lever.

The result (Ex. 24) of the experiment can be derived from the theory that the valence of the goal G, and therefore the force in its direction, is a function of the need of the individual

$$|f_{A,G}| = F(Va(G)) = F(t,G)$$

. . . and that the speed of locomotion is a function of the resultant force in its direction

$$(|v_{A,G} = F(|f^*_{A,G}|)$$

. . . For, the restraining force $f_{L^n,-L}n$ offered by the tapping of the lever probably can be considered to be relatively constant (and not very great) as soon as the animal is familiar with it. We have already mentioned that the driving force $f_{P,G} = F(Va(G))$. Therefore, the resultant

$$f_{P,G} + f_{L}n_{,-L}n = f^*_{P,G} = F(Va(G)).$$

If one applies these formulas in our case, one assumes that the velocity of consumption $v(cons)$ can be viewed as one type of velocity of locomotion. That means that formula (33) can acquire the form

$$\text{(Ex. 25)} \quad v(cons)_{P,G} = F(|f^*_{P,G}|) = F(t)$$

in case the other factors are kept constant. Skinner's results are fully in line with these deductions (12, pp. 141-144).

It is clear that this experimental situation, typical of those which have been the primary concern of learning theorists, can indeed be verbalized in Lewin's terms. It seems entirely likely that any learning situation can be described in these terms. It should be noted, of course, that in each new case, as in the illustration just quoted, new coordinating definitions must be set up as needed (e.g., the coordination of velocity of locomotion to speed of bar pressing). It is necessary to look more closely at the "deduction" that the rate of bar pressing is a function of the drive (tension). First we note that the learning involved is accounted for by the statement that after several days of experience the animal knows that tapping the lever will produce food. This statement must have its basis in the omniscience of the theorist, for it is certainly not derivable by logical (or topological) techniques from Lewin's concepts. The animal's knowledge must be inferred from the fact that the animal does come to press the bar rapidly; whether and at what pace a given animal will acquire this knowledge is unpredictable. The remainder of the derivation depends upon the "possible assumptions" (12, p. 135) that speed of locomotion is a joint function of the resultant force impelling the individual and of the construct h which represents the totality of other factors (e.g., means of locomotion, characteristics of the path) which might influence speed.

Several conclusions can be drawn from inspection of the dynamic concepts in use. (1) Any conceivable outcome of a bar-pressing experiment could be "deduced" in the same way as the result just cited, so there is no ground for claiming that the theory is confirmed by this sort of application. (2) The "deduction" yields no statement about relations among observables; the end result of the derivation is the virtually empty assertion that velocity of locomotion is some function of tension, i.e., that two theoretical concepts are related in an unknown manner. (3) In order to carry out the derivation at all it was necessary to introduce new informal coordinating definitions and to bring in assumptions involving metrical concepts. All in all we find here no very strong testimonial to the fruitfulness of topology or hodology in mediating theoretical accounts of learning phenomena. It is possible of course that we have merely selected an unfortunate example. It is our opinion, however, that this illustration is characteristic of the Lewinian mode of accounting for learning phenomena. The interested reader is referred to Lewin's monograph (12) for further illustrative material.

E. Lewin's Treatment of Conventional Learning Concepts

In order to be sure that we have not overlooked important ways in which Lewin's system might contribute to a science of learning, we shall round out our examination of the system by considering briefly Lewin's only publication devoted explicitly to learning theory—his chapter, "Field Theory and Learning," in the 1942 NSSE yearbook (13).

The critique of the conventional learning concept which opens this chapter expresses views surprisingly similar to those of recent learning theorists. He points out that "learning" is "a term with many meanings and a disturbing history" (13, p. 219). In the vernacular and in some psychological writing "learning" is a popular term which "refers in a more or less vague way to some kind of betterment." In earlier psychological systems learning seems to have been thought of as a unitary concept, the process which together with the complementary process of fatigue explained any change in behavior. Lewin notes that in practice the term learning is used in reference to many different phenomena and that there is no adequate theoretical justification for thinking of these empirically diverse phenomena as manifestations of a single underlying process.

Sometimes, we hope, psychological theory will be so advanced that, as in modern physics, a few very general formulae will permit the derivation of most psychological phenomena. However, a science cannot reach this state without first having developed more specific laws, each representing the nature of certain types of processes (13, p. 220).

This is a remarkable statement coming from the author of the not particularly modest topological and hodological systems. Since it was written several years after the publication of those systems, one may speculate that Lewin might not have found much room for disagreement with the principal conclusions of our critique.

Within the area generally called learning, Lewin proposes a number of distinctions: (1) learning as a change in cognitive structure (acquiring knowledge); (2) learning as a change in motivation (learning to like or dislike); (3) learning as a change in group belongingness or ideology; (4) learning in the sense of developing voluntary control of the body musculature (as in acquiring speed).

The first variety can be further categorized by reference to Lewin's system. (1) Differentiation of unstructured areas. Crudely, a situation is considered unstructured for an individual if he knows nothing about it. Lewin shows how changes in cognitive structure may be diagramed by means of the illustration of an individual learning his way about in a new town. It becomes clear that the system provides a rich vocabulary for describing the state of the individual's knowledge at any point. The difficult problem for the uninitiated, as in the case of Tolman's cognitive maps, is that of ascertaining how we are to know what the individual knows. In this paper, as in his other writings, Lewin does not make a serious attempt to deal with the question of how we are to infer the individual's cognitive structure from his actions or of how changes in cognitive structure are reflected in changes in behavior. One of the principal advantages claimed for the concept of differentiation is that it is "a basic biological concept related to such fundamental and familiar notions as the subdivision of the egg into smaller units of more specific character" (13, p. 226). The reasoning seems to be that taking over a term from another discipline automatically establishes a theoretical relationship. (2) Restructurization. It is conceded that not all instances of learning can be regarded as the differentiation of regions into smaller units. Sometimes a change in cognitive structure may occur without change in degree of differentiation. This point is illustrated by means of the detour problem. Lewin poses the question: "What psychological change occurs at the moment when the child has 'insight' into the solution for the first time?"

(13, p. 227). His answer is that the cognitive structure of the situation for the child changes so that the goal has a new "psychological direction" with respect to the starting point. It will be seen that here, as in many other situations, Lewin poses and solves a quite different problem than would a learning theorist. The latter would be more apt to ask what conditions make the solution possible or impossible, hard or easy for the child, and then to depend more upon the laboratory than the drawing pen to make progress toward handling the problem.

The section on learning as change in valence and values begins with a resumé of Lewin's views concerning reward and punishment. The treatment of conflict situations involving reward and punishment seems to be an advance over traditional law of effect thinking. Lewin emphasizes the necessity of analyzing the situations to ascertain the conflicting tendencies set up in the person, the barriers necessary to keep the individual in the conflict area, the role of threats and promises. Unfortunately, as in other areas, Lewin's "topological" diagrams of typical situations give an impression that all is understood, and it may be this illusion that has deterred workers in the Lewinian tradition from conducting many of the researches that would be needed to relate conflict behavior to experimental variables. In the remainder of this section it is pointed out that valences change with experience and that the factors which determine level of aspiration are important for learning.

In summary, it may be said that the article is illustrative and critical rather than constructive. Lewin makes the points that "learning" denotes a loosely defined class of diverse behavior changes, that learning in the child involves processes referred to in everyday speech by such terms as "organization" and "meaning"; that likes and dislikes, interests and aspirations are learned as well as simpler responses or skills. His constructive effort is limited to emphasizing problems which learning theories have not mastered and pointing out the variety of psychological processes and causal conditions which must be taken into account in attempting to understand and modify human behavior. In many cases this pointing up of problems and guessing at significant causal variables strikes one as extremely shrewd and penetrating and likely to lead to fruitful extensions of learning theory. It is well to keep in mind, however, that recognizing problems is not the same as solving them. Lewin has pointed out deficiencies in existing theory, but he has not constructed a theory that does handle complex learning processes. This feature seems to be characteristic of the gestalt and field theories in general. The theorists are typically acute observers with strong orientation toward everyday life problems; they provide a running barrage of criticism which serves to keep their colleagues up to date on the inadequacies of associationism and which may upon occasion have the effect of instigating learning theorists to extend their slower moving, experimentally geared theories to new areas.

CONCLUSION

In summary, how can we evaluate claims that field theory offers a more fruitful approach to the problems of learning than the systems we have termed collectively learning theory? About the field approach in general we have little useful to say, for it has proved difficult to define satisfactorily. Most of the alleged methodological and conceptual similarities between what are called field theories in psychology and field theories in physics have proved evanescent upon close examination, and the same can be said for many of the alleged differences between field and non-field theories in psychology. One of the most generally accepted tests of a theoretical approach, its value in directing research, is hard to apply in this instance. None of the so-called field theories have been developed in conjunction with programs of experimental research upon learning. Typically the field theorists have developed their systems in other areas, then have attempted to collect the psychology of learning as an extra dividend without much additional investment. The measure of their success seems to depend upon the criterion adopted. From the writings of Köhler, Koffka, Hartmann, and Lewin one would gather that field interpretations of learning are demonstrably superior to all others. From the experimental literature on learning, on the other hand, one would conclude that if this view is correct, then the most superior theories of learning have had the least influence upon research. Since it did not seem possible to clear up this disparity at a level of broad generalities, we have attempted a case study approach. Lewin's system, the most elaborately developed of the psychological field theories, was selected for this purpose and its structure and mode of operation have been analyzed in some detail in these pages.

Lewin's theoretical enterprise has understandably been of considerable interest, even fascination to psychologists and social scientists. There seem to be two main sources for Lewin's not inconsiderable influence. First, his theorizing was carried on in conjunction with a well-known program of research upon child behavior and group behavior. Second, Lewin capitalized upon the immense prestige of relativity theory, proposing to revolutionize psychological theory by wholesale application of what he conceived to be the concepts and methods of physical field theory.

A casual or hearsay acquaintance with Lewin's principal works (10, 11, 12, 13) could easily result in an impression that the revolution has already been effected. The topological steamroller seems to have run roughshod over the whole field of psychology, either crushing or geometrizing all varieties of old-fashioned theory. If a reader is led to wonder how a theory could cover so much ground, learning, motivation, conflict, child development, social processes, in so little time, and examines the system in detail, he finds that Lewin has not operated under the restraints accepted by most other theorists. Where most learning theorists consider successful predictions of behavior to be the principal test of a good theory, Lewin's system requires only an "adequate," according to the theorist, description and symbolic representation of a situation. Lewin's rationale for this unrestrictive methodology lay in his interpretation of the field concept. He frequently criticized other psychological systems for depending upon an outmoded view of causality which led to explanations of phenomena in terms of forces or other entities lying behind the phenomena, and held that the problem of explaining a phenomenon ended when the situation in which it occurred had been fully described. In practice this view was pressed so far that Lewin and his followers threw out not only the demons but also the predictive laws. Contemporary learning theorists (e.g., Skinner, Tolman, Guthrie, Spence) differ from Lewin, not in postulating underlying entities to explain behavior but in seeking functional relationships between observable aspects of the behavior and observable antecedent conditions.

The main conclusion from our analysis of Lewin's methodology is not that field theory has been found unsuitable in the treatment of learning but rather that the issue is still open because Lewin did not construct a field theory. By carrying over into psychology some of the verbal phraseology of physical field theories without the mathematics, Lewin has given us a facsimile of a field theory which resembles the real article in much the same way that a masterpiece of taxidermy resembles a live animal. Lewin's system looks like a field theory but it does not work like one. There seems to be no room for disagreement with Lewin's contention that in a field-theoretical representation of a process the events occurring at any instant depend upon the state of the field at that instant, but it is equally pertinent to emphasize that the same mathematical formalism that characterizes the field also prescribes how the field changes with changes in independent variables, and thus permits predictions and experimental tests of the theory. The fact that predictions from physical field theories have frequently been confirmed by observation may not be unrelated to the fact that the field theories did not appear on the scene in any area of physics until after considerable bodies of well-validated descriptive theory had become available. It may be necessary to wait patiently for the same chronology to run its course in the behavioral sciences.

Even though Lewin may not have succeeded in revolutionizing learning theory, he has contributed criticisms and discussions of method that will probably influence its course of development. By injunction and example Lewin emphasized that elaborating the properties and interrelationships of theoretical concepts is as important for scientific progress as providing operational definitions. At the same time, although possibly not by intention, Lewin illustrated the point that however well a theory has been garnished with the latest methodological devices, it will not be incorporated into the body of a science if its concepts are not securely linked to a body of observational data.

Upon concluding our review of Lewin's system in relation to learning theory it may not be out of place to ask what we have accomplished by it. Literary critiques of theories probably have little to do with the progress of a science. The experimenter rather than the critic is the final arbiter of the value of a theoretical contribution. In the case of Lewin's system in relation to learning, the verdict of the laboratory seems fairly clear. Lewin's theory has not been taken up by investigators of learning, and new theories now under development are quite different in character from Lewin's. Is there, then, any value in a formal review of the theory?

It would seem that the most important excuse for a formal critique is that it may contribute something toward the development of more adequate standards for appraising theoretical work. As the concepts used in our theories improve, so should the concepts we use in talking about the theories, the point being not to judge dead theories more accurately but to exhibit better craftsmanship in constructing new ones. In the Dartmouth conference we tried to bring together and organize somewhat the principles, concepts, and categories currently utilized in reviewing and criticizing theoretical works. The outcome of these efforts, as exhibited in the present report, may serve to shed light upon the adequacy of contemporary critical standards as well as upon the more morphological aspects of contemporary theories.

Bibliography

1. BARKER, R. G., DEMBO, T., and LEWIN, K. Frustration and regression: a study of young children. *Univ. Ia. Stud. Child Welfare,* 1941, 18, No. 1.
2. HARTMANN, G. W. The field theory of learning and its educational consequences. *Yearb. Nat. Soc. Educ.,* 1942, 41, Part II, 165-214.
3. HILGARD, E. R. *Theories of learning.* New York: Appleton-Century-Crofts, 1948.
4. HULL, C. L., HOVLAND, C. I., ROSS, R. T., HALL, M., PERKINS, D. T., and FITCH, F. B. *Mathematico-deductive theory of rote learning.* New Haven: Yale Univ. Press, 1940.
5. HULL, C. L. *Principles of behavior.* New York: Appleton-Century-Crofts, 1943.
6. KOCH, S. The logical character of the motivation construct. *Psychol. Rev.,* 1941, 48, 127-154.
7. KOFFKA, K. Principles of gestalt psychology. New York: Harcourt, Brace, 1935.
8. KÖHLER, W. *Gestalt psychology.* New York: Liveright, 1929.
9. LEEPER, R. *Lewin's topological and vector psychology, a digest and a critique.* Eugene, Oregon: Univ. Oregon Press, 1943.
10. LEWIN, K. *A dynamic theory of personality.* New York: McGraw-Hill, 1935.
11. ———. *Principles of topological psychology.* New York: McGraw-Hill, 1936

12. LEWIN, K. The conceptual representation and measurement of psychological forces. *Contrib. to Psychol. Theory,* I, No. 4, 1938.
13. ———. Field theory and learning. *Yearb. Nat. Soc. Stud. Educ.,* 1942, 41, Part II, 215-242.
14. ———. Defining the "field at a given time." *Psychol. Rev.,* 1943, 50, 288-290.
15. LONDON, I. D. Psychologists' misuse of the auxiliary concepts of physics and mathematics. *Psychol. Rev.,* 1944, 51, 266-291.
16. SKINNER, B. F. *The behavior of organisms.* New York: Appleton-Century-Crofts, 1938.
17. SPENCE, K. W. The nature of discrimination learning in animals. *Psychol. Rev.,* 1936, 43, 427-449.
18. TOLMAN, E. C. *Purposive behavior in animals and men.* New York: Appleton-Century, 1932.

SECTION 5

Edwin R. Guthrie

-》》》-》》》-》》》-》》》《《《-《《《-《《《-《《《-

CONRAD G. MUELLER, JR.,

and WILLIAM N. SCHOENFELD

INTRODUCTION

GUTHRIE is customarily included among the *S-R* learning theorists, and is frequently distinguished from other men in this category by reference to his adherence to a form of the "contiguity principle." The following account will show the reasons for both these characterizations. Nevertheless, it may be said of Guthrie that he has not really formulated a theory of learning; rather he has put forward two or three statements that serve as principles around which he builds his discussion of learning problems. These statements are the recurrent themes of his theoretical papers, but they have not been systematically developed by him in any detail.

Guthrie's work cannot, therefore, be analyzed fruitfully under the rubrics feasible in the case of other men treated in this volume. The broad outline followed here may be given in advance in order to clarify the course of the discussion:

I. Guthrie's orientative attitudes toward science in general, and toward psychology in particular.
II. The data language from which his theory starts, namely, the dependent and independent variables featured in his treatment of learning.
III. The theory's construct system, and some applications of the theory.
IV. An evaluation of Guthrie's contributions to the area of learning theory.

345

I. ORIENTATIVE ATTITUDES [1]

A. Orientation Toward Science and Psychology

1. Science is based upon information that is "public" in the sense of being accessible to, or acceptable by, all observers. In this sense, science is "founded on an interest in fact" (22, p. 2) and seeks to order or arrange facts. These "facts" are not equivalent to "nature" but rather to descriptions of nature acceptable by any observer; they are certain statements about events or objects that all can agree on—they are the "basis of human cooperation" (22, p. 1) in science. "There are . . . no absolute facts, and a universe without men and human discourse would be a universe without facts" (22, p. 1). Facts are addressed to an audience, and get their existence from the acceptance of hearers. Thus, the facts that men accept will determine their scientific theories, and, reciprocally, the theories of men may determine what observations they will make and accept as facts.

2. "Science cannot deal with unique events. Only in recurring events can we discriminate between mere antecedents and necessary and sufficient antecedents" (10, p. 194). A scientific "explanation of any event consists in stating the rule or generalization of which the event is an instance" (10, p. 12). Scientific psychology must go beyond the common sense explanations which often rely on "the act of an agent" (10, p. 13) as the causative factor, since "knowing that an event is an act of an agent does not give the rule of the act unless we know the ways of the particular agent" (10, p. 13).

Scientific explanations all have much the same form. They state the rule of which the event in question is an instance. A state of affairs which we may call "A" (for "antecedent") is followed in a certain proportion (say x per cent) of the cases observed by another state of affairs "C" (for "consequent"). If the law has to do with the degree or quantity of some state instead of merely with its presence or absence it would read: State "C" is a certain mathematical function of state "A," or $C = \phi(A)$, with an observed error of estimate, "z."

In such a law both the antecedent and the consequent may be anything whatever, provided that it is observable, describable, and recognizable. The consequent, "C," will be something which we are interested in anticipating or predicting; the antecedent, "A," will be anything that can conveniently serve as a warning of "C." The rule itself, if it is to qualify as scientific, must be the result of observation of cases of "A" and of "C" and it should be verified by further observation after it has been formulated (10, pp. 13-14).

---

[1] In the text, quotation marks will be used in two ways: (1) for direct quotations from Guthrie's writings in which case reference citations will be given, and (2) for single words or short phrases which are used with a Guthrian connotation. Particularly in the section on orientation attitudes, however, we have often found it necessary to paraphrase Guthrie and we hope it is clear where Guthrie is speaking and where we are commenting.

3. Science, in its attempt to arrive at explanations, relies upon analysis. In psychology, the "flow of behavior" is always "confused and intricate," (10, p. 9) and "infinitely complicated" (18, p. 22). "We cannot record or control all the conditions under which our experiments are made, or record all the details of any sample of behavior" (10, p. 10). Thus, Guthrie regards as trivial, albeit indisputable, the Gestalt assertion that "behavior is always a response to a total situation" (10, p. 19), since any attempt to predict from, or form a scientific rule to cover, a "total situation" is hopeless. This hopelessness arises partly from (a) the fact that total situations (including an organism's previous state and responses) are never repeated and cannot be reconstructed, hence are unique; and (b) the fact that total situations are not recordable in their entirety. What we must do, is to "select certain outstanding and conspicuous parts of the total stimulus situation and keep some record of their consequences" (10, p. 29). Similarly, on the response side, "total behavior" is not recordable and is always unique, hence it is not useful in arriving at a scientific generalization leading to prediction. We must select a segment of the continuing flow of behavior which will be a practical and useful C term in the explanation formula $C = f(A)$. Thus, a conditioned response may "never be the exact duplicate of the original behavior; but it will on many occasions be enough like the original behavior to make its prediction important" (10, p. 31). So long as we stick to "facts" in the sense of acceptable statements about events, our analysis leads to scientific laws in stimulus and response terms.

4. For Guthrie, theory is of central importance to any science. He holds that

. . . theories are the basis of working concepts. They enable men to confront new facts and deal with them successfully. Furthermore, theories are required to direct the search for relevant facts. It is theories that endure, not facts. Events are ephemeral and their descriptions also may be ephemeral. It is theory that lasts for years or for generations. It is theory rather than fact that leads to new controls over nature and events. From theory inferences can be made and new applications devised. Facts are likely to be local and temporary. Their applications are limited (22, pp. 3-4).

Furthermore,

. . . (to make progress in developing psychology as a science) . . . two things are necessary. One is that theory be continuously produced and continuously amended and continuously used to guide the collection of fact. The other is that we remember to conform to the rules that have been responsible for the remarkable achievement of the scientific tradition, the use of objective evidence which means a basis in facts open to the observation of all who are interested and described in public terms that must be accepted by other scientists. These requirements may bear heavily on many current movements in psychology, in which recognition of events is claimed to be an art not communicable by ordinary means, open only to the inner members of a cult and closed to outsiders. Facts may accumulate without theory; but they will prove to be unstable and of little profit in the end. Theories may flourish if their basis lies not in scientific fact but in opinions and interpretations acceptable only to the members of a limited faction; but they will be bad theories. Schools flourish only when theories are not carried back to public facts. Unless psychologists maintain an interest in general theory the fields of psychology will increasingly become independent collections of undigested information (22, pp. 19-20).

Guthrie acknowledges, however, that some facts can be useful without being ordered into a theory. Such would be various types of chemotherapy in medicine, or metallurgy in the hands of a blacksmith. In these cases, the absence of theory eliminates the chance for generalized knowledge, hence for extension and extrapolation to other, and perhaps novel, uses.

5. The aims of science are prediction and control. Thus:

Scientific explanations have placed upon them at the start a severe restriction. They are directed at the prediction and control of natural events. . . . (10, pp. 12-13).

The laws of learning are attempts to explain certain features of human and animal behavior. Like all other scientific laws, they make possible the anticipation of natural events from other events which serve as their signs or warnings. And, as with other scientific laws, their validity is measured by their success in prediction in instances other than those on which the generalization is based. An event is explained when it is shown to be an instance of such a law or generalization (6, p. 125).

6. From the foregoing sections, which are applicable to science in general, including psychology, we may extract, and perhaps add, a few of Guthrie's thoughts regarding psychology in particular.

a. There are certain things to be avoided in formulating psychological laws or constructing psychological theories:

(1) The laws are to be based on *observables*. This rules out physiological or neurological constructs, subjective determiners, etc. Thus, "The laws of science describe the *observable* conditions under which certain classes of events take place" (10, p. 187). "A great deal has been made of (the) theory of the brain as a dynamic electrical field in which any change in detail alters the whole pattern. The theory is quite safe, of course, from experimental verification or disproof by any technique so far developed and as an attempt to state the circumstances under which action or learning occurs it is quite useless because it calls on unobservable determiners" (10, p. 195). Similarly, Thorndike's assumption concerning the synaptic basis of *S-R* bonds "is a highly speculative and quite unnecessary assumption" (10, p. 152). The same point is raised concerning Dunlap's contention that the determining conditions of learning are "thoughts, desires and ideals" (10, p. 143). Guthrie comments that these are accessible only through the media of speech, gesture and other physical actions.

For Guthrie, only the observable conditions under which learning occurs are of any use for a theory or for an understanding of learning, and when these are described, the theory is already complete. His views of learning are independent of any special theories of the physiology of the nervous system.

(2) The primary interest of psychology cannot be in the utility or outcome of behavior, that is, not in teleological laws. This, he feels, is the error committed by the psychologists who deal with law-of-effect or reinforcement learning. "We must know *how learning occurs* as well as know *what it accomplishes*" (10, p. 240). More will be said below on Guthrie's attitude toward law-of-effect learning. We may note that he believes the description of learning in terms of outcomes may be important in a practical way at some times; and that he also believes that behavior as referred to effects can be predicted with some "crude" certainty.

Guthrie clearly feels that law-of-effect principles of learning should be derivable from primitive statements of conditioned *doings*—after all, he argues, an animal is wired nerve-to-muscle, not nerve-to-effect; moreover, prediction is better on the basis of *doings* (i.e., what the animal has last done) than on the basis of teleological principles like self-preservation. After all, an animal may also learn to do self-harming things. Not that effect principles are wrong; Guthrie believes they cannot and do not contradict empirically more basic laws, but they lead to different laws, ones which may not be as fundamental or useful for the "prediction and control" of behavior.

b. While science aims at the "prediction and control" of behavior, the nature of psychology's subject matter imposes limits upon the achievement of both these aims. Thus, the reproducibility of a previous situation is never perfect; hence we cannot control the response *exactly* (in the sense of getting the exact response we want) and we cannot predict the exact response that will be made. This lack of reproducibility arises from at least two considerations: (*a*) following a response, the organism can never return to exactly the same position with respect to the physical environment; and (*b*) the previous situation includes the response made in it, and every new response inevitably alters the situation by adding its own stimuli so that the prior situation can never be completely recaptured. Thus: "The psychologist must resign himself to the fact that no psychological event is ever really repeated. The second repetition of a stimulus is only roughly and for practical purposes equivalent to the first; his laboratory subject is only substantially or approximately the same person who sat in the chair the day before. Since that time he has slept, eaten a little, learned a little, and this will alter his response no matter what precautions have been taken to have conditions the same. No two responses are alike. Two trips through a maze, two conditioned salivary reflexes may be substantially the same, but they are always the same with a difference. As a result of this indescribable complexity of events we are limited to prediction with a high degree of error. We can attach only probabilities to expected events and the probabilities may be very slight. Our comfort lies in the fact that even slight probabilities in the expectation of human conduct may be better than complete ignorance" (10, pp. 10-11).

Predictability is, therefore, a matter of probability. The error of estimate in our psychological laws, $C = f(A)$, arises because, first, we can never know everything about (A), and, second, the very response itself changes (A) so that it is *a forteriori* unique and non-recurring. Thus, predictability, and the possibility of control, will forever be less than perfect, both for individuals and for groups.

7. Specifically with respect to learning, Guthrie feels that this is a central topic of psychology, since so much of what we want to know involves shifts, changes, and recombination of the behavior of organisms. It is not all of psychology, certainly, but by taste and conviction, Guthrie holds it to be one of the fundamental fields of psychological inquiry. He writes: "I have already expressed the opinion that learning and motivation represent the two fields most fundamental to an understanding of behavior and thought" (22, p. 9).

Guthrie does not attempt a single-statement definition of the term "learning." He does, however, try to indicate what behavioral phenomena he is interested in accounting for, and these he takes as defining the scope of learning. Learning consists in behavioral change, in modifications of behavior following behavior, in responding differently to a situation because of past responses to that situation.

Yet, "Learning, as so defined, does not include all changes in behavior tendencies" (10, p. 4). Thus, fatigue and sense organ adaptation are not to be included as learning, since they are "transient changes . . . (that) . . . disappear after brief intervals through physiological processes" (10, p. 4). Guthrie prefers a definition of learning based on the lasting effects of practice, since he believes these effects are permanent except as they are altered by new learning. In the end, the problem becomes one of deciding *what* changes resulting from *what* situations we *want* to account for. In his words:

Learning will be understood as change rather than as improvement. Our task is to understand the circumstances under which learning takes place and the nature of the changes that it involves. Our method should be to survey the experimental work on learning and to review what is common knowledge of learning and to try to discover any generalizations that can be made from our survey. Can we find any rule or uniformity in the phenomena? Can we describe any circumstances which regularly have a certain kind of outcome? Does the animal which has had one kind of history afterward tend to do certain things? *Under what circumstances do the specific changes in behavior we call learning take place?* (10, p. 6).

What Guthrie's reader emerges with is a sort of denotative definition of the theorist's interest.

B. *Some Comments on Guthrie's Orientative Attitudes*

Before proceeding to a discussion of the data language in Guthrie's system, let us return to several points raised in the preceding discussion. These points, while not chosen at random here, still represent only a selection and do not exhaust the possible starting points for methodological argument.

For example, we have seen that Guthrie believes scientific explanation of any event to consist of "stating the rule or generalization of which the event is an instance." It is these rules or generalizations that constitute scientific laws. Thus, laws are inductive, rather than deductive, generalizations. Moreover, "the laws of science describe the *observable* conditions under which certain classes of events take place." From this reasoning, it is not clear what Guthrie's intention is when he characterizes his own central principle of conditioning (that of association by contiguity in time: "stimuli acting at the time of a response tend on their recurrence to evoke that response"; 8, p. 199) as a "scientific law." His principle of association could be considered a descriptive generalization only if we invoke the broadest possible meaning of "tend" (see footnote, page 363), in which case stimulus and response might be regarded as data words. A later discussion, however, will attempt to show that it is truer to Guthrie's view to consider this "principle" as a postulate involving stimulus and response as construct words.

Second, Guthrie also regards theory as a mnemonic device on which facts may be strung for easier remembering or for easier teaching to other people. By this criterion, there would be no reason why the theorist could not tailor his theory to his audience, in order to suit its mnemonic value to their memory span. That this is not, indeed, wholly foreign to his intention is indicated in this passage:

Professional explainers regularly forget that there are two parties involved in an explanation, the one who offers the explanation and the one at whom it is directed. An explanation that does not make clear the event to the person seeking information is no explanation at all. It is not the explainer who must be satisfied but the listener (10, p. 12).

And again in this passage:

Explanations are, after all, statements addressed to persons and it is quite possible that an explanation that does not explain to the person to whom it is addressed is no explanation at all, and the hearer is quite within his rights in refusing to accept it. It is also quite conceivable that there may be more than one good explanation of the same event. Different hearers may have different requirements, and the same hearer may have at different times different uses for an explanation. No listeners can rid themselves of their cultural backgrounds or the limitations of their linguistic repertoires. Absolute and final explanations could only be addressed to celestial and timeless beings (6, pp. 124-125).

From such passages it is not clear what has become of the idea Guthrie expresses elsewhere that an explanation is a general inductive rule about facts accessible to all persons. Furthermore, we are not given the secret of how Guthrie might change his present theory of learning if his audience of fellow-theorists were of a different caliber from whatever he assumes it to be today. We may agree with Guthrie that the technical level of exposition should, for purposes of communication, conform to one's audience, but this is not to say that the substantive aspect of the theory can be permitted to change so as to yield an "explanation" for different hearers. Expositions may differ depending upon the audience, but must be inter-relatable if they are to be considered expositions of some common theory.

As a third example, the quotation and discussion of section 6(b) raise the question for Guthrie's readers of whether psychology is in a singular position with respect to the problem of the repeatability of events, or whether this is a problem for all sciences. If the quotation is intended as a general commentary on the problems of measurement in science, then psychology is not different from other sciences on this score. But if Guthrie considers psychology to be alone in this impasse of non-repeatability, then it is not clear from his writings what the characteristic of behavioral data is that marks them off from data in other sciences. If experimental and theoretical tools were actually available to establish that the organism or situation is not the same from trial to trial, then *pari passu* one could study this variability and the factors of which it is a function. As matters stand, however, Guthrie seems to regard this variability as synonymous with a form of chaos, or unlawfulness in nature; he does not hint that variability may have a lawfulness of its own as a dependent variable, open to the same scientific analysis as any other phenomenon. He simply offers this variability (experimental situations are never the same, and responses are never alike) as the preventer of perfect prediction and control.

Fourthly, in arguing for the measurement of behavior by movements rather than by effects on the environment (or "acts" defined in terms of the environment, such as pressing a bar, or taking a right turn in a T maze), Guthrie has frequently asserted that prediction is better in the case of movements than in the case of "effects." But if this is meant as an empirical statement, no references to data are given. Data such as presented in *Cats in a Puzzle Box* (27) are certainly not relevant to this point, since it was a response defined in terms of "effects" that was used to trigger the camera (see discussion, pages 357-358).

Lastly, let us consider Guthrie's attitude toward physiological constructs or constructs couched in physiological terms. It is undoubtedly true that behavioral theory can be developed without going outside the realm of behavioral data and constructs, and a clear rationale for this choice is readily statable. Guthrie, however, deplores physiologizing (e.g., Thorndike's synaptic nature of learning, Pavlov's cortical mechanisms, Gestalt theory's brain fields), mainly on the ground that the assumed physiological changes are not "visible." Thus, he argues that if one were to open a person's head, one would not be able to tell whether the individual had previously learned to play the piano. Accordingly, he regards assumed "cerebral hangovers" (10, p. 152) as being unobservable and untestable notions, and condemns any attention by learning theorists to them. Even if one were inclined to regard this criticism as being metaphorically worded (i.e., that Guthrie does not intend "visible" to mean visible to the naked eye), the fact remains that he holds physiological theorizing to be immune to proof or disproof because of this lack of visibility. The argument, however, fails to distinguish "visibility" (in some sense) and testability. In the context of such an argument, Guthrie is more likely to offer one figure of speech for another (for example, that learning may be likened to "setting a switch" rather than to "wearing a path" 5, p. 419) than he is to attack the logical problems involved.

II. THE DATA LANGUAGE

In examining Guthrie's data language—that is, the pre-theoretical descriptive and empirical terms in which are couched the observations that his theory undertakes to order—it will prove convenient to use categories linked to our customary ways of sorting out, or collecting, observations and data. These are the categories *dependent* and *independent variables*.

A. Dependent Variables

1. In Guthrie's language, "movement" is regarded as the primary datum of behavioral science, although in his own experimentation he has also used bodily positions and verbal responses as data. Movements are understood to be coordinated, in a general sense, with contractions of muscles, both smooth and striate, and both large and small. Included among responses are not only movements attended by visible displacement of the organism or its parts in space, but also glandular secretions, muscle tonus, simultaneous contraction of antagonistic muscles, and so on. Guthrie distinguishes repeatedly between movements and "acts," the latter being movements or classes of movements defined in terms of their effects or outcomes (e.g., catching a fish, sorting cards, getting to the goal box of a maze, pressing a lever). Thus:

The boy sharpens his pencil, writes in his book, walks to the door, signals a companion. These are acts, not movements. Writing can be done in many ways, with either a hand or a foot, and still be called writing. We speak of writing on the typewriter, which is done by very different movements from those demanded by a pen. Common sense does this because we are usually concerned more with the results of a movement than with its style or detail (18, p. 22).

For Guthrie, such descriptions in terms of effects are teleological; they attempt to "connect accomplishment and situation by psychological laws" (18, p. 22), and this "without regard to the means by which the effects are brought about" (10, p. 244). Attempts to predict behavior on this basis are bound to be, in his opinion, "inaccurate" and "extremely tentative" (18, p. 22). They have two limitations: "They remain extremely tentative because they predict success; and failure is both unfortunately common and important. Secondly, they fail to attempt to predict the movements by which results are accomplished . . ." (18, pp. 22-23). Some degree of prediction for "acts" is possible only because we have some common-sense grasp of the capacities and abilities of the species.

In place of such objectionable descriptions, Guthrie feels that we must recognize that:

. . . the boy's nerves connect his sense organs with his muscles, not with his notebook, the door, or his companion. The psychology of learning must therefore first apply to movements and not to accomplishments (18, p. 22).

Punishment and reward are, objectively viewed, stimuli acting on the animal's sense organs, and their effect must be mediated through the animal's nervous system and appear in muscular contraction or glandular secretion. Since levers and loops and mazes are not innervated, the operation of these devices are incidental to the actual learning which the living animal performs (22, p. 7).

But to use practical achievement, goal attainment, success, as the essential criterion of learning, and to turn our search for facts to the observation of success and the conditions under which it is attained is analogous to the use of money value by the chemist as his chief descriptive term in observing a chemical reaction, or the definition by the physicist of work in terms of useful work or valuable work. All the psychologies which are written in terms of "least effort" or of goal achievement are by that choice rejecting the possibility of developing an objective and scientific psychology (22, p. 5).

Consequently, Guthrie feels that we should look for the "facts" of psychology in the behavior of the organism rather than in the operation of the organism on its environment. He writes:

My first suggestion concerning the factual basis for learning theory was that we give more attention to the organism itself, and that we recognize that such classes of fact as improvement, success and failure, reward and punishment, are external and incidental features of learning. The mechanism of learning is within the organism. These external features should be examined only in their role as stimuli to sense organs (22, p. 9).

If we follow this lead, Guthrie feels, we would not neglect, as do effect-learning laws, "the most obvious source of information about the behavior of persons, their past histories" (10, p. 244). Only if we do these things—only if we study behavior *qua* behavior (read "movement"), and changes in behavior, and the circumstances leading to changes in behavior—will our understanding of (and prediction and control of) behavior get beyond the tentative and inaccurate stage. In short, Guthrie does not believe that "acts" constitute a proper data language from which learning theory can take off. Rather, it is the movements that have been learned, while acts are regarded as something to be derived or explained in terms of the movements composing them.

2. Guthrie's espousal of the movement as the dependent datum leads one to inquire how it is (a) defined, and (b) actually observed and recorded experimentally. Some comment may be appropriate at this point, even if we momentarily digress from the topic of data language and anticipate somewhat the next section on Guthrie's construct system. We will return to the matter later, but the digression may be helpful in exemplifying the problems faced by an analyst of Guthrie's system, and in indicating how close to the data level lies the first of those problems.

Responses or movements are viewed as effector activities; thus: "Responses, the answers to stimuli, are limited to the contraction of muscles or the secretion of glands" (18, p. 20). But this broad generic definition is not sufficient for any specific experimental case, since there we need to define the response or movement that is being observed, that is, the segment selected out of the flow of behavior for recording and study. To say that a response is conditioned to the stimuli present at its occurrence (Guthrie's principle of association by contiguity, which will be treated below), requires elaboration beyond the point of saying that the response is muscular activity. Rules must be set up for identifying the movement conditioned so that, for one thing, successive occurrences of the response may be duly noted. In this connection, there arises a fundamental question: How much must a later response resemble the chosen response before we will call it another instance of the same response? That is, how and where do we set the limits of the response segment we are studying? If we insist on identity, Guthrie has clearly indicated that he would not expect to observe response repetition; and, if this is so, are we not forced back to some conception of the class character of a "response"? (Cf. Skinner on the generic nature of the stimulus and response, 36; 37.) Accordingly, in each experimental situation the researcher must define the criteria he will accept for granting class membership to a response.

In the Guthrie-Horton cat studies, where photographic recording was used, responses (actually, positions) were classified on the basis of recognizability. The two experimenters took as instances of the "same response" those upon which they could agree by inspection of the pictures. They write that often they did not agree, or did so with great difficulty on many occasions. Thus:

Horton and I had a very considerable amount of fact-trouble in making our observations of our cats. Though we made notes and in a number of cases a motion picture record, there was often doubt whether or not a sequence of movements of the cat in the box could be reported as substantially the same as a previous sequence. The statement just made that the major determiner of the animal's actions is the present state of action or rest is an interpretation rather than a fact. It is an interpretation to which we found ourselves compelled; but it is not an interpretation to which we could be sure other psychologists would be forced. A large part of the time we could tell at any moment what this particular cat would do next. Our ability to do so was based on having seen it execute the same routine in a previous trial or earlier in the current trial. Having started any former routine, we could predict its continuance. . . . (22, p. 14).

Certain questions arise concerning the "recognizability" that figures so prominently in the Guthrie-Horton work. Whether by individual human observers or by agreement among observers, recognizability is a statistical matter. We are dealing here with the problem of the observer's responses which are initiated by stimuli arising from the behavior of the organism under observation. Leaving aside the regress that, were we able to account for the observer's behavior, we could also account for the organism's, we must at least accept the fact that this introduction of a recognizability criterion confronts us now with a *new* datum, namely the observer's behavior rather than the cat's. The criterion of recognizability means that we are employing human observers as the recording instruments in our experiment. But we do not know to what extent the action of these instruments is a function (nor what *sort* of function) of the phenomenon we are studying (or, more exactly in the Guthrie-Horton case, of the visual stimuli arising from the cats or their pictures). Recording instruments in the form of human observers may act in response to many variables which arise from their own past histories, their present thresholds, or their momentary state as determined by many factors. In the present instance, we do not have either adequate data or adequate theory regarding these instruments in the situation where Guthrie and Horton are now using them. The adequacy of recording devices in any given instance is a general question involving not only fineness of measurement, but adequate understanding of the theory and use of the recording device. Recourse is often had to machine recording in experimental work, but for our present argument it is important to keep in mind just what is achieved by this. Admittedly, the makers or users of machine recorders must "punch into" the machine the arbitrary standards which it will follow in tallying or recording events, and in this sense the machine, too, must "recognize" instances of the "same" response. We may also grant that the use of machines to make "impartial" judgments does not in itself guarantee either increased reliability or increased usefulness of the data it records. But these are not the crucial things. What one means to achieve in using machines is at least a better knowledge of *what* is being recognized and recorded, what the error of observation is, and so on. In short, to deal with the data adequately, one needs to know what the data *are;* and what they are depends partly on what gathers them, as Guthrie himself would admit in other contexts. The point being made is not the humanness or non-humanness of the recording device, but our understanding or ignorance of the recording device. With the recognizability criterion employed by Guthrie and Horton in their cat studies, this problem is an acute one, as Guthrie frankly states. The situation is somewhat better in other psychophysical situations which also involve human observers, but in which some degree of empirical and theoretical knowledge is available on stimulus-response relations.

From the point of view of Guthrie's theory, as opposed to his experimentation, the foregoing argument may seem a minor point. But it emphasizes a failure to meet the problem of the definition of the dependent variable in Guthrie's data language. The theory leads to statements that the organism will do now what he did the last time in this situation, but it gives us no rule by which we measure the "movements" on either occasion. Since Guthrie restricts us little on the side of the dependent variable it is difficult to define the response for measurement purposes without introducing our own restrictions.

Continuing our digression for a moment, we may consider another aspect of the results presented in the Guthrie-Horton work, *Cats in a Puzzle Box*. These studies represent Guthrie's most recent, and perhaps most extensive, experimental work and purport to attack the problem of "movement" versus "effect" specification of the response. As indicated earlier, the thesis is repeatedly presented that the best way to tell what an animal is going to do is to see what he did the last time. The basic question involved is that of defining the "doing." Guthrie rejects any "effect" definition of the response as "deflecting the rod." He holds that if the bar deflection leads to a change in stimuli such as would result if the animal is permitted to escape from the cage, then the particular set of movements of the animal, by virtue of which the stimuli were changed (via bar deflection), would be repeated on succeeding visits to the cage. If we now go to the Guthrie and Horton pictures to shed light on these two sets of attitudes we find the following: (1) on every trial a picture was taken of the animal as the rod was deflected; (2) although every picture taken was associated with a response defined in terms of the "effect" of rod deflection, fewer than all were associated with a particular movement (or, more exactly, posture), how much less than all being dependent upon the observers' criteria of what they would call the "same" posture. But regardless of our criterion of "sameness," we could never have more than 100 per cent of the stances classified as the same. Thus, by defining the response in terms of position or stance, we can do no more than match the replicability of response defined in terms of effect. Once the results are viewed in this way it becomes obvious that Guthrie and Horton have taken a restricted set of pictures. They photographed the set of all positions assumed by their cats at the moment of rod deflection, that is, the set of responses defined in terms of stance that are included in the set of responses defined in terms of a particular effect. This feature of the Guthrie-Horton experiment merely makes it possible (for someone who thinks there is any logical need to do so) to argue that to the extent that the pictures exhibit stereotyping, to that extent they show that responses defined in terms of effect may also be homogeneous with respect to position or stance.

The effect of this restriction in picture taking could be seen more clearly in an experiment that required the animal to stand on his hind legs and reach out of the upper corner of a cage in order to press a button to release the door and take the picture. In this way we further restrict the set of possible responses and achieve added stereotypy. On the other hand, other experimental situations could be constructed, which would reduce stereotypy. In either case, however, what is procured are data concerning responses defined in terms of effect. If the present argument can be generalized, then it is not obvious that the recording of a movement can be logically distinguished from an "effect" specification. If this be true then the issue of movement versus effect raised by Guthrie may be considered an ephemeral one.

B. Independent Variables

The difficulties encountered in Guthrie's treatment of the response, or dependent variable, are paralleled by difficulties with one of his major independent variables, namely the stimulus. We shall, however, reserve our discussion of this for the section on Guthrie's construct system, rather than anticipate it here as we have done with the above analysis of his response variable. In presenting the remainder of Guthrie's data language under the heading of independent variables, we shall simply exhibit the terms which fall wholly or in part into the category of data terms for him.

1. For Guthrie, movements or responses are contingent on stimuli, and one of the ways in which he uses the word stimulus suggests that it is a term in his data language. Thus: "movement, light, sound, pressure, skin contact, the contact of various substances with the olfactory membrane and with the taste papillae, these are what we mean by stimuli" (10, p. 29). In this connection, Guthrie elsewhere develops the argument that these stimuli must be defined in terms of some outstanding detail of the continuously changing environment. Such outstanding segments of the "total situation" must be selected for recording and for use in controlling and predicting behavior. Stimuli, so conceived, must be "observable, describable, and recognizable." Terms such as movement, light, and so on, presumably are to be defined in the language of physics.

As we search Guthrie's writings for further specification of the stimulus term, we find that other properties are given. One added property of stimuli is that the sense organ must respond to the energy change. Thus: ". . . the normal occasion for muscular contraction, and hence for all that an animal does, is the activation of sensory receptors" (22, p. 7). "Stimuli are changes in the world order to which sense organs or receptors respond by exciting impulses in sensory nerves" (10, pp. 27-28).

Further, as will be discussed in more detail in the following section, we find the term stimulus applied not only to the outstanding detail but to the totality of events at the time the outstanding detail is being recorded. For example, Guthrie asserts that stimuli vary, although the experimenter's measurement of it (i.e., the outstanding detail) may remain constant. We may not wish to view the stimulus as the outstanding detail, but rather consider the latter as an indicator of the stimulus. The stimulus in turn could then refer to the total flow of energy changes. In this case, however, the term indicator would fall in the data language while the term stimulus would clearly be a theoretical concept.

2. We must include as independent variables several other determinants of behavior than stimuli alone, according to Guthrie's view. These others include:

a. Species differences. Thus:

Observation of living organisms gives very little insight into the details of human behavior if it is confined to those traits which hold of all organisms. But if we patiently observe a species we can offer a great deal of important information concerning what to expect of members of that species. The work just published by Carpenter (1934) on the behavior and social relations of howling monkeys after two years observation of them in Panama makes us familiar with many of their ways, just as the work of Tolman and his associates has added to our information concerning what to expect of the white rat in a maze (10, p. 18).

b. Maturation. Thus:

We cannot go the whole distance with Holt (1931) and say that all stimulus-response associations are dependent on conditioning. Maturation of the nervous system appears to be the principal determiner of many classes of acts (10, p. 38).

c. Muscle tonus. Thus:

In many cases the response is not dependent on any one known original stimulus but on a complex situation in which the most important features are internal to the animal. In a recent monograph, Jensen (1932) reports that moderately full infants that had just stopped suckling resumed in all cases when the infant was dropped four inches, or when the large toe was pinched, or when hair was pulled. . . . Anything which will increase general tonus reinforces the suckling movements (10, p. 37).

Muscles when they contract stimulate their own sense organs and the resulting impulses are responsible for an additional contraction of the muscle itself, as well as contraction of allied muscles. Not only contraction, but stretching, and sudden resistance to contraction have this effect of addition to the original tension of the muscle. The contraction of any muscle thus leads to a sort of reverberation which tends to increase muscular tonus. The main feature of states of excitement is undoubtedly this general increase of muscle tonus which tends to be self-sustaining through the circular reflexes described, and to exaggerate or reinforce whatever action is taking place (10, pp. 105-106).

Nevertheless, the aforementioned variables seem to be regarded by Guthrie as setting up merely parametric problems in the analysis of behavior. Learning remains the central problem of psychology, and learning is to be considered the outcome of stimulus-response association.

III. CONSTRUCT SYSTEM

Guthrie has at no time attempted to formalize a theory of learning and he does not explicitly set forth his construct system. Only by observing the ways in which certain terms are manipulated can Guthrie's construct content be clarified. At first glance, Guthrie's treatment of learning phenomena seems to contain only the terms stimulus, response (defined as we have noted earlier, in terms of movements, not effects on the environment), and the assumption that once a stimulus and a response occur together the response will tend to occur again on recurrence of that stimulus. Closer examination reveals, however, that this simplicity is only apparent, and that a rather elaborate system of assumptions is required in order to cover logically the areas discussed by Guthrie.

An analysis of the use of the terms stimulus and response introduces the first complications. These terms have not been unambiguously defined by Guthrie; it is possible, however, to search for a definition implicit in his usage of them. In so doing, we are confronted with several concrete usages that seem to imply mutually exclusive definitions. As we shall see below the failure to anchor the stimulus and response terms unambiguously has introduced a flexibility that makes explanation by the theory deceivingly simple. It is not the simplicity that we are objecting to here, but rather the opposite; that, although it looks simple, the content of the theory turns out to be quite formidable when made explicit and given rigorous statement.

As we have seen, emphasis is put throughout Guthrie's writings on the movements of an organism rather than on the effects of these movements upon the environment. But what constitutes a movement or a response is not made clear. Movement as muscular activity could range from activities of small muscle groups to broad activities of the muscular system, and it is difficult to place Guthrie's position along this continuum. A few quotations may illustrate this difficulty. "Responses, the answers to stimuli, are limited to the contraction of muscles or the secretion of glands. In practice, when we actually observe the boy and speak of his response to a stimulus situation what we select is usually some outstanding detail of an infinitely complicated total response. We can discuss actual behavior only by choosing some nameable detail in which we happen to be interested" (18, p. 20). For Guthrie, a complicated flow of activity is present, and some detail of this flow must be selected to specify the response. But confusion results from his use of the word *response* for the "total response" (the infinitely complex movement patterns of all muscle groups), as well as for the "outstanding detail" that may be used to specify the occurrence or nonoccurrence of the "response." We find him saying that the process of conditioning mingles responses into new combinations, so that presumably the responses are enough of a unit that we may speak of combining them; yet we are never reassured that the assertion that responses are never the same is not to be extended to these units, which would have to be true if the units are to be regarded as units.

In view of our earlier discussion of Guthrie's response term in the data language section, as well as the added comments above, it is unnecessary to elaborate again on this failure to specify the terms response and movements. It is simply a fact that the unit in which responses are to be measured is not specified. The general tenor of his writings leads one to a response specification between the extreme of individual muscles and the total complex of muscle activity. On the basis of his attacks on Gestalt psychology's emphasis on wholes and totalities, Guthrie clearly does not mean to define the response in terms of total movement. He insists on some form of analysis. "Actions, like rising from (one's) seat, answering a question, or making a mistake in multiplication, we cannot do justice to. They occur in a total response that is infinitely complicated and merges into other responses. But total responses have no names and no description" (18, p. 22). That it is not Guthrie's intention to specify response in terms of individual muscle activity is also clear from his repeated emphasis on the observability of both stimulus and response, and his recurring use of notions like "compromise responses," "combination of responses," etc. (10, pp. 41, 215).

As will appear later, Guthrie actually assumes that all portions of the total response that occur are conditioned to all components present at the time of the stimulus, and the occurrence or nonoccurrence of certain of these portions presumably determines whether we say that a "response" has recurred (see above discussion on Guthrie-Horton criterion of response sameness); so it seems necessary to admit a concept of "component of a response," as an unspecified part of the observed or recorded response. Any use of such a phrase is an example of what may be called the concept of "sub-response." Certainly, Guthrie's usage would suggest that such components have existential properties, perhaps the action of smaller muscle groups, etc., and are possibly quantifiable, although a statement to the effect that "responses are never twice alike" would seem to imply a definition of response that defies complete measurability. Whether or not he regards it as ultimately measurable, the concept of the "sub-response" is frequently encountered by a reader of Guthrie.

A second and more heavily emphasized construct in Guthrie's analysis of learning appears in his use of the term stimulus. At one time he considers the stimulus as an observable.

What we can observe is the source of light, not the beam that enters our subject's pupil; or we hear or record the sound wave that must affect his ear, the same wave but on a different section of the wave front; we can see and record movements and changes in posture, but the sense organs that these movements affect are hidden from direct observation. Movement, light, sound, pressure, skin contact, the contact of various substances with the olfactory membrane and with the taste papillae, these are what we mean by stimuli (10, p. 29).

At another time, he places a restriction on the definition by saying that stimuli are "changes in the world order to which sense organs or receptors respond by exciting impulses in sensory nerves" (10, pp. 27-28). The extent to which this is observable in any experimental case is open to question. And finally, we find many references to smaller units of stimuli, with variations in these smaller units being appealed to in an important explanatory way in treating learning data. Thus, we find him saying that stimuli in a controlled conditioning experiment are "never the same" and "Thousands of stimuli accompany every response" (6, p. 134). Thus, stimuli are lights, sounds, etc., as conventionally specified and measured; but at the same time they are something of which there are thousands in every test situation and which are never repeated in the same pattern. We shall reserve the term stimulus for the first usage and refer to the smaller units, the number of which is indefinitely large, and the patterns of which may never be repeated, as sub-stimuli. The term sub-stimuli has the status of a construct, as does the term which designates the total population of these elements.

Our discussion of the stimulus and response terms in Guthrie's writings may seem labored, but it has important consequences for any analysis of Guthrie's system. The apparent simplicity of Guthrie's theory rests upon a failure to examine the many usages to which a small number of terms are put. We have seen already that stimuli and responses play the role of constructs as well as measurable variables, and even this observation does not do justice to the complexities. The ease with which the concept of sub-stimuli, for example, permits us to talk about different areas of data arises, in no small way, from the failure to specify the properties of these sub-stimuli and from the tendency to assign them properties *a posteriori* on the basis of the data to be "explained."

Thousands of stimuli accompany every response. What combination of these will bring about a repetition? I have in the past suggested that it is a question of their number and their pattern, but I must confess that I have never found any method by which they could be counted, or any rule for selecting effective patterns. Consequently I have no rule to offer by which it can be told in advance whether or not a certain group of stimuli accompanying a response will on a later occasion be followed by the response (6, pp. 134-135).

Guthrie recognizes the *ad hoc* nature of the "stimulus pattern," as shown in the above quotation, but this insight has not been used to improve the concept. One is forced to the conclusion that when time is taken to display the implicit assumptions involved in it, the simplicity of Guthrie's theory vanishes.

One possible starting place for a list of Guthrie's assumptions concerning the learning process in his *principle of association*, which states that, "A stimulus pattern that is acting at the time of a response will, if it recurs, tend to produce that response" (18, p. 23). While it is often taken as a point of departure for Guthrie's theory, because of its frequent occurrence in his writing, we shall choose not to start with this association principle for a number of reasons. One is that Guthrie's view of the status of this principle is not clear. Although association is "assumed to be the basic event in learning . . ." (18, p. 23), he later in the same article says that the "principle amounts to a convention that we shall use associated stimuli for the prediction of responses. It has no provision for measuring the relative effectiveness of different signals or the extent of similarity required in the practice and in the test situation" (18, p. 33). A second, and more important, reason is that the principle may easily be viewed as a consequence of certain other assumptions, either explicit or implicit, to be found in the theory.[2]

A less frequently stated, but more powerful, assumption is to the effect that "a stimulus pattern gains its full associative strength on the occasion of its first pairing with a response" (18, p. 30). If, for example, the frequency of occurrence of a response is taken as a measure of associative strength, we assume that frequency will not change with repeated presentations of the stimulus in the first sense above, i.e., stimulus as a measurable experimental variable. The assumption, if retained, will serve to define, partially at least, and by exclusion, what is meant by a stimulus pattern. Stimulus pattern then comes to mean something that is not

---

[2] In addition to these reasons, another objection to using this principle as a starting point is that no testable consequences flow from it. Presumably, the phrase "tend to produce the response" means that there will be a certain probability that the response will occur if the stimulus pattern recurs. Stated in this fashion there is no commitment that the probability will increase, decrease, or show no change. It may be argued that the point is trivial because in context Guthrie obviously implies more than he says, i.e., he implies that there will be an *increased* tendency to produce the response. Although possibly correct in its interpretation of Guthrie's mental content, this view would be hard to defend, since in the most extended explanation Guthrie has given of what he means by "tend," he leads up to the statement, "The principle of conditioning thus stated with the word 'tend' merely asserts that on the recurrence of the stimulus pattern we can expect the former response, but with what certainty it does not state" (10, p. 26).

guaranteed to be repeated when the measured and observable stimulus is repeated. Here we are led back to the view that each stimulus contains "thousands of stimuli" (our sub-stimuli) and it is only to the extent that we can expect duplication of the original pattern or number of these stimuli that we can expect the response to be duplicated.

Some of the assumptions implicit in a Guthrian treatment of conditioning might take the following form.[3]

A. A stimulus pattern (sub-stimulus set) is maximally conditioned on the occasion of its first pairing with a response.

B. The pattern and number of sub-stimuli are assumed to be a function of a large number of operations typically found as independent variables in experimental work. The pattern and number are dependent on: (a) environmental conditions, i.e., lights, sounds, and other experimentally manipulable stimuli; (b) movements and postures of the organism—these presumably are the observable correlates of propioceptive stimuli. The latter assume an important role in Guthrie under the heading of movement-produced stimuli. These stimuli are the conditioners, for example, in delay and trace conditioning; (c) deprivation schedules— food, water, and other rhythms are assumed to change the pattern and number of "maintaining stimuli"; (d) "emotion-producing" operations— certain operations such as using a very intense stimulus, repeatedly presenting a stimulus which leaves accumulated effects (as in "teasing"), interfering with an activity—these operations serve not only to change the pattern of exteroceptive stimuli but also change the pattern of internal and maintaining stimuli by producing an emotional state. This emotional state is one of increased muscle tension and carries with it characteristic stimuli of its own (10, pp. 103 ff).

C. The repeated presentation of a stimulus situation under constant experimental conditions involves variations in the patterns of sub-stimuli. (As stated earlier, this variability in the sub-stimulus pattern is said to arise from our inability to completely control and specify the sub-stimuli resulting from the experimentally manipulable stimuli and from the movements and postures of the organism.)

D. The tendency for a response to recur is some function of the similarity of the patterns of sub-stimuli in the conditioning and test presentation.

The set of assumptions we have listed is not to be taken as an exhaustive postulate set, nor is any implication intended that such could be written on the basis of what Guthrie has provided us. As a matter of fact, if an attempt were made to deduce rigorously *any* phenomenon in learning it would become obvious that still further restrictions would have to be placed on the ideas presented to this point. In some cases these addi-

---

[3] Recently, Voeks (39) has attempted a formal development of Guthrian theory.

tions are implied by Guthrie's treatment, but even the implication is usually uncertain, or too incomplete to permit the deduction of statements that Guthrie believes to follow directly from his principles.

Consider the acquisition of a conditioned response. Without making some statement about the nature of the variations in the pattern of stimuli present on successive applications of the stimulus, it is not obvious that acquisition would ever take place. In other words, without a specification of the kind of sampling of the total possible stimuli, we do not guarantee that overlap of sub-stimuli occurs from trial to trial. For example, our sets of sub-stimuli could be conceived of as being conditionally selected; sub-stimuli viewed as sensory events, or modeled after them, could easily be conceived as being dependent upon previous patterns in such a way as either to secure or to avoid overlap of stimulus samples on successive trials. The point being stressed is that not all ways of conceptualizing the sub-stimulus sets would generate a statement that acquisition does occur. The fact that Guthrie feels he can handle the phenomenon of acquisition, at least its presence or absence, and possibly its speed, implies that some particular kinds of sampling of sub-stimuli are involved.

When we get to the problem of extinction, new theoretical requirements appear. An operation will produce extinction if it insures that the conditioned response will not occur when the stimulus is presented. When coupled with the assumption that behavior is continuous, i.e., that some response always occurs contiguously with the stimulus, this means that a new response has been conditioned to the stimulus. In short, Guthrie views extinction as an interference phenomenon, i.e., that we get one response out of our repertoire by learning to give another response to the same stimulus. For Guthrie, the best procedures for extinguishing a response are those that (1) present the conditioned cue along with other stimuli for other inhibitory or antagonistic or interfering responses, (2) repeat the signal until the response gets fatigued to the point of response nonoccurrence, or (3) introduce the signal at intensities that do not elicit the response and gradually raise the intensity to a level at which the response would normally occur but now does not because of the graduated extinction. The impression is frequently created by Guthrie and others that extinction by interference can be deduced merely by granting that another response has been attached to the stimulus. This obviously is not the case, since such an assumption insures only that two stimulus-response connections (both involving the same stimulus) have reached their respective maximum strengths. The question of what will happen when the stimulus is presented without benefit of "stimulus for inhibitory responses," "fatigue," etc., remains to be answered. In order to treat the above three procedures as effective extinguishers, Guthrie's theory must take on at least one more postulate. A number of "Guthrian" possibilities present themselves, perhaps the most obvious being Guthrie's associative inhibition, or the negative version of assumption A. This might take the form:

> E. A stimulus pattern is maximally unconditioned on the occasion of its first occurrence that is not followed by the response in question.

An alternative assumption for handling extinction might be in the form of a recency postulate, for example:

> E_1. The last response attached to a given stimulus pattern is the only response attached to the stimulus pattern.

Parenthetically it may be noted that if we state the postulate in terms of greater strength (e.g., the last response is always the stronger), rather than in the all-or-none fashion used above, we are confronted with the problem of compatibility of responses since in this case there is some probability of getting both responses or a certainty of getting both responses with some ratio of magnitudes.

The stopping point in a list of implicit assumptions for Guthrie will depend upon the number of phenomena discussed. A few more examples will be given to demonstrate that the number of hidden assumptions is not small, but no attempt will be made to treat Guthrie's writings exhaustively in this manner. At each point in the discussion, a number of possible choices for assumptions would each seem reasonable from Guthrie's point of view, and in most cases there would be little reason for choosing one over the others. To select an assumption at each of these choice points would be to construct our own theory and not to reconstruct Guthrie, since he might or might not agree with our selection. We wish only to illustrate that many additional assumptions are required in order to generate statements about data, statements which Guthrie probably would regard as flowing obviously from his principle of association, or from one or more of our assumptions A-D.

One case in which Guthrie's discussion of a topic clearly requires an added assumption, and even suggests its nature, is that of spontaneous recovery. A quote will give the tenor of his discussion.

> There remains to be explained the reestablishment of the conditioned response after a lapse of time. We have a hint toward this explanation in the fact that a sudden extraneous and unusual stimulus may cause the conditioned response to recover its original strength and certainty. It is possible that the inhibiting stimuli in this case include the somewhat specific details of posture and environment which hold during the process of extinction. A sudden interruption disorganizes posture and orientation, removes many recently conditioned inhibitors, and allows the original posture and conditioners to prevail again (5, pp. 423-424).

This treatment of spontaneous recovery holds that the postures present during the first extinction period do not exhaust the supply of internal conditioners, and that an interruption of the extinction process by a time interval of no extinction restores some of the original internal conditioners. The question may arise as to the relative importance of the interruption and the time interval of no extinction; presumably the latter is important since the amount of spontaneous recovery is a function of this interval. Thus, some assumption about the change of specific postures with time would have to be made. Of course, the wording of the assumption would not have to take the form of changes with time but might be expressed in terms of a change in general posture and orientation as a function of the amount of intervening activity, but the intervening activity must then be some stated function of time. The interruption *per se* may also be a variable and this too might be stated in terms of postural changes. The present form of Guthrie could easily incorporate either.

Not all of the additions of assumptions are as obvious as the one just given, and an example at the other extreme of specifiability may be drawn from his discussion of experiments on changes in the type of experimental reward.

When, in the course of a number of trials the reward is changed, confusion is introduced. Readiness for bran mash is now confused with readiness for sunflower seed and the two are as incompatible as readiness for a high and for a low pitch on the part of a baseball catcher. The rat, encountering the changed reward is disappointed, which is only to say that the movements with which the rat approaches the food are not movements adjusted to the eating of this particular food and there is some resultant confusion (10, p. 174).

The attempt to define disappointment may be noteworthy, although the finality with which one can judge whether a movement toward food is adjusted to the eating of one food and not adjusted to the eating of another may be questioned. Similarly, the incompatibility of different readinesses is an assumption about the readinesses in question, and not a statement about observables. Finally, after these points are incorporated into theory, we might entertain in more detail questions concerning the status of the term "confusion." Is it another way of saying that something happens to the acquisition curve, is it another way of speaking about incompatibility of responses, or is it more than either of these? Once again, we do not mean this as a representative sample of Guthrie; nor do we mean to imply that other theorists have handled this particular problem more adequately. We present it to show that the steps from Guthrie's statements to a testable deduction may, and perhaps always do, involve considerable construction and invention.

All of the classical problems in psychology that Guthrie discusses are treated in terms of stimulus and response. The so-called "state" variables, such as emotion and drive, are stimuli. Thus, for example, "Motives are stimulus situations that keep the individual active until some specific goal is reached. By a goal we mean the removal of the maintaining stimuli responsible for the activity and excitement. . . ." (18, p. 59). The movements in the puzzle box situation "that attain the goal or that remove the maintaining stimuli for activity tend to be preserved from unlearning" (18, p. 59). Perception, thinking, and other classical topics are interpreted as responses. But, again, an adequate Guthrian treatment of these topics would require additional constructions and assumptions in order to be rigorous.

Among the theoretical developments considered in this volume, Guthrie's is among the least quantitative. Formal developments in general are non-existent. He has not explicitly axiomatized any part of the theory, nor have any formal derivations been presented. There are instances in which a statement, or group of statements, is treated as following from a particular assumption, where analysis shows this not to be the case. It is undoubtedly true that many reviews of Guthrie in the literature have mistaken incompleteness for simplicity.

Guthrie's writings suggest a kind of model for the patterning and sampling of units conceived variously as environmental (stimulus) or sensory events on the one hand, and motor events on the other. Presumably, this model or one close to it is what Guthrie would apply to the sampling of sub-stimuli or sub-responses during acquisition, extinction, spontaneous recovery, and other phases of conditioning. The model has not been elaborated by Guthrie, although others (e.g., Estes, 1) have presented more formal systems using the kind of model suggested by Guthrie's work. The kind of sampling model suggested by Guthrie is illustrated in the following quotation:

This statistical decrease in conditioners with time which is described by the forgetting curve would resemble, to use a frivolous illustration, the decreased expenditures of a certain artist whose method of protecting himself from starvation was to change the proceeds of his rare sales into dimes and broadcast these about his large and disordered studio. The following day dimes were retrieved easily in numbers. As time went on more and more search was required, though he seldom reached such a pass that an afternoon's search would not yield a dime (5, p. 422).

A discussion of Guthrie should include some consideration of at least two other topics, which are not unrelated as he treats them: first, the concept of contiguity, which figures centrally in the theory; and, second, the concept of reinforcement, which is prominent in current behaviorism and which Guthrie has attempted to subsume within his own theory.

At first glance, it would appear that the term "contiguity" in Guthrie's statement of the conditioning principle has the straightforward physical meaning of simultaneity or coincidence in time of the conditioned stimulus (CS) and the response (R). Thus, Guthrie (8) disputes with Pavlov the correctness of regarding the pairing of CS with the unconditioned stimulus (US) as the important consideration in conditioning, arguing rather that US simply serves to get out the response and that it is the temporal relation between CS and R that is crucial for the emergence of the new reflex. Again, Guthrie cites his own experimental studies of word-association learning as showing that "backward" conditioning is not as difficult or impossible as other theorists suppose (also see 10, p. 34), arguing rather that response contiguity with the "backward" CS is the important factor.[4] However, any attempt to deal with the bi-directional gradient obtained from CS-US asynchronism studies necessarily forces us to a much broader conception of what it is that is occurring simultaneously. Experimental evidence on the strength of conditioning as a function of (forward) CS-US interval indicates that placing CS at the time of US is largely, if not entirely, ineffective, and that a temporal gradient exists with an optimal CS-US interval ranging from somewhat below 0.5 sec. up to 7-10 sec. (e.g., 30)[5] depending upon the response measured and the conditioning procedure. In all cases, however, the optimal interval is in a forward direction rather than at simultaneity. By Guthrie's account, successful backward conditioning is achieved through an assumed persistence of response which allows contiguity between CS and R to occur; in forward conditioning, on the other hand, the important consideration is some unmeasured response to the CS that mediates the conditioning by providing movement-produced stimuli (m.p.s.) as new CS. Accepting this for the moment as an account that can be made to have some additional testable consequences, we may still ask the question why, if CS-R contiguity is this important factor, there would not be a maximum rate of conditioning at the point of CS-R contiguity with gradients on each side for the reasons admitted above. From the experimental evidence on optimal CS-US intervals for forward conditioning, however, Guthrie would seem almost forced to the assumption that m.p.s. are better conditioners (in some sense).[6] In any event, however, it seems apparent that the "contiguity" referred to in Guthrie's association principle is not to be construed in a literal, physical sense, but is rather employed by him as a construct word. M.p.s., and

---

[4] Note that Guthrie brings into his discussion, without distinction, data from experiments that other writers would regard as being of two different conditioning types: classical and instrumental, Type S and Type R, or however the dichotomy is labeled. His doing so, of course, flows from, and is consistent with, his view that all conditioning is of a single type based on the self-same contiguity principle being discussed here.

[5] No attempt has been made in the present paper to document all of our statements concerning experimental results. Only where the data cited are recent or not widely known, or where an article contains a summary of literature on a given point, have specific references been included.

[6] It may be recalled as an aside here that the important role generally assigned by Guthrie to the m.p.s. has been encountered earlier as one source of the uncontrollable variability of the stimulus, and is encountered also as providing a reason why the CR is not always the same and is not exactly like the R.

consequently contiguity, is another of the response-inferred terms featured in Guthrie's writings. It might perhaps be urged that Guthrie invents *m.p.s.* only to emphasize the idea that, in an objective science of behavior, conditioning must be conceived as being in relation to real, physical, present events, and not to imaginary traces of historical stimuli that are now absent; that is to say, that conditioning must involve *something* real here and now. Although one might agree with this position, Guthrie's *m.p.s.*, given their indeterminacy, are no less imaginary than other invented trace mechanisms which have been proposed by others to bridge the temporal gap between *CS* and *US*, or between *CS* and *R*. The defense of Guthrie on the ground that he is no more vulnerable on this score than, say, Hull, suggests two comments. The first is that it may be true; the second is that Hull specifically introduces similar terms (e.g., afferent neural actions) as construct words and attempts, albeit unsuccessfully, to assign them definable and testable properties. Thus, the present imperfections of Hull might be ascribed to incompleteness or to failure of a defensible effort. Guthrie, on the other hand, frequently, and on principle, criticizes the use of such terms particularly if they suggest a physiological mechanism such as a trace, and asserts that behavior is to be understood, and behavior theories to be complete, when a description of behavior and its observable relations to stimuli is provided.

Turning to the concept of reinforcement, we find that learning theories have generally treated this concept in two ways. The first considers reinforcement as a primitive empirical term defined with reference to an experimental operation and an observed effect upon response strength or upon the conditional relation between *S* and *R*. Skinner's use of the term is of this descriptive or positivistic sort, as seen in his "law of reinforcement" which, though often criticized as circular, is reducible to a definition (that the name reinforcement shall be applied to any stimulus operation having a specified effect upon *R*) and an empirical proposition (that the class of stimulus operations named as reinforcements is not a null class). The second alternative in handling reinforcement is to regard descriptive reinforcement as a derived phenomenon, to regard the reinforcing effect of any (empirically demonstrated) operation as being derivable from some still more primitive or fundamental process (either assumed or experimentally demonstrable). This second alternative involves asking the analytic question, *why* is a reinforcement reinforcing, or by virtue of *what* property is a stimulus capable of acting as a reinforcer? This question Hull has attempted to answer by introducing the concept of drive (or need) reduction. Guthrie has attempted to answer this question by indicating the manner in which reinforcement operations change the stimulus and response conditions to which the organism is exposed. Guthrie's concept of reinforcement is based upon the change in the stimulus situation following the response; the change serves to protect the last S-R bond in that situation, and thereby increases the probability that the same response will be made again when the same stimulus situation occurs again. The stimulus situation change that follows R prevents the possibility of unconditioning S and R by having S present with the organism not in a position to make R again immediately, hence of some other R being made which becomes conditioned to S and which displaces the first R by reason of incompatibility. Changes in the stimulus situation may be made by the experimenter (or his apparatus) following the occurrence of the response to be conditioned, or may be the result of the stimulus consequences of the organism's response itself.

Guthrie's statements on reinforcement are in absolute or universal form, leading one to expect that any and all changes in the stimulus situation will strengthen the last S-R bond. Nevertheless, his actual stand on whether any given change is reinforcing is an empirical one like Skinner's, since he provides no rule for saying how large a change, or what type of change, must be made to secure effective protection of the last S-R connection, with the result that the adequacy of the change must be inferred from its effect upon the conditioning. The fact that Guthrie's reinforcement is response-inferred provides us little basis for separating it from the positivistic treatment given by Skinner. Every Skinnerian "reinforcing stimulus" is perforce a "change in prior stimulus situation"; Guthrie, uncommitted as to details, requires nothing more, and no experiment in which conditioning occurs can conceivably contain anything less.[7]

Some implications for both concepts of reinforcement are contained in a recent experiment by Schoenfeld, Antonitis and Bersh (33), which indicated (or re-emphasized) that the discriminative and reinforcing stimulus functions of Skinner are closely related, if not identical. Subsequent data (e.g., 31; 40) also support the conclusions that a stimulus can act as a reinforcement for any S-R bond only if that stimulus itself gives rise to another response. From the Guthrian standpoint, there is no way of predicting whether any given S following an S-R will suffice as a bond-protecting reinforcement; more particularly one would have no reason to expect the finding that only that S will suffice which has a re-

---

[7] Guthrie does not attempt to differentiate among functions of a stimulus as Skinner does, but seems always to use the stimulus in the one sense of the antecedent clause in the conditional relation or proposition [If S, then R]. In point of fact, Skinner's use of S is also of this conditional sort, but for purposes of descriptive clarity (or purity?) he distinguishes the different S functions on the basis of the different sorts of R effects achieved by the different uses of S. Although disavowing such distinctions, here again Guthrie parallels Skinner closely, as when he speaks of a stimulus as producing an emotion, or when he speaks of S as protecting (read, reinforcing) a prior S-R bond without mentioning, or in any way utilizing, the response to the S itself, thus neglecting the conditional nature of S in favor of its effect upon a response other than its own. The matter of the response to the reinforcing stimulus comes up again in the following discussion.

sponse conditioned to it. One might perhaps intuit that Guthrie might use this experimental finding to emphasize once more the role of *m.p.s.* Thus, the response conditioned to the reinforcing *S* might be thought of as a necessary component in the "change in prior stimulus situation" which does the protecting of the *S-R*. But if, as we have assumed, Guthrie would accept this experiment, then how *m.p.s.* are different from other stimuli, why they have special status in conditioning as against other stimuli, why or when they are a necessary component of a bond-protecting change in prior stimulus situation, and so on with the general parameters of the case—none of this information can now, in advance of Guthrie's own discussion of the problem, be extracted or deduced from Guthrie's writings to date for reasons of the same lack of specificity which we have noted before.[8] The nature of Guthrie's treatment of reinforcement emphasizes again the positivistic nature of his approach to the problem. It appears that his actual treatment is indistinguishable in the last analysis from Skinner's.

IV. GENERAL EVALUATION

An attempt to evaluate Guthrie's work in the field of behavior theory may start with his orientative attitudes, at least to the extent that those attitudes actually leave their mark on his system. In well-developed sciences, a systematist's expressed philosophy need have little bearing on his actual theoretical productions, and in such cases any evaluation of his philosophy of science is, from the science's viewpoint, entirely *ad hominem*. Where theoretical developments in a man's work have not progressed far, however, the orientative attitudes of a theorist often fill in the gaps in his work and are likely to aid an understanding and evaluation of his work. This is true of contemporary psychology and behavior theorists, Guthrie included, so that some comments on his extra-theoretical attitudes seem in order.

---

[8] What is involved here is the definition of a "stimulus," a matter of general confusion and concern in all sectors of modern behavior theory. If Guthrie took the proximal rather than the distal view of the stimulus—that is, that a stimulus is not defined by what the experimenter does, but by the organism's response, in short, that a stimulus is a stimulus only when the organism tells us it is by its response to it—if Guthrie took that view, then the finding that an *S* must have a response made to it if it is to be a reinforcing *S*, would not create any difficulties on the conversational level at least. For in that case, Guthrie could still say that a reinforcing *S* is reinforcing because it changes the prior stimulus situation, and the only way it can be called an *S* is if it has an *R*, according to the conditional relation [If *S*, then *R*]. Needless to say, it is possible to find a quotation suggesting such a usage, but it is not clear from his writing whether Guthrie would choose such a response-inferred definition of stimulus despite the prevalence of response-inference in his theory; it is more likely that he prefers a definition of stimulus in physical or operational terms (see quotes, p. 358 herein). Admittedly, the confusion in usage of the word stimulus is not unique to Guthrie, and perhaps a re-examination of the stimulus concept by other theorists as well would be timely.

A reader of Guthrie certainly emerges with an impression of his hard-headedness. This is illustrated by his emphasis on the observable, public, non-unique nature of the data that science deals with; by his rejection of concepts in rival systems that are not open to test or the possibility of disproof; by his insistence (e.g., vis-a-vis Gestalt theories) that some level of analysis is required in the gathering of data and the construction of theory; by some of his criticisms of other systems (e.g., Tolman's rat, which Guthrie describes as being left "buried in thought"; 10, p. 172). Furthermore, Guthrie is sensitive to the place of theory in science: for him, it is a central endeavor in any science, and in several vigorous passages he expounds this theme as opposed to the mere collection of independent facts.

It is all the more surprising, therefore, to see the number and variety of points at which Guthrie's own work departs from the standards he sets. Among these lapses are the way in which his own data language slips quickly into the intricacies of an elaborate construct system while appearing to keep its feet firmly planted on observable experimental operations (stimuli) and on public responses (movements) of the organism; and, again, the way his basic principle of conditioning by contiguity lacks testability, since, as he himself avows, there is no way of independently specifying stimulus similarity on successive occasions except by the recurrence of the response. In considering the use to which the terms stimulus and response are put, we found that both have the status of constructs. At the same time we found that explicit definitions of these terms are not available although some implicit restrictions on an eventual definition are provided. In addition to the inadequate definition of terms, Guthrie's usage suggests that stimulus and response may not be separable; to the extent that the stimulus term is specified at all it is specified on the basis of the response.

These deficiencies probably do not arise solely from the fact that Guthrie has failed to attempt explicit definitions or has avoided quantitative analysis. Some of these difficulties are encountered in other accounts of the Guthrian type that have attempted to evolve quantitative statements concerning acquisition, extinction, etc. For example, in the formulation presented by Estes (1), assumptions necessary to mediate quantitative statements of the acquisition curve have been made explicit and concepts such as populations and samples of stimuli have been formalized. But the account has not yet related the "stimulus" terms to physical variables such as lights, sounds, etc., and barring such developments there still would seem to remain the difficulty of identifying the experimental operations on the stimulus side that are coordinated with stimulus assumptions involved in formal derivation on the response side, that is, derivations of one set of response data from others (2).

While we do not consider it fruitful to judge now the logical or quantitative adequacy of a theory by applying the standards prevalent at the time the original formulations were made, nevertheless, we feel that some comment is required concerning the historical setting in which many of the contributions discussed and criticized in this book were made. Most of the works considered in this and other chapters of this book can be considered to have had their beginning in the early 1930's. By 1935, Tolman had written his *Purposive Behavior in Animals and Men*, Guthrie his *Psychology of Learning*, Hull had published *Mind, Mechanism and Adaptive Behavior*, and *Knowledge and Purpose as Habit Mechanisms*, and Skinner had completed a number of experimental papers concerned with the bar-pressing situation and had offered his discussion of the generic nature of the stimulus and response concepts. Lewin's works had not been extensively translated, but were formulated and available in German and had already stimulated work by Hoppe, Brown, and others.

In the setting of the 1930's, many of the arguments in the literature sought to argue for a break with certain segments of the history of psychology, and, in Guthrie's case, for the acceptance of behaviorism. For such arguments to pass beyond the schools-of-psychology stage required that specific experimental situations be discussed and specific systematic or theoretical arguments be presented. Guthrie was one of the early champions of this cause. He discussed specific cases where he thought that a simple contiguity of a stimulus and a response was a sufficient principle for the description of the experimental results.

Perhaps it is unfortunate that Guthrie did not permit his own formulation to become more specific and exact as the empirical area grew and became more rigorously defined (compare 10 and 25), but the fact that his account of conditioning has not become more rigorous seems not to have interfered with the continued acceptance of Guthrie as one of the prominent learning theorists on the present scene. Since we have attempted to show that the account is not now, nor has it ever been, rigorous enough to handle even first order problems of conditioning without considerable elaboration on the part of the interpreter of the theory, it may not be amiss to suggest some reasons for the continued inclusion of Guthrie's formulations in the theoretical literature over the past twenty years.

First, Guthrie has unswervingly held to a monistic conception of learning, and has never accepted views like those of Skinner or Tolman that conditioning may be of different types. That he had based his position on the contiguity principle is almost irrelevant to the separate appeal of his reductionism. To reduce different types of learning to a single one is to deal in parsimony, and any effort along this line possesses an appeal for the scientist. Guthrie has been practically alone among modern theoreticians in this particular reductional stand, since he not only applies the same theoretical constructs to all learning situations, but also asserts that the same experimental operations (namely, *S-R* contiguity) are involved in all learning situations. Added to the appeal of Guthrie's reductionism, is that of the apparent simplicity of his version of the contiguity principle. As we have seen, the simplicity is only superficial, but the very fact that he has striven for a reductional solution has helped keep his theory alive.

Second, Guthrie and his students have always maintained the role of shrewd critics of other theories. One recalls, for example, Sheffield and Roby's (35) experimental demonstration that a saccharine solution, which is non-metabolizable and therefore presumably not "need-reducing," can serve to reinforce a response. Experiments of this sort have forced need-reduction theorists to introduce "higher order" drives and drive reducers. In a similar vein have been the Guthrian arguments and attempted demonstrations that, under suitable conditions, a response that is "punished" will persist even though the need-reduction hypothesis would require the response to cease.

Third, Guthrie's writings have contained a number of ideas and emphases which other writers either developed independently later, or found occasion to employ in their own thinking. Examples are: the movement-produced (propioceptive) stimuli to which Guthrie often had recourse, and which are now receiving renewed emphasis by others in treating avoidance conditioning, and in treating the effects of various reinforcement schedules in conditioning; the intervening response sequences or chains which Guthrie, in his argument against Hull and Robinson, assumed to mediate delay and trace conditioning, and which are receiving renewed emphasis in the analysis of delay-of-reinforcement conditioning.

And finally, Guthrie's doctrines have derived some viability from the very fact that reinforcement theory has flourished alongside them. This is true partly because Guthrie has devoted much critical attention to reinforcement theory as a rival, but even more, from the indistinguishability of the two theories on many counts. We have pointed earlier to several similarities, such as their concepts of reinforcement and their use of the stimulus term. Other examples come to hand quickly: (*a*) In treating escape conditioning, Guthrie holds that the organism passes from response to response under the prod of the not-yet-escaped-stimulus until the prescribed response is made which terminates the stimulus (that is, changes the prior stimulus situation), thereby insuring that the escape response is the last response made in the situation, and increasing the probability that it will be made again when the stimulus recurs; reinforcement theory, in one form (e.g., Skinner), holds that the stimulus is noxious and that its termination is (definable as) positive reinforcement for the terminating response, while in another form (e.g., Hull), the stimulus is need-inducing and its termination is reinforcing because it is need-reducing. (b) Both contiguity theory and reinforcement theory handle avoidance conditioning as a special case of escape training (e.g., 32, 34). (c) Reinforcement theory in Hullian hands treats drives as having associated stimuli, and phenomena of so-called drive conditioning are capable of being treated in this way; contiguity theory considers drives as maintaining stimuli, and would interpret the same data in similar fashion. (d) Guthrie accounts for extinction in terms of unconditioning of the response (and conditioning of new responses) to ever-increasing numbers of the sub-stimuli composing the stimulus population to which the response was originally conditioned; Skinner speaks of extinction in terms of stimulus novelty, that is, how much the extinction session differs, or comes to differ as it progresses, from the stimulus situation prevailing during the period of reinforcement (38). These examples will, perhaps, suffice to make the point. Though seeming to differ, contiguity and reinforcement theory make equivalent statements in key areas, and the prosperity of the one necessarily succors the other, since the two, with allowance for differences in vocabulary, take parallel positions on many problems. We do not intend to say that contiguity theory and reinforcement theory are identical throughout, for this is not so; but the inadequate elaboration of assumptions and consequences makes contiguity theory indistinguishable from reinforcement theory very soon after its introductory propositions are voiced and empirical data of minimal complexity are encountered. Add to these considerations, the existence in both contiguity and reinforcement theory of some inadequately specified, yet basic, terms such as drive or stimulus or response or simultaneity, and it may be seen how the two types of theories generate explanatory statements which allow, with some substitutions in vocabulary, easy passage back and forth. From one point of view, there is a gain for science in recognizing that two theories, commonly regarded as distinct, are really not so; but it should at the same time be recognized that the similarities flow from not altogether praiseworthy sources. In place of a convergence based on independent development and maturation of the two theories, we observe on logical analysis and repeated applications of the theories to empirical data, that it is difficult to distinguish the theories in the first instance. Be that as it may, it does appear that continued reference to Guthrie in contemporary theory may be attributed in part to the prosperity of a rival which enjoys a prominent place in that same contemporary scene.

V. SUMMARY

Guthrie's orientative attitudes concerning such topics as scientific method, the problems confronting psychology as a science of behavior, the role of theory in psychology, and the like, have been summarized.

Comments have been made with respect to some of these attitudes in an attempt to explore their content, their explicitness, and the extent to which they are reflected in Guthrie's contributions to learning theory.

Consideration has been given to the manner in which Guthrie specifies the experimental dependent and independent variables in the empirical domain to which he addresses himself. Attention has also been given to the nature of some of the empirical and theoretical terms employed by Guthrie in his discussions of experimental results. Certain important similarities between Guthrie and reinforcement theory have been noted which raise a question as to whether the two theories are actually distinguishable at many points.

Criticisms of Guthrie seem to cluster around a small number of points, in particular, the inadequate definition of key terms and the response-inferred character of many of his constructs and explanations. Guthrie's formulation is non-quantitative in development and prediction, and may be depicted more as a manner of speaking about experimental results, and as a suggestion concerning the general form that learning theory should take, than as a finished theory. While the principles of conditioning which he expands seem to have a parsimony that would be desirable in a theoretical formulation of behavior, a closer analysis reveals that this seeming simplicity is deceptive and that a formidable set of additional assumptions and constructs are required if his theory is to possess any real applicability to experimental data. In fact, there is basis in his writings for saying that Guthrie himself does not claim to have a theory, but rather would agree that his work proffers a few statements as a springboard for the elaboration of a behavioristic stimulus-response theory.

Finally, several comments were made concerning possible reasons for Guthrie's continued prominence over several decades as a learning theorist.

Bibliography

(For completeness, the following references contain all of Guthrie's publications, save some smaller items such as abstracts, the obituary of Janet, autobiographical items, and the like.)

1. ESTES, W. K. Toward a statistical theory of learning. *Psychol. Rev.*, 1950, 57, 94-107.
2. ———. Effects of competing reactions on the conditioning curve for bar pressing. *J. exp. Psychol.*, 1950, 40, 200-205.
3. GUTHRIE, E. R. Purpose and mechanism in psychology. *J. Phil.*, 1924, 21, 673-682.
4. ———. Measuring introversion and extraversion. *J. abn. soc. Psychol.*, 1927, 22, 82-88.
5. ———. Conditioning as a principle of learning. *Psychol. Rev.*, 1930, 37, 412-428.

6. GUTHRIE, E. R. On the nature of psychological explanations. *Psychol. Rev.,* 1933, 40, 124-137.
7. ———. Association as a function of time interval. *Psychol. Rev.,* 1933, 40, 355-367.
8. ———. Pavlov's theory of conditioning. *Psychol. Rev.,* 1934, 41, 199-206.
9. ———. Reward and punishment. *Psychol. Rev.,* 1934, 41, 450-460.
10. ———. *The psychology of learning.* New York: Harper, 1935.
11. ———. Thorndike's concept of "belonging." *Psychol. Bull.,* 1936, 33, 621. (Abstract.)
12. ———. Psychological principles and scientific truth. *Proc. 25th Anniv. Celeb Inaugur. Grad. Studies,* Univ. of Southern Calif., 1936.
13. ———. Tolman on associative learning. *Psychol. Rev.,* 1937, 44, 525-529.
14. ———. *The psychology of human conflict.* New York: Harper, 1938.
15. ———. The effect of outcome on learning. *Psychol. Rev.,* 1939, 46, 480-485.
16. ———. Association and the law of effect. *Psychol. Rev.,* 1940, 47, 127-148.
17. ———. German Psychological Warfare. *Infantry J.,* 1941, 49, 82-84.
18. ———. Conditioning: a theory of learning in terms of stimulus, response and association. *Yearbk. nat. Soc. Stud. Educ.,* 1942, 41, 17-60.
19. ———. The principle of associative learning. In Clarke, F. P. and Nahm, M. C. *Philosophical essays in honor of Edgar Arthur Singer, Jr.* Philadelphia: University of Pennsylvania Press, 1942.
20. ———. *Psychology of war time. Marriage and family living,* 1943, 5, 56-57.
21. ———. Personality in terms of associated learning. In Hunt, J. McV., *Personality and the Behavior Disorders.* New York: Ronald Press, 1944. Pp. 49-68.
22. ———. Psychological facts and psychological theory. *Psychol. Bull.,* 1946, 43, 1-20.
23. ———. The conditioned response. In Harriman, P. L., *Encycl. Psychol.* New York: Philosophical Libraries, 1946.
24. ———. The status of systematic psychology. *Amer. Psychologist,* 1950, 5, 97-101.
25. ———. *The Psychology of Learning,* rev. ed. New York: Harper, 1952.
26. ——— and MORRILL, H. The fusion of non-musical intervals. *Amer. J. Psychol.,* 1928, 40, 624-625.
27. ———, and HORTON, G. P. *Cats in a Puzzle Box.* New York: Rinehart, 1946.
28. ———, and EDWARDS, A. L. *Psychology: a first course in human behavior.* New York: Harper, 1949.
29. ———, and POWERS, F. F. *Educational Psychology.* New York: Ronald Press, 1950.
30. LIBBY, A. Two variables in the acquisition of depressant properties by a stimulus. *J. exp. Psychol.,* 1951, 42, 100-107.
31. NOTTERMAN, J. M. A study of some relations among aperiodic reinforcement, discrimination training, and secondary reinforcement. *J. exp. Psychol.,* 1951, 41, 161-169.
32. SCHOENFELD, W. N. An experimental approach to anxiety, escape and avoidance behavior. Chap. 5 in *Anxiety,* ed. by P. Hoch and J. Zubin. New York: Grune and Stratton, 1950.
33. ———, ANTONITIS, J. J. and BERSH, P. J. A preliminary study of conditions necessary for secondary reinforcement. *J. exp. Psychol.,* 1950, 40, 40-45.
34. SHEFFIELD, F. D. Avoidance training and the contiguity principle. *J. comp. physiol. Psychol.,* 1948, 41, 165-177.

35. SHEFFIELD, F. D., and ROBY, T. B. Reward value of a non-nutritive sweet taste. *J. comp. physiol. Psychol.*, 1950, 43, 471-481.
36. SKINNER, B. F. The generic nature of the concepts of stimulus and response. *J. gen. Psychol.*, 1935, 12, 40-65.
37. ———. *The Behavior of Organisms.* New York: Appleton-Century-Crofts, 1938.
38. ———. Are theories of learning necessary? *Psychol. Rev.*, 1950, 57, 193-216.
39. VOEKS, V. W. Formalization and clarification of a theory of learning. *J. Psychol.*, 1950, 30, 341-362.
40. WEBB, W. B., and NOLAN, C. Y. Cues for discrimination as secondary reinforcing agents: a confirmation. *J. comp. physiol. Psychol.*, 1953, 46, 180-181.